Crimes of Privilege

READINGS IN CRIME AND PUNISHMENT
Michael Tonry, *General Editor*

What Works in Policing
David H. Bayley

Criminology at the Crossroads:
Feminist Readings in Crime and Punishment
Kathleen Daly and Lisa Maher

Community Corrections:
Probation, Parole, and Intermediate Sanctions
Joan Petersilia

Incarcerating Criminals:
Prisons and Jails in Social and Organizational Context
Timothy J. Flanagan, James W. Marquart, and Kenneth G. Adams

Readings in Juvenile Justice Administration
Barry C. Feld

Crimes of Privilege:
Readings in White-Collar Crime
Neal Shover and John Paul Wright

Crimes of Privilege
Readings in White-Collar Crime

Edited by

Neal Shover
University of Tennessee, Knoxville

John Paul Wright
University of Cincinnati

New York   Oxford
OXFORD UNIVERSITY PRESS
2001

Oxford University Press

Oxford   New York
Athens   Auckland   Bangkok   Bogotá   Buenos Aires   Calcutta
Cape Town   Chennai   Dar es Salaam   Delhi   Florence   Hong Kong   Istanbul
Karachi   Kuala Lumpur   Madrid   Melbourne   Mexico City   Mumbai
Nairobi   Paris   São Paulo   Shanghai   Singapore   Taipei   Tokyo   Toronto   Warsaw

And associated companies in
Berlin   Ibadan

Published by Oxford University Press, Inc.,
198 Madison Avenue, New York, New York, 10016
http://www.oup-usa.org

Library of Congress Cataloging-in-Publication Data
Crimes of privilege : readings in white-collar crime / edited by Neal Shover, John Paul Wright.
p. cm. — (Readings in crime and punishment)
Includes bibliographical references.
ISBN 0-19-513621-7 (pb : alk. Paper)—ISBN 0-19-513620-9 (cl : alk. Paper)
1. White collar crimes. I. Shover, Neal. II Wright, John Paul. III. Series.
HV6768 C75   2000
364.16′8—dc21   00-26144

Printing (last digit): 9 8 7 6 5 4 3 2 1

Printed in the United States of America
On acid-free paper

For Lindsey Hale Shover
N. S.

For my daughters:
Kassi, LaChelle, and Whitnie
J. P. W.

Contents

List of Panels   *x*

Preface   *xi*

1. CONCEPTUAL ISSUES AND SKIRMISHES

Introduction   *1*

White-Collar Criminality   *4*
Edwin H. Sutherland

Is "White-Collar Crime" Crime?   *12*
Edwin H. Sutherland

Collaring the Crime, Not the Criminal: Reconsidering the Concept of White-Collar Crime   *21*
Susan P. Shapiro

Organizational Crime   *32*
Albert J. Reiss, Jr., and Michael Tonry

Crime and Capitalist Business Corporations   *35*
Frank Pearce

2. VICTIMS AND COSTS

Introduction   *49*

The Neglected Victims and Unexamined Costs of White-Collar Crime   *51*
Elizabeth Moore and Michael Mills

Personal Fraud and Its Victims   *57*
Richard M. Titus

White-Collar Crime Victimization   67
Michael Levi

Consequences of Victimization by White-Collar Crime   74
Neal Shover, Greer Litton Fox, and Michael Mills

Victims of Fraud: Comparing Victims of White-Collar and
Violent Crime   87
Linda Ganzini, Bentson McFarland, and Joseph Bloom

3. WHITE-COLLAR CRIMINAL OPPORTUNITIES

Introduction   96

"Heads I Win, Tails You Lose": Deregulation, Crime, and Crisis in the
Savings and Loan Industry   99
Kitty Calavita and Henry N. Pontell

From Fiddle Factors to Networks of Collusion: Charting the Waters of
Small Business Crime   127
Hugh D. Barlow

Transaction Systems and Unlawful Organizational Behavior   136
Diane Vaughan

Opportunity and Crime in the Medical Professions   144
John Liederbach

Fire in Hamlet: A Case Study of a State-Corporate Crime   156
Judy Root Aulette and Raymond Michalowski

4. DECISION MAKING

Introduction   173

The Poverty of Theory in Corporate Crime Research   175
Donald R. Cressey

A Rational Choice Theory of Corporate Crime   194
Raymond Paternoster and Sally Simpson

Organizational Culture and Organizational Crime   210
Andy Hochstetler and Heith Copes

Profits, Pressure, and Corporate Law Breaking   222
Anne Jenkins and John Braithwaite

Rational Choice, Situated Action, and the Social Control
of Organizations   234
Diane Vaughan

5. SOURCES AND CHARACTERISTICS OF WHITE-COLLAR OFFENDERS

Introduction   *255*

Who Is the White-Collar Criminal?   *257*
Hazel Croall

Gender and Varieties of White-Collar Crime   *276*
Kathleen Daly

Corporate Control, Crime, and Compensation: An Examination of Large Corporations   *297*
Diana Bilimoria

Toward Understanding Unlawful Organizational Behavior   *313*
Diane Vaughan

Characteristics and Sources of White-Collar Crime   *329*
Nicole Leeper Piquero and Alex Piquero

Competition and Motivation to White-Collar Crime   *341*
James William Coleman

6. CONTROLLING WHITE-COLLAR CRIME?

Introduction   *359*

On Theory and Action for Corporate Crime Control   *361*
John Braithwaite and Gilbert Geis

Prosecuting Corporate Crime: Problems and Constraints   *381*
Michael L. Benson

Corporate Crime and Criminal Justice System Capacity: Government Response to Financial Institution Fraud   *392*
Henry N. Pontell, Kitty Calavita, and Robert Tillman

An Evolving Compliance Model for Tax Enforcement   *405*
Valerie Braithwaite and John Braithwaite

Cooperative Models and Corporate Crime: Panacea or Cop-Out?   *419*
Laureen Snider

List of Panels

1.   Varieties of White-Collar Crime   5
2.   What Travel Brochures Do Not Tell You   13
3.   Abuse of Office   20
4.   A Dangerous Combination   50
5.   Financial Institution Fraud and Failure Investigations   58
6.   Theft of Natural Resources   75
7.   More White-Collar Crime   98
8.   Corporate Lawlessness   128
9.   Medical Fraud   137
10.   Extent of Corporate Crime   145
11.   Environmental Crime   157
12.   Charity Begins at Home?   195
13.   Money Talks   211
14.   Bhopal   222
15.   An Economy of Fraud   277
16.   Small Change   315
17.   Violent Corporate Crime   330
18.   Strategies for Getting Dangerous Products to Market   380
19.   Legal Reponses to Corporate Crime   392
20.   Critics Beware   405
21.   Criminal Interference?   420

Preface

Since its introduction more than six decades ago, the concept *white-collar crime* has taken firm root in everyday discourse. It is widely understood and used by academics, by criminal justice practitioners, and by lay citizens to denote a type of crime that differs fundamentally from street crime. One way it is different is the backgrounds and characteristics of its perpetrators; the poor and disreputable fodder routinely encountered in police stations and in studies of street crime are seldom in evidence here. White-collar crime differs also in its appearance; whereas street crime typically is committed by confronting victims or entering their homes or businesses, most white-collar crimes are committed by using guile, deceit, or misrepresentation to create and exploit for illicit advantage the appearance of a routine legitimate transaction. Fraud, defined generally as use of deception to secure unfair or unlawful gain, is the core component of many white-collar crimes. Others are behaviors abusive of organizational position or public office. When judges demand sex from criminal defendants' wives or girlfriends in return for favorable bail decisions, they commit white-collar crime. When employers knowingly or negligently subject their workers to an unsafe work environment, they also commit white-collar crime.

Evidence of serious white-collar crime is both abundant and, save for those who perhaps have a stake in doing so, difficult to ignore. The mass media, for example, routinely report accounts of respectable offenders and the consequences of their illicit conduct. Although the national media generally single out for coverage only the most egregious crimes and thereby perhaps convey a misleading picture of the problem, the one that is gained from the day-to-day lives of ordinary citizens is not appreciably different; regional and local newspapers also routinely report accounts of serious white-collar crimes.

As a companion to textbook treatments of the subject, this collection of readings provides to students a critical overview of issues and problems in the analysis and control of white-collar crime. Both the interpretation and organization of the readings employ a rational-choice theoretical framework. The notion of crime as choice has gained wide currency in recent decades, and it has been used both to interpret and to justify official responses to street crime. We believe it applies equally well to white-collar criminal conduct. Rational-choice theory has the additional advantage of being logically compatible with other theoretical approaches to understanding white-collar crime. Whatever the presumed sources of pressures or inducements to engage in crime, inevitably their effects operate through the calculus of decision making. Strain theory, for example, is used by some as a theoretical explanation for the distribution of white-collar crime, one that directs attention to inequities in the distribution of legitimate opportunities. But the fact that the options available to some may be unattractive and few while those available to others by comparison seem limitless is significant principally because of how this constrains and in other ways influences estimates of the likely consequences of decisions to commit discrete criminal acts.

With white-collar crime, as with all analytic problems, much depends upon how fundamental concepts are defined, but we believe Edwin Sutherland's definition captures its most important aspects. Viewed in this way, most if not all of those who commit white-collar crime are distinguished by lives of privilege, much of it with origins in class inequality. Fiscal precariousness and the relentlessly pressing need to generate income for basic material needs are alien to their worlds and lives. Their automobiles start on command; their refrigerators and wine cellars are amply stocked; their homes are commodious, comfortable, and secure; and their children are well-clothed, well-fed, and placed high on waiting lists for the best public and private schools.

The privileges of class are the most important characteristic of white-collar criminals, but they are privileged also by the respectable work they do. Apart from their location in a wealth-and-property hierarchy, white-collar criminals also occupy privileged positions in this moral hierarchy. Consequently, when they confront officialdom or mid-level bureaucrats, they receive a polite and sympathetic hearing. They are subjected infrequently to gratuitous, sanctimonious, and classist comments about their "inappropriate" behavior, and they stand a reasonable chance of prevailing.

Wealth, respectability, and privilege, however, are not dichotomous variables; the members of any population can be arrayed on a continuum from those with an assured if only adequate income and unexceptional respectability to the wealthiest and most respectable citizens. The expanse is extremely wide, encompassing university faculty members with annual incomes of less than $50,000, attorneys and medical doctors with investment accounts, and presidents of Fortune 500 corporations whose annual "compensation package" exceeds $10 million. The ranks of white-collar criminals represent an equally expansive range and variety of backgrounds, occupations, and incomes. What distinguishes all, however, is the privilege afforded by their favored class position and their respectable status. We differ with Sutherland on one point, however. Whereas he defined white-collar crime broadly, for present purposes we restrict it to acts that violate criminal statues. In other words, we do not treat as crime violations of administrative rules or adverse civil decisions.

Despite these definitional biases, however, we recognize that many others take issue with our approach. For this reason, our selection of readings for this volume reflects a definitionally eclectic approach. In order to conserve space and facilitate reader understanding, most of the previously published materials have been edited substantially, including omission of most footnotes and references. Readers who are interested in these materials can follow up by obtaining the original source. Interspersed throughout the book are panels that are meant to broaden the view of students beyond the readings or to summarize exemplary research into white-collar crime. In constructing panels that describe specific crimes, we generally avoided selecting high-profile cases of the kind that figure prominently in many textbook treatments of white-collar crime, preferring instead to use materials from regional newspapers. Our objective in doing so is to emphasize to students how much serious white-collar crime occurs close to home; it is not a problem confined to Washington, D.C., to Wall Street or to the highest reaches of the world's largest corporations.

Conceptual Issues and Skirmishes

Introduction

In his 1939 presidential address to the American Sociological Association, Edwin Sutherland introduced and defined white-collar crime, called for more attention to it, and criticized academic social scientists for the class bias in their near-exclusive focus on crimes of the disadvantaged. His efforts not only gave initial direction to investigations of white-collar crime and its perpetrators, but he also triggered the controversy that continues to surround it. Sutherland regarded the respectable social status of its perpetrators as the defining characteristic of white-collar crime, and the question of whether or not location in hierarchies of wealth and repute should be the basis for distinguishing it remains the bedrock issue in this area of criminological investigation. We have reprinted here Sutherland's now–classic statement of white-collar criminality.

Following Sutherland's lead, offender-based definitions emphasize as its essential characteristic the status and power of those who commit white-collar crime. In this view, differentials of wealth, power, and influence are key to identifying, framing satisfactorily, and unraveling fundamental questions about crime and crime control. Others, however, counter with offense-based definitions, arguing either that there is little reason to highlight offenders' privileged position or even to carve out a conceptual category designated white-collar crime. They opt instead for a definitional approach in which the focus is on crimes distinguished by specific formal characteristics without regard to the status of those who commit them. *Abuse of trust* is an example of a status-free category, one that includes much of what proponents of offender-based approaches instead call white-collar crime. This position has been argued most notably by Susan Shapiro. An abbreviated version of her efforts is reprinted here.

Other offense-based approaches to white-collar crime use the criminal code as the starting point. In their research on white-collar offenders, investigators at Yale University, for example, chose to include in their sample all persons who were convicted of or pleaded guilty to any of eight statutorily defined crimes: securities fraud, antitrust violations, bribery, bank embezzlement, postal and wire fraud, false claims and statements, credit and lending institution fraud, and tax fraud. The resulting sample of offenders included many of modest financial resources; a significant proportion, in fact, were unemployed at the time of their offense(s). This is the case with all offense-based definitions of white-collar crime; they lump together for theoretic and policy purposes both the corner television repairperson who fraudulently charges customers $20.00 for unperformed services and international bankers whose crimes can destabilize national economies. The fact that the two offenders differ conspicuously and consequentially in material resources and repute from this vantage point is irrelevant. Offense-based samples of white-collar criminals differ dramatically from the kinds of offenders at the core of offender-based definitional approaches.

A second area of conceptual skirmishing about white-collar crime stems from Sutherland's decision to restrict it to acts committed by women and men "in the course of their occupation." This excludes extravocational crimes committed by the respectable, whether these be spousal abuse or loan fraud, despite the fact these behaviors are statutorily indistinguishable from crimes they might commit in their occupational role. Particularly when offense-based definitions of white-collar crime are used, many offenses, in fact, are not committed as part of offenders' occupations. Providing false information on a loan application, for example, can be committed either apart from or in an occupational role; potential home buyers may commit loan fraud as well as businesses. Clearly, if white-collar crime is defined to include all crimes with designated characteristics regardless of whether or not they are committed in offenders' occupational role, both the forms it assumes and the ranks of those who pursue it will include few wealthy corporate executives or high-ranking state managers. This is the principal reason why offense-based definitions of white-collar crime have been dubbed by some as "crimes of the middle classes."

A third point of definitional dissension is raised by the question of whether the *crime* in white-collar crime—or in trust crime, for that matter—should be defined broadly or narrowly? Should it be restricted to acts for which offenders can be tried and convicted in criminal courts, or should a wider net be cast, one that includes acts punished by adverse civil or administrative decisions? Sutherland treated as white-collar crime not only violations of criminal law but also actions that resulted in adverse civil decisions or in administratively imposed penalties. He justified this by arguing that all are state-imposed sanctions for acts recognized as potentially harmful. Put differently, because all share with criminal offenses these formal characteristics, they can be treated as crime. This approach includes as white-collar crime both a corporate manager's negligent failure to post workplace safety regulations properly and intentional release of toxic chemicals into the environment. Many, however, believe it is inappropriate to extend the label of crime to include acts not proscribed by the criminal code for which legal strictures of culpability are not required or cannot be demonstrated. They further question the appropriateness of labeling as crime business practices that may be legal, albeit "sharp" or aggressive behaviors. Failure to distinguish violations of administrative rules and crime runs the risk, they contend, of treating as crime these technical violations and those who commit them as criminals. They suggest the designation *illegalities* or *unlawful behavior* for acts that violate rules for which there is limited moral consensus, negligible harm, and minor penalties. The label *crime* is thereby reserved for acts that violate the criminal code and are punishable in criminal courts. Following his initial work on white-collar crime, Sutherland was criticized for expanding the boundaries of crime to include adverse administrative and civil judgments. His response ("Is 'White-Collar Crime' Crime?") is reprinted here.

Regardless of how it is defined, however, white-collar crime encompasses a broad range of behaviors, most of which differ conspicuously from street crimes. The enormous diversity of white-collar crime is apparent from Panel 1. Many investigators have responded to this diversity by isolating for study specific types of white-collar crime and deviance. These include *economic crime, business crime, state crime,* and *elite crime.*

A high proportion of white-collar crimes are committed by free-wheeling, organizationally unattached predators, but others are committed by individuals or by groups employed by and in legitimate organizations. Many investigators refer to these as *organizational* white-collar crimes. The principal rationale for distinguishing organizational crime is the assumption that organizational dynamics, conditions, and constraints presumably play a major part in their onset and course. Examples of organizational crime include reports of bogus research findings by university-based scientists and crimes directed, encouraged, or condoned by state managers. Organizational crime, therefore, is distinguished from *occupational crime,* which typically is committed by individuals or groups for their own purposes or enrichment. The importance of and the case for examining organizational crime is made here by Albert J. Reiss Jr., and Michael Tonry.

Not content with the distinction between organizational and occupational white-collar crimes, other investigators further narrow their focus to *corporate crime.* The principal reason is belief that the pervasiveness, the power, and the inherent criminogenic dynamics of the corporate form are too important to treat as a subtype of organizational white-collar crime. The overriding importance of pure economic calculation coupled with other structural and cultural features of corporations makes them essentially criminogenic. We reprint here an exemplary statement of this position by Frank Pearce.

White-Collar Criminality

EDWIN H. SUTHERLAND

This paper[1] is concerned with crime in relation to business. The economists are well acquainted with business methods but not accustomed to consider them from the point of view of crime; many sociologists are well acquainted with crime but not accustomed to consider it as expressed in business. This paper is an attempt to integrate these two bodies of knowledge. More accurately stated, it is a comparison of crime in the upper or white-collar class, composed of respectable or at least respected business and professional men, and crime in the lower class, composed of persons of low socioeconomic status. This comparison is made for the purpose of developing the theories of criminal behavior, not for the purpose of muckraking or of reforming anything except criminology.

The criminal statistics show unequivocally that crime, *as popularly conceived and officially measured,* has a high incidence in the lower class and a low incidence in the upper class; less than two percent of the persons committed to prisons in a year belong to the upper class. These statistics refer to criminals handled by the police, the criminal and juvenile courts, and the prisons, and to such crimes as murder, assault, burglary, robbery, larceny, sex offenses, and drunkenness, but exclude traffic violations.

The criminologists have used the case histories and criminal statistics derived from these agencies of criminal justice as their principal data. From them, they have derived general theories of criminal behavior. These theories are that, since crime is concentrated in the lower class, it is caused by poverty or by personal and social characteristics believed to be associated statistically with poverty, including feeblemindedness, psychopathic deviations, slum neighborhoods, and "deteriorated" families. This statement, of course, does not do justice to the qualifications and variations in the conventional theories of criminal behavior, but it presents correctly their central tendency.

The thesis of this paper is that the conception and explanations of crime which have just been described are misleading and incorrect, that crime is in fact not closely correlated with poverty or with the psychopathic and sociopathic conditions associated with poverty, and that an adequate explanation of criminal behavior must proceed along quite different lines. The conventional explanations are invalid principally because they are derived from biased

---

"White-Collar Criminality" from *American Sociological Review* 5:1 (February 1940): 1–12. Reprinted by permission.

[1] Thirty-fourth Annual Presidential Address delivered at Philadelphia, Pa., Dec. 17, 1939, in joint meeting with the American Economic Society (its Fifty-Second) at which President Jacob Viner spoke on the relations of economic theory to the formulation of public policy.

samples. The samples are biased in that they have not included vast areas of criminal behavior of persons not in the lower class. One of these neglected areas is the criminal behavior of business and professional men, which will be analyzed in this paper. . . .

PANEL 1   Varieties of White-Collar Crime

Fraud
    False Advertising
    Consumer Fraud
    Financial Fraud
    Tax Evasion
    Professional Fraud

Labor Violations
    Violations of Privacy
    Political Harassment and Repression
    Dangerous Working Conditions
    Wage and Hours Violations

Manufacturing Violations
    Environmental Violations
    Unsafe Consumer Products

Unfair Business Practices
    Mergers and Acquisitions
    Conspiracies
    Collusion in the Professions
    Bid Rigging
    Commercial Bribery
    Industrial Espionage

Abuse of Authority
    Sexual Assaults
    Corruption in Criminal Justice
    Corruption and Bribery in Political Arena

Judicial, Regulatory, and Administrative Violations
    Perjury
    Failure to Obey Agency Orders
    Refusal to Produce Information
    Failure to Report Information
    Copyright, Trademark, and Patent Infringements

Adapted from James William Coleman, *The Criminal Elite: Understanding White-Collar Crime* (4th edition). New York: St. Martin Press, 1998.

White-collar criminality in business is expressed most frequently in the form of misrepresentation in financial statements of corporations, manipulation in the stock exchange, commercial bribery, bribery of public officials directly or indirectly in order to secure favorable contracts and legislation, misrepresentation in advertising and salesmanship, embezzlement and misapplication of funds, short weights and measures and misgrading of commodities, tax frauds, misapplication of funds in receiverships and bankruptcies. These are what Al Capone called "the legitimate rackets." These and many others are found in abundance in the business world. . . .

These varied types of white-collar crimes in business and the professions consist principally of violation of delegated or implied trust, and many of them can be reduced to two categories: misrepresentation of asset values and duplicity in the manipulation of power. The first is approximately the same as fraud or swindling; the second is similar to the double-cross. The latter is illustrated by the corporation director who, acting on inside information, purchases land which the corporation will need and sells it at a fantastic profit to his corporation. The principle of this duplicity is that the offender holds two antagonistic positions, one of which is a position of trust, which is violated, generally by misapplication of funds, in the interest of the other position. A football coach, permitted to referee a game in which his own team was playing, would illustrate this antagonism of positions. Such situations cannot be completely avoided in a complicated business structure, but many concerns make a practice of assuming such antagonistic functions and regularly violating the trust thus delegated to them. When compelled by law to make a separation of their functions, they make a nominal separation and continue by subterfuge to maintain the two positions. . . .

White-collar criminality in politics, which is generally recognized as fairly prevalent, has been used by some as a rough gauge by which to measure white-collar criminality in business. James A. Farley said, "The standards of conduct are as high among officeholders and politicians as they are in commercial life," and Cermak, while mayor of Chicago, said, "There is less graft in politics than in business." John Flynn wrote, "The average politician is the merest amateur in the gentle art of graft, compared with his brother in the field of business." And Walter Lippmann wrote, "Poor as they are, the standards of public life are so much more social than those of business that financiers who enter politics regard themselves as philanthropists."

These statements obviously do not give a precise measurement of the relative criminality of the white-collar class, but they are adequate evidence that crime is not so highly concentrated in the lower class as the usual statistics indicate. Also, these statements obviously do not mean that every business and professional man is a criminal, just as the usual theories do not mean that every man in the lower class is a criminal. On the other hand, the preceding statements refer in many cases to the leading corporations in America and are not restricted to the disreputable business and professional men who are called quacks, ambulance chasers, bucket-shop operators, dead-beats, and fly-by-night swindlers.[2]

The financial cost of white-collar crime is probably several times as great as the financial cost of all the crimes which are customarily regarded as the "crime problem." . . .

The financial loss from white-collar crime, great as it is, is less important than the damage to social relations. White-collar crimes violate trust and therefore create distrust, which lowers social morale and produces social disorganization on a large scale. Other crimes produce relatively little effect on social institutions or social organization.

White-collar crime is real crime. It is not ordinarily called crime, and calling it by this name does not make it worse, just as refraining from calling it crime does not make it better than it otherwise would be. It is called crime here in order to bring it within the scope of criminology, which is justified because it is in violation of the criminal law. The crucial question in this analysis is the criterion of violation of the criminal law. Conviction in the criminal court, which is sometimes suggested as the criterion, is not adequate because a large proportion of those who commit crimes are not convicted in criminal courts. This criterion, therefore, needs to be supplemented. When it is supplemented, the criterion of the crimes of one class must be kept consistent in general terms with the criterion of the crimes of the other class. The definition should not be the spirit of the law for white-collar crimes and the letter of the law for other crimes, or in other respects be more liberal for one class than for the other. Since this discussion is concerned with the conventional theories of the criminologists, the criterion of white-collar crime must be justified in terms of the procedures of those criminologists in dealing with other crimes. The criterion of white-collar crimes, as here proposed, supplements convictions in the criminal courts in four respects, in each of which the extension is justified because the criminologists who present the conventional theories of criminal behavior make the same extension in principle.

First, other agencies than the criminal court must be included, for the criminal court is not the only agency which makes official decisions regarding violations of the criminal law. The juvenile court, dealing largely with offenses of the children of the poor, in many states is not under the criminal jurisdiction. The criminologists have made much use of case histories and statistics of juvenile delinquents in constructing their theories of criminal behavior. This

---

[2]Perhaps it should be repeated that "white-collar" (upper) and "lower" classes merely designate persons of high and low socioeconomic status. Income and amount of money involved in the crime are not the sole criteria. Many persons of "low" socioeconomic status are "white-collar" criminals in the sense that they are well dressed, well-educated, and have high incomes, but "white collar" as used in this paper means "respected," "socially accepted and approved," "looked up to." Some people in this class may not be well-dressed or well-educated, nor have high incomes, although the "upper" usually exceed the "lower" classes in these respects as well as in social status.

justifies the inclusion of agencies other than the criminal court which deal with white-collar offenses. The most important of these agencies are the administrative boards, bureaus, or commissions, and much of their work, although certainly not all, consists of cases which are in violation of the criminal law. The Federal Trade Commission recently ordered several automobile companies to stop advertising their interest rate on installment purchases as 6 percent, since it was actually 11$\frac{1}{2}$ percent. Also it filed complaint against *Good Housekeeping,* one of the Hearst publications; charging that its seals led the public to believe that all products bearing those seals had been tested in their laboratories, which was contrary to fact. Each of these involves a charge of dishonesty, which might have been tried in a criminal court as fraud. A large proportion of the cases before these boards should be included in the data of the criminologists. Failure to do so is a principal reason for the bias in their samples and the errors in their generalizations.

Second, for both classes, behavior which would have a reasonable expectancy of conviction if tried in a criminal court or substitute agency should be defined as criminal. In this respect, convictability rather than actual conviction should be the criterion of criminality. The criminologists would not hesitate to accept as data a verified case history of a person who was a criminal but had never been convicted. Similarly, it is justifiable to include white-collar criminals who have not been convicted, provided reliable evidence is available. Evidence regarding such cases appears in many civil suits, such as stockholders' suits and patent-infringement suits. These cases might have been referred to the criminal court but they were referred to the civil court because the injured party was more interested in securing damages than in seeing punishment inflicted. This also happens in embezzlement cases, regarding which surety companies have much evidence. In a short consecutive series of embezzlements known to a surety company, 90 percent were not prosecuted because prosecution would interfere with restitution or salvage. The evidence in cases of embezzlement is generally conclusive, and would probably have been sufficient to justify conviction in all of the cases in this series.

Third, behavior should be defined as criminal if conviction is avoided merely because of pressure which is brought to bear on the court or substitute agency. Gangsters and racketeers have been relatively immune in many cities because of their pressure on prospective witnesses and public officials, and professional thieves, such as pickpockets and confidence men who do not use strong-arm methods, are even more frequently immune. The conventional criminologists do not hesitate to include the life histories of such criminals as data, because they understand the generic relation of the pressures to the failure to convict. Similarly, white-collar criminals are relatively immune because of the class bias of the courts and the power of their class to influence the implementation and administration of the law. The class bias affects not merely present-day courts but to a much greater degree affected the earlier courts which established the precedents and rules of procedure of the present-day courts. Consequently, it is justifiable to interpret the actual or potential failures of conviction in the light of known facts regarding the pressures brought to bear on the agencies which deal with offenders.

Fourth, persons who are accessory to a crime should be included among white-collar criminals as they are among other criminals. When the Federal Bureau of Investigation deals with a case of kidnapping, it is not content with catching the offenders who carried away the victim; they may catch and the court may convict twenty-five other persons who assisted by secreting the victim, negotiating the ransom, or putting the ransom money into circulation. On the other hand, the prosecution of white-collar criminals frequently stops with one offender. Political graft almost always involves collusion between politicians and business men but prosecutions are generally limited to the politicians. Judge Manton was found guilty of accepting $664,000 in bribes, but the six or eight important commercial concerns that paid the bribes have not been prosecuted. Pendergast, the late boss of Kansas City, was convicted for failure to report as a part of his income $315,000 received in bribes from insurance companies, but the insurance companies which paid the bribes have not been prosecuted. In an investigation of an embezzlement by the president of a bank, at least a dozen other violations of law which were related to this embezzlement and involved most of the other officers of the bank and the officers of the clearing house, were discovered but none of the others was prosecuted.

This analysis of the criterion of white-collar criminality results in the conclusion that a description of white-collar criminality in general terms will be also a description of the criminality of the lower class. The respects in which the crimes of the two classes differ are the incidentals rather than the essentials of criminality. They differ principally in the implementation of the criminal laws which apply to them. The crimes of the lower class are handled by policemen, prosecutors, and judges, with penal sanctions in the form of fines, imprisonment, and death. The crimes of the upper class either result in no official action at all, or result in suits for damages in civil courts, or are handled by inspectors, and by administrative boards or commissions, with penal sanctions in the form of warnings, orders to cease and desist, occasionally the loss of a license, and only in extreme cases by fines or prison sentences. Thus, the white-collar criminals are segregated administratively from other criminals, and largely as a consequence of this are not regarded as real criminals by themselves, the general public, or the criminologists.

This difference in the implementation of the criminal law is due principally to the difference in the social position of the two types of offenders. Judge Woodward, when imposing sentence upon the officials of the H. O. Stone and Company, bankrupt real estate firm in Chicago, who had been convicted . . . of the use of the mails to defraud, said to them, "You are men of affairs, of experience, of refinement and culture, of excellent reputation and standing in the business and social world." That statement might be used as a general characterization of white-collar criminals for they are oriented basically to legitimate and respectable careers. Because of their social status they have a loud voice in determining what goes into the statutes and how the criminal law as it affects themselves is implemented and administered. . . .

[This] should be regarded neither as an assertion that all efforts to influence legislation and its administration are reprehensible nor as a particularistic interpretation of the criminal law. It means only that the upper class has greater influence in moulding the criminal law and its administration to its own interests than does the lower class. The privileged position of white-collar criminals before the law results to a slight extent from bribery and political pressures, principally from the respect in which they are held and without special effort on their part. The most powerful group in medieval society secured relative immunity by "benefit of clergy," and now our most powerful groups secure relative immunity by "benefit of business or profession."

In contrast with the power of the white-collar criminals is the weakness of their victims. Consumers, investors, and stockholders are unorganized, lack technical knowledge, and cannot protect themselves. Daniel Drew, after taking a large sum of money by sharp practice from Vanderbilt in the Erie deal, concluded that it was a mistake to take money from a powerful man on the same level as himself and declared that in the future he would confine his efforts to outsiders, scattered all over the country, who wouldn't be able to organize and fight back. White-collar criminality flourishes at points where powerful business and professional men come in contact with persons who are weak. In this respect, it is similar to stealing candy from a baby. Many of the crimes of the lower class, on the other hand, are committed against persons of wealth and power in the form of burglary and robbery. Because of this difference in the comparative power of the victims, the white-collar criminals enjoy relative immunity.

Embezzlement is an interesting exception to white-collar criminality in this respect. Embezzlement is usually theft from an employer by an employee, and the employee is less capable of manipulating social and legal forces in his own interest than is the employer,. As might have been expected, the laws regarding embezzlement were formulated long before laws for the protection of investors and consumers.

The theory that criminal behavior in general is due either to poverty or to the psychopathic and sociopathic conditions associated with poverty can now be shown to be invalid for three reasons. First, the generalization is based on a biased sample which omits almost entirely the behavior of white-collar criminals. The criminologists have restricted their data, for reasons of convenience and ignorance rather than of principle, largely to cases dealt with in criminal courts and juvenile courts, and these agencies are used principally for criminals from the lower economic strata. Consequently, their data are grossly biased from the point of view of the economic status of criminals and their generalization that criminality is closely associated with poverty is not justified.

Second, the generalization that criminality is closely associated with poverty obviously does not apply to white-collar criminals. With a small number of exceptions, they are not in poverty, were not reared in slums or badly deteriorated families, and are not feebleminded or psychopathic. They were seldom problem children in their earlier years and did not appear in juvenile courts or child guidance clinics. The proposition, derived from the data used by the conventional criminologists, that "the criminal of today was the problem child of yesterday" is seldom true of white-collar criminals. The idea that the causes of criminality are to be found almost exclusively in childhood similarly is fallacious. Even if poverty is extended to include the economic stresses which afflict business in a period of depression, it is not closely correlated with white-collar criminality. Probably at no time within fifty years have white-collar crimes in the field of investments and of corporate management been so extensive as during the boom period of the twenties.

Third, the conventional theories do not even explain lower class criminality. The sociopaths and psychopathic factors which have been emphasized doubtless have something to do with crime causation, but these factors have not been related to a general process which is found both in white-collar criminality and lower class criminality and therefore they do not explain the criminality of either class. They may explain the manner or method of crime—why lower class criminals commit burglary or robbery rather than false pretenses.

In view of these defects in the conventional theories, an hypothesis that will explain both white-collar criminality and lower class criminality is needed. For reasons of economy, simplicity, and logic, the hypothesis should apply to both classes, for this will make possible the analysis of causal factors freed from the encumbrances of the administrative devices which have led criminologists astray. . . .

I have presented a brief and general description of white-collar criminality on a framework of argument regarding theories of criminal behavior. That argument, stripped of the description, may be stated in the following propositions:

1) White-collar criminality is real criminality, being in all cases in violation of the criminal law.

2) White-collar criminality differs from lower class criminality principally in an implementation of the criminal law which segregates white-collar criminals administratively from other criminals.

3) The theories of the criminologists that crime is due to poverty or to psychopathic and sociopathic conditions statistically associated with poverty are invalid because, first, they are derived from samples which are grossly biased with respect to socioeconomic status; second, they do not apply to the white-collar criminals; and third, they do not even explain the criminality of the lower class, since the factors are not related to a general process characteristic of all criminality.

4) A theory of criminal behavior which will explain both white-collar criminality and lower class criminality is needed. . . .

Is "White Collar Crime" Crime?

EDWIN H. SUTHERLAND

The argument has been made that business and professional men commit crimes which should be brought within the scope of the theories of criminal behavior.[1] In order to secure evidence as to the prevalence of such white collar crimes an analysis was made of the decisions by courts and commissions against the seventy largest industrial and mercantile corporations in the United States under four types of laws, namely, antitrust, false advertising, National Labor Relations, and infringement of patents, copyrights, and trademarks. This resulted in the finding that 547 such adverse decisions had been made, with an average of 7.8 decisions per corporation and with each corporation having at least 1.[2] Although all of these were decisions that the behavior was unlawful, only 49 or 9 per cent of the total were made by criminal courts and were *ipso facto* decisions that the behavior was criminal. Since not all unlawful behavior is criminal behavior, these decisions can be used as a measure of criminal behavior only if the other 498 decisions can be shown to be decisions that the behavior of the corporations was criminal.

This is a problem in the legal definition of crime and involves two types of questions: May the word *crime* be applied to the behavior regarding which these decisions were made? If so, why is it not generally applied and why have not the criminologists regarded white collar crime as cognate with other crime? The first question involves semantics, the second interpretation or explanation.

A combination of two abstract criteria is generally regarded by legal scholars as necessary to define crime, namely: legal description of an act as socially injurious, and legal provision of a penalty for the act.[3]

When the criterion of legally defined social injury is applied to these 547 decisions the conclusion is reached that all of the classes of behaviors regarding which the decisions were made are legally defined as socially injurious. This can be readily determined by the words in the statutes—"crime" or "misdemeanor" in some, and "unfair," "discrimination," or "infringement" in all the

---

Is 'White Collar Crime' Crime?" from *American Sociological Review* 10:132–39. Reprinted by permission.

[1] Edwin H. Sutherland, "White Collar Criminality," *American Sociological Review,* 5:1–12, February, 1940; Edwin H. Sutherland, "Crime and Business," *Annals of the American Academy of Political and Social Science.* 217:112–18, September, 1941.

[2] Paper on "Illegal Behavior of Seventy Corporations," to be published later.

[3] The most satisfactory analysis of the criteria of crime from the legal point of view may be found in the following papers by Jerome Hall: "Prolegomena to a Science of Criminal Law," *University of Pennsylvania Law Review.* 89:549–80, March, 1941; "Interrelations of Criminal Law and Torts," *Columbia Law Review.* 43:735–79, 967–1001, September–November, 1943; "Criminal Attempts—A Study of the Foundations of Criminal Liability," *Yale Law Review.* 49:789–840, March, 1940.

PANEL 2   What Travel Brochures Do Not Tell You

On July 22, 1999, Royal Caribbean Cruises Ltd., one of the world's largest cruise ship lines, pleaded guilty in six U.S. District Courts and was fined $18 million for routinely dumping oil and hazardous chemicals from nine ships in coastal waters around the United States. Royal Caribbean also admitted that it continued to dump criminally for a month after it was convicted earlier on similar charges and had promised to stop. The firm dumped oil and toxic solvents or toxic chemicals in New York Harbor, in Miami, in the Virgin Islands, in Los Angeles, and in the Alaskan Inside Passage. It pleaded guilty to 21 counts of polluting and lying about it as representative of many more illegal acts. U.S. Attorney General Janet Reno said Royal Caribbean cruise ships used "secret bypass pipes" to dump waste oil and toxic materials overboard, often at night. Ship personnel falsified log books that they referred to by a Norwegian word meaning "fairy tale book." By dumping the substances criminally, the company saved tens of thousands of dollars per ship per year on oil filters and the dockside disposal of hundreds of thousands of gallons of toxic substances. Ship engineers won bonuses for minimizing expenses. Steven P. Solow, chief of the environmental crimes section of the U.S. Department of Justice, said that the company had a "culture of crime." He added that crew members on Royal Caribbean ships wore buttons that said "Save the Whales."

Sources: New York Times, Los Angeles Times, and *Boston Globe,* July 22, 1999.

---

others. The persons injured may be divided into two groups: first, a relatively small number of persons engaged in the same occupation as the offenders or in related occupations, and, second, the general public either as consumers or as constituents of the general social institutions which are affected by the violations of the laws. The antitrust laws are designed to protect competitors and also to protect the institution of free competition as the regulator of the economic system and thereby to protect consumers against arbitrary prices, and to protect the institution of democracy against the dangers of great concentration of wealth in the hands of monopolies. Laws against false advertising are designed to protect competitors against unfair competition and also to protect consumers against fraud. The National Labor Relations Law is designed to protect employees against coercion by employers and also to protect the general public against interferences with commerce due to strikes and lockouts. The laws against infringements are designed to protect the owners of patents, copyrights, and trademarks against deprivation of their property and against unfair competition, and also to protect the institution of patents and copyrights which was established in order to "promote the progress of science and the useful arts." Violations of these laws are legally defined as injuries to the parties specified.

Each of these laws has a logical basis in the common law and is an adaptation of the common law to modern social organization. False advertising is related to common law fraud, and infringement to larceny. The National Labor Relations Law, as an attempt to prevent coercion, is related to the common law prohibition of restrictions on freedom in the form of assault, false imprisonment, and extortion. For at least two centuries prior to the enactment of the modern antitrust laws the common law was moving against restraint of trade, monopoly, and unfair competition.

Each of the four laws provides a penal sanction and thus meets the second criterion in the definition of crime, and each of the adverse decisions under these four laws, except certain decisions under the infringement laws to be discussed later, is a decision that a crime was committed. This conclusion will be made more specific by analysis of the penal sanctions provided. . . .

The Sherman antitrust law states explicitly that a violation of the law is a misdemeanor. Three methods of enforcement of this law are provided, each of them involving procedures regarding misdemeanors. First, it may be enforced by the usual criminal prosecution, resulting in the imposition of fine or imprisonment. Second, the attorney general of the United States and the several district attorneys are given the "duty" of "repressing and preventing" violations of the law by petitions for injunctions, and violations of the injunctions are punishable as contempt of court. This method of enforcing a criminal law was an invention and, as will be described later, is the key to the interpretation of the differential implementation of the criminal law as applied to white collar criminals. Third, parties who are injured by violations of the law are authorized to sue for damages, with a mandatory provision that the damages awarded be three times the damages suffered. These damages in excess of reparation are penalties for violation of the law. They are payable to the injured party in order to induce him to take the initiative in the enforcement of the criminal law and in this respect are similar to the earlier methods of private prosecutions under the criminal law. All three of these methods of enforcement are based on decisions that a criminal law was violated and therefore that a crime was committed; the decisions of a civil court or a court of equity as to these violations are as good evidence of criminal behavior as is the decision of a criminal court.

The Sherman antitrust law has been amended by the Federal Trade Commission Law, the Clayton Law, and several other laws. Some of these amendments define violations as crimes and provide the conventional penalties, but most of the amendments do not make the criminality explicit. A large proportion of the cases which are dealt with under the amendments could be dealt with, instead, under the original Sherman Law, which is explicitly a criminal law. In practice, the amendments are under the jurisdiction of the Federal Trade Commission, which has authority to make official decisions as to violations. The Commission has two principal sanctions under its control, namely: the stipulation and the cease and desist order. The Commission may, after the violation of the law has been proved, accept a stipulation from the corporation that it will not violate the law in the future. Such stipulations are customarily restricted to the minor or technical violations. If a stipulation is violated or if no stipulation is accepted, the Commission may issue a cease and desist order; this is equivalent to a court's injunction except that violation is not punishable as contempt. If the Commission's desist order is violated, the Commission may apply to the court for an injunction, the violation of which is punishable as contempt. By an amendment to the Federal Trade Commission Law in the Wheeler–Lea Act of 1938 an order of the Commission becomes "final" if not officially questioned within a specified time and thereafter its violation is punishable by a civil fine. Thus, although certain interim procedures may be used in the enforcement of the amendments to the antitrust law, fines or imprisonment for contempt are available if the interim procedures fail. In this respect the interim procedures are similar to probation in ordinary criminal cases. An unlawful act is not defined as criminal by the fact that it is punished, but by the fact that it is punishable. Larceny is as truly a crime when the thief is placed on probation as when he is committed to prison. The argument may be made that punishment for contempt of court is not punishment for violation of the original law and that, therefore, the original law does not contain a penal sanction. This reasoning is specious since the original law provides the injunction with its penalty as a part of the procedure for enforcement. Consequently all of the decisions made under the amendments to the antitrust law are decisions that the corporations committed crimes.[4] . . .

In the preceding discussion the penalties which are definitive of crime have been limited to fine, imprisonment, and punitive damages. In addition, the stipulation, the desist order, and the injunction, without reference to punishment for contempt, have the attributes of punishment. This is evident both in that they result in some suffering on the part of the corporation against which they are issued and also in that they are designed by legislators and administrators to produce suffering. The suffering is in the form of public shame. . . The design is shown in the sequence of sanctions used by the Federal Trade Commission. The stipulation involves the least publicity and the least discomfort, and it is used for minor and technical violations. The desist order is used if the stipulation is violated and also if the violation of the law is appraised by the Commission as wilful and major. This involves more public shame; this shame is somewhat mitigated by the statements made by corporations, in exculpation, that such orders are merely the acts of bureaucrats. Still more shameful to the corporation is an injunction issued by a court. The shame resulting from this order is sometimes mitigated and the corporation's

---

[4]Some of the antitrust decisions were made against meat packers under the Packers and Stockyards Act. The penal sanctions in this act are essentially the same as in the Federal Trade Commission Act.

face saved by taking a consent decree.[5] The corporation may insist that the consent decree is not an admission that it violated the law. For instance, the meat packers took a consent decree in an antitrust case in 1921, with the explanation that they had not knowingly violated any law and were consenting to the decree without attempting to defend themselves because they wished to co-operate with the government in every possible way. This patriotic motivation appeared questionable, however, after the packers fought during almost all of the next ten years for a modification of the decree. Although the sequence of stipulation, desist order, and injunction indicates that the variations in public shame are designed, these orders have other functions, as well, especially a remedial function and the clarification of the law in a particular complex situation.

The conclusion in this semantic portion of the discussion is that 473 of the 547 decisions are decisions that crimes were committed.

This conclusion may be questioned on the ground that the rules of proof and evidence used in reaching these decisions are not the same as those used in decisions regarding other crimes, especially that some of the agencies which rendered the decisions did not require proof of criminal intent and did not presume the accused to be innocent. These rules of criminal intent and presumption of innocence, however, are not required in all prosecutions under the regular penal code and the number of exceptions is increasing. In many states a person may be committed to prison without protection of one or both of these rules on charges of statutory rape, bigamy, adultery, passing bad checks, selling mortgaged property, defrauding a hotel keeper, and other offenses.[6] Consequently, the criteria which have been used in defining white collar crimes are not categorically different from the criteria used in defining other crimes, for these rules are abrogated both in regard to white collar crimes and other crimes, including some felonies. The proportion of decisions rendered against corporations without the protection of these rules is probably greater than the proportion rendered against other criminals, but a difference in proportions does not make the violations of law by corporations categorically different from the violations of laws by other criminals. Moreover, the difference in proportion, as the procedures actually operate is, not great. On the one side, many of the defendants in usual criminal cases, being in relative poverty, do not get good defense and consequently secure little benefit from these rules; on the other hand, the Commissions come close to observing these rules of proof and evidence although they are not required to do so. This is illustrated by the procedure of the Federal Trade Commission in regard to advertisements. Each year it examines several hundred thousand advertisements and appraises about 50,000 of them as probably false. From the 50,000

---

[5]The consent decree may be taken for other reasons, especially because it cannot be used as evidence in other suits.

[6]Livingston Hall, "Statutory Law of Crimes, 1887–1936," *Harvard Law Review* 50:616–53, February, 1937.

it selects about 1,500 as patently false. For instance, an advertisement of gum-wood furniture as "mahogany" would seldom be an accidental error and would generally result from a state of mind which deviated from honesty by more than the natural tendency of human beings to feel proud of their handiwork.

The preceding discussion has shown that these seventy corporations committed crimes according to 473 adverse decisions, and also has shown that the criminality of their behavior was not made obvious by the conventional procedures of the criminal law but was blurred and concealed by special procedures. This differential implementation of the law as applied to the crimes of corporations eliminates or at least minimizes the stigma of crime. . . .

Three factors assist in explaining this differential implementation of the law, namely, the status of the business man, the trend away from punishment, and the relatively unorganized resentment of the public against white collar criminals. Each of these will be described.

First, the methods used in the enforcement of any law are an adaption to the characteristics of the prospective violators of the law, as appraised by the legislators and the judicial and administrative personnel. The appraisals regarding business men, who are the prospective violators of the four laws under consideration, include a combination of fear and admiration. Those who are responsible for the system of criminal justice are afraid to antagonize business men; among other consequences, such antagonism may result in a reduction in contributions to the campaign funds needed to win the next election. Probably much more important is the cultural homogeneity of legislators, judges, and administrators with business men. Legislators admire and respect business men and cannot conceive of them as criminals, that is, business men do not conform to the popular stereotype of "the criminal." The legislators are confident that these business men will conform as a result of very mild pressures.

This interpretation meets with considerable opposition from persons who insist that this is an egalitarian society in which all men are equal in the eyes of the law. It is not possible to give a complete demonstration of the validity of this interpretation but four types of evidence are presented in the following paragraphs as partial demonstration.

The Department of Justice is authorized to use both criminal prosecutions and petitions in equity to enforce the Sherman antitrust law. The Department has selected the method of criminal prosecution in a larger proportion of cases against trade unions than of cases against corporations, although the law was enacted primarily because of fear of the corporations. From 1890 to 1929 the Department of Justice initiated 438 actions under this law with decisions favorable to the United States. Of the actions against business firms and associations of business firms, 27 per cent were criminal prosecutions, while of the actions against trade unions 71 per cent were criminal prosecutions.[9] This

---

[9]Percentages compiled from cases listed in the report of the Department of Justice "Federal Antitrust Laws, 1938."

shows that the Department of Justice has been comparatively reluctant to use a method against business firms which carries with it the stigma of crime.

The method of criminal prosecution in enforcement of the Sherman antitrust law has varied from one presidential administration to another. It has seldom been used in the administrations of the presidents who are popularly appraised as friendly toward business. . . .

Business men suffered their greatest loss of prestige in the depression which began in 1929. It was precisely in this period of low status of business men that the most strenuous efforts were made to enforce the old laws and enact new laws for the regulation of business men. The appropriations for this purpose were multiplied several times and persons were selected for their vigor in administration of the laws. Of the 547 decisions against the seventy corporations during their life careers, which have averaged about forty years, 63 per cent were rendered in the period 1935–43, that is, during the period of the low status of business men.

The Federal Trade Commission Law states that a violation of the antitrust laws by a corporation shall be deemed to be, also, a violation by the officers and directors of the corporation. However, business men are practically never convicted as persons and several cases have been reported, like the six per cent case against the automobile manufacturers, in which the corporation was convicted and the persons who direct the corporation were all acquitted.[10] . . .

White collar crime is similar to juvenile delinquency in respect to the differential implementation of the law. In both cases, the procedures of the criminal law are modified so that the stigma of crime will not attach to the offenders. The stigma of crime has been less completely eliminated from juvenile delinquents than from white collar criminals because the procedures for the former are a less complete departure from conventional criminal procedures, because most juvenile delinquents come from a class with low social status, and because the juveniles have not organized to protect their good names. Because the juveniles have not been successfully freed from the stigma of crime they have been generally held to be within the scope of the theories of criminology and in fact provide a large part of the data for criminology; because the external symbols have been more successfully eliminated from white collar crimes, white collar crimes have generally not been included within these theories.

A third factor in the differential implementation of the law is the difference in the relation between the law and the mores in the area of white collar crime. The laws under consideration are recent and do not have a firm foundation in public ethics or business ethics; in fact certain rules of business ethics, such as the contempt for the "price chiseler," are generally in conflict with the law. These crimes are not obvious, as is assault and battery, and can be appre-

---

[10]The question may be asked, "If business men are so influential, why did they not retain the protection of the rules of the criminal procedure?" The answer is that they lost this protection, despite their status, on the principle "You can't eat your cake and have it, too."

ciated readily only by persons who are expert in the occupations in which they occur. A corporation often violates a law for a decade or longer before the administrative agency becomes aware of the violation, and in the meantime the violation may have become accepted practice in the industry. The effects of a white collar crime upon the public are diffused over a long period of time and perhaps over millions of people, with no person suffering much at a particular time. The public agencies of communication do not express and organize the moral sentiments of the community as to white collar crimes in part because the crimes are complicated and not easily presented as news, but probably in greater part because these agencies of communication are owned or controlled by the business men who violate the laws and because these agencies are themselves frequently charged with violations of the same laws. Public opinion in regard to picking pockets would not be well organized if most of the information regarding this crime came to the public directly from the pickpockets themselves.

This third factor, if properly limited, is a valid part of the explanation of the differential implementation of the law. It tends to be exaggerated and become the complete explanation in the form of a denial that white collar crimes involve any moral culpability whatever. On that account it is desirable to state a few reasons why this factor is not the complete explanation.

The assertion is sometimes made that white collar crimes are merely technical violations and involve no moral culpability, i.e., violation of the mores, whatever. In fact, these white collar crimes, like other crimes, are distributed along a continuum in which the *mala in se* are at one extreme and the *mala prohibita* at the other.[12] None of the white collar crimes is purely arbitrary as is the regulation that one must drive on the right side of the street, which might equally well be that he must drive on the left side. The Sherman antitrust law, for instance, is regarded by many persons as an unwise law and it may well be that some other policy would be preferable. It is questioned principally by persons who believe in a more collectivistic economic system, namely, the communists and the leaders of big business, while its support comes largely from an emotional ideology in favor of free enterprise which is held by farmers, wage-earners, small business men, and professional men. Therefore, as appraised by the majority of the population it is necessary for the preservation of American Institutions and its violation is a violation of strongly entrenched moral sentiments.

The sentimental reaction toward a particular white collar crime is certainly different from that toward some other crimes. This difference is often exaggerated, especially as the reaction occurs in urban society. The characteristic reaction of the average citizen in the modern city toward burglary is apathy unless he or his immediate friends are victims or unless the case is very spectacular. The average citizen, reading in his morning paper that the home

---

[12]An excellent discussion of this continuum is presented by Jerome Hall, "Prolegemena to a Science of Criminal Law," *University of Pennsylvania Law Review,* 89:563–69, March, 1941.

of an unknown person has been burglarized by another unknown person, has no appreciable increase in blood pressure. Fear and resentment develop in modern society primarily as the result of the accumulation of crimes as depicted in crime rates or in general descriptions, and this develops both as to white collar crimes and other crimes.

Finally, although many laws have been enacted for the regulation of occupations other than business, such as agriculture or plumbing, the procedures used in the enforcement of those other laws are more nearly the same as the conventional criminal procedures, and law-violators in these other occupations are not so completely protected against the stigma of crime as are business men. The relation between the law and the mores tends to be circular. The mores are crystallized in the law and each act of enforcement of the laws tends to re-enforce the mores. The laws regarding white collar crime which conceal the criminality of the behavior, have been less effective than other laws in re-enforcement of the mores.

PANEL 3   Abuse of Office

In 1992, a federal jury convicted David Lanier, a chancery judge and former mayor of Dyersburg, Tennessee, on seven counts of sexually assaulting women who worked in his courthouse or came before him with legal matters. Evidence suggested that Lanier had engaged in this pattern of conduct over a period of years. One victim, a juvenile court supervisor, said that he grabbed her breasts and buttocks and pinned her to a chair. When she later confronted him about the incident, he demoted her. Another victim, a 26-year-old women with a child custody case before Lanier testified that she was forced to perform oral sex on him in his chambers. Prior to judicial imposition of sentence of 25 years confinement, the prosecutor cast Lanier as a criminal for whom "power was the aphrodisiac . . . [Victims'] crying turned him on." Two years after he began serving his prison term, the former judge was ordered released from prison after a federal appeals court ruled in favor of his appeal. When the U.S. Supreme Court ordered the appeals court to reconsider its decision, Lanier was ordered back to prison. The former judge went on the lam, however, and was not located until two months later in Mexico, where he was living under an assumed name. When arrested, Lanier was picking up mail-order false identification papers. Returned to the United States, he told the judge that his decision to flee was a "bad judgment call."

Sources: Memphis Commercial Appeal, December 19, 1992, page A1; *Washington Post,* August 16, 1997, page A14; *USA Today,* October 15, 1997, page 19A; and *The Buffalo News,* December 31, 1997.

Collaring the Crime, Not the Criminal
Reconsidering the Concept of White-Collar Crime

SUSAN P. SHAPIRO

. . . Over the years, Sutherland's definition of "crime committed by a person of respectability and high social status in the course of his occupation" (1949, p. 9) has been criticized, refined, and debated by several cohorts of scholars (for reviews see Shapiro 1980 and Braithwaite 1985b). Yet the concept of white-collar crime in general currency is virtually unchanged. Current usage centers on some combination of characteristics of lawbreakers, specifying that they be upper-class or upper-status individuals, organizations or corporations, or incumbents of occupational roles (Clinard and Quinney 1973; Schrager and Short 1978).

The corresponding "white-collar," "organizational/corporate," or "occupational" crime labels variously delimit the conceptual terrain, but share a fundamental problem: they confuse acts with actors, norms with normbreakers, the modus operandi with the operator.[1] "Crime" is defined as an *act* in violation of the penal law (Black 1979, p. 334). Although attributes of the perpetrator (e.g., age, or gender, or mental state) may, on occasion, be necessary conditions for the application of certain criminal labels, they are never sufficient. These concepts provide no guidance regarding the characteristics of the acts committed or norms broken by these upper-crust offenders that constitute white-collar, corporate, organizational, or occupational crimes. Surely not all their misdeeds and negligent or harmful acts are white-collar crimes. Moreover, defining crimes by the characteristics of their perpetrators results in "an unfortunate mixing of definition and explanation" (Braithwaite 1985b, p. 3) that precludes the possibility of exploring empirically the relationship between social class and crime—the very reason Sutherland coined the phrase (Shapiro 1980; Reiss and Biderman 1980, pp. 1, 39).

The first task in liberating the white-collar crime concept requires disentangling this identification of the perpetrators with their misdeeds. The seeds to a solution can be found in Sutherland's earliest work. In a transitional paragraph that recurs in his writing, Sutherland moves from presenting definitions based on attributes of offenders to anecdotes or descriptive data about specific misdeeds:

"Collaring the Crime, Not the Criminal" from *American Sociological Review* 55 (June 1990): 346–365. Reprinted by permission.
[1]There are some exceptions that move in the right direction. Several conceptualizations interweave notions of occupational status, institutional position, or structural location in the social organization of work with elements of deception, guile, exploitation, or cover-up in the commission of illicit activities (Edelhertz 1980; Katz 1979b; Moore 1980; and Reiss and Biderman 1980).

These varied types of white-collar crimes in business and the professions consist principally of *violation of delegated or implied trust,* and many of them can be reduced to two categories: (1) misrepresentation of asset values and (2) duplicity in the manipulation of power. The first is approximately the same as fraud or swindling; the second is similar to the double-cross (1940, p. 3, italics added; see also 1941, p. 112 and 1949, pp. 152–8).

Unfortunately, neither Sutherland nor later scholars pursued the implications of this promising lead.[2] In this paper, I flesh out this inchoate notion of white-collar crime as a violation of trust, develop a conception of trust, and specify the nature of the acts proscribed by norms of trust. . . .

A CONCEPTION OF TRUST

The conception of trust developed here mirrors legal definitions of the fiduciary role more closely than conventional sociological definitions.

> [A fiduciary relationship exists w]here a person has his interests served by another, but has not himself agreed with that other the powers and duties to be exercised and discharged for his benefit . . . [nor has he] the general right to say how they are to be exercised and discharged for his benefit. . . . Here [the fiduciary] is a functionary who, within the limits of his powers and duties, is independent of, and not controlled by, the person for whose benefit he acts. In this independence, *this freedom from immediate control,* lies the final and decisive characteristic of the fiduciary office (Finn 1977, pp. 12–13, italics added).

This notion of trust as the absence of beneficiary control in asymmetric relationships,[3] lays the groundwork for the major themes of this paper. The concept of "agency" provides a starting point. In agency relationships, individuals or organizations act on behalf of another (the "principal"). Using a somewhat different paradigm, Coleman (1974, 1982) describes this process as one by which actors invest "sovereignty" in another. Sovereigns (i.e., principals), who have ultimate rights of ownership to resources, transfer power and delegate usage rights over these resources to their agents.[4] By doing so,

---

[2]This is not to suggest that social scientists have not studied trust (see, for example, Lahmann 1979; Barber 1993; and Gambetta 1988) or recognized the relationship between trust and crime (Reiss 1984; Wheeler, Mann, and Sarat 1988, pp. 76–9). Cressey's (1953) work on the social psychology of embezzlers described their misdeeds as the "criminal violation of financial trust." But, like Sutherland, Cressey neither defined trust nor made its relationship to white-collar crime problematic.

[3]My argument draws primarily from the work of Coleman (1974), Jensen and Meckling (1976), Mitnick (1980), Frankel (1983), Moe (1984), Clark (1985) Pratt and Zeckhauser (1985), and especially Shapiro (1987) and Heimer (1988).

[4]In Coleman's treatment, sovereigns are natural persons and the holders of delegated usage rights (i.e., agents) and corporate actors. In my formulation, both principals and agents, sovereigns who own resources and those to whom they delegate usage rights, can be either persons or organizations.

agents can perform a diverse array of services. They offer differentiated labor markets, specialization and expertise to principals who entrust property and delegate responsibility to agents to perform tasks they are unwilling or unable to accomplish themselves. Other agents provide contacts, intermediation, and brokering, offering a conduit to property, information, or exchange otherwise inaccessible to principals owing to physical, temporal, or social distance. Principals also entrust agents in order to accomplish complex projects that they could not undertake with limited resources, to enjoy economies of scale, to spread risk, and to anticipate future contingencies. These principals collectivize and participate in charities, labor unions, insurance, stocks and bonds, credit institutions, or retirement funds, administered for them by other agents.

The structure of agency relationships is profoundly unbalanced. First, in providing access and expertise and in bridging physical and social distance, agents hold monopolies of information that cannot readily be verified or assessed by their principals. These information asymmetries are of two kinds: (1) hidden information available to the agent on which his or her actions are based—what economists call "adverse selection"—and (2) hidden action of the agent in discharging his or her obligations—what economists call "moral hazard" (Arrow 1985, p. 38; Moe 1984). Second, in acting as holder of usage rights to resources, repository for delegated power, property, collective assets, responsibility, and discretion, agents have custody and control over other people's property, "the capacity to create wealth, and discretion over the distribution of opportunity" (Shapiro 1987, p. 629). Third, these "acting-for" roles are structurally ambivalent; they institutionalize conflict between fidelity to principal interests and agent self-interest.

Principals who choose to participate in agency relationships devise a number of risk-abatement strategies to minimize these so-called "agency costs." Principals carefully select their representatives. They seek out familiar agents from embedded structures of personal relations with which they have repeated contract or ongoing relationships and whose past behavior is known and whose integrity is readily established (Granovetter 1985). They may recruit agents whose interests coincide with their own so that, as agents pursue self-interest, they will also be furthering the interest of their principals. Where interests do not naturally coincide, principals may manipulate incentive structures—devising performance fees, profit-sharing plans, compensation or joint ownership arrangements, and the like—that artificially couple the interests of principal and agent, giving the agent a stake in the outcome.

Where principals have little control over the selection or incentives of agents, they may seek to reduce their vulnerability by limiting agent discretion. Contractural arrangements specify their preferences in advance, the procedures agents are to follow or the desired outcomes of agency relationships and stipulate sanctions if these contractural obligations are not met. Principals also devise policing or monitoring measures to oversee and evaluate the output of agent behavior and the performance of contractual obligations and to deter or, if necessary, sanction misconduct. Finally, anticipating the occasional failure of these social control or risk-abatement strategies, principals make side-bets by employing insurance, bonding, collateral, or other risk-sharing arrangements to cushion the blow of agent abuse.

Ironically, the very factors that drive principals into agency relationships impede the exercise of control. First, agents provide expertise to those who do not have it and who are, therefore, unable to specify or evaluate agent performance. Second, agents bridge physical and social distance in social exchange and are often further separated from their principals "by a pyramid of indirect ties" with intervening agents (Heimer 1988, p. 12). Principals therefore typically lack the access necessary to install familiar candidates into agency roles, experience "difficulty conveying information to agents about their interests, difficulty figuring out what incentives are most appropriate for each agent, difficulty making certain that intervening links in the chain do not siphon off some of the rewards or distort the message about what the principal desires," difficulty monitoring these agents to determine whether contractural agreements have been met, and difficulty imposing sanctions on errant agents in the network (Heimer 1988, p. 13).

Third, agents such as banks, municipal governments, charities, publicly-held companies, or pension funds collectivize the discrete interests of dispersed, multiple, and often changing principals. These "collective" agents, therefore, remain insulated from the preferences, demands, incentives, or surveillance of each discrete principal and relatively unresponsive to them. Indeed, relationships that couple single agents with multiple principals show a "tendency toward reversal of control" (White 1985, p. 205). As Galanter (1974) has observed, "repeat-players"—the agents—typically set normative agendas, not the "one-shotter" principals who seek to constrain agent performance. So agents rather than their principals often design the agency contract.

The fact that organizations frequently serve multiple principals represents another liability of collective agency relationships. Principals experience difficulty maintaining relations with those who fill organizational roles, monitoring behaviors hidden behind corporate walls, and piercing the corporate veil in order to communicate their preferences or apply incentives or sanctions to the invisible functionairies responsible for servicing their needs. As Coleman observes, as principals' "interests change, the change is less and less easily reflected in the important activities of society, because the interests are cast into corporate structure, and the actions are insulated from the men who gave corporate actors their power" (1974, p. 50).

Temporal features of many of these collective agency relationships further impair the ability of principals to monitor their agents. "Futures transactions"—investment, credit, insurance, pensions, and the like—"demand that commitment be conferred far in advance of payoff without any necessary confirmation during the interim that the return on investment will eventually be honored" (Shapiro 1987, p. 628); as principals patiently await delivery on agent promises—often for decades—there may be nothing relevant to oversee.

Fourth, principals empower agents to exercise discretion on their behalf, but contractual and other controls on discretion erode the benefits of agency. There is an acute "tension between the need to restrict the [agent] in order to prevent injury to the [principal], and the need to leave the [agent] free to act in order to benefit the [principal]. . . . if the [principal] lessens his exposure to loss by reducing the delegated power, he may also reduce the benefit expected from the relation" (Frankel 1983, pp. 826, 809).

Finally, principals rely (often unwittingly) on myriad agency relationships every day, many of them indirect and relatively trivial. Even if contractual specification and assessment of the obligations of these agents were possible, the sheer number of negotiations quickly becomes paralyzing. The "transaction costs involved in drawing up a detailed prior agreement covering all discretionary uses of power over the life of the relation would not only be enormous, but also would probably exceed the benefits of the proposed relation" (Frankel 1983, p. 813).

The concept of agency encompasses a broad range of "acting-for" relationships that vary considerably with respect to the ability of principals to select and terminate their agents, the amount of power or discretion delegated to agents, the ability of principals to monitor and sanction their agents, and so on. Though principals, especially those which are themselves repeat-playing organizations, may be able to implement these various risk-abatement strategies and exercise considerable control over their agents, increasingly agency relationships are asymmetric, enfeebling principals (Coleman 1982, p. 88).

In legal jargon, "agency" is reserved for the more symmetric relationships "in which the principal retains the power to control and direct the activities of the agent" (Clark 1985, p. 56). Those in which "one party is at the mercy of the other's discretion (Weinrib 1975, p. 7) are labeled "fiduciary" or "trust" relations and subject to much stricter legal rules and intrusive moral rhetoric (Clark 1985, p. 76, Finn 1977).

These trust or fiduciary rules do not provide substantive guidance regarding the exercise of the myriad agency roles that proliferate in complex societies (Stinchcombe 1986). Indeed, the whole point of trust as an alternative to contract is that agents must be trusted to define the parameters of and to exercise their particular brand of service or discretion. Trust articulates generic procedural norms that seek to check the inherent opportunities and temptations for abuse (Shapiro 1987, pp. 636–8). These norms reflect the fundamental structural imbalances of agency relationships: asymmetries of information; usage rights to resources, delegated power, custody, and discretion; and expertise. . . .

The violation and manipulation of the norms of trust—of disclosure, disinterestedness, and role competence—represent the modus operandi of white-collar crime.

THE VIOLATION OF TRUST

Despite the enormous imbalances of many fiduciary relationships and their vulnerability to abuse, these relationships persist. The norms of trust, reinforced by a social-control system of second-order trustees or guardians—accrediting organizations: fidelity, malpractice, or deposit insurance; bonds, guarantees, warranties, and collateral; boards of directors; independent auditors and accountants; private inspectorates; government or self-regulatory organizations; etc.—support these acts of faith (Shapiro 1987). . . .

Manipulators readily prey on trust relationships, exploiting the custody, discretion, and access to information and property offered by trustees to principals. They have refined the modus operandi of pedestrian property crime. Ordinary robbers steal directly from their victims by threats or actual violence. Trustee "robbers" become *confidence* men, women, and organizations and induce victims to part with their money or property with lies, misrepresentations, and deceptions rather than with brute force. Ordinary burglars steal by break-in or trespass. Instead of cultivating mechanical technology to break into a secured building, trustee "burglars" cultivate social technology to become trusted organizations or insiders in organizations rich with opportunity for exploiting their positions for personal or corporate advantage. In short, wayward trustees lie (violating disclosure norms) and steal (violating disinterestedness norms).[5]

As noted earlier, most conceptions of white-collar crime or corporate crime are preoccupied with actors rather than with acts. As a consequence, much of the work in the area tends to depict a vast undifferentiated canvas of negligence, inadvertence, malevolence, and evil or what I once sarcastically labeled "Corporate Torts: or All the Bad, Offensive, Hurtful Things Corporations Do" (1983, p. 307). This paper is not about all the bad, offensive, hurtful things trustees do; for white-collar crime is not about trustees but about norms of trust. Rather, the paper concentrates on how fiduciaries exploit the structural vulnerabilities of trust relationships through deception, self-interest, and, to a lesser extent, incompetence.

Lying

Because of information asymmetries, virtually all types of fiduciary relationships are vulnerable to misrepresentation, deception, exaggeration, omission, distortion, fabrication, or falsification of information by those in positions of trust. Lies abound in the ordinary world of work, where differentiation creates dependencies on the disclosures of co-workers. . . .

---

[5]To Sutherland (1940), they engage in "misrepresentation of asset values," fraud, and swindling (i.e., lying or they commit "duplicity in the manipulation of power" or "the double-cross" (i.e., stealing).

Other trustees exploit the physical and social barriers to information and property they possess. . . .

Stealing

Some trustees have difficulty abiding by the norm of disinterestedness, instead abrogating their commitment to those who have placed them in positions of trust in favor of personal or organizational aggrandizement. Some engage in what economists call "shirking"—"consumption of leisure on the job" (Jensen and Meckling 1976, p. 355), neglect of duties, less than vigorous effort to maximize principals' interests, and the like. Others exploit their custody of other people's property by simply taking. But the complex social organization of agency relationships affords alternative, longer lasting, and generally safer and more lucrative forms of fiduciary theft—for example, the abuse of discretion to serve personal interests (self-dealing) or the sale of fiduciary loyalty (corruption).

Misappropriation. Trustees have ample opportunities to steal directly from those they represent. With custody of other people's money and property, fiduciaries can embezzle funds, pilfer supplies and merchandise, or apply property, staff, or equipment for personal use; in British usage, they "fiddle" (Mars 1982; Cressey 1953, Hollinger and Clark 1983).

Collective forms of agency that gather the wealth of individual and organizational principals in publicly-held corporations, pensions, banks, mutual funds, insurance companies, and the like provide especially deep pockets into which trustees may be tempted to dip. . . .

Self-dealing. Agents are not merely the custodians of property; many are entrusted with discretionary responsibility for the disposition of property and the allocation of corporate largess. Some wayward trustees exercise this responsibility for personal benefit; they "self-deal." . . .

Corruption. Some trustees have limited opportunities to misappropriate or self-deal. They have no personal use for mainframe computers or B-1 bomber parts that they might pilfer; they have no outside financial interests to which they can direct company investments, contracts, or loans; they have no use for the corporate secrets or inside information to which have access. But outsiders often do. . . . These outsiders, lacking access to lucrative positions of trust, endeavor instead to buy the trustees and thereby gain access to privileges fiduciaries enjoy. Corruption thus represents an alternative form of theft, in which positions of trust are essentially rented or sold to outsiders.

Role conflict. Complete disinterestedness is impossible. Incumbents of positions of trust bring multiple interests and role obligations to fiduciary relationships. Some of these conflicting roles can be stripped, divested, or silenced. . . . But competing interests and obligations cannot be silenced entirely. Indeed, the expertise essential to some fiduciary positions insures that the ablest and most experienced individual and organizational candidates arrive with considerable baggage; independence often comes at the price of inexperience. In short, trust relationships are structurally duplicitous; conflict of interest represents an intrinsic vulnerability that gives rise to stealing.

THE GUISE OF TRUST: IMPLICATIONS
FOR SOCIAL CONTROL

The social organization of trust provides ample opportunity for deception. In trust relationships, principals are rarely able to observe their fiduciaries. They do not have access to vital information. They often lack the expertise to evaluate the conduct of trustees. Principals exchange symbolic proxies—bank statements, stock certificates, mortgages, commodities futures contracts, etc.—for tangible property. These pieces of paper or electronic impulses can be hidden, fabricated, or distorted more easily than the real commodities they represent. The acts of trustees are frequently hidden within a vast inter-organizational matrix that impedes surveillance or the attribution of responsibility. These acts are embedded in long-term relationships that often require a considerable period of time before principals realize that they have been deceived; indeed, some never learn of the deception.

These structural opportunities to victimize principals offer rich fodder for opportunity theories of deviance (Cloward and Ohlin 1960; Weisburd, Wheeler, Waring, and Bode, forthcoming). Structures of agency relationships may promote misconduct by furnishing "mechanisms for carrying out illegal acts and minimizing the risk of deception and sanctioning" (Vaughan 1983, p. 67), thereby undermining deterrence and affording wrongdoers time to pull off a successful "futures" scam. Theories of so-called "white-collar" deviance require the marriage of a systematic understanding of the distribution of structural opportunities for trust abuse with an understanding of the conditions under which individual or organizational fiduciaries seize or ignore these illicit opportunities. . . .

"LIBERATING" THE CONCEPT OF
WHITE-COLLAR CRIME

The Sutherland legacy is not easily cast aside. The concept of white-collar crime is polemically powerful and, notwithstanding considerable imprecision, palpably self-evident. My amendment of the concept as the violation or abuse of trust boasts neither of these virtues and poses additional problems.

First, operationalizing the acts of deception, self-interest, and incompetence poses complicated questions about offender knowledge and intent and about how to differentiate between abuse and normal variability in talent, candor, honesty, conscientiousness, selflessness, or fidelity. Still, many defiant acts—commonly considered corporate or white-collar crimes—committed by persons and organizations in positions of trust clearly do not violate trust norms: "corporate violence" that ensues from negligence, carelessness, or deliberate decisions to pursue profits over safety (e.g., the Exxon oil spill or Union Carbide in Bhopal), abuse of power (the My Lai massacre, police brutality, sexual harassment, or child abuse), some kinds of espionage, antitrust violations, and so forth. The cover up of these misdeeds may lead to ancillary deceptions that *do* violate trust norms, though.

Second, trust is not binary; rather it is located on a continuum defined by the degree of principal control in asymmetric agency relationships. One might think of some abusive relationships as being more "trust-like" than others—the deception of IUD wearers by the makers of the Dalkon Shield compared to the victimization of the U.S. Government by military contractors—but, again, some will want to see precise boundaries imposed on the continuum. . . .

Third, the conception of trust proffered here is normatively flexible. Fiduciary relationships are found in the underworld (among illicit drug producers and consumers or members of organized crime networks) as well as the upper-world and in private normative subcultures (academe, religious institutions, families, etc.) where trust may not enjoy legal protection. Sutherland's solution to this problem was to limit white-collar crime to "respectable" persons. But that begs the question of what constitutes respectability, fails to appreciate the extent to which disreputable manipulators of trust feign respectability in order to pull off their crime, and ignores the more tantalizing dilemma of role conflict and the possibility that respectable normative cultures demand contradictory obligations of their trustees. . . .

Fourth, the normative flexibility embodied in the notion of trust also means that, like Sutherland's white-collar "crimes," not all trust abuses are crimes or civil or administrative violations or even torts. Indeed, because of asymmetries between principals and trustees, many victims will be unable to muster a legal offensive and will be forced to accept their losses, thereby shielding misdeeds from official deviant labels of any sort.

It is tempting to develop a simple conceptual scheme or taxonomy that precisely identifies trust violations on each of these dimensions. But the task is futile because points of demarcation are socially contingent and particularistic (e.g., the degree of deception treated as a benign white lie in medical care or mere puffery in consumer advertising may constitute fraud in a stock prospectus or income tax return) and misguided because the variation a more rigorous conceptualization seeks to define away is precisely what is most intriguing sociologically about trust. To indulge the temptation is to resurrect the Sutherland error of mixing definition and explanation. If abuse of trust is to be theoretically empowering rather than imprisoning . . . sociologists will have to tolerate some conceptual openness, however frustrating. . . .

CONCLUSION

. . . Liberating the concept of white-collar crime means reclaiming the sociological agenda. It means acknowledging that offender characteristics such as class or organizational position are consequential and play a more complex role in creating opportunities for wrongdoing (Weisburd et al., forthcoming) and in shaping and frustrating the social control process than traditional stereotypes have allowed. It also means acknowledging that the focus on the offender has hindered our understanding of the deviant act and the role of organizational processes and macro social forces—the problems of asymmetry in modern societies, for example—in theories of crime and social control. . . . The related concepts of white-collar, corporate, and occupational crime have created an imprisoning framework for contemporary scholarship, impoverishing theory, distorting empirical inquiry, oversimplifying policy analysis, inflaming our muckraking instincts, and obscuring fascinating questions about the relationship between social organization and crime. . . .

[I]t is time to integrate the "white-collar" offenders into mainstream scholarship by looking beyond the perpetrators' wardrobe and social characteristics and exploring the modus operandi of their misdeeds and the ways in which they establish and exploit trust.

REFERENCES

Arrow, Kenneth. 1985. "The Economics of Agency." Pp. 37–51 in *Principals and Agents: The Structure of Business*, edited by John W. Pratt and Richard J. Zeckhauser. Boston: Harvard Business School Press.

Barber, Bernard. 1983. *The Logic and Limits of Trust*. New Brunswick: Rutgers.

Black, Henry Campbell. 1979. *Black's Law Dictionary*. St. Paul: West.

Braithwaite, John. 1985b. "White Collar Crime." *Annual Review of Sociology* 11:1–25.

Clark, Robert C. 1985. "Agency Costs versus Fiduciary Duties." Pp. 55–79 in *Principals and Agents: The Structure of Business*, edited by John W. Pratt and Richard J. Zeckhauser. Boston: Harvard Business School Press.

Clinard, Marshall B. and Richard Quinney. 1973. *Criminal Behavior Systems: A Typology*. New York: Holt, Rinehart and Winston.

Cloward, Richard A. and Lloyd E. Ohlin. 1960. *Delinquency and Opportunity*. New York: Free Press.

Coleman, James S. 1974. *Power and the Structure of Society*. New York: Norton.

———. 1982. *The Asymmetric Society*. Syracuse: Syracuse University Press.

Cressey, Donald R. 1953. *Other People's Money: A Study in the Social Psychology of Embezzlement*. Belmont, California: Wadsworth.

Edelhertz, Herbert. 1970. *The Nature, Impact and Prosecution of White Collar Crime*. Washington, D.C.: U.S. Government Printing Office.

Finn, Paul D. 1977. *Fiduciary Obligations*. Sydney, Australia: The Law Book Company.

Frankel, Tamar. 1983. "Fiduciary Law." *California Law Review* 71:795–836.

Galanter, Marc. 1974. "Why the 'Haves' Come Out Ahead: Speculations on the Limits of Legal Change." *Law and Society Review* 9:95–160.

Gambetta, Diego (ed.). 1988. *Trust: Making and Breaking Cooperative Relations.* New York: Basil Blackwell.

Granovetter, Mark. 1985. "Economic Action and Social Structure: The Problem of Embeddedness." *American Journal of Sociology* 91:481–510.

Heimer, Carol A. 1988. "Dimensions of the Agency Relationship." Paper presented at the Public Choice meetings, San Francisco (March).

Hollinger, Richard C. and John P. Clark. 1983. *Theft by Employees.* Lexington, Mass: D.C. Health.

Jensen, Michael C. and William M. Meckling. 1976. "Theory of the Firm: Managerial Behavior, Agency Costs and Ownership Structure." *Journal of Financial Economics* 3:305–60.

Katz, Jack. 1979b. "Legality and Equality: Plea Bargaining in the Prosecution of White-Collar and Common Crimes." *Law and Society Review* 13:431–59.

Luhmann, Niklas. 1979. *Trust and Power.* Chichester: Wiley.

Mars, Gerald. 1982. *Cheats at Work: An Anthropology of Workplace Crime.* London: Unwin Paperbacks.

Mitnick, Barry M. 1980. *The Political Economy of Regulation: Creating, Designing, and Removing Regulatory Forms.* New York: Columbia University Press.

Moe, Terry M. 1984. "The New Economics of Organization." *American Journal of Political Science* 28:739–77.

Reiss, Albert J., Jr. 1984. "Selecting Strategies of Social Control over Organizational Life." Pp. 23–35 in *Enforcing Regulation,* edited by Keith Hawkins and John M. Thomas. Boston: Kluwer-Nijhoff.

Reiss, Albert, J., Jr. and Albert Biderman. 1980. *Data Sources on White-Collar Law-Breaking.* Washington, D.C.: U.S. Department of Justice.

Schrager, Laura Shill and James F. Short, Jr. 1978. "Toward a Sociology of Organizational Crime." *Social Problems* 25:408–19.

Shapiro, Susan P. 1980. *Thinking About White Collar Crime: Matters of Conceptualization and Research.* Washington, D.C.: U.S. Government Printing Office.

———. 1983. "The New Moral Entrepreneurs: Corporate Crime Crusaders." *Contemporary Sociology* 12:304–7.

———. 1987. "The Social Control of Impersonal Trust." *American Journal of Sociology* 93:623–58.

Stinchcombe, Arthur L. 1986. *Stratification and Organization: Selected Papers.* Cambridge: Cambridge University Press.

Sutherland, Edwin H. 1940. "White-Collar Criminality." *American Sociological Review* 5:1–12.

———. 1949. *White Collar Crime.* New York: Holt, Rinehart & Winston.

Vaughan, Diane. 1983. *Controlling Unlawful Organizational Behavior.* Chicago: University of Chicago Press.

Weinrib, Ernest J. 1975. "The Fiduciary Obligation." *University of Toronto Law Journal* 25:1–22.

Weisburd, David. Stanton Wheeler, Elin Waring, and Nancy Bode. Forthcoming. *Crimes of the Middle Classes.* New Haven: Yale,.

Wheeler, Stanton. Kenneth Mann, and Austin Sarat. 1988. *Sitting in Judgment: The Sentencing of White-Collar Criminals.* New Haven: Yale.

White, Harrison C. 1985. "Agency as Control." Pp. 187–212 in *Principals and Agents: The Structure of Business,* edited by John W. Pratt and Richard J. Zeckhauser. Boston: Harvard Business School Press.

Organizational Crime

ALBERT J. REISS, JR., AND MICHAEL TONRY

Perhaps the most striking revolution of the twentieth century was the rapid expansion of the population of organizations. As the century draws to a close, the population of profit, not-for-profit, and governmental organizations in the United States rivals in number the population of individuals.

Both organizations and individuals may be regarded as behaving under the law. Many organizations, created by the acts of individuals, of corporate organizations, or of governments, are given a legal identity. Under the law, organizations are accorded distinct properties, such as a corporate form, a domicile, and recognition as a not-for-profit, a profit-making, or a governmental entity. Organizations can be held accountable for their behavior under the law, without any of the individuals who took actions on behalf of the organization being held legally accountable. Capital and not-for-profit organizations, for example, can be fined for violations of law—even to the point of bankruptcy. They can be placed on probation for violations of laws and be required to meet special conditions or perform community service, much as is the case for sanctioned individuals. . . .

Violations by and within organizations are facilitated by the behavior of other organizations in their or other networks. For example, enforcers or regulators of organizational behavior in various ways may account for the pattern of violations by organizations in the network. . . .

From an organizational perspective, however, violations by a particular class of individuals—for example, the affluent or those at the top of an industry, or of the less affluent who often become involved in the commission of violations—are less important than how persons of any class may become enmeshed in the patterned violations and hence be open to individual prosecution under the criminal law, to tort liability and litigation, or to regulatory sanctions like fines, loss of licenses, or registrations. . . .

I. FOUR FEATURES OF THE LEGAL CONTROL OF ORGANIZATIONS

Most theories and conceptions of law violation and of victimization center on persons rather than on organizations. Most criminological theories, including subcultural, social learning, and structural opportunity theories, focus on individuals and attempt to explain their behaviors. . . . Any examination of different kinds of law violations, however, makes it clear that an emphasis solely

"Organizational Crime" from *Beyond the Law: Crime in Complex Organizations* in *Crime & Justice* 18 (1993):1–19. Reprinted by permission.

or preponderantly on individuals can provide only an incomplete and impoverished account of crime in America.

Once the search for improved understanding of the causes of crime is widened to include organizations, four implications stand out. One is that organizations are central offenders in many violations of law. Most major violations of environmental pollution laws, for example, are committed by public and private organizations rather than by private individuals. It is organizations that must be controlled in the public interest. . . . Likewise, fraudulent record keeping and billing is endemic in the American nursing home industry. To remain financially solvent, many operators bill Medicaid for services that are not rendered. Similarly, institutional neglect of the well-being of nursing home residents is more of a problem for nursing home regulation than is employee abuse of residents. . . .

Second, organizations and collectivities of individuals (such as taxpayers, or residents of a town or neighborhood, or members of an association) are a major class of victims of crimes by individual offenders and by organizations. Vandals who destroy public property, such as parks and schools and public transportation equipment and facilities, directly victimize a corporate entity and indirectly victimize collectivities of taxpayers and users. Organizations that collude in fixing the prices of commodities or services may target organizations as well as individuals as their victims. . . .

Third, many individual violations of law and almost all organizational violations involve use of an organization's position of significant power, influence, or trust to commit the violation (Biderman and Reiss 1968). The insider trader who uses a position of access to information that will affect the market price of shares is an example, as is the use of appraisal, loan officer, corporate officer, and directors' positions in the savings and loan crisis.

Finally, it is evident that many violations of law are committed neither by individuals nor by organizations acting separately. Much organizational lawbreaking involves the use of the organizational power created by a network of organizations or the coercive power of a syndicated network. Recent notorious examples include allegations of price-fixing in bidding on public construction projects in many cities, allegations of nationwide collusive bidding for military and public school supply contracts by dairy products companies, and allegations of price-fixing by domestic airlines. . . .

II. FIVE LIMITATIONS OF THE WHITE-COLLAR CRIME LITERATURE ON ORGANIZATIONAL WRONGDOING

Since Sutherland (1945), the empirical criminological literature on white-collar crime has abounded with examples of organizations as violators. Critiques of that literature have drawn attention to five limitations. . . .

The first . . . is the general neglect of organizations as victims of law violations. . . . There are many other examples of how minor crimes, such as employee theft, are more costly to organizations than are felonies; a retailer that suffers "shrinkage" of 2, 4, or 10 percent of its inventory bears far greater financial burdens from shoplifting and employee theft than from store robberies. . . .

A second major limitation of the white-collar crime literature is the tendency to focus solely or preponderantly on large profit-making organizations and on the behavior of corporate officers and managers as major offenders; many violations by and against organizations are committed by people in lower-ranking white-collar and blue-collar positions. The corruption of authority endemic in large public police organizations in the United States, for example, normally involves the rank and file and line supervisors rather than the top command. . . .

A third limitation has been the tendency to focus on particular named organizations and the violations of their white-collar employees rather than on how industrial and commercial organization creates and sustains particular patterns of violation. The focus should be on opportunities the legal, economic, and regulatory structure of an industry provide for patterned law-breaking by organizations. For example, an examination of the highway construction industry might concentrate on major changes in the structure of competition in the industry, in the public bidding process and its regulations, and in supervision of performance contracts awarded.

By focusing on industrial systems and the environments they create, such as the savings and loan industry, or on market organization, such as that of garbage and trash collection or stock transactions, one can better understand how particular organizations and their employees become violators as a consequence of system organization and change. . . .

This limitation is closely related to a fourth. Typically, the control of organizational law violations is investigated by studying the behavior of enforcement or regulatory agencies and their agents and only rarely by focusing on how enforcement or regulation interacts with an environment. . . .

Finally, there is a tendency to treat violations of administrative law as violations of criminal law . . . in part because willful, persistent, or extreme violations of administrative regulations can constitute criminal offenses, many violations of law involve administrative regulations and are subject to administrative rather than criminal law proceedings. The failure to distinguish these two bodies of public law usually carries over into treating all organizational violators as white-collar criminals and all organizational violations as white-collar crimes. . . .

Too often, scholars and policy analysts from different specialties look at different aspects of a large and complex problem. The cumulative result too often resembles the portrayal of an elephant as a horse built by a committee. Criminologists interested in organizational crime have tended to adhere to the white-collar-crime emphases described earlier and too seldom have learned from sociologists of organization and bureaucracy, from economists and organizational theorists, and from legal and regulatory literatures. Each of these in turn generally fails to benefit from each others' learning and from the criminologists. . . .

We hope . . . that the understanding of organizational law violations is enhanced by bringing an organizational and social system analysis to the study of the behavior of organizations rather than relying principally on the traditional criminological analyses of white-collar and organized crimes and criminals. . . .

REFERENCES

Biderman, Albert D., and Albert J. Reiss, Jr. 1968. "On Exploring the 'Dark Figure' of Crime." *Annals of the American Academy of Political and Social Science* 374:1–15.
Sutherland, Edwin H. 1945. "Is 'White-Collar Crime' Crime?" *American Sociological Review* 10:132–39.

Crime and Capitalist Business Corporations

FRANK PEARCE

While Edwin Sutherland broadly defined white-collar crime as "crime committed by a person of respectability and high social status in the course of his "occupation" (Sutherland, 1949, p. 7), his research tended to focus on crimes involving businessmen and corporations (Friedrichs, 1992, pp. 18–19). This is especially evident in the original unbowdlerized version of *White-Collar Crime,* where he describes the key characteristics of corporations. According to Sutherland:

> The corporation probably comes closer to the "economic man" and to "pure reason" than any person or any other organization. The executives and directors not only have explicit and consistent objectives of maximum pecuniary gain but also have research and accountancy departments by which precise determination of results is facilitated. . . . The rationalistic, amoral, and nonsentimental behavior of the corporation was aimed in earlier days at technological efficiency; in later days more than previously it has been aimed at the manipulation of people by advertising, salesmanship, propaganda and lobbies (Sutherland, 1983, p. 236).

Accordingly, the corporation selects crimes which involve the smallest danger of detection and identification and against which victims are least likely to fight.

Adapted by the author from "Corporate Rationality as Corporate Crime" in *Studies in Political Economy,* vol. 40 (1993). Reprinted by permission of the publisher.

This paper builds on Sutherland's insights and demonstrates that corporate crimes should be viewed as distinct from other types of organizational crime. While corporate crimes are similar to organizational crimes, there are specific organizational factors that contribute to its occurrence that makes it distinct from other types of organizational crimes, such as governmental crime. Namely, they pursue the overarching goal of profit. This paper examines different forms of corporate organization and the various ways that they generate crime. This elaboration will make the distinction between the two more evident. It is argued in the conclusion that the limited-liability business corporation is inherently antisocial in that it routinely acts in ways that are harmful, illegal, and criminal.

ORGANIZATIONAL CONTEXT OF CORPORATE CRIME

Since most contemporary businesses, and hence most perpetrators of business crimes, are organizationally complex limited-liability corporations, it is useful to conceptualize their illegal behavior as corporate crimes and to explore the significance of doing so. One starting point for this discussion is Kramer's argument that:

> By the concept of "corporate crime," then, we wish to focus attention on criminal acts (of omission or commission) which are the result of deliberate decision making (or culpable negligence) of those who occupy structural positions within the organization as corporate executives or managers. These decisions are organizationally based—made in accordance with the normative goals (primarily corporate profit), standard operating procedures, and cultural norms of the organization—and are intended to benefit the corporation itself (Kramer, 1984, p. 18).

It is important to note that Kramer's definition is overly restrictive because many laws that are enforced by administrative bodies through the civil courts also regulate actions that cause injuries to specific individuals or that undermine social institutions. Indeed, the content of laws and the nature of such legal distinctions as those between crimes, torts, and administrative sanctions and between acts *mala in se* and *mala prohibita*, are conventional, time-bound social products without an intrinsic substantive meaning that transcends their social or historical contexts. Thus Kramer's definition needs extending to encompass "any act committed by corporations that is punished by the state, regardless of whether it is punished under administrative, civil or criminal law" (Clinard and Yeager, 1980, p. 16; Box, 1983).

Through references to negligence and the use of the phrase "omission or commission," Kramer's definition avoids the trap of arguing that there must be *actus reus* and *mens rea* for corporate crime to exist. Given the organizational locus and origins of corporate crime, it is often inappropriate to emphasize either an illegal *act* or an *intention* because each term is anthropomorphic and individualizing and because intention implies an unproblematic link between an act or omission and its consequence. Such simplistic causal sequencing leads to an obscuring of the construction and maintenance of a situation or context that, as a consequence, is fertile ground for violations. Any focus upon corporate crimes requires us to examine acts and intentions in terms of their *organizational production.*

It has been argued that "most corporate crimes cannot be explained by the perverse personalities of their perpetrators" (Braithwaite, 1984, p. 2), and this claim calls into question the proclivity to locate the source of evil deeds in evil people (see also Shrager and Short, 1977; Snider, 1993). Corporate crime can be produced by an organization's structure, its culture, its unquestioned assumptions, or its very modus operandi. Thus its understanding requires a shift from an individual to a structural perspective. This shift involves a recognition that organizations are the sites of complex relationships between individuals and wider groups, between these groups themselves, between these groups and the "organization," and between the organization and its various operating environments. Some of this complexity is highlighted by Box:

> The pursuit of organisational goals is deeply implicated in the cause(s) of corporate crime. But it is important to realise that these goals are not the manifestation of personal motives cast adrift from organisational moorings, neither are they disembodied acts committed in some metaphysical sense by corporations. Rather, organisational goals are what they are perceived to be by officials who have been socialised into the organisational "way of life" and who strive in a highly co-ordinate fashion to bring about collectively their realisation (Box, 1983, p. 21).

To speak of organizational goals should not be read as implying that there necessarily exists an identified set of goals within a particular organization. Of course, referring to organizational goals is important because doing so separates corporate crime from occupational crime. However, the reference to the furthering or pursuit of organizational goals can be problematic, since it conjures up images of perfect rationality on the part of corporations; that is, it implies that corporations have unequivocal sets of goals, that they are aware of them, that they are consistent, and that they are strategically developed and operationalized. Nevertheless, it is worth noting here that whether or not corporations are rational actors, they certainly *represent* themselves as such (Keane, 1995)—and this representation is a key to corporations' claims that they can and should regulate themselves (Pearce and Tombs, 1998). If corporations *are* rational actors, as they generally claim, then they could be held strictly accountable for their actions and inactions, including illegal behaviors; moreover, a rational actor would be expected to respond to regulatory and sentencing policies aimed at deterrence. On the other hand, if corporations *are not* rational actors, that is, if they lack any "directing mind," if they are fundamentally disorganized and sites of competing rationalities, or if they lack internal structures of accountability and responsibility, then they can open themselves up to interventionist forms of regulation so that regulators can prevent future corporate crimes in various contexts (for example, in relation to health, safety, and environmental law). While there is a body of work that sensitizes us to the importance of organizational factors in the determination of corporate conduct, what is lacking is a developed enough analysis of the different forms of corporate organization and the various ways in which they help generate corporate crime. The intention of the remaining portion of this paper is to attend to the (varying) nature of organizational forms in the context of their articulation with different legal categories. By doing so the distinction between corporate and other organizational crime will become more evident.

CORPORATIONS IN THE LAW

According to legal reasoning and practice a limited-liability corporation is made up of five elements: (1) the corporation itself, with its own legal personality; (2) its shareholders who can buy or sell stakes in the company and who are entitled to shares of the profits but who are not personally liable for its actions or its debts; (3) its directors, who are legally responsible for determining the corporation's policy goals, organization, and the kind of business it does; (4) its managers who are responsible for the day-to-day activities of the corporation's factories, chemical plants, and supermarket stores; and (5) the corporation's lower-level employees who cannot commit the corporation to particular lines of action but whose actions can create vicarious liability for their employer.

One implication of this corporate form is that shareholders can reap large profits at relatively low risk to themselves and given the volume of corporate crime it is clear that shareholders routinely benefit from such illegal activities (Clinard and Yeager, 1980; Snider, 1993). Directors and managers also are usually not personally liable for what the corporation does, or are insured against such liability. Routinely, when corporations are prosecuted for environmental and health and safety violations, it is only the corporation as a juristic person that is prosecuted and given the resources of most corporations, the fines result in little more than a minor tax (Etzioni, 1993). In fact, the law, in its use of the corporate personality:

> is both naive and sophisticated. It is naïve because it does not, cannot, recognise the reality of corporate structure; it is sophisticated because its inclusive reasoning system enables it to do so with impunity. . . . The criminal law, rather than recognising the fact that decisions are the product of systemic processes, focuses instead on individual intentionality. Until conscious changes are made to the law through legislation (such changes are unlikely if not impossible within the law's own analogic reasoning system) this crass anthropomorphism will persist (Weait, 1992, pp. 59–60).

On the other hand, once the corporation is recognized as a legal personality there is a tendency to view it as being like a private individual, free to engage in lawful private transactions, with its internal life and actions equally private, privileged, and unregulated. In the United States this has even included the right of corporations to have protection under the first, fourth, fifth, sixth, seventh, and fourteen amendments, severely limiting governmental regulation, investigation, and intervention (Mayer, 1990).

Although corporations may be treated as if they are persons for legal purposes, they only share some of the attributes of human beings, and lack many others. The contradictions that derive from the differences between a naturalized person (an individual human subject) and the naturalized legal person (a legal construct) is exemplified clearly in the issue of aggregation (Moran, 1992). The focus on individual actors is entirely inappropriate for a large corporation "because the way that responsibilities are distributed through a corporate body makes it extremely unlikely that the necessary fault will ever reside entirely in a single identifiable individual. Companies gain many benefits from the principle of aggregation" (Slapper, 1993, p. 435). Thus it is notable that the two convictions for corporate manslaughter in England and Wales have both been against small companies where the identification of the controlling mind is straightforward. In this respect, as in so many others, larger, complexly organized corporations enjoy an unequal advantage (Cahill, 1997).

Both corporations and individual human beings may engage in actions that further some basic overall goal. Individuals, however, often also are concerned with such nonteleological elements as integrity, autonomy, and responsibility even when these concerns cannot be shown to further a basic goal such as happiness. We regard them as intrinsically important and valuable and not simply as means to other more basic ends. On the other hand, as formal organizations, with particular goals such as the maximization of profits, growth, and survival, other things have ethical value for business corporations only insofar as they are instrumental in furthering their ultimate goals. Honesty and keeping one's word when dealings with other members of the organization are important to the extent that these operating principles ensure overall efficiency and the realization of the organizations' goals. And in dealing with those outside the organization they are important only if they are seen to function as operating conditions that set the upper limits to an organization's operations, for example, the scarcity of resources, of equipment, and of trained personnel. In organizational decision-making and planning such conditions must be taken into account as *data*. In this respect information about them is logically consistent with other information utilized in planning and decision-making, for example, cost–benefit computations. It is therefore pointless to expect an industrial organization actively to avoid polluting the atmosphere on purely noninstrumental moral grounds. From the standpoint of the logic of organizational behavior such actions would be irrational (Benjamin and Bronstein, 1987). It is equally pointless to expect those managing such an organization for profit to be concerned with community interests out of an active communal identification with members of local communities. On the other hand, it is possible to include in the memoranda of association of organizations specific legally binding moral and political constraints—for example, that independent unions should be recognized and arms manufacture avoided.

THE CAPITALIST BUSINESS CORPORATION AND ITS ORGANIZATIONAL FORMS

In addition to the legal definition of a corporation, it can be defined as "an organization for the accumulation of capital in order to maximize profits, in order to accumulate more capital, leading to more profits . . ." (Glasbeek, 1988, p. 373). Thus its managers experience pressure to achieve high profits from the company's major shareholders and major creditors, from stock market evaluations of the corporation's performance *vis-á-vis* their competitors, and because their own interests are linked with the company's since significant components of their own remuneration is related to profit returns and/or is in shares in that company. They will therefore do everything possible to maximize output and to minimize costs and external constraints.

The relationships between corporations and profit maximization require some elaboration. First, precisely how "profitability" should be calculated has been, and remains, subject to dispute (Cutler et al., 1977; 1978). And there is little doubt that different positions on this question have real, practical consequences. What is not in doubt is that corporate management is under pressure to maximize profitability, however, the latter term is defined or calculated. Relatedly, the disciplines of business policy and business strategy reveal a range of competing arguments (in the form of techniques) as to how the aim of profit maximization might be secured (see, for example, Mintzberg and Quinn, 1996). Second, and related to the previous point, a key variable in terms of the calculation of profitability is the time span over which profitability in general, and returns on investment in particular, is calculated. The calculative attitude that is central to corporate decision-making and behavior can involve a commitment either to short-term profits or to long-term profits and to judgments regarding continuing economic viability. Thus a central element of corporate strategy may be to assume "the cloak of social responsibility" for actions that "are in the long-run interest of a corporation" (Friedman, 1970). Third, we should also be clear that while profit maximization is the key corporate goal, corporations do not necessarily make accurate calculations as to how this should be achieved, or manage to implement effective strategies and policies to reach this end. In other words, corporations do not always accurately or successfully calculate. They may be unsuccessful for a variety of reasons, and are sites of bounded, multiple, and competing rationalities. For these reasons, it is perfectly possible that corporations, operating as rational actors, might not appear as such.

It is more realistic to view the corporation not as a private person, but more as a political entity. In some senses it is a shareholder's republic in that every shareholder, usually, has the vote and the capacity to withdraw from what is, after all, a voluntary association. On the other hand, shareholders are many and relatively atomized compared to the top management who are few, unified, and in control of information. Do the latter, then, control the corporation?

If yes, are these managers socially conscious as Berle and Means (1967) believed or, as others less sanguine argue, do they use the corporation for their own advantage rather than that of anybody else, increasing the size of the organization to boost their salaries, for example (Marris, 1964). Now, there is a great deal of evidence that the management in many large corporations has significant relative autonomy from all or most shareholders but that, at the same time, top managerial groups are not simply self-selecting, but require the endorsement of key sections of capital, whether stock holders, shareholders, or large creditors, like the banks. The phenomena of corporate raiding, shareholder revolts, and massive dividend bonuses involve struggles between different groups of shareholders and between shareholders and top management. Such struggles despite "the rituals of a democratic contest" and "the deployment of the symbols of democracy" are often only "contests between adversary political machines" controlled by rival wealthy shareholders (Latham, 1961, p. 225). For example, in the United States, Zeitlin (1989, p. 89) has identified such ownership interests in 40 percent of the top 500 U.S. firms. Further, he has shown that the wealthiest one percent of American families own "a fifth of all the real estate (and over twice that much of commercial real estate), three-fifths of corporate stock, and over four-fifths of all the trust assets" (Zeitlin, 1989, p. 141). Moreover, the "major banks are major lenders of funds to the top corporations and own significant stock in them as do the major insurance companies" (Zeitlin, 1989, p. 29) and large corporations also own stock in the large banks and in each other. Zeitlin's empirical analysis provides strong arguments why, as a matter of course, "the corporate veil" should be pierced (Clark, 1986, pp. 71–74). Nevertheless, who is in control needs to be empirically established, and it is important to recognize that the exercise of control by large owners of stock is usually only partial, and won through struggle.

Thus the corporation is an aristocratic or oligopolistic republic, and one subject to bloody struggles between its elites. Like other political entities, the corporation pursues its goals through a system consisting of: "(1) an authoritative allocation of principal functions; (2) a symbolic system for the ratification of collective decisions; (3) an operating system of command; (4) a system of rewards and punishments; and (5) institutions for the enforcement of the common rules" (Latham, 1961, p. 220). The corporation's goals and its authoritative allocation of principal functions are specified, but only in part, by the "constitution" provided by the corporation's "Memorandum of Association" and its "Articles of Association." These are then interpreted in the interests of those who rule the organization, either by the rules themselves or by their representatives who govern for them. In either case, the controllers, as we have seen, are chosen politically.

The question then remains, how exactly does the organization function? Kreisberg (1976) has argued that, in practice, there are three "ideal-typical" forms of corporate organization. One is the "rational actor model." In this model the corporation is controlled in a centralized hierarchical authoritarian way. There is an imperative specification and co-ordination of, at least, the key tasks of "suitably" qualified employees. The control of employees is facilitated by the exploitation of their "bounded rationality" (shifting and unclear preferences, limited information, and limited knowledge of cause and effect relations) and by "premise setting" (i.e., by defining what are "reasonable" goals and "good" reasons for the "normal" ways of dealing with situations) (Perrow, 1986). The controllers of these corporate bureaucracies, however, are also subject to "bounded rationality." This can have positive consequences for those who control the organization, since it can generate unexpected but constructive changes which they can capitalize upon by modifying their tactics to take advantage of these new situations (Palmer and Pearce, 1983). On the other hand, the boundedness of their rationality may make it possible for subordinate groups within the organization to modify it in line with their own interests.

Those at the top of the hierarchy may also accept the impossibility of directly controlling all of a large organization's many activities and therefore deliberately decentralize their organization and let it function according to the second of Kreisberg's models, the "organizational process" model. In this model, while central management establishes goals and standard operating procedures, a great deal of immediate decision making takes place at the more local level.

Kreisberg's third model involves "bureaucratic politics," where the organization's structure, its goals, its criteria for success and for the selection of top management, may be affected by the struggles of the different professional groups within it—engineers, research scientists, lawyers, sales personnel, and accountants and of its different component divisions, whether functional, geographic, or product-based. Sometimes these conflicts may be so pervasive and unresolved that the organization itself is characterized by a general, and potentially dangerous, disorder. A number of theoretical and empirical analyses of capitalist corporations certainly suggest that such conflicts are common. This is not to say, however, that they never get resolved. First, as we have seen, whilst top management may have some flexibility, there is no evidence that they ever pursue anything but some combination of profits and growth. Second, a key to how leadership disputes within an organization are resolved is provided by turning to analyses of the problems posed for organizational priorities by changes in the external environment. These may raise questions about the competencies required of the top executives in order to achieve these goals of growth and profits.

Fligstein has argued that efficient corporations have successfully developed a series of different forms of organization and market control to produce a "relatively higher likelihood of growth and profits . . . given the existing sets of social and political and economic circumstances" (Fligstein, 1990, p. 295). Changes in their legal environment, particularly in the regulation of monopolies, have meant that for firms to remain or become economically powerful they need to change their organizational form, market relations, and the qualifications and experience of the groups from whom the top executives were recruited. Firms use four distinct modes of control: direct, manufacturing, sales and marketing, and finance. Even with the recent change of business organization, the finance mode of control still remains dominant (Kanter, 1989; Clegg, 1990; Pearce, 1995). It is of interest here that even the most sophisticated attempts to elaborate upon the variety of corporate forms, as variations upon organization, do so through reference to metaphor (Morgan, 1986; Fisse and Braithwaite, 1993). For while there is little doubt that there exists "a diversity of styles of organizational life" (Fisse and Braithwaite, 1993:122), and that these diverse styles do have real effects for the production and potential regulation of crime, once one examines a particular organization, the corporation, then there are equally some essential features of that organization that a focus upon complexity and difference tends to obscure. Thus more important than organizational *forms* are organizational *modes of control.*

Fligstein (1990) overstates the extent to which these changes have occurred simply because of external legal pressure, because large corporations also significantly influence the way that the law develops (Pearce, 1976; Zey, 1998). Nevertheless, his characterization of these modes of control is accurate and useful for this paper. Moreover, his analysis reminds us again that the top managerial groups are not simply self-selecting, but require the endorsement of key sections of capital.

Currently, the major corporate actors, particularly in the United States and Britain, are driven by a concern with short term gains (Fligstein, 1990; Williams et al., 1990), and a continuous obsession with "the bottom line," both are tendencies that are exacerbated by the finance conception of control. The major corporations are now involved in diverse markets, often with no long-term commitment to staying in many of them. The top corporate executives are characteristically financial experts who can most easily compare and assess the performance and potential of their corporation's radically different kinds of businesses by closely monitoring the rate of return on the capital invested in each. This may be efficient for some purposes, as Williamson (1975) claims, but from other points of view the consequences can be inefficient or literally disastrous. It can also have negative consequences for national economies—and it is significantly not so characteristic of Japanese and German companies (Fligstein, 1990; Williams et al., 1990). For the moment, at least, the latter appear to be oriented to their countries of origin more than are American or British companies that are more nearly "pure" multinationals (Reich, 1983).

ORGANIZATIONAL FORMS AND CORPORATE CRIME

How, then, do these differences in organizational form affect the occurrence of corporate crime? If we turn first to the finance mode of control, we find that this tends to treat dramatically different production processes organized according to diverse time scales as homogeneous, and to elide the effects on profitability of the radically different and frequently changing environments within which different businesses operate. These different corporations *organize production*, in accordance with Kreisberg's "organizational process" model, but the *assessment of their performance* is primarily financial and in a mode more akin to the "rational actor" model. And this explains why so many safety, health, and environmental violations are the effects of the policies of higher management without this necessarily being traceable to any specific decisions that they have made about product quality, health, and safety. It maximizes the likelihood of "willful blindness" (Wilson, 1979), since it allows those at the top to be ignorant of the activities of subordinates and to ignore the difficulties that subordinates face (Braithwaite, 1984; Pearce and Tombs, 1998). This is why, more generally,

> the most shocking safety and environmental violations are almost exclusively the product of decisions at lower managerial levels. . . . The directive from the top of the organization is to increase profits by fifteen percent but the means are left to the managerial discretion of the middle manager who is in operational control of the division. . . . The results of such a structure are predictable: when pressure is intensified, illegal or irresponsible means become attractive to a desperate middle manager who has no recourse against a stern but myopic notion of accountability that looks only to the bottom line of the income statement (Coffee, 1981, p. 389).

If a subdivision of a company is brought under rigid and effective fiscal control, it may for that very reason be *out of control* in other ways. One OECD (Organisation of Economic Co-Operation and Development) study found that the subsidiaries of large multinational corporations are allowed substantial autonomy in their decisions about day-to-day production, labor relations, and marketing strategies. Subsidiaries, however, are given much less autonomy over their use of cash flow and their ability to borrow from banks, and they have little control over the selection of their CEO (OECD, 1987). It is clear that strategic control, including the decision about acceptable profit levels, remains with the parent. A major cause of the Bhopal chemical plant disaster was pressure for a "normal" return on the capital invested in an overseas subsidiary, in the context of a declining market (Pearce and Tombs, 1998).

Thus we should be clear that all may not be as it appears with complexly organized corporations, within which independence, autonomy, diffuse accountability, and responsibility are represented as the norm. It is interesting that Braithwaite, who has focused at length upon the relationships between organizational forms and corporate crimes, has noted that

> the presumed diffusion of accountability in a complex organisation sometimes can be a hoax that the corporation plays on the rest of the world, especially courts and sociologists. When companies want clearly defined accountability they can generally get it. Diffused accountability is not always inherent in or-

ganisational complexity; it is in considerable measure the result of a desire to protect individuals within the organisation by presenting a confused picture to the outside world (Braithwaite, 1984, p. 324).

Thus we need to be clear: that corporate organization is not always accurately revealed through corporate forms; that if companies appear to be organized in a highly complex and decentralized form, that this is itself a consequence of organization; finally, that even the most decentralized, complexly organized corporations manage (internally) to distribute benefits in a clear, unambiguous (and usually hierarchical) manner—thus there are no reasons why they cannot, or do not, distribute disbenefits, and why this should not also be possible from an external standpoint.

These different forms of organizational decision-making represent ideal or pure types. In key functions, such corporations operate, or constantly strive to operate, in a way similar to Kreisberg's rational actor model. The dominant tendency must be towards the rational-actor model, given the need to achieve and maintain control as a precondition of maximizing profitability. Thus Kreisberg's "pure" rational actor mode of organization represents particular problems in terms of the production of crime.

Within its centralized hierarchical authoritarian structure, abstract criteria are used to judge the worth of people. In order to be successful within the organization, it will be necessary for individuals to be seen as contributing to the achievement of high profits, and to stay out of trouble. Individuals will thus try to control and limit the upward information flow, and then blame their subordinates for any problems that arise (Stone, 1973). These organizational arrangements produce both "organizational crimes" (Sherman, 1982) undertaken in line with the goals of the "organization's dominant coalition" (Ellis, 1987:86) and "occupational crimes," where rules are bent and information is concealed to facilitate individual career goals (Coleman, 1989; Green, 1990). In situations characterized by bureaucratic politics with different sectors and functional groups struggling to set organizational goals, policy making, implementation, and outcomes become contingent and problematic. There is a real sense in which, with the important exception of their pursuit of the bottom line, these organizations are out of control.

The limited-liability corporation has a strong proclivity to engage in antisocial, illegal, and criminal conduct. As a capitalist business it is essentially dedicated to making continuous and, if possible, ever-increasing profits. It is intrinsically indifferent to what commodities it produces as long as there is a market for them; thus in the United States the carcinogen tobacco was produced mainly for domestic consumption, but as this market has become smaller, tobacco firms began targeting overseas markets. In order to maximize profits, there is always a need to cut costs. This means that efforts are made to make it difficult for workers to join effective trade unions, or to demand safe workplaces. These tendencies are exacerbated by the limited-liability corporate form. Shareholders invest in a wide range of companies, and since their only concern is with the return of their investments they are indifferent to what occurs within different production processes and rarely live in the areas where these take place. They are legally protected from most of the negative consequences of company actions. Company executives are also fundamentally concerned with profitability, and with "willful blindness" are again often distanced from (and legally protected from the consequences of) production, conceive of it abstractly and, in turn, pressure managers to produce as much and as cheaply as possible. This creates a form of structural irresponsibility where it is often difficult to identify how decisions are made and how well or poorly they relate together. I have provided here and elsewhere (cf. Pearce, 1976) a great deal of evidence about the antisocial consequences of the routine activity of corporations, but I have also provided suggestions as to how, in theory at least, their conduct can be disciplined and modified (cf. Pearce and Snider, 1995; Pearce and Tombs, 1998). In the current phase of global politics the likelihood of this happened is somewhat remote, but this could be, and needs to be, accomplished.

REFERENCES

Berle, A. and G. Means. 1967. *The Modern Corporation and Private Property*. New York: Harcourt, Brace and World.

Benjamin, M. and D. A. Bronstein. 1987. "Moral and Criminal Responsibility and Corporate Persons." In W. J. Samuels and A. S. Miller (eds), *Corporations and Society: Power and Responsibility*. New York: Greenwood Press.

Box, S. 1983. *Power, Crime and Mystification*. London: Tavistock.

Braithwaite, J. 1984. *Corporate Crime in the Pharmaceutical Industry*. London: Routledge and Kegan Paul.

Cahill, S. 1997. "Killing for Company." *Company Secretary* March.

Clark, R. C. 1986. *Corporate Law*. Boston: Little, Brown and Company.

Clegg, S. 1990. *Modern Organizations: Organization Studies in the Postmodern World*. London: Sage.

Clinard, M. B. and P. Yeager. 1980. *Corporate Crime*. New York: Free Press.

Coffee, J. 1981. "No Soul to Damn, No Body to Kick: An Unscandalized Essay on the Problem of Corporate Punishment." *Michigan Law Review* (79).

Coleman, J. 1989. *The Criminal Elite*. New York: St. Martin's Press.

Cutler, A., B. Hindess, P. Q. Hirst, A. Hussain. 1977. *Marx's Capital and Capitalism Today: Volume 1*. London: Routledge and Kegan Paul.

Cutler, A., B. Hindess, P., Hirst, A. Hussain. 1978. *Marx's Capital and Capitalism Today: Volume 2*. London: Routledge and Kegan Paul.

Ellis, D. 1987. *The Wrong Stuff*. Toronto: Collier-Macmillan.

Etzioni, A. 1993. "The U.S. Sentencing Commission on Corporate Crime: A Critique." In G. Geis and P. Jesilow (eds), *White Collar Crime Special Issue of the Annals of the American Academy Political and Social Science* 525. Newbury Park, CA: Sage.

Fisse, B. and J. Braithwaite. 1993. *Corporations, Crime and Accountability*. Cambridge University Press.

Fligstein, N. 1990. *The Transformation of Corporate Control*. Cambridge, MA: Harvard University Press.

Friedman, M. 1970. "The Social Responsibility of Business is to Make Profits." In *New York Times Magazine*, 13th September.

Friedrichs, D. O. 1992. "White-Collar Crime and the Definitional Quagmire: A Provisionsal Solution." *Journal of Human Justice* 3(2).

Glasbeek, H. 1988. "The Corporate Social Responsibility Movement—The Latest in Maginot Lines to Save Capitalism." *Dalhousie Law Journal* 11(2) March.

Green, G. S. 1990. *Occupational Crime.* Chicago: Nelson Hall.

Henry, F. 1982. "Capitalism, Accumulation and Crime." *Crime and Social Justice* 18.

Kanter, R. M. 1989. *When Giants Learn to Dance.* New York: Simon and Schuster.

Keane, C. 1995. "Organization Theory and Corporate Crime." In F. Pearce and L. Snider (eds), *Corporate Crime: Contemporary Debates.* University of Toronto Press.

Kramer, R. 1984. "Corporate Criminality: The Development of an Idea." In E. Hochstedler (ed.), *Corporations as Criminals.* Beverley Hills: Sage.

Kreisberg, S. M. 1986. "Decision Making Models and the Control of Corporate Crime." *Yale Law Journal* 85.

Latham, E. 1961. "The Body Politic of the Corporation." In E. S. Mason (ed.), *The Corporation in Modern Society.* Cambridge, MA: Harvard University Press.

Marris, R. 1964. *The Economic Theory of Managerial Capitalism.* London: Macmillan.

Mayer, C. J. 1990. "Personalizing the Impersonal: Corporations and the Bill of Rights." *The Hastings Law Journal* 41.

Mintzberg, H. and J. B. Quinn, 1996. *The Strategy Process: Concepts, Contexts, Cases.* Upper Saddle River, NJ: Prentice Hall.

Moran, L. J. 1992. "Corporate Criminal Capacity: Nostalgia for Representation." *Social and Legal Studies* 1.

Morgan, G. 1986. *Images of Organization.* Beverly Hills, CA: Sage.

OECD. 1987. *International Investment and Multinational Enterprizes: Structure and Organization of Multinational Enterprizes.* Paris: OECD.

Palmer, J. and F. Pearce. 1983. "Legal Discourse and State Power: Foucault and the Juridical Relation." *International Journal of the Sociology of Law* 11.

Pearce, F. 1976. *Crimes of the Powerful.* London: Puto Press.

——— 1995. "Accountability for Corporate Crime." In P. Stenning (ed), *Accountability for Criminal Justice.* University of Toronto Press.

Pearce, F. and S. Tombs. 1998. *Toxic Capitalism: Corporate Crime and the Chemical Industry.* Farnborough: Ashgate.

Perrow, C. 1986. *Complex Organizations: A Critical Essay* (3rd edition). New York: McGraw-Hill.

Reich, R. B. 1983. *The Next American Frontier.* New York: Times Books.

Shrager, L. S. and J. F. Short. 1977. "Toward a Sociology of Organizational Crime." *Social Problems* 25.

Sherman, L. 1982. "Deviant Organizations." In D. Ermann and R. Lundman (eds.), Corporate and Governmental Deviance. New York: Oxford University Press.

Slapper, G. 1993. "Corporate Manslaughter: An Examination of the Determinants of Prosecutorial Policy." *Social and Legal Studies* 2.

Snider, L. 1993. *Bad Business: Corporate Crime in Canada.* Toronto: Nelson Canada.

Stone, C. D. 1973. *Where the Law Ends: The Social Control of Corporate Behavior.* New York: Harper and Row.

Sutherland, E. H. 1949. *White Collar Crime.* New York: Dryden Press.

———— 1983. *White Collar Crime. The Uncut Version.* New Haven: Yale University Press.

Weait, M. 1992. "Swans Reflecting Elephants: Imagery and the Law." *Law and Critique* (III).

Williams, K., J. Williams and C. Haslam. 1990. "The Hollowing out of British Manufacturing and its Implications." *Economy and Society* 19.

Williamson, O. 1975. *Markets and Hierarchies: Analysis of Antitrust Implications.* New York: Free Press.

Wilson, L. 1979. "The Doctrine of Willful Blindness." *University of New Brunswick Law Review* 28.

Zeitlin, M. 1989. *The Large Corporation and Contemporary Classes.* New Brunswick, NJ: Rutgers University Press.

Zey, M. 1998. "Embeddedness of interorganizational corporate crime in the 1980s: Securities frauds of banks and investment banks," in P. Bamberger and W. J. Sonnenstuhl, *Deviance and Organizations, Research in the Sociology of Organizations,* Volume 15, Stamford and London: JAI Press.

Victims and Costs

Introduction

White-collar crime exacts an astronomical toll in deaths, physical health, emotional suffering, and fiscal costs, one that dwarfs comparable losses to street crime. No one seriously disputes this fact, although it is also true that no one can estimate these costs with precision or confidence. Development of comprehensive reliable estimates requires systematically collected data on the prevalence of white-collar crime, the numbers of victims, and their losses. At present these data do not exist. In marked contrast to street crime, data on white-collar offenses, offenders, and victims are not routinely collected, collated, and disseminated by centralized offices of state or federal government. For white-collar crime investigators there is no counterpart of the Federal Bureau of Investigation's Uniform Crime Reporting program.

It is also the case that a great deal of white-collar crime goes unreported since many of its victims are unaware they have been victimized. Unlike robbery, burglary, and other street crimes, acts of white-collar crime frequently do not stand out in victims' experiences; often they have the look of routine legitimate transactions. Victims who realize or suspect what has happened may have no idea where to report the incident; it is characteristic also of white-collar crimes that the appropriate places or agencies to report to either are unknown or unfamiliar. Many victims do not report their victimization, frequently because they believe they should have been more careful in the first place or because they feel a sense of embarrassment and shame and prefer that others not learn what happened. The problems and misgivings of white-collar crime victims gives to those who commit these offenses a sizeable advantage over their less privileged criminal cousins.

Research into the problems faced by victims of white-collar crime lags far behind the more numerous and methodologically sophisticated studies of street-crime victims. Survey procedures, for example, are used routinely to examine the nature and aftermath of victimization by street offenders, but only limited efforts have been made to employ these procedures to study victimization by white-collar offenders. Past surveys have focused almost entirely on fraud and its victims. Thus the National Crime Victimization Survey, which is

---

PANEL 4   A Dangerous Combination

On April 11, 1996, Rockwell International pleaded guilty to three felony counts of hazardous waste mishandling. The corporation agreed to pay $6.5 million for a 1994 chemical explosion that killed two scientists. The firm admitted to illegally storing and burning chemicals that led to the explosion. In exchange for the settlement, Rockwell International receives immunity from any other federal charges in any case involving hazardous waste that may have occurred since 1991.

Source: Los Angeles Times, Friday, April 12, 1996.

---

funded by an extravagant outlay of public monies, makes no effort, for example, to explore death or injury caused by criminal workplace conditions. There are many excellent case studies of the impacts of white-collar crime, but most are journalistic in approach, descriptive in presentation, and feature sensational and, therefore, atypical criminal incidents. In a paper written specifically for this volume, Richard M. Titus reviews what investigators have learned about the victims and their experiences with crimes of personal fraud. It is worth noting that very few of the victims whose experiences Titus reviews were victimized by offenders of respectable social position and privilege.

Traumatic deaths and injuries caused by white-collar crime probably exceed the numbers for street crime, but employer failure to provide a safe and healthful working environment exacts an even heavier toll in health and shortened lives. Damage to health generally is incremental and long-term rather than catastrophic; high levels of workplace carcinogens, for example, take time off the end of lives, long after employees have been replaced or have retired. Estimates of the harm caused by crime are influenced heavily by whether the intangible and long-term costs are acknowledged, measured, and priced. A study by Linda Ganzini, Bentson McFarland, and Joseph Bloom, reprinted here, found that victims of both fraud and violent crime show similar psychological effects, including anxiety and major depressive disorders. The intangible costs of white-collar crime can ripple far beyond immediate victims. When organizations dispose of hazardous materials in reckless and criminal fashion, the costs may be increased risk of health problems for innocent parties as well as the financial costs of cleaning up their poisonous legacies.

More important than the psychological suffering, pain, and shortened lives caused by white-collar crime is the possibility that it has powerful delegitimation effects; particularly when it is permitted to go unchecked by public officials and agencies, white-collar crime can undermine citizen confidence in governmental and economic institutions and erode respect for law. Past indifference to the victims of white-collar crime and its potential delegitimation effects are discussed in the paper by Elizabeth Moore and Michael Mills. Despite the clear importance of its potential effect on trust and confidence in public institutions and leaders, this has received very little research attention. We also have reprinted a paper by Neal Shover, Greer Litton Fox, and Michael Mills that is one of the few efforts to explore the delegitimation effects of white-collar crime.

Discussions of the victims of white-collar crime typically begin with and do not extend beyond individuals, but organizations, both private and public, also are harmed by it. Where public agencies are concerned, the larger community of taxpaying citizens is the ultimate victim. They must pay the fare, for example, when local school districts are charged artificially high prices for products due to price fixing by ostensibly competitive suppliers.

The harmful effects on businesses caused by white-collar crime are easy to imagine, but little is known about their range and severity. Small businesses may be forced into bankruptcy and their employees onto unemployment rolls. It is reasonable to assume that many organizational victims have an interest in keeping quiet about their victimization. Knowledge of their apparent vulnerability and experience, particularly if it reaches competitors, creditors, or potential customers, could erode further an already precarious balance sheet. We have reprinted here a paper by Michael Levi that draws from research on victims of fraud in the United Kingdom. It is one of the few exceptions to past neglect of organizational victims of white-collar crime.

The Neglected Victims and Unexamined Costs of White-Collar Crime

Elizabeth Moore and Michael Mills

For decades the victims of crime were all but ignored by researchers, criminal justice professionals, and policymakers. Recent years have seen a dramatic reversal of this situation. As public officials and a victims' movement focused unprecedented attention on the financial loss, physical injuries, and suffering caused by street crimes, victim-rights legislation and assistance programs were developed across the nation. Although this victims' movement has spawned significant policy reforms, white-collar crime victims have been ignored. . . .

Research has documented the disruptive and sometimes devastating effects of street crime on its victims. Victims often report psychological and somatic problems triggered by their victimization, including stress, diminished

"The Neglected Victims and Unexamined Costs of White-Collar Crime" from *Crime & Delinquency* 36:3 (July 1990): 408–418. Reprinted by permission.

self-esteem, and helplessness. Many alternate between intense anger and increased feelings of vulnerability and fear (Burt and Katz 1985; Fischer 1984; Janoff-Bulman 1985; Leyman 1985; Maguire 1980; Wortman 1983). These reactions can be trivial or devastating, transitory or enduring.

The problems faced by crime victims do not end once their plight becomes known to authorities. Victims who come to criminal justice officials expecting protection and remedy often find something very different:

> They discover . . . that they [are] treated as appendages of a system appallingly out of balance. They learn that somewhere along the way the system has lost track of the simple truth that it is supposed to be fair and to protect those who obey the law while punishing those who break it. Somewhere along the way, the system began to serve lawyers and judges and defendants, treating the victim with institutionalized disinterest. (President's Task Force on Victims of Crime 1982, p. vi)

VICTIMS OF WHITE-COLLAR CRIME

. . . Whereas street crimes disproportionately victimize the poor and marginal, white-collar crime is more democratic in its impact. It harms not only well-heeled financial speculators but couples and individual citizens with few if any assets beyond a modest savings account. . . .

Like victims of street crimes, there is reason to believe that white-collar crime victims who seek redress by notifying public officials of their apparent victimization receive less than a satisfactory response (Geis 1975; McGuire and Edelhertz 1980). It may be necessary for them to negotiate a maze of agencies and institutions, most of uncertain jurisdiction and commitment. Often the process produces little beyond frustration and, eventually, angry resignation. Vaughan and Carlo (1975) discovered that a group of citizens victimized by an appliance repairman, hardly the most serious of white-collar offenders, "repeatedly expressed their indignation at being cheated and their frustration at being unable to get satisfaction from the offender, or from anyplace else" (p. 158). A study of fraud in California that victimized many elderly citizens pointed to the "callous indifference that the system demonstrates toward those whom it is particularly charged with assisting" (Geis 1976, p. 14). . . . Interviews with a sample of 42 individuals who filed complaints with the consumer fraud bureau of the Illinois Attorney General's office revealed that "dissatisfaction with and even hostility toward the Bureau were widespread." The Bureau was seen as "too slow, unaggressive, biased, disorganized, and 'bureaucratic'" (Steele 1975, p. 1179). In short, "just as the criminal-justice system has been termed a 'nonsystem,' the approach taken by the criminal-justice system to white collar-crime containment might be considered a 'nonapproach'" (Edelhertz and Rogovin 1980, p. 78). The fact that white-collar crime victims have been ignored by the justice system is only the latest example of this.

UNDESERVING VICTIMS

Like the post-1975 wave of criminal sentencing reform that swept over the nation, the victims' movement drew support from diverse sources. By focusing attention on women as targets of violence, the womens' movement promoted a new definition of their plight as victims. Angered by liberal U.S. Supreme Court decisions expanding the rights of the accused, politically conservative citizens and public officials seized the opportunity to redress this perceived imbalance by promoting *victims'* rights. This was not extended to victims of white-collar crime.

For conservative politicians, the victims' rights movement offered an opportunity to do something positive about crime, thereby undercutting criticisms that their crime control policies amount to nothing more than repression. By establishing restitution and compensation programs, conservatives could show they were willing to fund programs that would benefit women and minorities, groups typically not part of the conservative constituency. These political gains could be achieved at limited political cost and the only group not benefiting from expanded victim rights was street criminals.

The politics of government programs may explain the failure of the victim rights legislation to take explicit account of white-collar crime victims. Compensation and restitution programs for victims of street crime seem a natural extension of the traditional government responsibility to preserve public order. Innocent victims of street crime deserve to be compensated, if only because the state has failed in its responsibility to protect them. Street criminals, however, typically are poor and have few prospects of ever being able to repay their victims. Hence it follows that the state should help make good victims' losses.

This reasoning is harder to apply in the case of white-collar crime. Whereas its victims may or may not be poor, the offenders may, but need not, be part of the wealthy and powerful business establishment. In this situation, the argument that the state owes it to victims to defray the costs of victimization is not persuasive. If the offenders are not poor, why not have them pay for the costs of victimization? Why not set up programs requiring that perpetrators of consumer fraud, bank scams, securities fraud, and other such crimes automatically pay restitution to their victims? But at this point, we confront certain political and economic realities.

New programs facilitating victims' ability to recover from corporate white-collar offenses would necessarily impose costs on the business community. Attempts to legislate such programs will encounter resistance. The business community will point to the existing network of laws, regulations, and agencies and argue that mechanisms for redressing the wrongs suffered by white-collar crime victims are already in place; no new ones are needed. Given the antiregulation, probusiness sentiments increasingly evidenced by public officials, these arguments likely would be well received by many state and federal legislators. Ironically, the conservative political philosophy underpinning the original victims' rights movement may be responsible in part for its continued failure to address white-collar crime victimization.

Other reasons for continued neglect are rooted in prevailing notions about white-collar crime and its victims. Walsh and Schram (1980) suggested that white-collar crime, like the crime of rape, raises "double standard issues." Both crimes are characterized by widespread ambivalence toward the proscribed conduct, victim involvement, and victims' claims for redress. As a result, many white-collar victims do not "arouse the general sympathy reserved for those who have suffered harm, loss, or injury. Instead, these victims often are viewed with a mixture of skepticism, suspicion, and disbelief" and they are seen as "unworthy of society's protection" (pp. 46–47). Little wonder that simply reporting white-collar crime and seeing one's complaint through to resolution can be both exhausting and disillusioning.

BEYOND THE PRIMARY COSTS OF CRIME

Although the primary costs of white-collar crime are obvious, its *secondary* costs may be equally harmful. Sutherland (1949) noted, . . . that white-collar crime is harmful to the social fabric in ways uniquely its own. Because most white-collar offenses violate trust, they breed distrust, lower social morale, and "attack the fundamental principles of the American institutions" (p. 13). . . . Three areas of potentially significant secondary impact have been identified: (a) diminished faith in a free economy and in business leaders, (b) loss of confidence in political institutions, processes, and leaders, and (c) erosion of public morality.

Many have expressed fears about the potential impact of white-collar crime on our nation's economic life. They reason that restraint of trade, for example,

> tends to undermine the principles of free enterprise that the antitrust laws are intended to protect. [Thus,] the damage from the price-fixing conspiracy in the electrical equipment industry was not limited to the direct extra costs imposed. As Judge T. Cullen Ganey declared in sentencing a defendant: "This is a shocking indictment of a vast section of our economy, for what is really at stake here is the survival of the kind of economy under which this country has grown great, the free enterprise system." (President's Commission 1967, p. 48)

American citizens must have faith and confidence that corporate and business leaders are motivated by an ethic of responsible concern for others and for the common good. To the extent citizens believe otherwise, believe that business decisions are motivated by greed and selfishness, they may withhold financial support and economic investment.

Another secondary cost is the effect of white-collar crime on faith in and support for political institutions, public officials, and governmental processes. Citizens, for the most part, expect public officials to be honest themselves and also to deal unflinchingly with those who employ deceit and exploitation to prey on the public. In a word,

> [citizens] want to see evidence that the criminal-justice system will treat deception and abuses of institutional position as harshly as stealth and physical attack and that it is willing to punish privileged and powerful offenders as well as those who are relatively powerless (Moore 1980, p. 44)

This is true especially in the U.S., whose economy is based largely on trust in the honesty and legitimacy of agencies that regulate financial markets and activities. The Internal Revenue Service, for example, depends greatly on voluntary, honest compliance by American citizens. The viability of banks and thrifts greatly depends on citizens' confidence in regulatory officials and agencies. Whenever citizens see corrupt public officials and other white-collar offenders violate the law with impunity they inevitably must question official integrity and commitment to fairness. In many ways, the greatest harm to the victims of white-collar crime may be this loss of faith in the very possibility of fair, impartial government. Surely this problem is exacerbated and cynicism intensified when victims' efforts to enlist the aid of political officials in the pursuit of simple justice lead only to frustration. The result may be increased citizen apathy and feelings of *delegitimation*. In one of the few empirical investigations of this hypothesized relationship, Peters and Welch (1980) found that charges of corruption apparently had little effect on net voter turnout and election outcomes in five Congressional elections from 1968 to 1978. They suggested, however, that individual-level studies would be more appropriate for examining whether official corruption or other forms of white-collar crime cause delegitimation.

The state's failure to mete out swift and appropriately severe punishment to white-collar criminals may erode not only victims' confidence in and support for American political and social institutions but also their commitment to and willingness to play by "the rules." Thus, the final secondary impact of white-collar crime is its potentially deleterious effect on public morality. As the President's Commission on Law Enforcement and Administration put it:

> It is reasonable to assume that prestigious companies that flout the law set an example for other businesses and influence individuals, particularly young people, to commit other kinds of crime on the grounds that everyone is taking what he can get. If businessmen who are respected as leaders of the community can do such things as break the antitrust laws or rent dilapidated houses to the poor at high rents, it is hard to convince the young that they should be honest. (1967, p. 48)

In other words, by violating citizens' sense of equity, lenient treatment of white-collar criminals may provide them with easy rationalizations for personal misconduct. This reaction may be understandable particularly among poor and minority citizens who see the stark contrast between our harsh response to street criminals and our limp response to white-collar criminals.

Moore (1980) suggests that, "given the intensity of our attack on street crime, there seems to be a *special* obligation to prosecute respectable people who use their position and reputation to steal through deception and exploitation" (p. 30) . . .

REFERENCES

Burt, Martha R. and Bonnie L. Katz, 1985. "Rape, Robbery, and Burglary: Responses to Actual and Feared Victimization, with Special Focus on Women and the Elderly." *Victimology* 10:325–358.

Edelhertz, Herbert and Charles Rogovin, eds., 1980. *A National Strategy for Containing White-Collar Crime.* Lexington, MA: D. C. Heath.

Fischer, Constance T. 1984. "A Phenomenological Study of Being Criminally Victimized: Contributions and Constraints of Qualitative Research." *Journal of Social Issues* 40: 161–178.

Geis, Gilbert. 1975. "Victimization Patterns in White-Collar Crime." Pp. 89–105 in *Victimology: A New Focus. Exploiters and Exploited.* Vol. 5, edited by I. Drapkin and E. Viano. Lexington, MA: D. C. Heath.

———, 1976. "Defrauding the Elderly." Pp. 7–19 in *Crime and the Elderly,* edited by J. Goldsmith and S. Goldsmith. Lexington, MA: D. C. Heath.

Janoff-Bulman, Ronnie. 1985. "Criminal vs. Non-criminal Victimization: Victims' Reactions." *Victimology* 10:498–511.

Leymann, Heinz. 1985. "Somatic and Psychological Symptoms after the Experience of Life Threatening Events: A profile Analysis." *Victimology* 10:512–538.

Maguire, Mike. 1980. "The Impact of Burglary upon Victims." *British Journal of Criminology* 20:261–275.

McGuire, Mary and Herbert Edelhertz. 1980. "Consumer Abuse of Older Americans: Victimization and Remedial Action in Two Metropolitan Areas." Pp. 266–292 in *White-Collar Crime: Theory and Research,* edited by G. Geis and E. Stotland. Beverly Hills, CA: Sage.

Moore, Mark H. 1980. "Notes toward a National Strategy to Deal with White-Collar Crime." Pp. 21–53 in *A National Strategy for Containing White-Collar Crime,* edited by H. Edelhertz and C. Rogovin. Lexington, MA: D. C. Heath.

Peters, John G. and Susan Welch. 1980. "The Effects of Charges of Corruption on Voting Behavior in Congressional Elections." *American Political Science Review* 74:697–708.

President's Commission on Law Enforcement and Administration of Justice. 1967. *The Challenge of Crime in a Free Society.* Washington, DC: U.S. Government Printing Office.

President's Task Force on Victims of Crime. 1982. *Final Report.* Washington, DC: U.S. Government Printing Office.

Steele, Eric H. 1975. "Fraud, Dispute, and the Consumer: Responding to Consumer Complaints." *University of Pennsylvania Law Review* 123:1107–1186.

Sutherland, Edwin H. 1949. *White Collar Crime.* New York: Holt, Rinehart & Winston.

Vaughan, Diane and Giovanna Carlo. 1975. "The Appliance Repairman: A Study of Victim Responsiveness and Fraud." *Journal of Research in Crime and Delinquency* 12: 153–161.

Walsh, Marilyn E. and Donna D. Schram. 1980. "The Victim of White-Collar crime:

Accuser or Accused?" Pp. 32–51 in *White-Collar Crime: Theory and Research,* edited by G. Geis and E. Stotland. Beverly Hills, CA: Sage.
Wortman, Camille B. 1983. "Coping with Victimization: Conclusion and Implications for Future Research." *Journal of Social Issues* 39:195–221.

Personal Fraud and Its Victims*

Richard M. Titus

Fraud is the intentional deception or attempted deception of an individual with the promise of goods, services, or things of value that do not exist or in other ways are misrepresented. The element of deception in this definition implies an interaction between victim and offender; this interaction can be anything from a false billing to an elaborate promotional charade. In this paper we are concerned with *individuals* as victims of fraudulent acts, for which we employ the term *personal fraud.* Examples include credit assistance or loan consolidation scams, offers for "free" prizes at overstated value or odds of winning, unnecessary or useless goods such as beauty products or home repairs, deceptive acquisition of bank or credit card numbers, and charity scams. This paper reviews what is known about victimization by personal fraud, the magnitude and nature of victim losses, and the characteristics of citizens disproportionately victimized by personal fraud. It concludes with comments on the prevention and control of personal fraud.

EXTENT OF FRAUD VICTIMIZATION

Prior to the introduction of the National Crime Victimization Survey (NCVS) in 1973, the only national statistical source of crime victimization data was the Federal Bureau of Investigation's Uniform Crime Report (UCR). The UCR is the most widely cited source of aggregate criminal statistics and provides a nationwide view of crime based on data provided by local law enforcement agencies throughout the United States. Despite its importance and wide use by criminologists, the UCR has been criticized for issues related to reporting practices, law enforcement practices, and its methodological problems. Specifically, surveys of crime victims show that fewer than half of all criminal incidents are reported to the police, which indicates that the UCR data significantly underestimates the total number of annual criminal events.

Fraud is defined by the *Uniform Crime Reports* as the "fraudulent con-

---

*The views expressed are those of the author and not necessarily those of the U.S. Department of Justice or the National Institute of Justice.

PANEL 5   Financial Institution Fraud and Failure Investigations

The Federal Bureau of Investigation is charged to investigate fraud committed by and against financial institutions, such as banks. Given the complexity of these cases and the resources required to complete the investigations, the FBI has developed a White-Collar Crime Program. Each year the FBI publishes the results of investigations within the White-Collar Crime Program. The following are the results taken from the 1997 report, "The Financial Institution Fraud and Failure Report."

1) Estimates of amount of money lost to the S&L crisis have topped over 500 billion dollars. The FBI found that "approximately 60 percent of the fraud reported by financial institutions related to bank insider abuse." Employees, managers, and executives were responsible for almost two-thirds of the fraud cases reported by banks, S&Ls, and credit unions during this time period.

2) Loan frauds have become more complex and are expanding to multitransactional frauds involving groups of people from top management to industry professionals who assist in the loan application process. These professionals include loan brokers, appraisers, accountants, and real estate attorneys. Such transactions are sometimes hidden against a backdrop of genuine transactions which give them an appearance of legitimacy. These cases now involve large-scale fraud operations comprising hundreds of subjects in multiple jurisdictions.

3) FIF investigations ranged in number from 404 in 1989 to a high of 740 in 1992—the peak year for S&L failures. The number of investigations has dropped every year since 1992, to a low of 200 investigations in 1997. Moreover, the number of FDIC insured "problem" institutions has declined from 1426 in 1991 to only 98 as of 1997.

4) Even so, the number of pending FIF cases investigated by the FBI ranged from a high of 10,088 in 1993 to 8,512 in 1997. Of the 8,512 pending cases, 3,859 were considered "major" cases, or cases that involved the failure of an institution or where the loss exceeded $100,000.

5) In 1997, 2551 individuals were convicted in cases related to financial institution fraud. Moreover, 1342 people were convicted in "major" cases where the loss exceed $100,000. These included 528 bank employees, 204 bank officers, 19 corporations, and 7 local, state, or federal law enforcement officers.

6) In 1994 over 240 million dollars was recovered, over 864 million was paid as restitution, and over 10 million dollars was ordered in fines. In 1995, over 185 million dollars was recovered, over 1.1 billion dollars was paid as restitution and over 16 million dollars was ordered in fines. In 1997, the FBI recovered 41.2 million dollars, 537 million dollars through restitution, and 25.6 million dollars through fines.

Adapted from U.S. Department of Justice, Federal Bureau of Investigation, Financial Crimes Section. "Financial Institution Fraud and Failure Report."

version and obtaining money or property by false pretenses," and it includes "confidence games and bad checks, except forgeries and counterfeiting" (Federal Bureau of Investigation, 1997). The UCR Handbook indicates that fraud "consists of some deceitful practice or willful device, resorted to with the intent to deprive another or in some way to do an injury" (Federal Bureau of Investigation, 1984). UCR data for 1996 show that 324,776 persons nationwide were arrested for fraud while the numbers for robbery and burglary were 121,781 and 264,193, respectively (Federal Bureau of Investigations, 1997). This converts to a rate of 171.0 persons arrested for fraud per 100,000 persons in the population, 64.1 for robbery, and 139.1 for burglary (not all the fraud arrests are for personal fraud). Although the UCR does collect arrest information on the prevalence of fraud, the UCR is an imperfect indicator since many fraud victimizations are not reported and many reports do not lead to arrest. Compilations of national data on prosecutions, convictions, sentences, and time served suffer from the same limitations.

The shortcomings of the UCR led to development of the National Crime Victimization Survey (NCVS), a joint venture by the U.S. Bureau of Census and the Bureau of Justice Statistics of the U.S. Department of Justice. Because it collects information about victims, offenders, and crime (including criminal events that go unreported to the police), the NCVS provides a picture of crimes that are missed by the UCR. The most recent NCVS obtains data on over 110,000 individuals from 66,000 households (Bureau of Justice Statistics, 1996). While the NCVS provides an extremely valuable source of information on crime victimization, this survey does not contain questions about fraud victimization.

The absence of systematic data about fraud victimization was a major stimulus to household surveys. One of the first, conducted in 1992, found that one in three Americans reported having been cheated out of money through various deceptive means (Bass and Hoeffler, 1992). Fewer than one-third of those victimized reported the incident to anyone, and only one-third of those surveyed believed that they knew whom to contact to determine whether an offer or promotion was legitimate. A national telephone survey was administered to a representative probability sample of 1246 respondents ages 18 and older (Titus et al., 1995). This survey provided the first national estimate of the incidence and prevalence of personal fraud victimization, the characteristics of the victims involved, and the impacts and effects of these offenses. Respondents were asked whether they had been victims of fraud or if an attempt had ever been made to victimize them by 21 specific types of fraud plus a category of "other" types of fraud. Fifty-eight percent of the respondents reported that they had been the victim of a successful fraudulent act or the victim of an attempted fraudulent act during their lifetime. Within the previous 12 months from the time of the survey, 31% of the respondents reported one or more fraud attempts and of these, 48% were reported to be successful. Therefore, 15% of the entire sample had been successfully victimized by personal fraud within the previous year. Even more startling, 8% of the sample reported a victimization or attempted victimization for five or more of the fraud categories, which indicates that there is a substantial proportion of individuals who are repeat victims of this crime.

In 1996, a random sample of 865 persons aged 50 and older participated in a telephone survey that focused on telemarketing fraud for the American Association of Retired Persons (AARP, 1997). This same survey was replicated with a random sample of 882 individuals in 1997. Fifty-seven percent of the 1996 sample and 52% of the 1997 sample reported that they received a telemarketing call at least once a week from an unknown organization asking them to make a donation or investment, requesting them to buy something or to enter a sweepstakes or contest. Fourteen percent of the 1996 sample and 12% of the 1997 sample responded to these telemarketing calls by giving a credit card number, sending in money to make a purchase, investment, donation, or entering a contest. These figures show that a large proportion of the population (of those ages 50 and older) are in fact contacted quite frequently by telemarketers and are responding to such calls. Forty percent of the 1996 sample and 43% of the 1997 sample reported that they did not know how to identify whether a call was fraudulent. Finally, nearly two-thirds of the respondents from both surveys (64% of the 1996 sample of 65% of the 1997 sample) were unable to name any organizations that are working to protect people from being victimized by telephone fraud.

In addition to national surveys, regional studies have been carried out. In 1995, for example, residents from Delaware and Pennsylvania were surveyed for AT&T Corp. (Princeton Research Associates, 1995). Seventeen percent of those surveyed reported that they had been victims of fraud at least once during their lives. Individuals over the age of 50 were least likely to have succumbed to potentially fraudulent sales techniques; however, significant differences in fraud victimization were not found based on age.

LOSSES TO PERSONAL FRAUD

We have already referred to the scarcity of good data on the incidence and prevalence of fraud victimization; the same applies to data on the dollar losses. According to one of the national surveys of fraud victimization, the total annual losses exceed $40 billion. The average amount of money and property loss victims incurred was $216; there was large variation in loss experienced by these victims—the overall loss range for victims was from $0 to 65,000 (Titus et al., 1995).

There is also variation in the types of fraud that are attempted or completed most often. The types of fraud, for example, that were frequently mentioned by subjects in the Titus survey ("pigeon drop," fake bank official, fake ticket, phony inspector, credit repair) were not very common, and others, while mentioned frequently, usually were not successful ("free" prize, credit card number scam, fake charity). The fraud types that occurred most often and were more likely to have been successful were Appliance/Auto Repair, Fraudulent Price, 900 Number, Other Types, Subscriptions, and Warranty. Mean losses for these crimes were in excess of $280.00. It is important to note that some types of fraud (e.g., investment, insurance, broker/planner, and credit card number), while relatively infrequent and not usually successful, involved high losses for victims. If a similar survey were conducted today, Internet-related frauds and identity theft would most likely appear on this list.

Successful most often was a byproduct of consumer transactions that might have involved misunderstandings or "bad shopping experiences" rather than true fraud. The survey was designed throughout to cue the reporting of events that were criminal and fraudulent, involving the elements of deception, false and misleading information, impersonation, misrepresentation, abuse of trust, and failure to deliver. Furthermore, the legal elements of fraud were incorporated as appropriate into the wording of each screener question; the response option of "Not sure if it was legal" was available on every screener item. Thus it appears that the respondents *believed* that they were defrauded. Moreover, the evidence provided by congressional hearings and consumer protection agencies indicates that consumer transactions often do involve deception and abuse of trust for financial gain, which are key elements of economic crimes, as in the case of fraud.

Case studies of high-profile crimes also shed light on the financial toll exacted by fraud. In 1994, Shichor and colleagues mailed questionnaires to 152 victims of an oil and gas partnership telephone investment scam that ended in early 1991 (Shichor et al., 1996). Individuals who completed the surveys were selected randomly from the 8527 victims who lost money from this scam. The majority of the victims were between the ages of 52 and 63 years old, well educated, and male. Sixty-five percent of the victims invested less than $30,000, 17% between $30,000 and $74,999, and 18% invested more than $75,000. Victims were promised to receive between a 15 to 1 and 37 to 1 return on their investments within a few years. None of them received any returns.

In response to the recognition by United Kingdom's Home Office Crime Prevention Unit that credit and check card fraud have significant social and economic consequences, a telephone survey of victims was conducted by Barclaycard's Market Research Division in 1991 (Levi, 1991). Of the 200 individuals surveyed, 84% of the respondents reported that their credit cards were stolen, while the remainder reported that their cards had been lost. Of these individuals, 57% of the lost or stolen cards were used fraudulently. Fifteen percent of the sample were repeat victims of fraud or loss on one or more occasions. In over 40% of the cases of lost or stolen cards, other forms of personal identification, other credit cards, or check books were also stolen. Of these additional items that were stolen or lost, almost half of them were fraudulently used. Of this sample of 200 Barclaycard losses, for those who were victims of fraud as a result of the loss, an average of 12 fraudulent transactions were made using the lost or stolen card.

VICTIM CHARACTERISTICS

In personal fraud, as it is defined here, the victim's facilitation is required for the crime to occur. This may include one or more of several actions:

1) The victim either makes the initial contact with the offender or takes steps that lead to the initial contact (e.g., by mailing in a coupon in response to a "free vacation" advertisement, or by visiting a website that promises extravagant returns on investment), thus providing means of contact and signaling some receptivity to the "pitch."

2) The victim provides information about him/herself (e.g., desires, tastes, financial capacity) that helps the offender carry out the scam.

3) The victim allows the offender to convert what should be a business relationship into a personal relationship, to create a sense of trust, and to get a waiver of customary safeguards.

4) The victim allows the offender to create a scenario or version of events (e.g., specially selected, rare good fortune, unique opportunity, insider information, need for prompt action) that when believed sets the stage for fraud.

5) The victim writes checks, gives out credit card or bank account numbers, and in other ways provides the offender with access to his/her funds.

Personal frauds can be based on good citizenship (e.g., "bank inspector"), compassion and generosity (e.g., charity), or respect for authority (e.g., "building inspector"); however, an important component of many scams is a receptivity to the scam and to participation in it. Some scams increase the lure by painting themselves as a bit shady and the victim as something of a co-conspirator (Delord-Raynal, 1983). The lure of something free, absurdly cheap, or unrealistically lucrative is integral to many fraud pitches, and there seem to be large numbers of Americans ready to believe that business can turn a profit by giving things away.

Because of the ease with which con artists can accumulate, access, and utilize available information about us, there are also behaviors and life events that not only increase the likelihood of legitimate sales pressure but also increase the likelihood that a fraudulent solicitation will be received. These behaviors include: having been a fraud victim before; signing up for "free offers" and "prizes"; entering contests or sweepstakes; being on catalogue mailing lists or "junk mail" lists; belonging to organizations; buying things over the phone; using a 900 number; making purchases on the Internet; registering with many of the sites or groups on the Internet; engagement, marriage, birth, graduation, or death in the family; retiring or turning 65; moving, purchasing a house, car, or major appliance; having a major medical treatment or operation; buying stocks, bonds, some other investment or insurance; giving to a charity; and requesting information about an advertisement.

It appears that one of the surest ways to become a personal fraud victim is to have been a victim. Typically the names of fraud victims are added to "mooch" lists that are exchanged and sold among con artists for "reload" schemes (the same or similar scams) and "recovery" schemes (an offer to assist the victim recover his/her losses). Prior victims are targeted again and again because they are the very opposite of a "cold call"; they have given clear evidence of their vulnerability (Schulte, 1995). In the 1995 AARP study of fraud victims, 42% of victims reported receiving 20 or more telemarketer calls involving sale of a product, contribution to charity, or a contest or sweepstakes; 82% received one or more such calls within the past 6 months and 46% within the past week (AARP, 1996).

The media typically portrays the elderly population as prime targets of con artists, but Titus et al. (1995) found that those 65 and older were less likely to report being fraud victims, and that the probability that the recipient of a fraud attempt will succumb cannot be predicted by any demographic variable, including age. This finding is consistent with the AT&T survey discussed below, and with a 1993 survey by the AARP that examined older consumer behavior. According to the AARP survey, individuals who are ages 50 and older reported receiving fewer calls than the general population for "prize notifications" (AARP, 1993). In a second survey, AARP interviewed 745 victims of telemarketing fraud in 1995 and found that they are "besieged by telemarketers" (AARP, 1996). Specifically, 99% of the victims interviewed reported that they had been contacted by a telemarketer who was notifying them that they had won a prize or sweepstakes, or were selected as one of a few people who were eligible for a prize. Forty-two percent of the victims interviewed reported that they had received 20 or more calls during the past 6 months by telemarketers who asked for a charity contribution, tried to sell the victim something, or were notifying them about a contest or sweepstakes. In fact, 82% of the victims received one or more attempts within the past 6 months, and 46% within the past week. Contrary to the national survey by Titus et al. (1995), this research found that older individuals were more likely to be victimized by telemarketing fraud than younger people. Fifty-six percent of the victims were age 50 years and older, while only 36% of this age group comprised the general population. However, some of this over-representation could be explained by the findings of Titus et al. (1995) that older fraud victims were more likely to report to authorities.

Consistent with Titus et al. (1995), fraud victims interviewed in the AARP (1996) study were more likely to be well educated, well informed, relatively affluent, and not socially isolated. Interestingly, half of these victims reported sending in money for participation in a sweepstakes offer at some point in their lives, and nearly two-thirds of these individuals reported doing so more than once. However, the majority of the victims said that as a result of their experience, they would change their behavior in the future if they received a similar pitch.

The evidence from this limited set of fraud victimization surveys is unanimous that greater education is not a protective factor; instead, the evidence points to the reverse. Much of the evidence also suggests that older individuals are not at greater risk for fraud victimization. It may be that younger and better-educated people have wider interests, engage in a broader range of activities, and have more consumer participation in the marketplace than other demographic groups. If so, they may increase their exposure to fraudulent solicitations and transactions.

VICTIM IMPACTS

When thinking about or discussing crime, most people have images of robbery, assault, rape, and similar street crimes. As a result, a large amount of research in criminology and criminal justice has focused on the financial and physical consequences of these criminal actions on victims (Shichor et al., 1996). According to this research, victims experience self-blame, anxiety, and worry about their continued safety over a long period of time (Greenberg and Ruback, 1992). Unfortunately, criminological research has devoted much less attention to the aftermath of fraud victimization. This is an interesting fact, because many investigators believe that experience with fraud and other forms of white-collar crime have more devastating effects on victims than street crime does (e.g., Edelhertz, 1980). Fraud offenses involve issues such as a violation of trustworthiness and honesty—basic values that are not typically associated with street crime victimization. In fact, according to a survey of public attitudes in Illinois on the costs of white-collar crime, 55.2% of the respondents believed that white-collar crimes do more to undermine the morality in society than do regular street crimes (Cullen et al., 1983).

Financial and property loss is not the only consequence of fraud (Ganzini et al., 1990). This is clear from interviews with victims of a failed financial institution confirm this (Shover et al., 1994). Victims who lost investments in this institution (Southland Industrial Banking Corporation) due to the criminal activities of its officers and employees harbored feelings of bitterness and anger even 10 years following the victimization. In addition, a small proportion of the victims were completely devastated by their experiences, became severely depressed, and felt intensified feelings of anger and resentment by their belief in the injustice of their situation. These findings are mirrored in results from subsequent studies. In the study conducted by Titus et al. (1995), 10–20% of the victims reported health problems, lost time from work, and harm to other family members. In the Shichor et al. study (1996), when victims were notified that they would be losing their investments, they felt "anger," "enraged," "sick," "depressed," "devastated," and other variations of these responses of emotional outrage. Even after being contacted years after the scheme, victims continued to have feelings of anger and distress, and many of the victims still remained in serious financial jeopardy as a result of the scam. Interestingly, victims of this particular telephone scam felt that their experience was sufficient protection from repeat fraudulent victimization experiences of this nature.

PREVENTION AND CONTROL OF PERSONAL FRAUD

There is a saying among bunco squad detectives that "If you want to know what tomorrow' scams will be, watch tonight's news." This is only partially true; with fraud there is not so much that is new under the sun; indeed, the "swoop and squat" staged automobile accidents that were recently featured on two TV news magazines first made their appearance in the very infancy of the automobile (Dornstein, 1996). And while some con artists are sadists or sociopaths, others simply see it as a line of work that pays well, is not boring or particularly demanding, differs but little from other forms of business, and poses very few risks of punishment.

In order to have an impact on individual behavior for the prevention of personal fraud victimization and to develop policies for the criminal justice system's reaction to such crime, it is imperative for the criminological community accurately to estimate the nature and extent of fraud victimization. Unfortunately, studies of fraud victimization are few in number and statistical estimates of these crimes are under-represented in the literature (Moore and Mills, 1990). Of the few studies that have been conducted, many suffer methodological problems such as the utilization of small samples and a reliance on samples of convenience. Criminology has devoted less attention to the aftermath of fraud victimization, though some believe that victims' experiences with fraud and other forms of white-collar crime can have more devastating effects than street crime on victims. In fact, according to a survey of public attitudes in Illinois on the costs of white-collar crimes, 55.2% of the respondents believed that white-collar crimes do more to undermine the morality in society than do regular street crimes; 76% believed that the amount of money lost through white-collar crime is more than that lost as a result of street crimes such as robberies, burglaries, and thefts (Cullen et al., 1983). However, the element of danger, and the threat of death, bodily injury, confrontation, or the violation of one's person or property are not present in fraud, as in these other crimes. The criminals do not invoke the same amount of loathing and fear, nor the victims the same amount of compassion. Fraud cases are also much more difficult cases to investigate, prosecute, convict, and get meaningful sentences for.

Research aimed at prevention of fraud victimization would benefit from enhanced and routine data collection on a national level. Currently, the criminological community has incomplete data on the types of fraud that are occurring, who the victims of fraud victimization are, the costs of fraud victimization to victims and society, and what strategies have been effective in controlling and preventing fraud victimization. In addition to routine and comprehensive data collection, another research priority is to examine the operations of con artists with a view to interdicting them; most of what we know today comes from the practitioner literature. For example, more knowledge is needed on how con artists develop their lists of potential victims for purposes of preventing individuals from appearing on these lists and to remove victims' names from these lists. Another priority would be to explore research of a preemptive nature, which involves predicting what new scams will be committed by con artists, how new technologies will be used to carry them out, and how these events can actually be prevented. A final item for a future research agenda includes a measure of the effectiveness of public information campaigns that aimed at teaching people how to recognize scams, and how to terminate attempted scams quickly and effectively. According to the national survey by Titus et al. (1995), fraud attempts were less likely to succeed if the potential victim had heard of this type of fraud before or had tried to investigate the person or proposition before responding. There may be a preventive role for public information campaigns to increase general understanding of how frauds are perpetrated, what current frauds are, how to decrease one's exposure and risk, how to investigate a solicitation before participating in it, and how to report if victimized. There is some research evidence that these general campaigns can be effective (AARP, 1997), but we need to know more about how best to conduct them for different populations and against different types of scam. For example, given that a powerful predictor of future victimization is past victimization, how can more targeted campaigns aimed at known victims be mounted for fraud, as is already done for such crimes as burglary.

REFERENCES

American Association of Retired Persons. 1993. *The AARP Report on the 1993 Survey of Older Consumer Behavior.* Conducted by Princeton Survey Research Associates.
———. 1996. *Telemarketing Fraud and Older Americans: An AARP Study.* Conducted by Princeton Survey Research Associates.
———. 1997. *Comparative Findings from the 1996 & 1997 Omnibus Surveys on Telemarketing Fraud.* Evaluation Research Services, Research Division, June.
Bass, Ron, and Lois Hoeffler. 1992. *Telephone-Based Fraud: A Survey of the American Public.* New York: Louis Harris and Associates.
Bureau of Justice Statistics. 1996. *Criminal Victimization in the United States 1994.* Washington, D.C.: Office of Justice Programs, U.S. Department of Justice.
———. 1997. *1996 Sourcebook of Criminal Justice Statistics.* Washington, D.C.: Office of Justice Programs, U.S. Department of Justice.
Cullen, Francis T., Richard A. Mathers, Gregory A. Clark, and John B. Cullen. 1983. "Public support for punishing white-collar crime: Blaming the victim revisited?" *Journal of Criminal Justice* 11:481–93.
Delord-Raynal, Yvette. 1983. "Les victimes de la delinquance d'affaires." *Victimology: An International Journal* 8:68–79.
Dornstein, Ken. 1996. *Accidentally, On Purpose: The Making of a Personal Injury Underworld in America.* New York: St. Martin's Press.
Edelhertz, Herbert. 1980. "Appendix B: White Collar Crime." Pp. 119–32 in *A National Strategy for Containing White Collar Crime,* edited by Herbert Edelhertz and Charles Rogovin. Lexington, Mass.: D. C. Heath.

Federal Bureau of Investigation. 1984. *Uniform Crime Reporting Handbook.* Washington, D.C.: U.S. Government Printing Office.

———. 1997. *Crime in the United States, 1996.* Washington, D.C.: U.S. Government Printing Office.

Ganzini, Linda, Bentson McFarland, and Joseph Bloom. 1990. "Victims of fraud: Comparing victims of white collar and violent crime." *Bulletin of the American Academy of Psychiatry and the Law* 18:55–63.,

Greenberg, M., and R. B. Ruback. 1992. *After the Crime: Victim Decision Making.* New York: Plenum.

Levi, Michael. 1991. *Credit and Cheque Card Fraud: Some Victim Survey Data and Their Implications.* London: Home Office Research and Statistics Department.

Moore, Elizabeth, and Michael Mills. 1990. "The neglected victims and unexamined costs of white collar crime." *Crime & Delinquency* 36:408–18.

Nelson, James F. 1980. "Multiple victimization in American cities: A statistical analysis of rare events." *American Journal of Sociology* 85:871–91.

Princeton Research Associates. 1995. *Consumer Rights and Technology Survey.* March.

Schulte, Fred. 1995. *Fleeced!: Telemarketing Rip-offs and How to Avoid Them.* Amherst, N.Y.: Prometheus Books.

Shichor, David, J. Doocy, and Gilbert Geis. 1996. "Anger, disappointment, and disgust: Reactions of victims of a telephone investment scam." Pp. 105–11 in *International Victimology: Selected Papers from the 8th International Symposium,* edited by Chris Sumner, Mark Isreal, Michael O'Conner, and Rick Sarre.

Shover, Neal, Greer Litton Fox, and Michael Mills. 1994. "Long-term consequences of victimization by white-collar crime." *Justice Quarterly* 11:75–98.

Sparks, Richard F. 1981. "Multiple victimization: Evidence, theory, and future research." *Journal of Criminal Law and Criminology* 72:762–78.

Titus, Richard M., Fred Heinzelmann, and John Boyle. 1995. "Victimization of persons by fraud." *Crime & Delinquency* 41:54–72.

Tomlin, John W. 1982. "Victims of white-collar crimes." Pp. 274–78 in *The Victim in International Perspective,* edited by Hans Joachim Schneider. New York: Walter de Gruyter.

Walsh, Marilyn E., and Donna D. Schram. 1980. "Victims of white-collar crime: Accuser or accused?" Pp. 32–52 in *White-Collar Crime: Theory and Research,* edited by Gilbert Geis and Ezra Stotland. Beverly Hills, Calif.: Sage.

White-Collar Crime Victimization

MICHAEL LEVI

Crime victimization surveys and the standard debates concerning "what should be done about the victims" almost invariably exclude discussion of corporate and white-collar crime. In this sense victim movements, like victim sur-

"White-Collar Crime Victimization" from *White-Collar Crime Reconsidered* (Northeastern University Press, 1992), pp. 169–94. Reprinted by permission.

veys, reinforce traditional ideologies of what crime is and who offenders are. While accepting that corporate health and safety and environmental violations are more serious in their social impact than financial white-collar crime and are perceived seriously by the general public, this article aims to redress that victimization research imbalance slightly by discussing some recent modest . . . attempts to examine the extent of fraud against business and business attitudes toward fraud in Britain. . . .

. . . [T]he frauds in this chapter occupy a complex moral arena in which wealthy corporations and individuals and—less rewardingly because they have less to steal—the poor are defrauded by the relatively poor, and by the wealthy criminal professionals and professional criminals. My analysis will draw primarily upon a recent study carried out for the Economic and Social Research Council (Levi and Pithouse, forthcoming); on two modest, exploratory, corporate-fraud victimization surveys conducted in 1985 and 1989 in collaboration with the accounting firm Ernst & Young (Levi, 1987; Levi and Sherwin, 1989); and on a study of check and credit-card fraud for the Home Office (Levi et al., 1991).

METHODOLOGY AND SOURCES OF EVIDENCE

The regulation of fraud is a messy activity. Governmental and quasi-governmental agencies that are engaged in investigating it include the police—both fraud squads and divisional criminal investigation departments—the Post Office, Department of Trade and Industry, H.M. Customs and Excise, the Inland Revenue, the Serious Fraud Office, the Office of Fair Trading, the Bank of England, Lloyd's of London, the Securities and Investments Board, and self-regulatory organizations such as the Securities and Futures Association and the Financial Intermediaries, Managers, and Brokers Regulatory Association. In addition, there is a vast array of commercial bodies—from Visa International and Dun & Bradstreet to gumshoes in pokey offices—whose investigation and recovery services are purchased by victims. Officials from all of these types of agencies were interviewed.

Also interviewed were a sample of victims of fraud drawn from court records at the London Central Criminal Court (1984–1985) and Cardiff Crown Court (1983–1984) and a more ad hoc set of victims known to my private-sector "police" contacts. The former were selected so as to represent both "repeat players"—larger commercial organizations such as insurance companies, who were generally multiple victims—and "one-shot players," generally private individuals such as investor fraud victims. We (Levi and Pithouse, forthcoming) were able to discuss fraud with representatives of prominent companies in banking, credit finance, insurance, and building-society sectors. Victims in our court sample who were not interviewed were given postal questionnaires regarding the impact of fraud and their experience with the criminal justice system. The years were selected as the most recent two-year periods for which full records were available: examining the records was a very time-consuming process.

The corporate-victimization survey conducted by Levi and Sherwin (1989) involved (1) an anonymous survey sent to the chairpersons of 200 corporations representative of all large-quoted companies, of which 67 (drawn from all sectors asked) returned questionnaires, and over 20 others replied stating basically that since they had experienced no fraud, they saw little point in completing the questionnaire; and (2) a telephone survey of 144 companies, stratified to include a disproportionate number of financial-services firms, which was devised and conducted by a market research company. However, cold calling even senior executives with complex questions about levels of fraud experienced in their organizations and about their responses to it seems to be of very limited value. My detailed discussions indicate that few such executives know all the details of corporate victimization due to the segmentation of such knowledge because of diffuse responsibilities and intraorganizational cover-ups of fraud. Moreover, informal feedback suggests that telephone personnel were sometimes given data of doubtful validity simply to terminate the interviews. Consequently, I shall refer to the telephone survey findings only where I judge the results to be reasonably valid and will refer explicitly to the origins of the data.

Finally, the check and credit card fraud study by Levi et al. (1991) involved extensive interviews with all major financial institutions and security printers in the U.K., as well as an analysis of their officially reported and unreported fraud data. I also interviewed three professional fraudsters in the course of this latter study, to supplement the dozens of fraudsters I have interviewed since 1973.

RESEARCH FINDINGS

Although the term "white-collar crime" is usually treated—at least by non-criminologists—as a synonym for fraud, most frauds taken to court would be depicted more accurately as "blue-collar crime," being committed by people of modest social origin (see Weisburd et al., 1991, for U.S. data drawn from federal cases that comes to similar conclusions). On the other hand, looked at in terms of average sums involved and total costs, the major fraud victims were financial services firms and the major offenders were white-collar males.

Most victims whose cases were prosecuted were organizations: only 15 percent were private individuals. The smaller frauds were typically what might be described as "hit-and-run" thefts against banks and credit card companies by "blue-collar" males. The larger ones typically involve more social and commercial interaction between victims and offenders, and are carried out by white-collar males using business organizations who defraud, on average, twice as many victims as do the others.

The Victims

The victims at both Cardiff Crown Court and the London Central Criminal Court (Old Bailey) were typically businesses providing financial services. Private citizen victims were a distinct minority in both places: they comprised just 36 out of 291 at Cardiff, and among this group those that lost most did so at the hands of family and friends (or former friends!). Frauds by kith and kin constituted just 3 of the 36 cases, and averaged £4,500 compared with £300 for the average individual victims defrauded by outsiders. At the Old Bailey, there were only 10 private citizens among 116 victims: 4 were relieved of an average of £11,500 by "close friends"; 2 lost (but later recovered) their family home from relatives who forged documents to remortgage their property without their knowledge; and the remainder lost an average of £1,000 in various business encounters. In short, friends and family seem to be in a better position than strangers to defraud large sums from private citizens. As one fraudster interviewed in an earlier study expressed it, "Do your friends first; they're easier" (Levi, 1981). It appears also that friends are more profitable!

In both courts, the majority of victims were commercial organizations. Those who lost most were (in descending order): banks, customers or clients in an assumed fiduciary relationship with the fraudster, employers, suppliers of goods and services, insurance companies, finance companies, building societies, and retail services. Since then, there has been a spate of revelations regarding rings of mortgage frauds, with multiple mortgages on the same—or even a nonexistent—property. So building societies (savings and loans in the U.S.) will have increased their market share as fraud victims, even prior to their wider involvement in the supply of financial services as part of the deregulation process. Likewise, there have been several large pension fund frauds, such as those concerned with the late Robert Maxwell. The retail sector suffered less because unless negligence or conspiracy is shown, many frauds in this sector impact not on them but on the credit card and hire-purchase companies whose credit facilities are misused. (Though the artificially low ceiling on check guarantee cards set by the banks means that many losses on larger checks are borne not by the bankers, but by the sellers of the goods and services, or by international organizations such as Transax, which use their databases to guarantee—or refuse to guarantee—checks in exchange for a fee proportionate to the transaction.) Banks lost a total of £3.2 million: £170,000 of this was stolen by 13 blue-collar fraudsters, the remainder by 23 white-collar ones. Eleven white-collar fraudsters relieved their trusting clients or customers of £1.8 million. Employers lost £1.7 million, mainly to 28 white-collar employees. Suppliers of goods and services lost £1.1 million to 10 white-collar, and £10,000 to 3 blue-collar defendants. Insurance companies lost £230,000 to 9 white-collar fraudsters, and £60,000 to 16 blue-collar ones.

To place these cost data in context, in 1986, excluding attempts and cases where nothing was taken, the average losses of nonfraud property crime were £644 for burglary dwelling; £578 for burglary other than in a dwelling; £1,191 for robbery; and £150 for thefts, excluding auto theft. The median figures are much lower than this. These findings on the sectoral distribution of fraud victimization correspond reasonably well with the survey by Levi (1988) of cases handled by fraud squads nationally in 1985 (though these exclude the normally smaller cases handled by the Criminal Investigation Department officers on division, as well as frauds dealt with by other public sector agencies).

However, there is one sense in which looking at costs in absolute terms is misleading: the impact of fraud (and other crimes) should properly be seen in terms of the victim's means, net of insurance costs and benefits. In other words, a fraud of £100 upon a poor person may be more damaging than a fraud of £10 million upon an asset-rich insurance company, though the latter appears to be more serious and, unlike the £100 fraud, is likely to receive the attention of the Serious Fraud Office launched in April 1988 under the Criminal Justice Act of 1987, which normally will not handle a fraud unless at least £2 million has been lost. (And properly so, since small frauds do not need the attention of specialist accountants and lawyers. On the other hand, in practice, the allocation of regulatory resources is a zero-sum game, and more go into cases with a high media and/or political profile than into those with "needy" but unsensational victims.) An alternative method of judging seriousness is to look at how seriously the victims regard their loss. In our survey, 37 percent of all victims thought that their frauds were serious or very serious losses to themselves or to their organizations; the remainder thought the loss was either moderate or not significant at all (Levi and Pithouse, forthcoming).

The 1989 Corporate Victimization Findings on the Amount of Fraud against Large Companies

In the past five years, a third of large U.K. companies in our sample reported to the authorities at least one fraud involving over £50,000; 6 percent reported more than two such frauds (Levi and Sherwin, 1989). Since 1986, 7 percent of the companies surveyed reported a fraud involving more than £500,000. The reporting of fraud tended towards extremes: companies made either extensive use, or almost no use, of the police and other regulatory agencies.

In order not to have findings distorted by small frauds, we asked companies to give us some details about the worst fraud cases that they had reported since January 1986, the date of the previous fraud survey (see Levi, 1987). In these cases, the average amount actually obtained was £215,180, and the average amount attempted was £232,487. The average losses to financial services companies were substantially greater. Of the companies reporting fraud, the median sum of money obtained in the worst fraud was £40,000, thus emphasizing the importance of examining medians in modest samples, for a small number of million-pound frauds can distort the mean. (In 1985, Levi had asked a slightly different question about the most recent fraud they had reported, which screened in small check and credit card frauds. There, the mean was £89,537 and the median £15,000; see Levi, 1987.)

How did these worst frauds come to light? Only one came to light during an external audit (and the telephone survey found only four frauds of whatever seriousness that came to light during external audits). This confirms other studies of auditor nondetection in the U.K. and the U.S. The poor record of the auditors of savings and loan corporations in detecting and/or reporting frauds that caused their downfall was the rationale for the decision in 1990 not to permit five out of the six largest audit firms to carry out work on the rescue of savings and loans. Levi and Sherwin (1989) found that by far the most common source of detection was internal checks and internal audit—occasionally on the systems advice of external auditors—followed by information from junior employees and information from customers. Less orthodox sources of enlightenment came when (1) a bribe was (unsuccessfully) offered to a new employee to keep quiet, (2) when research was carried out to decide whether or not to close down a subsidiary, and (3) when the offender was away on holiday! Disgruntled lovers—a phenomenon observed in our 1985 survey as a salient source of reports—did not feature in the 1989 survey. Perhaps this is a reflection of the heavier executive workload in the late 1980s, unless executives learned from our previous survey that they should retain them or "cool them out" more subtly!

Clearly, these studies of fraud victims are predicated upon the selection processes used to sample them. The corporate and individual victim sample in Levi and Sherwin (1989) did go beyond the court-derived one of Levi and Pithouse (forthcoming), and, to the extent that changes in the policing and prosecution process—described by Levi (1987) and Wood (1989)—broaden the base of prosecutions, one might anticipate changes in victim sets in the future, particularly in the corporate manipulation case where there are fewer clear-cut victims. At all stages, however, we are propelled to utilize some implicit or explicit concept of "white-collar crime" when deciding who is and is not a legitimate sample member. (See, further, Shapiro, 1980; Levi, 1989; Weisburd et al., 1991.) In 1989, arrests were made following a vast fraud upon mainly elderly investors who were induced to believe that they were investing in government securities when, in reality, it appears that they were investing in speedboats and speculative corporate ventures (LeQuesne, 1988). On some occasions, this would merely have led to a decision that no crime had occurred, or that there was insufficient evidence to yield more than than a 50 percent probability of conviction (however such a judgement is made), or that prosecution was not "in the public interest" (whatever that is!). However, public and political pressure assisted in the prioritization of this case, making it into a crime. (In February 1992, the principal was jailed for ten years, though two codefendants were acquitted. Had they all been acquitted, should this have been classified as a crime?) After an enormous amount of lobbying and massive media support, and a critical report by the parliamentary commissioner, the losers were mainly repaid by the Department of Trade and Industry, which had continued to license the British part of the investment firm when it (or, more precisely, some officials within it) had received strong representations that the firm was misleading investors. However, even though repaid, the victims still suffered emotional and physical hardship in a way not entirely related to the materiality of their financial losses as a proportion of their liquid and illiquid assets (Levi and Pithouse, forthcoming). The measurement of this damage, except in terms of general-health questionnaires and sad tales, is, however, extremely difficult to ascertain. This issue of measuring victim impact raises problems for retributivists that lie outside the scope of this article. . . .

Business Motives for Reporting Fraud and Confidence in the Authorities

When asked what their motives had been for reporting frauds, the order of priorities given was as follows: (1) to get the money back; (2) to deter others from committing fraud against one's company in the future; (3) to stop the offenders from doing it again to others; and (4) out of social obligation. Other reasons given included to publicize details of those involved and to punish the offender. Almost a third of financial services and two-thirds of other companies stated that they would be more likely to report fraud in the future if there was a great likelihood of obtaining compensation. . . .

What about reasons for not reporting frauds of which one believes oneself the victim? Overall, the most common reason cited for not reporting frauds was that too much management time was tied up in reporting one. Embarrassment at the revelation of the fraud was far more significant to financial services companies than to others, while the additional burden of reporting upon expensive management time was more salient to companies outside the financial sector than to those inside it. The supposed softness of the courts played almost no role in decisions not to report . . . interviews support that this is beginning to affect prosecution decisions.

REFERENCES

Levi, M. (1981). *The phantom capitalists: The organisation and control of long-firm fraud.* Aldeshot, England: Gower.

———. (1987). *Regulating fraud: White-collar crime and the criminal process.* London: Routledge.

———. (1988). The prevention of fraud. Home Office Prevention Unit Paper 17. London: Home Office.

———. (1989). Recent texts on white-collar crime: An overview. *British Journal of Criminology, 29* (4), 412–415.

Levi, M., and Sherwin, D. (1989). *Fraud '89: The extent of fraud against large companies and executive views on what should be done about it.* London: Ernst & Young (accountants).

Levi, M., Bissell, P., and Richardson, T. (1991). The prevention of cheque and credit card fraud. Home Office Crime Prevention Unit Paper. London: Home office.

Levi, M., and Pithouse, A. (forthcoming). *The victims of fraud.* Milton Keynes, England: Open University Press.

Shapiro, S. (1980). *Thinking about white-collar crime: Matters of conceptualization and research.* Washington, D.C.: Department of Justice, National Institute of Justice.

Weisburd, D., Wheeler, S., Waring, E., and Bode, N. (1991). *Crimes of the middle classes: White-collar offenders in the federal courts.* New Haven: Yale University Press.

Wood, J. (1989). The serious fraud office. *Criminal Law Review,* March, 175–184.

Consequences of Victimization by White-Collar Crime*

Neal Shover, Greer Litton Fox, and Michael Mills

"[After] the mid-1970s the victims' rights movement emerged as a powerful force in America's response to crime. Testimony to the symbolic and political strength of this movement is the initiation of victim assistance and victim compensation programs in states across the nation and, more recently, in amendments to state criminal codes giving crime victims a voice in the prosecution and sentencing of offenders (Davis and Henley 1990; Elias 1993). Political activity has been matched by new interest in the impact of crime on its many victims. Investigators have documented the physical injuries, suffering, and financial loss caused by offenders and thereby have provided justification for victim compensation programs. Investigators, however, largely have ignored problems faced by victims of white-collar offenders. . . .

THE PROBLEM

. . . [A]part from the immediate impact of white-collar crime on individual victims, the wider *delegitimation effects* may be serious. Some 40 years ago Sutherland suggested that it may be harmful to the social fabric in ways uniquely its own. Because it violates trust, white-collar crime breeds distrust, lowers social morale, and "attack[s] the fundamental principles of American institutions" (Sutherland 1949:13).

Sutherland may have been the first to call attention to the costs of white-collar crime, but he is not alone (eg., President's Commission 1967; Shichor

"Consequences of Victimization by White-Collar Crime" from *Justice Quarterly* 11:1 (March 1994): 75–98. Reprinted by permission.

*Support for this research was provided by the Social Science Research Institute and the Department of Sociology, University of Tennessee, Knoxville. Points of view or opinions expressed here do not necessarily reflect the policies or positions of the Institute.

PANEL 6   Theft of Natural Resources

On July 25, 1998, the Tennessee Shell Company, a subsidiary of Kogen Trading of Japan, pleaded guilty to purchasing thousands of pounds of freshwater mussels harvested illegally from rivers in Michigan, Ohio, Kentucky, and West Virginia. The shells were sent to Japan, where they are cut up into small beads and inserted into live oysters. Secretions from the oysters then cover the implant and result in a cultured pearl. Although Tennessee Shell is licensed to export legally harvested shells, it knowingly bought shells that were taken from protected waters. Of some 300 species of freshwater mussels, 30 are extinct and 70 are listed as endangered. According to a U.S. wildlife official, they are an important source of early warning of environmental pollution. The U.S. attorney characterized the crime as "plundering America's wildlife for profit." As part of its plea agreement, Tennessee Shell also agreed to pay a $1 million restitution payment to be used for mussel research and restoration of freshwater mussel beds.

Sources: Columbus Dispatch, July 25, 1998, page 1A; and *Knoxville News-Sentinel,* July 25, 1998, page A5.

1989). Nor is he alone in suggesting that these costs may include the erosion of legitimacy for prevailing institutions and persons who hold high-level positions in those institutions. . . .

Observers have identified two potentially significant areas of delegitimation caused by white-collar crime. One is loss of confidence in *political* institutions, processes, and leaders. Crimes committed by public officials and agencies or with their acquiescence may damage the public faith in and regard for political leaders and institutions. The second potential effect is diminution of trust in business leaders and *economic* institutions. "Trust," as Shapiro (1984:2) notes, "is truly the foundation of capitalism." In its absence, "people would not delegate discretionary use of their funds to other entrepreneurs . . . [and] capitalism would break down as funds were stuffed into mattresses, savings accounts, and solo business enterprises rather than invested in the business ventures of American corporations." This may be true particulary when white-collar crime becomes integrated closely with the structure of legitimate business (Conklin 1977:7).

In view of the importance of these arguments, it is remarkable that the delegitimation effects of white-collar crime have been the focus of so little research. In one of the few investigations of this subject, Peters and Welch (1980) examined the electoral consequences of charges of official corruption. Analyzing data from five congressional elections held from 1968 to 1978, they found little apparent effect on voter turnout and election outcomes. In contrast to the aggregate-level approach taken by those authors, we present an individual-level analysis based on personal interviews with former investors in a financial loan institution that failed largely because of criminal conduct by its officers and employees. We pursue two objectives. First, we describe the array of effects experienced by victims, and suggest an interpretation. Second, we explore the personal and institutional delegitimation effects produced by the crime-facilitated collapse of the loan company. We conclude with brief interpretive comments that underscore the importance of sociohistorical and ideological contexts in constructing meanings of white-collar criminal victimization and the potential contributions of social science inquiry.

BACKGROUND

The Southland Industrial Banking Corporation (SIBC) chartered in 1929, operated for many years as a small loan company in a southeastern state. Under a "grandfather" clause it was permitted to use the word *banking* in its name, even though other industrial loan and thrift companies were prohibited from doing so. The business of SIBC, which some people referred to as a "bank impersonator," consisted of making loans to individuals and business entities. The most important source of funds for SIBC was money received through the sale of investment certificates; these were remarkably similar to certificates of deposit (CDs) offered by commercial banks and savings and loan institutions. Unlike CDs, the certificates of investment offered by SIBC were not insured, although they generally earned a higher rate of interest than similar accounts at commercial banks and savings and loans. SIBC grew during the 1970s, and eventually operated nine separate branches located in six counties in the eastern part of its home state. In February 1983, some 4,000 individuals and businesses held investment certificates or passbook accounts in SIBC totaling nearly $51 million (R.J. Fast, personal communication, May 28, 1991).

On March 10, 1983, three weeks after the collapse of a local bank whose operations were entangled with its own, SIBC filed a petition to reorganize under Chapter 11 of the Bankruptcy Code. The Federal Deposit Insurance Corporation (FDIC) conducted a special examination of SIBC's assets as of April 4, 1983 to determine whether SIBC might qualify for federal deposit insurance. FDIC revealed "gross mismanagement" of SIBC's resources, including numerous examples of abusive and extremely complicated insider dealings. A variety of state and federal criminal indictments were returned against officers and employees of SIBC. Subsequently the defendants were acquitted of some charges, were found guilty of others, and pleaded guilty to still others. Eventually H.C. Baker, SIBC's former president and the principal defendant in the case, was sentenced to 20 years' federal imprisonment.

The Bankruptcy Code vests in the bankruptcy judge substantial discretion in resolving Chapter 11 petitions (Lebowitz 1986). Once SIBC's Chapter 11 bankruptcy petition was filed, the fate of SIBC and its investors was largely in his hands. The bankruptcy judge is authorized either to oversee a plan for corporate reorganization (if one is submitted) or, alternatively, to order the liquidation of the failed institution and the distribution of its assets to creditors. In this instance, to represent the interest of investors and other creditors, the judge appointed a creditor's committee consisting of seven persons whose investments in SIBC were among the largest. A plan of reorganization was developed by a group of out-of-state investors, their attorneys, the bankruptcy trustee, and the creditor's committee. The plan called for formation of the East State Bank Corporation (ESBC) as successor in interest to SIBC, thus allowing it to be awarded SIBC's remaining assets. These assets, along with capital from the out-of-state investors, would be used to place ESBC on a sound financial footing. A liquidating trust also would be established to recover SIBC's outstanding loans and other debts, which then would be forwarded to ESBC. Underlying the reorganization plan was the assumption that with SIBC's assets as a foundation, with funds provided by the new investors, with the infusion of recovered funds from the liquidating trust, and with competent and honest new management, ESBC would succeed where SIBC had failed. This arrangement would allow ESBC eventually to repay SIBC's victimized depositors and would allow the out-of-state investors to realize a profitable return on their risk capital.

Under the terms of the plan of reorganization, which gained approval from all quarters, businesses and individuals with funds invested at the time of the collapse were defined and treated as "unsecured creditors," and were divided into three categories. Those with less than $1,000 invested or deposited in SIBC received full return of their funds; those with $1,001 to $5,000 invested received a three-year certificate of deposit for the full amount of their investment, albeit at a rate of interest lower than promised by SIBC. Those with more than $5,000 invested or deposited received a 10-year certificate of deposit for 30 percent of their investment; for the remaining 70 percent they received stock claims in the new bank and an interest certificate in the liquidating trust.

Ten years after the collapse of SIBC, these interest certificates have yielded no return to holders. The same is true of the stock claims; in view of the present financial condition of SIBC's successor, there is little chance that they will ever generate any income for victims (T. Du Voisin, personal communication, March 16, 1993). That is, persons with more than $5,000 invested in SIBC have received only 30 percent of their investment, with no guarantee that they ever will receive the remaining 70 percent. Because many of the investors are approaching old age, this outcome seems increasingly likely with the passing years.

The bankruptcy process and the plan of reorganization are central to understanding the outcome of the SIBC case and its impact on former investors. Not only could investors be subject to victimization through direct loss of funds that were tied up in investment certificates and passbook accounts at the time of the SIBC collapse (loss victimization); in addition, for some investors, the bankruptcy process itself became a second source of victimization (resolution victimization). From the outset, former investors and other interested parties were assigned legal statuses and definitions that distorted and (in a minority of cases) greatly intensified the impact of their loss victimization. Exercising his discretionary power (Treister 1986), the bankruptcy judge ruled that SIBC was insolvent 90 days before the bankruptcy petition was filed. He ruled further that depositors and investors who withdrew funds during this 90-day period were "preferential creditors," and ordered them to return the funds to the liquidating trustee. His decision was applied even to investors who redeemed investment certificates that happened to mature during the 90-day period. As a result, these investors could be treated in the same fashion as any who may have acted on "inside information" and who withdrew funds before the collapse. Those who failed to comply with the judge's order to return funds withdrawn during this period were subject to legal action by the liquidating trustee. The judge's "90-day ruling" affected some 1,000 individual account holders. Some of these persons returned their funds voluntarily; the remainder promptly were sued by the trustee.

The trustee obtained summary judgments against all but a fraction of the victims affected by the "90-day rule." He also sued for, and was awarded, interest on the disputed funds. Many victims who initially resisted the trustee's efforts to reclaim their funds eventually negotiated settlements with him, but actions against others remain unconcluded 10 years after the process began. These investors, opposed by the trustee's attorneys, met with nothing but frustration and unfavorable judicial decisions. Because of accumulating interest charges, the sums of money they owed the liquidating trustee eventually far exceeded their original SIBC accounts. The trustee is empowered by the Bankruptcy Code to scrutinize their assets—home, land, automobiles, wages, and the like—for recovery of the contested funds plus interest charges. Their property was subject to seizure by the trustee and could be sold at public auction to satisfy all or part of outstanding judgments. Property belonging to some former investors, in fact, was seized and sold; the wages of other investors were garnished; and liens were placed on property belonging to still others.

METHODS AND DATA

Interview data for this study were collected during 1990–1991. To select a sample of SIBC victims we began by examining a list of the names, the 1983 addresses, and the amount of the deposits or investments of SIBC's former customers that was generated and maintained in the office of the U.S. Bankruptcy Court in the city where SIBC was based. Although it would have been desirable to collect data from a random sample of investors on the list, practical difficulties made this impossible: in the years after 1983, many investors either moved out of the area or died.

Taking care to include ample numbers of persons with large and small investments, and excluding investors who lived outside the immediate metropolitan area where SIBC had its headquarters, we selected approximately 300 names from the 1983 list. We then searched the telephone directory for their telephone numbers, telephoned those persons we could locate, explained the research project, and asked them to grant us a brief interview at a time and place convenient for them. Our selection of respondents was guided by the desire to include a wide range of investors. Investments by members of the interview sample ranged from $1,400 to $205,000 (mean = $33,251; median = $16,000). Of approximately 150 persons contacted, we eventually conducted interviews with 45 investors and two close relatives of now-infirm or deceased investors. The 47 respondents ranged in age from 26 to 89, and averaged 63 years of age. They had completed an average of 15 years of education. Although 69 percent were retired from employment when interviewed, most had spent their later working lives as blue-collar craftsmen, as owner/operators of small businesses, or as public-sector professionals. We do not know how closely the interview sample resembles the total group of former SIBC investors.

Employing qualitative research procedures, we developed an interview guide, used it during the interviews, and revised it several times during the course of the study in response to ongoing analysis. Topics covered included the history and extent of respondents' investments in SIBC, their reactions upon hearing that it had filed for bankruptcy protection, the effects of victimization and financial loss in specific areas of their lives and finances (e.g., physical health and medical care), and the impact of the experience on their respect for and confidence in prevailing economic and political institutions. We conducted the interviews by asking respondents questions designed to elicit their assessments retrospectively before 1983 and at the time of the interview.

Despite the passage of years, most respondents spoke readily about their reactions to the bankruptcy, although they seemed less clear in remembering the details of the process and of the settlement itself. Even so, we cannot rule out the possibility that selective, potentially biasing recall may have been operating when respondents reported their experiences. Nor can we state confidently that any negative recollections of the SIBC experience do not reflect period effects, particularly because we collected our data at a time when the mass media almost daily reported crimes in the savings and loan industry.

We continued contacting and interviewing victims until we were confident of our understanding of the victimization experience. During interviews with the first 29 respondents the interviewer recorded notes on a standardized form; the final 18 interviews were audio tape-recorded and later transcribed. During later interviews we also endeavored to include several standardized questions, such as: "Overall, is your confidence in American business leaders today greater, about the same, or less than it was [seven] years ago?" and "Why?"

To obtain a clearer picture of the range of variation and to determine how closely the interview sample approximated the universe of former SIBC accounts, we also selected from bankruptcy court records, after a random start, a systematic sample of 275 former savings accounts and investment certificates. The records contained no information except the amount of each account and the account holder's name and address. Accounts in the sample ranged in value from $.06 to $190,000 (mean = $9,922; median = $3,768). We used data from this sample of records to estimate the distribution of financial loss victimization among individuals who held SIBC accounts. Comparison of data from the records sample with the characteristics of the interview sample shows that the latter includes a greater number of larger investments, and therefore of investors who lost large sums of money when SIBC collapsed. Therefore the impact of sampling on our findings may be twofold: 1) the interview sample may yield a richer array of evidence of the most serious effects of loss victimization, and 2) to the extent delegitimation parallels loss victimization (i.e., increases with dollar loss), the interview data may be biased somewhat toward discovery of delegitimation effects.

We have no systematic data on the perspectives or experiences of those who declined to be interviewed. They did so for many reasons, chiefly lack of interest, advanced age, embarrassment about their investment in SIBC, and unwillingness to revisit unpleasant memories. One individual, for example, explained that "it's something in the past. Talking about it would just make me more bitter, fill me with hatred again. . . There's not a thing in this world you can do about it now." If the refusals reflect discouragement, futility, and disgust with the system rather than mere lack of interest, we may underestimate the impact of white-collar crime victimization on delegitimation. Although we are not certain, we think that those for whom the issue was most salient were willing to talk with us; for most nonrespondents, we believe, the refusal to participate reflected caring too little about the matter rather than caring too much. Delegitimation is not a likely outcome for those for whom the episode was "no big deal."

All but two respondents were interviewed in their homes or workplaces. We also interviewed the bankruptcy trustee and a local attorney who represented investors in litigation over the plan of reorganization.

FINDINGS

Personal Effects

We found enormous variation in investors' reactions to the bankruptcy of Southland Industrial Banking Corporation and in its impact. This variation is evident, for example, in their attitudes toward the reorganization plan and settlement process. Most respondents did not contact or retain an attorney, voted to accept the plan and the settlement formulas it contained, and have managed more or less successfully to put the experience behind them. Other SIBC victims, however, actively sought to protect their interests throughout the various stages of the bankruptcy process; some refused to surrender to the bankruptcy trustee the funds they were ordered to return. For individual investors, the decision to accept or to resist the settlement process was one of two principal determinants of the long-term impact of the SIBC experience. The other was the victims' potential to recover financially from their losses. . . .

Delegitimation Effects

After exploring the personal impacts of victimization, we questioned the members of the interview sample to determine whether the experience had diminished their confidence in prevailing political and financial leaders and institutions. Did this series of white-collar crimes produce the delegitimation effects hypothesized by scholars? This question is not easy to answer, largely because our data lack strictly comparable information from all respondents, and thus will not permit us to disentangle confidently possible antecedents of declining trust in leaders and institutions. Some respondents, for example, gave unmistakable evidence of growing disenchantment with political leaders. A subsequent opinion poll of the state's adult population showed that their concerns were shared by a substantial number of their peers ("Results," 1991). Topics of critical evaluation by respondents included intercession by five U.S. Senators—the "Keating Five"—in threatened federal regulatory action against a large savings and loan institution that subsequently collapsed, charges of criminal conduct by officials of the Department of Housing and Urban Development, and action by members of Congress to raise their annual salary during a time of national belt tightening. One respondent commented on

> . . . the complete arrogance, as I see it, of an organization [Congress] that passes itself [pay] raises when people are being laid off from work left and right, [their] inability to even address, to even admit that there is a problem. It's like the king with no clothes—the kid's story—he thinks everything is fine. And nobody's gonna tell him any different, except the children, who tell the truth.

Victims were particularly disappointed with government's response to the problems of Southland Industrial Banking Corporation. A clear majority ranked state banking regulators just behind SIBC's principal officers when apportioning blame for the collapse of SIBC. They faulted state officials especially for permitting SIBC to continue operating past the point when its freewheeling operating style and fiscal problems should have been apparent to competent regulatory overseers:

> I feel like the state of Tennessee banking department, or insurance department, I guess it was, didn't do a very good job. And [they] let that go on without doing something, they were remiss in what they should have done, you know. To me, it's negligence on their part, that it ever got that far.

Despite this backdrop of increasing dissatisfaction and frustration with political leaders, most victims reported little, if any, loss of support for political institutions which can be attributed solely to crime committed by SIBC officers. They distinguished between evaluations of specific political leaders and evaluations of political institutions; their decline in confidence in the former rarely extended to the latter. Pressed to explain why they did not suffer stronger persisting effects of institutional delegitimation, a number of respondents said "It [American institutions] may not be perfect but it's the best there is." Most vote as often today as before the collapse of SIBC, and no subjects attributed their decline in voting to that experience.

The story is entirely different, however, for those who were targets of actions by the liquidating trustee:

> Q: Do you feel the same way about the law today as you did before this incident?
>
> A: See, I never had much [experience] with the law. I never gave it much thought. . . . If I was speeding, and I was caught, hey, so I was speeding. I'd pay the fine. I don't hold the law in as high esteem as I used to. I don't think we were given any protection under the law, be it state or federal.

Similar comments were offered by another respondent:

> [Action by the bankruptcy trustee to seize his assets] was the first in a series of occurrences that . . . to a great extent changed my view of what this country really stands for. . . . [Previously] I believed much more readily in the philosophies, the theories that we have these basic rights that are inviolate. I don't believe that anymore. Now I believe that *money* rules. And occasionally public opinion can sway.

How did their experiences effect respondents' confidence in business institutions and leaders? Here we elicited evidence of substantial disillusionment and declining confidence. The combination of massive crime in the savings and loan industry (Calavita and Pontell 1990) and Wall Street investment scandals has left the respondents confused and not so confident that financial institutions and safeguards are in good hands. Just as when they discussed confidence in political institutions and leaders, most respondents did not always find it easy to distinguish the effects of victimization from the overall effect of these contextual developments. As one man stated, "You think about it more or less all together. They're all out to make a fast buck. And they don't care how they get it, legally or what." Several, however, distinguished carefully between the effects of context and the impact of the SIBC experience as causes for their admitted decline in confidence in American business leaders:

> Q: Overall, is your confidence in American business leaders today greater, about the same, or less than it was seven years ago?
>
> A: I'd say it's less than it was. Because the more I see, and the more I read, and the more I hear, it appears that—this savings and loan thing—the people that handle and loan money aren't "purists." They don't give a hoot whether they do it properly or improperly, as I see it. Now [that is] not caused from my experience [with SIBC], it's just developed that way.

Most respondents told us that the crimes of SIBC and the bankruptcy reorganization process served as "a focus" for growing concern or "sensitized" them to national political and economic conditions that they found unsettling.

Like their assessments of political leaders and institutions, the victims' loss of confidence in business leaders did not extend to business institutions. We explored, for example, whether victimization affected their subsequent investment behaviors and their participation in financial institutions and processes. Does victimization by white-collar crime cause victims to withhold investment and participation in economic institutions and markets? The data suggest that in this case it did not, although victims reported that they now invest more cautiously by first "checking things out more carefully" and by dispersing their investments throughout several institutions and programs. Nearly all subjects also said that they invest only in federally insured programs or institutions; this response attests either to their continuing faith in government or to their general unawareness of investment options. We can summarize by saying that loss of trust and confidence in political and financial leaders was commonplace, although institutional delegitimation was rare. The strength of delegitimation effects was influenced heavily by the severity of victimization impact and by the requirement that investors return funds to the bankruptcy trustee.

We suggest two reasons for failure to find evidence of widespread or persisting institutional delegitimation effects: (1) victims' tendency to individualize responsibility for institutional failure and personal misfortune, and (2) cohort or generational effects. Subjects' responses to questions about the shortcomings of political institutions reveal a distinct tendency to invoke individual-centered attributions of responsibility. The subjects spoke readily about the faults of individual officials who happen to occupy positions in state and federal government, but they generally reserved criticism of political institutions:

> Like I said, I don't have nearly the faith in the people who are holding positions now. I think we have the best system in the world. . . . It just depends on who is in positions of making decisions. I think, right now, just to be blunt about it, we've got a bunch of self-serving—I hesitate to use the word, but I'd love to. They're just self-serving [and] that's why they got into the positions they are in.

Even while we emphasize our respondents' tendency to fault individuals rather than institutions, we acknowledge that it may be related to important characteristics of the SIBC case. The crimes of SIBC were crimes of readily identifiable *individuals* whose families were known personally to many of its investors. The effects of white-collar crime, whether on individual well-being or on institutional legitimacy, may differ according to the specific nature of the crime. Crimes committed by large, remote, impersonal corporations, as in the Ford Pinto case (Cullen et al. 1987), for example, may produce stronger condemnation of institutions.

Perhaps it is noteworthy that the SIBC incident occurred in a region of the United States with a long tradition of political conservatism, whose inhabitants value and celebrate individual responsibility and self-reliance. Historically, for example, workers in this region resisted labor unions because they feared the unions would be a meddlesome force and would limit or interfere with employees' prerogatives to work under conditions and terms of their own choosing. In light of this cultural heritage, individualistic interpretations of misfortune may be particularly appealing.

Whatever its sources, the tendency to individualize responsibility is evident also in responses to the question "Who is to blame for what happened to you?" We noted earlier that victims blame SIBC officers, state regulators, and political figures for the collapse of SIBC. Their apportionment of responsibility does not stop there, however; they reserve a major share for themselves:

> Q: Has this experience affected the way you think about the government, in any way?
>
> A: I don't think the government was to fault, I think we were. We were gullible. And we were greedy, because we wanted the big interest.
>
> Q: You blame yourself?
>
> A: I blame myself. . . . I should have known better. I've done business, I know better than that.

Another said simply, "I think I was greedy, in trying to get 'super maximum interest' on that money I had." Indeed, the words *greedy* or *greed* are used more often than any others in spontaneous self-attributions elicited in response to questions about responsibility for the incident:

> I'm disgusted with me, that I could have been such a dope, you know. And not really looked a little deeper and been a little more careful. . . . I should have been more careful. . . . And I should have been a little more responsible than I was, really. . . . [And] I'm still just kinda mad at Mr. Baker.

Ten years after the incident occurred, the self-blaming and embarrassment felt by some victims of the SIBC case borders on stigma:

> You know, we've never even told our kids that it happened. We would hate for them to know that we were that dumb.
>
> Q: You've never told your kids?
>
> A: No, we never have.
>
> Q: Now you said, before I turned on the tape recorder, that you really don't want *anyone* to know?
>
> A: That's right.
>
> Q: You feel that bad about it, yourself?
>
> A: I just feel *stupid!* That's the way I feel about it. I feel madder at myself than I do [at] Southland Industrial Banking . . .

Q: Did you go to any of the public meetings that were held?

A: No! We stayed away from them. We were afraid somebody would see us there.

Victims looked to the shortcomings of *individuals*, including themselves, and less to political and economic institutions as the primary cause of their misfortune.

Cohort effects also may contribute to respondents' tendency to avoid blaming institutions. The majority grew up during the Great Depression (Elder 1974), products of economically depressed circumstances, and their achievements in life surpassed their childhood prospects and expectations. They experienced a measure of success and mobility. Their generation also helped defeat the Axis powers in World War II. Several of our respondents served in World War II combat, returned to a grateful nation, and together with their peers set to work to manufacture and consume the products that fueled postwar prosperity. For them, as for most of their generation, the years of work and child rearing were the years of the "American celebration" (Mills 1958). In those years as well, political leaders waged a cold war with communist states, and encouraged citizens to define the American experience and American institutions as exemplars for all nations. Although our interview notes and transcripts contain no indication of any mention by respondents, most were interviewed at a time when the Soviet Union and its eastern European alliances, America's politically defined opponent through nearly all of their adult years, were disintegrating. We cannot speculate whether these developments affected their responses to victimization by Southland Industrial Banking Corporation, but it is doubtful that respondents' faith in and support for American institutions could be shaken easily.

IMPLICATIONS AND INTERPRETATION

Most studies of criminal victimization not only focus on street crimes but also, because of limited follow-up, report only short-term effects. In our study of white-collar crime victims, we found enduring and pervasive effects, for some individuals, nearly a decade after their victimization. . . .

The findings of our research suggest, further, that the delegitimation effects of victimization by white-collar crime are moderated by aspects of the cultural and ideological context in which it occurs. Particularly important may be the presence of values of individualism and ideologies that foster and support constructions of blame which almost exclusively emphasize failure on the part of the individual, often of the victim. We are not alone in finding evidence of this situation. In reviewing evidence from many public opinion polls over nearly three decades, Lipset and Schneider note that "the public has shown a tendency to personalize social problems, that is, to attribute them to inept leaders and corrupt powerholders. . . . [As a result] people lose faith in leaders much more easily than they lose confidence in the system" (1987:378–79). "Individualism," according to Bellah et al. (1985:142), "lies at the very core of American culture." An important consequence is that Americans generally lack a vocabulary to articulate the overarching moral or political implications and significance of their experiences. To the extent that victims of white-collar crime are limited by language to explanations expressed in terms of individual culpability, to that extent institutions are immune both to eroded confidence and to demands for reform.

A similar preference for individual-centered attributions of responsibility finds expression in victims' self-blaming, which other investigators also have reported. Interviews with victims of fraud showed that they are "conscious of the primacy of the *caveat emptor* principle in relation to commercial transactions" and the *"prima facie* assumption of negligence" on their part (Levi 1991:5). They experienced great "concern about their own failings in being caught out, and about how foolish other people would think them if they discovered that they had been conned" (p. 11). Victimization "was a blow not only to their pockets but also to their self-esteem and (where others had been told about it) to their social reputation" (p. 5). Walsh and Schram (1980) argue that the experiences of rape victims and victims of white-collar crime share several important characteristics—among others, that questions about guilt or responsibility often turn on the victim's behavior. Like rape victims, persons victimized by white-collar crime have been prepared by socialization and life experiences to accept these pervasive attributions of personal culpability. They often look inward to explain their misfortunes. . . .

REFERENCES

Bellah, R., R. Madsen, W.M. Sullivan, A. Widler, and S.M. Tipton (1985) *Habits of the Heart.* Berkeley: University of California Press.

Calavita, K. and H.N. Pontell (1990) "'Heads I Win, Tails You Lose': Deregulation, Crime, and Crisis in the Savings and Loan Industry." *Crime and Delinquency* 36:309–41.

Conklin, J.E. (1977) *Illegal but Not Criminal.* Englewood Cliffs, NJ: Prentice-Hall.

Cullen, F.T., W.J. Maakestad, and G. Cavender (1987) *Corporate Crime under Attack.* Cincinnati: Anderson.

Davis, R.C. and M. Henley (1990) "Victim Service Programs." In A.J. Lurigio, W.C. Skogan, and R.C. Davis (eds.), *Victims of Crime,* pp. 157–71. Newbury Park, CA: Sage.

Elder, G.H. (1974) *Children of the Great Depression.* Chicago: University of Chicago Press.

Elias, R. (1993) *Victims Still: The Political Manipulation of Crime Victims.* Newbury Park, CA: Sage.

Lebowitz, H.M. (1986) *Bankruptcy Deskbook.* New York: Practicing Law Institute.

Levi, M. (1991) "The Victims of Fraud." Paper presented at the second Liverpool Conference on Fraud, Corruption, and Business Crime, University of Liverpool.

———. (1992) "White-Collar Crime Victimization." In K. Schlegel and D. Weisbard (eds.), *White-Collar Crime Reconsidered,* pp. 169–92. Boston. Northeastern University Press.

Lipset, S.M. and W. Schneider (1987) *The Confidence Gap.* (Revised ed.). Baltimore: Johns Hopkins University Press.

Mills, C.W. (1958) *The Sociological Imagination.* New York: Oxford University Press.

Peters, J.G. and S. Welch (1980) "The Effects of Charges of Corruption on Voting Behavior in Congressional Elections." *American Political Science Review* 74:697–708.

President's Commission on Law Enforcement and Administration of Justice (1967) *The Challenge of Crime in a Free Society.* Washington, DC: U.S. Government Printing Office.

"Results of the Tennessee Poll." (1991) Knoxville *News-Sentinel,* November 17, p. A1.

Shapiro, S. (1984) *Wayward Capitalists.* New Haven: Yale University Press.,

Shichor, D. (1989) "Corporate Deviance and Corporate Victimization: A Review and Some Elaborations." *International Review of Victimology* 1:67–85.

Sutherland, E.H. (1949) *White Collar Crime.* New York: Holt, Rinehart and Winston.

Treister, G.M. (1986) *Fundamentals of Bankruptcy Law.* Philadelphia: American Law Institute and American Bar Association.

Walsh, M.E. and D. D. Schram (1980) "The Victim of White-Collar Crime: Accuser or Accused?" In G. Geis and E. Stotland (eds.), *White-Collar Crime,* pp. 32–51. Beverly Hills: Sage.

Victims of Fraud: Comparing Victims of White Collar and Violent Crime.

LINDA GANZINI, BENTSON MCFARLAND, AND JOSEPH BLOOM.

In recent years sociologists, criminologists, and mental health professionals have focused attention on crime victims. Mental health professionals have begun to describe the emotional distress and recovery patterns following criminal victimization. The majority of studies have examined the sequelae of violent crimes such as rape.[1] Little research has been conducted on the victims of white collar crimes.

This article reviews the literature on the psychiatric sequelae of criminal victimization, with particular emphasis on white collar victimization. Forms of white collar victimization will be described, and the similarities and differences between the victims of white collar and violent crime will be discussed. Emphasis is given to data obtained from interviewing 77 victims of a fraudulent financial scheme.

"Victims of Fraud" from *Bulletin of the American Academy of Psychiatry and Law,* Vol 18 (1990): 55–63. Reprinted by permission.

WHITE COLLAR CRIME

. . . Fraud takes many forms including work at home schemes, securities fraud, illegal franchises and distributorships, land fraud, illegal commodities, home improvement schemes, funeral abuses, and pension and insurance fraud.[3]

Many frauds are illegal investment schemes such as swindles which take the form of Ponzi (pyramid) schemes. In a Ponzi (pyramid) scheme clients place their money in supposedly low risk investments. Early investors report substantial gains to friends and coworkers who then eagerly invest capital. In fact, this capital is used to pay interest to those early investors who "test" the credibility of the scheme by withdrawing their money. Many of these schemes last for years. Most of the funds are never invested but are in fact diverted.[4–6]

An important element of a Ponzi scheme is an affinity group, that is a group of friends and coworkers who trust each other and communicate regarding their investment earnings. The confidence man who perpetrates the scheme is usually a member of the affinity group. For example, a disproportionate number of these swindles occur in church-affiliated groups. The Utah attorney general's office investigates approximately 80 such swindles per year, the majority occurring among and perpetrated by members of the Church of Latter Day Saints (Mormons). The numbers of investors bilked range from 50 to 1200 per fraud with losses as high as $67 million per scheme (Mike Hines, Utah Attorney General's Office, personal communication). The number of these schemes nationwide is unclear but is estimated to be in the hundreds with $40 billion bilked from investors annually.[7] Although swindling comprises only three percent of all white collar felony dispositions, the magnitude of the problem may be underestimated, as a single confidence man can victimize hundreds of investors and victims are frequently embarrassed to report their losses.[2]

Four Ponzi schemes perpetrated in Oregon between 1984 and 1986 are described in Table 1.[8] We recently completed a study of 77 victims of one of these Ponzi schemes. A description of this fraud illustrates the complexity and the extent of deceit in these schemes. In April of 1985, 450 investors in First Colonial Bank of the Marshall Islands (Pac Rim, Inc.) were notified that the bank was fraudulent and their investments were lost. Eighty percent of the investors were employees or recent retirees of a northwest electronics firm with an average length of employment at that firm of 19.4 years. The perpetrator of the fraud was a 23-year employee of the firm who had been a high level manager and president of the company's credit union. After he retired in 1982 he received a license to sell securities from the Securities and Exchange Commission and made several successful investments for his former coworkers. In 1983 the electronics firm, seeking to decrease its work force, offered generous lump sum cash retirement packages to long-time employees in exchange for early retirement. Many retirees placed their money in Pac Rim. Forty-six percent of the Pac Rim victims lost more than $40,000, and 14 percent of the victims lost more than $100,000 in this scheme. A detailed description of

TABLE 1
Ponzi Schemes in Oregon, 1984 to 1986

Affinity Group	Number of Investors	Confidence Man	Bank	Losses
Tektronix Inc.	450	Former Tektronix manager	First Colonial Bank of Marshall Islands (Pac Rim, Inc.)	$5–7 million
Oregon Department of Education	60	Former Department of Education manager	Merchants International Bank Ltd.	$3 million
Mormon Church	100	Bishop of Mormon Church	International Bank of South Pacific	$3.5 million
Seventh Day Adventist Church	100+	Church member	Republic Overseas Bank	$4.5 million

Source: Portland Oregonian.[8]

the psychiatric disorders experienced by the victims following this loss and the methodology used to examine this group has been presented elsewhere.[9]

COMPARISON OF WHITE COLLAR AND VIOLENT CRIME VICTIMS

Victims of white collar crime can be compared with victims of violent crime (rape, robbery, and assault) on several parameters, including statistical risk of victimization, psychiatric outcome and recovery rates after victimization, and the effects of crime-related variables on subsequent psychiatric disorders. We will use data obtained from interviews with the Pac Rim victims for illustrative purposes. The experience of the Pac Rim victims shares the common elements of deceit and financial loss with other white collar victims. However, our equation of the experience of the Pac Rim victims with that of other white collar victims remains speculative pending further studies in this area; to our knowledge the study of Pac Rim victims and Blum's study of con game victims represent the only studies of the psychiatric outcome after white collar victimization.[10]

Statistical Risk of Victimization

Table 2 compares some risk factors associated with white collar and violent victimization. Victims of the Pac Rim scheme were demographically homogenous: all were Caucasian, lived in a three county area surrounding Portland, and 83 percent earned more than $20,000 in 1984. Eighty-seven percent were married at the time of the interview. The average age was 53, and 88 percent were between 40 and 65 years of age. Forty-eight percent were female. Sixty percent had some college education, and 33 percent were somewhat or very religious. Blum, in a study of 24 individuals who were deceived in non-Ponzi frauds (which were perpetrated by strangers and did not involve an affinity group), also found that victims tended to be older (median age 60 to 69 years), disproportionately female, predominately widowed, and deeply religious. Unlike the Pac Rim victims, his group was predominately lower middle class and somewhat less educated than the city average.[10]

Persons with demographic characteristics similar to those of the Pac Rim victims are at low risk for violent crimes such as rape, robbery, and assault. The risk of violent crime decreases with increasing financial assets. The segment of the population with an income greater than $15,000 per year has half of the criminal victimization risk of those with an income less than $9000 per year.[11] Sixty-nine percent of rape victims come from households with income less than $15,000 per year.[12] Increasing age is also associated with decreased risk of violent victimization. Persons over the age of 50 are at the lowest risk for violent victimization with one-sixth of the risk for this kind of victimization relative to those between the ages of 16 and 24.[11] On the other hand, the elderly, although making up 11 percent of the population, constitute 30 percent of the victims of fraudulent investment schemes.[3] Females over age 65, although equally at risk for white collar crime in our study and predominantly at risk in Blum's study, have only half the risk of violent crime as males in the over age 65 group.[13] Despite the increased risk of rape in females, males have a higher risk of violent victimization in all age groups due to higher rates of such crimes as homicide and assault.[11]

Pac Rim victims were compared to 66 age, sex, and residential area matched controls. Names of controls were obtained from a list of 20,000 drivers generated by the Oregon Department of Motor Vehicles. Victims and controls were interviewed using the Diagnostic Interview Schedule (DIS) which generates current and lifetime prevalences of psychiatric disorders as defined by DSM-III.[14] Among the Pac Rim victims, cognitive impairment, alcohol

TABLE 2
Risk Factors for Violent and White Collar Victimization

Risk Factor	WHITE COLLAR CRIME		Violent Crime
	Ponzi Schemes[9]	Other Frauds[10]	
Social network	Strong	Weak	Varies
Age	Middle-aged	Elderly	Young adult[11]
Sex	F = M	F > M	F > M (rape)[12]
			M > F (other violent crimes)[11]
Yearly income	83% > $20,000/year	Lower than city average	69% < $15,000/year (rape)[12]
Mental disorder	None	Depression	Major mental illness, alcohol and drug abuse[15]
Marital status	83% married	Predominantly widowed	14% married (rape)[12]
Religiosity	33% religious	Very religious	Unknown

abuse, and a history of mental disorder prior to the loss were rare and were not risk factors for financial deception. There were no differences between Pac Rim victims and their controls in lifetime prevalences of any DSM-III disorder. Ten percent of Pac Rim victims had seen a mental health professional at any time in their lives, not significantly different from controls. Blum also found that alcohol abuse was rare in his study of victims of frauds not based on affinity groups. He observed that many appeared depressed and lonely, but he did not distinguish between depression occurring before or after victimization.[10]

In contrast, mental disorders, cognitive impairment, and alcohol abuse have all been demonstrated to be risk factors for violent criminal victimization.[15] Several studies show that many rape victims, the most well characterized of the criminal victimized, have previous histories of psychiatric care, although this was not confirmed in a more recent controlled study.[16–21] Alcohol abuse and intoxication have been implicated as risk factors for rape.[16,17,20,22,23]

Psychiatric Outcome and Recovery

Twenty-nine percent of the Pac Rim victims experienced a major depressive episode as defined by DSM-III criteria in the first 20 months after their loss as compared to two percent of controls during the same time period (McNemar's test, $p < .0001$). Five Pac Rim victims developed suicidal ideation after the loss. Generalized anxiety disorder was found in 45% of the Pac Rim victims as compared to 15% of the controls (McNemar's test, $p = .004$). Blum was also impressed by depressive characteristics in the fraud victims he interviewed.[10]

The emotional and behavioral consequences of violent criminal victimization have been studied, especially for rape in women and assaults in the elderly. However, different approaches have been used in describing these groups with the emphasis on emotional sequelae in the rape victim, and fear and avoidance in the elderly. Rape victims have been the most extensively characterized. Of course, when comparing fraud victims with rape victims one must recognize the vast demographic differences that exist between the groups. In studies of rape victims rarely are subjects stratified by age, and studies of male rape are rare.

Frank et al. used the DIS to evaluate 60 female rape victims with an average age of 23. Thirty-eight percent met the DSM-III criteria for major depressive disorder (MDD) in the first six weeks after the rape, and 82 percent met DSM-III criteria for generalized anxiety disorder (GAD). (DSM-III duration criteria were removed which may increase the prevalence of the disorder.) Thus, GAD was the most frequently experienced disorder in both Pac Rim victims and rape victims, followed by MDD. Use of alcohol did not change following the stressor in either group.[21]

Atkeson et al., in their study of rape victims, found that levels of anxiety and depression, although initially high, were not significantly different between victims and control subjects four months after the rape.[24] Other studies that follow up rape victims also show recovery by one year.[18,25] In contrast, studies by Nadelson et al. and McCahill et al. indicate that many rape victims continue to have fearfulness, depression, fatigue, sleep disturbance, and difficulties with sexual adjustment for more than one year after the rape.[26,27] None of these studies reports the length of clinical depression. Among the Pac Rim victims, 48 percent of those who suffered a major depressive episode continued to have depressive symptoms six months after the loss as compared to two percent of controls during the same time period. In the Pac Rim victims, persistence of symptoms may be the result of a domino effect whereby the initial financial loss resulted in subsequent catastrophes such as loss of home or difficulty paying debts and taxes.

There is virtually no literature addressing the risk of psychiatric disorder in the elderly after violent criminal victimization. For example, the British Crime Survey showed that eight percent of victims of burglary suffered depression and sleeplessness, but results were not stratified by age.[28] Criminologists have instead focused on measuring levels of fear, avoidance, and isolation in the elderly after assaults. Most studies have shown that all of these behaviors are increased.[1] There was no evidence of an increase in avoidance or isolation after fraudulent victimization. Pac Rim victims and their controls had similar levels of social involvement as measured by frequency of socialization and number of contacts, church attendance, encounters with friends and relatives, and use of confidantes following the stressful events. It is not surprising that the elderly may perceive avoidance and isolation to have some deterrence value after assault or robbery. Pac Rim victims, on the other hand, were from the outset at increased risk of fraudulent victimization due to their high levels of social contact and affiliation, and most continued to be socially active even in the face of depression. Blum in his study of nonaffinity group based fraud victims found that loneliness and isolation preceded victimization, and that widowhood and lack of offspring were risk factors for deception. He hypothesized that isolation results in failure to "test ideas and lack of controls for foolish adventures."[10] In the Pac Rim fraud the sophistication of the fraud and the trust in the confidence man and other investors resulted in "idea testing" that led, in fact, to further fraudulent investing.

Determinants of Outcome Extent of victimization and other crime related factors can be examined as independent variables in determining outcome and recovery after violent crime. Sales et al. demonstrated that the degree of victimization as measured by the amount of violence in the attack was the most important contributor to short term emotional response, but this has not been duplicated in other studies.[29,30] Frank et al. found that increased pre-rape levels of psychiatric symptomatology and a history of suicidal ideation were associated with poorer adjustment and more depression after the trauma.[20] Subjects with prior psychiatric diagnoses were significantly more likely to meet criteria for a mental disorder in the aftermath of assault compared to subjects with no such history.[21] Burgess and Holstrom also found that women with a past psychiatric history were more likely to develop symptoms of depression and suicidality than those without such a history.[31] Atkeson et al. found that decreased support after assault was associated with increased depression four and eight months after rape.[24] Burgess and Holmstom also noted a significant association between the level of support and recovery from stress both several months and 4 to 6 years after rape.[32] Similarly the degree of victimization (as measured by increased financial loss and decreased financial resources) and a previous history of major depressive disorder were the most important variables in predicting the development of major depressive disorder in Pac Rim victims after the fraud. However, there were no differences between depressed and nondepressed Pac Rim victims in measures of social support, including numbers and types of visits to friends and relatives, memberships in clubs and groups, and uses of confidantes.

There are no studies that assess the importance of financial loss associated with burglary or robbery in determining psychiatric outcome. However, only 18 percent of personal crimes and 25 percent of household crimes resulted in financial losses greater than $250 for those over age 65 earning annual incomes greater than $25,000.[13] This financial loss is several orders of magnitude less than those incurred by the Pac Rim victims.

DISCUSSION

Despite the limited research on the psychiatric sequelae of criminal victimization and the differences in study design, several tentative conclusions can be drawn in the comparison of white collar crime victims with the victims of violent crime.

First, victims of white collar crime, as opposed to victims of violent crime, tend to be older, more affluent, and relatively more likely to be female. Thus, the term "white collar" not only describes the deceivers but the deceived.

Second, both similarities and differences between these victim groups may have implications for assessment and treatment by the clinician. Generalized anxiety disorder and major depressive disorder are the most common psychiatric complications of both types of victimization. The incidence of posttraumatic stress disorder (PTSD) after violent victimization is unknown as systematic examination for PTSD symptoms has not been done. Dementia and mania, which need to be excluded in cases of financial loss, were absent in the Pac Rim victims. In both white collar and violent victimization, a previous history of psychiatric illness and the degree of victimization are important variables in predicting risk of psychiatric disturbance. More specifically in the case of fraud victims, the clinician should be aware that a previous history of depression, a large financial loss, and a decreased standard of living may increase the risk for major depressive disorder and suicidality and that the depression may be lengthier and more severe than most "reactive depressions."

Treatment of alcohol abuse may improve coping and prevent recidivism after violent victimization such as rape; however, alcohol abuse was rare in Pac Rim victims and was not a risk factor for depression.

After violent victimization such as rape, adequate social support is an important predictor of good recovery and remittance of psychiatric symptoms. Victims of Ponzi schemes, on the other hand, have been noted by criminologists to be at risk for victimization due to membership in affinity groups. The study of the Pac Rim victims indicates that this strong social network remains intact after victimization and offers no apparent protective value against depressive disorders. Thus, therapeutic strategies that attempt to increase social support may be of little value after this kind of financial loss.

. . . Education of groups at risk such as members of churches and employees of government agencies and large businesses, regarding the existence and dangers of such speculative investments, may be a valuable and cost effective approach to the prevention of fraudulent victimization.

REFERENCES

1. Burt MR, Katz BL: Rape, robbery and burglary: responses to actual and feared criminal victimization with special focus on women and the elderly. Victimology 10:325–58, 1985
2. Manson DA: Tracking offenders: white-collar crime. Bureau of Justice Statistics. United States Department of Justice, Nov. 1986, p 2
3. Pepper C: Abuse of the elderly, in Abuse and Maltreatment of the Elderly. Edited by Kosberg JI. Boston. PSG, 1982
4. Nettler G: Lying, Stealing and Cheating. Cincinnati, Anderson, 1982
5. Leff AA: Swindling and Stealing. New York, Free Press, 1976
6. Shapiro S: Wayward Capitalists: Targets of the Securities and Exchange Commission. New Haven, CT, Yale Univ Press, 1984
7. Sacramento Bee, February 17, 1986
8. Portland Oregonian, June 16, 1985; June 17, 1985; December 29, 1986
9. Ganzini LK, McFarland B, Cutler D: Prevalence of mental disorders following catastrophic financial loss. J. Nerv Ment Dis, In press, 1989
10. Blum RH: Deceivers and Deceived. Springfield, IL, Charles Thomas, 1972, pp. 61–80
11. Langan PA, Innes CA: The Risk of Violent Crime, Bureau of Justice Statistics. United States Department of Justice, May 1985, p 3
12. Klaus PA, DeBerry M: The Crime of Rape. Bureau of Justice Statistics. United States Department of Justice, Mar 1985, p 3
13. Whitacker CJ: Elderly Victims. Bureau of Justice Statistics. United States Department of Justice, Nov 1987, p 6
14. Eaton WE, Holzer CE, VonKorff M, et al: The design of the epidemiologic catchment area surveys. Arch Gen Psychiatry 41:942–8, 1984
15. Carmen EH, Rieker PP, Mills T: Victims of violence and psychiatric illness. Am Psychiatry 141:378–83, 1984

16. Miller, Moeller D, Kaufman A, et al: Recidivism among sexual assault victims. Am J Psychiatry 135:1103–4, 1978
17. Myers MB, Templer DI, Brown R: Coping ability of women who become victims of rape. J Cons Clin Psychology 52:73–8, 1984
18. Katz S, Mazur MA: Understanding the Rape Victim: A Synthesis of Research Findings. New York, John Wiley, 1979
19. Peters JJ: Social, legal, and psychological effects of rape on the victim. Penn Med 78:34–36, 1975
20. Frank E, Turner SM, Stewart BP, et al: Past psychiatric symptoms and the response to sexual assault. Comp Psychiatry 22:479–87, 1981
21. Frank E, Anderson BP: Psychiatric disorders in rape victims: past history and current symptomatology. Comp Psychiatry 28:77–82, 1987
22. Amir M: Patterns of Forcible Rape. Chicago, Univ of Chicago Press, 1971
23. Hayman C, Lanza R. Fuentes R, et al: Rape in the District of Columbia. Am J Obstetr Gyn 113:91–7, 1972
24. Atkeson BM, Calhoun KS, Resick DA, et al: Victims of rape: repeated assessment of depressive symptoms. Cons Clin Psychology 50:96–102, 1982
25. Sutherland S, Scherl DS: Patterns of response among victims of rape. Am J Orthopsychiatry 4:503–11, 1970
26. Nadelson CC, Noteman MT, Zackson H, et al: A follow-up study of rape victims. Am J Psychiatry 139:1266–70, 1983
27. McCahill TW, Meyer LC, Fischman AM: The Aftermath of Rape. Lexington, MA, Lexington Books, 1979
28. Hough M: The impact of victimisation: findings from the British Crime Survey. Victimology 10:488–97, 1985
29. Sales E, Baum M, Shore B: Victim readjustment following assault. Journal of Social Issues 40:117–36, 1984
30. Frank E, Turner SM, Stewart BD: Initial response to rape: the impact of factors within the rape situation. J Behav Assess 2:39–53, 1980
31. Burgess AW, Holstrom LL: Rape trauma syndrome. Am Psychiatry, 131:981–6, 1974
32. Burgess AW, Holmstrom LL: Recovery from rape and prior life stress. Res Nurs Health 1:165–74, 1978

3

White-Collar Criminal Opportunities

Introduction

Rates of street crime vary across time and place, and the same is true for white-collar crime. Why rates of crime fluctuate over time and why some neighborhoods, occupations, and industries are plagued by more crime than others draws attention to the distribution of criminal opportunities and of those predisposed to exploit them. Criminal opportunities are arrangements or situations individuals and groups encounter that offer attractive potential for criminal reward, largely because they are accompanied by little apparent risk of detection or penalty. For street criminals, attractive targets are homes filled with portable electronic equipment that are unoccupied much of the day. Opportunities to engage in household burglary and other street crimes are widely distributed throughout the general population, but opportunities for many white-collar crimes require access to restricted social networks and information or to positions of organizational power. We have reprinted a paper by Hugh Barlow that illustrates how access to networks of people and information shape available opportunities to commit crime. Owing to their respectable positions, white-collar offenders can commit crimes beyond the reach of less privileged citizens.

Both the number and the nature of white-collar criminal opportunities respond to changes in the wider society. Just as rates of burglary increased following the "miniaturization" and mass marketing of home electronic products, changing technology has created new opportunities for the privileged to steal and to harm. Through the use of high-speed data networks, telephone lines, and satellite networks, for example, funds from banks and business accounts can be manipulated instantaneously over great distances. The development of these technologies coincided with and hastened the emergence of "finance capitalism," a form of productive enterprise distinguished not by the manufacture of goods or services for consumption, but instead by "production" of paper profits through the manipulation of financial accounts. Finance capitalism is the production of wealth at the computer keyboard, increasingly from the privacy of the home. The merger of new technologies with finance capitalism made more attractive the temptation of white-collar crime; the crimes of those who exploit the new opportunities are cloaked by the real and the felt anonymity that comes from working at a computer terminal. The fact that few resources are dedicated to detecting and prosecuting their crimes only heightens the allure.

Similarly, the emergence of new communications technologies has transformed the ways individuals relate to one another and to organizations, thereby increasing the supply of white-collar criminal opportunities. Generally, communications have become more impersonal and difficult to monitor effectively as exchanges based on face-to-face interaction yield to impersonal contact over digital networks. Interpersonal trust between individuals, once thought to be a cornerstone of business transactions, has been supplanted by cybercommunication via impersonal passwords and screen names. Offenders and their victims may know one another outside these transactions, but increasingly they do not. Nor is the process of verifying credentials the easy matter it was when parties interacted personally or within geographically circumscribed and culturally shared worlds. White-collar criminals are quick to exploit the growth of impersonal trust. Diane Vaughan describes changes in transaction systems. She then suggests that these encourage unlawful behavior either by making available to remote others valuable resources with little threat of detection for criminal exploitation or by frustrating the reach for legitimate goals.

The state and its programs are a major source of white-collar criminal opportunities. State actions and programs increase the supply of white-collar criminal opportunities either by changing the supply of *lure* or by relaxing its oversight of individuals and organizations who might be tempted by it. By lure we mean anything that turns the heads of potential offenders and makes them sensitive to whether or not anyone is monitoring their actions. We shall delay until Chapter 6 presentation of materials on variable state oversight and controls, and here we take only passing note of its importance as a key component of criminal opportunities. Their case study of a poultry processing plant fire led Judy Root Aulette and Raymond Michalowski to argue that lax state enforcement of workplace safety regulations was an important cause of the criminal behavior; the plant had not been inspected in more than 7 years. With oversight of this kind, the plant owner likely did not fear civil or criminal penalties when he criminally padlocked the plant doors, an act that caused the deaths of 25 people.

In the United States, and in other countries, fundamental shifts following World War II in the states's public welfare functions expanded government largesse for citizens across the income spectrum. Some of the ways this increases criminal opportunities are seen in state programs and actions to promote business interests, a process that can make available new monies, generally in the form of tax incentives, subsidies, low-interest loans, or access to new streams of revenue. In this way, presidential decisions and congressional legislation during the 1980s helped transform and increase opportunities for criminal behavior in the U.S. savings and loan industry. These developments

---

PANEL 7   More White-Collar Crime

On May 14, 1999, Gerald Draper, a Washington D.C. government official, was sentenced to a two-year prison term and ordered to pay $88,000 in restitution. Draper befriended a fire department employee responsible for the purchase of equipment for the city's ambulance crews. The two men then billed the fire department for supplies that were never delivered.

Source: Washington Post

On April 9, 1998, Ann Eppard, a transportation lobbyist, was indicted by a federal grand jury for allegedly taking $230,000 in illegal payments to influence a Boston highway project. Eppard was House Transportation Chairman Bud Shuster's top aid. Eppard was also charged with embezzling $27,500 from Shuster's campaign committee. She allegedly arranged phony payments for a consultant who then returned the money to Eppard through a relative.

Source: Washington Post

On January 16, 1996, Peter Caserta, former president of Spectrum Information Technologies, Inc., pleaded guilty to federal charges of mail fraud and conspiracy. He conned numerous companies out of hundreds of thousands of dollars. Caserta would tell business officials to pay a fee in order to be approved by a highly selective, and fictitious, executive financing committee. Caserta was ordered to pay $625,000 in restitution and $375,000 in fines.

Source: Wall Street Journal

On April 27, 1999, ten people from New York, including two state senators, two former state senators, and two former education officials, were indicted on a variety of racketeering, mail fraud, and money laundering charges. Senator Nick Wilson, the group's leader, initiated and supervised four schemes to obtain $5 million in state money diverted from child support enforcement, workers' compensation for the state school board, and a program to provide legal counsel for children in divorce cases.

Source: New York Times

---

and their consequences are highlighted in the paper by Kitty Calavita and Henry N. Pontell. Their work shows how the burgeoning supply of criminal opportunities, particularly when coupled with deregulation of the S&L industry, resulted in one of the costliest public frauds in modern history. The S&L bandits are among the few who managed to exceed the level of fraud and abuse in Medicaid and Medicare programs. The profits can be substantial for those inclined to exploit criminal opportunities provided by state-supported health programs. The risk of detection is minimal and the temptation, therefore, great. The perpetrators of these crimes include respectable professionals and health-care corporations. The paper by John Liederbach shows how the privileges extended to physicians creates opportunities for them to steal from taxpayer-funded programs.

"Heads I Win, Tails You Lose"; Deregulation, Crime, and Crisis in The Savings and Loan Industry

KITTY CALAVITA AND HENRY N. PONTELL

In the winter of 1989, reports of the biggest set of white-collar crimes ever uncovered hit the news. According to the reports, some savings and loan operators across the United States had brought their institutions to financial ruin while pocketing untold millions of dollars in personal profits, passing the tab on to the American taxpayer.

The savings and loan crisis provides an important opportunity for the study of white-collar crime. First is its mere size. Official estimates of the cost of the rescue effort to bail out insolvent savings and loans are placed at $200 billion over the next decade, and range from $300 billion to $473 billion by the year 2021 (U.S. Congress. House Committee on Ways and Means 1989, p. 20; U.S. Congress, Senate Committee on Banking, Housing, and Urban Affairs 1989, p. 9). Government reports suggest that criminal activity was a central factor in 70 to 80% of these insolvencies (General Accounting Office June, 1989; U.S. Congress House Committee on Government Operations 1988, p. 51). Second, the case brings into sharp relief the mechanisms of the production and reproduction of white-collar crime, and the role of the state in those processes. . . .

DESCRIPTIVE BACKGROUND

Underpinnings of the Crisis

The federally insured savings and loan system was established in the early 1930s, both to promote the construction of new homes during the depression

"'Heads I win, Tails You Lose'" from *Crime & Delinquency* 36:3 (July 1990): 309–341. Reprinted by permission.

and to protect financial institutions against the kind of devastation that followed the panic of 1929. The Federal Home Loan Bank Act of 1932 (12 USC 1421 *et. Seq.*) established the Federal Home Loan Bank Board (FHLBB) whose purpose was to create a reserve credit system to ensure the availability of mortgage money for home financing and to oversee federally chartered savings and loans. Two years later, the second principal building block of the modern savings and loan industry was put in place when the National Housing Act of 1934 (12 USC 1724 *et. Seq.*) created the Federal Savings and Loan Insurance Corporation (FSLIC) to insure deposits in savings and loan institutions.

The FHLBB has been (until the 1989 reform, to be discussed later) the primary regulatory agency responsible for federally chartered savings and loans. It is an independent executive agency made up of a Chair and two members appointed by the President. This agency oversees 12 regional Home Loan Banks that serve as the conduit to the individual savings and loan institutions that comprise the industry. It is the function of these regional district banks to provide a pool of funds for their member institutions at below market rates, in order to disburse loans and cover withdrawals. In 1985, the FHLBB delegated to the district banks the task of examining and supervising the savings and loans within their regional jurisdiction. Thus, although the FHLBB is formally responsible for promulgating and enforcing regulations, agents of the district banks oversee the thrifts' operations and have discretion to initiate corrective measures and/or to notify the Bank Board of savings and loan misconduct. As will be shown, this dual role of the district banks and the Bank Board to both promote *and* regulate the savings and loan industry is a potentially critical factor in explaining their curiously complacent response to ongoing indications of fraud in the industry.

The National Housing Act of 1934 provided for federal insurance on savings and loan deposits through the FSLIC, also under the jurisdiction of the FHLBB. In exchange for this protection, thrifts were regulated both geographically and in terms of the kinds of loans they could make, essentially being confined to the issuance of home loans within fifty miles of their home office. The 1960s brought a gradual loosening of these restraints—for example extending the geographical area in which savings and loans could do business and slowly expanding their lending powers—yet did not significantly alter the protection/regulation formula.

A confluence of economic factors in the 1970s radically changed both the fortunes of the savings and loan industry and ultimately the parameters within which they were to operate. Most important, "stagflation" hit the savings and loan industry particularly hard, as the "double whammy" of high interest rates and slow growth squeezed the industry at both ends. Locked into relatively low-interest fixed mortgages from previous eras, limited by regulation to pay no more than 5.5% interest on new deposits, and with inflation at 13.3% by 1979, the industry suffered steep losses. Not surprisingly, thrifts found it difficult to attract new money when inflation outpaced the meager 5.5% return on deposits. Even worse, the new Money Market Mutual Funds allowed middle-income investors to buy shares in large denomination securities at high money market rates, triggering "disintermediation," the euphemism for massive withdrawals from savings and loans.

In 1979, Paul Volker, head of the Federal Reserve Board, tightened the money supply in an effort to break the back of inflation, sending the interest rate up to its highest levels in this century, and ultimately contributing to a serious recession. Faced with defaults and foreclosures resulting from the recession, combined with increasing competition from high-yield investments given the new hikes in the interest rate, savings and loans were doomed. The net worth of the industry fell from $16.7 billion in 1972 to a *negative* net worth of $17.5 billion in 1980, with 85% of the country's savings and loans losing money (Pizzo, Fricker, and Muolo 1989, p. 11).

Deregulation: The Cure that Killed

Coinciding with these economic forces, a new ideological movement was afoot. Since the early 1970s, policymakers had been considering significantly loosening the restraints on savings and loans so that they could compete more equitably for new money and invest in more lucrative ventures. However, it was not until the deregulatory fervor of the early Reagan administration that this strategy gained political acceptance as a solution to the rapidly escalating savings and loan crisis. Throwing caution to the wind and armed with the brashness born of overconfidence, the deregulators undid most of the regulatory infrastructure that had kept the thrift industry together for four decades.

The conviction of deregulators was that the free enterprise system works best if left alone, unhampered by perhaps well-meaning but ultimately counterproductive government regulations. The bind in which the savings and loan industry found itself seemed to confirm the theory that government regulations imposed an unfair handicap in the competitive process. The answer then was to return the industry to what these policymakers saw as the self-regulating mechanisms of the free market. In 1980, the Depository Institutions Deregulation and Monetary Control Act (DIDMCA; P.L. 96-221) began to do just that, phasing out restrictions on interest rates paid by savings and loans. It is important to point out, however, that the move to the free market model was incomplete and accompanied by a decisive move in the *opposite* direction. For, at the same time that the law unleashed savings and loans to compete for new money, it bolstered the federal protection accorded these "private enterprise" institutions, increasing FSLIC insurance from a maximum of $40,000 to $100,000 per deposit.[1]

The 1980 law was followed by devastating losses in the industry. In the

---

[1] This change, which some critics argue is the single most expensive mistake in the "deregulatory" series, was made in the absence of Congressional hearings on the subject and with very little debate. Apparently a concession to the U.S. League of Savings Institutions, one of the most powerful lobbying groups in Washington, one House staff person reported later that "It was almost an afterthought" (quoted in Pizzo et al. 1989, p. 11).

first place, it triggered an even more pronounced "negative rate spread." Savings and loans did attract more new money at the higher interest rates they could now offer, but the discrepancy between the high rates they had to pay to attract short-term deposits and the low rates at which they had invested in long-term home mortgages widened. The law's primary effect was to precipitate larger losses on more money.

When these deregulatory measures did not work, Congress prescribed more of the same. In 1982, the Garn-St. Germain Depository Institutions Act (P.L. 97-320) did away with the differential between permissible interest rates for commercial banks and savings and loans, and accelerated the phase-out of the ceiling on interest rates initiated in the 1980 law. Probably more important, it dramatically expanded the investment powers of savings and loans, moving them farther and farther away from their traditional role as a provider of home mortgages. They were now authorized to increase their consumer loans, up to a total of 30% of their assets; make commercial, corporate or business loans; and invest in nonresidential real estate worth up to 40% of their total assets. Furthermore, the Garn-St. Germain Act allowed thrifts to provide 100% financing, requiring no down payment from the borrower, in an apparent effort to attract new business to the desperate industry.

Industry regulators soon joined Congress in the deregulation. In 1980, regulators removed the 5% limit on "brokered deposits," allowing thrifts access to unprecedented amounts of cash. Brokered deposits were placed by middlemen who aggregated individual investments that were deposited as "Jumbo" certificates of deposit (CDs). Since the maximum insured deposit was $100,000, these brokered deposits were packaged as $100,000 CDs, on which the investors could command high interest rates. So attractive was this system to all concerned—brokers who made hefty commissions, investors who received high interest for their money, and thrift operators who now had almost unlimited access to funds—that between 1982 and 1984, brokered deposits as a percentage of total assets increased 400% (General Accounting Office September, 1985, p. 7). These brokered deposits turned out to be a critical factor both in creating pressure to engage in misconduct and in providing unprecedented opportunities for fraud.

In 1982, regulators dropped the requirement that thrifts have at least 400 stockholders, with no one owning more than 25% of the stock, opening the door for a single entrepreneur to own and operate a federally insured savings and loan. Furthermore, single investors could now start thrifts with noncash assets, such as land or real estate. Presumably hoping that the move would halt the dying off of savings and loans as innovative entrepreneurs bought them up, the deregulators seemed unaware of the disastrous potential of virtually unlimited new charters in the vulnerable industry.

The deregulatory process was complicated and accelerated by the fact that federal and state systems of regulation coexisted and not infrequently overlapped. State-chartered thrifts were regulated by state regulatory agencies and governed by their regulations, but could be insured by FSLIC if they paid the insurance premiums, which most did. (By 1986, 92.6% of the country's savings and loans—holding 98.5% of the industry's assets—were insured by FSLIC [Federal Home Loan Bank System 1987, p. 11]) This dual structure, which had operated smoothly for almost fifty years, had disastrous consequences within the context of federal deregulation. Because the funding for state regulatory agencies was provided in large part from "member" institutions, state agencies that were perceived by savings and loans as more rigorous or enforcement-oriented than the federal system risked losing their funding. The experience of the California Department of Savings and Loan serves as a good example of the effect of the regulatory competition that resulted.

Beginning in 1975, the California Department of Savings and Loan had been staffed by no-nonsense regulators who imposed strict rules and tolerated little deviation. The California thrift industry complained bitterly, and when federal regulations were relaxed in 1980, they switched en masse to federal charters (U.S. Congress. House 1987a, pp 12–13). With the exodus, the California Department lost over half of its funding and more than half of its staff. In July 1978, the California agency had 172 fulltime examiners; by 1983, the number of examiners had shrunk to 55 (U.S. Congress. House Committee on Government Operations 1988, p. 62).

It seemed that California policymakers had learned the hard way that if the state's Department of Savings and Loan was to survive (and if California state politicians were to continue to have access to the industry's lobbying dollars), they had to make it more likeable. On January 1, 1983, the Nolan Bill (Cal. Stats. 1983c. 1091) passed with only one dissenting vote, making it possible for almost anyone to charter a new savings and loan, and virtually eliminating any limitations on investment powers. Similar state legislation around the country followed the federal initiative, as state legislatures and regulators deregulated for their survival. Some states—Texas, for example—already had thrift guidelines that were even more lax than the new federal regulations, but those that did not quickly enacted "me-too" legislation (U.S. General Accounting Office 1989a, p. 25).

At the same time as this deregulation zeal gained momentum, Congress passed a Joint Current Resolution in 1982, putting the full credit of the U.S. government behind the savings and loan industry. Although by law (12 USC 1435), the federal government is not obligated to rescue the FSLIC to cover insured deposits, Congress acted with this joint resolution to appease the fears of depositors. Once again, the free market deregulators had applied their principles selectively, setting in place the ultimately fatal formula of deregulation and protective insurance.

Losses continued to mount. In 1982, the FSLIC spent over $2.4 billion to close or merge insolvent savings and loans, and by 1986 the federal insurance agency was itself insolvent (U.S. Congress. Subcommittee on Financial Institutions Supervision, Regulation and Insurance of the House Committee on Banking, Finance and Urban Affairs 1989, p. 286). As the number of insolvent and ailing thrifts climbed, the FSLIC, knowing that its resources were inadequate to cope with the financial disaster, began to slow the pace of closures. Hoping against hope that windfall profits or an innovative buyer might reverse the decline of these institutions, the fateful decision compounded the crisis. In 1988, the FSLIC closed or sold 220 defunct savings and loans, and 300 other insolvent institutions were waiting in the wings (U.S. General Accounting Office 1989a, p. 2). In the first six months of 1988, the industry lost an unprecedented $7.5 billion (Eichler 1989, p. 119).

MAJOR FORMS OF THRIFT CRIME AND THEIR CAUSAL STRUCTURE

In 1987, the Federal Home Loan Bank Board referred 6,205 savings and loan cases to the Justice Department for possible criminal prosecution, and an additional 5,114 cases were referred in 1988 (testimony before the Senate Committee on Banking, Housing and Urban Affairs, quoted in U.S. General Accounting Office 1989a, p. 11). It has been estimated that crime or misconduct played a significant role in 80% of the insolvent savings and loans destined to be bailed out by the U.S. government (U.S. Congress. House Committee on Government Operations 1988, p. 51). A GAO study of 26 of the nation's most costly thrift failures found evidence of "numerous and sometimes blatant violations of laws and regulations" in every one of the thrifts in the sample (U.S. General Accounting Office 1989c, pp. 2, 51). Furthermore, the GAO concluded that criminal activity was the central ingredient in the collapse of all of these institutions. By October, 1988, the FSLIC had sued the officers or directors of 51 failed thrifts for misconduct and estimated that these cases alone had cost the government over $8 billion (U.S. Congress. House Committee on Government Operations 1988, pp. 4–5).

The Federal Home Loan Bank Board, in a report to Congress in 1988 defined fraud as it relates to the savings and loan industry:

> Individuals in a position of trust in the institution or closely affiliated with it have, in general terms, breached their fiduciary duties; traded on inside information; usurped opportunities or profits; engaged in self-dealing; or otherwise used the institution for personal advantage. Specific examples of insider abuse include loans to insiders in excess of that allowed by regulation; high-risk speculative ventures; payment of exorbitant dividends at times when the institution is at or near insolvency; payment from institution funds for personal vacations, automobiles, clothing, and art; payment of unwarranted commissions and fees to companies owned by a shareholder; payment of "consulting fees" to insiders or their companies; use of insiders' companies for association business; and putting friends and relatives on the payroll of the institutions. (U.S. General Accounting Office 1989c, p. 22).

The varieties and possible permutations of criminal activity perpetrated by thrift operators are seemingly endless. By and large, however, fraud in the savings and loan industry falls into three general categories, classified here as "unlawful risk-taking," "looting," and "covering-up." Although these categories of fraud are analytically distinct in their makeup and in terms of the incentives, pressures, and facilitating factors that produce them, in practice they are often found as interacting parts of the same complex money machine.

Unlawful Risk-Taking

The GAO, in its study of 26 insolvent savings and loans, found that "all of the 26 failed thrifts made nontraditional, higher-risk investments and in doing so . . . violated laws and regulations and engaged in unsafe practices" (U.S. General Accounting Office 1989c, p.17). Deregulation made it legal for thrifts to invest in "nontraditional, higher-risk" activities, but regulations and laws were often broken in the process, either by extending these investment activities beyond permissible levels or by compounding the level of risk by, for example, inadequate marketability studies or poor supervision of loan disbursements. In order to explain the prevalence of this unlawful risk-taking, it is important to understand the new deregulated environment in which it was taking place, the pressures that this environment exerted, and the opportunities that it accorded. Two related thrift activities—brokered deposits and Acquisition, Development, and Construction (ADC) loans—were an integral part of this environment and will serve as good examples of both the incentive to commit fraud and the disastrous consequences for the industry.

The deregulation of savings and loans' investment powers unleashed an escalating competitive process in which brokered deposits were a key ingredient. Overnight, ailing savings and loans could obtain huge amounts of cash to stave off their impending insolvency. But the miracle drug had a downside. Like a narcotic, the more these institutions took in brokered deposits, the more they depended on them, and the more they were willing to, and had to, pay to get them. As brokerage firms shopped across the country for the best return on their money, thrifts had to offer ever-higher interest rates to attract them. And, like a drug, the most desperate institutions needed the most and paid the highest interest rates. In a perverse contortion of the theory of the survival of the fittest to which the free market deregulators subscribed (and tenaciously clung in spite of all the contrary evidence), in this environment it was the weakest thrifts that grew the fastest.

By 1984, Edwin Gray, Chair of the FHLBB, was so alarmed over the rate of growth of brokered deposits that he attempted unsuccessfully to reregulate the handling of these accounts.[2] Referred to in the business as "hot money," brokered deposits often entail huge sums, at high rates for the short term—not infrequently passing through an institution in twenty-four hours, then

---

[2] The U.S. League of Savings, Treasury Secretary Donald Regan, and a coalition of powerful brokerage firms led by Merrill Lynch, reportedly stymied the effort and successfully discredited Gray as a pessimist and a naysayer (Pizzo et al. 1989, pp. 77–83).

moving on to the next highest bidder. Institutions whose survival depends on such jumbo deposits are clearly vulnerable to the effects of unexpected withdrawals. But the problems associated with brokered deposits go far beyond this simple vulnerability factor.

The FHLBB today claims that "a large influx of brokered savings" is an "abuse flag," in recognition of the high probability of misconduct related to dependence on these deposits (U.S. Congress. House Committee on Government Operations 1988, p. 41). Given the addictive quality of brokered deposits and the high cost of obtaining them, it should not be surprising that they are associated with what is called here "unlawful risk-taking." Not only do the large cash infusions facilitate risky speculative ventures, but conversely and more importantly, long-shot investments with the potential for high payoff are undertaken by desperate institutions to offset the costs of high-interest deposits.

Among the most popular of the high-risk strategies used in conjunction with brokered deposits are Acquisition, Development, and Construction (ADC) loans. The power of federally chartered savings and loans to invest in commercial real estate projects was expanded with the deregulation of 1982, so that thrifts could invest up to 40% of their total assets in such ventures. Increasingly, high-risk loans were made to developers to acquire and develop projects for commercial use, more than tripling such loans between 1980 and 1986 (U.S. Congress. House 1987a, p. 265). As long as high-risk ADC loans remained within the 40% limit stipulated by federal regulation, they did not, by themselves, constitute misconduct. The problem was that, given the competitive pressure exerted on thrifts by the new deregulation and the proliferation of high-interest brokered deposits that it triggered, some thrifts exceeded the federal ceiling on ADC loans and/or committed misconduct in handling them.

Because these high-risk loans have the potential (although are unlikely) to be very profitable in the long run, and because they provide a desperately needed cash flow in the short run (in the form of "points" paid up front), they are an extremely attractive source of investment for the brokered money to which faltering savings and loans increasingly turned in the early and mid-1980s. But it was the "no-risk," federally insured, nature of these "high-risk" investments that ensured their proliferation and abuse. For, should developers default on these loans, they suffered no personal liability, as deposits were protected by FSLIC insurance. William Black, the San Francisco regional counsel for the newly created Office of Thrift Supervision, referring to the enormous cash flow generated by such loans, observed that "it was as simple as 'ADC'" (Quoted in *the Los Angeles Times* October 28, 1989b). The short-term and long-term potential of these ADC loans, in combination with their low risk for the investor, triggered a scramble among savings and loans to enter the world of speculative development (particularly in Texas and other states where no ceiling existed for ADC lending).

The scramble was often accompanied by inadequate marketability studies of project potential, violations of the loans-to-one-borrower limitations, and other such regulatory misconduct. The GAO concluded that of the 26 failed institutions it examined, 19 engaged in ADC lending, and two-thirds of these performed either no marketability studies or inadequate studies, in violation of federal regulations (U.S. General Accounting Office 1989c, p. 27).[3]

In some cases, thrift operators dropped any pretense of caution. Tyrell Barker, owner and operator of State Savings and Loan in Texas, who has since pleaded guilty to misapplication of bank funds, told speculators in Dallas in the early 1980s, "You bring the dirt, I bring the money. We split 50-50" (quoted in Pizzo et al. 1989, p. 191). When one Barker-backed speculator was asked how he determined which property to buy, he replied flippantly, "Wherever my dog lifts his leg I buy that rock and all the acreage around it." So common are such arrangements that they have come to be known colloquially in the industry as "cash-for-dirt" loans. With the caution of a state official and the clarity of overdue hindsight, the U.S. Attorney for the Central District of California described the motive: "It appears that there have been institutions . . . that have been sufficiently desperate for income in the competitive arena for loan money, that they have become less conscious and vigilant than one would like" (quoted in U.S. Congress. House 1987a, p. 334).

The House Committee on Government Operations concludes that in some cases, "normally honest bankers (including thrift insiders) have resorted to fraud or unsafe and unsound practices in efforts to save a battered institution. In those cases an incentive existed to turn an unhealthy financial institution around by garnering more deposits and then making even more speculative investments, hoping to 'make it big'" (1988, p. 34). The Commissioner of the California Department of Savings and Loan described the pressure to engage in fraud in the competitive environment dominated by brokered deposits: "If you have got a lot of money, high-cost money pushing you, and you have to make profits, you have to put it out awful fast" (U.S. Congress. House 1987a, p. 13). FHLBB Chair M. Danny Wall described the bind of thrift operators on a "slippery slope of a failing institution trying to save probably their institution first and trying to save themselves and their career" (U.S. Congress. House Committee on Government Operations 1988, p. 46). But, the words of an unidentified witness best summed up the formula that produced an epidemic of unlawful risk-taking in the thrift industry: "If you put temptation and the opportunity, and the need in the same place, you are asking for trouble" (U.S. Congress. House 1987a, p.9).

Deregulation was heralded by its advocates as a free market solution to the competitive handicap placed on thrifts by restraints on their investment powers and interest rates. But the "cure" turned out to be worse than the dis-

---

[3]The overbuilding that resulted from ADC lending practices has been cited as a critical factor in the collapse of the commerical real estate market in areas where the activity is concentrated (U.S. General Accounting Office 1989a, p. 23). Although the decline in oil prices was in part responsible for the real estate glut in Texas, the excess supply resulting from the logic of ADC lending compounded the crisis.

ease. Deregulation itself triggered an ever-escalating competition for deposits, and pressed some thrift operators into high-risk, even unlawful, loan arrangements. Dennis Fitzpatrick, Chair of Beverly Hills Savings and Loan in the early 1980s, told the Congressional Committee investigating wrongdoing at the thrift whose insolvency cost the FSLIC almost $1 billion (apparently with no irony intended), "We could not survive if we continued to do business in the traditional fashion" (quoted in Eichler 1989, p. 108).

As deregulation lifted the ceiling on interest rates and intensified competition, it provided a primary incentive for fraud, and by opening up investment powers, it provided the opportunity; by simultaneously deviating from the free market model upon which these moves were ostensibly based, and increasing the level of protective FSLIC insurance, would-be "deregulators" added the irresistible force of temptation.

In many respects, the factors that generate this unlawful risk-taking are similar to those highlighted in other analyses of white-collar crime. Most obviously, Sutherland (1949), Farberman (1975), Geis (1967), Hagan (1985), and others, have cited the importance of the force of competition in the profit-making enterprise as a major incentive to commit corporate crime. According to these analyses, the corporate criminal violates laws and regulations in the pursuit of the maximization of profits within the context of a competitive economy. Thus executives at Ford Motor Company in the 1970s decided to design and build the Pinto with a defective rear assembly, in spite of their knowledge that even minor rear-end collisions would cause death, injury, and burned vehicles. Spending the $11 per vehicle that it would cost to correct the defect, they reasoned, would cut into profits and impair their competitive position (Dowie 1979, p. 26). At about the same time, the president of General Motors explained his refusal to use safety glass in Chevrolets: "You can say perhaps that I am selfish, but business is selfish. We are not a charitable institution—we are trying to make a profit for our stockholders" (quoted in Mintz and Cohen 1976, p. 110). How similar is the refrain of a Houston savings and loan consultant and developer, explaining regulatory violations in the thrift industry: "If you didn't do it, you weren't just stupid—you weren't behaving as a prudent businessman, which is the ground rule. You owed it to your partners, to your stockholders, to maximize profits. Everybody else was doing it" (quoted in Lang 1989, p. 21).

In addition, the opportunity structure has been cited as a facilitating factor in the commission of corporate crime. Some analyses, for example, have emphasized the ease with which these crimes can be committed as complementary to the profit motive in the production of such crime (Wheeler and Rothman 1982). The infamous electrical company conspiracy of the 1940s and 1950s, in which employees of the heavy electrical manufacturing industry engaged in price-fixing, is exemplary (Geis 1967). Clearly, the reduction of competition and the maximization of profits were the motives for the price-fixing, but the relatively small number of very large companies such as General Electric and their domination of the industry (in a sense, the relative *lack* of competition) provided the opportunity structure for, and facilitated, the criminal conspiracy.

But the unlawful risk-taking in the savings and loan industry described here is distinct from such corporate crimes in a number of very important ways. Probably most fundamental is the way in which the savings and loan industry itself resembles the gambling casinos that they financed so heavily in the early 1980s. Whereas corporate crime in the industrial economy virtually automatically "pays off" in increased profits and long-term liquidity for the company, unlawful risk-taking in the thrift industry is a gamble—and one with very bad odds. It should not be surprising, then, that unlike more traditional corporate crimes in the manufacturing sector, these financial crimes often result in the bankruptcy of the firm.

Furthermore, although the logic of the economic structure (i.e, the inexorable drive for profits in a competitive economy) is primarily responsible for traditional corporate crime, in the case of thrift crime, the state itself has in large part set in place the generating components, in the form of deregulation, enhanced competition, and cushioned losses. The following discussion of "collective embezzlement"—a crime unique to the economic structure of finance capitalism—underscores the opportunities and temptations that this peculiar mix of deregulation and protectionism produces, the seemingly endless variety of scams devised to capitalize on it, and the havoc that it unleashes on the thrift industry.

Collective Embezzlement

In its report on crime and fraud in financial institutions, the House Committee on Government Operations (1988, p. 34) concluded, "Usual internal controls do not work in this instance." Elaborating, the Committee quoted the Commissioner of the California Department of Savings and Loans: "We built thick vaults; we have cameras; we have time clocks on the vaults; we have dual control—all these controls were to protect against somebody stealing the cash. Well, you can steal far more money, and take it out the back door. *The best way to rob a bank is to own one*" (quoted in U.S. Congress. House Committee on Government Operations 1988, p. 34; emphasis in original).

"Collective embezzlement," also called here "looting," refers to the siphoning off of funds from a savings and loan institution for personal gain, at the expense of the institution itself *and with the implicit or explicit sanction of its management*. This "robbing of one's own bank" is estimated to be the single most costly category of crime in the thrift industry, having precipitated a significant number of the thrift insolvencies to date (U.S. Congress. House Committee on Government Operations 1988, p. 41; U. S. General Accounting Office 1989c, p. 19). In characteristic understatement, the GAO reports that of the 26 insolvencies it studied, "almost all of the 26 failed thrifts made transactions that were not in the thrift's best interest. Rather, the transactions often personally benefitted directors, officers, and other related parties" (U.S. General Accounting Office 1989c, p. 19).

In discussing various forms of white-collar lawbreaking, Sutherland noted that "the ordinary case of embezzlement is a crime by a single individual in a subordinate position against a strong corporation" (1983, p. 234). Cressey, in his landmark study, *Other People's Money* (1953), developed an explanatory model of the behavior of the lone white-collar embezzler, stealing from his or her employer. Traditionally, then, embezzlement has been considered an isolated act of individual employees.[4] The "collective embezzlement" described here is a relatively new form of corporate crime that has yet to be closely studied. Previous analyses have differentiated between corporate crime (in which fraud is engaged in *by* the corporation *for* the corporation) and embezzlement (in which crime is committed *against* the corporation), but the "collective embezzlement" discussed here is a hybrid—perhaps "crime *by* the corporation *against* the corporation."

In some cases, thrift embezzlement takes the form of "buying sprees" (Pizzo et al. 1989, p. 36), in which thrift operators and others with inside access to thrift funds, purchase luxury goods and services and charge them to the institution. Examples abound. When Erwin Hansen took over Centennial Savings and Loan in California at the end of 1980, one of the industry's most expensive shopping sprees began. "Erv" Hansen threw a Centennial-funded, $148,000 Christmas party for 500 friends and invited guests that included a 10-course sitdown dinner, roving minstrels, court jesters, and pantomimes. Hansen and his companion Beverly Haines, a senior officer at Centennial, travelled extensively around the world in the thrift's private airplanes, purchased antique furniture at the thrift's expense, and "renovated" an old house in the California countryside at a cost of over $1 million, equipping it with a gourmet chef at an annual cost of $48,000. A fleet of luxury cars was put at the disposal of Centennial personnel, and the thrift's offices were adorned with art from around the world (Pizzo et al. 1989, pp. 25–37; U.S. General Accounting Office 1989c, p. 22). Hansen died before he could be formally charged, but Haines was convicted of having embezzled $2.8 million. Centennial's inevitable insolvency cost the FSLIC an estimated $160 million (U.S. Congress. House Committee on Government Operations 1988, p. 38).

Don Dixon similarly operated Vernon Savings and Loan in Texas as if it were his own personal slush fund. He and his wife Dana divided their time between a luxury ski resort in the Rocky Mountains and a $1 million beach house north of San Diego, commuting on one of two Vernon jets that cost the thrift

---

[4]In Sherman's (1978) terms, such embezzlement constitutes deviance *in* an organization, as distinguished from deviance *by* an organization (such as the corporate price-fixing discussed above).

$100,000 apiece to operate. They went on luxury vacations across Europe, in one case running up a bill of $22,000, paid for with Vernon funds. Dixon bought a 112-foot yacht for $2.6 million, with which he wooed Congressmen and regulators on extravagant boating parties. In March, 1987, Vernon Savings and Loan was declared insolvent; it was estimated that the Vernon debacle would cost FSLIC $1.3 billion. Regulators argued in court that Dixon and others connected with Vernon had "wrongly extracted" up to $40 million from the thrift's coffers (quoted in Pizzo et al. 1989, p. 193).

Other more subtle forms of collective embezzlement include a variety of schemes to obtain "excessive compensation" for the institution's directors and officers (U.S. General Accounting Office 1989c, p. 21). As defined by the General Accounting Office, "compensation includes salaries as well as bonuses, dividend payments, and perquisites for executives" (1989c, p. 21). Although a federal regulation limits permissible compensation for thrift personnel to that which is "reasonable and commensurate with their duties and responsibilities," the GAO found instances of excessive compensation in 17 of the 26 failed thrifts they studied (U.S. General Accounting Office 1989c, p. 21).

At one thrift, the chairman of the board of directors resigned his formal position in January 1985, whereupon he arranged a "services agreement" with the institution to carry on all his previous responsibilities. According to this agreement, he was to be paid $326,000 plus a percentage of profits in the form of a bonus. Six months later, the thrift paid him a bonus of $500,000 in "special employee compensation," even though it reported a loss of approximately $23 million during the course of 1985 (U.S. General Accounting Office 1989c, p. 21).

The most widespread techniques of looting discovered thus far, however, involve an array of "special deals." For example, in "nominee loan" schemes (U.S. Congress. House Committee on Government Operations 1988, p. 41), a "straw borrower" outside of the thrift obtains a loan for a third person, who is usually affiliated with the thrift from which the loan is received. Such nominee loans are a popular devise for disguising violations of the regulation which limits unsecured commercial loans to "affiliated persons" to $100,000. Don Dixon, of Vernon, was particularly adept at this, setting up an intricate network of at least 30 subsidiary companies for the express purpose of making illegal loans to himself.

A related system for violating the loans-to-affiliated-persons regulation is "reciprocal loan arrangements" (U.S. Congress. House Committee on Government Operations 1988, p. 41). Hearings before the House Subcommittee on Commerce, Consumer, and Monetary Affairs in 1987 described four investigations in Wyoming that "revealed a pattern of complex activities . . . [which] include reciprocal loans in which the insiders from one bank authorize loans to the insiders of another bank in return for similar loans" (U.S. Congress. House 1987b, pp. 79–80, 129–130). The scam resulted in losses to taxpayers of $26 million when the loans defaulted and the institutions failed.

So-called "land flips" (U.S. Congress. House Committee on Government Operations 1988, p. 41) use real estate deals as the mechanism for looting. Land flips are defined as "transfers of land between related parties to fraudulently inflate the value of the land. The land is used as collateral for loans based on the inflated or fraudulent valuation. Loan amounts typically greatly exceed the actual value of the land" (U.S. Congress. House Committee on Government Operations 1988, p. 42). Hansen of Centennial Savings and Loans, his friend and high financier Sid Shah, and Dutch investor Neik Sandmann, regularly used this technique to mutual advantage. According to reporters Pizzo et al. (1989, p. 46), the three "flipped" one property worth $50,000 back and forth in the early 1980s until it reached the inflated value of $487,000, upon which they received a loan from Atlas Savings, the "sucker" institution of choice for Hansen.

Similarly, loan broker J. William Oldenburg bought a piece of property in Richmond, California, in 1979 for $874,000. Two years later, after a number of "flips," he had the land appraised at $83.5 *million*. After buying State Savings and Loans in Salt Lake City for $10.5 million, he sold the property to the newly acquired thrift for $55 million (Pizzo et al. 1989, p. 177; U.S. Congress. House Committee on Government Operations 1988, pp. 180–181). In 1985, the ill-fated thrift went under, leaving the FSLIC responsible for $416 million in outstanding deposits.

"Linked financing," or "daisy chains" as they are known in the industry, is perhaps the most subtle and complex of the "special deals" used for embezzling. Linked financing is "the practice of depositing money into a financial institution with the understanding that the financial institution will make a loan conditioned upon receipt of the deposits" (U.S. Congress. House Committee on Government Operations 1988, p. 42). It often involves large brokered deposits, made by a deposit broker who then receives a generous loan from the bank or thrift for his business. The brokers can then default on their loans, essentially obtaining free cash (these are called "drag loans," because the borrower simply drags away the loan, with no intention of repayment); middlemen obtain a generous "finder's fee"; and thrift operators record hefty deposits and inflated assets, which spell extra bonuses and dividends for thrift executives.

Looting is not confined to inside operators of thrifts. More often than not, the scheme requires intricate partnerships with those outside the industry, usually in real estate or loan brokerage (U.S. Congress. House 1987a, p. 332). In some cases the outsiders themselves initiate the fraud by identifying weak thrifts as "easy targets" that are "ripe for the plucking" (U.S. Congress. House Committee on Government Operations 1988, p. 12). In one infamous deal, loan broker Charles J. Bazarian, Jr. engaged in fraudulent real estate transactions that contributed to the insolvency of two large California thrifts—Consolidated Savings Bank of Irvine and American Diversified Savings Bank of Costa Mesa. According to charges brought against Bazarian, in one instance he borrowed more than $9.5 million from Consolidated, putting close to $5 million of it into a partnership in which the owner of the thrift, Robert Ferrante, had a direct interest. The same year, Bazarian arranged a reciprocal transaction with American Diversified in which the thrift bought $15 million of "worthless" investor notes from Bazarian's brokerage firm, in exchange for Bazarian's purchase of $3.85 million in promissory notes and two pieces of real estate from the thrift. When federal regulators finally closed the two thrifts, together they registered close to $200 million in losses (*Los Angeles Times* September 19, 1989).[5]

"Daisy chains," "dead cows for dead horses," "land flips," "cash for trash," "cash for dirt," "kissing the paper," "white knights"—their playful jargon reflects the make-believe, candy-store mentality of this new breed of white-collar criminal and belies the devastating consequences of their actions. In Arkansas, where one-third of all thrifts have collapsed since 1986, taking with them $4 billion in deposits (a sum which is more than the state's annual budget), local residents have developed a jargon of their own. "S&L," they say, stands for "Squander and Liquidate" (quoted in Bates 1989, p. 17).

As looters were shoplifting goods and pilfering cash out the back door of thrifts, more shady characters were being welcomed in the front door. Increasingly, the word spread that deregulation of thrifts had offered up a money machine to the unscrupulous. At the federal level, new charters, which had averaged 45 a year in the 1970s, shot up to an average of 96 per year in the 1980s (Federal Home Loan Bank Board 1987, p. A29). In states such as Texas and California where regulations were especially lax, the number of new charters increased even more sharply. In California, 235 applications for new thrift charters were received by the California Department of Savings and Loan in a little over a year between 1982 and 1984, and most were quickly granted (U.S. Congress. House 1987a, p. 18).

Summarizing the looting epidemic, the House Committee on Government Operations (1988) lamented the opportunities opened up for the con artist: "We have even got organized crime types taking a look at thinly capitalized institutions which are candidates for takeover and then using [various specified fraud schemes] . . . to create a paper financial asset which they can pull the plug on after a year-and-a-half or two, and leave the FDIC or FSLIC, i. e., the taxpayers, holding the bag" (pp. 5–6).

Deregulation and subsequent intense competition had produced the incentive for those on the "slippery slope of a failing institution" to try to save that institution via unlawful, but in the end not very "risky," risk-taking. As deregulation had thus opened the doors to gambling risk-free with depositors' money, it simultaneously opened them to crooks and swindlers whose inten-

---

[5]Bazarian has also been accused of siphoning money off of two housing projects of the Department of Housing and Urban Development (HUD), thus providing a human link between two of the biggest scandals of the 1980s—corruption at HUD and the savings and loan debacle.

tion was to embezzle funds. Not infrequently, the gamblers and swindlers were the same people. Whether the motive was to keep the doors open for further sport, or to get in and out with as much of the pot as possible, the game was the same: "Heads I win. Tails you lose."

Covering up

As savings and loans teetered on the brink of bankruptcy, broken by negligent loan practices on one hand and outright looting on the other, their operators struggled to hide both the insolvency and the fraud through a manipulation of their books and records. This "covering up" was, and is, perhaps the most widespread criminal activity of thrift operators. Of the alleged 179 violations of criminal law reported in the 26 failed thrifts that the GAO studied, 42 were for such covering-up activity, constituting the largest single category of fraud (U.S. General Accounting Office 1989c, p. 51). Furthermore, every one of the 26 failed thrifts had been cited by regulatory examiners for "deficiencies in accounting" (U.S. General Accounting Office 1989c, p. 40).

In some cases, the cover-up comes in the guise of deals similar to those discussed above—the difference being that the primary purpose of the transactions is to produce a misleading picture of the institution's state of health. Most important, thrifts are required to have on hand a specific amount of capital, as well as a given capital-to-assets ratio; when they fail to meet these standards, they are subject to enforcement actions. U.S. Attorney Anton R. Valukas describes a number of cover-up deals and the motivation for them:

> In the prosecuted cases of Manning Savings and Loan, American Heritage Savings and Loan of Bloomingdale and First Subruban Bank of Maywood, when the loans ("nominee loans") became non-performing the assets were taken back into the institution, again sold at inflated prices to straw purchasers, financed by the institution, in order to inflate the net worth of the bank or savings and loan. The clear purpose was to keep the federal regulatory agencies . . . at bay by maintaining a net worth above the trigger point for forced reorganization or liquidation. (U.S. Congress. House 1987b, pp. 99–100)

In some cases, deals can be arranged that include a built-in cover-up. For example, in cases of risky insider or reciprocal loans, a reserve account can be included in the original loan to be used to pay for the first few months (or years) of interest. Thus if a real estate developer, or for that matter a straw borrower, wants to borrow $500,000, he can be extended $750,000, putting the additional $250,000 into a special account from which the interest payments can be drawn. The effect is to make a loan appear current whether or not the real estate project has failed or was phony in the first place.

Probably most common, however, is simply adjusting the books to shield the thrift from regulatory action. At one savings and loan studied by the GAO, three irreconcilable sets of records were kept—two on two different computer systems and one manually (U.S. General Accounting Office 1989c, p. 41). At another, $21 million of income was reported in the last few days of 1985 in transactions that were either fabricated or fraudulent, allowing the thrift to report a net worth of $9 million, rather than its actual worth of negative $12 million (U.S. General Accounting Office 1989c, pp. 44–45). Noting the prevalence of such cover-up devices, the president of one savings and loan testified in Congressional hearings that, "instead of attempting to remedy the problems which were so apparent, they [industry operatives] spent all of their efforts in proposing intricate schemes which . . . would appear to aid in maintaining the equity at a proper level" (U.S. Congress. House 1987a, p. 546).

Having perpetrated fraud and brought their institutions to ruin, thrift operators had to cover their tracks, both to protect themselves from prosecution and to keep their money machine running. Ironically, they were aided and, some would say, encouraged in their efforts by the same agencies from which they were presumably hiding. The Federal Home Loan Bank Board set in place a number of bookkeeping strategies during the deregulatory period that simultaneously provided the industry with the tools to juggle their books to present themselves in the best possible light, and implicitly relayed the message that in trying to keep afloat, "anything goes."

Most important, in 1981 the FHLBB devised and encouraged the use of new accounting procedures known as "regulatory accounting procedures" (RAP). The new procedures entailed a complex formula that allowed for the understating of assets and the overstating of capital (Eichler 1989, pp. 72, 77). The sole purpose of the new RAP techniques was to inflate an institution's capital-to-assets ratio, thereby bolstering its image of financial health, and warding off reorganization, which the FSLIC increasingly could not afford. Not only did the procedures supply the industry with a "gray area" within which they could commit fraud with little chance of detection, but it sent the message that the Bank Board itself promoted deceptive bookkeeping.

In addition, the Bank Board in the early 1980s sent a more general message that it condoned discretionary reporting by thrifts. The GAO, for example, cites the Board's failure to provide appropriate guidelines for recording ADC transactions until 1985, thereby implicitly encouraging accounting treatments that inflated thrifts' net worth. ADC transactions can be classified as loans or investments; "Thus, a thrift could possibly forestall regulatory action by using whichever classification resulted in the most favorable portrayal of its financial condition" (U.S. General Accounting Office 1989c, p. 42). Nonetheless, the Bank Board issued no guidelines for the recording of these important transactions. One district bank official who sought advice from the Board as to how these transactions should be reported "was told that the Bank Board was not going to act on this issue" (U.S. General Accounting Office 1989c, p. 42).

Deregulation, based on a free market model of capitalism, had provided the economic pressure and the opportunity for thrift operators and their partners to make a fortune fast. But the free market model was by no means uniformly applied. As deregulators busily dismantled restrictions on thrifts, protections were not only left intact, but were increased, providing a risk-free environment for the white-collar heist of the century. In the following section, we address the question asked pointedly by one of the most prolific of thrift embezzlers, Charles Bazarian: "So where were the regulators?" (quoted in Pizzo et al. 1989, p. 14).

SAVINGS AND LOAN ENFORCEMENT: IDEOLOGY, NETWORKS OF INFLUENCE, AND STRUCTURAL FACTORS

Deregulation Ideology and Limited Resources

According to the House Committee on Government Operations (1988, p. 8), "serious deficiencies" exist in the way the federal banking regulators and the Justice Department have handled fraud in the banking and thrift industry. The Committee Report points out that in the early 1980s, many thrifts were able to avoid timely examination altogether (U.S. Congress. House Committee on Government Operations 1988, p. 69), and that those that were found to be violating the law, were treated too leniently to offer any deterrence (U.S. Congress. House Committee on Government Operations 1988, pp. 16, 34–39). The Committee faults the "graduated response" strategy of enforcement, describing the system as follows:

> An agency uncovers abuse and issues a directive or letter; the abuse continues and becomes worse, and the agency then issues a MOU [Memoradnum of Understanding] or a supervisory agreement; and then, as the situation worsens, the agency issues one or more supervisory directives, and possibly a C&D [Cease and Desist] order or removal [of management], but by then the institution is failing. This committee specifically criticized this practice in its 1984 report. With certain exceptions, the agencies' approach has not changed. (U.S. Congress. House Committee on Government Operations 1988, p. 16)

Both the House Committee and the GAO report a general lack of "formal enforcement actions" against even the most serious offenders. One GAO study (1989b) examined 424 "Significant Supervisory Cases," that is, thrifts that both have serious internal control problems and are in imminent danger of insolvency, and found that formal actions had been taken by regulators in fewer than 50% of the cases; in most of these cases the formal actions involved placing the thrift into receivership *after* it had become insolvent. Another GAO report (1989c, p.4) concludes that "numerous safety and soundness problems" had been documented by examiners in 26 of the nation's most costly insolvencies over the course of five years or more. Despite the examiners' notes that these thrifts required "urgent and decisive corrective measures," in most cases nothing substantive was done before it was too late (U.S. General Accounting Office 1989b, p. 4). The House Committee on Government Operations (1988, pp. 75–77) reports that enforcement actions, which they had argued in a 1984 report (U.S. Congress. House Committee on Government Operation 1984) were already too rare to constitute a deterrent, declined further after 1986.

Not only did thrift fraud go relatively undetected by regulators, and was generally not dealt with through formal actions, but those offenders who were prosecuted typically received lenient sentences. According to the report of the House Committee cited above, "The message to culpable insiders and outsiders is: 'Crime does pay'" (U.S. Congress. House Committee on Government Operations 1988, p. 35). Every U.S. Attorney who testified before the Committee complained of the light sentences handed down in financial fraud cases. The U.S. Attorney for Southern California reported that in his district since January 1986, 60% of the convictions under the bank fraud statutes have brought sentences of probation; 10% received less than a year in custody; and fewer than 5% of the defendants were given five years or more in prison (U.S. Congress. House Committee on Government Operations 1988, p. 36). The House Subcommittee on Commerce, Consumer, and Monetary Affairs (1989b, pp. 982–1014) conducted its own examination of the sentences of 38 serious offenders in 28 thrifts and found that 16 received probation, and that only 8 of these were ordered to pay significant restitution. As one U.S. Attorney put it, responding to such lenience, "If someone had walked in the door of the bank with a note saying this is a robbery . . . and walked out with $1500, I dare say he would have received 5 to 10 years in prison" (U.S. Congress. House 1987b, pp. 110–111).

The lack of meaningful enforcement in the savings and loan industry in the 1980s is partly the result of ideological imperatives in the deregulatory era. In the first place, deregulators believed wholeheartedly in the intrinsically healthy nature of intense competition and in the healing power of entrepreneurial innovation. Regulators themselves had invented and encouraged the use of Regulatory Accounting Procedures that would camouflage thrifts' actual state of declining health. The perpetrators of thrift fraud were, in a sense, only carrying this message of the deregulators to an extreme. Second, having deregulated the thrift industry, policymakers and industry regulators were undoubtedly reluctant to intervene while the new deregulated thrift environment was presumably working its magic and revitalizing the industry. If a few thrift operators were getting carried away, and their institutions were on the brink of insolvency, this was merely a transitional period on the road to a reinvigorated industry.

Related to these ideological imperatives of deregulation, inadequate resources compounded the problem. The size of the examination staff of the FHLBB remained constant for almost 20 years, despite dramatic increases in workload. In 1966, when the total assets of thrift institutions was $133.8 billion, FHLBB had a field examination staff of 755 persons; by, 1985, when total assets had soared to $1 trillion, the examination staff stood at 747. The House Committee on Government Operations (1988) remarks on this shortage of inspectors: "No one questions that this contributed to untimely detection of misconduct in numerous institutions which subsequently failed" (p. 69).

Despite repeated requests by the FHLBB for budget increases commensurate with the growth of the industry, the Office of Management and Budget

(OMB) was determined to maintain existing low levels of funding in the first half of the 1980s. Citing OMB's "disdain for the examination process," the former deputy director of the FSLIC told the House Subcommittee on Commerce, Consumer, and Monetary Affairs (1987a, p. 175) that OMB budgetary policies were directly responsible for the lack of supervision in the thrift industry. In July 1985, the FHLBB decentralized its examination process in the quasi-independent FHL District Banks, thereby taking it outside the budgetary control of OMB. As a result, the examination staff doubled in two years (U.S. Congress. House Committee on Government Operations 1988, p. 15).

Networks of Influence

The increase in budget and enforcement personnel after 1985 proved insufficient to offset the impact of political influence and favor-trading that dictated against strict enforcement. A revolving door between the state and federal regulatory agencies and the thrift industry itself provides one dimension of these networks of influence. For example, it is commonly understood that the U.S. League of Savings Associations, a powerful lobbying group of thrift executives, had virtual veto power on the nomination of the head of the FHLBB, and that members of the regulatory board are drawn almost entirely from the industry itself (Eichler 1989, p. 131). Richard Pratt, head of the FHLBB at the time, in a moment of candor told his subordinates at an agency conference that the Bank Board was "perhaps too closely allied to the industry that it regulates" (1982, p. 46). At the lower levels, it is not uncommon for thrifts to woo examiners and regulators with job offers in the industry (see *Los Angeles Times* September 1, 1989). Journalists Pizzo et al. (1989, p. 47) put it bluntly, describing the strategy of "Erv" Hansen, owner and embezzler of Centennial Savings and Loan: "Hansen had his own way of appeasing regulators. He'd hire them." Hansen, for example, hired Pat Connolly, former deputy commissioner of the California Department of Savings and Loan, making him an executive vice president of the thrift and doubling his $40,000 a year government salary.

In one of the most infamous cases of personal intrigue in the savings and loan crisis, it has been charged that M. Danny Wall, head of the FHLBB at the time, met personally with Charles Keating, owner of Lincoln Savings and Loan, and intervened on behalf of Keating to ward off FHLB regulators in the San Francisco district who were investigating the thrift (*Los Angeles Times* October 21, 1989; *Los Angeles Times* October 25, 1989). Wall managed to move the investigation from the San Francisco office to Washington and to delay closure of the insolvent thrift for two years—a delay that is estimated to have cost the FSLIC insurance fund $2 billion (*Los Angeles Times* October 25, 1989). Once the investigation had been moved to Washington, according to Congressional testimony, Rosemary Stewart, head of the enforcement office in Washington, signed a "memo of understanding" with Lincoln. This "understanding" was bitterly referred to by examiners in the San Francisco office as "Rosemary's Baby," because it essentially permitted Lincoln to continue its high risk-taking and misconduct for a full year before it was finally closed (testimony reported in *Los Angeles Times* October 27, 1989).

Similar networks of influence have been documented between members of Congress and the thrift industry, with significant repercussions on enforcement. For example, just before the Lincoln case was moved to Washington, five U.S. Senators (Cranston, Glenn, DeConcini, McCain, and Riegle) who had received campaign and other contributions from Charles Keating, called San Francisco regulators to Washington to discuss their prolonged examination of Lincoln (a memorandum of notes of the meeting is quoted in Pizzo et al. 1989, pp. 392–404). According to a racketeering lawsuit brought against accountants in the Lincoln case, the intervention of the Senators "protracted the examination process and afforded [operators] additional time in which to exacerbate their frauds" (quoted in *Los Angeles Times* September 21, 1989).

In other well-publicized cases, former House speaker Jim Wright and former Democratic Whip Tony Coelho have been linked to the savings and loan industry in Texas, intervening on behalf of Dixon's Vernon Savings and Loan, and attempting to devise more "flexible" regulatory policies (*U.S. News and World Report* June 12, 1989). Republicans are by no means exempt from the maneuverings. According to one report, the republican National Committee put together an exclusive group of high financiers and named them the "Team 100" (Lang 1989, p. 24). A prominent member of this group, and one who donated heavily to the Bush campaign in 1988, was Texas billionaire Trammel Crow. Crow has managed the Texas real estate repossessed by the FSLIC for years. As thrift failures have increased, Crow and other members of the "Team" have been offered the insolvent S&Ls at bargain-basement prices, suggesting a link between thrift failures in Texas and the financial fortunes of the Republican's "Team 100" (Lang 1989, p. 24).

Structural Conflicts and Enforcement

Besides these networks of personal influence and corruption, more general structural forces sabotaged regulation. According to the GAO, a "basic structural flaw" permeated the FHLB system (U.S. General Accounting Office 1989a, p. 80). This structural flaw consisted of the complex division of labor and overlapping responsibilities of thrift regulators and, related to this, the "conflicting responsibilities for promoting the thrift industry while at the same time regulating and insuring it" (U.S. General Accounting Office 1989a, p. 80), Prior to the reform of 1989, the FHLB regulatory system included the following layers: the 12 district banks' examiners, to whom primary field-level responsibility was delegated in 1985; the Office of Regulatory Activity (ORA), established in 1986 to oversee these district bank examiners; the Office of Enforcement (OE) within the central FHLBB in Washington, DC, to whom the district examiners made recommendations for formal enforcement actions;

the three-member Federal Home Loan Bank Board itself; and, finally, the FSLIC, which had ultimate responsibility for liquidating or reorganizing insolvent thrifts.

In addition to the potential for overlapping responsibilities inherent in this system, the structural problems were two-fold. First, the FSLIC, which insured the thrifts and had to pay the tab for insolvencies, had no legal authority to monitor or supervise the institutions and had to receive approval from the Bank Board before it could take any final action. Making matters worse, a "fundamental conflict" existed in the Bank Board and district banks' "roles in both promoting and regulating the industry" (U.S. General Accounting Office 1989a, p. 80). The Bank Board was responsible for chartering new thrifts and promoting the general welfare of the savings and loan system, yet at the same time was the main thrift regulator. The district banks, whose field examiners had to uncover any potential problems or misconduct, had as their primary role the provision of banking services to the member institutions and depended on these institutions for their livelihood. The thrift industry executives who made up the vast majority of district bank board members (U.S. General Accounting Office 1989a, p. 81) were the personal embodiment of this symbiotic relationship between the district banks and the thrift industry that they were supposed to regulate. Previous analyses have used the concept of "captive agencies" to refer to regulatory agencies that are subordinate to, and cater to, the industries they are charged with regulating (Lowi 1969, Rourke 1969). The dual functions of the FHLBB effectively *institutionalized* the "captive agency" syndrome.

But there are other, even more fundamental, structural problems. First, not only was the FSLIC dependent on the Bank Board for approval for its actions, but the insurers faced a catch-22 situation: The worse the crisis in the thrift industry, the less likely it was that the FSLIC could respond. This dilemma has plagued the insurers for years, but by the mid-1980s it paralyzed them. By 1986, the FSLIC itself was insolvent (its liabilities exceedee its assets by an estimated $3 billion to $7 billion), drained of its resources by the epidemic of thrift failures (U.S. General Accounting Office May, 1987, p. 3).

Throughout the 1980s, the FHLBB had extended "forebearance" to ailing thrifts, forestalling their closure or reorganization, "either because it believed the thrift to be capable of recovery" in the new deregulated environment, or "because the regulators desired to postpone using insurance fund reserves" (U.S. General Accounting Office May, 1987, p. 1). When the fund itself became insolvent in 1986, forebearance became a matter of necessity. As the FSLIC stopped closing insolvent thrifts, not only did the final costs escalate, but fraud—which in many cases had contributed to the insolvency in the first place—went undeterred. With nothing to lose, careless risk-taking and looting permeated the brain-dead institutions until they were finally, mercifully, put out of their misery.

Finally, and perhaps most importantly, a contradiction inherent in the structure of finance capitalism underlies the inability of regulators to respond effectively to the widespread fraud in the thrift industry. Clues as to the nature of this contradiction occasionally surface in government reports on the crisis. For example, the U.S. Attorney for the Southern District of Texas testified before the House Subcommittee on Commerce, Consumer, and Monetary Affairs (1987, p. 126) that "the public's faith in the security and integrity of their banking institutions is considered so vital to the continued viability of the banking system that Congress has promulgated laws to prevent people from even starting rumors about a bank's solvency or insolvency." Although the official concluded from this that the state must act quickly to deter crime and restore public confidence in the banking system, quite a different conclusion could be drawn. In fact, the House Committee on Government Operations (1988) reports that "Although every other Federal regulatory agency discloses final enforcement actions, the banking agencies continue to refuse to routinely disclose the existence or a summary of final civil enforcement orders taken against individuals or institutions". The FHLBB argument against the "adverse publicity" that such disclosure would generate is that it would damage public confidence in the institution, worsening its condition. The Committee points out that this reluctance of the agency to act decisively and openly, in the interest of protecting the banking industry, has exacerbated thrift misconduct (U.S. Congress. House Committee on Government Operations 1988, p. 17).

An essential characteristic of finance capitalism is that its product is illusory—based on collectively agreed upon, but fundamentally arbitrary, values and shared faith. In this context, the "market" works so long as all of the players agree to pretend. Alan Webber, managing editor of the *Harvard Business Review*, points to this make-believe quality of our "soap-bubble" economy and explains, "That's why the slightest whiff of smoke can so easily spook the crowd to rush for the exits" (*Los Angeles Times* October 18, 1989). The banking industry is a clear and simple example of the importance of the collective agreement to have faith, since its success, indeed its very survival, depends on our illusion that banks in fact can pay off their debts (our deposits). Any "whiff of smoke" to the contrary sets off a run on the bank. For the regulator caught between sending up this smoke and shattering the collective illusion, or ignoring fraud and insolvency, the name of the game may be "Heads I Lose, Tails You Win."

DISCUSSION

The House Committee on Government Operations (1988) summed up the testimony of senior Justice Department officials on the topic of bank fraud, reporting "(a) that financial institution fraud has reached epidemic proportions, [and] (b) that the number of criminal cases is increasing at an alarming rate" (p. 5). Federal Bureau of Investigation figures reveal that Financial Institution Fraud and Embezzlement (FIF & E) cases make up 45.2% of all white-collar crime convictions or pretrial diversions, and that more than 80% of these involve insider fraud (U.S. Congress House Committee on Government Operations, Subcommittee on Commerce, Consumer, and Monetary Affairs, 1987b, pp. 991–992, 592–593).

The argument presented here has been that the epidemic of financial fraud in the thrift industry can be traced in large part to state policies and related ideologies of the 1980s that set in place a formula of deregulation and protectionism that unleashed unprecedented incentives and supplied tempting opportunities to commit fraud. Furthermore, it has been shown that the economic structure of the deregulated and protected thrift industry has generated a new breed of white-collar crime, called here "collective embezzlement," in which the systematic embezzlement of company funds is *company policy*.

But a more general point is implicit in this analysis: Both this new hybrid of white-collar crime—crime by the corporation against the corporation—and the role of the state in its generation and proliferation, are products of a new economic structure. French economist and Nobel prize winner, Maurice Allais, has called finance capitalism in the United States a "casino" economy (quoted in the *Los Angeles Times* October 26, 1989). Profits in this economy are made from speculative ventures designed to bring windfall profits from having placed a clever bet. In contrast to industrial capitalism where profits are dependent on the production and sale of goods and services, profits in finance capitalism increasingly come, as one commentator has put it, from "fiddling with money" (*Los Angeles Times* October 4, 1989). Corporate takeovers, currency trading, loan swaps, land speculation, futures trading—these are the "means of production" of finance capitalism. Only one thing is missing: Nothing is being produced but capital gains.

Maurice Allais underlines the magnitude of this shift from an economy based on the circulation of goods to one circulating money itself, by pointing out that "more than $400 billion is exchanged every day on the foreign exchange markets, while the flow of commercial transactions is only about $12 billion" (*Los Angeles Times* October 26, 1989). Nothing epitomizes the new financial era like the junk bond. The irony of its name should not be lost. The device transforms debt into wealth, and "junk" into "one of the greatest fortunes in Wall Street history" (Grant 1989, p. 61).

The advent of finance capitalism has clearly created new opportunities for fraud, because the amount that can be reaped from financial crime is confined only to the limits of one's imagination. Furthermore, as we have seen, state policies in the form of deregulation multiplied the opportunities in the savings and loan industry. But there is a way in which the new economic structure more generally encourages fraud, or at least fails to discourage it. A number of analysts have delineated the constraints placed on entrepreneurs in industrial or manufacturing capitalism, focusing on the contradiction between the simultaneous need to maximize surplus value and to minimize labor unrest and other forms of economic and political instability (Miliband 1969; Weinstein 1968; Wiebe 1967). Weinstein (1968), for example, explains Progressivism in the early 20th century as the product of capitalists' pressing need for stability dictated by long-term investments in the costly infrastructure of capitalist production versus the potential instability of an escalating class struggle. Industrial capitalism clearly presents incentives and opportunities for serious crime, as several generations of students of white-collar crime have documented. Nonetheless, these corporate criminals are generally pressed into crime to advance their corporation and are constrained by a vested interest in its long-term survival. By contrast, perpetrators of financial fraud in the thrift industry and throughout the "casino" economy, have little to lose by their reckless behavior. With no long-term investment in the infrastructure of production and no labor relations (since there are no workers in this "production" process) to inhibit them, the casino capitalists' main concern is to get in and out of the "house" with as much of the pot as possible. The effect of their crimes on the health of the casino, or even its long-term survival, are unimportant to these financial gamblers. Not surprisingly, then, the repercussions of these crimes, unlike more traditional white-collar crimes, have the potential to extend far beyond their direct costs to wreak havoc throughout the economy.

The structure of finance capitalism not only has contributed to the unprecedented proportions and far-reaching consequences of savings and loan and other financial fraud, but has limited the state's ability to respond to it effectively. One reason for this paralysis of the state in treating thrift fraud has to do with outdated assumptions and ideologies that were the product of industrial capitalism, but which are anachronistic in the new economic environment. Most important is the notion that individual profit-making activity is intrinsically beneficial to the general economy, and that the spillover will eventually "trickle down" to the public at large in the form of increased jobs, better wages, and an overall improved standard of living. Thus, in 20th century America, it became a truism that "What's good for General Motors is good for the country." There was a certain, albeit limited, logic to this trickle-down axiom within the framework of early 20th century capitalism. State actions calculated to provide conditions favorable to capital accumulation, while exacting brutal sacrifices from workers, at least had the *potential* to pay a return on those sacrifices in the form of an expanded economy. Given the right conditions (a strong and active labor movement being a central one), trickle-down theory could, and sometimes did, work.

This trickle-down ideology born of industrial capitalism has had direct implications for the treatment of corporate crime. Policymakers and regulators have reasoned that an overly punitive approach to corporate crime is counterproductive if it cuts into profits or discourages aggressive business practices. Theorists of the state have thus noted a structural contradiction between the need of the capitalist state to encourage the maximization of profits versus the threat to profit maximization entailed in, for example, the rigorous enforcement of occupational safety and health standards (Berman 1978; Donnelly 1982; Stearns 1979).

But the logic of finance capitalism is such that capital gains based on speculative ventures are, at best, irrelevant to the welfare of the general population. Unlike the production of goods and services, "fiddling with" money produces few new jobs and no consumer goods. Policies based on outdated assumptions about the intrinsically beneficial nature of entrepreneurial activity tend to exacerbate the situation. Thus, for example, deregulation—rooted in notions of the inherent desirability of profit maximization—within the context of the new casino economy not only did not solve the thrift crisis, but compounded it by condoning fraud as simply aggressive business practices that would eventually stimulate recovery. In the case of savings and loans, the abstract theory of "trickle down" yielded the harsh reality of "trickle up," as taxpayers foot the bill for the casino extravaganza.

As policymakers are mired in the old ideologies of a past era, a new contradiction adds to the paralysis. As we have seen, a fundamental contradiction between profit maximization and enforcement of standards and regulations permeates industrial capitalism and limits the state's ability to respond to corporate crime. The logic of finance capitalism contains its own set of contradictions, with even more disastrous consequences. The new economy is built on "soap-bubbles" and illusion, where prosperity is based on debt, and the collective agreement to ignore the emperor's nakedness not only staves off collapse but is the very motor that drives the economy. In this context, the role of the state is not to establish optimal conditions for productive activity, as it was in industrial capitalism, but to shore up the illusion and minimize the potential for panic. Thus it makes sense that the same deregulators who dismantled all restrictions on the savings and loan industry in the name of the free market deviated so dramatically from their own convictions and *increased* deposit insurance. The contradiction underlying the thrift debacle, then, is that the casino economy is based on illusion but that that illusion must be preserved at all costs. As losses were covered by federal insurance, and regulators were discouraged from publicizing fraud and insolvencies, the state response to the thrift crisis and financial fraud inevitably contained within it the seeds of its own destruction.

The future is likely to bring more of the same, because the savings and loan reform act passed by Congress in August, 1989, leaves untouched the major causal factors in both the thrift crisis and the crime that contributed to it. The Financial Institutions Reform, Recovery, and Enforcement Act of 1989 (FIRREA), among other things, raises the capital-to-assets ratio required of thrifts, reorganizes the regulatory apparatus by creating a new Office of Thrift Supervision, and sets up the Resolution Trust Corporation to manage and sell an estimated $500 billion worth of assets from failed thrifts. However, the deregulation and protectionism that in the early 1980s provided the unprecedented incentives and opportunities for white-collar crime in the thrift industry, and the underlying contradictions upon which these policies were based, remain fundamentally unchanged. Having been bailed out with huge subsidies from taxpayers and their coffers replenished, the savings and loan casino is once again open and ready for business.

REFERENCES

Bates, Eric. 1989. "Outrage in Little Rock." *Southern Exposure* 17:16–18.
Berman, Daniel M. 1978. *Death on the Job. Occupational Health and Safety Struggles in the United States.* New York: Monthly Review Press.
Cressey, Donald. 1953. *Other People's Money: A Study of the Social Psychology of Embezzlement.* Glencoe, IL: Free Press.
Donnelly, Patrick. 1982. "The Origins of the Occupational Safety and Health Act of 1970." *Social Problems* 30:13–25.
Dowie, Mark. 1979. "Pinto Madness." Pp. 26–34 in *Crisis in American Institutions,* 4th ed., edited by J. Skolnick and E. Currie. Boston: Little, Brown.
Eichler, Ned. 1989. *The Thrift Debacle.* Berkeley: University of California Press.
Farberman, Harvey A. 1975. "A Crimogenic Market Structure: The Automobile Industry." *Sociological Quarterly* 16:438–457.
Federal Home Loan Bank Board. 1987. *Savings & Home Financing Source Book.* Washington, DC: Author.
Federal Home Loan Bank System. 1987. *A Guide to the Federal Home Loan Bank System.* Washington, DC: Federal Home Loan Bank System Publishing.
Geis, Gilbert. 1967. "The Heavy Electrical Equipment Antitrust Cases of 1961." Pp. 140–151 in *Criminal Behavior Systems: A Typology,* edited by M. Clinard and R. Quinney. New York: Holt, Rinehart & Winston.
Grant, James. 1989. "Michael Milken, Meet Sewell Avery." *Forbes 400* (October 23):60–64.
Hagan, John. 1985. *Modern Criminology, Crime, Criminal Behavior, and Its Control.* New York: McGraw-Hill.
Lang, Curtis J. 1989. "Blue Sky and Big Bucks." *Southern Exposure.* 17:20–25.
Los Angeles Times, September 1, 1989, sec. 4, p. 1.
Los Angeles Times, September 19, 1989, A3, A23.
Los Angeles Times, September 21, 1989, sec. 4, p. 3.
Los Angeles Times, October 4, 1989, sec. 2, p. 7.
Los Angeles Times, October 18, 1989, B7.
Los Angeles Times, October 21, 1989, D1.
Los Angeles Times, October 25, 1989, D2.
Los Angeles Times, October 26, 1989, D1.
Los Angeles Times, October 27, 1989, A1, A31.
Los Angeles Times, October 28, 1989a, B7.
Los Angeles Times, October 28, 1989b, D1.
Lowi, Theodore. 1969. *The End of Liberalism.* New York: Norton.
Miliband, Ralph. 1969. *The State in Capitalist Society.* New York: Baisc Books.
Mintz, Morton and Jerry Cohen. 1976. *Power, Inc.: Public and Private Rulers and How to Make Them Accountable.* New York: Viking.

Pizzo, Stephen, Mary Fricker, and Paul Muolo. 1989. *Inside Job. The Looting of America's Savings and Loans.* New York: McGraw-Hill.

Pratt, Richart T. 1982. "Perspective of the Chairman." Paper presented at the Eighth Annual Conference of the Federal Home Loan Bank Board, San Francisco, December.

Rourke, Francis E. 1969. *Bureaucracy, Politics and Public Policy.* Boston: Little, Brown.

Sherman, Lawrence. 1978. *Scandal and Reform.* Berkeley: University of California Press.

Stearns, Lisa. 1979. "Fact and Fiction of a Model Enforcement Bureaucracy: The Labor Inspectorate of Sweden." *British Journal of Law and Society* 6:1–23.

Sutherland, Edwin. 1949. *White Collar Crime.* New York: Dryden.

U.S. Congress. House. Committee on Banking, Finance and Urban Affairs. Subcommittee on Financial Institutions Supervision, Regulation and Insurance. 1989. *Financial Institutions Reform, Recovery, and Enforcement Act of 1989 (H.R. 1278).* Hearings before the Subcommittee, March 8, 9, and 14.

U.S. Congress. House. Committee on Government Operations. 1984. *Federal Response to Criminal Misconduct and Insider Abuse in the Nation's Financial Institutions* (House Committee on Government Operations No. 98-1137).

———. 1988. *Combatting Fraud, Abuse, and Misconduct in the Nation's Financial Institutions: Current Federal Reports Are Inadequate.* (House Committee on Government Operations No. 100-1088).

U.S. Congress. House. Committee on Government Operations. Subcommittee on Commerce, Consumer, and Monetary Affairs. 1987a. *Fraud and Abuse by Insiders, Borrowers, and Appraisers in the California Thrift Industry.* Hearings before the Subcommittee, June 13.

———. 1987b. *Adequacy of Federal Efforts to Combat Fraud, Abuse, and Misconduct in Federally Insured Financial Institutions.* Hearings before the Subcommittee. November 19.

U.S. Congress. House. Committee on Ways and Means. 1989. *Budget Implications and Current Tax Rules Relating to Troubled Savings and Loan Institutions.* Hearings before the Committee. February 22; March 2 and 15.

U.S. Congress. Senate. Committee on Banking, Housing and Urban Affairs. 1989. *Problems of the Federal Savings and Loan Insurance Corporation (FSLIC).* Hearings before the Committee. Part 3. March 3, 7, 8, 9, and 10.

U.S. General Accounting Office. 1985. "Thrift Industry Restructuring and the Net Worth Certificate Program." Report to Congress. GAO/GGD-85-79.

———. 1987. *Thrift Industry. Forebearance for Troubled Institutions, 1982–1986.* Briefing Report to the Chairman, Committee on Banking, Housing and Urban Affairs. U.S. Senate, GAO/GGD-87-78BR.

———. 1989a. *Failed Thrifts. Internal Control Weaknesses Create an Environment Conducive to Fraud, Insider Abuse and Related Unsafe Practices.* Statement of Frederick D. Wolf, Assistant Comptroller General, before the Subcommittee on Criminal Justice, Committee on the Judiciary. House of Representatives. GAO/T-AFMD-89-4.

———. 1989b. *Troubled Thrifts. Bank Board Use of Enforcement Actions.* Briefing Report to the Honorable Henry B. Gonzales, Chairman, Committee on Banking, Finance, and Urban Affairs. House of Representatives. GAO/GGD-89-68BR.

———. 1989c. *Thrift Failures. Costly Failures Resulted From Regulatory Violations and Unsafe Practices.* Report to the Congress. GAO/AFMD-89-62.

U.S. News and World Report, June 12, 1989, 21–22.

Weinstein, James. 1968. *The Corporate Ideal in the Liberal State, 1900–1919.* Boston: Beacon.

Wheeler, Stanton and Mitchell Lewis Rothman. 1982. "The Organization as Weapon in White Collar Crime." *Michigan Law Review* 80:1403–1426.

Wiebe, Robert H. 1967. *The Search for Order, 1877–1920.* New York: Hill and Wang.

From Fiddle Factors to Networks of Collusion: Charting the Waters of Small Business Crime

HUGH D. BARLOW

CRIMINOGENIC FACTORS AFFECTING SMALL BUSINESS ACTIVITY

In his Ph.D. dissertation on the hidden economy in England, Stuart Henry (1978) concentrated on the amateur trade in cheap, often stolen goods, where things are bought and sold usually for little more than a beer or a promise of favors returned. Many participants in Henry's study were employed in small businesses, to be sure, and some were owners (Henry, 1978; 24). On the whole, however, the picture Henry paints is of small businesses providing "cover" or otherwise facilitating illegal trading by employees who are acting on their own behalf. The benefits, if any, to the businesses are left obscure.

Anthropologist Gerald Mars (1982) refocused Henry's analysis in two ways: first, by examining how different occupational structures facilitate or inhibit particular types of workplace crime, and second, by demonstrating that the attitudes and inclinations of workers support and encourage routinization of those illegal activities facilitated by the occupational structure in which they work.

Mars's work is especially interesting because he singles out small businesses and small businessmen as illustrative of a distinct type of occupation/worker: the "Hawk." Hawk *jobs,* Mars (1982) tells us, stress initiative, autonomy, competition, and control. Hawk *people* are described as follows:

> Hawks, like their feathered counterparts, are individualists. . . . Their aim is "to make it". . . . Hawks . . . are independent; swooping to their oppor-

---

"From Fiddle Factors to Networks of Collusion" from *Crime, Law and Social Change* 20 (1993): 319–337. Reprinted by permission.

PANEL 8   Corporate Lawlessness

Investigators from *Fortune* magazine inspected the records of 1043 companies that appeared on its list of the 800 largest industrial and non-industrial corporations in the 1970s. They examined the companies' involvement in five offenses—bribery (including kickbacks and illegal rebates); criminal fraud; illegal political contributions; tax evasion; and criminal antitrust violations. They purposely excluded crimes directed against the corporation, such as embezzlement, and "questionable" behavior committed abroad. All the cases they reviewed resulted in conviction on criminal charges, in consent decrees, or in administrative settlements in which the company neither confirmed nor denied past transgressions but agreed not to commit them in the future. Of the 1043 firms, 117 (11%) were involved in at least one major offense where a successful federal case was brought against them. A total of 188 citations were issued covering 163 separate offenses. Nearly 52% of these offenses were antitrust violations; 15% were cases of kickbacks, bribery, or illegal rebataes; 11% were instances of illegal political contributions; and 6% were cases of fraud.

Source: Irwin Ross, "How Lawless are Big Companies?" *Fortune* (December 1, 1980): 56–64.

---

tunities, energetic, adaptable, and resourceful. . . . [E]veryone is free to make his *own* way. . . . In this type of job, entrepreneurial, frontier principles make fellow travellers of small businessmen and big fixers, of the more independent professionals and the most successful managers and executives. All share certain attitudes: the most common are a resistance to external constraints and a high value placed on independence. Our small businessman is, therefore, typically and almost by definition a hawk. (Mars 1982, pp. 42–43).

Small business crimes stem from and reinforce the autonomy and entrepreneurialism central to hawk occupations. Tax fiddles are the archetypal offense. One of Mars's informants describes a simple, seemingly trivial form of small business tax evasion:

> We fiddle part of our workers' wages. All the very small businesses that I know have to be in on this kind of fiddle. If you employ someone and he earns below the amount that allows him to get the maximum supplement as a low wage-earner—then you make sure he gets the supplement. You pay him just enough to qualify for the maximum and you make the rest of his wages up in cash. This is possible because we've got a lot coming through the till. (Mars 1982, p. 40).

Cash is the key here, as it is in other common tax fiddles such as avoidance of sales tax. Cash transactions by-pass bookkeeping and therefore are difficult to monitor and trace.

In conjunction with by-passing the checks and controls of the official economy, small businessmen may become involved in networks of collusion. Besides supporting the shadow economy, these networks bridge the worlds of compliance and crime while providing opportunities and incentives for a wide range of illegal activities. I shall have more to say on networks of collusion in the next section.

Mars's anthropology of workplace crime identified an extensive list of routine crimes located throughout the occupational structure from shortchanging customers to tax avoidance to kickback schemes. In addition, Mars uncovered "fiddle-prone" factors, things that "so structure economic activity as to facilitate the regular payment of a significant part of people's total reward in the form of fiddles. . . ." According to Mars (p. 138), "these factors depend on the underlying structural differences of knowledge, control, power, and ability held by some groups over others."

Consider, for instance, businesses in high traffic areas catering primarily to the tourist and convention trade. Such contexts are fiddle-prone because they involve "passing trade": the parties to a transaction typically meet only once. Furthermore, because business customers are usually strangers in the community, possibly also of dirrerent class, race, gender or ethnicity than "regulars," the conventional morality governing exchange is suspended or modified, thus increasing the likelihood of fraudulent behavior.

Another fiddle factor favoring small business crime in the retail and service economy results from the widespread ignorance of customers regarding what they need and don't need, how to satisfy a need, and what to pay. This imbalance in knowledge is often exacerbated by an imbalance in power, exemplified when the customer cannot for one reason or another go elsewhere. Automobile repair and maintenance are prime settings for fraud (see Tracy and Fox, 1989) though the fraudulent opportunities represented by these fiddle factors are not lost on doctors, lawyers, dentists, and a host of other professionals (see Jesilow, Pontell and Geis 1993; Vaughan 1983).

Passing trade and the imbalance in knowledge and power probably tip the market economy toward crime independently of the supply and demand for goods and services. Yet supply and demand, and the levels of business competition associated with them, are also potential fiddle factors. When demand for products and services is low or erratic, or when supply is excessive, competition grows and rates of business failure increase. Under these conditions, the gatekeepers who control the flow of business opportunities as well as a firm's access to them, and the entrepreneurs who need the business, are encouraged to form collusive relationships through which industrial espionage, bribery, kickbacks, and other corrupt practices are facilitated. It is interesting to note in this connection that during the Reagan years, the rate of business failures skyrocketed, from 42 per 10,000 businesses in 1980 to 120 in 1986 [U.S. Bureau of the Census 1990, p. 530]; unfortunately, appropriate data do not exist to show whether there was a corresponding jump in business crime, but the foregoing suggests what the hypothesis would be.

If gatekeepers facilitate crime in a competitive market economy, this role is probably even more prominent in the *redistributive economy* which deals with the collection and disbursement of taxes. In the United States, federal contracts with small businesses are worth over $25 billion annually, and this is only part of the story; contracts from state and local governments, outright grants of various sorts, and certification, licensing, and other work regulation should also be added in. In relations with small businesses, the gatekeepers of the annual torrent of public funds hold a powerful hand which is made even more powerful, of course, during hard times when many businesses are struggling.

If the incentives for racketeering and corruption are greater during hard times, the risks are less. There are at least three reasons for this: (1) economic decline results in reduced enforcement resources; (2) consequently, the enforcers themselves feel increasingly vulnerable, and are more susceptible to temptation; and (3) economic declines affect decisions about where to direct enforcement efforts.

The third point is documented in a recent American survey of district attorneys. Apparently, these officials made greater efforts to control business crime when the economy improved. Even though the research in question focused on the prosecution of corporate crime, the following observation surely applies equally well to small business crime; "[w]hen general economic conditions are good communities may perceive less threat from street crime and be able to afford greater control of corporate crime" (Benson, Cullen, and Maakestad 1990, p. 21).

Of course, corruption does not disappear just because there is plenty of business to be had. Consider the case of Baltimore County, Maryland, during the 1960s. The county population was growing rapidly; huge amounts of public money were being spent on schools, sewers, and streets; zoning decisions and construction permits were being issued at a growing pace. Contractors, architects, engineers and other firms routinely kicked back five percent to county officials in exchange for lucrative contracts and other favorable decisions (Simon and Eitzen 1993, p. 215). Regardless of the state of an economy, concentrations of economic resources provide lucrative criminal opportunities for those with access to them, and it is often difficult, if not simply bad for business, for entrepreneurs to resist them (for more on this, see Braithwaite 1990, Cohen and Machalek 1988).

Finally, there is (in America, at least) the criminogenic impact of machine politics. Referring once again to the Baltimore County experience, Simon and Eitzen (1993, p. 215) observe that "[t]he practice of kickbacks was not new. In fact, it was a time-honored Maryland custom." As in many other jurisdictions across America, local politics had long been dominated by the party machine. The resulting symbiotic relationship between corrupt urban politicians, organized crime, and the business community has been documented quite extensively (see, e.g., Haller 1990; Chambliss 1988, and Tarr 1967). . . .

CRIME NETWORKS

One important feature of the criminogenic environment of small business touched on earlier consists of networks of collusion that organize and promote criminal enterprise. While it is true that a small business may be actively engaged in crime without hooking up with others for that purpose—tax evasion can be accomplished in private, for example, and short-changing customers does not require confederates outside the business—many business crimes do require collusion and collusion itself promotes crime in various ways: for example, providing normative support, offering protection, disseminating information, and forging connections between participants. The enumeration of these aspects of collusive networks points up a rather obvious fact: crime networks are largely indistinguishable from networks fo legitimate exchange, and that makes them all the more insidious and difficult to investigate. Indeed, as I emphasize below, crime networks and networks of legitimate exchange are superimposed, each feeding off the other as well. As opportunity theory predicts, noncriminal opportunities create opportunities for crime, and vice versa. . . .

It is precisely because networks of collusion (e.g., on-the-side trading, bidrigging conspiracies, drug trafficking) and of compliance (e.g., legitimate trading) are superimposed one on the other that stories from the inside are indispensable to understanding small business crime (and white-collar crime generally—see Jackall 1988; Reichman 1990; Simpson 1990; Vaughan 1983, 1990). Furthermore, the social and moral order of exchange relations among network participants—concerning power and control, distributive justice, rights, understandings, and obligations, and membership itself—are *ongoing* matters of discovery and negotiation, not conveniently frozen in time and space and readily observable from the outside. There is no reason to believe that collusive networks are any different in this regard.

Yet these observations and those of the preceding section tell us little about how individual small businesses find their way into criminal activities, nor about the dynamics of collusive networks—how they emerge, prosper, and spread; how they support, influence, and control the actions of members, and how they collapse. Nor do they address the "sensual dynamics of crime" (Katz 1988, p. 5), the seductions and compulsions that help us understand what small businessmen are trying to do when they commit crime. If we are to understand small business crime we need answers to these questions as well. To find them, criminologists must turn to the proximate causes of illegal behavior, that is, the causes closest to the decisions of people actually committing small business crime. One promising strategy is the use of autobiographical accounts by small business employers and employees who have participated in crime networks. . . .

ILLUSTRATIONS FROM AN AUTOBIOGRAPHICAL ACCOUNT

Joining the network

Networks of collusion emerge tentatively and awkwardly. They may also take years to evolve into anything like a persistent arrangement. For this reason it is probably rare that members of an established network know how it first got started. There may well be more fortuity than design in its origins, of course, and this characterization apparently describes how many small businessmen get involved in collusion in the first place. Chambliss (1988, p. 85) provides the following illustration from one of his Seattle informants:

> I met Jay (P) at the Rainier Club. We liked each other. We both played sports in college and had a lot in common. We also liked to drink and horse around. Then one day he called and told me he knew of a possibility for turning a nice profit if I had some unused cash lying around. It was a perfectly natural thing. Businessmen are always doing things like that.

The informant invested money, doubled it in two months, later discovered that he had helped finance a heroin shipment, and recounts: "naturally, I didn't want to ask too many questions with that kind of profit."

Joining the inner circle

John returned from the second hockey game feeling he had scored in a big way and was "on my way" even though he made no money out of the deal. When he took the $4,500 kickback money to the architect as instructed he was invited to meet the mayor. The two went over to the mayor's house.

> The mayor takes the money, counts it, and the mayor's secretary is right there. She doesn't bat an eyelid. He than says "Do you think John can help us stop these guys fucking with our money?"
>
> I found out that ["B.B."] was supposed to be the bagman; ["A.D."] was supposed to pay and didn't; ["A.F.J."] was supposed to be paying, and wasn't, ["B.B."] was in between, the bagman. The others contended they were paying and that ["B.B."] was not delivering it where it was supposed to go. It got to be a pissing contest between ["B.B."] and these subcontractors.
>
> We go out to the mayor's car and he pulls out a Thompson submachine gun and says "This is what I've got to stop people from fucking with our money."

John decides he's getting in deep. "I couldn't believe that these people were going to kill anyone, but I didn't know. The mayor also said that if people didn't take him seriously there were others on the Teamster's [union] payroll who will do the work if necessary."

John is impressed; he believes they all mean business, and he decides to take B.B.'s place as the bagman. "I knew I was now in the rackets." Other companies now give John envelopes with money to deliver around town. Within a few days his company also gets work at the hospital site.

I asked John why he thought he was chosen for the trusted role of bagman, which brought him into direct criminal contact with both gate-keepers and businesses. He put it down to a number things: his reputation as "steady:" he could keep his mouth shut; he didn't drink and others did; and the network was desperately in need of someone. It turned out that John got nothing from the contracts and he was expected to kick back his own ten percent from any work he got in the future. The gatekeepers had a good thing going.

Escalation

Word quickly got around that John was the new bagman. He kept track of all his transactions in a little notebook; he estimates that in the period of one month he paid the mayor around $25,000 in connection with the hospital job.

But his own fortunes turned on the development of his relationship with the architect who had invited him to the hockey games. He gradually became involved in all projects the architect was working on. Federal construction money was pouring into the area, and John's company began to prosper. He also joined other members of the network in forming corporations specifically for the purpose of rigging bids on projects. Most of them were hidden partners. Since the same people owned the companies bidding on the same contracts, they were assured of winning. To get money through the Model Cities program they installed a local Black man as a front, and John's own company qualified for minority contracts because it was in his wife's name.

Within six months of joining the network John's companies are doing jobs for the hospital board, which always included a kickback, divided equally among the five board members. He also did city hall construction work in two communities, built a public swimming pool and a skating rink, and became heavily involved in work on school district projects. For these he kicked back directly to the school board president.

By now John's job as a bagman is producing its own profits: five to ten percent of all the money he handled. He becomes a small-time moneylender as well, further broadening his role in the network and, he thought, increasing his status in the eyes of the inner circle. A lot of partying goes on, and John walks around with $2,000 in his pocket at all times.

Network regulars

John Believes that ten people formed the inner circle of the network: the county board chairman, the mayors of two cities, the president of the levee district, a township supervisor and school board member, the school board president, two plumbing contractors, a supplier, and the architect who had invited him to the hockey games. Yet John insists there was no kingpin. "Everyone who handled a piece of paper got a kickback so it would flow."

From this inner circle the network spread out across state lines, and even reached New York City, 1,200 miles away. Within the immediate area, John had personal criminal dealings with, or knew the network association of, 63 individuals—including a nun on the school board. (John likes to point out "If you can corrupt a nun you can corrupt anybody.") And more network members were identified through court testimony and subsequent federal and state investigations. Thirty-two local companies, most of them small businesses, were subpoenaed to testify.

Collapse of the network

As I mentioned earlier, aggressive reporting by a local newspaper was instrumental in bringing about the federal investigation that eventually broke up the network. The reporter who pursued the story was contacted by "W," the brother-in-law of the county board chairman. Though nepotism had worked well for him, "W" swore that he had never participated in kickbacks or bidrigging. John used to work for him and confirms the claim.

According to John. "W" came to the office of "RAP," one of the companies in which John was a hidden partner, seeking specifications for a job he planned to bid on. The secretary told him she would have to check with John before giving them out. This was not the correct procedure. "I'm not supposed to have anything to do with RAP. That's collusion," John points out. "W" tipped off the local reporter who then began asking questions around town, and the local State's Attorney—himself a member of the network according to John—had no choice but to begin his own "investigation."

Tipped off to the State's Attorney's investigation by a mutual friend and network member, who told him it would cost $25,000 to get the official investigation dropped, John went to the inner circle and asked them to contribute $5,000 each. They refused. John then "wired" his office and telephone.

> So when [the mutual friend] came back I recorded him; made about three recordings of him. I called [the state] organized crime strike force and they took it to the U.S. Attorney. I went along with them. The FBI was brought in. Their sole purpose at that time was to catch [the State's Attorney] in the act of collecting $25,000 from me.

John made the mistake of telling his own attorney that he was making tapes and word got out, so the state's attorney did not take the pay-off. After the state's attorney bowed out of the payoff, the FBI asked if John was interested in recording for them. According to John, they promised him that his material would be used without anyone ever knowing its source. John agreed and recorded conversations between himself and other inner circle participants for eleven months. Finally, the case got too hot:

> I got shot at and then "M" wanted me to have "CJ" killed. That's what brought the whole case to a climax; it had to end there, as far as the undercover work.

Three years later, seventeen people had been indicted for crimes ranging from bribery, extortion, bid-rigging, and a variety of other corrupt practices. Fourteen were convicted, eleven spent time in prison, including the nun. John escaped conviction, but the IRS took his assets and his business collapsed. The architect who first brought John into the network was never indicted.

SUMMARY

In this paper I have argued that relatively little criminological research has been undertaken on small business crime. That is surprising given the extent of small business activity and the many opportunities there are for unlawful behavior. When one looks at serious offending such as bid-rigging, bribery, extortion, and other activities that subvert the economic, political, and legal processes, the picture is even worse. . . .

REFERENCES

Benson, Michael L., Francis T. Cullen, and William J. Maakestad. 1990. "Community Context and the Prosecution of Corporate Crime. Paper presented at the *Edwin H. Sutherland Conference on White-Collar Crime: 50 Yrars of Research and Beyond.* May 12–15, Indiana University.

Braithwaite, John. 1990. "Poverty, Power and White-Collar Crime: Sutherland and Three Paradoxes of Criminological Theory." Paper presented at the *Edwin H. Sutherland Conference on White-Collar Crime: 50 Years of Research and Beyond.* May 12–15, Indiana University.

Chambliss, William J. 1988. *On the Take: From Petty Crooks to Presidents.* Bloomington: Indiana University Press.

Cohen, Lawrence E., and Richard Machalek. 1988. "A General Theory of Expropriative Crime: An Evolutionary Ecological Approach." *American Journal of Sociology* 94: 465–501.

Haller, Mark H. 1990. "Policy Gambling, Entertainment, and the Emergence of Black Politics: Chicago from 1900 to 1940." Unpublished paper.

Henry, Stuart. 1978. *The Hidden Economy: The Context and Control of Borderline Crime.* Oxford: Martin Robertson.

Jackall, Robert. 1988. *Moral Mazes: The World of Corporate Managers.* New York: Oxford University Press.

Jesilow, Paul, Henry N. Pontell, and Gilbert Geis. 1993. *Prescription for Profit.* Los Angeles: University of California Press.

Katz, Jack. 1988. *Seductions of Crime: Moral and Sensual Attractions in Doing Evil.* New York: Basic Books.

Mars, Gerald. 1982. *Cheats at Work: An Anthropology of Workplace Crime.* London: Unwin Paperbacks.

Reichman, Nancy. 1990. "Moving Backstage: Uncovering the Role of Compliance in Regulating Securities Trading." Paper presented at the *Edwin H. Sutherland Conference on White-Collar Crime: 50 Years of Research and Beyond.* May 12–15. Indiana University.

Simon, David R. and D. Stanley Eitzen. 1993. *Elite Deviance,* 4th Edition, Boston: Allyn and Bacon.

Simpson, Sally S. 1990. "Corporate Crime Deterrence and Corporate Control Policies: Views from the Inside." Paper presented at the *Edwin H. Sutherland Conference on White-Collar Crime: 50 Years of Research and Beyond.* May 12–15, Indiana University.

Tarr, Joel. 1967. "The Urban Politician as Entrepreneur." *Mid-American Historical Review* 49:55–67.

Tracy, Paul E., and James Alan Fox. 1989. "A Field Experiment on Insurance Fraud in Auto Body Repair." *Criminology* 27: 589–603.

U.S. Bureau of the Census. 1990. *Statistical Abstract of the United States.* Washington D.C.: U.S. Government Printing Office.

Vaughan, Diane. 1983. *Controlling Unlawful Organizational Behavior: Social Structures and Corporate Misconduct.* Chicago: University of Chicago Press.

———— 1990. "The Macro-Micro Connection in 'White-Collar Crime' Theory." Paper presented at the *Edwin H. Sutherland Conference on White-Collar Crime: 50 Years of Research of Research and Beyond.* May 12–15, Indiana University.

Transaction Systems and Unlawful Organizational Behavior

Diane Vaughan

. . . Transactions between complex organizations have four distinguishing characteristics: (1) formalization; (2) intricate and highly specialized processing and recording methods; (3) reliance on trust; and (4) general, rather than specific, monitoring procedures. Considered separately, the four factors commonly associated with transactions between complex organizations may each present opportunities for unlawful behavior. However, it is reasonable to assume that the potential for violations increases when the factors combine. For example, complex methods for recording and processing transactions present opportunities for violation. Sorensen et al. (1980:235) note how highly diversified companies with numerous businesses have complex accounting procedures which allow "creative accounting"—and thus fraud. The tendency of accounting procedures to facilitate unlawful behavior has been exacerbated by the advent of computer and other electronic equipment, which have come to dominate the daily operation of nearly all large organizations. While these new technologies complete and record transactions with increased speed and

"Transaction Systems and Unlawful Organizational Behavior" from *Social Problems* 29:4 (April 1982): 373–79. Reprinted by permission.

efficiency, they simultaneously offer faster and more efficient ways to gain resources unlawfully.

Computers are a direct link to organizational resources. Theft can be accomplished without breaking and entering. Records, secret information, funds, and programs can be stolen. Assets can be shifted from one location to

---

PANEL 9 Medical Fraud

To shed light on physician misconduct, Paul Jesilow, Henry Pontell, and Gilbert Geis interviewed 60 Medicare/Medicaid and AMA officials, 42 physicians convicted of medical scams, and a control group of 32 physicians with no record of criminal conviction. They also examined the cases of 358 medical providers suspended from Medicare/Medicaid between 1977 and 1982. While the annual cost to Americans of physician fraud is unknown, estimates range from 10 to 25% of the total cost of the Medicaid program ($61 billion in 1989). Only a small number of physicians are convicted of fraud because their status and power permit them a measure of freedom from prosection. Of those convicted, foreign-trained and minority physicians account for a disproportionate number. The high conviction rate for these doctors probably reflects the heavier concentrations of black and foreign medical graduates in inner-city work, where there are more Medicare/Medicaid patients and where enforcement resources are aimed, rather than personal characteristics of the doctors. Conditions that facilitate Medicaid fraud include: "(1) the perpetrator's ability to redefine the violation, both in private and to others, in benign terms; (2) the perpetrator's feeling that insensitive external forces are interfering with his or her just deserts; (3) the availability of opportunities to violate the law easily; and (4) the perpetrator's belief that the violations are unlikely to be discovered or, if found out, are unlikely to result in serious penalties" (p. 186). Physicians caught violating Medicaid programs generally commit four categories of crime: (1) billing schemes, which include billing for services not rendered and charging for nonexistent office visits; (2) poor quality of care, which includes unnecessary tests, treatments, and surgeries; (3) illegal distribution of controlled substances; and (4) sex with patients whereby physicians, under the guise of therapy, receive payments for sexual liaisons with their patients. The majority of convicted physicians see themselves as "sacrificial lambs led to slaughter because of perfidy, stupid laws, bureaucratic nonsense, and incompetent bookkeepers" (p. 148).

Source: Paul Jesilow, Henry Pontell, and Gilbert Geis, *Prescription For Profit.* Berkeley: University of California Press, 1993.

another. Large amounts can be taken in minutes, or resources can be slowly drained away over long periods. The presence of the offender is not required at the scene of the offense: electronic action can happen in the future, separated by time as well as space from the action of the individual. Nonetheless, offenders weigh the risks of detection when using computers or complex acconting procedures to secure desired resources unlawfully. Hence, trust and general monitoring procedures also precipitate the unlawful conduct.

The factors that characterize transactions between organizations may combine in many forms to provide opportunities for unlawful behavior. However, when the four factors in combination repeatedly generate violations, then the *transaction system* of an organization may be said to be at fault. A transaction system may encourage unlawful behavior between organizations in two ways. First, it may *directly* encourage misconduct by providing convenient access to resources with little risk of detection by the other party to the exchange. Spence's (1974) notion of market signaling illustrates ths possibility. Second, a transaction system may *indirectly* encourage the choice of unlawful behavior to attain organizational goals because the system itself blocks completion of the exchange, thus creating an impetus to search for alternative and, perhaps, unlawful methods. The Revco case illustrates this system interface problem.

MARKET SIGNALING AND UNLAWFUL ORGANIZATIONAL BEHAVIOR

Spence (1974:6) notes that the nature of transactions inhibits an organization's ability to discriminate in decision-making. Organizations make decisions in a world of incomplete information-gathering. Because of the number and complexity of transactions in which they engage, and the amount of information necessary to complete each one, organizations are unable to thoroughly know each individual case. As a result, signals and indexes are used as criteria to make decisions when the organization considers a transaction about which product uncertainty exists.

Spence uses transactions in the job market as an example. An employer, confronted with a pool of potential employees, is unable to gather complete information on each one in order to assess the competence of the applicant. Though the information is obtainable, in most cases the employer is unwilling to conduct a thorough search because of cost. Instead, the organization relies on readily observable characteristics to make the decision. Of those characteristics that are observable to the employer, some are subject to manipulation by the individual applicant and some are not. *Signals* are observable, alterable characteristics, such as years of education, or performance, as measured by grades. In sociological terms, signals are achieved characteristics, and therefore capable of manipulation. *Indexes,* on the other hand, are observable, unalterable characteristics, such as race. In a competitive situation, applicants make those adjustments which will make them appear more favorable to an employer. This is called "signaling" (1974:10). Herein lies an opportunity for fraud: some signals can be falsified, and incomplete information-gathering and broad monitoring procedures may permit false signals to pass unnoticed.

Though Spence's examples are limited to individual signaling, the model is appropriate for organizations. The key elements are: (1) a transaction between organizations; (2) a decision-maker and a pool of applicants (organizations); (3) product uncertainty; and (4) high observation costs, necessitating reliance on signals and indexes. The delivery of Medicaid benefits illustrates the model. Medicaid services are provided to recipients through contractual arrangements between federal, state, or local government agencies and third parties (providers) for specialized goods and services to be delivered from the private sector. Organizations under contract as providers to recipients include pharmacies, dental clinics, hospitals, ambulance services, and nursing homes. To become and remain eligible to participate in the program, providers submit eligibility data (signals) on their own behalf. Due to excessive red tape, burdensome paperwork, inadequate verification of data, and poor quality control, some providers manipulate the system to their advantage. Lange and Bowers provide three examples of willful misrepresentation of eligibility signals by providers:

> Major fraud and abuse occurred in the summer food service program where prime sponsors claimed to establish several feeding sites within the inner-city and these sites subsequently were shown to be duplicative. Since feeding sites are created on the basis of demographic data on potential eligible children to be served, providers would create sites on paper, never serve meals at some of the sites, and yet fraudulently collect reimbursement for each meal claimed to have been served (1979:25).

> Misrepresentation of service abilities may occur separately or in conjunction with misrepresented eligibility data for those whom third parties intend to serve. For example, some providers serving the Rural Housing Program for the USDA have misrepresented the eligibility of recipients. Program regulations allow providers of large housing developments of tenant housing to submit the applications of potentially eligible borrowers in a single package, thereby presenting a number of applications to USDA county offices at a time. As the program is currently structured, high volume offices have come to rely on "packaged applications" to speed the benefit delivery process. The problem is that falsified and misrepresented eligibility information which is submitted without verification is frequently taken at face value by administrative personnel (1979:26).

> Third parties submit eligibility data for non-existent clients they claim to serve. They then collect benefits for "ghost" eligibles. Bogus eligibility data to create a "ghost" client may be drawn form identification from the living or deceased. Duplicate social security numbers, forged obituary data, abandoned residence addresses, or falsified wage reports illustrate ways of establishing "ghosts." The Unemployment Insurance, CETA, SBA 8(a) and Vocational Education programs have documented incidences of this pattern of provider offense (1979:26).

Thus, to enter and remain in an exchange agreement with the welfare department, providers (organizations and individuals) may falsify market signals concerning service abilities, client eligibility, and even the existence of clients. Of course, the misrepresentation of market signals by recipients in order to obtain benefits is well-known (Lange and Bowers, 1979). However, we are primarily concerned with signaling by organizations. When legitimate avenues to resources are blocked or appear uncertain, an organization in a market signaling situation may falsify signals in order to obtain strategic resources. Hence, the opportunities for unlawful behavior by organizations in a market signaling situation may be extended to other examples: organizations competing for government defense contracts, private firms negotiating a merger or sale, or organizations seeking accreditation (Wiley and Zald, 1968) or approval of a product (Vandiver, 1978).

The Medicaid examples raise another point: false signaling may regularly occur in transactions with certain organizations. The degree to which the focal organization defines it as a chronic rather than infrequent problem might be estimated by the amount of resources the organization allocates to detect false signaling. When a focal organization is repeatedly the victim of false signaling as other organizations in its set attempt to gain resources fraudulently, the factors associated with transactins may, in combination, create a *criminogenic transaction system* in which violations are regularly produced in the course of organizational exchange.

THE SYSTEM INTERFACE PROBLEM AND UNLAWFUL ORGANIZATION BEHAVIOR

A system interface problem occurs when the language, rules, procedures, and recording and processing systems of two organizations fail to mesh, so that a transaction is inhibited rather than facilitated. Resource exchange may stall and become difficult to complete to the satisfaction of both parties. One or both of the organizations concerned may have to adjust their system. Negotiations may often flounder in a between-system lag induced by formalized communications. The problem may be short- or long-term, depending on the two organizations, the nature of their interdependence, their frequency of interaction, the task around which the specific exchange revolves, and the resources each can devote to correcting the difficulty. Should one of the organizations be unwilling or unable to devote resources to legitimate resolution, or require immediate completion of the exchange in order to gain resources, the transaction system itself may be the chosen mechanism for bypassing the system interface problem. The result may be unlawful behavior, as the Revco case illustrates (Vaughan, 1980, 1983).

In 1977, Revco Drug Stores, Inc., one of the largest discount drug chains in the United States, was found guilty of Medicaid-provider fraud: specificially, a computer-generated double-billing scheme that resulted in the loss of over half a million dollars in Medicaid funds to the Ohio Department of Public Welfare. Revco was engaged in exchange on a contractual basis with the welfare department, as a provider of pharmacy goods and services to Medicaid recipients. Prescriptions were given to recipients by Revco pharmacists, then submitted to the welfare department for reimbursement. That a system interface problem existed is indicated by the history of high rejection rates for Revco claims submitted to the welfare department for reimbursement. Documents and memos showed that Revco had experienced reimbursement problems since the welfare department first began processing and paying claims by computer in 1972.

According to representatives of both organizations, Revco's high rejection rates were a function of welfare department rules for allowable Medicaid recipient claims and procedures for claim-filing on the part of providers. The number of rules and procedures was overwhelming; they changed frequently, and providers received periodic notification of how computer claims submission procedures should be altered to suit new criteria. The modifications could be costly and time-consuming, and, in addition to the computer changes, required assimilation by pharmacists in each store. Errors were common, and computer modifications either lagged behind or were not made. Claims were rejected for all three reasons. As a consequence, Revco was not reimbursed for filling the prescriptions which had been dispensed to recipients in the belief that the reimbursement would be forthcoming. When a claim is rejected, reimbursement is withheld until the error is corrected, and the claim successfully resubmitted. In Revco's case, rather than correct the rejected claims for resubmission, rejected claims accumulated. Over 50,000 claims, rejected by welfare department computers and representing more than half a million dolars in accounts receivable, accumulated at Revco headquarters.

Two Revco officials initiated a plan to bring the company's outstanding accounts receivable back into balance. A temporary clerical staff of six was hired to alter the rejected claims to make them acceptable to the welfare department computer. According to Revco officials, the decision to falsify prescription claims was influenced by four factors. (1) They had faced this situation before. Revco had a history of stalled negotiations with the welfare department which impeded reimbursement for provider services. Revco executives believed the corporation had repeatedly been victimized in this same manner by the welfare department (Vaughan, 1980). (2) The two executives believed that the rejected claims represented resources legitimately owed to Revco. (3) They calculated that the cost of legitimate correction and resubmission would be more than the average amount of the claims. (4) They believed that the funds could be retrieved without being detected by the department's screening system. This belief was based on the skills possessed by the two executives. One was a licensed pharmacist and the other a computer specialist who knew the welfare department's computer system well. They thoroughly understood the intermesh between the two organizations transaction systems. To take back resources they believed belonged to the corporation, the executives falsified prescriptions equal in number to those rejected, and submitted them through the transaction system.

The Revco case suggest that when a system interface problem ties up resources or inhibits resource delivery, unlawful attainmnet of resources may be a function of: (1) demand for the resources; (2) legitimate access blocked by cost and delay; (3) structured opportunity to secure the resources through the transaction system; (4) low probability of detection and sanctioning (Vaughn, 1983); and (5) redefinition of property rights concerning possession of organizational resources (Dynes and Quarantelli, 1974).

Because the Revco incident is a case study, no conclusions can be drawn about the extensiveness of the system interface problem. In exchange between Medicaid providers and the welfare department in Ohio, all providers routinely had claims rejected. This fact might indicate that in this particular welfare department, the system interface problem runs rampant. However, the department monitors the rate of provider rejection for two reasons: to work out system interface problems, and to detect fraud. If a provider's rejection rate is higher than the average for all providers, or from its own rejection history, either system interface difficulties or intentional fraud could be the explanation. The Revco case is an example of a system interface problem which led to fraud. System interface difficulties can exist without fraud, or as in the market signaling example, fraud may be the principle purpose of a transaction, rather than the solution to a bureaucratic snag.

Without examing rejection rates of other providers and identifying the facts of each case, generalizations cannot be made about system interface problems in the Ohio Medicaid system. In this case, a system interface problem did occur, and unlawful behavior was used to resolve it. System interface problems occasionally occur for nearly all organizations, demanding varying amounts of resources to complete transactions that stall. With transactions encumbered by formalization, complex processing methods and mechanisms, and general rather than specific monitoring practices, some organizations may resolve their difficulties unlawfully. For some organizations, system interface problems may be the rule, rather than the exception, increasing the likelihood of fraudulent resolution. When this is the case, the transaction system itself may be labelled criminogenic.

SUMMARY AND IMPLICATIONS

Transaction systems which develop to cope with the complex legitimate exchanges between complex organizations can also be used to secure gains unlawfully. Because transactions of complex organizations are characterized by high degrees of formalization, intricate processing and recording methods, exchange based on trust, and general monitoring procedures, illegal conduct can be carried out with little risk of detection. Not only are opportunities for unlawful behavior present in each of these four characteristics, but also in the ways they combine in a transaction system. Indeed, the transaction systems of some organizations may be criminogenic, repeatedly generating violations between organizations. Unlawful conduct may occur regularly when exchange between organizations relies upon market signals as the basis for decision-making. Signals can be falsified, and transaction systems with incomplete information gathering and broad monitoring procedures facilitate the fraudulent attainment of resources. Transaction systems may also systematically generate illegality by creating system interface problems. Unlawful conduct may occur because the transaction system itself blocks legitimate access to resources.

Opportunities for violations multiply as transaction system complexity increases. While not all organizations in a market signaling situation or confronting system interface problems will resort to unlawful behavior,[1] some organizations may be more likely to become offenders, depending upon the complexity of their transaction systems and those of the various organizations in their set. This variability across organizations is important, for the Medicaid system examined here is highly-complex: a criminogenic transaction system plagued by violations as a result of the four factors functioning individually to generate illegal behavior, as well as acting in combination to present opportunities for violations both through a market signaling situation and system interface problems.

Of the organizational characteristics believed to be associated with unlawful organizational behavior (Gross, 1980; Needleman and Needleman, 1979; Stone, 1975; Vaughn, 1980; 1983), the transaction systems of organizations have been least addressed by scholars and activists, and yet are perhaps the most vulnerable to manipulation. Because the complexity of inter-organizational exchange appears to have systematic consequences for illegality, reducing the complexity of transactions may also reduce rates of violations. To realize this possibility, organizations must assume a social responsibility to recognize the relationship between transaction complexity and unlawful conduct and, hence, to monitor and adjust their own transaction systems to minimize the possibility that they are the source of violations. Reducing transaction complexity between organizations may result in fewer violations by decreasing opportunities for illegality, improving the risk of detection, and/or decreasing the probability of system interface problems, thus eliminating a source of motivation to pursue resources unlawfully. . . .

REFERENCES

Dynes, Russell R. and E. L. Quarantelli. 1974. "Organizations as victims in mass civil disturbances." Pp. 67–77 in Israel Drapkin and Emilio Viano (eds.), *Victimology: A New Focus.* Lexington, Massachusetts: D. C. Heath.

---

[1] For an analysis of the variation in patterns of organizational behavior under circumstances conducive to illegality, see Vaughn, 1983.

Gross, Edward. 1980. "Organizational structure and organizational crime." Pp. 52–76 in Gilbert Geis and Ezra Stotland (eds.), *White-Collar Crime: Theory and Research*. Beverly Hills: Sage.

Lange, Andrea G. and Robert A. Bowers. 1979. *Fraud and Abuse in Government Benefit Programs*. Washington, D.C.: U.S. Government Printing Office.

Needleman, Martin L. and Carolyn Needleman. 1979. "Organizational crime: Two models of criminogenesis." *Sociological Quarterly* 20:517–528.

Sorensen, James E., Hugh D. Grove, and Thomas L. Sorensen. 1980. "Detecting management fraud: The role of the independent auditor." Pp. 221–251 in Gilbert Geis and Ezra Stotland (eds.), *White-Collar Crime: Theory and Research*. Beverly Hills: Sage.

Spence, Michael. 1974. *Market Signaling*. Cambridge: Harvard University Press.

Stone, Christopher D. 1975. *Where the Law Ends: The Social Control of Corporate Behavior*. New York: Harper and Row.

Vandiver, Kermit. 1978. "Why should my conscience bother me?" Pp. 80–101 in M. David Ermann and Richard J. Lundman (eds.), *Corporate and Governmental Deviance: Problems of Organizational Behavior in Contemporary Society*. New York: Oxford University Press.

Vaughan, Diane. 1980. "Crime between organizations: Implications for victimology." Pp. 77–97 in Gilbert Geis and Ezra Stotland (eds.), *White-Collar Crime: Theory and Research*. Beverly Hills: Sage.

——— 1983. *On the Social Control of Organizations*. Chicago: The University of Chicago Press.

Wiley, M. G. and Mayer N. Zald. 1968. "The growth and transformation of educational accrediting agencies: An exploratory study of the social control of institutions." *Sociology of Education* 41:36–56.

Opportunity and Crime in the Medical Professions

John Liederbach

Over time, health care has grown into a trillion dollar a year enterprise. The delivery of patient services involves not only physicians, but also large-scale insurance companies, government-financed benefit programs, and Health Maintenance Organizations (HMOs). Estimates of the cost of health-care fraud range from fifty to eighty billion dollars annually (Witkin, Friedman, and Doran 1992). In the Medicare program alone, some seventeen billion dollars a year is lost (Shogren 1995). The financial cost of medical crime has led one observer to characterize the situation as "white-collar wilding" (Witkin, Friedman, and Doran 1992).

The consequences of medical crime are not merely financial. Unnecessary medical procedures, negligent care, prescription violations, and the sexual abuse of patients exact an enormous physical toll as well. Each year some

---

PANEL 10   Extent of Corporate Crime

Marshall Clinard and Peter Yeager analyzed administrative, civil, and criminal actions initiated or completed during 1975 and 1976 by 25 federal agencies against the 582 largest publicly owned manufacturing, wholesale, retail, and service corporations. Like Sutherland, they employed a broad definition of crime that included not only criminal acts but also administrative violations and adverse civil decisions. Their data sources included federal agencies, law service reports, annual 10-K corporate financial reports to the SEC, and newspaper articles. A total of 1553 cases were filed against the 582 corporations, or an average of 2.7 violations per firm. Of the 582 corporations, 350 (60.1%) had at least one federal action brought against them, and of those with at least one violation, the average was 4.4 per corporation. Of the 477 manufacturing firms in the sample, 38 of the 300 firms that were cited for violations (13%) accounted for 52% of all violations, an average of 23.5 violations per firm. In order to examine the relationship between violations and firm size, they divided the manufacturing firms on the basis of annual sales into three size categories: small, medium, and large. Violations were far more likely to be committed by the large corporations: 10% of all violations were by small firms, 20% by medium firms, and nearly 75% by large firms. Large corporations were also more likely than smaller firms to commit serious offenses, averaging 3.0 serious or moderately serious violations each. Firms in the oil, pharmaceutical, and motor vehicle industries were the most likely to violate the law. Oil refining firms were charged in 20% of legal cases brought in 1975–1976, and accounted for 10% of all serious and moderately serious violations.

Source: Marshall B. Clinard and Peter Yeager, *Corporate Crime.* New York: Free Press, 1980.

400,000 patients become victims of negligent mistakes or misdiagnoses. One Harvard researcher estimates that 180,000 patients die every year, due at least in part to negligent care (Harvard Medical Practices Study 1990). Up to two million patients are needlessly subjected to physical risks through unnecessary operations each year; the resulting price tag approaches four billion dollars (Jesilow, Pontell, and Geis 1993).

THE "PROTECTIVE CLOAK": STATUS, ALTRUISM, AND AUTONOMY

Physicians are recognized as a special group in society—a privileged caste able to decipher puzzling ailments and able to fix broken-down bodies. The privilege is hard won through years of education and exhaustive training. The physician's honored rank, however, sponsors opportunities for doctors to commit crimes within their profession. Attributes synonymous with medical practice, such as high social status, trustworthiness, and professional autonomy, have provided doctors with what some have termed a "protective cloak" that has shielded doctors from scrutiny and legal accountability (Jesilow, Pontell, and Geis 1993; Parsons 1951).

One element of the "cloak," high social status, has helped to afford doctors the protections necessary to commit medical crimes. Doctors' traditional high status derives from two related elements, namely, lucrative salaries and occupational prestige. Physicians remain one of the most highly compensated occupational groups, with median annual incomes exceeding $120,000 (Ruffenach 1988). Aided by the prestige that typically accompanies high slaries in American culture, physicians have been able to retain an elite social position.

Historically, there has also been a general reluctance in American society to use the criminal law against high-status offenders, and criminologists have long recognized the important role that status plays in shaping the criminal opportunities afforded to professional groups. Professionals possess the financial and political wherewithal to influence the manner in which criminal statutes are written and enforced, and they are more apt to "escape arrest and conviction . . . than those who lack such power" (Sutherland 1949). While scholars debate whether this reluctance stems from public apathy and/or ignorance concerning the costs connected to elite crimes (Cullen, Maakestad and Cavender 1987; Evans, Cullen, Dubeck 1993; Wilson 1975), the typically lenient sanctions currently imposed on doctors who pillage government benefit programs, provide negligent care, or otherwise physically abuse their patients points to a historical reluctance to treat as criminal even the most egregious forms of physician malfeasance (Jesilow, Pontell, and Geis 1993; Rosoff, Pontell, and Tillman 1998; Tillman and Pontell 1992; Wolfe et al. 1998).

A second protective element is the altruistic and trustworthy image projected by doctors. This image is cemented in the physician's code of ethics. The oath serves to define doctors as selfless professionals who perform an invaluable service without regard to personal financial gain (Jesilow, Pontell, and Geis 1993). The image structures criminal opportunities in several ways: the image creates an assumption of good will on the part of doctors that makes charges of intentional wrongdoing difficult to justify. Prosecutors may find it too challenging to prove intentionally fraudulent or harmful behavior in cases against highly respected and trusted doctors. Also, the physician's altruistic image has traditionally engendered a certain level of trust from patients (McKinlay and Stoeckle 1988; Stoeckle 1989). Trusting patients who are victims of fraudulent medical schemes or negligent care may fail to hold doctors accountable for their crimes. One observer has defined the impact of these factors more generally as a "pattern of deference" to doctors—a prevailing unwillingness to question their presumed trustworthiness (Bucy 1989).

Third, doctors have been relatively immune from legal scrutiny because of the medical professions' historical preference for self-regulation. State medical review boards, whose members are predominantly physicians themselves, are supposed to provide a "first line of defense" against doctors who violate legal or ethical codes (Wolfe et al. 1998). These boards can revoke medical licenses or otherwise discipline doctors who fail to meet professional or legal standards. Doctors argue that self-regulation and autonomy characterize any profession—that is, doctors alone possess the specialized expertise and unique qualifications to judge the actions of other physicians. The medical community regards the imposition of civil and/or criminal penalties as both unwarranted and unnecessary, especially in cases that involve errors in clinical judgement (Abramovsky 1995). The profession's reliance on self-regulation, however, may facilitate criminal opportunities by shielding its members from more effective punishments. State medical boards, for example, have continually failed to identify doctors who are chronically incompetent, and often punish them with "slaps on the wrist" (Wolfe et al. 1998). The case of one New York doctor illustrates the dangers of relying solely on professional controls:

> During the mid-1980s [Dr. Benjamin] was investigated by the Department of Health in connection with numerous medical irregularities. In 1986, after a medical review board convicted him on 38 counts of gross negligence and incompetence, the New York State Health Commissioner asked the Board to revoke his license. . . . The doctor's punishment was reduced to a three-month suspension and three years probation. In June 1993 . . . the Department revoked Dr. Benjamin's license for five botched abortions performed in one year. However, Dr. Benjamin was allowed to continue performing abortions pending appeal. Less than a month later (patient) Gaudalupe Negron met her death from another of Dr. Benjamin's botched procedures (Abramovsky 1995).

The lax enforcement typically provided by state medical boards has created an inviting opportunity structure for doctors to commit fraud and abuse within their profession. The problems realted to professional control are exacerbated by the well-documented "code of silence" that exists among medical professionals (Rosoff, Pontell, and Tillman 1998). Doctors are often hesitant to report fraud and abuse for fear of professional recriminations (Karlin 1995; Levy 1995). Still, some in the medical community recognize the extent of the problem: "The profession has done a lousy job of policing its own," acknowledges Arthur Caplan, chairman of the Center for Bioethics at the University of Pennsylvania (Grey 1995).

SELECTED MEDICAL OFFENSES

Medical "Kickbacks": Fee Splitting and Self-Referrals

"Kickbacks" are generally defined as payments from one party to another in exchange for referred business or othr income-producing deals. Their acceptance by doctors is considered unethical, and in most cases illegal, because they create a conflict of interest between the physicians' commitment to quality patient care and their own financial self-interest. Doctors who are primarily concerned with financial gain compromise their loyalty to patients, as well as their independent professional judgement. Two well-recognized types of medical kickbacks include fee splitting and self-referrals.

Fee splitting occurs when one physician (usually a general practitioner) receives payment from a surgeon or other specialists in exchange for patient referrals. Fee splitting artificially inflates medical costs, provides incentives for unnecessary tests and specialized treatment, and can also endanger the quality of patient care (Stevens 1971). As Sutherland (1949) explained, the fee-splitting doctor "tends to send his patients to the surgeon who will split the largest fee rather than to the surgeon who will do the best work." Early observers regarded fee splitting as an "almost universal" practice, and estimated that 50–90% of physicians split fees (MacEachern 1948; Williams 1948). Despite the advent of more secure payment sources provided by the spread of health insurance coverage in the post–World War II years, congressional investigations in the 1970s continued to recognize fee splitting as a problem (Rodwin 1992; U.S. Congress 1976). While it remains difficult to determine whether the prevalence of fee splitting has increased or decreased over time, it clearly has persisted (Rodwin 1992).

Alternatives to fee splitting have developed more recently, including self-referrals. Self-referrals involve sending patients to specialized medical facilities in which the physician has a financial interest. Between 50,000 and 75,000 doctors have a financial stake in ancillary medical services (quoted in Rosoff, Pontell, and Tillman 1998). Recent research identifies the problems associated with self-referrals, including higher utilization costs and unnecessary services (Hillman et al. 1990; Mitchell and Scott 1992; Rodwin 1992). Self-referring doctors refer patients for laboratory testing at a 45% higher rate than noninvesting physicians (U.S. Department of Health and Human Services 1989). Physicians' utilization of clinical laboratories, diagnostic imaging centers, and rehabilitation facilities was found to be significantly higher when physicians owned these facilities (Hillman et al. 1990).

The medical profession's traditional response to financial conflicts of interest has been less than overwhelming. While most states had declared fee splitting illegal by the mid-1950s, the medical profession did not explicitly address financial conflicts in ethical codes until the 1980s (Rodwin 1992). One newspaper characterized the profession's response with embarrassing clarity: "Fee splitting has been like a venereal disease . . . it exist(s), but nice people do not talk about it" (quoted in Rodwin 1992). The legal and professional response to self-referrals has been more ambivalent. Despite recent legislative attempts to prohibit self-referrals, the practice remains legal. Likewise, professional standards have not been effective in curtailing abuses:

> Unlike other professionals who are the subject to extensive conflict of interest regulation . . . physicians have addressed these issues largely on their own, and have been subject to minimal regulation by state and federal laws or even

professional codes. . . . The American Medical Association addresses these issues primarily by relying on professional norms, individual discretion and subjective standards . . . (the profession) lacks an effective means to hold physicians accountable (Rodwin 1992, 734).

Prescription Violations

Only doctors possess the education and specialized expertise required to safely prescribe dangerous and often addictive drugs, including narcotics, amphetamines, tranquilizers, and other controlled substances. The privilege is entrusted with the legal responsibility to limit access to these drugs on the basis of medical need. While the vast majority of physicians uphold these responsibilities, an alarming number of doctors violate this trust. Between 1988 and 1996, 1521 doctors were disciplined for misprescribing or over prescribing drugs (Wolfe et al. 1998). Numerous doctors were caught selling blank prescriptions to known addicts. One physician dispensed expired drugs from old, unlabeled spice jars. Another doctor prescribed dangerous weight loss pills to a patient for four years without even examining her—eventually resulting in the patient having a stroke (Wolfe et al. 1998). Some prescription violations are coupled with fraudulent billings schemes designed to maximize profits from illegal prescriptions. Jesilow, Pontell, and Geis (1993) relate one of the most appalling cases:

> In Los Angeles, one investigator reported a Medicaid doctor who saw so many patients daily that red, blue, and yellow lines had been painted on his office floor to expedite traffic. Each color represented a different kind of pill (22).

Similar to the case of medical kickbacks, the medical profession has also largely failed to adequately discipline doctors who violate prescription laws. At least 69% of the doctors cited between 1988 and 1996 were not even temporarily suspended from practicing medicine (Wolfe et al. 1998).

Unnecessary Treatments

Doctors who intentionally subject patients to medically unnecessary treatments violate the law in two ways. First, unnecessary treatments are fraudulent because they result in compensation that is deceptively gained. More important, unnecessary procedures that are invasive, such as surgery, may be considered a form of assault because they needlessly expose patients to physical risks (Lanza-Kaduce 1980). The highly publicized case of one California ophthalmologist clearly illustrates how unnecessary treatments can result in serious physical harm to patients. The doctor preformed unneeded cataract surgery on patients solely to collect a $584 operation fee. In the process, the doctor admitted needlessly "blinding a lot of people" (Pontell, Geis, and Jesilow 1984).

Determining the prevalence of "unnecessary" treatments is often difficult given the inherent uncertainties involved in diagnosing and treating patients. Green (1997) has outlined several methods used by researchers to estimate the extent of unnecessary surgeries: (1) geographical variations in surgical rates, (2) studies of second surgical opinions, (3) variations in surgical rates between payment plans, and (4) expert opinions based on predetermined criteria. Although these studies present mixed findings, wide geographical variations in surgical rates can be used to suggest that unnecessary surgeries occur with some frequency. For example, hysterectomies are performed at an 80% higher rate in Southern states, and 1000% rate variations in pacemaker operations have been identified in Massachusetts (quoted in Green 1997). Similarly, one government-sponsored study found a 120% higher surgical rate for patients enrolled in fee-for-service plans versus patients enrolled in HMOs (U.S. Department of Health, Education, and Welfare 1971).

Sexual Misconduct

Sexual misconduct by doctors can take a variety of forms (Jacobs 1994). Doctors may engage in sexual misconduct in exchange for professional services. Alternatively, doctors may allow relationships with patients to escalate beyond what is ethically acceptable. Finally, doctors may sexually assault patients while they are under the control of anesthesia or otherwise incapable of consenting to a sexual act (Green 1997). These offenses are especially abhorrent, because they represent an abuse of power by the doctor in situations where the patient is particularly vulnerable. From 1987 to 1996, 393 doctors were disciplined by state medical boards for sexual misconduct with patients. At least 34% of those doctors were not forced to even temporarily stop practicing (Wolfe et al. 1998).

MEDICAID FRAUD AND ABUSE

Medicaid began in 1965 as one of the "Great Society" programs initiated during the Lyndon B. Johnson administration. The program extended health coverage to needy Americans who could not otherwise afford it. Perhaps overshadowed by the nobility of this goal, the program's costs were not considered a primary concern (Jesilow, Pontell, and Geis 1993). Since its inception, fraud and abuse has been endemic to the program (see panel). Jesilow, Pontell, and Geis (1993), in their exposé on Medicaid crime, identify several reasons why the introduction of Medicaid has surreptitiously expanded the scope of the medical crime problem.

The medical profession opposed the initial Medicaid legislation. Doctors perceived Medicaid as a threat to their professional autonomy, because the program dictated the price of their professional medical services (Jesilow, Pontell, and Geis 1993). The Medicaid program introduced an unwelcome influence—the government—into decisions that were traditionally left to the independent professional discretion of doctors. This intrusion into the professional autonomy of doctors created widesparead dissatisfaction within the medical community, and served to facilitate fraud and abuse within the program in at least two important ways (Jesilow, Pontell, and Geis 1993). First, the medical community's initial opposition led to certain flaws in the program's design that created easy opportunities to violate the law. For example, the original Medicaid legislation did not include provisions for punishing doctors who violated program rules (Jesilow, Pontell, and Geis 1993). The omission was not an accident, but an attempt to placate doctors, without whose cooperation the program could not be launched. As a result, the program lacked the effective sanctions necessary to police an additional design flaw, the program's fee-for-service payment structure. The fee-for-service plan reimbursed doctors a fixed amount for each procedure, but the doctor could earn additional income by double-billing for the same patient, billing for more expensive procedures than those performed, or even charging the program for services that were never done (Jesilow, Pontell, and Geis 1993). A significant number of Medicaid providers could not resist the combination of easy opportunities and lenient sanctions.

Second, the government's intrusion on the professional autonomy of doctors gave rise to an aggressively defiant attitude among some practitioners against the rules that governed Medicaid work. As Jesilow, Pontell, and Geis (1993) explain, this militant defiance "dramatically reduced one of the most powerful deterrents to crime, especially for middle and upper class perpetrators: the sense of guilt and the force of conscience associated with depredations against known human victims." Because they believed Medicaid to be an illegitimate intrusion on their professional autonomy, some Medicaid violators "redefined" their criminal behavior in a positive light. As a result, many of these doctors did not view their actions as wrong (Jesilow, Pontell, and Geis 1993).

This combination of opportunities, motivations, and lax sanctions has produced a dizzying array of violations related to the Medicaid program (see panel). Perhaps the most striking example of Medicaid fraud, however, is the discovery of Medicaid "mills" by fraud investigators (Jesilow, Pontell, and Geis 1993).

> Located in dilapidated areas, often in storefronts, and catering almost exclusively to patients on Medicaid rolls, the mills resemble clinics in that doctors with different specialties are gathered under one roof. But the mill's providers often rent space in the building and bill Medicaid individually. . . . Criminal activities flourished in the Medicaid mills. Some employed "hawkers" to round up customers. Several catered to drug traffic. Various government agents, all claiming to be suffering from nothing more than the common cold, had been seen by eighty-five doctors in Medicaid mills. They underwent eighteen electrocardiograms, eight tuberculosis tests, four allergy tests, as well as a hearing, glaucoma, and electroencephalogram tests (50).

The inception of the Medicaid program posed one of he first significant challenges to the professional autonomy of physicians. Although this challenge did serve to extend health benefits to many of the nations' most indigent citizens, the program also altered the traditional opportunity structure for medical crime, and created new and unique avenues for physicians to commit offenses relating to their medical practice.

HMOS AND THE "CORPORITIZATION" OF MEDICINE

The healthcare landscape has changed dramatically over the last two decades with the advent of "managed care" and the Health Maintenance Organization (HMO). HMOs incorporate doctors and hospitals into networks designed to decrease the costs associated with health care. Contrary to traditional fee-for-service arrangements, HMOs provide care through a flat-rate payment structure (Wrightson 1990). Some observers have generally described these sweeping changes as a movement toward the "corporatization" of medicine (McKinlay and Stoeckle 1988; Stoeckle 1989). The growing influence of these large-scale bureaucracies may impact opportunities for medical crime and deviance in two important ways. First, the HMOs profit-oriented strategies may foster incentives to reduce costs by lowering the quality of patient care. Second, the introduction of corporate influences may increase the vulnerability of physicians to legal attacks by eroding the physician's protective professional environment.

HMOs employ a variety of procedures that are designed to increase the economic productivity of physicians, including flat-rate fees, incentives to reduce costs, limiting access to specialized care, and mandatory case reviews by nonphysicians (Wrightson 1990). HMOs also reward doctors for *not* using diagnostic tests and *avoiding* patient referrals (Rodwin 1992). For example, a recent twist on the traditional fee-split is the "premium-split," whereby the HMO compensates doctors who refuse to make referrals. There is empirical and anecdotal evidence to suggest that profits are increasing at the expense of quality patient care. The RAND Health Insurance Experiment correlated HMO care with reduced costs, lower patient satisfaction, and poorer health status among low-income enrollees (Wagner and Bledsoe 1990; Ware et al. 1986). The use of financial incentives by some HMOs has been found to significantly alter physician treatment decisions (Hillman, Pauley, and Kerstein 1989). Newspaper anecdotes compiled by the National Health Insurance Citizens Network provide additional evidence that corporate influences may be inducing patient neglect:

> A 27-year-old man from central California was given a heart transplant, and was discharged from the hospital after only four days because his HMO wouldn't pay for additional hospitalization. Nor would the HMO pay for the bandages needed to treat the man's infected surgical wound. The patient died (Mitchell 1996).
>
> A 12-year-old girl had to wait six months for a back operation to correct severe scoliosis. The reason: the HMO rejected the parents' bid to have a spe-

cialist perform the procedure, insisting instead on an in-network surgeon. After taking six months to determine that no one in its own network was capable, the HMO relented (Sherman 1995).

In 1995 the Florida Attorney General's office decertified 21 of the state's 29 Medicaid managed care plans, citing widespread incidence of poor care (Himmelstein 1996).

Although far from conclusive, the evidence suggests an inherent conflict of interest between the HMO's cost-containment measures and the physician's commitment to the best interests of the patient. Physician loyalty is divided between the patient and the HMO. Similar to problems associated with fee splitting and self-referrals, the existence of such a conflict increases the risk of professional neglect—a compromised physician may not perform effectively or may exploit their position and harm patients (Rodwin 1992).

While providing incentives for lower-quality care, the HMO movement may also be chipping away the "protective cloak" that has traditionally insulated doctors from punitive legal sanctions. For example, one significant outcome of the movement has been weaker relationships between doctors and patients. Physicians report diminished gratification from patient relationships, and they see patients as more critical, adversarial, and less committed to long-term associations with doctors (Stoeckle 1989). Managed care seems to have de-personalized the doctor-patient relationship (McKinlay and Stoeckle 1988). Indeed, doctors and patients have been replaced by "providers" and "enrollees" in the new HMO lexicon (Wrightson 1990). Weakening doctor–patient relationships may result in a breach of patient trust, a central element of the "cloak" that has traditionally protected doctors from criticism and harsh legal scrutiny.

HMOs may also increase the vulnerability of physicians more directly. The public may increasingly view physicians simply as employees of an impersonal corporation, working in part to maximize shareholder profits (Hillman, Pauley, and Kerstein 1989; Wagner and Bledsoe 1990; Ware et al. 1986). Research suggests that the public is more willing to sanction corporate offenders as an entity than individual actors, viewing corporate offenses as more deserving of harsh civil and criminal penalties (Frank, Cullen, Travis, and Borntrager 1989; Hans and Ermann 1989). Moreover, public disdain for managed care seems to have peaked, fueling congressional debates and calls for a "patients bill of rights." The physician–employee of an impersonal corporation seems more vulnerable to harsh legal sanctions than the trusted family doctor of bygone days.

One indication of increasing physician vulnerability is the recent spate of criminal prosecutions against doctors who have killed or maimed patients through negligent or reckless medical care. Because of the protections traditionally afforded to doctors, errors in clinical judgment—even if they resulted in the death of patients—have traditionally been sanctioned exclusively through civil actions or peer-oriented sanctions. The filing of *violent* criminal charges, such as manslaughter, assault, reckless homicide, or murder, against doctors who victimize patients in the course of their medical practice had been an exceedingly rare occurrence (Abramovsky 1995; Crane 1994; Green 1997). However, at least seven doctors have been criminally prosecuted for their violent victimization of patients over the last ten years (Liederbach, Cullen, Sundt, and Geis 1998). The case against Dr. Joseph Verbrugge is indicative not only because of the gravity of his mistakes, but also because he is believed to be the first doctor to stand trial in Colorado accused of a violent crime related to a medical procedure:

> Verbrugge was charged with reckless manslaughter in connection with the death of eight-year-old Richard Leonard during ear surgery. The normally routine procedure went awry when the boy's heart rate jumped significantly after Verbrugge administered the anesthetic. During the surgery, the patient's breathing became irregular and his temperature soared to 107 degrees. Prosecutors contended that Verbrugge failed to react to those danger signs because he had fallen asleep during the operation. The patient died after three hours in surgery. His reaction to the anesthesia had increased the level of carbon monoxide in his blood to four times the normal level (Liederbach, Cullen, Sundt, and Geis 1998).

It remains to be seen how prevalent criminal prosecutions against doctors for medical "mistakes" will become. However, the recent cluster of these cases may suggest the beginning of a trend toward increasing physician vulnerability. These cases may be a signpost indicating that the traditional protections afforded to doctors have eroded. In particular, as long-term doctor–patient relationships wane and as HMOs increasingly influence the delivery of medical services, patient trust in doctors—especially when things go badly in a medical procedure—will decline, and the ability to see reckless doctors as *criminals* may increase (Liederbach, Cullen, Sundt, and Geis 1998).

REFERENCES

Abramovsky, A. 1995. "Depraved Indifference and the Incompetent Doctor." *New York Law Journal,* November 8, pp. 3–10.

Bucy, P. H. 1989. "Fraud by Fright: White Collar Crime by Health Care Providers." *North Carolina Law Review* 67: 855–937.

Crane, M. 1994. "Could Clinical Mistakes Land You in Jail? The Case of Gerald Einaugler." *Medical Economics* 71: 46–52.

Cullen, F. T., W. J. Maakestad, and G. Cavender. 1987. *Corporate Crime under Attack: The Ford Pinto Case and Beyond.* Cincinnati: Anderson.

Evans, D. T., F. T. Cullen, and P. J. Dubeck. 1993. "Public Perceptions of White Collar Crime." Pp. 85–114 in *Understanding Corporate Criminality,* edited by M. B. Blankenship. New York: Garland.

Frank, J., F. T. Cullen, L. F. Travis III, and J. Borntrager. 1989. "Sanctioning Corporate Crime: How Do Business Executives and the Public Compare?" *American Journal of Criminal Justice* 13: 139–69.

Green, G. S. 1997. *Occupational Crime,* 2nd ed. Chicago: Nelson Hall.

Grey, B. 1995. "Medical Scandal." *Baltimore Sun,* August 21.

Hans, V. P., and M. D. Ermann. 1989. "Response to Corporate versus Individual Wrongdoing." *Law and Human Behavior* 13: 151–66.

Hillman, A. L., M. V. Pauley, and J. J. Kerstein. 1989. "How Do Financial Incentives Affect Physician's Clinical Decisions and the Financial Performance of Health Maintenance Organization?" *New England Journal of Medicine* 321: 86–92.

Hillman, B. J., V. A. Joseph, M. R. Mabry, J. H. Sunshine, S. D. Kennedy, and M. Noether. 1990. "Frequency and Costs of Diagnostic Imaging in Office Practice—A Comparison of Self-Referring and Radiologist Referring Physicians." *New England Journal of Medicine* 323: 1604–8.

Himmelstein, D. V. 1996. "US Health Reform: Unkindest Cuts." *The Nation,* January 22.

Jacobs, S. 1994. "Social Control of Sexual Assault By Physicians and Lawyers within the Professional Relationship: Criminal and Disciplinary Actions." *American Journal of Criminal Justice* 19(1): 43–60.

Jesilow, P., H. N. Pontell, and G. Geis. 1993. *Prescription for Profit: How Doctors Defraud Medicaid.* Berkeley: University of California Press.

Karlin, R. 1995. "Selective Silence Is under Scrutiny." *The Time Union* (Albany, NY), August 28, p. B1.

Lanza-Kaduce, L. 1980. "Deviance among Professionals: The Case of Unnecessary Surgery." *Deviant Behavior* 1: 333–59.

Levy, D. 1995. "Physicians Can Run, Hide from Deadly Errors." *USA Today,* September 11, p. 1D.

Liederbach, J., F. T. Cullen, J. Sundt, and G. Geis. 1998. "The Criminalization of Physician Violence: Social Control in Transformation?" Paper presented at the annual meeting of the American Society of Criminology, Washington, D.C.

MacEachern, M. 1948. "College Continues Militant Stance against Fee-Splitting and Rebates." *Bulletin of the American College of Surgeons* 33: 65–67.

McKinlay, J. B., and J. D. Stoeckle. 1988. "Corporatization and the Social Transformation of Medicine." *International Journal of Health Services* 18: 191–200.

Mitchell, J. M., and E. Scott. 1992. "New Evidence on the Prevalence and Scope of Physician Joint Ventures." *Journal of the American Medical Association* 268: 80–84.

Mitchell, L. 1996. "Butte Urged to Immunize against HMO Ills." *The Enterprise Record,* January 21.

"Patients, Doctors, Lawyers: Medical Injury, Malpractice Litigation, and Patient Compensation." 1990. *Harvard Medical Practices Study.* Boston: President and Fellows of Harvard University.

Parsons, T. 1951. *The Social System.* Glencoe, IL: Free Press.

Pontell, H. N., G. Geis, and P. D. Jesilow. 1984. "Practitioner Fraud and Abuse in Government Medical Benefit Programs." Washington, D.C.: U.S. Department of Justice.

Rodwin, M. A. 1992. "The Organized American Medical Profession's Response to Financial Conflicts of Interest: 1890–1992." *Milbank Quarterly* 70(4): 703–41.

Rosoff, S. M., H. N. Pontell, and R. Tillman. 1998. *Profit without Honor: White Collar Crime and the Looting of America.* Upper Saddle River, NJ: Prentice Hall.

Ruffenach, G. 1988. "No Need to Worry, Doctors Do Just Fine." *Wall Street Journal,* October 10.

Sherman, W. 1995. "Girl Waited 6 Months for Spine Surgery." *New York Post,* September 19.

Shogren, G. 1995. "Rampant Fraud Complicates Medicare Cures." *Los Angeles Times,* October 8, p. 1.

Stevens, R. 1971. *American Medicine and the Public Interest.* New Haven: Yale University Press.

Stoeckle, J. D. 1989. "Reflections on Modern Doctoring." *Milbank Quarterly* 66: 76–89.

Sutherland, E. H. 1949. *White-Collar Crime.* New Haven: Yale University Press.

Tillman, R., and H. N. Pontell. 1992. "Is Justice Color Blind?: Punishing Medicaid Provider Fraud." *Criminology* 30(4): 547–74.

U.S. Congesss. Senate Subcommittee on Long-Term Care, Special Committee on Aging. 1976. *Fraud and Abuse among Practitioners Participating in the Medicaid Program.* Washington, D.C.

U.S. Department of Health, Education, and Welfare. 1971. *The Federal Employees Health Benefit Program—Enrollment and Utilization of Health Services 1961–1968.* Washington, D.C.: U.S. Government Printing Office.

U.S. Department of Health and Human Services. 1989. *Financial Arraignments between Physicians and Health Care Businesses.* Washington, D.C.: U.S. Government Printing Office.

Wagner, E. H., and T. Bledsoe. 1990. "The RAND Health Experiment and HMO's." *Medical Care* 28: 191–200.

Ware, J. F., W. H. Rogers, A. R. Davis, G. A. Goldberg, R. H. Brooks, E. B. Keeler, C. D. Sherbourne, P. Camp, and J. P. Newhouse. 1986. "Comparisons of Health Outcomes at an HMO with Those of Fee-for-Service Care." *Lancet* 1: 1017–22.

Williams, G. 1948. "The Truth About Fee-Splitting." *Modern Hospital* 70: 43–48 (reprinted in *Reader's Digest,* July 1948).

Wilson, J. Q. 1975. *Thinking about Crime.* New York: Basic Books.

Witkin, G., D. Friedman, and G. Doran. 1992. "Health Care Fraud." *US News and World Report,* February 24, pp. 34–43.

Wolfe, S., K. M. Franklin, P. McCarthy, P. Bame, and B. M. Adler. 1998. *16,638 Questionable Doctors Disciplined by State and Federal Governments.* Washington, D.C.: Public Citizens Health Research Group.

Wrightson, C. W. 1990. *HMO Rate Setting and Financial Strategy.* Washington, D.C.: Health Administration Press.

Fire in Hamlet: A Case Study of a State-Corporate Crime

JUDY ROOT AULETTE AND RAYMOND MICHALOWSKI

On September 3, 1991, an explosion and fire at the Imperial Food Products chicken processing plant in Hamlet, North Carolina, killed 25 workers and injured another 56. This human disaster, which devastated the small working-

"Fire in Hamlet" from *Political Crime in Contemporary America,* Kenneth D. Tunnell, ed. (New York: Garland Publishing, 1993): 171–206. Reprinted by permission.

PANEL 11   Environmental Crime

On December 4, 1998, the Burlington Northern and Santa Fe Railway Company pleaded guilty to charges that it dumped lead residue near a creek in the Ozark foothills and agreed to pay $19 million in criminal fines, restitution, and cleanup costs. From 1968 to 1994, the railway company had operated a rail siding in Crawford County, Missouri, where it cleaned rail cars used in lead mines, and gondolas containing lead residue concentrate also were dumped. The railroad discharged lead sulfide into a creek without a federal permit, and lead residue was moved to various parts of Crawford County and used as fill materials. The company pleaded guilty to one felony count of violating the federal Superfund law and to one misdemeanor violation of the Clean Air Act. Tests found lead in some private water supplies, but no evidence of lead in any public drinking water supply was found. In a public statement, the company said the settlement would not affect its fourth-quarter earnings.

Source: St. Louis Post-Dispatch, December 12, 1998, p. 8.

---

class community of Hamlet, immediately became the subject of both controversy and investigation. Shortly after the fire there was speculation that Imperial might face felony manslaughter charges in the deaths because fire doors that would have led the workers to safety were deliberately kept locked. According to a number of workers at the plant, fire doors were "routinely locked to keep employees from stealing chicken nuggets" (Drescher and Garfield, 1991:1). Subsequent inquiry indicated that not only did the company lock the fire doors, one of which displayed the bloody footprints of workers who tried to batter it open before they died, but also that an interwoven pattern of regulatory failure on the part of several state and federal agencies played a significant role in creating the conditions that led to the tragedy. This regulatory failure was facilitated by the State of North Carolina through its refusal to fund and support the state's Occupational Safety and Health Program even to the limits of *available* Federal monies. In 1990, a year before the Imperial plant fire, the State of North Carolina returned $453,000 in unspent OSHA money to the Federal government, even though its OSHA program was "underfunded and overwhelmed" and state safety inspections had fallen to their lowest level in 16 years (Parker et al., 1991:1).

The fire at the Imperial Food Processing plant and the regulatory environment that made it possible underscore the importance of the interplay between corporations and government in the production of life-threatening criminal conduct by businesses. The *technical cause* of the Imperial plant fire was the rupture of a hydraulic line near a deep fryer. This resulted in an explosion and a fireball that not only destroyed the plant and the lives of 25 workers, but also shattered the social make-up of an entire town. Those who died or were injured in the Hamlet fire, however, were the victims of much more than a simple mechanical breakdown. They were the victims of a series of *social decisions* made by a broad array of institutions. These include Imperial Food Products, the U.S. Occupaional Safety and Health Administration, the U.S. Food and Drug Administration, the legislature and governor of the State of North Carolina, the North Carolina Occupational Safety and Health Administration, and, finally, local agencies responsible for building inspection and fire protection. These organizational units pursued a pattern of actions and relations that made it possible and routine that workers in the Imperial chicken processing plant would be denied adequate escape routes in case of fire. This pattern does not represent an aberrant moment in North Carolina labor history. Rather, we argue it is only a current reflection of North Carolina's long-standing commitment to a development policy based on attracting industry by offering low taxation and, particularly relevant in the immediate case, a lax regulatory environment.

In this chapter we will examine the ways in which the interplay of government and business interests in North Carolina culminated in the disastrous fire at the Imperial chicken processing plant. Specifically, we will argue that the deaths and injuries in Hamlet represent an example of what Kramer and Michalowski (1990) term *state–corporate crime,* and we will explore three nested contexts—the societal context, the organizational context, and the control context—that shaped the conditions which produced 25 new graves in Hamlet, North Carolina in the fall of 1991. . . .

THE SOCIETAL CONTEXT

. . . Since the emergence of the "New South" at the end of the 19th century, North Carolina's ability to attract capital investment in industry has been linked to the state's ability to offer what state officials like to refer to as an "attractive business environment." In practice this meant high rates of return due to lower production costs, preferential tax policies for industry, and most importantly, extremely low rates of unionizaion which, in turn meant, both a lower wage bill for investors, and a limited ability of workers to press for improvements in working conditions.

The pro-business/anti-labor characteristics of the North Carolina political economy are not the outcome of simple market forces. They are the fruits, first, of a war on progressive political organizations in the late 19th-century, and then, of a concerted battle against unionization throughout the 20th century (Key, 1950; Crow, 1984; Bloom, 1987; Luebke, 1990). Regarding the destruction of 19th century political movements that might have developed as a force for the protection of the industrial and agricultural labor force in North Carolina, Tomaskovic-Devey (1991:20) says:

> The only effective challenge to capitalist elite rule occurred during the populist period in which black and white farmers created a populist party, the Farmers Alliance. The Populist and Republican parties created a fusion alliance in the 1890s, in 1894 won two-thirds of the seats in the General Assembly, and in 1896 elected a reformist Republican Governor [Crow, 1984]. The Democrats, the party of the planter-industrialist elites, countered with a violent white supremacy campaign, successfully institutionalizing Jim Crow legislation and disenfranchised blacks and many poor whites and led to nearly complete conservative pro-business, anti-labor Democratic control of the state for the entire twentieth century.

The destruction of populist parties, although setting the stage for North Carolina's 20th-century labor policy, was not the final struggle. Throughout the 20th-century business and political leaders in North Carolina struggled against unionization, an effort that was punctuated by a number of bitter and often bloody labor battles in which the police powers of the state, and the state-supported moral authority of dominant religious institutions, usually weighed in heavily on the side of capital, and against labor (Pope, 1942).

The consequences of this political history have been a pattern of economic development in contemporary North Carolina characterized by low wages, violent discouragement of unionization by the state officials as well as employers, enduring racial inequalities, little protective legislation for workers, transfer payments to the poor lower than the national averages, and fewer controls over business activity than found in many other states. . . .

In recent years, in pursuit of investment, North Carolina's state government has developed a wide number of agencies, divisions, departments, and programs whose purpose is to attract "external" capital to the state by publicizing North Carolina as a "promised land" for high-yield capital investment. The Industrial Development Division of the State of North Carolina, which was established in the late 1970s, employed sixteen full-time industrial recruiters whose role was to "sell" North Carolina to corporate executives outside the state. Wood (1986:164) argues that these recruiters are not pursuing *all* industries, but specifically those that would be best suited to and attracted by North Carolina's labor climate—that is labor intensive, low-wage industries seeking to escape unionization, labor market competition, and higher wages in other regions.

It is important to note that the kinds of industries that fit this description, and which North Carolina has actively recruited and attracted, are most heavily concentrated in the competitive sector of the economy. Industries in this sector find it more difficult to pass on every increase in wages, taxes, or regulatory costs to consumers as easily as businesses in the oligopopolistic sector such as automobiles, metals, rubber, and petroleum production. Thus, competitive-sector industries frequently operate on a narrow margin of profitability. For this reason they are particularly attracted to states that can promise reduced labor, regulatory, and tax costs. As a relatively small, family-run operation, Imperial Foods was an ideal target for North Carolina's industrial recruitment. In 1980, Imperial responded to the attraction of a nonunionized labor force that enjoyed few labor market options, and that would consequently be willing to accept low wages and marginal working conditions, by moving its operation from Pennsylvania to North Carolina.

North Carolina's public industrial policy is not merely a passive one, promising a hands-off attitude toward business and business regulation. The State is also proactive in providing businesses special benefits. North Carolina state laws allow local city and county governments to issue revenue bonds to finance branch plant recruitment, and allows counties to negotiate property tax abatements with potential industrial recruits (Tomaskovic-Devey, 1991: 15). As one example of the extremes to which the state will go to attract low-wage industry, in 1989 John Martin, Governor of North Carolina, eliminated the inventory tax on *all* manufacturers in order to lure a *single* cookie plant to the state (Tomaskovic-Devely, 1991:16).

Altogether, these forces have produced a form of growth with only limited benefit for workers. Wood (1986), however, suggests that there were two key institutions that might have placed pressure on North Carolina's political establishment in ways that would have resulted in a closer linkage between economic growth and economic advancement for workers. The first of these is unionization, and the second is Federal regulation. Both of these mechanisms for improving wage and working conditions, however, have been effectively blocked by the political–economic arrangements within North Carolina.

Blocking Worker Organization

The most consistent specific vehicle by which unions have been undercut in North Carolina is the state's right-to-work law. This law hinders the ability of unions to organize, and legally limits the strength of unions by outlawing union shops. Under the right-to-work law, which is more appropriately named a "right-not-to-unionize law," if a union wins the right to represent a plant, only those workers who wish to join the union, pay union dues and abide by union decisions, such as a strike vote, do so. In states without such laws, when a union wins recognition, all of the workers in the plant must join the union, pay dues and abide by union decisions.

Because it is a right-to-work state, even a unionized plant in North Carolina may have up to 49 percent of its work force who are not union members. Consequently, the economic strength of the union is diminished because not all workers pay dues, and its bargaining strength is substantially weakened because employers know that even if there is a strike vote, only the union members will walk out. Thus, while strikes may be an inconvenience, in many plants they do not threaten a total shutdown of operations. Moreover, in a plant that is significantly split between unionized and nonunionized workers, managers have to employ far fewer strike breakers in order to maintain near-full levels of operation than they would if they were faced by a union-shop strike. . . .

In North Carolina not only are unions kept from organizing by the combined efforts of state government and industry, but already organized companies are kept out by a similar constellation of forces. In order to insure North Carolina remains an employers' paradise, members of the business community have often actively worked to discourage investment that they felt might raise the value of labor by creating too many job opportunities, or by establishing a higher wage scale, particularly if the industry seeking relocation to North Carolina was a unionized one. In one instance, in 1976 the owners of Cannon Mills sought to keep a Philip Morris plant from being built in their county because they feared it would create competition for workers and would drive up the price of labor (Luebke, 1990). In another instance, the Raleigh Chamber of Commerce has a written policy against recruiting companies that do not agree to resist unionization, and throughout the 1970s and 1980s they have rejected companies such as the Miller Brewing Company, Brockway Glass, and Xerox because they would bring union jobs (Wood, 1986:163). "As recently as 1991 groups of businessmen actively discouraged United Airlines from locating a major maintenance facility in Greensboro, North Carolina, for fear that the 1,500 unionized high skill jobs would drive up wages and increase unionization" (Tomaskovic-Devey, 1991:24). . . .

What all of this means for industrial workers, as well as other working people in North Carolina, is that they operate in a societal context hostile to worker protection, a context created by a state that has actively blocked the ability of workers to make their collective voices heard through effective labor organization, and which additionally is now facing a fiscal crisis that threatens to exacerbate these conditions.

Blocking Worker Safety: The Case of NC-OSHA

The second factor Wood (1986) suggests might be an avenue for North Carolina workers to improve their situation is through Federal regulation. In the case of workplace safety, a relatively strong Federal law has been in place since 1970 in the form of the Occupational Safety and Health Act. The act's stated goal is "to assure as far as possible every working man and woman in the Nation safe and healthful working conditions." The Act requires that each employer furnish each employee "a place of employment which is free from recognized hazards that are causing or likely to cause death or serious physical harm" to employees (Public Law 91–596, quoted in Noble, 1986:3).

The law gives impressive rights to American workers. First it obliges companies to reduce the risks in the workplace. While other labor laws limit businesses from preventing efforts by workers to make improvements in the safety of their workplace, the OSH Act not only allows workers to fight for safety and health, it places the burden of responsibility on the employer, demanding that the company take action to improve the workplace in ways that benefit the worker. The second way in which the Act is impressive is in its breadth of coverage compared to other protective legislation. Nearly all workers are protected by the OSH Act. Public-sector employees are the only group of workers who are not protected by the Act (Noble, 1986).

The OSH Act was not the first attempt to protect American workers' health and safety. Massachusetts passed the first worker safety law in 1877 and all other states eventually had some kind of legal protection of at least some workers. The OSH Act, however, was the first Federal law to protect workers' health and safety, and it was the first law to require Federal inspectors and a Federal system of fines. The OSH Act also differs from all previous worker health and safety legislation because it gives employees the right to participate in agency inspections (Noble, 1986).

Despite its positive potential for American workers, the OSH Act is not as progressive as similar legislation in other countries. For example, U.S. employers, unlike those in some other nations, are not required to establish health and safety committees, nor are they required to involve workers in decision making about health and safety issues. In addition, some property rights of the employer are protected through an appeal system that facilitates employer challenges to cited violations (Noble, 1986).

The establishment of OSHA, nevertheless, threatens the interests of investors because it can make inroads into profits. In order to maintain profit levels employers need to either keep their production costs low, or be able to pass on any increase in costs to consumers. Profit pressures can inhibit the development of a safe workplace because minimizing costs usually means foregoing the establishment of safety measures that absorb workers' time or the company's money (Noble, 1986). The OSH Act, which insists that safe practices be implemented, even if they have a negative impact on profits, is particularly threatening to competitive-sector industries, which as previously mentioned, are less able to pass on the cost of a safe workplace to consumers.

The OSH Act potentially restructures the relations between workers and managers of capital by insisting that profits are not the only standard by which businesses will be judged. It creates new rights to health and safety for employees and empowers the Federal government to enforce them. . . .

In addition, Congress sought to appease states'-rights advocates by allowing states to create their own version of OSHA that was to be controlled by the state rather than the Federal government. In a last minute compromise during the passage of the bill, state governments successfully lobbied for this joint program. According to the hearings held by the Committee on Education and Labor of the House of Representatives to inquire into the Hamlet fire (hereinafter designated as CEL, 1991), North Carolina was one of the 23 states to opt for a state-run program. By establishing the North Carolina Occupational Safety and Health Administration (NC-OSHA) in 1974, North Carolina become one of 23 states with their own OSHA program. Of these 23, 10 have only been conditionally approved because they are not in compliance with Federal OSHA regulations. North Carolina is one of these ten on probation. No state OSHA, however, has ever been decertified and placed under Federal control because of non-compliance, regardless of their performance record, and no specific criteria have been established to determine whether or not a state should be decertified (CEL, 1991:104).

If a state chooses to establish its own OSHA operation, it has the option of setting its own penalties and priorities. NC-OSHA has used this prerogative to minimize the effect of penalties for violations of safety and health standards. In 1991, for instance, North Carolina increased the fines for OSHA violations for the *first time* since the establishment of NC-OSHA in 1974. The current maximum fine in North Crolina (and by no means the most common one) is $14,000, just a fraction of the Federal maximum fine of $70,000 (Parker, Menn and O'Brien, 1991).

Workers in North Carolina, like other American workers could be protected by Federal regulation under the OSH Act. The implementation of the OSH Act, however, has been diluted at the Federal level by the executive branch. In addition, the option of states' rights has allowed the state of North Carolina to organize its own version of OSHA, one that is even less effective than the Federal version. In this way, the potential for protection of North Carolina workers by Federal regulation has been successfully blocked in North Carolina by the mutual efforts of business and government in North Carolina. These efforts frequently intersect in significant ways as businesses, particularly competitive sector industrial operations, pursue their profit goals through limiting worker power, and the State pursues its development goals by offering a haven for industries fleeing more unionized states with more stringently enforced occupational health and safety regulations.

INSTITUTIONAL CONTEXT

The history of North Carolina's political economy reveals a state in which workers have been most often blocked in their efforts to control their work environment by a business-government coalition favoring a relatively *laissez faire* industrial policy. But this political-economic climate alone does not explain the complex dynamics that led to the fire at Hamlet. Word *could* have reached authorities about the unsafe practices in the plant, and NC-OSHA *did have* the legal authority to unlock the doors. What then kept these things from happening? This question is partially answered by examining the institutional context in which the fire took place, and by delineating the specific pattern of industrial relations among Imperial's management, workers and NC-OSHA.

By the late 1980s Imperial Foods was under considerable pressure because of the general economic decline and because of specific fiscal problems within the corporation. Even before the fire in Hamlet, it appears that Emmett Roe, the owner of Imperial Foods, was facing financial difficulty. In 1990 he had closed a plant in Alabama without giving his employees proper notice. The courts had awarded the laid-off workers $250,000 in severance pay, although by the time of the fire no payments on this obligation to the Alabama workers had been made. Roe was facing suits for $350,000 in debts owed to his creditors and a $24,000 bill for unpaid taxes (Greif and Garfield, 1991). The financial difficulty which Roe faced may have increased the likelihood of decisions that placed profitability ahead of the health or safety costs to workers. This interpretation would be consistent with the findings of Clinard and Yeager (1980) which suggest that the greater the financial strain faced by businesses, the greater the likelihood that they will engage in regulatory violations.

Regardless of what decisions Roe's financial pressures or management policies may have provoked, NC-OSHA could have intervened in a way that would have ultimately protected the workers in Hamlet. What were the factors that disrupted the ability of NC-OSHA to regulate the conditions at Hamlet? Two issues stand out. First, there is some evidence to suggest that workers who recognized hazards at the plant found it difficult to make their concerns for a safe workplace heard. Second, NC-OSHA failed to effectively regulate Imperial's safety practices because it was not adequately funded, and because, at least according to some observers, it was not efficiently organized. . . .

The Failure of OSHA

Had the concerned workers at Imperial chosen to contact OSHA instead of bringing their complaints directly to the plant's management, they, like many other workers in North Carolina, would not likely have met with success. First of all, they would have been informed by a poster in the plant to call an 800 number. Three-fourths of the 160,000 workplace posters publicizing the phone number for safety complaints, including the posters at Imperial, listed a number that had been disconnected, with no forwarding number. Thus, the basic requirement of being able to contact the safety agency could not be met. Certainly, a highly motivated worker, familiar with the process of hunting through a bureaucratic tangle of phone numbers and disconnected lines, might have reached OSHA. But the more likely response of the average worker who called the NC-OSHA number only to be told it was disconnected would be to conclude that the office was no longer in operation. At the very least, the incorrect posters, and the failure to replace them with correct ones, constituted a serious limitation on the accessibility of OSHA to the workers at Imperial and elsewhere in North Carolina.

The incorrect posters and other problems faced by NC-OSHA reflect in part the organization's inadequate level of funding. Nationally, OSHA is seriously underfunded, and NC-OSHA is comparatively even less well funded. North Carolina Governor James Martin testified before Congress that although a minimum of 64 safety inspectors were required to be working in the state according to Federal OSHA guidelines, the legislature had authorized only 34. He went on to say that in January of 1991 he attempted to have 19 more inspectors authorized, but that the legislature had denied his request.

Even if Martin's request had been granted, however, North Carolina would have remained 11 short of the minimum number of required OSHA inspectors. Only nine states in the United States have fewer inspectors than is recommended by Federal OSHA regulations. Of these nine, North Carolina falls the farthest below the recommended number, funding only 53% of the total number of inspectors required. As a consequence, for instance, although North Carolina has 83 poultry plants, only half of them have ever been inspected since the inception of NC-OSHA.

In 1980 North Carolina had 1.9 million workers and 47 OSHA safety inspectors. Ten years later, when North Carolina's work force had grown by 37 percent, to a total of 2.6 million, the number of OSHA inspectors had declined by 12 percent, to 42 inspectors. According to the Bureau of Labor Statistics, between 1977 when John Brooks, Commissioner of the Department of Labor and head of the NC-OSHA, first took office, and 1988, the number of North Carolina workplace injuries grew from 120,000 a year to 177,300 (Menn, 1991). This rate of growth in workplace injuries outstripped the growth in the actual number of workers, suggesting that between 1977 and 1988 North Carolina actually lost ground in workplace safety despite the fact that the purpose of the OSH Act was to ensure just the opposite. The record of NC-OSHA in improving worker safety in North Carolina is not commendable.

In addition to the inadequate numbers of inspectors, Brooks reported to the Congressional committee that until late in 1991 the inspectors NC-OSHA did have were able to work in the field only four days a week because the department lacked sufficient travel funds. Since then they have been able to work in the field only three days a week because of further cuts in NC-OSHA funding. Brooks also noted that even if he hired additional staff there would be difficulty training them because the closest training center is in Chicago and it is constantly booked up (CEL, 1991:168).

At the Congressional hearings on the fire it was also revealed that $453,000 which could have been used for salaries for OSHA inspectors in North Carolina was returned to the Federal government in 1991 (CEL, 1991:129). Moreover, this was not a one-time budgetary aberration. According to testimony, in five of the six years preceding the Imperial fire, Federal OSHA money had been returned to Washington by NC-OSHA. These funds were returned to the Federal government because in order to accept them, the state would have been required to match them. For example, in 1991, because the state legislature was unwilling to provide the state OSHA with $243,000, they were unable to accept the matching $453,000 from the Federal government (CEL, 1991:223). . . .

FAILURE OF CONTROLS IN CONTEXT

A competitive economy dominated by profit-seeking investors, a government committed to offering an attractive profit-making climate and consequently far from aggressive in protecting the health and safety of workers, and workers with very limited ability to shape the safety and health conditions of their work place, all contributed to the fire in Hamlet. These things alone, however, did not cause the tragedy at Imperial. In order to understand how these things interacted to produce the outcome they did, it is important to examine the ways in which the activities of government regulatory agencies intersected with the activities of the management of Imperial. The fire and the locked doors may have resulted from actions taken by management at Imperial, but those actions were made possible by the failure of several control agencies.

Kramer and Michalowski (1991) suggest that state-corporate crime can be understood as the result of an interaction between elements of government and elements of the private-production system. They offer the destruction of the space shuttle Challenger as a prototypical example of state corporate crime, emphasizing the relationship between several governmental units (NASA, Congress, and the Administration), and a private corporation, Morton Thiokol, the builder of Challenger's rocket motors. We argue that the Hamlet fire was likewise a case of state-corporate crime. But unlike the prototype offered by Kramer and Michalowski, the events leading to the Hamlet fire were more the consequences of socially injurious omissions on the part of governmental agencies, rather than direct consequences of the pursuit of specific goals, as was the case with governmental actions surrounding the building and launching of the ill-fated Challenger.

In the case of the Hamlet disaster, the critical intersections were between a private business, Imperial Foods, and several government agencies at the Federal level (US-OSHA and the USDA), at the state level (NC-OSHA, the office of the governor, and the state legislature), and at the local level (the county building inspectors and the city of Hamlet fire department). For a variety of reasons each of these agencies, by omission—that is, by failing to perform the control functions assigned to them—made possible the continuation of the hazardous conditions at the Imperial plant in Hamlet that led to the deaths of 25 workers. To unravel this skein of ultimately destructive decisions and omissions we will first examine the specifics of the fire and then discuss the ways in which each of the controls failed within the specific context of Imperial's operation in Hamlet.

The Imperial Fire

The accumulated evidence in the Hamlet fire indicates that the single most important factor leading to the 25 deaths was the lack of readily accessible routes to safety. All but 1 of the 25 deaths resulted from smoke inhalation. Only one person died of extensive burns (CEL, 1991:233). The fire itself and the heat it produced was not large enough within the 30,000 square foot building Imperial occupied to kill the number of people it did. Rather, people died because they could not escape the smoke the fire produced. Particularly telling is the fact that a number of the dead were found in a large freezer where they had retreated to escape the fire. Once inside the freezer they were protected from the heat and fire, but unfortunately they were unable to close the door tightly enough to keep out the toxic smoke (CEL, 1991:118). Considering that these workers had sufficient time to reach the freezer, in all likelihood they would also have had sufficient time to escape the building, *if* there been adequate pathways to safety. This point is underscored by the example of one woman who survived because, although she could not get out of a blocked door, she was able to put her face out of the door where a friend who was outside fanned away the smoke with his baseball cap.

There were eight entrances to the building. Four were locked from the outside and one other was probably blocked from the outside. Three doors were not locked. One was the main plant entrance which is where most of the employees who did escape exited, and which was the only door marked with an exit sign. One door was blocked by the fire. And one door, that could only be reached by walking through a freezer, was unmarked and unknown to most employees because they were not allowed in the freezer unless that was their work station (CEL, 1991:102).

Workers testified that most employees assumed that the doors were not locked because of fire laws (CEL, 1991:52). And in fact that is the law. The OSHA law reads, "Every exit must be well lit. Door passages and stairways that might be mistaken for access should be so marked. Doors shoud be unobstructed so that employees can always get out" (CEL, 1991:100).

There were two reasons given for why the doors were locked; one was that it was to keep the flies out, and one was that it was to keep the employees from stealing the chicken.

Approximately a dozen current and former plant workers told news reporters that doors were routinely locked to keep employees from stealing chicken nuggets. Police records show the company reported employee thefts three times in recent years. "Hamlet police records show Imperial employees stole chicken valued at between $24 and $245 (Drescher and Garfield, 1991). If the theft of chicken was, in fact, the reason for locking the doors, it suggests that Imperial management operated according to a frightening calculus wherein preventing the theft of several hundred dollars worth of chicken parts justified risking human lives by cutting off what would be escape routes in case of fire, and doing so in violation of the law. It is also disturbing that in all of the discussion and reportage about the locking of the doors, there appears little evidence that the simple solution of installing fire doors with alarms that sound whenever the door is opened, a commonplace installation in many buildings and a solution that would have both insured safe exits *and* minimized the use of these doors for illicit commerce, was ever seriously considered.

In addition to locked doors, exits were unmarked and employees were not made aware of where exits were and whether they were locked or not. There had never been a fire drill in the plant nor any fire safety instruction of employees.

The fire itself started because of the unsafe practice of repairing hoses carrying hydraulic fuel while continuing to maintain cooking temperatures with gas flames under large vats of oil. To minimize down-time, Imperial Food Products routinely left its gas-fired chicken fryer on while repairing adjacent hoses carring flammable hydraulic fluid, a maintenance worker testified (Trevor and Williams, 1991). Bobby Quick testified at the Congressional hearings that on the day of the fire he heard Brad Roe tell a maintenance worker to hurry repairs to the line in order to avoid down-time (Trevor and Perlmutt, 1991).

The vats of oil are 27 feet by 4 feet and are kept at 390–405 degrees. The flash point of cooking oil is 460 degrees (CEL, 1991:49). On the day of the fire, repairs were being made on hoses carrying hydraulic fuel to the cooking vats. The cooking was not stopped as the repairs were made. The insurance department of the state of North Carolina filed a report describing how the fire started.

> The cause of the fire was determined to be the ignition of hydraulic oil from a ruptured line only a few feet from a natural-gas-fueled cooker used in preparation of the chicken. Investigators determined that during a repair operation, the incoming hydraulic line separated from its coupling at a point approximately 60 inches above the concrete floor and began to discharge the fluid at high pressure. This high pressure and subsequent flow resulted in the hydraulic fluid being sprayed against the floor and onto the nearby cooker. Ignition of the fuel was immediate; likely from the nearby gas burners. . . . The intense fire also impinged upon a natural gas regulator (located directly above the ruptured hydraulic line) on the supply line to the burners which soon failed and added to the fuels being consumed (CEL, 1991:112).

To make matters worse, there were no automatic cutoffs on the hydraulic or gas lines, there was only one fire extinguisher in the plant, and there were no working telephones to call the fire department when the fire broke out. An employee had to drive several blocks to the fire station to inform them that there was a serious fire at the plant (CEL, 1991:57).

How did these conditions come about, and what were the acts of omission on the part of governmental agencies that helped make it possible?

Omission by the Federal Government

Two Federal agencies failed the workers at Hamlet in important ways. The first of these is OSHA. OSHA was statutorily responsible for insuring the quality of services provided by state-run NC-OSHA. As previously discussed, while Federal OSHA had known for quite some time about the inadequacy and ineffectiveness of the North Carolina agency's operations, no effective effort was taken to remedy the situation, except to file a report.

The second agency that could have, but did not act to prevent the disaster in Hamlet came as a surprise to most people—the United States Department of Agriculture (USDA). Because Imperial Foods in Hamlet is a meat-processing plant, a USDA agent visited the plant *daily* in order to make sure that the meat was being handled properly. . . .

The Failure of North Carolina State Government

Three components of the state government in North Carolina contributed to the circumstances that led to the fire and deaths at the Imperial plant. First of all, the state legislature refused to match funds with the Federal OSHA. The actual decision-making process of the individual legislators who voted not to fund OSHA to the required level is difficult to know for sure. The general political climate of North Carolina suggests, however, that probably some combination of four views on worker safety—(1) expanding NC-OSHA would contradict the interests of key constituents in the business community, (2) mandatory safety inspections are an unacceptable intrusion of the state into the rights of private enterprise, (3) inspections are not worth the money they would cost in the light of North Carolina's budget crisis, or (4) expanding NC-OSHA would give the wrong signal to industries that might relocate in North Carolina—played a role in the history of the North Carolina legislature's refusal to adequately fund NC-OSHA. Not only did the legislature fail to fund NC-OSHA's inspector staff to required levels, but it even failed to provide adequate travel and training funds for the limited number of NC-OSHA inspectors it did authorize. In addition, the state legislature was apparently quick to interpret the state's hiring freeze as an absolute barrier to the expansion of NC-OSHA's staff of inspectors, when exceptions to this freeze were allowed in other areas deemed "critical." Additionally, the governor appeared to be reluctant to use the weight of his office to pressure the legislature toward expanding the number of NC-OSHA inspectors. While the Governor did request funds from the legislature in 1991 for additional inspectors, this was the first time in six years he had done so. In the previous five years of his tenure in office he took no lead in attempting to bring NC-OSHA up to Federal standards.

The internal operations of NC-OSHA itself may have also contributed to the situation in Hamlet in ways that are not entirely attributable to the lack of financial support NC-OSHA received from the state. While the underfunding of NC-OSHA was undoubtedly the critical factor in limiting its effectiveness, employees of NC-OSHA have also suggested that the management style of John Brooks, its director, may have been a contributing factor. Four current safety inspectors and five recent retirees from NC-OSHA discussed Brooks with news reporters. All expressed frustration with the department's performance over the past 10 years. "A lot of people have come in, seen what was going on, and left," said Bryan McGlohon, who retired in 1987 after 14 years as a safety inspector and consultant. McGlohon said he left in part because of Brooks' "lack of skill in human resources. I can't put up with bureaucracy and inefficiency." Each of the other eight inspectors said he knew of at least one person he considered qualified rejected by Brooks for a job in the past few years (Menn, 1991). It is difficult to know to what extent internal management difficulties further limited NC-OSHA's effectiveness, or to what extent these difficulties were themselves the consequence of the stress resulting from an inadequate budget, but the testimony of current and former NC-OSHA workers suggests that the organization may not have been functioning as effectively as it might have, even in the face of its limited budget.

Taken together, these factors suggest that the State of North Carolina, for a variety of reasons, simply did not take the issue of worker health and safety seriously, or at least did not take them seriously enough to insure that NC-OSHA was adequately funded and effectively run.

Local Government

The operations of local government agencies also played their part in contributing to the Hamlet fire. Hamlet is located in Richmond County, which is responsible for regularly conducting inspections to identify unsafe or unlawful buildings in the county. According to the North Carolina Insurance Department, the Hamlet plant was in violation of building codes because it did not have a sprinkler system, did not have enough doors, workers had to walk more than the allowable 150 feet to exit the building, one door opened to the inside, four doors were locked, and there were no exit signs. Some of these violations were a result of Imperial management having made changes in the building without requesting inspections and without obtaining building permits.

Another issue regarding local inspection concerns the question of whether or not the building code violations at Imperial were inappropriately "grandfathered" as permissible under Richmond county law. According to this law the Building Code Council cannot require existing buildings to meet new and tougher codes unless the building is substantially renovated. In 1983 a new $125,000 roof was put on the building after a fire damaged the plant, an expenditure that could have been viewed as a substantial renovation. The Richmond County inspector, under the wide latitude provided by the building code, however, chose to conclude that despite the new roof, the Imperial plant had not been substantially renovated, and that it did not have to bring the entire building up to code (Drescher, 1991a).

Richmond building inspector Jack Thompson examined the new roof put on in 1983 but not the building. "I just figured the roof wouldn't be more than 50 percent of the property's value." He said he did not check property value records and only guessed at Imperial's worth. "I did look around but as far as digging around looking to see what was holding the building up, I didn't do that. Didn't nothing stand out to me that wouldn't meet the code" (Williams and Drescher, 1991). What can be said of Thompson's testimony is that it is relatively clear he did not take a proactive stance toward building safety. This minimalist approach to building safety inspections is consistent with the climate of business regulation in North Carolina generally, and in industry-hungry Richmond county in particular, and is another example of the velvet-glove treatment given to industry in North Carolina.

The other local government agency that played a role in the deaths of the 25 workers, although perhaps a minor one, was the Hamlet Fire Department. Here the story takes a racial twist. The town of Hamlet is predominately white, and its fire department is all white. Although Hamlet is a small town, it has a suburb—the town of Dobbins—which, as a reflection of the continuing patterns of residential racial segregation in North Carolina, is predominately black and has a black fire department. When the fire at the plant started, the Dobbins Fire Department arrived at the scene. They were not, however, allowed to assist in the rescue and were asked to leave. Members of the Dobbins Fire Department claim they were asked to leave for racial reasons. Specifically, they contend that members of the Hamlet Fire Department believe that because the members of the Dobbins Fire Department are black, they are not qualified fire fighters (*Charlotte Observer,* 1991). It will never be known for sure whether or not the added aid of the Dobbins Fire Department might have saved additional lives, but the simple fact that they were not allowed to assist in the rescue raises serious questions about the relative priorities that guided the Hamlet Fire Department in attempting to assist the workers trapped inside the Hamlet plant.

CONCLUSION

The fire in Hamlet was caused by an array of actors, actions, omissions, and social circumstances that surrounded the workers in concentric circles from the closest supervisors and owners to local, state and Federal agencies, and finally to the organization of both the North Carolina and the U.S. political economy itself. Like a noose, these concentric circles closed around Hamlet and interacted in a way that brought about the death of 25 workers. When the list of factors arrayed against worker safety in North Crolina are tallied, it is surprising that there are not more workplace disasters such as the one at Imperial. It also suggests that many other industrial employees in North Carolina work on the fine edge of potential disaster. The Hamlet fire was not an aberration. It was almost predictable. In fact, it had been predicted by some workers.

In the final analysis, what is particularly disturbing and particularly telling is that *so many* components of the system designed to protect the health and safety of workers, from Federal OSHA, to NC-OSHA, to local inspectors *had to fail* in order for this killing fire to have occurred. The deaths in Hamlet are clear evidence that laws alone are not sufficient to protect worker safety. They require political will for their effective enforcement. Without this will, they become more symbolic than real. The Hamlet fire constitutes a clear instance of state-corporate crime precisely because it was the absence of this *political will* and the omissions on the part of *politically constituted agencies* that enabled the management of Imperial to continue violating basic safety requirements at the plant in its pursuit of private profit.

REFERENCES

Bloom, Jack. 1987. *Class, Race and the Civil Rights Movement*. Bloomington: Indiana University Press.

Charlotte Observer. 1991. "Firefighters Near Plant Not Called: Chief Cites Racism." September 6, 4a.

Clinard Marshall and Peter Yeager. 1980. *Corporate Crime*. New York: The Free Press.

Committee on Education and Labor, House of Representatives. 1991. *Hearing on H.R. 3160, Comprehensive OSHA Reform Act, and the fire at the Imperial Food Products Plant in Hamlet, North Carolina* Serial No. 102–47, September 12, Washington, D.C.: U.S. Government Printing Office.

Crow, Jeffrey. 1984. "Cracking the Solid South: Populism and the Fusionist Interlude." In L. Butler and A. Watson (eds.), *The North Carolina Experience: an Interpretive and Documentary History*. Chapel Hill: University of North Carolina Press.

Drescher, John. 1991a. "In Hamlet Fire Government Safety Nets Gave Away." *Charlotte Observer,* September 22, A1, 7.

Drescher, John and Ken Garfield. 1991. "Workers: Doors Kept Locked." *Charlotte Observer,* September 12, A1, 11.

Greif, James and Ken Garfield. 1991. "Debt Dogged Imperial's Owner—Then the Fire." *Charlotte Observer,* September 15, A1, 12.

Key, V. O. 1950. *Southern Politics in State and Nation*. New York: Alfred A. Knopf.

Kramer, Ronald and Raymond Michalowski. 1990. "State-Corporate Crime." Paper presented at the American Society of Criminology, November.

Luebke, Paul. 1990. *Tar Heel Politics: Myths and Realities*. Chapel Hill: University of North Carolina Press.

Menn, Joseph. 1991. "North Carolina Official Puts Blame on Legislature." *Charlotte Observer,* September 6, A1, 4.

Noble, Charles. 1986. *Liberalism at Work: the Rise and Fall of OSHA*. Philadelphia: Temple University Press.

Parker, Jennifer, Joseph Menn, and Kevin O'Brien. 1991. "North Carolina Inspection Program Ranks Last in U.S." *Charlotte Observer,* September 5, A1.

Tomaskovic-Devey, Donald. 1991. *Sundown on the Sunbelt? Growth Without Development in the Rural South, A Report to the Ford Foundation*. Raleigh: North Carolina State University Press.

Trevor, Greg and David Perlmutt. 1991. "Worker to Testify of Order to Rush Repair." *Charlotte Observer,* September 12, A1, 10.

Trevor, Greg and Paige Williams. 1991. "Worker: Repairers Left Fryer On." *Charlotte Observer,* September 10, A1, 9.

Wiliams, Paige and John Drescher. "Plant Not Inspected as Authorized." *Charlotte Observer,* September 21, C1.

Wood, Phillip. 1986. *Southern Capitalism: The Political Economy of North Carolina, 1880–1980*. Durham, N.C.: Duke University Press.

4

Decision Making

INTRODUCTION

In contrast to Chapter 3, where we discussed the distribution of criminal opportunities as one of the keys to understanding aggregate-level variation in crime rates, in this chapter we turn our attention to the challenge of accounting for individual and organization-level decisions to commit white-collar crime. We understand that there is an objective, common-sense quality to criminal opportunities; this is the reason we are cautioned, for example, not to leave our automobile keys in the ignition switch or to leave attractively wrapped gifts in plain sight while away from our cars. Still, even when surrounded by abundant criminal opportunities and indications that others are exploiting them, not all individuals and organizations do so. Why?

In the logic of rational-choice theory, decisions to engage in crime are products of cognition and calculation in which decisions makers pursue desired goals, select between various options, and weigh consequences. In this view, white-collar crime is purposeful, chosen behavior designed to advance the interests of the individual or the organization, albeit at the expense perhaps of the health of citizens across the globe.

A rational-choice perspective also sensitizes us to the fact that organizational crimes are the result of decisions made by managers and executives. Corporate crimes, for example, are not the products of reified but faceless corporate actors but take shape instead in executive boardrooms and in the decisions of individuals. The notion of crime as choice directs attention to the complex of structural, cultural and situational factors that influence their decision making. We reprint here Donald Cressey's well-known treatment of this issue. It is important precisely because Cressey calls into question the utility and logic of attributing criminal decisions to corporations, which are only legally created entities, and not to their executives.

Many decision makers surrounded by criminal opportunity presumably either are unaware of or are insensitive to it, while others, who may sense the potential at hand, lack the knowledge, the access to criminal networks, or the motivation required to exploit them. Even among those who are wise to criminal opportunity, many simply do not weigh and calculate equally the potential consequences of rule breaking. The paper by Paternoster and Simpson draws attention to factors that influence the criminal calculus. They present a causal model of variation in criminal decision making by corporate officials.

Two variables—performance pressure and the presence of criminogenic cultural conditions—have been linked repeatedly to an increased likelihood that criminal choices will be made. Performance pressure means anxiety or fear induced in individuals or in employees of an organization by the felt need to maintain or increase standards of performance. This can be the need to increase profit margins or to improve a university athletic team's win–loss record, but in all cases it stems from belief that performance has not measured up in the eyes of peers or superiors. This may be coupled with the belief that continued failure to meet perceived expectations means that "time is running out." Particularly in the corporate world, pressure to maintain profits is thought to be an important source of criminal motivation. The paper by Anne Jenkins and John Braithwaite demonstrates the explanatory power of performance pressure. Their analysis of nursing homes found that for-profit homes are significantly more likely than voluntary homes to break the law and to deliver substandard care. Top-down pressure to meet the bottom line in for-profit homes creates an incentive to cut corners in patient treatment, to leave necessary maintenance unfinished, and to look the other way when dangerous conditions are apparent. Jenkins and Braithwaite further show how values, beliefs, and guiding principles shape workplace decision making.

Despite their collective nature, workplace cultures are constructed, enacted, and continuously reconstructed by individuals who populate the organization. Cultures conducive to criminal decision making generally include rationalizations, excuses, and justifications for illicit behavior, all of which increase the odds of criminal choices. When invoked by individuals or corporate managers, these shared linguistic constructions operate to blunt the moral force of the law and to neutralize the guilt of criminal participation. They serve not only as post hoc rationalizations for involvement in criminal conduct, but they also may precede and facilitate its commission. Andrew Hochstetler and Heith Copes note the contemporary appeal of the concept *organizational culture*. They also show how criminal culture shapes decision making, and they highlight the importance of hierarchical dynamics in shaping its content.

It is one thing to conjure in the abstract the criminal decision maker and another thing entirely to make sense of and accommodate theoretically the calculus of real-life offenders. More than two decades of research into the lives and decisions of street offenders has shown, for example, how both the influence of peers and drug-induced states of altered consciousness often distort the thought process. White-collar criminal decision making may be subject to influences of a comparable, if empirically distinctive, nature. Employees, for example, are subject to the restrictive influences of hierarchical relations and are expected to defer to or in other ways take account of the preferences and biases of superiors. Not surprisingly then, research on street offenders and privileged offenders alike suggest not that the notion of crime as choice must be rejected, but that the decision-making process defies simple analysis and description as *rational* choice.

This point figures prominently in the paper by Diane Vaughan. One of the few investigators to examine organizational decision making. Vaughan explored how officials at the National Aeronautics and Space Administration made the decision to launch the space shuttle Challenger, which resulted in the death of all crew members. Her analysis led Vaughan to suggest than an organizational bias toward risky decisions can become established by a confluence of factors and thereby shape individual decisions. NASA scientists, engineers, and mangers, Vaughan contends, gradually defined certain risks to flight safety as acceptable, which ultimately led officials to authorize a shuttle launch under dangerous conditions. Both her use of retrospective interview data and her focus on an incident that was neither criminal nor deviant means that Vaughan's interpretation should not be generalized to criminal decision making. Nevertheless, she is led to conclusions about the bounded rationality of organizational decisions that differ little from what is known about the rationality of robbers and burglars.

The Poverty of Theory in Corporate Crime Research

Donald R. Cressey

. . . Consistently, social scientists have written volumes on "organizational behavior." They have done so because it is easy to assume that corporations and other organizations act like humans. Sociologists and experts on business administration say, for example, that corporations and other formal organizations formulate goals and the means to achieve them, just as do human members of committees, teams, and other action groups. Political scientists assert that states, legislatures, and court systems make decisions and seem to have lives of their own. Public administration specialists insist that cities behave, as do their police departments, fire departments, and sewer departments. Historians studying foreign relations treat entire nations as corporations when they analyze actions of "the United States," not of Americans. Anthropologists and sociologists say they can observe the behavior of societies and cultures themselves, not just the behavior of a society's members or of the participants in a culture. And economists, of course, have projected the characteristics of a rational, calculating "economic man" onto many organizations, ranging from mom-and-pop grocery stores to entire nations. To them, the corporation is an ideal "economic man" because it persistently pursues profits and, ideally, lets nothing distract it from that pursuit.

Criminologists, being interdisciplinary, do and say all of these things, and more. For example, a recent review of an important book on controlling white-collar crime anthropomorphized as follows: "Corporations do after all have consciences, and they can be pricked by publicity. That is the conclusion of this first-rate study by two Australian legal scholars" (Maitland, 1986). I myself have asserted that juvenile gangs (Sutherland and Cressey, 1978:196, 98), La Costa Nostra "families: (Cressy, 1969) and even prisons (Cressy, 1965), as well as corporations (Cressey, 1976) and other organizations, behave as units, like persons. More significantly, criminologists rather routinely, unthinkingly, erroneously assert that corporations have the psychological capacity to be guilty of crime and to suffer from punishment. Assuming such a capacity is what, after all, makes it possible for criminologists to hold that corporations, as corporations, ought to follow ethical and legal "rules of the game," thus displaying social responsibility.

For at least a century, U.S. courts have regarded every corporation as a person. This legal fiction is essential to fairness. For example, if corporations were not assigned the legal characteristics of persons, no one could sue them or make contracts with them. And if corporations were not said to reside in a city, state, and nation—as do persons—they would be "outlaws" in the true sense of the word, for no government would have jurisdiction over them. A citizen could not even be employed by a corporation if the corporation were not viewed as a person who lives somewhere and has a right to make contracts and otherwise conduct business.

But anyone who tries to understand white-collar crime is severely handicapped by the fiction that corporations are disembodied political, social, and economic persons who behave just like ordinary men and women. As Arthur Selwyn Miller, the noted constitutional law scholar, has said, "The corporation is obviously more than a person, however characterized in law" (Miller, 1968:9). This assertion can be validated by making just two commonsense observations.

In the first place corporations are allowed to do many things persons are not permitted to do. They can buy and sell each other legally, as though the "person" being bought or sold were a slave. (According to the October 4, 1985, issue of the *Wall Street Journal*, "Revlon agreed to go private by selling itself for $56 a share, or about $1.77 billion.") They also can exterminate each other legally by methods resembling those of homicidal maniacs (cutthroat competition).

In the second place the makeup of a corporation is quite different from the makeup of a human being. For this reason, corporations can do things that are not humanly possible: growing from infant to adult in a year, shrinking from giant to midget, merging two or more bodies into one, achieving immortality on earth.[5]

Even more relevant to criminologists is the fact that legal fiction notwithstanding, the corporation is obviously *less* than a person. It cannot learn, contemplate, feel guilty or proud, intend, or decide. For this reason, none of the social machinery—including the social contract—that controls real persons has any effect on corporations. Writing ethical codes, preaching social responsibility, noting the wisdom of the Golden Rule, or even depicting the horrors of hellfire and damnation that await evil persons can have no influence on fictitious persons who do not have the psychological makeup of real ones.

These observations about the nature of the corporation have some counterparts in everyday life. For example, auditors and accountants call corporations "entities," which is another name for "things," not "persons."[6] And even though the language of ordinary citizens endows corporations with human attributes, this language also suggests that everyone knows the difference between a "person" and a "thing." Thus, the gas company is never referred to as "she" or "he." It, like other companies, is always called "it." This usage characterizes legal language too, suggesting that the regulation of corporations might be more effective if corporation codes of ethics as well as regulatory laws pertained to the real persons in charge of inanimate objects, not to the objects themselves.

Everybody knows that automobiles really do not behave, even if "Motor Vehicle Codes" and "Automobile Safety Rules" imply that they do. (Out west, we even have a California Auto Body Association.) Motorists, pedestrians, legislators, police, court officials, jail officials, and criminologists all recognize that the reference in such codes and rules is to drivers and passengers, not to cars. Similarly, a citizen who is indignant about an incorrect gas bill will, sooner or later, attribute the error to humans. "The bastards at the gas company don't know what they are doing," the victim of a bureaucratic snafu is likely to claim. In other bailiwicks, too, people with common sense recognize that "entities" do not behave. Saying that the United States has declared war is recognized as just a shorthand way of saying that the president and a majority of the members of Congress have decided to go to war. Reports stating that the White House has spoken, that the city of New York has made a decision, or that a police department has changed its tactics also are readily recog-

---

[5] In the famous Dartmouth College case, decided by the Supreme court in 1819, Chief Justice John Marshall commented on the immortal character of corporations as follows: "Among the most important [properties of corporations] are immortality, and, if the expression may be allowed, individuality; properties by which a perpetual succession of many persons are considered the same, and may act as a single individual" [Dartmouth College v. Woodward, 17 U.S. 518 (1819)].

[6] Ironically enough, auditors nevertheless treat their own firms as persons, not as entities. Stockholders reading the annual reports of corporations rarely note that the signatures following the auditors' statements are obviously fictitious; the reports are "signed" by firms such as Peat, Marwick, Mitchell & Company rather than by a real auditor. In accepting such reports about or by fictitious persons, we overlook the fact that in each case a real person or group of persons has made a decision.

nized as poetic license, as a lazy observer's way of substituting vagueness for needed precision, or as a canny reporter's way of concealing true authorship of the actions.

Although criminologists cannot be expected to crack down on all the poetic license in the world, it is time for them to put their common sense to work when confronting reports indicating that a corporation or other organization has committed a crime. Typical of such reports is a statement recently made by Representative John D. Dingell (Associated Press, 1985). In a five-page letter to Defense Secretary Caspar W. Weinberger, Dingell accused two huge corporations of conspiring to cheat a third organization, the U.S. Air Force:

> General Dynamics knew full well that the Air Force had already paid Westinghouse for the development of these tools. This is not sloppy business practice on the part of General Dynamics—it is fraud. The entire acquisition was clearly double-billed. It is fraud on the part of Westinghouse to plot with General Dynamics. It is also not the finest hour of the Air Force for having allowed this to happen.

In real life, if not in the academic world, criminologists realize that such anthropomorphism is misleading. Firms really do not "know," "plot," and "allow," as the legislator's statement suggests. They are "entities" that are owned, managed, and administered by *people*. Each of these persons talks, decides, intends, agrees, disagrees, deliberates, buys, sells, works, thinks, estimates, errs, and otherwise behaves. Each can be coerced by threats of punishment and persuaded by promise of reward. Except for the few who, due to mental disability, cannot tell right from wrong, each is responsible for individual actions, including violations of the penal code. The corporation itself does not behave. It just sits there. Its so-called actions are but manifestations of actions by real persons, as Hayworth argued years ago (1959), and as the Australian Trade Practices Act, enacted in 1974, makes abundantly clear:

> Any conduct engaged in on behalf of a body corporate by a director, agent or servant of the body corporate or by any other person at the direction or with the consent or agreement (whether express or implied) of a director, agent or servant of the body corporate shall be deemed, for purposes of this Act, to have been engaged in also by the body corporate [quoted by Hopkins, 1978:226].

The main criminological complication is this: to say that a real person rather than a corporation made a decision or acted in a certain way is to say that this individual should be held responsible for the costs as well as the benefits of the decision. Under this procedure corporations would commit no crimes—*executives* who commit the crimes now called crimes of corporations would be arrested, prosecuted, and convicted. This seems reasonable in light of the fact that executives and others whose decisions and behavior make money for the corporation, not the corporation itself, are praised and rewarded when total profits soar. On the other side, however, the policy unreasonably asks law-enforcement officers to detect the crimes of executives who are masters at using the corporate form to mask their misbehavior. As Jack Katz (1980) has noted, it also unreasonably asks prosecutors to convict managers who skillfully use the corporate entity to make their criminality almost impossible to prove.[7] Finally, a former United States attorney has correctly observed that corporations are often prosecuted because it would be unjust to try to establish the criminal liability of "individuals who, under normal standards of prosecutorial discretion, should not be prosecuted" (Martin, 1985). This is not meant to imply, however, that conviction of corporations is an easy matter, even under strict liability statutes (Shudson, Onellion, and Hochstedler, 1984).

Against these practical complications must be weighed the intellectual cost to criminology of the existence of a category of criminal behavior that criminologists' causal theories cannot explain. Although it is possible to find significant correlations between rates of corporate crime and structural variables, such as industry, financial status, and size, it is not possible to go beyond these statistical relationships to statements about causation. Most damaging is the fact that there can be no social psychology of so-called corporate or organizational crime because corporations have no biological or psychological characteristics. I pointed out a quarter of a century ago (Cressey, 1960) that an effective model of crime causation must have two parts: a statement about the way crime is distributed in the social order, and a logically consistent statement about the social psychological process by which criminal behavior is manifested. The latter is necessarily missing in explanations of so-called corporation crime or organizational crime. For reasons of expediency, it might be necessary for legislators, prosecutors, and judges to maintain that imaginary persons commit crimes. But it does not make sense for scientists to maintain that these fictitious persons do so because they are in poverty, are frustrated, are labeled as troublemakers, have poor attachments to the social order, or have had an excess of associations with criminal behavior patterns. Clearly, corporate criminality cannot be explained by the same causal principles used to explain the criminality of real persons.

The work of criminological pioneer Edwin H. Sutherland is especially revealing in this regard. Sutherland invented the concept of white-collar crime and introduced criminologists and others to white-collar criminality. He declared that his motive was "to reform the theory of criminal behavior, not to reform anything else" (1949:v). His discovery of white-collar crime, during the

---

[7] According to newspaper accounts, the indignation of members of Congress about the recent E.F. Hutton scandal stemmed principally from their belief that the white-collar police officers in the U.S. Department of Justice could not detect crimes by any corporate executive, even though the corporation pleaded guilty to 2,000 crimes, or from their belief that the prosecution in Justice either could not or would not prosecute either low-level personnel who executed the crimes or high-level executives who knew or should have known what their subordinates were up to (Pasztor, 1985).

1930s and 1940s—theories stressing personal and social pathologies—are defective because they pertain, at most, to working-class criminals alone. Accordingly, he developed a new causal theory—differential association and differential social organization—that made sense of the crime of high status persons as well as those of poor people.

It is rather ironic to find, therefore, that Sutherland considered corporations as persons but did not so much as give a hint about how the differential association process, a process of learning, could affect them. There is a great difference between what Sutherland said and what he did (Cressey, 1976). He defined white-collar crime as "a crime committed by a person of respectability and high social status in the course of his occupation," but he studied the crime rates of *corporations* not of live persons. His writings show that he viewed the executives of corporations as persons who are respectable and of high social status and, thus, as white-collar criminals if they violated the law in the course of their duties as executives. But the same writings show that Sutherland frequently but rather casually treated corporations as high status persons too, just as did the authors of the codes of ethics described earlier (Hopkins, 1980).

As Geis pointed out long ago, "The major difficulty in *White Collar Crime* as criminological research lies in Sutherland's striking inability to differentiate between the corporations themselves and their executive and management personnel" (1962). For example, Sutherland's demonstration of the relevance of differential association theory to white-collar crime begins with a discussion of documents relating to how businessmen are inducted into illegal behavior by other businessmen (1949:234–41). But soon the discussion moves to diffusion of illegal practices, and here the object of inquiry is corporations, not business personnel. Sutherland unthinkingly attributes human capabilities to these corporations: "When one firm devises (an illegal method) of increasing profits, other firms become aware of the method and adopt it, perhaps a little more quickly and a little more generally if the firms are competitors in the same market than if they are not competitors" (1949:241). He never asked the significant theoretical question, "By what process does a firm 'become aware of' and 'adopt' illegal processes?" Had he done so, he would have been reminded that humans behave but entities do not.

Vacillation between concern for the criminality of business personnel and the criminality of anthropomorphized corporations also appears in Sutherland's discussion of the psychological characteristics of offenders. This discussion appears, significantly enough, in a chapter entitled "Variations in the Crimes of Corporations" (1949:257). Sutherland first notes that corporations, being fictitious, obviously cannot suffer from human psychiatric disorders such as feelings of inferiority, regression to infancy, and Oedipus complexes. Then he assaults his own common sense by assuming that as corporations commit crimes they do so without acting through their officers, directors, employees, or agents. This assumption comes as he shows that variations in the crime rates of individual corporations are associated with variations in the positions of these corporations in the economic structure and then argues that the corporations, not their executives, are the significant actors:

> Manufacturing and mining corporations seldom violate laws regarding advertising because they seldom engage in advertising for sales purposes. This variation in practices is related to the position they hold in the economic structure rather than to the personal traits of the executives of the corporations . . . p. 262 Two facts are especially significant. First, many corporations violate the antitrust law in certain industrial areas and not in others, although the officers and directors are the same in all these areas . . . That is, behavior as to violations of law varies without variations in persons involved in the behavior. Second, many corporations which violated the antitrust law forty years ago are still violating that law, although the personnel of the corporation has changed completely. That is, variations in persons occur without variations in behavior as to the antitrust law [1949:264], p. 264.

Sutherland's materials on the criminal careers of businessmen suggest that a corporation's crimes are but manifestations of the crimes of its executives. In retrospect, it seems incredible that he did not use these materials in his discussions of what is now known as corporate crime on organizational crime. The fact remains, however, that he did not formally attribute similarities and consistencies in law violation among corporations to socialization into criminal behavior of new executives by old ones, as Marilyn Cash Mathews recently did (1984).[8] Such attribution is consistent with the theory of differential association and differential social organization.

It appears that *White Collar Crime* has become an influential criminological classic as much because Sutherland anthropomorphized corporations as because he defined white-collar crime as crime committed by persons of respectability and high social status. The work showed that the prevailing causal theories were incorrect, being based on biased samples, but it really was not much of a theoretical contribution. Thus, as I just indicated, Sutherland neglected to show how differential association or any other social psychological

---

[8]Sutherland often made this attribution in conversations and correspondence, however. For example, in a letter written to Frederic M. Thrasher on September 18, 1944, Sutherland said:

> Up to the present time I have done very little work on case histories of white-collar criminals but have made studies of corporations rather than of persons. The paper which I gave in Chicago was a statistical analysis of records of courts and administrative commissions as to the 70 largest industrial and commercial corporations in the U.S. (excluding the petroleum corporations, and also public utilities and financial corporations). I am enclosing a tabulation of the results. . . . The persons responsible for the actions on which courts and commissions made decisions against the corporations are the executive officers and the boards of directors. They include persons such as John D. Rockefeller, J.P. Morgan, Henry Ford, Julius Rosenwald, Harold Swift, etc.

But then Sutherland vacillates, just as he was to do in White Collar Crime, published five years later:

> My general inclination is to conclude that the criminal record of a corporation is a function of its opportunity to violate the law rather than of the personnel concerned. This makes big business an area of criminal culture, so far as the laws covered are concerned, with everyone participating who has been subjected to that culture, provided he has opportunity.

process might possibly work to produce criminal conduct in the fictitious persons called corporations. His macrolevel (sociological, epidemiological) hypothesis that rates of corporate crime are associated with structural conditions, such as position in the economic world (differential social organization), seems reasonable enough. But that is as far as one can go when the object of study is not a human being.

By drawing a distinction between "occupational crime" and "corporate crime," Clinard and Quinney (1973) tried to reduce the confusion introduced by Sutherland. The former was defined as "violation of the criminal law in the course of activity in a legitimate occupation," so that, in fact, only some occupational crime is white-collar crime in the Sutherland sense of "crime committed by a person of respectability and high social status in the course of his occupation." Occupational crime differs from corporate crime principally in that it consists of "offenses committed by individuals for themselves in the course of their occupations and the offenses of employees against their employers," and corporate crime consists of "the offenses committed by corporate officials for their corporation and the offenses of the corporation itself" (1973:188).[9] Braithwaite consistently defines corporate crime as "the conduct of a corporation, or individuals acting on behalf of the corporation, that is proscribed by law" (1982:1466)

Note that these definitions of corporate crime really show no concern for the differences between corporate crimes committed by persons and crimes committed by organizations. In their recent monumental work, Clinard and Yeager seem to correct this defect by deleting "corporate officials" from the definition: "A corporate crime is any act committed by corporations that is punished by the state, regardless of whether it is punished under administrative, civil, or criminal law" (1980:16). Almost immediately, however, they reintroduce Sutherland's ambiguity by going back to the idea that corporate crime also is perpetrated by real persons:

> Corporate and occupational crime can be confused. If a corporate official violates the law in action for the corporation it is corporate crime, but if he gains personal benefit in the commission of a crime against the corporations, as in the case of embezzlement of corporate funds, it is an occupational crime [1980:18].

This blurring of the distinction between corporate crimes committed by persons and corporate crimes committed by organizations asks theoreticians to use one causal theory to explain both, an impossible task. The meddling is

---

[9]Five years after the appearance of Clinard and Quinney's publication, Andrew Hopkins of the Australian National University could discern that it had a bandwagon effect: "Most writers . . . use the term [corporate crime] to refer to crime committed by the corporation itself or on behalf of the corporation by its employees, in furtherance of the corporate interest" (1978:214). Similarly, Georges Kellens of the University of Liège, Belgium, recently declared. "It is generally accepted now that white collar crime designates acts committed against business, for instance a computer fraud within a company, while organizational crime means acts committed by business against others" (1985:15).

reflected in much of Clinard and Yeager's prose, just as it is in Sutherland's. For instance, in a single paragraph these authors first discuss "corporations whose executives have knowingly concealed" unsafe products or occupational hazards, and then give two examples: (1) "Firestone officials knew that they were marketing a dangerous tire in their radial '500s.'" (2) "Allied Chemical also knew from its own laboratory research that Kepone is a potential carcinogen. It went ahead and marketed the deadly substance anyway." The first example reports on real people, the second on a fictitious person. But then Clinard and Yeager blur the distinction even more by using the plural *their,* not *its,* to refer to a corporation's possessions: "Many workers were subsequently poisoned, and miles of Virginia's James River ruined due to Allied's dumping of their Kepone wastes" (1980:10–11). This compromise nicely avoids the question of whether the action was that of the corporation or of corporation executives.

Clinard and Yeager's one short reference to organizational crime also blurs the distinction between crimes by persons and crimes by organizations: "Corporate crime actually is *organizational* crime occurring in the context of complex relationships and expectations among boards of directors, executives, and managers, on the one hand, and among parent corporations, corporate divisions, and subsidiaries, on the other" (1980:17). Consistently, their chapter on corporate organization and criminal behavior (pp. 43–73) vacillates between the view that the corporation (or parts of it) is a rational actor and the view that so-called corporate actions actually are the actions of managers. When the latter view prevails, causal explanation of executive criminality is stressed, and "the making of a corporate criminal" is said to be a matter of socialization of subordinates by elites (differential association). When the corporation itself is considered the actor, Clinard and Yeager's stress is on explaining crime rates, and variation in them is attributed to organizations' differing economic and political environments. This explanation is not very nourishing: "Economic pressures and other factors operate in a corporate environment that is conducive to unethical and illegal practices" (1980:132).[10]

---

[10]Reference to vague "pressures," "factors," "forces," and "tensions" is a popular way of "explaining" corporate crime, be it the crimes committed by executives or those said to be committed by organizations. Clinard and Yeager write about "pressures" on management and "forces" driving executives to violate the law. They use one or the other of these words seven times on the first several pages of a discussion of managers' illegal behavior (1980:273–76). Gross also accounts for executive misconduct with these atmospheric concepts (1980:64), which are synonymous for ignorance about the actual schedules of rewards and punishments that are used by people to modify other people's behavior.

Here, Clinard and Yeager's attempt to account for variations in the crimes said to be committed by corporations is obviously weak and uninformative because they rely on the same mystical "pressures" and "factors" that they use to account for crimes perpetrated by managers. Other criminologists who use these terms have produced equally lame "explanations" of why corporations violate the law. Diane Vaughan, for example, asserts that organizations seek economic success by unlawful means because they experience "pressures" to make money and also experience "social pressures" to stay in business (1983:62). She also uses "factors," "tensions," structural factors," and "structural tensions" (p. 67) to refer to these "pressures" for organiza-

Sutherland's vacillation between concern for the criminality of business personnel of respectability and high social status and the criminality of anthropomorphized corporations also has been duplicated in the writings of several other sociologists. The most noteworthy of these, perhaps, is Edward Gross, a distinguished scholar who specializes in the study of organizations, not crime. In an attempt to educate criminologists on the subject of organizational crime, Gross asserts that "all organizations are inherently criminogenic" (1978:56). In documenting this theoretical assertion, he shifts back and forth between the notion that organizations commit crimes and the notion that organizational personnel commit them. On the one hand, he says, "there is built into the structure of organizations an inherent inducement for the *organization* itself to engage in crime" (1978:56). On the other hand, he insists that organizations do not behave: "Although organizations are here held to be criminogenic and although courts no longer exhibit much hesitation in charging the organization itself with crime, organizations of course cannot themselves act—they must have agents who act for them" (1978:65).

Once people accept the fiction that organizations behave, they tend to promote it. Gross is no exception. His principal point is one adapted from Hayworth (1959), namely that an organization may be considered as acting when "what is meant is that the organization is *responsible* for the outcome" (1980:59). But a corporation is not responsible, at least in the sense of the criminal law, until the law declares it to be a person. Moreover, even if events represent the outcome of the patterns of activities that make up the "behavior" of this fictitious person, and even if the quality of the outcome "depends minimally on the peculiar qualities of the [biological] persons who make it possible," as Gross put it (1980:59), the fact remains that biological persons are responsible for establishing and maintaining the patterns and, thus for the action. "If [a human] were to arrange the workers differently, something different would happen," Gross concedes. But he then argues, in contradiction, that organizations, not humans, commit crimes because they require that persons be able to implement criminal patterns and then socialize them in ways such that they become willing to do so. He attributes all of this to the performance emphasis found in complex organizations, saying that when organizations (not people) face difficulty in meeting their profit

---

tions to engage in "unlawful organizational behavior." In addition, she says, "structure, process and transactions systems" are "factors" that "create opportunities for organizations to act as offenders" (p. 68). Further, she insists, the "regulatory environment" also is a "factor" in violation (pp. 96, 101).

In the world of "pressures," "forces," and "factors" there is no causality, so much uncritical use of atmospheric and hydraulic concepts can only lead to the conclusion that crime can be forever studied but never explained. Vaughan draws this conclusion, thus displaying an attitude of scientific despair shared by many criminologists:

The conditions and combinations of factors that do or do not result in unlawful behavior cannot yet be unraveled. They cannot, therefore, be discussed in the language of causality, but rather in terms of factors that facilitate, generate, encourage, or present opportunities to attain resources through unlawful conduct [1983:68; also see Vaughan, 1986].

goals they resort to crime. His criminological theory, then, is a simple one: poverty causes crime.

After presenting this macrolevel theory, Gross turns to the social psychological processes involved as the "agents" (corporation executives) of organizations come to commit crimes. Again, his key idea is that criminality stems from stress on performance and goal attainment. Ambitious, shrewd, and morally flexible managers are most likely to make it to the top, Gross says, and these are the persons who commit crimes on behalf of corporations (1978:71). Moral flexibility is especially significant, he continues, because socialization to the attitudes, values, and behavior patterns of successful superiors is the active crime producing process. But this idea, which is consistent with differential association theory, is soon garbled because, to Gross, the demand for a nondemanding moral code is made by an anthropomorphized organization, not by the corporation executives he has been discussing. Managers are socialized to change their moral beliefs, he says, "so that they match whatever is called for by the organization" (1978:69).[11] But organizations, being only entities, do not make demands; people do.

At the beginning of the follow-up essay (1980) Gross seems to correct his error by noting once more that organizations cannot act:

> Although the law has created these "persons," they cannot, of course, act autonomously; agents must act for them. Hence when we speak of corporate "actors" it must be recognized that there are always biological persons who act, in the manner of puppeteers, to put the show on the road [1980:54].

Still, Gross insists, a theoretical problem of disentangling people and organizations remains (1980:52). His proposed disentanglement is rather snarled, however, because it includes the legal fiction that corporations are persons and, moreover, that these persons "run afoul of the law" even if they do not deliberately break it (1980:52). More generally, corporations "take on lives of their own" (1980:58), and corporate crime follows from their need to create an orderly market (1980:53), their ways of integrating persons (1980:61), and their performance emphasis (1980:64). Consistently, Gross describes Staw and Szwajkowski's study of antitrust law violations (1975) and then concludes: "When these organizations faced difficulty in meeting their profit goals, they resorted to crime in order to do so" (1980:64; also see Gross, 1978:57).

Sets or organizations, such as sports leagues, cartels, trusts, industries, and oligopolies, also are clothed with the attributes of people: "The organiza-

---

[11] Vaughan, too, erroneously insists that organizations, not executives, socialize employees: "The tendency for organizations to select members like those already there, to devote resources to socializing employees . . . produces employees willing to act in the organization's behalf" (1986:7). Her discussion of policy implications nevertheless seems consistent with criminological theory that locates the cause of criminal behavior in social learning and differential social organization: "In order to alter the behavior of individuals, policy must aim at altering structural determinants of individual choice: the competitive environment, organizational characteristics, and the regulatory environment" (1986:12).

tions not only know of one another's existence, their own success depends further on a continuous monitoring of one another's behavior" (Gross, 1980:69). The crime of price fixing, too, is discussed as though it were an arrangement between organizations, not people: "The companies seem to have tacitly recognized that once they get into a battle about prices, they can easily destroy each other: (1980:70). But a U.S. attorney, noting that corporations can act only through their officers, directors, employees or agents, has come to a more realistic conclusion: "Corporations don't commit crimes, people do" (Martin, 1985).[12] In one famous case illustrating this point, Robert L. Crandall, president and chief operating officer of American Airlines, suggested in a telephone conversation with Howard Putnam, president of Braniff Airways, that price fixing might solve the financial problems that both were experiencing: "I think it's dumb as hell . . . to sit here and pound . . . each other and neither of us making a [word deleted] dime," Crandall said. When Putnam asked, "Do you have a suggestion for me?" Crandall replied, "Yes, I have a suggestion for you. Raise your goddamn fares 20 percent. I'll raise mine the next morning. . . . You'll make more money and I will too" (Rothbart, 1983).

A profound criminological problem is raised by Gross's, Clinard and Yeager's, Sutherland's, and many others' blurring of the distinction between crimes committed by corporations and crimes committed by executives and other managers. This is the problem of intentionality. In courthouses, the rise of the legal fiction that corporations commit crimes gave a severe jolt to the traditional criminal-law principle that performing an outlawed act does not alone make the doer guilty of crime. The actor also must have intended the act to be a crime. The legal fiction also stops theoretical criminologists in their tracks because it undermines every social psychological theory about the causation of crime that has been formulated and every theory that might be formulated in the future. Even if corporations are called persons for purposes of arguments, these juristic persons—unlike real people—cannot have criminal intentions.[13] It is not unreasonable to conclude that the corporation therefore

---

[12]William Safire, the famous columnist, agrees with Martin but notes the negative implications for general deterrence. In a column titled "Companies Don't Swindle Banks, People Do," he refers to the 1985 scandal in which "a gang of E.F. Hutton & Co . . . systematically bilked tens of millions of dollars out of 400 banks." Safire goes on to disagree with Attorney General Edwin Meese, who had announced that the conviction of the company "makes it clear that white-collar crime will not be tolerated." "On the contrary," Safire concluded, "the pretense that no humans beings operate E.F. Hutton makes it clear to the business world that if your company is shot through with managers involved in a huge swindle, the Meese Justice Department will limit the liability to the corporation. None of the guilty officers will have to pay" (Safire, 1985).

[13]Behaviorists, including the author, do not accept routine assumptions about the effects on human behavior of mentalistic mechanisms such as "mind" and "will,." I long ago tried to show (Cressey, 1953, 1954) that a person's attempts to achieve a criminal goal (called "intentions" in the criminal law) are linguistic rather than mentalistic, as are the person's reasons for such action ("motives"). At the criminal law level, the defendant's intent ("I am going to kill my neighbor") but not the defendant's motive ("because he let his dog run in my garden") is officially considered by judges and juries as they make decisions about guilt. Considerations of motives is officially permissible only when deciding on the proper sentence of persons who have been found guilty.

is incapable of committing a crime (Mueller, 1957; Valesquez, 1983). But this logical conclusion is not drawn in the criminal courts and, as we have seen, it is not drawn by some criminologists either.

Some people unthinkingly claim that corporations deliberately commit crimes. A science reporter, for example, recently used the following language to describe a case involving the Eli Lilly Company: "According to the Justice Department, Lilly was fully aware of, but delayed telling U.S. authorities about, ten cases in which patients taking Oraflex had suffered fatal or debilitating liver or kidney disease" (Marshall, 1985). Sometimes people hold, alternatively, that corporations are guilty of crimes even if they are incapable of formulating criminal intent. For example, the just-quoted reporter also says, "On 21 August, Eli Lilly & Co. wrote to its stockholders to say that it had negotiated an end to a federal investigation that 'puts to rest any speculation regarding intentional misconduct on the part of the company' in the marketing of Oraflex, an arthritis medicine suspected of causing liver and kidney failure . . . Lilly's strong emphasis [was] on the fact that it was guilty only of 'technical misdemeanors.'"

The Lilly Company could be guilty of "technical misdemeanors" even if no one intended to do wrong because legislatures have enacted statutes which hold persons, including fictitious corporate ones, liable for certain crimes, even if there is no psychological state such as criminal intent or *mens rea*. These strict liability statutes modify the ancient legal principle holding that, by definition, every crime involves an intentional act. Appelate courts have ruled that such statutes are constitutional, despite their radical character.

The best example of a strict liability crime is murder under the felony-murder doctrine of criminal law. Under the rule of strict liability (called "straight liability" in British courts), if someone dies because the defendant committed a felony, the defendant is guilty of murder. For example, a defendant who intentionally committed arson in order to defraud an insurance company is guilty of murder if a firefighter dies trying to knock down the flames. So far as murder is concerned, the defendant's intent is not considered. Another example is so-called statutory rape. If a man has sexual intercourse with a girl who is beneath the age of consent, he is guilty of a crime, even if she eagerly cooperates. He is strictly liable. The fact that he might have believed the girl to be of legal age is not officially considered. Criminal intent or *mens rea* is not an element of statutory rape.

Corporations, not being real persons, cannot intentionally commit crimes such as larceny, murder, or even fraud. Accordingly, most of the crimes said to have been committed by them are, like felony-murder and statutory rape, strict liability offenses. This means that the corporation is held criminally liable for the offense if the offense occurs.

Consider, for example, violations of the Sherman Antitrust Act of 1890, a law that stipulated that "every contract, combination in the form of trust or otherwise, or conspiracy in restrain of trade" is a crime (misdemeanor) punishable by a fine of $5,000. At first federal judges took this statement literally, and corporations were held strictly liable for their violations. But then, as I have shown elsewhere, the "rule of reason" came to replace strict liability; this was a way of insisting that criminal intent must be present before there can be a finding of guilt (Cressey, 1976:225). For example, what appellate courts were fifty years ago calling a "conscious parallelism" in the pricing of products by "competing" corporation executives was not taken to be evidence of "conspiracy in restraint of trade." The U.S. attorney general at the time (1937) complained that the courts refused to adopt the only practical criterion of restrain of trade—price uniformity and price rigidity—and insisted, instead, on trying to determine whether a fictitious personality has an evil state of mind.

The substitution of an evil intent for strict liability made it difficult to convict corporation executives of violating the Sherman Act, and it made it all but impossible to convict corporations themselves. Probably the substitution was made because, in the cultures of federal courthouses, there was, and is, a sympathetic understanding of corporations and their executives. But it is possible, too, that judges have resisted holding corporations guilty under strict liability statutes because they believe that courts have a duty to defend the traditional principle that an act is not criminal unless the actor intended it.[14] Even today, "monopolizing" in violation of antitrust law must be "nasty monopolizing" to be illegal; "no-fault" (strict-liability) restraint of trade is not enough (Clinard and Yeager, 1980:137–38).

Sutherland's treatment of criminal intent and strict liability is consistent with, but just as confusing as, the fact that he defined white-collar crimes as crimes committed by real, high-status persons but conducted his research on the crimes of fictitious persons called corporations. On the one hand, he argued that corporations or corporation executives (he was not clear about which of these he had in mind) intend at least some fraudulent ("patently false") advertisements: "For example, an advertisement of gum-wood furniture as 'mahogany' would seldom be an accidental error and would generally result from a state of mind which deviated from honesty by more than the natural tendency of human beings to feel proud of their handiwork" (1949:42). On the other hand, he noted that due to strict liability statutes, white-collar crime is like ordinary crime in the sense that a showing of criminal intent is not required in all prosecutions of either kind of crime. "The important consideration here," he said, "is that the criteria which have been used in defining

---

[14]In our culture, with its emphasis on due process of law, citizens demand that they be notified in advance of the precise nature of any deviation that is punishable by state officials so they can avoid it. When strict-liability statutes make them criminally liable for behavior that they could not avoid or in some other way did not intend, they are righteously indignant. Accordingly, strict-liability statutes must be administered very gingerly. Pollner (1970, 1979) long ago showed, for example, that traffic-court judges find it necessary—in the interest of justice—to let persons who are guilty under strict-liability statutes enter unofficial but exonerating pleas of "guilty with excuse." By the same token judges seem to look with a fishy eye at strict-liability statutes that ask them to hold even fictitious persons criminally liable for behavior that was not intended by any person, real or fictitious.

white collar crime are not categorically different from the criteria used in defining some other crimes" (1949:41).

This consideration governed Sutherland's research on the crimes of corporations. He did not acknowledge, in *White Collar Crime* or elsewhere, that most if not all the laws violated by the seventy corporations he studied had strict liability provisions. More important, he did not even speculate about how differential association theory might make sense of criminal behavior that was not intended by a real person, let alone by a juristic one. As already noted, no social psychological theory can make sense of behavior that is not intended, be it an ordinary crime such as felony murder or a white-collar crime such as restraint of trade, false advertising, or unfair labor practices.

Schrager and Short have recently walked in Sutherland's footsteps on this issue (1978). The legal literature teams with discussions of criminal intent, strict liability, and corporate criminal liability (Hall, 1982; 266–94). By and large, however, Schrager and Short's discussion of organizational crime ignores the criminological implications of these discussions. They note, clearly enough, that "the white-collar crime perspective does not deal adequately with unintended consequences of organizational behavior," but they do not really remedy this in their discussion of "organizational crimes," defined as "illegal acts committed by an individual or a group of individuals in a legitimate formal organization, consumers or the general public" (1978:411–12). This because they first make the puzzling claim that strict liability is rarely used in criminal prosecutions, follow that with an assertion that "lack of intention is typical of organizational offenses having physical consequences: (1978: 409–10), and then assert further that the law's requirement of criminal intent is met by their definition's stipulation that, to be organizational crime, the action must be committed in accordance with the operative goals of the organization (1978:412).

There are at least three fuzzy points in their definition and their commentary on it. First, *crime* and *criminal* are technical legal terms. Behavior cannot be a "crime" unless it is in violation of criminal law, meaning that it has been declared to be punishable by the state. And, as I have already noted, if a man does not intend his harmful act and if statute holds him strictly liable for the act, then his behavior is not an "illegal act" or an "offense"—at least not a criminal one—because he is not guilty. Obviously, it therefore cannot be an "organizational crime."

Second, the last part of Schrager and Short's definition is gratuitous because no act is a crime unless it does harm of some kind. "Serious physical or economic impact" is a characteristic of all felonies. Schrager and Short seem not to have noticed that violations of occupational health and safety regulations, for example, do not always have a *serious* impact but are crimes nevertheless. The issue is not one of seriousness. It is one of whether the offense is properly called "organizational."

Finally, to discern that an act was performed in accordance with organizational goals—as Schrager and Short's definition of organizational crime requires—is to deal with the legal problem of motivation, not of intent. That this is an error can be made obvious by use of a fictitious, but illustrative, case: Suppose the leaders of a terrorist organization announced that one of their operational organizational goals is to overthrow the government of the nation in which they reside. They agree that they need automatic weapons to do so. Suppose, further, that three members of the organization, hearing of a machine gun for sale, plot a bank robbery in which they will work as a three-person team to pull off the job. Then they harm the bank's investors by robbing them of $23,142.33, and they use the money to buy the gun. Now the *intent* of each of these three members was to rob. The *motive* of each was to acquire some money that could be used for revolutionary purposes, in accordance with the announced operational organizational goals. Each of the three is guilty of robbery and, perhaps, conspiracy, but the motive for the robbery and conspiracy is not what makes them guilty.

To underline the importance of the distinction between intent and motive, suppose that after the robbers in this fictitious case have been arrested, convicted, and sent to prison, they send a note to the editor of *Crime and Social Justice* asserting they are political prisoners. The assertion is based on the fact that their robbery was carried out in accordance with the operative goals of their organization, which are political in nature. At law, however, they are not political criminals or "organizational criminals," for that matter. Their crime was very much unlike the crime of political criminals who have violated laws stating, for example, that "harming the patriotic interests of the people" is punishable by imprisonment. Moreover, their motive (to get money with which to advance their political cause) could not have been officially taken into consideration by the judge or jury deciding their guilt. Instead, a judge or jury necessarily found that their intent was to rob, and a combination of this *mens rea* and a harmful act, prohibited by law, is what got them convicted. If motives are used to determine guilt, as Schrager and Short seem to recommend, then anyone whose motives were not acceptable to judge or jury would be guilty of organizational crime.

It could be argued that all this law talk is beside the point because Schrager and Short are merely saying, in a fuzzy way, that criminological theorists ought to (1) note that organizational crime is an important variety of white-collar crime, itself not a legal category, and then (2) use the organizational criminals' motives ("in accordance with the operative goals of the organization") to explain their behavior. I have been criminology's principal proponent of the notion that this kind of explanation is consistent with differential association theory and ought to be encouraged (Cressey 1954). But Schrager and Short actually do not use the concept of organizational crime in this social psychological way. This is clear in their discussion of intentionality. They want to shift the focus of inquiry *away* from motives, such as "I kept my mouth shut about the dangerous design of the brakes because I knew the boss would fire me if I didn't," and *toward* the objective characteristics of criminal acts. Significantly, this shift would make organizational crimes into strict liability offenses which are not explainable in differential association terms or in any other social psychological framework:

> In view of the often impenetrable difficulty of evaluating the motives behind illegal organizational actions, the definition shifts the focus of inquiry to the objective characteristics of these actions. The logic is similar to that employed in the legal concept of strict liability, which holds an offender responsible for illegal behavior without regard to the existence or absence of *mens rea* (a guilty mind) [Schrager and Short, 1978:412].

In conclusion, let it be said that it is just as ridiculous for criminologists to try to explain criminal behavior that was not intended as it is for judges to try to determine whether a fictitious person has an evil state of mind. Because corporations cannot intend actions, none of their criminality can be explained in the framework of behavioral theory. It is time for criminologists to eradicate this embarrassment by acknowledging that corporation crimes and organizational crimes are phantom phenomena. Such acknowledgment will not lead to abandoning criminological concern for white-collar offenses and offenders. On the contrary, the strength of this area of criminological research and theory will grown in proportion to the degree to which criminologists first recognize that only real persons have the psychological capacity to intend crimes, and then focus their analytical and theoretical skills on these persons.

Auditors and other accountants have already found an appropriate name for much of the behavior in question: management fraud.[15] This is deliberate deception by managers that injures others through misleading financial statements (Elliot and Willingham, 1980:4). Fraud of this kind is by definition perpetrated by corporation executives and other managers rather than by organizations. It is committed on behalf of corporations, not against them. For example, income obtained for firms by means of price fixing, bribery, and false advertising as well as profits obtained for firms by means of industrial pollution of air and water, violations of labor laws, and the manufacture and marketing of dangerous products are all maintained or increased by use of false (and thereby fraudulent) books and records. The techniques that managers use to commit crime on behalf of corporations are the same as those used by embezzlers to commit crimes against corporations. (For an illustration, see Clinard and Yeager, 1980:162). The verbalizations (motives) probably are the same in both cases, too (Cressey, 1980). Robert Elliot and John Willingham, partners in one of the world's largest auditing firms, have noted that there is a practical reason for determining why such behavior is so widespread: "Management frauds are of primary importance in the family of business improprieties because to a large extent the health of the capital markets rests on confidence that financial statements are not fraudulent. Thus, the detection and

---

[15]The term was coined in the later 1970s by Stanley Sporkin, then chief of the enforcement section of the Securities and Exchange Commission.

prevention of fraudulent financial statements goes to the heart of the functioning of the economy" (Elliot and Willingham, 1980, viii).

Despite my emphasis on explaining the criminality of biological persons, not of fictitious ones, I am not here proposing that corporations do not commit crime. Criminologists, like everyone else, must use the only permissible definition of crime, the legal one. This means that criminologists must accept the fact that the criminal law treats corporations as persons and says that these persons commit crimes.

What I am proposing is that criminologists acknowledge that no theory dealing with crime causation can make sense of strict-liability criminality or any other criminality that is not intended. Corporations and organizations, being inanimate, cannot formulate criminal intent. Accordingly, as Geis pointed out a quarter of a century ago, "For the purpose of criminological analysis . . . corporations cannot be considered persons, except by recourse to the same type of extrapolatory fiction that once brought about the punishment of inanimate objects" (1962:163).

It is not reasonable to try to locate the cause of unintentional, accidental, behavior that is called murder under the felony-murder doctrine. By the same token, it is not reasonable to try to identify the cause of crimes that are said to be committed by organizations. These crimes are by definition exceptional to any behavioral theory. Once criminological theoreticians acknowledge that fact they will be able to concentrate more attention, time, and energy on the question of why managers steal for the company as well as from it. As Michael Levi has put it, "There has been much sententious discussion of the need for an organizational perspective in the analysis of corporate crime, but adequate theorizing must mediate organizational norms through individual actors who make decisions . . ." (1985:45).

REFERENCES

Associated Press. 1985. "Military Contract Fraud Charged." *Santa Barbara News Press*, November 22.

Braithwaite, John. 1982. "Enforced Self-Reguylation: A New Strategy for Corporate Crime Control." *Michigan Law Review* 80: 1466–1507.

Clinard, Marshall B., and R. Quinney R. 1973. *Criminal Behavior Systems: A Typology*. 2d ed. New York: Holt Rinehart & Winston.

Clinard, Marshall B., and P. Yeager. 1980. *Corporate Crime*. New York: Free Press.

Cressey, Donald R. 1953. *Other People's Money: A Study in the Social Psychology of Embezzlement*. Glencoe, Ill.: Free Press.

———. 1954. "The Differential Association Theory and Compulsive Crime." *Journal of Criminal Law, Criminology, and Police Science* 45:49–64.

———. 1960. "Epidemiology and Individual Conduct: A Case from Criminology." *Pacific Sociological Review* 3:847–58.

———. 1965. "Prison Organizations." In *Handbook of Organizations*, edited by James G. March, pp. 1023–70. Chicago: Rand McNally.

———. 1969. *Theft of the Nation: The Structure and Operations of Organized Crime in America*. New York: Harper & Row.

————. 1976. "Restraint of Trade, Recidivism and Delinquent Neighborhoods." In *Delinquency, Crime and Society*, edited by J.F. Short, Jr. Chicago: University of Chicago Press.

————. 1980. "Management Fraud, Accounting Controls, and Criminological Theory." In *Management Fraud: Detection and Deterrence*, edited by R.K. Elliott and J.J. Willingham, pp. 117–47. New York: Petrocelli.

Elliott, Robert K., and J.J. Willingham. 1980. *Management Fraud: Detection and Deterrence.* New York: Petrocelli.

Geis, Gilbert. 1962. "Toward a Delineation of White-Collar Crime Offenses." *Sociological Inquiry* 32:160–71.

Gross, Edward. 1978. "Organizational Crime: A Theoretical Perspective." In *Studies in Symbolic Interaction*, vol. 2, edited by D. Denzin. Greenwich, Connecticut: JAI Press.

————. 1980. "Organizational Structure and Organizational Crime." In *White-Collar Crime: Theory and Research*, edited by G. Geis and E. Stotland. Beverly Hills, Calif.: Sage Publications.

Hall, Jerome. 1982. *Law, Social Science and Criminal Theory.* Littleton, Colo.: Rothman.

Hayworth, L. 1959. "Do Organizations Act?" *Ethics* 70:59–63. (Cited by Gross, 1980.)

Hopkins, Andrew. 1978. "The Anatomy of Corporate Crime." In *The Two Faces of Deviance*, edited by J. Braithwaite and P. Wilson. Brisbane, Australia: University of Queensland Press.

————. 1980. "Controlling Corporate Deviance." *Criminology* 18:198–214.

Katz, Jack. 1980. "Concerted Ignorance: The Social Psychology of Cover-up." In *Management Fraud: Detection and Deterrence*, edited by R.K. Elliott and J.J. Willingham. New York: Petrocelli.

Levi, Michael. 1985. "A Criminological and Sociological Approach to Theories and Research into Economic Crime." In *Economic Crime: Programs for Future Research*, edited by D. Magnusson, pp. 32–72. Stockholm: The National Council for Crime Prevention.

Maitland, Ian. 1986. Review of *The Impact of Publicity on Corporate Offenders* by Brent Fisse and John Braithwaite. *Contemporary Sociology* 15:380–81.

Marshall, Eliot. 1985. "Guilty Plea Puts Oraflex Case to Rest." *Science* 229:1079.

Martin, John S. 1985. "Corporate Criminals or Criminal Corporation?" *Wall Street Journal*, June 19.

Mathews, Marilynn Cash. 1984. "Corporate Crime: External vs. Internal Regulation." Ph.D. dissertation, University of California, Santa Barbara.

Miller, Arthur S. 1968. *The Supreme Court and American Capitalism.* New York: Free Press.

Mueller, Gerhard O.W. 1957. "Mens Rea and the Corporation." *University of Pittsburgh Law Review* 19:21–50.

Pasztor, Andry. 1985. "Bell's Probe of Illegal Overdrafts Is Disputed by Lawmakers, Regulators." *Wall Street Journal*, September 13.

Pollner, Melvin. 1970. "On the Foundations of Mundane Reasoning." Ph.D. dissertation, University of California, Santa Barbara.

————. 1979. "Explicative Transactions: Making and Managing Meaning in Traffic Courts." In *Everyday Language: Studies in Ethnomethodology*, edited by G. Psathas, pp. 227–48. New York: Irvington.

Rothbart, Dean. 1983. "American Air, Its President, Get Trust Suit Voided." *Wall Street Journal*, September 14.

Safire, William. 1985. "Companies Don't Swindle Banks, People Do." *Santa Barbara News-Press*, May 12.

Schrager, Laura Shill, and J.F. Short, Jr. 1978. "Toward a Sociology of Organizational Crime." *Social Problems* 125:407–19.

Shudson, Charles B., Ashton B. Onellion, and Ellen Hochstedler. 1984. "Nailing an Omelet to the Wall: Prosecuting Nursing Home Homicide." In *Corporations as Criminals*, edited by E. Hochstedler, pp. 128–56. Beverly Hills, Calif.: Sage Publications.

Staw, Barry M., and E. Szwajkowski. 1975. "The Scarcity-Munificence Component of Organizational Environments and the Commission of Illegal Acts." *Administrative Science Quarterly* 19:345–94.

Sutherland, Edwin H. 1949. *White Collar Crime*. New York: Dryden, 1946.

Sutherland, Edwin H., and Donald R. Cressey 1978. *Criminology*. New York: J.B. Lippincott.

Vaughan, Diane. 1983. *Controlling Unlawful Organization Behavior*. Chicago: University of Chicago Press.

———. 1986. "Organizational Misconduct: The Connection between Theory and Policy." Paper read at the Annual Meetings of the Law and Society Association, Chicago.

Velasquez, Manuel. 1983. "Why Corporations Are Not Morally Responsible for Anything They Do." *Business and Professional Ethics Journal* 3:1–18.

A Rational Choice Theory of Corporate Crime

RAYMOND PATERNOSTER AND SALLY SIMPSON

FORMAL DETERRENCE AND CORPORATE CRIME

. . . There are many reasons to believe that a traditional model of deterrence should be helpful in understanding corporate crime. It has been argued that white-collar (and especially corporate)[3] offenders are less committed to offending than conventional criminals (Chambliss 1967). Further, in their business and personal lives, managers are risk-averse, "unwilling to engage in ac-

[3]White-collar crime is defined by Sutherland (1949:9) as "crime committed by a person of respectability and high social status in the course of his occupation." Corporate crime, as a subtype of white-collar crime, is "any act committed by corporations that is punished by the state, regardless of whether it is punished under administrative, civil, or criminal law" (Clinard and Yeager 1980:16). In the latter, criminal actors include individual decision makers (typically corporate managers) and organizations that violate the law in the pursuit of corporate objectives.

PANEL 12   Charity Begins at Home?

In April 1995, a federal jury in New York City found guilty William Aramony, former president of United Way of America. Prosecutors alleged that Aramony had fraudulently diverted for his own use nearly $2 million of the charity's money. The stolen funds were used to pay for vacations, chauffeurs, luxury apartments, and exotic vacations for the defendant and his teenage girlfriend. Other monies were given to a friend who operated a charitable company, and large sums were funneled into Aramony's personal accounts. His attorney unsuccessfully argued that Aramony's crimes were caused by shrinkage in the area of the brain that controls impulses and inhibitions. He also argued in mitigation that Aramony had "given more to this country than any man I have ever known. . . . [H]e has fed the hungry, clothed the naked [and] given homes to the homeless." Convicted of multiple charges, the 67-year-old Aramony was sentenced to seven years in prison.

Source: New York Times, June 23, 1995, p. A14.

---

tivity that poses even minimal threats to the future of the corporation or their own position in it" (Schlegel 1990:16). Therefore, formal sanctions such as fines or incarceration provide a meaningful threat to potential corporate offenders.

Another argument for the deterrability of corporate crime is the nature of the offense. Corporate crimes are instrumental and strategic. Typical crimes are described as "calculated and deliberative and directed to economic gain" (Kadish 1977:305). They are "almost never crimes of passion; they are not spontaneous or emotional, but calculated risks taken by rational actors" (Braithwaite and Geis 1982:302). Accordingly, these offenses are presumed to be more amenable to a cost-benefit calculus on the part of the perpetrator (Chambliss 1967; Braithwaite and Geis 1982). The utilitarian calculus assumed by the deterrence model, in which threats are weighted against potential gains, seems particularly ideal for these offenders and circumstances.

Finally, public opinion plays an important role in the justification for corporate deterrence. The public is generally supportive of harsher sanctions for white-collar offenders, particularly in cases of corporate violent offenses (Cullen and Dubeck 1985). The public believes that "stiff jail sentences will stop most white-collar criminals from breaking the law" (Cullen, Mathers, Clark, and Cullen 1983:485). However, they discriminate between organizations (where harsh sanctions are generally favored) and business executives (where support depends on the degree of harm and individual culpability; See Frank, Cullen, Travis, and Borntrager 1989).

These justifications for corporate deterrence are more philosophical and ideological than scientific (Schlegel 1990; Simpson and Koper 1992). The general public, regardless of any evidence to the contrary, believes that deterrence works (Gibbs 1975). Yet, among conventional offenders, data show that informal sanctions are a more effective means of social control than the threat of formal sanctions.[4] There is only one study, to our knowledge, that explicitly tests a perpetual deterrence model for corporate executives (Braithwaite and Makkai 1991).[5] It is to this study that we turn for empirical tests of a deterrence model.

Formal Deterrence and Corporate Crime: Empirical Evidence

Braithwaite and Makkai (1991:11) posit a simple expected utility model of organizational compliance that assumes compliance to be a function of (1) the probability that noncompliance will be discovered; (2) the probability of punishment given discovery; and (3) the cost of punishment. The focus of their research was a sample of 410 Australian nursing home executives (essentially CEOs) who were asked to estimate the chances that discovery and sanctioning would occur under a condition of continual violation of six "standards" and "regulations." Sanction source was allowed to vary, tapping both state and commonwealth regulatory efforts. Executives were asked to gauge the costs to their organization of several sanction types in the event that they were caught and disciplined.

Using cross-sectional self-report and official measures of compliance, the authors estimated both individual and multiplicative deterrent effects, controlling for a variety of demographic, regional, and organizational factors. Zero-order correlations revealed only one variable—probability of state detection—to have a significant relationship with either self-reported or official indicators of rule compliance. In their fully specified models (including controls, additive and multiplicative deterrence factors), the formal deterrence model was revealed as a "stark failure" (1991:29). The authors concluded that formal deterrence

> fails under a variety of ways of specifying additive and multiplicative models. It fails even after an attempt to excise from consideration actors who do not give much thought to sanctions, actors who are high in emotionality, actors who believe strongly in the standards, and actors who are not proprietors of the nursing home as well as directors of nursing. (p. 35)

---

[4] See Paternoster (1987) for a review of these findings.

[5] We wish to be clear about this claim. There are a number of deterrence studies that might be deemed white-collar or corporate in accordance with Sutherland or Clinard and Yeager's definitions (see, e.g., Hollinger and Clark 1983; Jesilow, Geis, and O'Brien 1986; Lewis-Beck and Alford 1980; Block, Nold, and Sidak 1981; Simpson and Koper 1991; Stotland, Britnall, L'heureux, and Ashmore 1980). However, none of these studies exclusively focus on the perceptions of sanction threat by managers/executives whose primary responsibility is to pursue organizational objectives. In some cases, objective sanction risk is assessed; in others, the organization rather than the individual is examined for deterrent effects.

Why Formal Deterrence Fails

The lack of a discernable deterrent effect in Braithwaite and Makkai's (1991) study may be due to research design flaws or to more general limitations of the deterrence doctrine. First, the researchers employed a cross-sectional rather than a panel design. Consequently, perceptions may be the consequence of past experience with sanctions (Saltzman et al. 1982), instead of tapping true deterrent effects (Paternoster 1987). Second, a key assumption of a subjective utility model is that risks and consequences will be weighed against the perceived benefits of illegality. The benefits of crime are not modeled in this or other traditional deterrence studies. Third, respondents were queried about perceived organizational risks absent questions about their personal sanction risks. Since both can be sanction targets, a true test of corporate deterrence must incorporate threats to the individual as well as to the corporation.

Finally, Braithwate and Makkai's simple utility model failed to measure nonpenal consequences, that is, threats to self-esteem, future opportunities, respect of significant others, and so forth. These informal factors may inhibit corporate criminality independently or in conjunction with legal sanctions. For instance, moral imperatives may keep most managers from violating the law regardless of legal sanction risk or consequence. For others, however, threats to self-respect or job mobility may be activated by the threat of formal processing (see, e.g., Benson 1984).

A RATIONAL CHOICE MODEL OF CORPORATE CRIME

The preceding section has suggested that a strictly deterrence model, one that only includes formal sanction threats, is likely to be inadequate to explain corporate crime. This, of course, does not mean that those seeking explanations for corporate offending must abandon all utility-based models. In this section, we will offer a competing, and much more general, model of corporate crime. This model is based on a more inclusive understanding of social control than deterrence alone—rational choice theory. Our rational choice model of corporate crime will include, but will not be restricted to, formal sanction threats.

The Elements of a Rational Choice Theory of Crime

As suggested in the paragraph above, the rational choice perspective is a utility-based theory of criminal offending that is more inclusive than a strictly deterrence-based model. Although there are variations of rational choice theory, there are a few common elements. First, the decision by would-be offenders to commit a crime is a rational decision that is affected by the perceived costs and benefits of the action.[6] The costs of offending include, but are not restricted to, the possibility and severity of formal legal sanctions. Other costs include the certainty and severity of informal sanctions, lost legitimate alternatives to action, moral costs, and self-imposed costs such as a loss of self-respect. Also included in most rational choice models of offending, but not most deterrence models, are the perceived benefits of offending. Second, rational choice models of offending should be crime-specific since the kind of information both needed and employed by offenders varies considerably across crimes. The third common element is that decisions to offend in a specific instance (the "criminal event") are effected by the immediate contextual characteristics of the crime (Clarke and Cornish 1985; Cornish and Clarke 1986). For street crimes, the decision to offend is influenced by such situational considerations as how accessible a crime target is, the ease with which an escape may be made, the existence of security devices or the perceived likelihood of an armed or resisting victim. For corporate crimes, offending decisions are probably affected by such considerations as the profitability of the firm and the size of the corporation.

Rational Choice Theory and Corporate Crime

. . . Our rational choice theory of corporate crime presumes that the decision of a corporate employee to commit a crime is influenced by the perceived costs and benefits of the offense. This simple proposition includes several additional assumptions. First, we are constructing a *subjective utility theory* of corporate offending. That is, we hypothesize that what is important are not the objective costs and benefits of corporate offending, but the subjectively perceived costs and benefits, that is, what persons believe they stand to gain or lose by committing offenses. This, of course, implies that tests of our theory (to be discussed below) must be conducted at the individual level (persons as decision makers) rather than at the organizational level (corporations) of analysis.

This focus can seem contradictory when corporate crimes are considered; yet, many personal costs and benefits may accrue to the individual though the act ostensibly serves organizational ends. For instance, Gandossy (1985) describes an extensive fraud perpetrated by top executives and middle managers at OPM (Other Peoples' Money), a computer leasing company that grew to be one of the largest in the world. The company was insolvent from its inception and was kept afloat through bribery, laundered money, and extensive bank frauds. Not only did the firm "benefit" from the illegal activities, but the

---

[6]The belief that the commission of a crime involves a rational decision does not, however, imply the notion that would-be offenders are strictly rational calculators, that is, that they are utility maximizers. Rational choice theorists recognize that humans are limited in the amount and kind of information they are able to process, the amount of information they are able to store, and in how the information gets processed and interpreted. This is the notion of bounded or minimal rationality (Simon 1957; Cherniak 1986).

original partners amassed extensive personal fortunes, business perks such as chauffer-driven limousines, officers' loan accounts, and the status that comes from "rubbing shoulders with giants." The personal costs for the OPM executives were equally high. Criminal charges were brought against five officers; four served prison terms.

It is important to note that the subjective utility of corporate crime will vary by crime type and organizational position. For instance, corporate personnel who violate environmental protection standards are less apt to receive the extensive financial and status rewards that the fraud garnered top executives at OPM, but may feel rewarded by the peer admiration and the attention of the boss for "pulling one over on the EPA." We are offering, then, a social-psychological model of corporate rule compliance.

The fact that we are focusing on the individual decision maker, however, does not restrict the scope of our model, or any empirical tests of this model, solely to corporate executives. Rather, we believe that since decisions related to corporate rule compliance occur at many levels in a business organization, any rational choice model of corporate crime must focus on decision makers at those different levels. Empirical tests of our model would therefore be directed to upper level executives, plant managers, accountants, quality control experts, scientists, and others whose decisions are related to rule compliance.

Second, our discussion assumes that a general model of corporate social control should include *both* the benefits and costs of offending. In the past, deterrence models have considered only the costs of offending, and only a select few of those possible costs (formal legal sanctions). A more general and fully specified rational choice model of corporate crime should incorporate the benefits of offending and the costs corporations must absorb when they comply with rules and regulations.

COSTS AND BENEFITS OF CORPORATE CRIME

There are several different kinds of costs that are included in our rational choice model of corporate crime. One type of cost is the *perceived certainty and severity of formal sanctions.* These are the "typical" deterrence variables. The perceived certainty of formal punishment reflects would-be offenders' estimation of the likelihood of different legal sanctions should they commit a proscribed behavior. Since previous deterrence research has shown that self-referenced measures of formal sanction threats (what is the chance that *you* would be caught/arrested/punished) are a more potent source of deterrence than a generalized measure (Jensen et al. 1978; Paternoster 1987), the most appropriate indicator of the perceived certainty of sanction threat would come from the individual decision maker involved.

This underscores our belief that any rational choice model of corporate crime should focus on the individual rather than the organization. We contend that decision makers are influenced more by what they believe to be the risk and benefits of noncompliance to themselves than to the organization. That is, both risks and benefits are more salient when the individual decision maker is *personally at risk*.

The perceived severity of punishment would reflect the estimated cost (to the individual) should the pertinent sanction be imposed. In the past, this concept has been operationalized in terms of "how much of a problem would it be if you (were arrested)?" (Grasmick and Bryjak 1980). Comparable operationalizations could be employed for the possible sanctions that may be imposed on corporate decision makers (fines, arrest, and prison).[7]

In addition to perceived formal sanction threats, our rational choice model of corporate crime includes a measure of *perceived informal sanctions*. Previous deterrence research with "street crimes" has consistently demonstrated that the possibility of informal costs is far more effective in inhibiting offending than formal sanction threats (Paternoster 1987). Ethnographic and survey research of corporate offending has also suggested the potency of informal sanctions (Fisse and Braithwaite 1983; Benson 1984; Kagan and Scholz 1984; Simpson 1992). Informal sanctions would include such things as negative publicity for the corporation; a perceived loss of the company's "good name" and reputation; the possibility that colleagues, close friends, or family would devalue and disapprove of the individual. Collectively, these informal sanctions constitute a kind of social censure for would-be offenders, and are included in what Braithwaite (1989) has recently referred to as "shame." Separate measures of the perceived certainty and severity of different types of informal sanctions could be constructed. These measures would refer to the perception of informal costs that may accrue to the individual as a result of noncompliance to the rules and regulations binding on the corporation. The important point is that previous constructions of corporate crime deterrence models have neglected to consider the possibility of perceived informal costs. To the extent that these costs are effective in inhibiting corporate crime, such models are misspecified.

A consideration of formal and informal sanctions does not, however, exhaust the kinds of costs that may accrue to corporate offenders. Another potent inhibition for would-be offenders is the imposition of sanctions by oneself. Persons may refrain from offending not because they fear the social reaction to their behavior, but because they wish to avoid losing self-respect in their own eyes. Braithwaite (1989) has suggested that such self-imposed sanctions may be a potent source of social control, a suggestion given some credence by the recent deterrence research of Williams and Hawkins (1989) and Grasmick and Bursik (1990). Another element in our rational choice model of corporate crime, then, would include the perceived certainty and severity of a *loss of self-respect* for breaking rules.

---

[7]We recognize that organizations may be sanctioned for the action of their agents, but argue that even this aggregate level punishment is salient to individuals primarily in terms of how they are personally affected by it.

Our rational choice model of corporate offending also includes the *perceived costs of rule compliance* and the *perceived benefits of rule violation*. These factors are included because would-be offenders' decisions are doubtlessly affected by their estimate of the expense of not violating the law and the perceived advantages they would reap from noncompliance. The corporate crime literature has repeatedly suggested that many corporate crimes are committed not in direct anticipation of gain but to avoid what is perceived to be an avoidable expense of compliance. Some regulations may be perceived as simply too costly for some corporations to abide by, and they are subsequently violated. In addition, offenders consider the direct benefits of violating the law. This is an important instrumental consideration that has unfortunately been absent from most deterrence models (for exceptions, see Piliavin et al. 1986 and Klepper and Nagin 1989a, b). Some of the perceived benefits of corporate noncompliance include market control, higher prices, greater worker productivity, lower cost per commodity unit, and reduced safety expenses.

MORAL BELIEFS AND PERCEIVED LEGITIMACY AS INHIBITIONS ON CRIME

Supplementing the formal and informal costs of punishment in our rational choice model of corporate crime are considerations of moral belief and the perceived legitimacy of the law. *Moral beliefs* refer to the extent to which persons perceive a particular criminal act to be morally offensive. It is presumed that those who view an act with opprobrium will be less likely to commit the offense than those who are more morally tolerant. In criminological research with ordinary street crimes, moral inhibitions have consistently been found to be strong correlates of offending (Paternoster 1987; Grasmick and Green 1980, 1981), and there is no reason not to hypothesize that would-be corporate offenders are also inhibited by their moral evaluations of possibly criminal actions.

Two things should be emphasized here. First, moral beliefs constitute a noninstrumental consideration for a would-be offender's decision to commit a crime. Those with strong moral inhibitions are predicted to refrain from committing a particular offense no matter what the formal or informal costs or the perceived benefits of offending. Second, our reference to moral beliefs in the context of corporate crime does not necessarily refer to an organized and fully developed ethical system that corporate employees develop and important into their working environment. Rather, we suggest that those who work in corporations develop moral rules about the acceptability of *particular* conduct within a *particular* context. These moral rules will change somewhat depending upon the specific situation. Our notion of contextually anchored moral rules is comparable to Jackall's (1988:6) notion of the "rules-in-use" employed by corporate managers:

What matters on a day-to-day basis are the moral rules-in-use fashioned within the personal and structural constraints of one's organization. As it happens, these rules may vary sharply depending on various factors, such as proximityf to the market, line or staff responsibilities, or one's position in a hierarchy. Actual organizational moralities are thus contextual, situational, highly specific, and, most often, unarticulated.

To capture or measure a decision maker's rules-in-use, then, would require the stipulation of a contextually specific and relevant situation in which an offense is contemplated.

Moral beliefs or moral rules-in-use, are related to but conceptually distinct from the notion of a *perceived sense of the legitimacy of the rules and rule enforcers*. We argue that corporate decision makers will be less inclined to comply with rules and regulations that they perceive as unreasonable or capricious (Kagan and Scholz 1984:75). Kagan and Scholz have also suggested that an important consideration for businesspersons is the degree to which they are treated with respect and dignity by those who would regulate them. Furthermore, in an extensive empirical study of the etiology of rule compliance, Tyler (1990) found that people comply with rules because in large measure they believe them to be proper, independent of any instrumental concerns. He also noted that rules are more likely to be obeyed when people perceive them to be fairly administered and when they feel that they have been treated with respect and dignity. This would suggest that an important variable in any rational choice model of corporate offending would be the degree to which decision makers perceived the rules to be rational, reasonable, and perceive themselves to be fairly treated.

CHARACTERISTICS OF THE CRIMINAL EVENT

The preceding paragraphs have suggested that would-be corporate offenders are influenced by the costs and benefits of rule compliance (both formal and informal), the moral implications of their behavior, and perceptions of legitimacy and respect. In addition to these concerns, the decision not to comply with a law or business regulation is doubtlessly also affected by various situational and contextual factors.

One of the things that makes corporate crime distinct from other crimes is the context of the criminal event. Offenders are situated within formal organizations that are characterized by distinct cultures and structural features—*the internal organization of the firm*. The organizations themselves operate within and attempt to influence *external environments* comprising political, economic, and cultural forces (Fligstein 1987). Both can affect corporate offender motivations and crime opportunities (Coleman 1987).

Empirical research has identified a number of factors that are correlated with corporate offending (see Yeager 1986; Finney and Lesieur 1982 for summaries of this literature). However, these factors vary by organizational context considerably in their respective influences on the decision to commit corporate crime. For instance, unanticipated or costly changes in legal regulations, coupled with managerial cost-reduction policies, may produce greater pressure to offend in marginally profitable companies than in firms that can more easily absorb the increased costs of compliance. Larger firms may be more able to control their environments (say, through lobbying efforts or aggressive competitive practices) than smaller firms, thus reducing compliance costs and pressures to offend. On the other hand, the greater autonomy and invisibility that accompanies firm size and diversification may offer criminals greater protection from discovery and sanction. Thus, threats to profitability alone are not sufficient to cause managers across firms, or even the majority of managers within a firm, to violate the law (Simipson 1986). Nor are factors like business type (Sonnenfeld and Lawrence 1978), the degree of firm delegation (Braithwaite 1978), division strength (Ross 1980), scarce economic environments (Staw and Szwajkowski 1975), or "criminogenic cultures" (Sutherland 1949; Geis 1967; Zey-Ferrell and Ferrell, Weaver, and Ferrell 1979) satisfactory as causal mechanisms. Instead, the crime process is best understood as developmental and contingent in nature.

> Not only does [criminal] . . . action involve a temporal sequence, but as commonly put, one thing leads to another; events in the sequence are causally associated or interlinked. Viewed retrospectively, such links involve numerous situational contingencies. Strategically important steps in the process won't be taken *unless* prior pressures exist or potential controls are inoperative; illegal solutions to problems won't be perceived as feasible *unless* the problem cannot be solved in other ways or only in significantly less profitable ways. (Finney and Lesieur 1982:260, emphasis in original)

Managers located in different structural positions within the firm (hierarchical or task-specific) will sift through a set of distinct contingencies, progressively narrowing the decision choice of crime or noncrime. Thus, situational and contextual factors may be specified in general and manager-specific terms.

Finally, since criminological research has consistently shown that the best predictor of future offending is past offending, we include the latter in our model. Some persons within business organizations, because of personal attributes that are consistent over time or the unique pressures and opportunities of their position, may be generally inclined to noncompliance with rules and regulations. We expect some stability and consistency in offending, therefore, above and beyond what is explained by the other exogenous variables in the model.

In sum, we are offering a rational choice model of corporate crime that includes the following as possible explanatory variables:

1. Perceived certainty/severity of formal legal sanctions
2. Perceived certainty/severity of informal sanctions
3. Perceived certainty/severity of loss of self-respect

4. Perceived cost of rule compliance
5. Perceived benefits of noncompliance
6. Moral inhibitions
7. Perceived sense of legitimacy/fairness
8. Characteristics of the criminal event
9. Prior offending by the person

We schematically show these possible explanatory factors in figure 2.1. It can be seen that we are suggesting a more general model of the social control of corporate crime than has previously been described and empirically tested.

SPECIFYING THE RELATIONSHOPS AMONG THE EXPLANATORY VARIBLES

Our discussion to this point has suggested that the decision to commit corporate crime is affected by numerous considerations—the formal and informal costs and benefits of offending, moral considerations and perceptions of legitimacy, and the context within which the organization operates. The question to address now is the process through which these explanatory variables affect would-be offenders' decision to commit a corporate crime. There are two competing hypotheses, both of which are a priori plausible.

The first of these hypotheses states that the effect of formal sanctions, informal sanctions, and moral considerations are additive and independent. Blake and Davis (1964:477–81) for example, describe five sources of social control: (1) internalization of norms (moral beliefs), (2) desire for social approval (informal sanctions), (3) anticipation of formal punishment (legal sanctions), (4) anticipation of nonreward (failure to achieve the benefits of deviance, and (5) lack of opportunity. Blake and Davis's position is that each of these has a distinct effect on the inclination to commit a deviant act, that is, the effect of one source of social control does not depend upon the level of any other. This theoretical position hypothesizes an additive effect for each explanatory variable. For example, the effect of perceived formal sanction threats is presumed to produce the same amount of social control regardless of the level of moral beliefs or informal sanctions.

An alternative, second hypothesis about the effect of different sources of social control would predict that the effect of one source of the inclination to commit an offense is related to the level of another source. Contrary to the above, then, this alternative hypothesis suggests a multiplicative or interactive effect. A specific example of one derivation of this hypothesis can be found in the work of Talcott Parsons. In *The Structure of Social Action* (1937:402–3), Parsons suggests that the "principal basis" of social control is an internalization of the norms. In this hypothesis, those who have strong moral inhibitions are thought to conform to the requirements of rules no matter what the costs

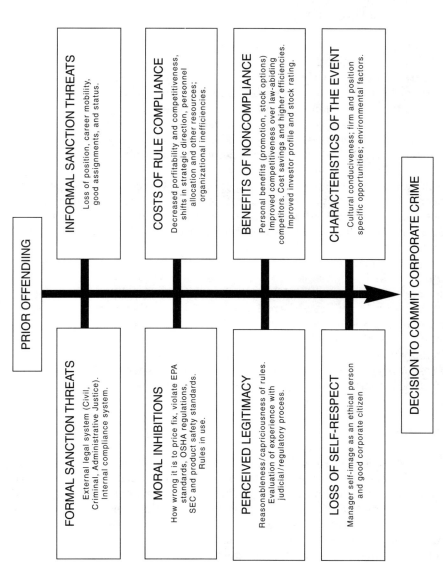

FIGURE 1 A General Rational Choice Model of Corporate Crime

or consequences. For such morally inhibited persons, there is no cost-benefit analysis in the contemplation of conformity, and instrumental considerations are irrelevant. For those unbound by moral inhibitions, however, instrumental factors are highly salient and may be the only source of conformity. Parsons's hypothesis would predict, then, that formal sanction threats are irrelevant for those with strong moral beliefs but highly significant for those with weak moral beliefs.

A related, but slightly different, interactive effect has recently been suggested by Williams and Hawkins (1986). They argue that formal legal sanctions deter best when they are contemplated by informal costs, such as social censure and a loss of material opportunities. Where such possible informal costs are absent, they contend, the law cannot effectively control behavior. Their hypothesis, then, is that there is an interaction between formal and informal sanctions; formal sanctions deter only at high levels of informal sanctions.

The empirical literature with respect to these two competing hypotheses is inconsistent, with some studies indicating an interactive effect between different sources of social control (Silberman 1976; Teevan 1976) and others revealing an independent, additive effect (Grasmick and McLaughlin 1978; Grasmick and Green 1981; Nagin and Paternoster 1991).

It is also conceivable that both hypotheses may be correct. For example, it may be that instrumental concerns are irrelevant within the subgroup effectively restrained by moral inhibitions. For those with weaker moral inhibitions, however, the effect of formal and informal sanction costs may be additive. We offer no judgment as to whether or not the rational choice model of corporate crime sketched out here presumes additive or interactive effects. We simply note the alternative specifications and suggest that the exploration and resolution of these issues must await empirical research conducted on the theoretical model we are suggesting here. . . .

CONCLUSION

It has often been presumed that, due to the risk-aversive nature of businesspersons and the instrumental nature of the types of crimes that they have the opportunity to commit in their business roles, corporate crime would be the quintessential deterrable offense. Perceptions of the certainty and severity of formal legal sanctions should, therefore, inhibit corporate employees from committing business crimes. In the most rigorous empirical test of this hypothesis to date, however, formal sanction threats were found to be unrelated to the frequency of rule violations. In fact, the authors of this study concluded that a formal deterrence model was a "stark failure" (Braithwaite and Makkai 1994:29).

In trying to understand this seeming anomaly, we have suggested in this chapter that a strictly deterrence model of corporate crime, that is, one that includes only formal sanction variables, is incomplete. We have suggested that corporate offending could best be understood with a more general model of social control and have suggested the contours of just such a model.

In constructing this preliminary model of corporate crime, we have drawn upon the rational choice perspective. Our proposed rational choice model of corporate crime includes a broad range of both utilitarian (instrumental) and nonutilitarian (moral) sources of social control. More specifically, our model contains perceived formal sanction threats, perceptions of diverse forms of informal sanctions such as social censure, loss of professional status and reputation, a perceived loss of self-respect, the perceived benefits of both rule compliance and noncompliance, moral inhibitions, and characteristics of the criminal event itself. In describing the conceptualization of our model, we have stressed the idea that it is a social-psychological model of corporate crime control. That is, it is premised on the perceptions that decision makers have about the personal costs and benefits of their behavior and its possible moral implications.

We also indicate that the specific elements of the model may vary for different decision makers within the corporate structure and, therefore, for different types of corporate crimes. We believe that this preliminary model is more fully specified, and therefore more theoretically accurate, than previous models of corporate crime.[11]

In addition, we have offered one possible research strategy for empirically testing our proposed theoretical model. We have emphasized the fact that tests of our model must be conducted at the individual level of analysis since it is predicated upon subjective, that is perceptual, understandings of utilities, disutilities, and moral positions. Influenced by recent critiques of traditional cross-sectional and panel research designs we have proposed a hybrid approach that includes the use of hypothetical offending scenarios supplemented with survey-type questions. Important contextual dimensions of the criminal event would be deliberately manipulated in these scenarios, and would provide a specific referent for queries regarding the certainty and severity of sanctions. With these scenarios, researchers would be able to examine the instantaneous relationship between key theoretical variables and self-reported intentions to commit a corporate offense. . . .

BIBLIOGRAPHY

Benson, Michael L. 1984. "The fall from grace." *Criminology* 22:573–93.
Blake, Judith, & Davis, Kenneth. 1964. "Norms, values and sanctions." In R. Faris (Ed.), *Handbook of modern sociology* (456–84). Chicago: Rand McNally.

---

[11] We acknowledge that our model may be overly reductionist. For instance, it is difficult to assess how individuals evaluate and respond to organizational costs and benefits that do not directly affect them, but matter nonetheless (e.g., organizational loyalty). Rational choice theory, as currently developed, offers little direction for sorting out and calibrating such factors.

Block, Michael K., Nold, Frederick C., & Sidak, Joseph G. 1981. "The deterrent effect of antitrust enforcement." *Journal of Political Economy* 89:429–45.

Braithwaite, John. 1978. "Corporate crime and the internalization of capital." Unpublished manuscript, Australia Institute of Criminology, Canberra.

———. 1989. *Crime, shame and reintegration.* Cambridge: Oxford University Press.

Braithwaite, John, & Geis, Gilbert. 1982. "On theory and action for corporate crime control. *Crime and Delinquency* 28:292–314,.

Braithwaite, John, & Makkai, Toni. 1991. "Testing an expected utility model of corporate deterrence." *Law and Society Review* 25:7–39.

Chambliss, William J. 1967. "Types of deviance and the effectiveness of legal sanctions." *Wisconsin Law Review* (Summer): 705–19.

Cherniak, Christopher. 1986. *Minimal rationality.* Cambridge, MA: MIT Press.

Clarke, Ronald V., & Cornish, Derek B. "Modeling offenders' decisions." In M. Tonry & N. Morris (Eds.), *Crime and justice* (Vol. 6, 147–85). Chicago: University of Chicago Press 1985.

Coleman, James William. 1987. "Toward an integrated theory of white-collar crime." *American Journal of Sociology* 93:406–39.

Cornish, Derek B., & Clarke, Ronald V. 1986. *The reasoning criminal.* New York: Springer-Verlag.

Cullen, Francis T., & Dubeck, Paul J. 1985. "The myth of corporate immunity to deterrence." *Federal Probation* 49:3–9.

Cullen, Francis T., Mathers, R., Clark, G. & Cullen, J.B. 1983. "Public support for punishing white-collar crime." *Journal of Criminal Justice* 2:481–93.

Finney, Henry C., & Lesieur, Henry P. 1982. "A contingency theory of organizational crime." In S.B. Bacharach (Ed.), *Research in the Sociology of Organizations* (Vol. 1, 255–99). Greenwich, CT: JAI Press.

Fisse, Brent, & Braithwaite, John. 1983. *The impact of publicity on corporate offenders.* Albany, NY: State University of New York Press.

Fligstein, Neil. 1987. "The intraorganizational power struggle." *American Sociological Review* 52:44–58.

Frank, James, Cullen, Francis T., Travis, Lawrence F., III, & Borntrager, John L. 1989. "Sanctioning corporate crime." *American Journal of Criminal Justice* 13:139–69.

Gandossy, Robert P. 1985. *Bad business: the OPM scandal and the seduction of the establishment.* New York: Basic Books.

Geis, Gilbert. 1967. In M.B. Clinard & R. Quinney (Eds.), *Criminal behavior systems: A typology* (140–51). New York: Holt, Rinehart, & Winston.

Gibbs, Jack P. 1975. *Crime, punishment and deterrence.* New York: Elsevier.

Grasmick, Harold G., & Bryjak, George J. 1980. "The deterrent effect of perceived severity of punishment." *Social Forces* 59:471–91.

Grasmick, Harold G., & Bursik, Robert J. 1990. "Conscience, significant others, and rational choice: Extending the deterrence model." *Law and Society Review* 24:837–61.

Grasmick, Harold G., & Green, Donald. 1980. "Legal punishment, social disapproval and internalization as inhibitors of illegal behavior." *Journal of Criminal Law and Criminology* 71:325–35.

———. 1981. "Deterrence and the morally committed." *Sociological Quarterly* 22:1–14.

Grasmick, Harold G., & McLaughlin, Steven D. 1978. "Deterrence and social control: Comment on Silberman." *American Sociological Review* 43:272–77.

Hollinger, Richard C., & Clark, John P. 1983. "Deterrence in the workplace." *Social Forces* 62:388–418.

Jackall, Robert. 1988. *Moral mazes: The world of corporate managers.* New York: Oxford University Press.

Jensen, Gary F., Erickson, Maynard L., & Gibbs, Jack P. 1978. "Perceived risk of punishment and self-reported delinquency." *Social Forces* 57:57–78.

Jesilow, Paul, Geis, Gilbert, & O'Brien, Mary Jane. 1986. "Experimental evidence that publicity has no effect in suppressing auto repair fraud." *Sociology and Social Research* 70:222–23.

Kadish, Sanford H. 1977. "The use of criminal sanctions in the enforcement of economic regulations." In G. Geis & R.F. Meier, (Eds.), *White-collar crime* (296–317). New York: The Free Press.

Kagan, Robert A., & Scholz, John T. 1984. "The 'criminology of the corporation' and regulatory enforcement strategies." In K. Hawkins & J.M. Thomas (Eds.), *Enforcing Regulation* (67–95). Boston: Kluwer-Nijhoff.

Klepper, Steven, & Nagin, Daniel. 1989a. "Tax compliance and perceptions of the risks of detection and criminal prosecution." *Law and Society Review* 23:209–40.

———. 1989b. "The deterrent effect of perceived certainty and severity of punishment revisited." *Criminology* 27:721–46.

Lewis-Beck, Michael S., & Alford, John R. "Can government regulate safety?" *American Political Science Review* (1980):746.

Nagin, Daniel S., & Paternoster, Raymond. 1991. "The preventive effects of the perceived risk of arrest: Testing an expanded conception of deterrence." *Criminology* 29:561–87.

Parsons, Talcott. 1937. *The structure of social action.* New York: McGraw-Hill.

Paternoster, Raymond. 1987. "The deterrent effect of the perceived certainty and severity of punishment." *Justice Quarterly* 4:173–217.

Piliavin, Irving, Gartner, Rosemary, Thorton, Craig, & Matsueda, Ross. 1986. "Crime, deterrence and rational choice." *American Sociological Review* 51: 101–19.

Ross, Irwin. 1980. "Illegal corporate behavior: Big companies?" *Fortune* (December):57–61.

Saltzman, Linda, Paternoster, Raymond, Waldo, Gordon P., & Chiricos, Theodore G. 1982. "Deterrent and experimental effects." *Journal of Research in Crime and Delinquency* 19:172–89.

Schlegel, Kip. 1990. *Just deserts for corporate criminals.* Boston: Northeastern University Press.

Silberman, Matthew. 1976. "Toward a theory of criminal deterrence." *American Sociological Review* 41:442–61.

Simon, Herbert. 1957. *Models of man.* New York: John Wiley.

Simpson, Sally S. 1986. "The decomposition of antitrust." *American Sociological Review* 51:859–75.

———. (1992). "Corporate crime deterrence and corporate control policies." In K. Schlegel & D. Weisburd (Eds.), *White-Collar Crime Reconsidered* (289–308). Boston: Northeastern University Press.

Simpson, Sally S., & Koper, Christopher C. 1992, "Deterring corporate crime." *Criminology* 30:347–75.

Sonnelfeld, Jeffrey, & Lawrence, Paul R. 1978. "Why do companies succumb to price-fixing?" *Harvard Business Review* 56:145–57.

Staw, Barry N., & Szawajkowski, Eugene. 1975. "The scarcity-munificence component of organizational acts." *Administrative Science Quarterly* 20:245–354.

Stotland, Ezra, Britnall, Michael, L'heureux, Andrew, & Ashmore, Eva. 1980. "Do convictions deter home repair fraud?" In G. Geis & E. Stotland (Eds.), *White-collar crime: Theory and research* (252–65). Beverly Hills, CA: Sage.

Sutherland, Edwin. 1949. *White-collar crime.* New York: The Dryden Press.

Teeven, James J. 1976. "Subjective perception of deterrence (cont'd)." *Journal of Research in Crime and Delinquency* 13:155–60.

Tyler, Tom R. 1990. *Why people obey the law.* New Haven: Yale University Press.

Williams, Kirk R., & Hawkins, Richard. 1989. "The meaning of arrest for wife assault." *Criminology* 27:163–81.

Yeager, Peter C. 1986. "Analyzing corporate offenses." In J.E. Post (Ed.), *Research in Corporate Social Performance and Policy* (Vol. 8, 93–120). Greenwich, CT: JAI Press.

Zey-Ferrell, Mary K., Weaver, Mark, & Ferrell, O.C. 1982. "Predicting unethical behavior among marketing practitioners." *Human Relations* 32:557–69.

Organizational Culture and Organizational Crime

ANDY HOCHSTETLER AND HEITH COPES

At the dawn of a new century, the number and power of bureaucratic organizations in private and public life continue to increase. In the United States alone, the number of corporations grew fivefold between 1917 and 1969 (Coleman, 1982), and in the past three decades, the total number of business concerns increased from 2.4 million to more than 9 million (U.S. Department of Commerce, 1996). Rapid growth of a world economic order has only escalated the significance and potential impact of organizations as they now do business and compete in countries around the globe. The appearance in particular of large corporations, whose wealth and budgets dwarf most nation states and whose operations span multiple countries, raise profound issues of accountability and control. With the number of corporations and other organizations growing daily, the potential for them to cause harm to innocent parties increases as well. And when innocent parties are harmed by the actions of organizations, frequently it results from crime.

ORGANIZATIONAL CRIME

Investigations of crime in the workplace have a long history in sociology, albeit one that has focused overwhelmingly on individuals and their misdeeds. Investigators by contrast were slow to recognize and to take seriously the fact

---

PANEL 13   Money Talks

Empire Sanitary Landfill recently pleaded guilty to funneling $129,000 in illegal corporate donations to political candidates. The company would recruit employees to make contributions that were then reimbursed with corporate funds. By saying the reimbursements were for entertainment expenses or other legitimate corporate expenses, the company was able to hide the illegal donations. The money was used to lobby for a trash transportation bill pending in Congress. Empire officials agreed to pay an $8 million fine, the largest penalty ever for campaign finance violations.

Source: Los Angeles Times, October 8, 1997.

Managed health care companies are pouring money into congressional campaigns in hopes of electing a sympathetic Congress. So far, 72% of the $2.1 million given by health care companies has gone to Republicans. Brenda Becker, Blue Cross/Blue Shield Association's chief fundraiser, stated that health care companies "are giving more to Republicans because they've been carrying our water on a lot of issues, and they are also in the majority."

Source: Los Angeles Times, October 30, 1998.

---

that a great deal of crime is organizational in nature. The concept *organizational crime* refers to illegal acts by officers, managers, or employees of legitimate formal organizations in furtherance of their conception, however far fetched or erroneous, of organizational interests and goals (Ermann and Lundman, 1978). Organizational crime also may take the form of acts of omission, as when supervisors react with indiferrence or tacit endorsement to crime by subordinates. This is the case, for example, where military commanders permit to go unchecked widespread sexual harassment of personnel. Although individuals frequently benefit from it, organizational crime is distinguished principally by the subsidiary importance of individual reward in favor of organizational benefit (Clinard and Quinney, 1973). For perpetrators of organizational crime, self-interest is of less concern than a desire to "get the job done" for their employer, their supervisors, or their fellow workers.

The rationale for distinguishing organizational crime principally rests in the belief that organizational forces play an important part in its genesis, in its course, and in reactions to it. Included here are differential authority, organizational goals, indoctrination and incentive programs, and formal channels of communication. To talk of organizational crime, however, is neither to reify a collectivity nor to endow it with volitional properties; organizations act through human agents (Cressey, 1995). Still, because organizational properties and dynamics may function to diffuse or obscure responsibility for misconduct, they can facilitate individual willingness to participate in crime. Alternately, they may cause individuals to make criminal choices because of pressure from supervisors intent upon getting the results they want without regard for other considerations. Here and elsewhere, when organizations repeatedly offend, organizational conditions frequently are an important reason, and the pathologies of individuals, business cycles, and abstract market forces fail as explanations for it.

Five decades of research into the prevalence of various forms of crimes by corporations has shown indisputably that rates vary both temporally and spatially. Some industries, for example, are rife with crime, while in others it is comparably rare (Clinard and Yeager, 1980; Shover and Bryant, 1993). Explanations of aggregate organizational offending rates typically rely on variation in the munificence of markets and available criminal opportunities. Proponents of these explanations assert that the demands on organizations and the means to achieve goals legitimately vary by industry, place, and time. There is considerable empirical substantiation that when organizations are struggling to compete for scarce resources, they are more likely to offend (Staw and Szawajowski, 1975; Clinard and Yeager, 1980; Simpson, 1986). Firms in depressed industries and firms performing poorly relative to others in the same industry violate the law to a greater degree (Clinard and Yeager, 1980:129).

Regardless of whether the aggregate-level rate of crime by organizations is high or low, some organizations maintain exemplary records of compliance with ethical and legal norms even as others habitually violate (Clinard and Yeager, 1980; Stover and Bryant, 1993; Sutherland, 1983). Market forces create conditions that make crime attractive to some organizations but are insufficient as an explanation for firm-level variation. Although structural factors undoubtedly contribute to organizational offending, they reveal little about the internal worlds and dynamics of organizations where decisions to offend are made.

ORGANIZATIONAL CULTURE

When investigators turn to describing and explaining the internal workings of organizations, they often employ the concept *organizational culture*. Variation in organizational culture has been linked hypothetically to an array of variables, including financial performance, productivity, and adaptability. For managers, awareness of and sensitivity to the culture of their organizations is touted as a powerful tool for achieving organizational goals and potential (e.g., Kilmann, Saxton and Serpa, 1985). Although initial explications of the notion of organizational culture is nearly 50 years old (Jaques, 1952), it did not begin attracting attention until nearly three decades later. Reflecting its quick and enthusiastic reception, the sister concept *corporate culture* was indexed in the *Business Periodicals Index,* and by 1990 the number of listings had increased to the current level of approximately 100 per issue (Yank, 1997). The titles of dozens of books devoted to organizational analysis now include the word *culture (Books in Print,* 1977). It and the concept of organizational culture are given prominent treatment in leading textbooks on formal organization and bureaucracy, although they are conspicuously absent from earlier editions of the same books (e.g., Pugh and Hickson, 1977; Scott, 1992).

The animus for its continuing appeal is the belief that organizational culture is a "social force that controls patterns of organizational behavior by shaping members' cognitions and perceptions of meanings and realities" (Ott, 1989:69). Deal and Kennedy (1982:4) claim that organizational culture has "a powerful influence throughout an organization; it affects practically everything—from who gets promoted and what decisions are made, to how employees dress and what sports they play."

Culture has not escaped the notice of students of organizational crime, but early use of the concept in criminology occurred independent of the subsequent wake of interest from management scholars. Geis (1967:143) described agreed upon "reasonable" divisions of markets worked out by firms in the heavy electrical equipment industry that guided their bidding on ostensibly competitive contracts. Sonnenfeld and Lawrence (1978) indict the "culture of the business" as an important cause of differential participation in price-fixing behavior by firms in the folding-box industry during the 1970s. They point specifically to "anticompetitive norms" and suggest that price fixing became a "way of life" in guilty firms (1978:149). Denzin (1977:918) concluded that "below the articulated legal structure" of the American liquor industry there exists a consensual *"informal structure . . .* which often contradicts or supersedes" the law and may be used as "an *a priori* justification for breaking or bending" it (1977:919). On the basis of interviews with retired corporate managers, Clinard (1983:65) reported that "[a]bout two-thirds . . . felt that some corporations do have a generally ethical or unethical culture." These and similar reports underpin the claim that "consistently, scholars have assigned great importance to culture as a cause of organizational deviance and misconduct" (Vaughan, 1996:406).

CRIMINOGENIC ORGANIZATIONAL CULTURE

Despite the fact that culture is a mainstay of sociological analysis, it is used in a variety of ways. Crime researchers have avoided debating which aspects of an organization are encompassed in its culture by pragmatically and consistently limiting the scope of the concept. Barnett (1986:555) defines it as a "set of commonly shared attitudes, techniques, and rationalizations." Similarly, Hills (1987) points to the strength within organizations of techniques of neutralization, linguistic devices that serve as moral justification for crime, and Braithwaite (1989) singles out as critical the proportionate mix of symbolic definitions favorable to violation of law and definitions unfavorable to violation. For purposes of understanding the origins of crime, legitimized and taken-for-granted rhetorical scripts invoked beforehand to minimize guilt and self-rejection caused by participation in crime are key components of organizational culture. Their ready availability within an organization facilitates crime and increases its incidence.

The importance of culture in shaping an organizational actor's behavior is widely accepted among criminologists. But how does the presence of a criminogenic organizational culture make criminal decisions attractive where they would otherwise not be? Or, as Hills (1987: 190) asks, "How is it possible that men who are basically moral and decent in their own families—perhaps even generous in civic and charitable contributions—are able to engage in corporate acts that have extraordinary inhumane consequences?"

The significance of culturally shared definitions of situations lies in how they influence individuals' decisions in ways that change either the likelihood or the frequency of crime. Through interaction with other members of the organization, employees are socialized into the culture of the organization; that is, they learn the techniques, motivations, and rationalizations of criminal behavior. Part of the socialization process involves learning how to filter deviant acts "through a sanitizing, ideological prism, which gives them the appearance of not bring criminal" (Simon and Eitzen, 1993:300). This sanitizing ideology in criminogenic cultures includes the adoption of a vocabulary of motives and acceptance of various techniques of neutralization.

While vocabulary of motives and techniques of neutralization are similar, there are subtle differences between them. Members of organizations use a specialized vocabulary of motives to shield themselves from the guilt associated with illegal acts. This is done by adopting a specialized vocabulary so that they are allowed the pretense that their behavior is not a crime. A convicted insider trader remembers that his peers referred to their questionable and illegal tactics with humorous names like the "poison pill," the "pac-man defense," "greenmail," "shark repellant," and the "golden parachute" (Levine, 1991). Savings and loans crooks referred to the practice of hiding bad loans from bank regulators by exchanging them between institutions as "flip-flopping," a lighthearted term considering that its meaning is a serious criminal fraud (Calavita, Pontell and Tillman, 1997). Vocabulary of motives also allow organizational offenders to redefine their behavior as commonplace and ordinary. After being convicted of antitrust violations an offender stated, "It was a way of doing business before we even got into the business. So it was like why do you brush your teeth in the morning or something. . . ." (Benson, 1985:591).

Some offenders recognize that they are flirting with or committing criminal behavior and must therefore find a way to rationalize their actions or to neutralize the guilt associated with it. Techniques of neutralization are linguistic devices that, when invoked by corporate managers or employees, blunt the moral force of the law, and neutralize the guilt of criminal participation (Hills, 1987). These justifications, or neutralizing techniques, are rationalizations that precede behavior and make criminal conduct possible. Through their use, "social controls that serve to check or inhibit deviant motivational patterns are rendered inoperative, and the individual is freed to engage in delinquency without serious damage to his self-image" (Sykes and Matza, 1957:667). This allows the organizational actor to remain committed to the dominant normative system and yet so qualifies its imperatives that violations are acceptable; it allows organizational offenders to "deny the guilty mind" (Benson, 1985).

Organizational offenders commonly use one or more of the following techniques of neutralization. *Denial of responsibility* is the belief that individual offenders are blameless because responsibility for their criminal actions lie elsewhere or with higher-ranking employees of the corporation. The hierarchical structure of organizations diffuses responsibility for actions that may harm consumers or the public. For example, when asked to inform the chief engineer of the reporting of false documents at B. F. Goodrich, Vandivier's superior told him, "I learned a long time ago not to worry about things over which I have no control. I have no control over this. . . . Why should my conscience bother me?" (Vandivier, 1996:118). Responsibility within an organization is diffused because organizational decisions are made incrementally. Organizational offenders also deny their responsibility by claiming that they were "forced" to engage in the illegal acts to keep their jobs or for their businesses to survive.

Denial of injury is the contention that the wrongfulness of an act is determined by whether anyone was hurt by it. If no one is harmed by a specific act of organizational crime, then those who have committed it can maintain that they acted properly. When asked whether he knew that meeting with competitors was illegal, a witness in the heavy electrical price-fixing case stated: "Illegal? Yes, but not criminal. . . . I assumed that a criminal action meant damaging someone, we did not do that" (Geis, 1967:122).

Denial of victim is the belief that the victims of crime are responsible for their own harm and suffering. For example, corporate officials indicted for marketing the harmful intrauterine contraceptive device (IUD) stated that the life-threatening infections caused by it were not caused by a design flaw; rather, it was the result either of improper insertion or the promiscuous behavior of women who used it (Hills, 1987). Similarly, automotive manufacturers blame road conditions and unsafe drivers for deaths and injuries rather than defective automobile designs (Frank, 1985).

Condemnation of the condemners finds expression by denying the legitimacy of the law and government regulatory agencies that enforce the unfair laws. Often, organizational members insist that regulatory agencies not only invite cheating but demand it. Thus some doctors who defraud Medicaid claim that they were forced to file false claims because Medicaid rules were changed frequently, were ambiguous, and were created by people who knew nothing about the practice of medicine (Jesilow, Pontell, and Geis, 1993).

Appeal to higher loyalties is the belief that those who breach legal conduct are doing so in pursuit of broader or more important objectives and, therefore, should not be held responsible for their transgressions. Some of the "higher" goals that organizational offenders pursue include profit for their stockholders and financial stability for their own families. After being convicted of price-fixing, an employee of a folding-box company stated "I've always thought of myself as an honorable citizen. We didn't do these things for our own behalf . . . [but] for the betterment of the company" (Sonnenfeld and Lawrence, 1978). Another common linguistic construction is to insist that management has a responsibility to the company's stakeholders to increase profits. Frequently, economic theories that emphasize the social importance of the profit motives are used to lend legitimacy to this belief. Free-market economists who obviously are not endorsing crime nevertheless provide convenient rationalizations: "Few trends could so thoroughly undermine the very foundation of our free society as the acceptance of a social responsibility other than to make as much money for their stockholders as possible" (Friedman, 1962:133). Others, usually lower in the hierarchy, indict family responsibilities for their participation in illegal behaviors. Vandivier (1996:215) describes a dilemma one of his colleagues at B. F. Goodrich faced: "I've been an engineer for a long time, and I've always believed that ethics and integrity were every bit as important as theorems and formulas. . . Now this. . . . Hell, I've got two sons to put through school."

ORGANIZATIONAL COMPLEXITY AND CULTURE

Culture largely exists in the oral tradition and off-the-record communications within an organization. Therefore, no organization has a single set of cultural values that all its members reference when making their decisions. The more organizational cultures are examined, the more doubt is cast on the assumption, for example, that computing technicians and maintenance workers share significant cultural beliefs and characteristics because their checks are cut in the same office (Hofstede et al., 1990; Trice, 1993). In contrast to depictions of organizational cultures as static, finite in number, and clearly demarcated from one another, sociological investigations show them to be emergent and fluid constructions grounded in choices, repetitive actions and ongoing processes of interaction among diverse groups. Despite this observation, most studies of organizational culture start from a monolithic bias that concentrates the search for its sources and consequences on variables that characterize organizations in their entirety.

Reflecting misguided portrayals of organizations as culturally homogenous, investigators often emphasize only the external environment of an organization in their search for the constraints on organizational culture. Where corporations are the focus of attention, this includes a culture of competition and overarching economic conditions and trends. Some firms are said to be more prone to develop crime facilitative cultures because they exist in competitive environments where customer requirements and societal expectations are high, for example (Gordon, 1991).

The environment of an organization clearly is an important contributor to its culture, but these external conditions do not convert effortlessly into cultures with invariant qualities. Instead, it is managers and their policies that convert environmental exigencies and organizational goals into shared objectives and ways of conducting business. Those assigned to commit organizational crimes raise doubt that cultures emerge spontaneously from consenually shared responses to the business environment where the organization operates. In testimony hearings before the U.S. Senate, a reluctant participant in the heavy electrical equipment price fixing scandals of the early 1960s explained that upon employment he began to be "indoctrinated properly" into the intricacies and history of administering prices in the industry (Senate Committee on the Judiciary, 1961:16822). His learning included the rationalizations commonly invoked in his company. For example, erratic fluctuations in the market were said to endanger U.S. enterprise, and stable profits were said to be necessary to continue research and development needed to move the country and his corporate organization forward. He also was educated in evasive language (vocabulary of motives), like "price stabilization" and "industry cooperation" so that collusion could be discussed comfortably, as well as in techniques for cloaking price-fixing behind legitimate trade meetings. Part of his cultural education also included oft-repeated stories about the lack of job security during "white sales," the industry name for competitive price wars, and of managers being reassigned to unrewarding jobs because their moral convictions were insufficiently flexible. This manager recalled that the importance of learning the ropes of the conspiratorial culture for career advancement was made clear, "I think the best way I can express this, Senator, is that every direct supervisor that I had directed me to meet with competition" (Senate Committee on the Judiciary, 1961:16869). His experience of culture bolstered by authority is not unique. An aircraft engineer told to write a misleading test report on a faulty aircraft break recounts how subtle directives came to a head when his superior finally advised "write the goddam thing and shut up about it" (Vandivier, 1996:132).

Investigators are in agreement that the stance towards ethical conduct and compliance with law taken by top management is a critical determinant of organizational culture (Coleman and Ramos, 1998). With regard to police compliance with legal restraints on their behavior, for example:

> Once they are inside, new officers' behavior, perceptions, and values are influenced enormously by their administrators, and there develops within police departments a shared view of the world and the police in it. To be sure, the routine policing is governed in large measure by peer pressures and by the desire for peer approval, but, whether through act or omission, the chief is the main architect of police officers' street behavior. This is so because the strength and direction of street-level police peer pressures ultimately are determined by administrative definitions of *good* and *bad* policing and by the general tone that comes from the top (Skolnick and Fyfe, 1993: 136).

As moral exemplars, top management's beliefs about the legitimacy, credibility, and efficacy of control measures is particularly important (Clinard, 1983; Hambrick and Mason, 1984; Sonnenfeld and Lawrence, 1978). When they signal that compliance with the law is not a primary organizational objective, subordinates take note. Crime conducive signals may be sent through rewards for those who achieve organizational goals by illicit means or by failing to put in place or support effective control measures. Gradually, hiring and firing decisions cultivate a culture in accord with organizational priorities.

Long-running conspiracies have been used to evidence the mundane and nondeliberative contexts in which acts of organizational crime occur. Proponents of this view point out that where criminal decisions are banal and ordinary, they may appear, both to outsiders and participants, indistinguishable from normal business transactions. Entrenched conspiracies are evidence also of the strategic lengths to which organizational managers sometimes will go to hide criminal behavior from authorities and to ensure that subordinates need not think of themselves or other organizational members as criminals. Management decisions by some make crime seem routine and easy for others. Despite attempts to mask criminal acts as acceptable, it is doubtful whether actors are so constrained by crime-conducive cultures that they do not recognize criminal activity. Evasive language and directives, meticulous avoidance of documentation and accountability, and concerted ignorance by management, while criminally useful, are signs to those with experience working in organizations that their firm is engaging in action that is unscrupulous if not illegal.

CONCLUSION

Some of the strongest evidence for the impact of organizational culture comes from those few white-collar offenders who have come around to acknowledging that they broke the law but point out that their actions did not seem criminal at the time. They admit that in their former view of the world their behavior seemed necessary or even heroic. Only when confronted with the views of those outside their organization or with the realization that their organization abandoned them in the face of prosecution, do they see their crime from the perspective of an organizational outsider. These offenders' accounts of the ease and the acceptance of criminal behavior in their organizations lends intuitive support to cultural explanations.

Nevertheless, there are reasons also to question the power of culture as an explanation of organizational crime. After the first decade of research into the nature and consequences of organizational culture, one observer charged that "[c]ulture research remains an unpaid promissory note in the field of organizational behavior . . . [and] we are still in the earliest phases of understanding . . . [its] role in organizations" (Rousseau, 1990:186). Imprecise and multiple definitions of organizational culture have impeded theoretical understanding of its effects. Although advocates for the explanatory and predictive power of organizational culture have wrestled with the problem of how to conceptualize its core meaning, success has been limited. Even casual examination reveals a bewildering array of definitional approaches. Whereas all apparently agree that organizational culture is shared, precisely what is shared is less clear; by one count, more than 73 constructs have been used to define it (Ott, 1989).

Matters are no different where cultural explanations of crime are concerned. Although improved conceptual clarity is evident, that has not translated into better focused or methodologically more rigorous research. Today, as more than a decade ago, there are no studies "that develop systematic and independent measures of both business illegalities and corporate or industry cultures" (Yeager, 1986:100). The explanatory merits of organizational culture are conducted in an ad hoc fashion without appeal to a body of empirical evidence or adequate attention to the origins of culture in organizations and its influence on criminal action of individuals and their choices.

Cultural interpretations too often evoke an oversocialized conception of actions; culture is sketched as a force that drives behavior rather than a context in which volitional agents construct lines of action. As such, they fail to capture the complexity of cultures that often are ambiguous, contradictory, and contested. Actors do not "adhere slavishly to a script written for them by the particular social category that they happen to occupy" simply because their "attempts at purposive action are . . . embedded in concrete ongoing systems of social relations" (Granovetter, 1985:487). Organizational culture constrains actors' choices, but it also enables them by providing convenient rationalizations and situationally appropriate behaviors. Cultures emerge from patterened interaction and learning between organizational **actors and** units. They also may be constructed with intent and perhaps with criminal intent. Cultural scripts often are selected according to the advantages they offer. When it is difficult to attribute the origin of a decision to a single actor or policy, it is tempting to explain it with culture; however, culture is a context for choices.

REFERENCES

Barnett, Harold C. 1986. "Industry culture and industry economy: Correlates of tax noncompliance in Sweden." *Criminology* 24:553–74.

Benson, Michael. 1985. "Denying the guilty mind: Accounting for involvement in a white-collar crime." *Criminology* 23:583–607.

Books in Print. 1997. R. R. Bowker.

Braithwaite, John. 1989. "Criminological theory and organizational crime." *Justice Quarterly* 6:333–58.

Calavita, Kitty, Henry N. Pontell, and Robert Tillman. 1997. *Big Money Crime: Fraud and Politics in the Savings and Loan Crisis.* Berkeley, CA: University of California Press.

Clinard, Marshall B. 1983. *Corporate Ethics and Crime.* Beverley Hills, CA: Sage.

Clinard, Marshall B., and Richard Quinney. 1973. *Criminal Behavior Systems: A Typology* (2nd ed.) New York: Holt, Rinehart and Winston.

Clinard, Marshall B., and Peter C. Yeager. 1980. *Corporate Crime.* New York: Macmillan

Coleman, James S. 1982. *The Asymmetric Society.* Syracuse, NY: Syracuse University Press.

Coleman, James W. 1987. "Toward an integrated theory of white-collar crime." *American Journal of Sociology* 93:406–39.

Coleman, James W., and Linda L. Ramos. 1998. "Subcultures and deviant behavior in the organizational context." Pp. 3–34 in *The Sociology of Organizations: Deviance in and of Organizations,* edited by Peter A. Bamberger and William J. Sonnenstuhl. Vol. 15. Stamford, CT: JAI.

Cressey, Donald R. 1995. "Poverty of theory in corporate crime research." Pp. 413–31 in *White-Collar Crime: Classic and Contemporary Views* (3rd edition), edited by Gilbert Geis, Robert F. Meier, and Lawrence M. Salinger. New York: Free Press.

Deal, Terrence E., and Allan A. Kennedy. 1982. *Corporate Cultures: The Rites and Rituals of Corporate Life.* Addison-Wesley.

Denzin, Norman K. 1977. "Notes on the criminogenic hypothesis: A case study of the American liquor industry." *American Sociological Review* 42:905–20.

Ermann, M. David, and Richard J. Lundman. 1978. "Deviant acts by complex organizations: Deviance and social control at the organizational level of analysis." *Sociological Quarterly* 19:55–67.

Frank, Nancy. 1985. *Crimes Against Health and Safety.* New York: Harrow and Heston.

Friedman, Milton. 1962. *Capitalism and Freedom.* University of Chicago Press.

Geis, Gilbert. 1967. "White-collar crime: The heavy electrical equipment antitrust cases of 1961." Pp. 139–51 in *Criminal Behavior Systems: A Typology,* edited by Marshall B. Clinard and Richard Quinney. New York: Holt, Rinehart, and Winston.

Gordon, George G. 1991. "Industry determinants of organizational culture." *Academy of Management Review* 16:396–415.

Granovetter, Mark. 1985. "Economic action and social structure: The problem of embeddedness." *American Journal of Sociology* 91:481–510.

Hambrick, Donald C., and Phyllis A. Mason. 1984. "Upper echelons: The organization as a reflection of its top managers." *Academy of Management Review* 9:193–206.

Hills, Stuart L. 1987. "Epilogue: Corporate violence and the banality of evil." Pp. 187–206 in *Corporate Violence,* edited by Stuart L. Hills. Totawa, NJ: Rowman & Littlefield.

Hofstede, Geert, Bram Neuijen, Denise Daval Ohayv, and Geert Sanders. 1990. "Measuring organizational cultures: A qualitative and quantitative study across twenty cases." *Administrative Science Quarterly* 35:286–316.

Jaques, Elliot. 1952. *The Changing Culture of a Factory.* New York: Dryden.

Jesilow, Paul, Henry Pontell, and Gilbert Geis. 1993. *Prescription for Profit.* Berkeley: University of California Press.

Levine, Dennis B. 1991. *Inside Out: An Insider's Account of Wall Street.* New York: Putnam

Kilmann, Ralph H., Mary J. Saxton, and Roy Serpa, eds. 1985. *Gaining Control of the Corporate Culture.* San Francisco: Jossey–Bass.

Minor, W. 1981. "Techniques of neutralization: A reconceptualization and empirical examination." *Journal of Research in Crime and Delinquency* 18:295–318.

Ott, J. Steven. 1989. *The Organizational Culture Perspective.* Belmont, CA: Brooks/Cole.

Paternoster, R., and Simpson, Sally. 1993. "A rational choice theory of corporate crime." Pp. 37–58 in Ronald V. Clarke and Marcus Felson, eds. *Routine Activity and Rational Choice,* New Brunswick, NJ: Transaction.

Pugh, Derek L., and David J. Hickson. 1997. *Writers on Organizations* (5th edition). Thousand Oaks, CA: Sage.

Rousseau, Denise M. 1990. "Assessing organizational culture: The case for multiple methods." Pp. 153–92 in *Organizational Climate and Culture,* edited by Benjamin Schneider. New York: Jossey–Bass.

Scott, W. Richard. 1992. *Rational, Natural and Open Systems* (3rd edition). Englewood Cliffs, NJ: Prentice-Hall.

Senate Committee on the Judiciary. 1961. Administered Prices: Price Fixing and Bid-Rigging in the Electrical Manufacturing Industry. Testimony of George E. Burens before Subcommittee on Antitrust and Monopoly. Washington D.C.: GPO.

Shover, Neal, and Kevin A. Bryant. 1993. "Theoretical explanations of corporate crime." Pp. 141–76 in *Understanding Corporate Criminality,* edited by Michael Blankenship. New York: Garland.

Simon, David R., and Stanley Eitzen. 1993. *Elite Deviance* (4th edition). Boston, MA: Allyn and Bacon.

Simpson, Sally. 1986. "The decomposition of antitrust: Testing a multi-level, longitudinal model of profit-squeeze." *American Sociological Review* 51:859–75.

Skolnick, Jerome and James J. Fyfe. 1993. *Above the Law: Police and the Excessive Use of Force.* New York: Free Press.

Sonnenfeld, Jeffrey, and Paul R. Lawrence. 1978. "Why do companies succumb to price fixing?" *Harvard Business Review* 56:145–57.

Staw, Barry M., and Eugene Szwajkowski. 1975. "The scarcity–munificence component of organizational environments and the commission of illegal acts." *Administrative Science Quarterly* 20:345–54.

Sutherland, Edwin H. 1983 [1949]. *White Collar Crime: The Uncut Version.* New Haven, CT: Yale University Press.

Sykes, Gresham, and David Matza. 1957. "Techniques of neutralization: A theory of delinquency." *American Sociological Review* 22:667–70.

Trice, Harrison M. 1993. *Occupational Subcultures in the Workplace.* Ithaca, NY: Cornell University Press.

U.S. Department of Commerce. 1996. *Statistical Abstract of the U.S.* Washington, D.C.: U.S. Government Printing Office.

Vandivier, Kermit. 1996. "Why should my conscience bother me?" Pp. 118–38 in *Corporate and Governmental Deviance,* 5th ed., edited by M. David Ermann and Richard J. Lundman. New York: Oxford University Press.

Vaughan, Diane. 1996. *The Challenger Launch Decision: Risky Technology, Culture, and Deviance at NASA.* Chicago: University of Chicago Press.

Yank, Hiyol, ed. 1997. *Business Periodicals Index.* H. W. Wilson

Yeager, Peter C. 1986. "Analyzing corporate offenses: Progress and prospects." Pp. 93–120 in *Research in Corporate Social Performance and Policy,* Vol. 8, edited by J. E. Post. Stamford, CT: JAI.

Zimring, Franklin E., and Gordon S. Hawkins. 1993. "Crime, justice and the savings and loan crisis." Pp. 247–92 in Michael Tonry and Albert J. Reiss, eds. *Beyond the Law: Crime in Complex Organizations.* University of Chicago.

PANEL 14   Bhopal

In 1984, the Union Carbide Corporation, one of the largest companies headquartered in the United States, released methyl isocyanate and hydrogen cyanide gas into the atmosphere from their plant in Bhopal, India. According to the Indian government's count, the incident killed 3,329 people and seriously injured some 20,000. Immediately following the disaster, the chairman of the company indicated that the chemical plant had not complied with standard safety protocols and had used procedures that were not permitted in the United States. His statement soon was retracted, however, and the company now blamed unidentified saboteurs and inadequate Indian regulations. In 1987, Indian prosecutors filed criminal charges against Union Carbide, its CEO and eight officers of its Indian subsidiary. Union Carbide, however, won a judgment in U.S. courts establishing that Indian courts had sole jurisdiction over all civil litigation resulting from the disaster. Observers speculated that company lawyers believed they would receive favorable treatment and less costly judgements from Indian courts. The case was settled for $470 million in 1989, a sum that included payments of approximately $1,000 per claimant. It was also agreed in the settlement that Carbide would be immune from all pending litigation and that criminal charges against officers of the company would be dropped. The Indian Supreme Court subsequently ruled that criminal charges would stand, but it is unlikely that any of those charged will be extradited from their first-world homes to face manslaughter charges.

Sources: Los Angeles Times, February 15, 1989, p. D3; Frank Pearce and Steven Tombs, *Toxic Capitalism: Corporate Crime and the Chemical Industry.* Brookfield, Conn.: Dartmouth, 1998.

Profits, Pressure, and Corporate Law Breaking

ANNE JENKINS AND JOHN BRAITHWAITE

There are not many themes in the empirical literature on corporate crime that are repeatedly reported. A recurrent one, however, is that pressure for the worst types of corporate crimes comes from the top. Organizations, like fish,

"Profits, Pressure, and Corporate Lawbreaking" from *Crime, Law and Social Change* 20 (1993): 221–232. Reprinted by permission.

rot from the head down. This was a recurrent theme in Braithwaite's interviews with 131 pharmaceutical industry executives:

> [The Chief executive] sets the tone and the rest of management fall in line. The ethical standards of anyone other than him don't matter so much. Well, unless you have one of those companies where an old guy at the helm has a right hand man making all the real decisions [U.S. executive].[1]

Baumart[2] found that executives ranked the behavior of their superiors in the company as the principal determinant of unethical decisions. In a fifteen-year follow-up of Baumart's work, Brenner and Molander[3] found that superiors still ranked as the primary influence on unethical decision-making. Half of the 1977 sample of executives believed that superiors often do not want to know how results are obtained, so long as the desired outcome is achieved. Clinard's middle managers also repeatedly argued that it was "top management, and in particular the chief executive officer (CEO) who sets the ethical tone."[4] Similarly, Cressey and Moore's interviews with auditors supported the conclusion that the pressure for lawbreaking that counts comes from the top.[5] While it is often, even typically, middle managers who carry out corporate crimes, these crimes are frequently the result of pressure from the top to "get this done, but don't tell me how you do it." Obversely, one of the characteristics found in firms that have exemplary records of compliance with laws of a certain type, is top management commitment to and backing for internal compliance systems.[6]

A second recurrent theme has been that it is greed or the profit motive that is responsible for corporate crime.[7] While this seems almost a banal observation, it has actually been contested in various ways by scholars who have pointed to the ubiquitous organizational crime of state run bureaucracies in both the East and the West.[8] Gross, for example, concluded: "Some organizations seek profit, others seek survival, still others seek to fulfil government-imposed quotas, others seek to serve a body of professionals who run them, some seek to win wars, and some seek to serve a clientele. Whatever the goals might be, it is the emphasis on them that creates the trouble."[9]

In this paper, we explore these two hypotheses about corporate lawbreaking—that pressure from the top and pressure to make profits causes lawbreaking—using quantitative data of a sort that has not been applied to these hypotheses in the past. We embark on this research as scholars who basically agree with Coleman's lament that "reliable statistical analysis:" has not been possible on the basis of corporate offending rates available from U.S. government agencies: "The best work done so far in this field is the case studies that carefully analyze the conditions in particular organizations or industries, and I would suggest that lacking the development of a significant new data base, this approach offers the brightest hope of future progress . . ."[10] The data presented in this paper are indeed based on a "significant new data base," albeit one that will seem obscure to scholars in the Northern hemisphere. So we suggest that the analyses do not justify our being included among Coleman's researchers who have been "seduced into carrying on empirical research based on unreliable data."[11] Rather, we have discovered a kind of data on corporate lawbreaking much more reliable than traditional measures of either corporate or street crime. We use these data to test whether widely reported conclusions from qualitative research are quantitatively sustainable.

AUSTRALIAN NURSING HOME COMPLIANCE

In 1987, our research team seized an unusual opportunity to get in on the ground floor with the establishment of a completely new regulatory program for the Australian federal government to regulate quality of care in nursing homes. Previously this had been primarily a state government responsibility. The federal program involved a radical shift to 31 outcome-oriented standards away from the enforcement of inputs. Our research team has had a significant effect on the design of the emerging new regulatory process during the past six years. Part of the agreement reached by the two peak (profit and non-profit) industry associations in relation to the new program was to urge their members to cooperate with the research described in this paper. Part of our agreement with the federal government was that they would inspect a random sample of 242 nursing homes, stratified by size (number of beds), ownership (for-profit vs. non-profit), and the mean level of disability of the residents, on an agreed schedule. Interviews were conducted with directors of nursing, inspectors, staff, and proprietors not only for these nursing homes, but also at all other nursing homes inspected in the four study regions (in New South Wales, Victoria, Queensland, and South Australia) during the period of the study. Addition of this non-randomly selected supplementary sample increased the number of nursing homes included in the first wave of the study to 410.

The federal government and the industry also agreed to cooperate with follow-up inspections being completed within 18–20 months of the first inspection wherever possible for the random sample and also to do as many of the supplementary sample as they could manage within 18–24 months of the first inspection.

The commitments on the random sample, but not the supplementary samples were delivered with impressive diligence. For the first wave random sample only nine nursing homes refused to cooperate in the study, a 96 per cent response rate. The industry associations were extremely helpful in urging the cooperation of homes that were reluctant. We even received a message of cooperation from a proprietor who was in hiding in the United States at the time of the study, being pursued by the Australian Federal Police in relation to nursing home fraud allegations! Similarly, completed inspectors' questionnaires were received for 406 of the 410 first wave inspections.

A number of factors such as closures and ownership changes caused a considerable attribution of cases between the first and second waves, however. By far the most important cause of attrition was the inspectors not managing to get to most of the supplementary sample on time.[12] Repeatedly, analyses have not found results to be significantly different for randomly selected versus supplementary homes. Hence, we have adopted the practice of combining the random and supplementary samples. Nevertheless, a control dummy for random versus non-random selection is included in the regressions reported here as a check on selection bias affecting results.

What is most innovative about the new Australian nursing home regulation the way its compliance ratings are based on a systematic dialogue among number of participants—an inspection team (usually only two, but three and more in the more difficult cases), nursing home staff and management and the residents. By a systematic dialogue, we mean one that sees debate about the positives and negatives under each standard, addressed one after the other until all standards are completed. Australian nursing home regulation is far more resident-centered, relying more on interviews with residents, than nursing home regulation in the other countries where we have conducted research—the United States, Canada, England, and Japan.

An unexpected and exciting finding of the research program has been that this participatory-dialogic approach to regulatory inspection generates unprecedented reliability in ratings of compliance with the law. Test–retest reliabilities on total compliance scores when inspectors employed by our research team visited nursing homes at the same time as the government inspection teams ranged from 0.93 to 0.96, depending on the point in the process where agreement was calculated.[13] When chief executives of the organization were asked what ratings they should have received on a three-point rating scale on each of the standards, 84 per cent of the time they gave themselves the same rating as the team gave them. In short, the dialogic regulatory process generated an unusual degree of consensus on what was the true status of the facility's compliance with the law.

For most of the nursing homes in this study, most of the standards have the status of criminal law, the federal standards having been wholly incorporated into state law in New South Wales and many of them have been incorporated into Victorian state law. However, the operational effectiveness of these standards comes from the National Health Act, from the fact that the federal government can and does impose sanctions on non-compliant nursing homes by cutting off universal federal government per-patient benefits that are payable to all Australian nursing homes.

Compliance with the National Health Act is measured in the present study by adding compliance scores for each of the 31 standards (met scores 1, met in part scores 0.5, not met 0) to generate a total compliance score of 31, a procedure shown by earlier multivariate analyses to be sound.[14] In addition, the self-reported ratings given by directors of nursing to their own home were used as an alternative measure of compliance.

MEASURING PROFIT ORIENTATION AND PRESSURE FROM THE TOP

Profit orientation is measured simply by classifying nursing homes as non-profit (33 percent of cases) versus for-profit (66 percent). For-profit homes are then classified according to whether the director of nursing (the chief executive) is also the owner or a joint owner (often a couple are joint owners, with the wife being the director of nursing). For almost a quarter of for-profit homes, the director of nursing is an owner or joint owner. For another slightly larger group of homes, the owner is a private individual other than the director of nursing and for the largest group of for-profit homes (almost half), the owner is a corporation. Three-quarters of the non-profit homes are run by churches, with the remainder being run by charitable institutions such as lodges. Government-run nursing homes, which are small in number, were not subject to this regulatory program at the time of the study except in unusual circumstances.

The measure of pressure from the top is less reliable than the measurement of either compliance or for-profit status. We have only a three item scale (alpha = 0.61) based on an interview with the director of nursing after the first wave inspection. The items are "My proprietor sets me goals that can only be achieved by breaching the standards"; "My proprietor sometimes puts me under a financial squeeze that makes it impossible to meet the standards"; and a reverse scored item. "My proprietor has the attitude that the government's standards and regulations must be met no matter what the costs." These items are rated on a five-point scale: strongly disagree, disagree, neither agree nor disagree, agree, or strongly agree. In order to ensure that a particular item did not dominate the scale, individual items were divided by their standard deviation prior to summing their scores. In order to facilitate interpretation, the scores were rescaled to run from 0 to 10. The mean of the scale was 3.29, and the standard deviation 1.87.

CONTROLS

When examining the relationship between financial pressures and nursing home compliance, it is important to take into account the influence of a number of antecedent factors which, the literature suggests, also affect nursing home compliance. Characteristics of the home such as its size and age may influence the quality of care provided. In general, larger homes provide poorer quality care.[15] As Fottler, Smith, and James suggest, larger homes with high occupancy rates require a proportionately larger amount of nursing service. One of the major dilemmas that nursing home administrators face, however, is that profits can be increased by decreasing the intensity of patient care service and thereby decreasing the quality of service provided.[16] Clearly, then, it is necessary to control for both the size of the home and the amount of nursing care required by residents. Homes in older buildings are also be more likely to provide inadequate care to residents. In older buildings, maintenance requirements are greater and there is a greater likelihood of encountering design problems which require costly alterations in order to meet standards such as those relating to fire and physical safety.[17]

Apart from the characteristics of the home itself, factors associated with the inspection teams also have an impact on the compliance ratings given to a home. Inspection teams vary in size. While there is no hard and fast rule, the policy of the government has been to send larger inspection teams to larger homes in order to adequately cover the ground. The smaller the team, the greater the likelihood that instances of non-compliance will go unnoticed. The effect of team size is controlled in the analyses. Each state of Australia has its own teams which carry out the inspection of homes in that state only. Inspectors rarely work with teams based in other states. Although the standards for nursing home compliance are the same across the country, previous work suggests that significant variation on compliance ratings occurs across the states.[18] The pattern of compliance ratings suggested that state teams varied in the degree of toughness or permissiveness shown with regard to some standards. To control for geographical location, three dummy variables representing Queensland, New South Wales, and Victoria, were entered into the regression equations.

As indicated previously, nursing homes participating in this study were drawn from a random and supplementary sample. A dummy variable for the sample from which the home is drawn is included in analyses. Table 1 de-

TABLE 1.
Definitions, means, and standard deviations for background variables.

Variable	Coding	Mean	SD
Non-profit home[a]	1 = yes, 0 = no	0.34	0.47
Number of beds in the home[b c]	Number	49	36
Age of home[a]	Years	36.4	30.6
Mean disability of residents[b]	Mean hrs care	19	2.11
Number on inspection team[a]	Low 2 - high 9	2.49	0.60
Queensland home[a]	1 = yes, 0 = other	0.18	0.39
Victorian home[a]	1 = yes, 0 = other	0.23	0.42
New South Wales home[a]	1 = yes, 0 = other	0.41	0.49
Sample home	1 = yes, 0 = no	0.59	0.49

[a]These variables were taken from the interviews with directors of nursing.
[b]This variable was taken from the Commonwealth Department of Health, Housing and Community Services data base, which contains demographic information about nursing home residents. Each resident entering a home is allocated to one of five service need categories (resident's classification index, or RCI), according to the average number of hours of nursing and personal care (NPC) required per week. Residents allocated to level one require an average of 27 NPC hours; those at level two require 23.5 NPC hours; those at level three require 20NPC hours; those at level four require 13 NPC hours; and those at level five require 10 NPC hours. To calculate the mean weekly hours of nursing care per resident provided by each home, the average number of NPC hours, according to the RCI, were calculated across all residents in the home.
[c]The number of beds in the home was a highly skewed variable, with most homes having around 50 beds but some having as many as 200 or, in one case, 510. Residual analysis confirmed the need for a log transformation of this variable. The interpretation of the effect of this transformed variable in regression is that larger homes tend to have more incidences of non-compliance, but that as home size increases, larger differences in bed numbers lead to smaller increases in predicted non-compliance.

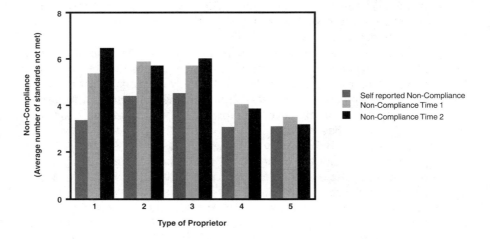

FIGURE 1. Incidence of non-compliance according to type of proprietor.
Type of proprietor:

1. DON is owner or joint owner
2. Private individual
3. Private company
4. Church group
5. Other charitable

scribes the scoring used for each of the control variables along with means and standard deviations.

RESULTS

Three measures of compliance are available: self-rated compliance at time 1 as assessed by the director of nursing, governmentally rated compliance at time 1 and governmentally rated compliance at time 2. The data in Fig. 1 show that for-profit homes on all three measures break the law more often than non-profit homes. While on the wave 1 data, non-compliance is only 47 percent higher among the for-profits, at wave 2, it is 60 percent higher.

There are many possible interpretations of why for-profit homes should have lower compliance than non-profits. One is simply based on the level of government funding support. Historically, though not today, non-profit homes attracted greater financial support from the government than for-profits and even today non-profits get more favorable tax treatment. Conversely, one of the arguments as to why residents get poorer care in for-profit nursing homes is that money is diverted from resident care to profits. A previous study found that directors of nursing in non-profit homes have a stronger commitment to nursing professionalism than for-profit directors of nursing.[19]

The question of particular interest in this paper is whether pressure for non-compliance from the top is greater in for-profit than in non-profit homes. Figure 2 shows that it is the effect is not but top-down pressure for non-compliance is significantly ($t = 3.36$, $df = 408$, $p < 0.001$) greater in for-profit homes than in non-profits.

At the bivariate level there is also a significant association between top-down pressure and non-compliance ($4 = 0.32$, $p < 0.001$). Table 2 summarizes how these associations hold up after entering the controls discussed above, fitting an ordinary least squares regression model to the data.

Table 2 shows that top-down pressure for non-compliance has a significant effect in reducing compliance after entering the appropriate controls, including the control for the ownership of the nursing home. The significant effect of perceived pressure at time 1 on compliance at time 2 is the more compelling result than the significant effect of time 1 pressure on time 1 compliance. This is because the latter result might conceivably be discounted as time 1 non-compliance causing the perception of pressure than the reverse. Any such in-

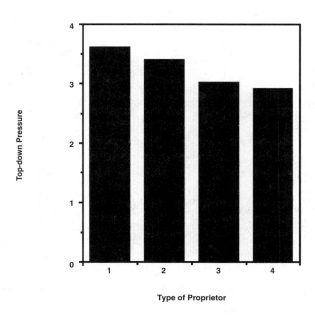

Type of Proprietor

FIGURE 2. Perceived top-down pressure on Director of Nursing according to type of proprietor.
Type of proprietor:

1. Private individual (cases where DON is proprietor are excluded)
2. Private company
3. Church group
4. Other charitable

TABLE 2.
Regression results for the effect of top-down pressure experienced by the Director of Nursing on three measures of compliance.

Variable Controls	Compliance time 1				Compliance time 2	
	Government rated		Self-rated		Government rated	
	b	beta	b	beta	b	beta
Number of beds in the home	-2.85	(-0.14)**	-0.01	(-0.10)*	-2.66	(-0.14)*
Age of the home	-0.57	(-0.15)***	-0.03	(-0.20)***	-0.03	(-0.18)**
Mean disability of residents	0.23	(0.09)	0.24	(0.12)*	0.26	(0.12)
Number of inspectors	-0.95	(-0.11)*	-0.49	(-0.07)		[a]
Queensland home	5.18	(0.41)***	3.98	(0.38)***	4.33	(0.42)***
Victoria home	4.79	(0.39)***	4.09	(0.40)***	1.29	(0.13)
New South Wales home	4.49	(0.45)***	4.01	(0.48)***	5.52	(0.67)***
Sample home	-0.94	(-0.09)	-0.75	(-0.09)	-0.58	(-0.07)
Non-profit home	1.15	(0.11)*	0.71	(0.08)	1.21	(0.15)*
Top-down pressure	-0.62	(-0.24)***	-0.57	(-0.26)***	-0.36	(-0.15)*
Constant		28.41		26.98		24.08
R^2 (adjusted)		0.346		0.349		0.304

[a]Information not available.
*$p < 0.05$, (two tailed), ** $p < 0.01$. (two tailed). *** p 0.001, (two tailed).

terpretation is untenable with the time lagged data. Being a for-profit nursing home significantly reduces compliance net of the effect of top-down pressure for compliance at both points in time. However, the effect of for-profit status in reducing compliance is not significant when the self-reported measure of compliance is used.

CONCLUSION

U.S. data on nursing home compliance, while it is inferior to the Australian data in terms of reliability of the measurement of compliance,[20] generally support the conclusion that for-profit homes have lower compliance and/or lower quality of care than non-profits.[21] Overall, our own impressionistic observations from visiting over 50 U.S. nursing homes, reading the literature and interviewing the key players in the industry is the same as Valdeck's:

> [O]n the average, voluntary facilities are somewhat better than proprietary ones. The best voluntary facilities are the best there are. The worst nursing homes are almost exclusively proprietary. But in the middle ranges, there is substantial overlap.[22]

The Australian data support a similar conclusion. However, we would say that some of the church homes have very poor compliance indeed with residents' right standards; these are church homes with an ideology of paternalistic caring that brings them into conflict with the regulators and advocacy groups.[23] Certainly, there are good for-profit and non-profit nursing homes, even though the latter are better on average. While pressure for profits does motivate law breaking, non-profits have their own pressures, including financial ones:

> Profit for us is not different from an increase in the 'general fund' for not-for-profits. [Administrator of a New York for-profit nursing home]

During our fieldwork, we did indeed encounter the odd case of a church using nursing home revenues to cross-subsidize other church activities. This does lead us back to Gross's critique of profit or greed as the pre-eminent explanation of organizational crime. Since before the Inquisition, it has been clear that churches have objectives so important to them that terrible crimes can be committed when attainment of those objectives is frustrated. Compliance differences between for-profit and non-profit institutions are not so great as to justify systematically lower regulatory scrutiny of non-profit providers. Indeed, given a choice between regulated private provision and unregulated voluntary or state provision of care to vulnerable people, prudent advocates might opt for the former. Yet there is an irony here, as political pressure for regulation only becomes effective when traditionally public or voluntary provision is shifted in the for-profit sector (as with aged care in Britain during the 1980s). This happens after decades of misplaced trust in public and voluntary providers to care ethically for vulnerable people who are difficult to manage.

At the same time, these unique quantitative data confirm what qualitative corporate crime researchers have consistently reported: that pressure for profits matters and what when the pressure for profits is greatest, the boss is more likely to say: "This is the bottom line I want. I don't care (and I don't want to know) what you have to do to get there." But just as business tycoons sometimes say this, so too do bishops. The policy implication of this would seem to be the importance of individual criminal liability of proprietors for serious regulatory offences, be they businessmen or bishops.

NOTES AND REFERENCES

1. John Braithwaite. *Corporate Crime on the Pharmaceutical Industry* (London: Routledge and Kegan Paul, 1984). 351.
2. R,.C. Baumart, "How Ethical are Businessmen?" in Gilbert Geis (ed.) *White-Collar Criminal* (New York: Atherton, 1968).
3. S.N. Brenner and E,A. Molander, "Is the Ethics of Business Changing?" *Harvard Business Review,* 1977 (55): 59–70.
4. Marshall Clinard. *Corporate Ethics and Crime: The Role of Middle Management* (Beverley Hills: Sage 1983).

5. Donald R. Cressey and Charles A. Moore. *Corporation Codes of Ethical Conduct* (Santa Barbara: Department of Sociology. University of Santa Barbara, 1980).

6. John Braithwaite. *To Punish or Persuade: Enforcement of Coal Mine Safety* (Albany: State University of New York Press, 1985).

7. See, for example, Harold C. Barnett. "Corporate Capitalism, Corporate Crime." *Crime and Delinquency,* 1981 (27). 4–23.

8. See, for example, P.N. Grabosky. *Wayward Governance: Illegality and its Control in the Public Sector* (Camberra: Australian Institute of Criminology, 1989); Ronald C. Kramer, "The Space Shuttle Challenger Explosion: A Case Study of State-Corporate Crime," in Kip Schlegel and David Weisburd (eds.), *White-Collar Crime Reconsidered* (Boston: Northeaster University Press, 1992); John Braithwaite, "White-Collar Crime Competition and Capitalism: Comment on Coleman." *American Journal of Sociology,* 1988 (94), 627 631; and see the rejoinder, James William Coleman, "Competition and the Structure of Industrial Society: Reply to Braithwaite." *American Journal of Sociology* 1988 (94), 632–636.

9. Edward Gross, "Organizations as Criminal Actors," in P.R. Wilson and J. Braithwaite (eds.) *Two Faces of Deviance: Crimes of the Powerless and Powerful* (Brisbane: University of Queensland Press, 1978), 209.

10. James William Coleman, "The Theory of White-Collar Crime: From Sutherland to the 1990s," in Kip Schlegel and David Weisburd (eds.) *White-Collar Crime Reconsidered* (Boston: Northeastern University Press, 1992), 71.

11. Ibid., p. 71.

12. For complete details on the sampling and other methodological issues, see John Braithwaite, Toni Makkai, Valerie Braithwaite, and Diane Gibson, *Raising the Standard: Resident Central Nursing Home Regulation in Australia* (Canberra: Australian Government Publishing Service, 1993).

13. John Braithwaite, Valerie Braithwaite, Diane Gibson, Miriam Landau, and Toni Makkai. *The Reliability and Validity of Nursing Home Standards* (Canberra: Australian Government Publishing Service, 1992).

14. Valerie Braithwaite, John Braithwaite, Diane Gibson, and Toni Makkai, "Assessing the Quality of Australian Nursing Home Care", *Australian Journal of Public Health,* 1992 (16), 89 97.

15. For example, S.R. Greenwald and M. W. Linn. "Intercorrelation of data on nursing homes," *The Gerontologist,* 1971 (11). 337–346.

16. Myron D. Fottler. Howard L. Smith, and William L. James. "Profits and patient care quality in nursing homes: Are they compatible?" *The Geronologist* 1981 (21), 532–538.

17. See Vernon L. Green and Deborah J. Monahan, "Structural and operational factors affecting quality of patient care in nursing homes," *Public Policy,* 1981 (29:4), 399–415.

18. See John Braithwaite, Toni Makkai, Valerie Braithwaite, Diane Gibson and David Ermann, *The Contribut9ion of the Standards Monitoring Process to the Quality of Nursing Home Life: A Preliminary Report* (Canberra: Department of Health, Housing and Community Services, 1990).

19. Toni Makkai and Valerie Braithwaite, "Professionalism, Organizations and Compliance," *Law and Social Inquiry,* 1993.

20. See John Braithwaite, Valerie Braithwaite, Diane Gibson, Miriam Landau and Toni

Makkai, *The Reliability and Validity of Nursing Home Standards* (Canberra: Australian Government Publishing Service, 1992).

21. The New York State Moreland Act Commission on Nursing Homes and Residential Facilities. Report 1: *Regulating Nursing Home Care: The Paper Tigers.* (Albany: New York, 1975), 37; V.L. Green and D.J. Monahan, "Structural and Operational Factors Affecting Quality of Patient Care in Nursing Homes," *Public Policy,* 1981 (29) 399–415; F. Elwell, "The Effects of Ownership on Institutional Services," *The Gerontologist,* 1984 (24), 77–83; Yong S. Lee, "Nursing Homes and Quality of Health Care: The First Year Result of an Outcome-Oriented Survey," *Journal of Health and Human Resources Administration, 1984 (7), 32–60; Sonne Lemke and Rudolf H. Moos, "Quality of Residential Settings for Elderly Adults," Journal of Gerontology.* 1986 (41). 268–276; Catherine Hawes and Charles D. Phillips, "The changing structure of the nursing home industry and the impact of ownership on quality cost and access," in Bradford H. Gray (ed.), *For-Profit Enterprise in Health Care* (Washington D.C.: National Academy Press, 1986); Pamela Paul-Shaheen and Andrew J. Hogan, *Identifying Cost Effective Nursing Homes: A Benefit/Cost Tradeoff Analysis* (Lansing: Bureau of Health Facilities, Michigan Department of Public Health, 1988). Sonne Lemke and Rudolf H. Moos, "Ownership and Quality of Care in Residential Facilities for the Elderly." *The Gerontologist,* 1989 (29), 209–215; Riportella-Muller and Slesinger found that in general Wisconsin non-profits had fewer code violations and complains than for-profits, but that large non-profits had more violations than large for-profits (Roberta Riportella-Muller and Doris P. Slesinger, "The Relationship of Ownership and Size to Quality of Care in Wisconsin Nursing Homes," *The Gerontologist,* 1982 (22), 429–434). Some studies have not found poorer quality care in for-profit nursing homes; R.H. Holmberg and N. Anderson. "Implications of Ownership for Nursing Home Care," *Medical Care,* 1968 (6), 300–307; S. Levey, H.S. Ruchlin, B.A. Stotsky, D.R. Kinloch and W. Oppenheim "An Appraisal of Nursing Home Care," *Journal of Gerontology,* 1973 (28), 222–228; and S. Winn, "Analysis of selected characteristics of a matched sample of non-profit and proprietary nursing homes in the state of Washington," *Medical Care,* 1974 (12), 221–228. A study of Detroit homes by Gottesman suggested that the quality of care in church-related nonprofit homes was largely due to the socially and in many cases, economically advantaged group which used such facilities (Leonard E. Gottesman, "Nursing home performance as related to resident traits, ownership, size and source of payment," *American Journal of Public Health,* 1974 (64), 269–276. An important study by Koetting found that while non-profits provided substantially superior care than for-profits, this was because non-profits spent more on their residents. For-profits were more efficient in providing care with the discretionary dollars available to them, so that for any given quality level, for-profits were less expensive (M. Koetting, *Nursing Home Organization and Efficiency: Profit Versus Nonprofit.* (Lexington, Mass: Lexington Books, 1980).

22. Bruce Vladeck. *Unloving Care: The Nursing Home Tragedy* (New York: Basic Books, 1980). 123.

23. One of Australia's most outstanding directors of nursing, who has worked in both the for-profit and non-profit sectors made this point in a somewhat different way: "Some of the church homes are too much into the caring role. They're not enough into independence. They encourage the sick role, dependency."

Rational Choice, Situated Action, and the Social Control of Organizations

Diane Vaughan

Management decisions in the business world that value competitive and economic success more highly than the well-being of workers, consumers, or the general public so often have come to public attention that today's most widely accepted model of corporate criminality portrays managers of profit-seeking organizations as "amoral calculators" whose illegal actions are motivated by rational calculation of costs and opportunities (Kagan & Scholz 1984). Driven by pressures from the competitive environment, managers will violate the law to attain desired organizational goals unless the anticipated legal penalties (the expected costs weighed against the probability of delaying or avoiding them) exceed additional benefits the firm could gain by violation. The amoral calculator model locates the cause of business misconduct in the calculations of individual decisions makers. It reflects the logic of sociological rational choice theory (Hechter 1987; Friedman & Hechter 1988; Cook and Levi 1990; J. S. Coleman 1990a; Hechter & Kanazawa 1997), but with one important distinction. When decisionmakers' calculations of costs and benefits are tainted by self-interest, economics, or politics so that *intentional* wrongdoing and/or harm result, their calculation becomes amoral. . . .

RESEARCH CHALLENGES TO THE RATIONAL CHOICE/DETERRENCE MODEL

The tendency for the legal and administrative apparatus to prioritize a rational choice/deterrence model for the social control of organizations no doubt originates in a belief fundamental to American culture: the value placed on individualism that locates responsibility for achievement, accountability, and responsibility in the single actor (Tocqueville 1969; Bellah et al. 1985). This cultural belief has been reinforced by sociolegal research on structural variables related to white-collar and other forms of organizational misconduct. Quantitative studies using organizations as the units of analysis (usually corporations) consistently have identified a correlation between competition, economic strain, and violative behavior (Sutherland 1949; Staw & Swajkowski 1975; Clinard & Yeager 1980; Simpson 1986). The impossibility of micro-analysis of choice in this research notwithstanding, the persistent relationship between economic strain and violative behavior has lent credibility to an amoral

"Rational Choice, Situated Action, and the Social Control of Organizations" from *Law & Society Review* 32:1 (1998): 23–61. Reprinted by permission.

calculator model of decisionmaking that goes like this: When an organization experiences structural strain to achieve its goals, individuals acting in their organization roles weigh the costs and benefits of their actions, choosing to violate laws and rules to attain organization goals. . . .

Are violations a result of rational calculation of costs and benefits of some harmful social act? Recently, scholars have attempted to map this unexplored terrain. Some have studied decisionmaking indirectly, using violative behavior as an indicator of the presence or absence of deterrence. Simpson and Koper (1992) analyzed recidivism of corporate offenders, finding weak support for deterrence. Weisburd et al. (1995), examining recidivism after incarceration of individual white-collar offenders, found no specific deterrent effect over a 126-month follow-up period. One project showed that legalistic deterrent strategies can have negative unintended consequences: Grabosky (1995:351–53) reviewed several studies showing that in some cases a deterrent regulatory posture actually reduced compliance. Even when research examines decisionmaking more directly, support for the amoral calculator model remains unimpressive. Grabosky (1989) analyzed 17 case studies of misconduct by public sector organizations, finding evidence of careful assessment and weighing of costs and benefits in only 2 of the 17. Several studies used interviews to examine managerial decisionmaking. Simpson (1992:303) concluded that "managers, for the most part, do not think in deterrence terms." Braithwaite and Makkai (1991) found no support for deterrence. Paternoster and Simpson (1993, 1996) and Simpson (1998) tested deterrence in surveys that used offense-specific models of corporate crime in a vignette design. They found some indication of a deterrent effect in some situations.

At the same time that these recent interview-based studies break new ground with innovative approaches, they also demonstrate the difficulties of research on decisionmaking and illegality. The research designs make the meaning of the results unclear. Testing the deterrent effects of punishment is the sated goal of this research. That individual decisionmakers knowingly and rationally calculate the costs and benefits of punishments is *assumed* at the outset and becomes the basis for the design. Respondents not only are informed that the behavior in question is a violation, but also the researchers make the costs and benefits clear, conditions that seldom hold in real-life decisionmaking in the workplace (Simon 1957, 1976; Gross 1980; Weick 1979, 1995). Further, social context matters: Organizational socialization, culture, financial dependence on the organization, and organizational mandates have known effects on the thoughts and actions of members (Van Maanen & Schein 1979; Finney & Lesieur 1982; Van Maanen & Barley 1985; Jackall 1988; Martin 1992). Consequently, a person responding to an interview, questionnaire, or vignette is not subject to the same contingencies that would apply when making routine decisions in the workplace. The outcomes, which show either minimal or no deterrent effects, are taken by the researchers as challenges to the study design, not the decontextualized rational choice assumptions on which the designs are based.

Research raises additional reasons for questioning the priority of a rational choice/deterrence model over other possible regulatory options. In contrast to the amoral calculator model, some managers violate for reasons other than instrumental action directly tied to achieving competitive success: incompetence, misunderstanding of laws, or improper attention to regulatory requirements (Kagan & Scholz 1984). Also, how managers actually assess risks in the workplace is far from the systematic calculation the rational choice model implies: Decisionmakers do not weigh all possible outcomes but instead rely on a few key values; the magnitude of possible bad outcomes is more salient, so that there is less risk taking when greater stakes are involved; in practice, quantifying costs and benefits of a line of action is not easy (March & Shapira 1987). Finally, the laws, rules, and administrative regulations designed to guide organizational behavior are likely to be *mala prohibita* rather than *mala in se*; thus the standards to which organizations are expected to adhere and the consequent punishments are not clear to either organization decisionmakers or the public (Stinchcombe 1965:174–75; Calavita, Pontell, & Tillman 1997).

When the effect of the organization as a locus of choice is taken fully into account, social context becomes obvious as an influence in decisionmaking, shaping what an individual perceives to be rational at a given moment. Because of specialization and division of labor, employees may be unaware of their illegality because their action was part of a chain of actions by invisible others: Each individual act was legitimate, but together all the acts constituted a violation of which some individual participants were ignorant (Gross 1980; Finney & Lesieur 1982; Vaughan 1983). Also, an extensive body of research and theory on decisionmaking in organizations shows that the weighing of costs and benefits does occur, but individual choice is constrained by institutional and organizational forces: Decision practices and outcomes are products of external contingencies, political battles, unacknowledged cultural beliefs, and formal and informal internal pathologies that undercut both the determination of goals and their achievement (Dalton 1950; Allison 1971; Zucker 1977; Feldman & March 1981; Wildavsky 1987; Feldman 1989).

These constraints on choice are reinforced in organizations as executives set the premises for decisionmaking through organizational routines that reduce uncertainty. Decisionmaking is more an example of rule following than of calculation of costs and benefits. Rationality is constrained further: The organization has limited abilities to search for information and solutions to problems; individuals have limited knowledge of alternatives, access to and ability to absorb and understand information, and computational capacity; the decisionmaking process is influenced by deadlines, limited participation, and the number of problems under consideration. Rather than a model of perfect rationality, decisionmaking in organizations is characterized by "bounded rationality"; performance is described as "satisficing" rather than optimizing (Simon 1957, 1976; March & Simon 1958). The notion of individual rationality has become so circumscribed and discredited that some organization theorists even have described the decision process by the "garbage can model" (March & Olsen 1979) and characterized managers as "muddling through" (Lindblom 1959)—a far cry from the imagery of cool, calculated managerial capability suggested by the ideology of rational choice theory. In fact, Weick (1979, 1995) argues that often the only rationality that might be credited to the process is imposed retrospectively by participants in order to justify a particular decision. Wilensky's (1967:vii) observation sums up the case against a decontextualized rational choice model from an organizational behavior perspective:

> Too many critics of the organizational and political sources of our troubles see diabolical plots where there is only drift, a taste for reckless adventure where there is only ignorance of risks, the machinations of a power elite where there is, in William James' phrase, only a "bloomin' buzzin' confusion."

This review of decisionmaking research shows many reasons to be skeptical about prioritizing a rational choice/deterrence model for the social control of organizations. In particular, the research on organizational behavior points to an alternative model of decisionmaking demonstrating the ties between social context and rational choice. A second challenge to the rational choice/deterrence model comes from sociological theory articulating social life as situated action. The situated action schema contests the consequentialist, means-ends orientation that typifies rational choice theory, showing that (1) social contingencies influence decisionmaking by narrowing options and shaping preferences, and (2) purposive social action can have unintended consequences. Even more convincingly than the decisionmaking literature, this schema suggests that a social control strategy that manipulates the consequences of choice does not go far enough.

SITUATED ACTION: THE STRUCTURE/CULTURE/AGENCY NEXUS

A fundamental sociological understanding is that interaction takes place in socially organized settings. Rather than isolating action from its circumstances, the task of scholars is to uncover the relationship between the individual act and the social context. This argument appears in the history of sociological thought as a common thread running through the work of such otherwise diverse thinkers as Herbert Blumer, Erving Goffman, Max Weber, George Herbert Mead, Harold Garfinkle, George Homans, and Talcott Parsons. Five recent theoretical developments allow us to build on these understandings about the situated character of social action, showing a more complex and complete picture. These developments suggest that the merging of levels of analysis is required for a full theoretical explanation of any particular behavior; they also provide a conceptual apparatus that indicates what needs to be included in research to make full explanation possible.

The first development is the extensive theoretical literature that establishes the relationship between structure and agency. At the same time these debates ferret out the complexity of the macro-micro relationship, they lay the groundwork for research examining it (Maines 1977; Giddens 1979, 1984; R. Collins 1981; Knorr-Cetina & Cicourel 1981; Alexander et al. 1987; Fine 1992; Sewell 1992; Emirbayer & Mische 1998). The second development is that culture has entered the picture as a mediating link in the structure/agency relationship. Theorists are refining the link between an individual's position in a structure and interpretive practices, meaning, and action at the local level (Bourdieu 1977; Hall 1987; Smith 1987; Haraway 1988; P. Collins 1990, 1991; Emirbayer & Goodwin 1994; Hays 1994). This nexus is identified in phenomenology as "lifeworld," by Michel Foucault as "episteme," by Pierre Bourdieu as "habitus," by Dorothy Smith and Patricia Collins as "standpoint." Although differing in important ways, each perspective draws attention to culture: the tacit understandings, habits, assumptions, routines, and practices that constitute a repository of unarticulated source material from which more self-conscious thought and action emerge. Also significant is the role of history: Both the macro-level historic moment, as its normative and legal standards affect individual tacit understandings, and micro-level individual history/ experience are critical to individual interpretation and meaning (Elias 1993; Emirbayer & Mische 1998).

The important role of culture in situated interpretation, meaning, and action is reinforced by a third development: the new institutionalism, which explains that organizational forms and behaviors take the form they do because of prevailing values and beliefs that have become institutionalized to varying degrees (Meyer & Rowan 1977; Zucker 1977; Powell & DiMaggio 1991). New institutionalists argue that cultural rules constitute actors (state, organizations, professions, and individuals), thus defining legitimate goals for them to pursue and therefore affecting action and meaning at the local level. Decision-making, from this perspective, is always rational; however, institutionalized categories of structure, thought, and action shape preferences, directing choice toward some options and not others (Douglas 1987; Wildavsky 1987; DiMaggio & Powell 1991:10–11). Because the generalized rules of the institutionalized environment are often inappropriate to specific situations, outcomes may be less than optimal and, to some extent, unpredictable (Meyer & Rowan 1977). The fourth development is Granovetter's (1985, 1992) work on the socially embedded character of economic action. Granovetter points to the relative autonomy and/or relative dependent between the forms of economic action and social organization and the institutionalized cultural belief systems within which they are located. In contrast to the new institutionalism, agency is at the heart of this analysis. Agents can be individuals or organizational forms, but the embeddedness perspective prohibits reduction to a decontextualized rational actor. Because agency is central, economic action can take a variety of forms, so in a common cultural system variations will exist that cannot be explained in cultural terms only.

The fifth recent theoretical development is the sociology of mistake. It was prefigured by Merton's (1936) argument that purposive social action produces unanticipated consequences. Purposive action is "conduct" as distinct from "behavior," conduct being "action which involves motives and consequently a choice between various alternatives" (p. 895). Merton observed that individual action can result in unintended consequences that can be differentiated into consequences to the actor(s) and consequences to others that are mediated through social structure, culture, and civilization (ibid.). His point is that the results of purposive action can be *unexpected*, not that they are suboptimal. Merton focuses at length on the social influences on choice. Unintended outcomes have many sources, including (1) limited knowledge (p. 900) and (2) the taken-for-granted aspects of cognition that may lead to error (pp. 896, 901).

Merton's theorizing finds reinforcement in several complementary strands of work that combine to build a sociology of mistake (Vaughan 1999). The possibility of mistake is scripted into the layered situated action schema, showing that social context can decouple rational choice from outcomes as follows. The structural preconditions of unexpected outcomes are etched into the relational and cultural frames of the embeddedness perspective and the new institutionalism (Granovetter 1985; Powell & DiMaggio 1991). Both articulate a taken-for-granted rationality that leaves room for unexpected outcomes. At the organization level, rational choice leading to unintended consequences finds support in the Carnegie School (e.g., Simon 1957, 1976; March & Simon 1958; March & Olsen 1979), classic studies of informal organization (e.g., Roethlisberger & Dickson 1947; Giallombardo 1966; Bosk, 1979), research on work as error-ridden activity (Hughes 1951; Paget 1988), and the now-burgeoning literature on risk accidents, and disaster (for a review, see Turner & Pidgeon 1997:169–95). At the micro-level, agency is further contextualized in ongoing work in cognitive psychology and cognitive sociology that joins culture and cognition (for a review see DiMaggio 1997). This work also affirms the possibility of mistake; moreover, it affirms culture as a mediating link between structure and agency (see especially Zucker 1977.

This complex conceptual package illuminates many aspects of situated action. Decisionmaking, in this schema, cannot be disentangled from social context, which shapes preferences and thus what an individual perceives as rational. Moreover, the situated action paradigm acknowledges that purposive social action can regularly produce unexpected outcomes, thus challenging all rational actor accounts of social behavior. Finally, it draws attention to the need for research that examines the structure/culture/agency nexus. A full theoretical explanation of the action of any social actor needs to take into account, to the greatest extent possible, its situated character: Individual activity, choices, and action occur within a multilayered social context that affects interpretation and meaning at the local level. Not only the nested character of social action (Jepperson 1991) but also the dynamic interplay between structure and agency (Fombrun 1986; Smith 1987; Friedland & Alford 1991) begin to suggest the difficulty of doing empirical work that targets the situated interpretative work that precedes every social act. Moreover, doing research that encompasses all these elements requires (1) researcher expertise at studying both structure and agency and (2) data that make a full analysis of situated action possible—two resources often absent. It is easy to understand why the theoretical debates about the relationship between structure and agency have not spawned a flurry of empirical work aimed at bridging the macro-micro gap. Instead, what is happening is that numerous scholars carve out a particular locus of inquiry: Researchers cast their studies at either the macro- or micro-level, but not both. They take a slice of the whole, thus offering a measured but nonetheless partial view—and thus a partial explanation—of the socially organized character of group life. . . .

The Connection between Cause and Control

To be effective, strategies for social control should target the causes of a problem. The closer we come to establishing the relationship between situated action, rational choice, and organizational misconduct, the better the understandings on which social control can be based. Research and theoretical explanations that isolate one level of analysis for attention automatically and implicitly suggest strategies for control that do not take into account relevant factors at other levels. This is not to say that isolating a particular level of analysis for research is no longer a worthy enterprise: Doing so helps us flesh out the details of situated action. Yet we need to bear in mind both the practical and political implications of our work. When we restrict our analysis to the individual, social-psychological, or structural level of explanation, we have isolated one element from the many that make up situated action. A partial explanation, no matter how important the finding, leads to a partial, or incomplete, strategy for social control. A decontextualized rational choice model locates cause at the individual level of analysis, suggesting strategies for control that target responsible individuals: ethic training, punishment, forced resignation, and so forth. While these are appropriate strategies, they are incomplete: They leave the social context untouched, tending to systematically reproduce misconduct. . . .

HOW DEVIANCE BECAME NORMAL: THE *CHALLENGER* CASE

In the aftermath of the tragedy, the historically accepted explanation of the controversial 1986 *Challenger* launch decision conformed to the amoral calculator model. Warned by contractor engineers that launching was risky in the unprecedented cold temperatures that were predicted at launch time, NASA managers nonetheless proceeded with the launch because the schedule had become all-important at the space agency. Underfunded by Congress, the Space Shuttle program depended on income from commercial satellite companies: the greater the number of flights per year, the greater the number of commercial payloads, the greater the income. Realizing the importance of schedule (the historically accepted explanation went), the managers who were immediately responsible for the decision responded to these pressures by disregarding the advice of their own engineers, knowingly violating rules about passing safety concerns up the hierarchy in the process. Seven astronauts, including Christa McAuliffe, Teacher-in-Space, lost their lives. The conjunction of competitive pressures, scarce resources, rule violations, and overriding of the objections of engineers suggested intent: managerial decisionmaking as volatile behavior—a calculated, amoral, consequentialist, rational choice.

Production pressure played a critical role in the fatal decision, but the historically accepted explanation of why *Challenger* was launched was wrong. Many key assumptions supporting it were flawed. Most critical for establishing the intent implicit in an amoral calculator explanation. NASA documents describing rules and procedures showed that managerial actions identified as rule violations by the Presidential Commission were in fact actions that conformed to NASA rules. The data forced me to conclude that the disaster resulted from mistake, not misconduct. Because no rules were violated, the case does not conform to traditional understandings of organizational misconduct that have employees violating laws and rules in pursuit of organization goals, nor does it exhibit the intent to do wrong implied in the amoral calculator model of decisionmaking. However, the analysis resulted in a discovery of even greater significance for theories of organizational misconduct than anything I originally envisioned. My case study shows that in the years preceding the *Challenger* launch, engineers and managers together developed a definition of the situation that allowed them to carry on as if nothing were wrong when they continually faced evidence that something *was* wrong. This is the problem of the normalization of deviance.

The story begins, not on the eve of the *Challenger* launch, when managers and engineers argued about whether to go forward or not, but nearly 10 years earlier. The past—previous engineering analysis, conclusions, and launch decisions—was an all-important context for decisionmaking on the eve of the launch. Prior to the *Challenger* launch, the Solid Rocket Boosters (SRBs) were often damaged on shuttle missions. After each incident, the work group recommended to their superiors to accept risk and fly. After the disaster, continuing to launch despite evidence of damage on many flights seemed not only deviant but an amoral, calculated choice to a public shocked by the death of the astronauts. Why didn't they stop launching until they had solved the problem? Because at the time decisions were being made, each technical anomaly was first defined as an escalated risk; then, after engineering analysis, decisionmakers redefined it as normal and acceptable. Each decision seemed logical, rational, and noncontroversial as cumulatively they expanded the amount of technical deviation that was acceptable. Flying with frequent and increasingly serious anomalies became routine and officially condoned. Three factors, in combination, explain the normalization of technical deviation at NASA: the production of a cultural belief system in the work group, the culture of production, and structural secrecy.

The Production of Culture

Risk assessment was a bottom-up process at NASA. The managers and engineers assigned to do the technical work on Space Shuttle component parts assessed risk daily, using NASA guidelines and relying on engineering tests, post-flight analyses, and calculations. Then, in a formal pre-launch decision process known as Flight Readiness Review (FRR), these work groups presented their risk assessments and recommendations about launching to superiors in what was a multilayered, multiparticipant, adversarial review process. Because the shuttle design had no precedent, risk was always negotiated and often controversial. But in order to launch shuttles, work groups had to assay each technical component and find it an "Acceptable Risk," following prescribed NASA and engineering methods. Arriving at this official designation had them routinely converting technical uncertainty into certainty.

Culture can be thought of as a set of solutions produced by a group of people as they interact about the situations they face in common. These solutions become institutionalized, remembered, and passed on as the rules, rituals, and values of the group (Van Maanen & Barley 1985). As the members of the SRB work group interacted about their task, their interpretive work became the basis for an official definition of the boosters as an "Acceptable Risk." The SRB work group's definition of the situation became an institutionalized cultural belief. To understand how this cultural belief originated and continued as returning flights showed continual signs of booster damage, we start with microlevel influences on decisionmaking. Two were important: social context and patterns of information. They affected the interpretive work of the work group, so that what appeared to the public in the aftermath of 28 January 1986 as clear and undeniable signals of danger were interpreted as weak signals, mixed signals, or routine signals by the engineers making risk assessments as the decisions were being made.

Initially, no technical deviations in booster performance were predicted by engineers. When anomalies began occurring, social context affected the SRB work group's interpretation of the damage. The immediate social context was one in which having technical problems was normal and expected because (1) the design was unprecedented and therefore untested in flight and (2) the shuttle was designed to be reusable. Consequently, having booster anomalies was not deviant because engineers and managers expected that all returning flights would have some damage that had to be fixed prior to the next launch. Patterns of information as boosters were inspected after each mission also affected the definition of the situation. Most launches had no booster anomalies. When they occurred, they seemed to be random. Post-flight engineering analysis indicated these technical deviations were shaped by "local conditions": peculiarities that were nonsystemic in origin. Each time, engineers were able to identify the cause of the failure and fix it, assuring themselves by tests, calculations, and scientific methods that the problem was within the bounds of acceptable risk. Subsequent missions would have no anomalies. Then a new incident would occur.

The preexisting definition of the situation, and the scientific procedures and engineering analysis on which it was based, became the context against which the risk of each succeeding anomaly was measured. Each incident was assessed in light of a gradually developed engineering analysis about conditions that might occur and the boosters' ability to tolerate those conditions. The incremental character of damage also had a normalizing effect. Had all the changes occurred at once, had damage been occurring on every flight due to a common cause, or had there been a discernable pattern of damage, the work group would have had some strong, clear signals with the potential to challenge the cultural belief in risk acceptability. Instead, the damage occurred incrementally, each incident's significance muted by social context and a learning-by-doing approach that had engineers interpreting each episode as separate and local.

The immediate social context and patterns of information explain *how* the cultural belief in acceptable risk developed. But *why* did their official definition of the situation persist, in the face of evidence of continuing problems? This is the problem of cultural persistence. Macro-level factors—the culture of production and structural secrecy—contributed to and affirmed the work group's belief in acceptable risk prior to *Challenger.*

The Culture of Production

The culture of production reinforced and maintained the work group's belief in acceptable risk because their actions conformed to its mandates. Thus, they saw continuing to launch under the conditions they faced as normative and conforming, not deviant. By culture of production, I mean institutionalized cultural belief systems that shaped interpretation, meaning, and action at the local level (Van Maanen & Barley 1985; Zucker 1977). These cultural meaning systems affect choice by functioning as institutionalized scripts that convey to people what is normal and acceptable in particular situations. In contrast to the historically accepted explanation that depicted a unidimensional NASA culture dominated by production concerns, the culture of production incorporated three cultural imperatives: the original technical culture of excellence created during the Apollo era (methodological rigor and quantitative science), political accountability (production and cost concerns), and bureaucratic accountability (attention to rules and procedures). Production pressure does not lose salience in this revisionist account but gains importance because of its seductive influence: Production pressures affected the choices of managers and engineers alike, by affecting decisionmaking at a prerational level.

The culture of production existed outside the work group's daily negotiation of risk but had a layered, or nested, character that permeated the group's risk assessment processes (Jepperson 1991). It originated in institutionalized cultural beliefs of the engineering profession that were elaborated in distinctive ways in the NASA organization, permeating Marshall Space Flight Center at Huntsville, Alabama, home of the Solid Rocket Booster Project. Of the cultural meaning systems that typify engineering as a profession, three were influential in work group decisionmaking. First, in the engineering of unprecedented large-scale technical systems, uncertainty, learning by experience, and developing ad hoc rules to guide technical decisions are taken-for-granted understandings about how work gets done (Wynne 1989). Second, "satisficing," not "optimizing," was normal and acceptable in the engineering profession (Simon 1957, 1976). The education of engineers prepares them to work in production systems where technology is product-oriented and cost/safety trade-offs are routine, so satisficing on design is common and nondeviant (Petroski 1985; Meiksins 1988; Kunda 1992). Third, technical assessments are grounded in "trust in numbers" and "trust in rules": Quantitative methods and scientific objectivity in risk assessment hold sway over intuitive sensibilities (Jasanoff 1986; Porter 1995); engineers are trained to work in hierarchical organizations where rule following is associated with safety (Meiksins 1988; Petroski 1985).

These institutionalized beliefs of the engineering profession materialized in the NASA organization in distinctive ways that contributed to the normalization of technical deviation on the SRBs. During the Apollo program of the 1960s, NASA's original technical culture was founded on a mandate for technical excellence (McCurdy 1993). The emphasis was on the "dirty hands" approach: Contractors were only used occasionally, and most work was done in house so that top administrators and technicians alike got their hands "dirty" by staying in close touch with the technology. This approach was joined by a near-obsessive emphasis on technical excellence, scientific positivism, and rigor in both method and data analysis. However, at the inception of the shuttle program in the 1970s, NASA's purist technical culture was joined by an additional cultural mandate: political accountability that called for attention to costs and schedule (Romzek & Dubnick 1987). As the Apollo program neared its end, consensus for the U.S. space program was undermined by the U.S. involvement in Vietnam. The war created a drain on the budget, raising questions about continued space explorations.

NASA administrators developed the Space Shuttle Program as the post-Apollo goal. Confronted by congressional recalcitrance and opposition, agency administrators proposed that the shuttle would not be a drain on the budget because it would be, to a great extent, self-funding. NASA officials pushed the vehicle as a reusable "space bus" that could fly many missions a year. Designed with a large payload bay, the shuttle would carry experiments from aerospace R&D firms and commercial satellites to be put in orbit, thus collecting money for each mission. When the proposal went to Congress, the projected number of missions assured a continued source of income from a space vehicle that administrators insisted would make space flight "routine and economical." The shuttle was endorsed on this basis. Reduced funding had converted the R&D space agency into one that operated like a business, complete with production cycles and concerns about cost and efficiency.

A second alteration in NASA culture that occurred was that bureaucratic accountability rose in importance (Romzek & Dubnick 1987). Bureaucratic accountability had always been esteemed: Rules were essential for coordinating work and for safety. However, in the 1980s, the agency became bureaupathological. Contracting out, formerly an occasional practice, became institutionalized. The consequence was that an immense new rule structure was necessary to coordinate NASA/contractor relations. The dirty hands approach was compromised: Many NASA engineers and technicians now had contractor oversight responsibilities, so were burdened with procedural tasks and huge amounts of paperwork. Soon after shuttle missions began in 1981, still another layer of bureaucracy was added. The 1980s were notable for the decreased regulation of business and the increased regulation of government agencies, which imposed another system of accountability on the space agency. The result of these changes was that rule following and procedural conformity rivaled the original technical culture and political accountability. History and politics had not eliminated the original technical culture of the Apollo era, but added political accountability and bureaucratic accountability to it. The result was that engineers and managers assigned to the shuttle hardware were struggling to conform to the mandates of the original technical culture while also conforming to political accountability (cost and schedule) and bureaucratic accountability (procedural requirements).

The Macro-Micro Connection

The work group conformed to the culture of production, which had an impact on cognition (Zucker 1977). It contributed to the normalization of technical deviation of the SRBs as follows. Post-flight analyses of the Space Shuttle missions produced quantitative evidence (the original technical culture) convincing the work group that the booster design was officially an "Acceptable Risk." Although they understood that the boosters were working, they did not understand why there were working as they were. Growing doubt, uncertainty, and anxiety about the unknown notwithstanding, concern about cost and schedule (political accountability) inhibited the work group from halting missions for the lengthy period necessary for additional tests. Following the rules, which they unfailingly did (bureaucratic accountability), had a social-psychological effect. Conforming to every rule and procedure—going by the book—assured them that their official risk assessments were correct, sustaining the cultural belief that the design was an "Acceptable Risk." Repeatedly and officially, they recommended "Go." As the problem unfolded in the years prior to *Challenger*, each decision seemed logical, correct, and rational. The social context and patterns of information that affected the definition of the situation were reinforced by the institutionalized cultural frame within which the interpretive work was done.

Structural Secrecy

Because the process of deviance normalization went on from 1977 until the fatal *Challenger* launch, we must wonder why no one outside the work group noticed and acted. Structural secrecy was the third factor that contributed to the persistence of the work group's cultural belief in acceptable risk. The effect of structural secrecy was to inhibit people outside the work group from overturning the definition of the situation. Structural secrecy refers to the way that the structure of organizations and their regulatory relations impedes knowledge and understanding of activities in the workplace. In the aftermath of the *Challenger* tragedy, managers were wrongly accused of individual secrecy: intentionally violating rules to hide information about booster problems from others in the organization. No rule violations occurred. Instead, it was routine characteristics of inter- and intra-organizational relationships—conditions common to all organizations—that concealed the seriousness of the technical problem on the Solid Rocket Boosters from people outside the work group, preventing them from identifying the trend and intervening in some way that might have altered the decisionmaking pattern prior to the *Challenger* launch decision.

Secrecy is built into the very structure of organizations. As organizations grow large, actions that occur in one part of the organization are, for the most part, not observable in others. Division of labor between subunits, hierarchy, and geographic dispersion segregate knowledge about tasks and goals. Distance—both physical and social—interferes with the efforts of those at the top to "know" the behavior of others in the organization—and vice versa. Specialized knowledge further inhibits knowing. The language associated with a different task, even in the same organization, can conceal rather than reveal. Changing technology also interferes with knowing, for assessing information requires keeping pace with these changes—a difficult prospect when it takes time away from one's primary job responsibilities. Also—and ironically— rules created to communicate more information can result in knowing less. Rules that generate wide distribution of information can increase the paperwork n individual desks so that a lot is not read. Executive summaries, although effectively conveying major points, condense and omit information, selectively concealing and revealing.

Paradoxically, NASA had developed both a pre-launch decisionmaking procedure and a safety regulatory system designed to protect against structural secrecy. The formal, hierarchical, prelaunch decision chain known as Flight Readiness Review (FRR) was designed to maximize information exchange by pulling all parts of the organization together for risk assessments prior to a launch. All engineering risk assessments were distributed in advance and orally presented in FRR, where they were critiqued aggressively by people outside the work groups whose sole responsibility was to uncover flaws in the analyses. Moreover, NASA had both internal and external safety review panels designated as safety regulatory agencies with oversight responsibilities in every aspect of technical work. However, structural secrecy remained (Vaughan 1990). While structural secrecy had many unanticipated negative consequences for safety, here I will isolate only one: information dependencies and how they kept people outside the work group from identifying the pattern of normalizing technical deviation and intervening.

In NASA's bottom-up risk assessment system, it was the work groups' construction of risk—and the engineering evidence support of their assessments—that were the basis for all launch decisions. FRR and safety regulatory systems were designed to challenge and oversee existing risk assessments and the scientific procedures and technical knowledge that went into work group launch recommendations. But the shuttle was made up of 60 million component parts. FRR participants and regulators were inundated with information about each part. Instead of enlightening upper-level managers, the deluge of information obfuscated many problems (Feldman & March 1981). Hence, people with oversight responsibility relied on oral interpretation and briefings in FRR and other inquiries. Removed from the hands-on work and reliant on work groups for the engineering on which risk assessments were based, these others could only challenge what was presented to them. When the SRB work group repeatedly defended its position with quantitative data, as those assigned to the Solid Rocket Booster Project did in the years preceding the *Challenger* tragedy, top NASA administrators and safety officials became persuaded the design was an acceptable risk. The work group's construction of risk was affirmed up the hierarchy, becoming the official organizational construction of risk prior to each launch.

NASA's oversight structure functioned effectively as a review system, but information dependencies interfered with its ability to identify basic assumptions that were in error. The House Committee on Science and Technology, whose investigation followed that of the Presidential Commission, concluded that administrators and regulators only knew what work groups told them:

> Flight Readiness Reviews are not intended to replace engineering analysis, and therefore, they cannot be expected to prevented a flight because of a design flaw that Project management [*read:* the SRB work group] had already determined represented an acceptable risk. (U.S. House of Representatives 1986:70–71, 148)

Thus, the official definition of the boosters as an "Acceptable Risk" persisted through the end of 1985. *Challenger* was the first launch of 1986. The decision to launch *Challenger* was one decision in a stream of decisions about the boosters. The debate that night was situated in history and social organization: The interplay of the production of culture in the work group, the culture of production, and structural secrecy affected the interpretive work and action of all participants.

The Eve of the Launch

The *Challenger* launch had been approved in FRR two weeks before the 27 January eve-of-launch discussion. But this was an emergency meeting, called because the temperature forecast resulted in a revised assessment of risk acceptability for the boosters before launch the next morning. So the 34 participants, located at agency and contractor facilities in Utah, Alabama, and Florida, held the discussion on a teleconference. It was unprecedented in several ways: the predicted cold temperature, the no-launch recommendation that the contractor engineers made, and the geographic locations of the participants. The purpose of the teleconference was to weigh the new circumstances to determine whether the engineering rationale for flight they had developed in preceding years was threatened by the cold. First, history mattered. All who were present that night were assessing new information within a historic and official definition of the situation: the production of scientific/technical knowledge in the work group that supported accepting the risk of previous flights. Second, the interaction took place within the same culture of production that had systematically contributed to the normalization of anomalous incidents in the past. The original technical culture, political accountability, and bureaucratic accountability affected the discussion, shaping the construction of risk on which the *Challenger* launch decision was based. Finally, although a relatively small number of people participated, they reproduced the specialization, hierarchy, and geographic distribution of the larger NASA/contractor structure. So it is not surprising that structural secrecy inhibited the proceedings that night as it had before, creating obstacles to information exchange, knowledge, and understanding.

NASA's cultural mandate for political accountability undermined the proceedings at the outset. Contractor engineers in Utah, aware of deadlines and cost concerns, immediately set a deadline for their preparations so the teleconference might begin and a decision reached before midnight, when time-consuming and expensive pre-launch procedures would begin at the launch site at Cape Kennedy, Florida. Rushing to meet their own deadline, contractor engineers divided up responsibility for the charts of engineering analysis, faxing them to other places without collectively assessing them. The result? NASA managers identified errors in the charts that contradicted the argument contractor engineers were making, so the analysis did not live up to the rigorous quantitative standards of NASA's original technical culture. Political accountability showed itself a second time when NASA managers, surprised that a flawed engineering analysis would be the basis for a no-launch decision when schedule was so important, gave their usual adversarial challenges in unusually harsh ways, intimidating contractor engineers and managers.

Throughout the discussion, structural secrecy blocked understanding. Engineering launch recommendations were always face to face in FRR. However, this night the participants were in three facilities of the NASA/contractor structure, an unreflexive choice that went unquestioned because teleconferences had become a normal way of doing business between contractors and NASA. In separate locations, with no video hook-up, words and inflections had to convey everything. Body language, facial expression, who was present or absent—additional information that adds to interpretive abilities and conveying meaning—were unavailable. At a critical moment, the effect of structural secrecy was increased when the contractor representatives went off the tele-conference line for a caucus. During that period, contractor administrators reversed their own engineers' recommendation. They returned to the teleconference with a recommendation to accept risk and fly. Separated by distance and a mute button, no one at the other two locations knew that the contractor engineers still objected. Further, the contractor engineers were unaware that people in the other two locations were expecting the launch to be stopped.

The cultural mandate of bureaucratic accountability had people going by the book, which also had a deleterious affect on the discussion. First, conformity to normative expectations about specialized knowledge and hierarchical relations affected talk: Some people were silent who had information that might have altered the outcome. Some deferred to authority; others, concluding that they had not worked on the booster problems recently enough or were insufficiently informed for other reasons, kept their insights to themselves, deferring to the few engineers presenting the analysis. Second, in unprecedented conditions, all participants followed all the usual NASA rules and procedures about how launch decisions were to be made. As in the past, conforming to rules had the latent social-psychological effect of affirming the correctness of the decision: All contractor engineers but one left the teleconference believing that the boosters would incur addition damage, not expecting a catastrophe. The one person who did fear the worst said nothing on the teleconference, abiding by NASA's bureaucratic norms about who legitimately could speak during an engineering decision and under what circumstances.

But conformity had a still greater consequence. Immediately following the disaster, many of the participating engineers admitted their analysis was flawed, stating that "we didn't have the data to convince NASA," so the preexisting engineering analysis that supported acceptable risk stood. However, retrospection and the luxury of hindsight show that they *did* have the data. After the disaster, two investigators (nonengineers) working for the Presidential Commission did a trend analysis of all launches, examining the relationship between temperature and booster damage. The quantitative data conclusively proved the correlation between cold temperature and damage (Vaughan 1996:382–83). But the work group did not create that chart, which would have conformed to the positivistic mandates of the original technical culture, thereby stopping the launch. Customarily, in conditions of uncertainty, people fall back on habits and routines (Mileti, Sorenson, & Bogard 1985). In unprecedented circumstances, with time to think things through, the engineers and managers in the work group followed all the mandates of the culture of production. No one had the idea to proceed in a different way.

Consider this. Whereas a rigorous, quantitative engineering analysis may assure safety in a pro-launch decision, in a no-launch decision under unprecedented, uncertain launch conditions, accepting qualitative observations and intuitive insight from technical experts closest to the technology would have been appropriate. Whereas hierarchical, adversarial FRR discussion style is suitable for pro-launch recommendations, a democratic sleeves-rolled-up let's-

all-put-our-heads-together-to-see-what-we-can-make-of-these-data   strategy
would have been a logical response. Again, we have the luxury of hindsight.
The situation looked very different to them at the time. The work group conformed to the triumvirate of cultural imperatives, resulting in an official decision that incorporated yet another anomalous condition, thus extending the
bounds of acceptable risk a final time.

ON THE SOCIAL CONTROL OF ORGANIZATIONS

. . . NASA made a decision that caused extensive social harm, but absent was
any evidence of intent to do that harm, or the calculated, knowing violation of
rules or ethical or normative standards essential to the amoral calculator
model of organizational misconduct. This was true not only for the SRB work
group but also for political elites inside and outside the space agency: top
NASA officials, Congress, and the Administration. These powerful elites set
up the tragedy in the years preceding *Challenger* by making political bargains
that (1) made routine and economic space flight a priority, interjecting production pressures into the culture; (2) institutionalized contracting out, altering
organization structure and adding layers of bureaucratic accountability, interjecting another dimension to the culture; (3) allowed civilians to fly on the
shuttle to promote the agency and its goals. Yet missing from the original
media-generated, historically accepted explanation of amorally calculating
managers were the invisible workings of power and politics that contributed
to the outcome. At the time they were made, these elite decisions, too, were
absent intent to do harm or violate laws, defined as normal and acceptable by
the top officials who made them. . . .

The lesson suggested by the *Challenger* case and these others is that the
legal and regulatory apparatus might better investigate and elevate the importance of additional strategies of social control. The potential deterrent impact of sanctions cannot figure into individual calculations when history, culture, and structure congeal in a worldview under which behavior that is
objectively deviant to outsiders is normal and legitimate within a particular
social context. When deviance becomes normalized, individuals see their actions as conforming, not deviant; consequently, they see their actions as conforming, not deviant; consequently, they see their actions as accruing benefits,
not costs. By definition, the potential deterrent impact of negative sanctions is
mitigated by the situated character of social action. Punishment is appropriate; people must be held responsible for action resulting in social harm. It may
be used against offending organizations and/or their employees to accomplish
other than deterrence: to make people publicly accountable for their actions,
to assure restitution or retribution, for example (Schlegel 1990). However, as a
strategy of social control, punishment does not go far enough. It decontextual-
izes decisions to violate, neglecting the social context that leads people to
make the choices that they do. The organization may be fined; the responsible

individuals may be incarcerated, fined, fired, transferred, or offered early retirement, but if the social context of decisionmaking is not altered, the next position incumbent's decisionmaking will be subject to the same organizational contingencies. Without attention to these other factors, the legal and administrative apparatus—and the public—are wrongly persuaded that once the responsible person is punished, the problems is solved. But the more difficult to diagnose goals, policies, cultures, and structures that create definitions favorable to harmful social acts remain unchanged, perpetuating the possibility of recurrence. . . .

REFERENCES

Alexander, Jeffrey C. Bernhard Giesen, Richard Munch, & Neil J. Smelser, eds. (1987) *The Micro-Macro Link.* Berkeley: Univ. of California Press.

Allison, Graham T. (1971) *The Essence of Decision: Explaining the Cuban Missile Crisis.* Boston: Little, Brown.

Bellah, Robert N., Richard Madsen, William M. Sullivan, Ann Swidler, & Steven Tipton (1985) *Habits of the Heart.* Berkeley: Univ. of California Press.

Bosk, Charles (1979) *Forgive and Remember.* Chicago: Univ. of Chicago Press.

Bourdieu, Pierre (1977) *Outline of a Theory of Practice.* Cambridge: Cambridge Univ. Press.

Braithwaite, John, & Toni Makkai (1991) "Testing an Expected Utility Model of Corporate Deterrence," 25 *Law & Society Rev.* 7–40.

Calavita, Kitty, Henry N. Pontell, & Robert H. Tillman (1997) *Big Money Crime: Fraud and Politics in the Savings and Loan Crisis.* Berkeley: Univ. of California Press.

Clinard, Marshall B., & Peter C. Yeager (1980) *Corporate Crime.* New York: Free Press.

Coleman, James S. (1990a) *Foundations of Social Theory.* Cambridge: Harvard Univ. Press.

Collins, Patricia Hill (1990) *Black Feminist Thought.* London: Harper Collins.

——— (1991) "Learning from the Outsider within," in M. M. Fonow & J. Cook, eds., *Beyond Methodology: Feminist Scholarship as Lived Research.* Bloomington: Indiana Univ. Press.

Collins, Randal (1981) "On the Micro-Foundations of Macro-Sociology," 86 *American J. of Sociology* 984–1014.

Cook, Karen Schweers, & Margaret Levi, eds. (1990) *The Limits of Rationality.* Chicago: Univ. of Chicago Press.

Dalton, Melville (1950) *Men Who Manage.* New York: Wiley.

DiMaggio, Paul J. (1977) "Culture and Cognition," 23 *Annual Rev. of Sociology* 163–87.

DiMaggio, Paul J., & Walter W. Powell (1991) "Introduction," in Powell & DiMaggio, eds. 1991.

Douglas, Mary (1987) *How Institutions Think.* London: Routledge & Kegan Paul.

Elias, Norbert (1993) *Time: An Essay.* Oxford: Blackwell.

Emirbayer, Mustafa, & Jeff Goodwin (1994) "Network Analysis, Culture, and the Problem of Agency," 99 *American J. of Sociology* 962–1023.

Emirbayer, Mustafa, & Ann Mische (1998) "What Is Agency?" 103 *American J. of Sociology* 962–1023.

Feldman, Martha S. (1989) *Order without Design.* Stanford, CA: Stanford Univ. Press.

Feldman, Martha S., & James G. March (1981) "Information in Organizations as Sign and Symbol," 26 *Administrative Science Q.* 171–84.

Fine, Gary Alan (1992) "Agency, Structure, and Comparative Contexts: Toward A Synthetic Interactionism," 15 *Symbolic Interaction* 87–107.

Finney, Henry, & H. R. Lesieur (1982) "A Contingency Theory of Organizational Crime," in S. B. Bacharach, ed., *The Social Psychological Process* (Research in the Sociology of Organizations). Greenwich, CT: JAI Press.

Fombrun, Charles (1986) "Structural Dynamics within and between Organizations," 31 *Administrative Science Q.* 403–21.

Friedland, Roger, & Robert Alford (1991) "Bringing Society Back in: Symbols, Practices and Institutional Contradictions," in Powell & DiMaggio, eds. 1991.

Friedman, Debra, & Michael Hechter (1988) "The Contribution of Rational Choice Theory to Macrosociological Research," 6 *Sociological Theory* 201–18.

Giallombardo, Rose (1966) *Society of Women.* New York: Wiley.

Giddens, Anthony (1979) *Central Problems in Social Theory.* Berkeley: Univ. of California Press.

Grabosky, Peter N. (1989) *Wayward Governance.* Woden, ACT: Australian Institute of Criminology.

——— (1995) "Counterproductive Regulation," 23 *International J. of the Sociology of Law* 347–69.

Granovetter, Mark (1985) "Economic Action and Social Structure: The Problem of Embeddedness," 91 *American J. of Sociology* 481–510.

——— (1992) "Economic Institutions as Social Constructions: A Framework for Analysis," 35 *Acta Sociologica* 3–12.

Gross, Edward (1989) "Organization Structure and Organizational Crime," in G. Geis & E. Stotland, eds., *White-Collar Crime: Theory and Research.* Newbury Park, CA: Sage Publications.

Hall, Peter M. (1987) "Interactionism and the Study of Social Organization," 28 *Sociological Q.* 1–22.

Haraway, Donna (1988) "Situated Knowledges: The Science Question in Feminism as a Site of Discourse on the Privilege of Partial Perspective," 14 *Feminist Studies* 575–99.

Hays, Sharon (1994) "Structure and Agency and the Sticky Problem of Culture," 12 *Sociological Theory* 57–72.

Hechter, Michael (1987) *Principles of Group Solidarity.* Berkeley: Univ. of California Press.

Hechter, Michael, & Satoshi Kanazawa (1997) "Sociological Rational Choice Theory," 23 *Annual Rev. of Sociology* 191–214.

Hughes, Everett C. (1951) "Mistakes at Work," 17 *Canadian J. of Economics & Political Science* 320–27.

Jackall, Robert (1988) *Moral Mazes: The World of Corporate Managers.* New York: Oxford Univ. Press.

Jasanoff, Sheila (1986) *Risk Management and Political Culture.* New York: Russell Sage Foundation.

Jepperson, Ronald (1991) "Institutions, Institutional Effects, and Institutionalism," in Powell & DiMaggio, eds. 1991.

Kagan, Robert A., & John T. Scholz (1984) "The 'Criminology of the Corporation' and Regulatory Enforcement Strategies," in Hawkins & Thomas, eds. 1984.

Knorr-Cetina, Karen, & Aaron Cicourel, eds. (1981) *Advances in Social Theory and Methodology: Toward and Integration of Micro- and Macro-Sociologies.* Boston: Routledge & Kegan Paul.

Kunda, Gideon (1992) *Engineering Culture: Control and Commitment in a High-Tech Corporation.* Philadelphia: Temple Univ. Press.

Maines, David R. (1977) "Social Organization and Social Structure in Symbolic Interactionist Thought," 3 *Annual Rev. of Sociology* 235–59.

March, James G., & Johan P. Olsen (1979) *Ambiguity and Choice in Organizations.* Bergen: Universitetsforlaget.

March, James G., & Zur Shapira (1987) "Management Perspectives on Risk and Risk Taking," 33 *Management Science* 1404–18.

March, James G., & Herbert A. Simon (1958) *Organizations.* New York: Wiley.

Martin, Joanne (1992) *Cultures in Organizations: Three Perspectives.* New York: Oxford Univ. Press.

McCurdy, Howard (1993) *Inside NASA: High Technology and Organizational Change in the U.S. Space Program.* Baltimore: Johns Hopkins Univ. Press.

Meiksins, Peter (1988) "The Revolt of the Engineers Reconsidered," 29 *Technology & Culture* 219–46.

Merton, Robert K. (1936) "The Unanticipated Consequences of Social Action." 1 *American Sociological Rev.* 894–904.

Meyer, John, & Brian Rowan (1977) "Institutionalized Organizations: Formal Structure as Myth and Ceremony," 83 *American J. of Sociology* 340–63.

Mileti, Dennis, John Sorenson, & William Bogard (1985) *Evacuation Decision-Making: Process and Uncertainty.* Oak Ridge, Tenn.: Oak Ridge National Laboratory.

Paget, Marianne A. (1988) *The Unity of Mistakes.* Philadelphia: Temple Univ. Press.

Paternoster, Ray, & Sally S. Simpson (1993) "A Rational Choice Theory of Corporate Crime," in R. V. Clarke & M. Felson, eds., 5 *Routine Activity and Rational Choice: Advances in Criminological Theory.* New Brunswick, NJ: Transaction Publishers.

——— (1996) "Sanction Threats and Appeals to Morality: Testing a Rational Choice Model of Corporate Crime," 30 *Law & Society Rev.* 549–83.

Petroski, Henri (1985) *To Engineer Is Human: The Role of Failure in Successful Design.* New York: St. Martin's.

Porter, Theodore M. (1995) *Trust in Numbers.* Princeton, NJ: Princeton Univ. Press.

Powell, Walter W., & Paul J. DiMaggio, eds. (1991) *The New Institutionalism in Organizational Analysis.* Chicago: Univ. of Chicago Press.

Roethlisberger, F. J., & William J. Dickson (1947) *Management and the Worker.* Cambridge Harvard Univ. Press.

Romzek, Barbara S., & Melvin J. Dubnick (1987) "Accountability in the Public Sector: Lessons from the *Challenger* Tragety," 47 *Public Administration Rev.* 227–38.

Schlegel, Kip (1990) *Just Deserts for Corporate Criminals.* Boston: Northeastern Univ. Press.

Sewell, William H., Jr. (1992) "A Theory of Structure: Duality, Agency, and Transformations," 98 *American J. of Sociology* 1–29.

Simpson, Sally S. (1986) "The Decomposition of Antitrust: Testing a Multi-level Longitudinal Model of Profit Squeeze," 51 *American Sociological Rev.* 859–79.

——— (1992) "Corporate Crime Deterrence and Corporate-Control Policies," in Schlegel & Weisburd, eds., 1992.

——— (1998) *Why Corporations Obey the Law.* New York: Cambridge Univ. Press.

Simpson, Sally S., & Christopher Koper (1992) "Deterring Corporate Crime," 30 *Criminology* 347–75.

Simon, Herbert A. (1957) *Models of Man: Social and Rational* New York: Wiley.

———— (1976) *Administrative Behavior: A Study of Decision-Making Processes in Administrative Organizations.* 3d ed. New York: Free Press.

Smith, Dorothy (1987) *The Everyday World as Problematic.* Boston: Northeastern Univ. Press.

Staw, Barry M., & Eugene Swajkowski (1975) "The Scarcity Munificence Component of Organizational Environments and the Commission of Illegal Acts," 20 *Administrative Science Q.* 345–54.

Stinchombe, Arthur L. (1965) "Social Structure and Organizations," in J. G. March, ed., *Handbook of Organizations.* Chicago: Rand-McNally.

Sutherland, Edwin H. (1949) *White-Collar Crime.* New York: Dryden Press.

Tocqueville, Alexis de (1969) *Democracy in America,* trans. G. Lawrence, ed. J. P. Thayer. New York: Doubleday.

Turner, Barry A., & Nick F. Pidgeon (1997) *Man-Made Disasters.* Oxford: Butterworth-Heinemann.

U.S. House of Representatives (1986) *Investigation of the Challenger Accident: Hearings; Report.* 3 vols. Washington, DC: GPO.

Van Maanen, John, & Steve Barley (1985) "Cultural Organization: Fragments of a Theory," in P. J. Frost et al., eds, *Organizational Culture.* Beverly Hills, CA: Sage Publications.

Van Maanen, John, & Edgar H. Schein (1979) "Toward a Theory of Organizational Socialization," in B. Staw & L. L. Cummings, eds., *Research in Organizational Behavior.* Greenwich CT: JAI Press.

Vaughan, Diane (1983) *Controlling Unlawful Organizational Behavior.* Chicago: Univ. of Chicago Press.

———— (1990) "Autonomy, Interdependence, and Social Control: NASA and the Space Shuttle *Challenger,*" 35 *Administrative Science Q.* 225–57.

———— (1996) *The Challenger Launch Decision: Risky Technology, Culture, and Deviance at NASA.* Chicago: Univ. of Chicago Press.

———— (1999) "The Dark Side of Organizations: Mishap, Mistake, Misconduct, and Disaster," 25 *Annual Rev. of Sociology* (forthcoming).

Weick, Karl E. (1979) *The Social Psychology of Organizing.* Reading, MA: Addison-Wesley.

———— (1995) *Sensemaking in Organizations.* Thousand Oaks, CA: Sage Publications.

Wildavsky, Aaron (1987) "Choosing Preferences by Constructing Institutions: A Cultural Theory of Preference Formation," 81 *American Political Science Rev.* 3–21.

Wynne, Brian (1988) "Unruly Technology: Practical Rules, Impractical Discourses, and Public Understanding," 18 *Social Studies of Science* 147–67.

Zucker, Lynn (1977) "The Role of Institutionalization in Cultural Persistence," 42 *American Sociological Rev.* 726–43.

5

Sources and Characteristics of White-Collar Offenders

Introduction

The rate of white-collar crime varies not only with the supply of criminal opportunities but also with the supply of individuals and organizations predisposed to exploit them. From decades of research on street offenders we know that disorganized urban neighborhoods contribute disproportionately to the pools of individuals who commit burglary, robbery, and similar crimes. By contrast, the conditions that generate proportionately few or many motivated white-collar offenders have received less attention, and, therefore, we are much less confident we understand them properly. What distinguishes times and places that produce alternatively many or few white-colar offenders?

As wtih street crime, males flood the ranks of white-collar criminals. Patriarchal notions of masculinity probably contribute in some way to explaining this gender imbalance, but what is clear is that despite several decades of legislation and policies meant to increase gender and racial equality, white males predominate in occupational positions of power and respectability. This stubborn fact not only helps to explain gender and racial differences in rates of white-collar crime but also differences in the kinds of crimes committed by men and women. Kathleeen Daly describes gender differences in the seriousness of white-collar crime and locates its causes in continuing gendered access to positions of power and authority.

Fluctuation in the business cycle has been linked repeatedly to changes in the size of the pool of white-collar offenders. Economic downturns, the reasoning goes, depresses income and pushes increasing numbers of citizens and organizations closer to insolvency. The resulting desperation causes them to consider behavioral options, including criminal ones, they normally would not find acceptable. And it may not be only the economic and personal pressures produced by fiscal downturns that increase the population of potential offenders; paradoxically, rapid economic growth and rising income may do the same. Periods of sustained economic expansion may raise expectations and cause individuals and business firms to venture into uncharted and volatile markets where the risks of failure are high. The relationship between changing economic conditions and the population of predisposed white-collar offenders remains unclear, but further research may show it to be curvilinear; severe upturns and downturns alike may expand the pool of motivated offenders. Hazel Croall suggests that while it may be similar for powerful business firms and neighborhood markets, small businesses particularly are susceptible to changing market prssures. Her research also teaches us that, in contrast to the impression gained from high-profile cases of white-collar crime, a great deal of it is mundane and committed by people of limited economic means.

Many believe that the odds of offending may be greater for large firms as compared with smaller ones. The reasons for this are largely speculative, but increasing size may increase the internal complexity of the organization, with the result that in large organizations, decisions are made incrementally across groups of workers who see and are responsible for only part of larger plans, objectives, and processes. Consequently, in large firms it can be nearly impossible to affix on specific, identifiable individuals responsibility for ill-conceived or criminal activities.

In response to the discovery of criminal or morally questionable business practices, corporations frequently publish a code of ethics or business principles that outlines their goals and self-imposed moral boundaries. Increasing size, however, may increase the challenge of establishing and maintaining consistent normative controls and effective supervision in organizations. Increasing size may stimulate the emergence of multiple cultures and normative ambiguities and conflicts. The sales division of a major corporation, for instance, likely maintains a different set of goals, values, and expectations than their counterparts in product development.

Finally, as organizations increase in size, their power may increase as well. Because they employ hundreds of thousands of people across multiple continents and generate enormous profits, large corporations wield substantial clout. Their executives meet and interact with national leaders, and they are made privy to potentially important and even classified information. When this is coupled with their privileged status and enormous personal wealth, it can set the stage for criminal behavior. If "power corrupts and absolute power corrupts absolutely," the historically unprecedented power of modern conglomerates is an invitation to crime. For a variety of reasons, then, there may be a positive relationship between organizational size and willingness to choose criminal behavior. These and other considerations are the focus of the original paper by Nicole Leeper Piquero and Alex Piquero, which documents the prosaic sources of white-collar offending.

The size of the white-collar offending pool may swell during periods when disparities in wealth increase. Both income data on American workers and recent trends in executive pay by American corporations point in one direction: The "rich are getting richer," while those below them struggle to maintian their standard of living. This growing income gap between America's wealthiest and its working citizens may promote white-collar crime either by engendering feelings of relative deprivation in those further down the pay scale or by emboldening some to climb the status hierarchy toward greater pay and privilege by using the most expedient means possible. The internal reward structure in some complex organizations may function to increase irresponsible and criminal conduct. Research by D. Bilimoria, reprinted here, lends support to this conclusion. Her analysis of 91 Fortune 500 companies found greater criminal behavior in companies where managers, as opposed to owners, controlled executive pay packages.

According to James W. Coleman, temporal and spatial cultural variation also play a part in determining the supply of predisposed white-collar offenders. Coleman's description of the qualities and consequences of cultures of competition is consistent with notions of criminogenic cultures that stimulate crime by providing individuals with perspectives and rationalizations that conflict with or call into question ethical and legal norms. The culture of competition elevates and rewards success above all else, and individuals feel driven to strive for success. Pervasive insecurity can be a powerful motivation, argues Coleman, for crime for both poor and rich alike. During economic boom peiods, competitive culutres stimulate excess and crime due to the widespread belief that "everyone is getting rich." In these circumstances, many come to believe that to pass up any opportunity is to miss the boat.

While Coleman explores how individuals assess and construct appropriate workplace behaviors, Diane Vaughan explores some of its structural sources. The goals of survival, prestige, and profit are paramount for corporate executives. Corporations must return profits, and the pressure to survive filters down the organization. According to Vaughan, this can cause them to select technically effective, if illegal, means to goal achievement.

Who Is the White-Collar Criminal?

HAZEL CROALL

. . . This paper is based on a study of "crimes against the consumer" that examined offences under aspects of consumner protection legislation (Croall 1987), which aims to protect the health, safety, and economic interests of consumers. Offences include the adulteration of food, selling food from unhygienic premises, the use of misleading descriptions of goods and prices, and the sale of goods with short weight or measure. These offences are typical of white-collar crime as traditionally characterized in that they are committed by persons "in the course of trade and business," and consumers are diffuse victims, poorly organized and often ignorant of their victimization. Although the

"Who Is the White-Collar Criminal?" from *British Journal of Criminology* 29:2 (Spring 1989): 157–74. Reprinted by permission.

net profits from illegal practices may be substantial, the loss of any one consumer is often small, leading to the underreporting of offences and a lack of perceived victimization. Offenders are often assumed to be large corporations making huge profits at the expense of the consumer by placing profit above health and safety considerations or by "conning" consumers through misleading marketing and advertising strategies. Thus Braithwaite and Condon (1978) comment that "apart from workers, the main victims of 'institutional violence' are consumers," and Box (1983) argues that "whether we are consumers or citizens we stand more chance of being robbed by persons who roam corporate suites than we do by those who roam public streets."

While not denying the large toll of human misery caused by corporate crime, it will be suggested that such imagery is far from the reality uncovered by empirical investigation. Attending cases in court, the observer is immediately struck by lists of seemingly trivial and routine cases involving dirty milk bottles and mouldy food. Particularly noticeable is the absence of corporate offenders and the prevalence of small shopkeepers, restaurateurs, market traders, and second-hand car salesmen. This could suggest that the "powerful" are more immune from prosecution, as the characteristics of convicted offenders may reflect enforcement decisions rather than "real" crime rates. It will be argued, however, that while smaller businesses may be more vulnerable to enforcement, other factors are involved. This has several implications for the depiction of the white-collar criminal, which arguably disguises the wide variety of white-collar offending.

SOURCES OF INFORMATION

"Official data" are available in annual reports of the Office of Fair Trading and of individual Trading Standards, Environmental Health, or Consumer Protection departments. However, the Office of Fair Trading merely tabulates annual prosecutions by category of offence (Director-General of Fair Trading 1984), and local reports cite only the name of an offender or company and broad categories of offences. Information about offenders is even sparser. Offenders may be described as a "company," which could be a small ("one-person") retail outlet, a subsidiary of a large corporation, a local concern with two or more outlets, or a national or international corporation. Accordingly, a variety of methods were employed to obtain more "qualitative data."

Additional information was initially gained by observing cases in court. In all, fifty cases were observed, this total representing almost all cases appearing in three areas over a period of fifteen months. All enforcement departments involved were subsequently approached and further details of cases obtained. Through court observation and subsequent visits to enforcement departments, informal contacts were built up. In addition, all chief officers willing to co-opeate were interviewed about the policies of their departments. A further enforcement department granted access to prosecution files, enabling a larger sample of cases. This latter department was "strategically" chosen as it was undertaking a well-publicized "crack down" on offenders that resulted in a large number of prosecutions. One further department was also visited and its annual report used in compiling figures. Thus through court observation, use of files, annual reports, and discussions with officers, the rudimentary information obtained from overall statistics about the nature of offences was supplemented by a variety of data. For food offences, use was also made of the *British Food Journal*, which contains press reports of prosecutions on a national basis and an annual review of prosecutions.

All the areas studied were urban and metroploitan boroughs; this had certain implications for the range of offences, but it is not felt that this affects the overall conclusions.

THE OFFENCES

. . .

Trade Desriptions Offences

The largest group of prosecutions under the Trade Descriptions Act of 1968 is for false description of goods, with smaller numbers being prosecuted for false price indications and false statements about services. In 1982/3 there were 1,484 prosecutions under the Trade Descriptions Act, 1,178 for false descriptions of goods, 142 for false price indications and 164 for false statements about services. (Director-General of Fair Trading 1984.) Motor vehicles and large items are frequently involved in prosecutions, as are misleading "flash" and "bargain" offers. These mislead the consumer by comparing a "sale" price with a "normal" price which may never have been charged, or indicating a "special offer" when the price has not been reduced. Such practices are often regarded by traders as involving "normal marketing strategies," jusitified on the grounds of competition. In the areas studied, 45 per cent of Trade Descriptions prosecutions were for "flash" or "bargain" offers.

The cosmopolitan nature of the geographical areas investigated was reflected in the wide variety of cases, including a false description of the services of a model agency which was in fact a "clip joint," and an "unbeatable" roulette system. While offences may on the surface appear rather trivial and are covered by strict liability, many involve fraud and dishonesty, and others systematically mislead the consumer. Indeed, one chief trading standards officer interviewed felt that there was an element of dishonesty in all cases prosecuted.

An example of a fraudulent practice is "clocking"—the practice of turning back odometers, thus giving a false indication of mileage, estimated by the Director-General of Fair Trading to cost the consumer "millions of pounds a year," which has assumed the proportions of a widespread fraud (Cranston 1984). A chief consumer protection officer (*Monthly Review,* 1983: 91/6) cites one case where a trader made £100,000 illegal profits in ten months. Fraud and deliberate organization are present in other offences. For example, the "passing off" of cheap scents as being expensive brand names was described by the *Observer* (13 Dec. 81) as "big business," and the sale of falsely described "gold" jewellery, the false use of hallmarks, and counterfeiting also involve fraud.

Weights and Measures Offences

In 1982/3 there were only 455 prosecutions under the Weights and Measures Act 1963, more than half involving short-weight food and drink. Bread, meat, and alcoholic drinks were the main items concerned (Director-General of Fair Trading 1984). As there are few prosecutions under this legislation, it is difficult to make generalizations. While in general offences appear trivial—one file recorded a magistrate's comment that the offence was "not really very serious"—this is not sustained on closer examination of the nature of offences. Selling goods with short measure often implies a degree of deliberateness, and one charge may conceal systematic practices. In the hotel industry, "fiddles," including the sale of short-measure drinks, are so institutionalized that they represent part of an "informal reward structure" (Mars 1973; Mars and Nicod 1984). Bakers are also common offenders, as bread falling short of the legally required weight involves extra profits. Large companies can be involved; in one case, an assortment of pricing and short-weight offences resulted from the practices of a large chain responsible for catering at occasional sporting matches. Staff were employed casually and little control exercised over prices charged.

Weights and Measures offences can also involve defrauding the government. In cases involving excess froth in beer, the publican pockets excess tax on the "extra" pints generated (*Which?* Apr. 1983, p. 139).

Food Offences

Offences under the Food Act 1984 involve food "not of the nature substance or quality demanded," which includes food containing foreign matter or mouldy; food "unfit for human consumption" (mainly, old and decomposed food), and food-labelling regulations. The latter involve breaches of information and compositional standards and foods containing excess preservatives or additives. While routine cases involving dirty milk bottles, mouldy pies, and out-of-date items may make offences appear trivial, underlying many practices are threats to consumer safety, fraudulent practices, and other methods of "misleading" the purchaser. In 1982/3, there were 1,822 prosecutions for food offences: 955 for food "not of the nature, substance, or quality demanded," 219 for food "unfit for human consumption," and 648 for breaches of food labelling regulations.

Food laws are principally concerned with the potential danger of bad or damaged food. Many will remember the Spanish cooking oil scandal where the use of industrial oils in cooking oil claimed over 200 lives and seriously crippled many thousands more, and the well-publicized use of anti-freeze and methyl alcohol in wine. In 8 out of 256 cases analysed from reports in the *British Food Journal*, actual injury resulted from the presence of "foreign bodies" (including metal, glass, stones, sticking plasters, sawdust, and wood), one victim requiring surgery to remove a piece of metal. Nine further cases involved victims being "generally ill," including a case where paint was used in a child's birthday cake. Other cases causing concern involved stones or metal being found in baby foods, and the supply of "unfit" meat to schools and hospitals.

Fraud is also involved. A large number of prosecutions resulted from "meat rackets" where meat taken from knackers' yards intended for pet food, including kangaroo, horse, and goat meat, were passed into the legitimate meat trade. When frozen, such illegal meat is similar to legal meat and is thus easily substituted. According to the Institute of Environmental Health Officers (1981), so widespread was this trade that it was estimated to amount to about 2 per cent of the meat market; therefore "the majority of people have at some stage eaten products made from unfit or knacker meat." Other "frauds" included what the *Daily Mail* (1 July 1984) termed "The Great Food Racket"—a highly organized trade in food from major stores past its sell-by date sold by various other outlets and market stalls. The use of additives, meat substitutes, and water in excess of legal limits in processed foods, which appears rather "technical," also involves practices criticized as fraudulent (see e.g. Cannon and Walker 1985).

Food Hygiene Offences

A further group of offences are those under food hygiene regulations, estimated to have constituted 28.1 per cent of all food offences in 1984 (*British Food Journal*, 1984). Offences mainly involve the presence of dirt and grease in food preparation or storage areas, and also include the absence of hot water, suitable clothing, sanitary facilities, first-aid boxes, and smoking by employees in food establishments. More serious cases involve infestation by insects or the presence of mice and rodents. In one of the worst cases, a small supermarket was found to have "mice, moths, biscuit beetles, larder beetles, cockroaches and slugs . . . filthy shelves, rusty tins and toilet walls smeared with human faeces." Other cases involved restaurants, some with a very high reputation. The underlying concern of the law is to prevent the spread of disease, particularly through food poisoning. Given that cases in court are often preceded by a long history of warnings, visits, exhortations, and threats, negligence is often a strong factor. Cutting costs may also be involved, as the cost of equipment or structural alterations to improve hygiene may be high. Thus, hygiene offences are far from trivial, especially when the dangers of food poisoning are considered. Offences are not often directly related to food poisoning, due to the difficulties of establishing the "chain of evidence" necessary to link a case of illness to the establishment concerned. None the less, 6 out of 144 hygiene cases analysed from the *British Food Journal* involved food-poisoning outbreaks. In one case, a bride and groom had to spend their honeymoon recovering from the wedding reception. In extreme cases, food poisoning can cause death, as shown in the case of the Stanley Royd Hospital, where an outbreak of salmonella killed nineteen patients (*Guardian*, various, 1986). Thus the potential impact on the victim of hygiene offences is severe. . . .

THE OFFENDERS

Table 1 illustrates the prevalence of small businesses among the establishments prosecuted: restaurants, food stores, grocers, bakers, butchers and garages. Other businesses included a night club, a roulette system, two large department stores, and a mock auction. Such a distribution undoubtedly reflects both the nature of the geographical areas studied and enforcement policies. For example, one department was undertaking a crack-down on restaurants, another on street-market traders. Overall, the range of establishments is similar to that found by Cranston (1979), and the pattern of offending in food offences is consonant with analyses in the *British Food Journal.*

Size of Businesses

Court observation enabled further exploration of the size of offending businesses. About half of all establishments prosecuted were described as companies; however, out of 57 defendants seen in court, only 9 were large companies.[1] A further 6 were medium-sized companies, and 33 were small businesses. Twelve employees were prosecuted, some "managers."[2]

The information in files and reports was less detailed, but none the less a broadly similar picture emerged. Out of eleven Weights and Measures files, only two concerned large companies. Slightly more large companies appeared in hygiene prosecutions, a feature perhaps of the area studied, which contained a large number of restaurants and hotels, belonging to chains of national repute. In only four cases involving unfit food were large companies involved: two food manufacturers, a supermarket branch, and a large bakery. The most "typical" offenders were therefore small establishments.

Unfortunately, due to the scarcity of comparative data, it is difficult to estimate the representativeness of such figures. In general, results, were similar to those found by Cranston (1979). An analysis of cases reported in the *British Food Journal* gave the distribution shown in Table 2. The proportion of large

---

[1] As information about the size of businesses was not always available, a "common sense" definition was employed. Companies identified as "large" were in fact defined as such on the basis of their being "household names"—for example, supermarket or catering chains and large food manufacturers. There is thus inevitably some underestimation of larger companies as their scope may not have been sufficiently described or their name not recognized.

[2] The discrepancy in total numbers between 50 cases seen and the number of defendants was due to multiple prosecutions.

companies is slightly greater, but they are still in the minority. Proportionately more appear in the "nature, substance and quality" of food category, which would be expected as foreign bodies are more likely to originate in the manufacturing process. Many well-known companies were involved, including large chains of restaurants, supermarkets, and food manufacturers. However, the majority of offenders were again individual food stores, restaurants, butchers, meat suppliers, market traders, and corner shops.

The Ethnicity of Offenders

Of the individual offenders for whom details were available, there were in all 15 Asian defendants, 15 English, 1 Chinese, I Italian, and 1 Irish. A further 16 were companies, for which such characterizations are inapplicable. Details

TABLE 1
Main Types of Establishment Prosecuted, by Main Offence Categories

	Food	Hygiene	Trades Description	Weights and Measures
Food stores/ grocers	12	4	1	0
Dairies	4	0	0	0
Bakeries	8	0	0	2
Restaurants	5	29	4	0
Bars	3	0	3	6
Butchers	7	2	0	3
Garages	1	0	6	0
Wholesalers	2	0	0	0
Supermarkets	4	1	3	0
Street markets	0	1	4	3
TOTAL	46	37	21	14

TABLE 2
Cases Cited in the *British Food Journal,* 1982–1984, by Offence and Size of Company

	"Unfit" Food	Food not of Nature etc. Demanded[a]	Hygiene
Proprietors	37	34	86
Companies (size unspecified)	23	64	38
Large companies	22	71	19
Managers/employees	5	0	1
TOTAL	87	169	144

[a] Food not of the nature, quality, or substance demanded by the consumer.

were more difficult to establish for cases not directly seen. Files made no reference to ethnic status, but this could on occasion be deduced from the description of the business, for example, "Indian restaurant" or "kebab house." In the 34 files involving hygiene, while in 20 cases the ethnic origin of the proprietors was unknown, 7 of the remainder were Asian and a further 4 non-English. This is likely to be an underestimation, as only those known to be non-English or Asian were counted as such. The owners of many other corner shops and small supermarkets could be assumed to be from diverse ethnic backgrounds.

This is not unique to the area studied. In annual prosecution surveys in the *British Food Journal*, the same characteristics are noted each year. In 1978 hygiene prosecutions were seen as "mainly a problem of Asiatic caterers," and in 1984 the continuing rise in hygiene prosecutions was attributed to increasing foreign ownership of food buisnesses. From reports received by the *Journal* of hygiene prosecutions in 1984, two-thirds of restaurants were foreign owned, mainly "Asiatic," as were the majority of take-aways (*British Food Journal*, Mar.–Apr. 1984).

Criminal Businesses

Offenders varied from the conventional picture of the white-collar criminal in another respect. Some, particularly those involved in more "serious" offences, could not be described as "respectable" but rather as "criminal businesses," in that their activities were organized primarily around illegal ends. The large-scale meat frauds and "passing off" trades indicate "illegal businesses," and perpetrators can be described as "shady operators" (Sutton and Wild 1985). Large legitimate corporations, as we shall see, are the *victims* of such frauds rather than the perpetrators.

Thus, while large companies are not totally absent, and their numbers, as will be seen, are likely to be an underrepresentation of their rates of offending, the above analysis suggests that significant numbers of white-collar criminals are small businesses, and a further minority of offenders could more properly be described as "criminal businesses." Employees are also involved, sometimes being charged along with companies. Before discussing the significance of these findings, the likely effect of underreporting of offences by victims and the activities and policies of enforcement agencies must be considered. In common with other regulatory offences, the well-documented compliance strategy of enforcers (see, e.g., Hawkins 1984; Cranston 1979) leads to few prosecutions in relation to detected offences. To what extent therefore does the relative scarcity of the corporate offender result from such processes?

REPORTING TRADING OFFENCES

The attitude of the victim is a vital factor affecting the reporting of any offence and is crucial in respect of the crimes under consideration. Thus, while consumers are not likely to purchase an obviously faulty product, eat in a restaurant which has insects all over the floor, and can tell if a bag of potatoes marked "5 lbs" only contains 2 lbs, they cannot test the contents of food; nor do they inspect the kitchens of apparently clean restaurants or weigh bread. Even if they could test the contents of food they would most likely not be aware of the standards laid down for the particular food item, which can be extremely technical. Serious offences are no more likely to be obvious as they may be undetectable by individual consumers, as in the case of the addition of excess water to processed food, or the use of substitutes in meat products. Thus one can safely assume that large numbers of victims are unaware of their victimization, even where serious and persistent offending may be involved.

Many offences, even if detected, are unlikely to be reported. Frequently, there is only a minimal effect on individual consumers, and they may seem too trivial to warrant further action, as for example the purchase of a mouldy sandwich. In other cases, consumers may consider themselves responsible for their own victimization. If, for example, food "goes off" the day after it is bought, a consumer might think that he or she did not store it properly. Indeed this is often the case, and is one factor inhibiting formal action. The deficiencies of cheap goods bought at a sale or market stall may be dismissed as a "bad buy." In this respect the seriousness of a complaint is relevant, as, for example, action is more likely to be taken if a major item of expenditure is involved. This is illustrated by the predominance of cars, major household appliances and furniture in complaints reported (Director-General of Fair Trading 1983).

If action is taken it may not involve enforcement agencies, and complaints not treated as potential offences. Harvey (1982) lists many possible avenues of redress including Citizens' Advice Bureaux, MPs, legal advice from solicitors, and, as only one avenue among many, the relevant Local Authority department. Many consumers complain directly to the shop or manufacturer concerned (Cranston 1979). Thus, the number of offences drawn to agencies' attention is likely to represent only a tiny proportion of the "real" volume of offences, and those eventually reported may not necessarily be the most serious.

ENFORCEMENT POLICIES

The proactive role of enforcers is therefore crucial, and this in turn is affected by departmental policies, the technicalities of the offence, and by manpower and resource considerations. Departments had different policies and priorities: the frequency of inspections varied, and different groups were "targeted" for attention. One department carried out "purges" of particular problems at different times—for example, concentrating on the weight of "punnets" of strawberries in the summer and on toy safety at Christmas. Another department was engaged in a crack-down on food establishments which involved inspecting all establishments over a period of time and prosecuting all offenders, leading to a "crime wave." Technical factors are also important. As production of consumer goods and food processing becomes more complex, more technical knowledge and equipment is needed to check compliance, and many of the most serious offences only come to light in this way. Such testing and the "test purchases" involved are very costly, and resource and manpower considerations are crucial. Thus, enforcement policies clearly affect the pattern of offences eventually reaching the courts.

One major question is to what extent different groups are more likely to be the "target" of enforcement officers. This could occur in different ways. In analysis of non-white-collar crimes, lower class offenders are the most likely targets of law enforcement activities, partly due to their higher visibility; and within the lower class, certain groups, for example, black unemployed youth, are more likely to be stopped, searched, and arrested (see, e.g., Smith and Gray 1985; Reiner 1985). In general, this results from a combination of factors such as the presence of greater numbers of such groups "on the streets," the use by police of stereotypes associating unemployed status and ethnic characteristics with "deviance," and the occupational culture of policing, which contains a degree of racism and thus affects such stereotypes (Reiner 1985; Lea and Young 1984). To what extent might this also be the case with trading offenders?

While regulatory enforcement is often differentiated from "policing," there are similarities. In their inspection role, officers proceed very much like police, calling on establishments according to their own discretion. Thus, they may be drawn to those that they associate with offending on their "patch," and some talked of having "black books." High street and corner shops are easier and quicker to inspect, and their operations are more "visible" than those of a food manufacturer. Officers recounted one case when they were drawn to an establishment by the height of boxes of fruit off the ground; in another they were attracted to an establishment by its smell. Hutter (1986) reports an instance in which enforcement officers noticed unsafe building work on a premises near one they had visited.

Cranston (1979) found that officers' stereotypes affected their decisions. Second-hand car dealers were seen as "rogues," and coal merchants also suffered an adverse stereotype. This meant more frequent inspection of premises, and if inspection revealed a problem, a greater likelihood of prosecution as these types of traders were considered persistent offenders. Such assumptions may well vary according to the area concerned, with departments having a conception of "normal offenders" (Sudnow 1965). Chief officers, when asked about the main problems in their areas, referred to particular groups. One officer referred to market traders as "villains," and another to a tendency to prosecute car dealers and coal merchants to "teach them a lesson." Some, though not all, felt that Asian shopkeepers were also a particular problem. Departmental policies involving "crack downs," "purges," or "blitzes" on particular groups are also crucial, as indicated above, and have been found to affect patterns of offending elsewhere (Braithwaite and Vale 1985).

In respect of the ethnicity of offenders, similar questions arise. The

British Food Journal (1981) emphatically denies any claims of racial discrimination: "occasionally ill-informed meddlers suggest an element of racial prejudice, but the facts . . . [the amount and seriousness of charges] . . . speak for themselves." In some of the areas studied, there was clearly a perception that Asian restaurants and shops dominated hygiene offences. Claims of discrimination, occasionally made by offenders, were strongly denied, although the problem was recognized and discussed. Some officers saw the proliferation of Asian traders in court as inevitable given the nature of the areas, all characterized by high concentrations of ethnic minorities and large numbers of foreign-owned shops and businesses. Others considered that they constituted a special problem. Ignorance of regulations and different cultural standards of hygiene were some factors mentioned in connection with this. This is echoed somewhat crudely by the editor of the *British Food Journal* (Mar.–Apr. 1985) who attributes the predominance of "foreign-owned" businesses in hygiene prosecutions to "indifference, obsession to outwit those in authority, ignorance of what hygiene really means, and language." Such strong sentiments were not encountered in this research, although as there was no participant observation, their absence cannot be taken as definitive; the attitudes of chief officers may not be shared by those "on the street." Several departments have attempted to tackle perceived problems with ethnic-minority businesses. Many publish hygiene regulations in the languages of ethnic communities, some have appointed officers from such communities, and run special educational programmes targeted at particular types of business (*Environmental Health,* Sept. 1980 and Jan. 1982).

A further question is the extent to which enforcers may be more sympathetic towards corporations. Some argue that large companies are "shielded" by enforcers' partiality towards high-status offenders. Cranston (1979) found different attitudes towards large companies in different departments. One department had a policy of *only* prosecuting large companies; another fought shy of such prosecutions, fearing a complex defence. In this study, some aspects of "differential treatment" did emerge. One senior environmental health officer felt that some officers might be afraid of being "grilled" in court by the barristers brought in by large companies. Another department acknowledged this problem and brought in specialist prosecuting staff for inportant cases. Others showed a certain pride in having brought particular large concerns to court. In one department, large companies were singled out as a group more likely to be prosecuted as "they should know better," and another chief officer felt that instead of pursuing "villains," small concerns that in his view would "never comply," they should "go and chase after big firms."

One area noted for a strong attitude to prosecution admitted to using more stringent tactics for large companies, especially chains of restaurants: if conditions in one restaurant of a chain were unsatisfactory, others would be visited. If the problem was found to be common to all outlets, then an approach to top management was made. One senior officer proudly recounted having berated a prominent businessman about the state of his kitchens. Prosecution would follow if action was not immediately forthcoming, sometimes despite high-level intervention by the company through prominent local councillors. Another prosecution attracted a newspaper comment to the effect that "premises which enjoy public prestige should not be prosecuted just to show an example."[3]

Adopting different policies for large concerns did not always work against them. Thus whereas small establishments may be inspected on a random basis, without warning, arrangements have to be made in advance for the inspection of large establishments, because of the technicalities involved for the development concerned. This does not indicate leniency—to quote the chief officer, "they can hardly run round cleaning the whole factory"—but such differential treatment may well have the effect, however unintended, of making the smaller concern more vulnerable to inspection and prosecution.

An important consideration in any public service department is the deployment of scarce resources and the consequent need to allocate priorities. Hutter (1986) found that environmental health departments with scarce resources devoted less attention to proactive work. Most departments in this study complained that manpower shortages made their inspection and testing duties less comprehensive than they would wish. This could affect the pattern of prosecutions in various ways. Departments acknowledged that testing programmes were limited. These include detecting substitutions or excess water content in processed foods, and the safety or quality of consumer goods, both involving manufacturers. Thus, the low priority accorded to expensive testing programmes could result in proportionately more offences of larger concerns escaping detection.

Both the victim's propensity to report offences and the decisions and attitudes of enforcers do therefore affect the pattern of prosecutions. Large companies and serious offences, not necessarily related, are likely to be underrepresented; however, it could equally well be argued that many small concerns commit offences which are undetected by consumers and enforcers alike. Such an underrepresentation does not appear to arise out of the "capture" of enforcement agencies by business, for which little evidence could be found. Rather it results from differences between large and small businesses which affect their vulnerability to enforcement and may also affect their propensity to offend. Nelken (1983) suggests that the pattern of prosecutions and the characteristics of offenders results from an interaction between structural factors, the law, and its enforcement. These "structural" factors will now be discussed.

STRUCTURAL FACTORS AND PATTERNS OF OFFENDING

Nelken's (1983) discussion of harassment legislation illustrates the importance of structural factors. The law was aimed at wealthy landlords and at ille-

---

[3]Specific quotes and examples must be withheld in order to preserve the anonymity of the area.

gal evictions known as "Rachmanism," but in practice, large landlords could "minimise the extent to which the law impinges on their activities." Residential landlords, letting only one or two rooms, were most regularly prosecuted. Large landlords could vet tenants carefully and had resources to employ legitimate means of getting rid of unwanted tenants, such as "winkling out" (offering large sums of money as an inducement to quit). They could also afford to improve properties, justifying an increase in rent which tenants could not afford. Smaller residential landlords, often Asian, had fewer of these resources at their disposal and frequently shared accommodation with tenants, leading to potential friction. Large landlords are thus "protected" by the scope of legislation, in part because they are large and do not *need* to use illegal tactics; in other words, the "application of universal standards produces unequal results" (Nelken 1983).

Similar processes can be identified for trading offences. A statutory defence is possible if a company can establish that it has a "system of checking" that abuses do not occur. Such systems include the (often expensive) scanning machinery used in dairies and food manufacture, the employment of quality-control staff, and in respect of pricing, a system whereby price schedules are communicated to all outlets. These, however, require both resources and manpower, and equipment may be too costly for smaller companies. In court, the ability to establish such "systems" clearly distinguished between large and small businesses (Croall 1988), and Cranston (1984) and Borrie (1984) both argue that large companies can more easily persuade the court that systems are present. They also employ legal and scientific staff to ensure that breaches of regulations do not occur, and to advise on the complexities of the law.

Small companies are more vulnerable. Many small traders may be ignorant of the precise details of regulations. They are more likely to receive goods pre-packaged, and to use cash-and-carry warehouses which, according to environmental health officers, makes them more likely to receive unsatisfactory goods. Low profit margins may make costly equipment difficult to afford. They are also less likely to establish an elaborate system of instructions and checking. In a small supermarket, written instructions about pricing or stock rotation are inappropriate, whereas large companies produce circular letters to management as a matter of course. Further, many face problems with hygiene regulations due to the cost of structural alterations. The *British Food Journal* (Mar.–Apr. 1984) comments that many problems in food shops are due to inadequate space for food storage, and many offenders complained of the capital needed to structurally alter kitchen areas. While not discussing hygiene specifically, Aldrich et al. (1981) found that the accommodation of Asian shops was often substandard, frequently located in deteriorating buildings and combining retailing with residence. This, they add, is a problem not only of the Asian shopkeeper but also of the "independent white ratailer." In addition, many small food stores rely on providing a large range of goods, yet may not be able to ensure adequate rotation. The special requirements of ethnic populations, such as special meats and cooking techniques, may create even more problems. The problems of installing and cleaning "tandoor" ovens were mentioned in court cases, as were habits of storing dried vegetables in sacks, attracting infestation. Ignorance of regulations may compound these difficulties, although on the whole, despite some variations between different groups, ethnic businesses appear no more ignorant of business matters generally (Aldrich et al. 1984).

The role of "market forces" has recently attracted attention in analyses of white collar and corporate crime (see, e.g., Box 1987; Clinard and Yeager 1980). In respect of small business offending, some offenders have been portrayed as "victims of circumstance," where the necessity of competing with large corporations creates a "criminogenic market" (Sutton and Wild 1985). In their analysis of fraud in the motor industry, Leonard and Weber (1977) argue that large motor manufacturers, operating in an oligopolistic market, control dealers through franchises and exert pressure for sales. However, pricing arrangements result in minimal profits from such sales, leaving servicing and second-hand car sales as the main area of profitability for such dealers. This encourages a variety of illegal activities, such as altering odometers and tendering false accounts of services. Thus unethical actions of dealers and mechanics are "coerced occupational crime." Braithwaite (1978) offers a similar analysis of used-car fraud in Australia, where salesmen pressured mechanics to alter odometers. Intense competition also encouraged false or deceptive advertising. Dealers interviewed were clear about their motives: the desire for profits. Car dealers were found to have no independent code of ethics, and, according to Braithwaite, were "groping in a moral fog." He concludes that the "used car dealer is a rational human being responding in a normal way to a market and society which has built into its structure of social relations a propensity to take advantage of the other."

While it would be impossible to analyse fully market considerations relevant to the many industries involved here, food retailing could be a market where structural factors may affect illegal activities. Large supermarkets can obtain favourable prices from food manufacturers for "bulk orders" (Smith 1982). These price reductions can then be passed on to the consumer. The small grocery, dependent for supplies on the wholesaler or the "cash and carry," not the manufacturer, cannot compete. Therefore profit margins are reduced if prices are not to be higher. This could create certain pressures—for example small grocers may be dependent on selling all goods irrespective of whether or not they become out of date. Similarly, they may be tempted to stock too large a range of goods for their available space, creating possible hygiene problems. Aldrich et al. (1981) argue that "irrespective of ethnicity, small retail business is characterised by high failure rates and rapid turnover," thus many shopkeepers are likely to be "preoccupied with survival." The constraints within which such businesses operate may well contribute to some offences, and it is possible that fuller analysis would find other "criminogenic" market situations.

Legal factors also play a part. The role of the "system" defence has already been mentioned. Further, the brunt of enforcement, and therefore prosecution, falls at the point of sale, not production. A small corner shop found selling an offending item is liable to be prosecuted for failing to exercise "all due diligence"—a more difficult task for a small concern. It is difficult to institute a third-party defence as this would require proof that the defect was caused through omissions on the manufacturer's part. This difficulty is compounded by the manufacturer's "system." As consumer complaints and inspections of establishments more often involve the actual seller, the latter is thus more vulnerable.

All these factors would in any case lead to an underrepresentation of large companies as offenders, without considering the enforcement process. They reflect the superior resources of large companies, the operation of "market forces," and the nature of legislation, which puts the onus of enforcement mainly at the point of sale, and requires proof of "systems" as a defence.

DISCUSSION

A combination of enforcement policies and structural factors affects the distribution of offenders. This has significance not only for the stereotype of the white-collar offender but also for comparisons between different "types" of offending, which indicate more clear-cut distinctions than those emerging from empirical investigation. Within the broad category of "crimes against the consumer," some offences involve widespread and deliberate frauds, others negligence shading into culpability, and others consist of misleading the consumer through "normal trading practices." Small businesses constitute a large proportion of offenders, other offences could be classified as "employee" crime, and yet other offenders are "criminal businesses." Corporations are the victims of many offences, along with consumers. There is a clear difference between the large food manufacturer systematically adding water to processed food in excess of the legal limits, and the organized "fiddles" of employees which may involve adding water to gin. One can also differentiate between the large manufacturer negligent in respect of quality control, the small shopkeeper preoccupied with the struggle for survival leaving out-of-date food on the shelves, and the market trader who obtains supplies of questionable food which he markets quickly for a quick sale. While not wishing to enter into tortuous definitional debates or attempting yet another typology, some general patterns of offending can be identified.

It has been argued that small businesses are likely to represent a significant group of offenders, and that this is not only the result of selective enforcement. However, Sutton and Wild (1985) recognize that small businesses are not a homogeneous category and identify two "models" of small business crime: an "interactional or agency view, which interprets their activities as individual, small-scale confidence tricksters" or "shady operators"; and a "structural" view in which they are seen as "victims of circumstance." In their view, neither model fully explains the complexities of small business crime, but they do provide a means of distinguishing broadly different types of offenders.

Sutton and Wild identify "shady operators" operating on the fringe of the market, "peripheral individuals manipulating the system" who conform to a "con-man" or "confidence trickster" image. These include the "phantom capitalists" described by Levi (1981) in his study of long firm fraud, and the "fly by night" operations and "shaky businesses" involved in consumer fraud depicted by Rothschild and Throne (1976). Producers and sellers of falsely hallmarked jewellery or fake perfumes, counterfeiters, and traders in the various meat rackets could also be characterized as "shady operators." Such systematic offending is clearly distinguishable from the occasional offending of the otherwise legitimate business, and victims are consumers and legitimate manufacturers alike. Other analyses of criminal organization (e.g., McIntosh 1974) point out that such activities are "rational" economic behaviour in a favourable market. Thus, such offenders are likely to form a significant minority in much economic crime.

The second group discussed by Sutton and Wild are the "victims of circumstance," businesses whose maginality may leave them preoccupied with a "struggle for survival." Their offences are likely to be affected by economic factors, coupled with neglect (or ignorance) of the finer points of the law. Negligence, often of a persistent nature, characterizes such offences. Because they cater largely for lower socio-economic groups, their victims are likely to be those least able to protect themselves. While "marginal," such businesses show little signs of disappearing (Ward and Jenkins 1984), and are thus likely to continue to be a significant group of offenders within categories of white-collar crime. Indeed, Box (1987) argues that in a recession such criminality may well increase.

Another group of offenders are "employees." Due to the well-known difficulty of attributing blame to any one level within a company, prosecution of employees could be seen as a denial of corporate responsibility. In attempting to "blame" employees, many companies attribute offences to "human error," "carelessness," "staffing difficulties," and occasionally to "sabotage" (Croall 1988). These excuses can be interpreted as "techniques of neutralisation" (Box 1983), as it is ultimately the responsibility of management to ensure that "human error" is designed out of production processes. Such arguments may however oversimplify the relationship between corporate responsibility and employee "deviance." Excuses may have some basis (Clinard and Yeager 1980), and many offences can be attributed to a lack of regard for safety precautions by workers, which may in turn be related to work processes and managerial policies. Industrial sociologists point out that many "accidents" are caused by the form of work organization in large enterprises. Braithwaite (1984) suggests that the lack of discretion accorded to workers arising from tight regulations surrounding the manufacture of drugs can lead to alienation, carelessness, and even sabotage. Ditton (1972) describes well the boredom of working on a mass production line producing cakes and bread, where workers resorted to day-dreaming and, as an "escape," occasionally dipped other workers in the confectionery mix—obviously running the risk of "foreign bodies" entering it! As much food is now mass-produced, these factors may account for seemingly "accidental" offences. Sabotage can also be related to work organization and can be an indication of poor industrial relations or boring work (Taylor and Walton 1971).

Other offences described as "employee crime," such as overcharging or watering down alcoholic drinks, may be related to managerial policies and pay. Ditton (1974, 1977) found bread salesmen's "fiddles" to be related to managerial systems, and in part motivated by a perceived desire to secure a "fair day's pay." In the hotel industry, widespread fiddles are accepted as a means of improving low earnings (Mars 1973; Mars and Nicod 1984). Such employee offending is deliberate and economic in motivation, and both employer and consumer are the ultimate victims. It is therefore misleading to separate consideration of "employee crime" from corporate crime, or to dismiss employee offences as an attempt by corporations to escape responsibility. Corporate policies may produce the conditions in which employees may neglect safety and quality regulations or engage in "fiddles," a more complex relationship than often assumed.

The prevalence of offending by small businesses and employees does not detract from the significance or impact of corporate offending, which may also be related to market and organizational factors (Clinard and Yeager 1980; Box 1983, 1987). Of relevance to this study is the example of food-manufacturing, an extremely competitive business where the search for cheap food substitutes and "efficient" techniques has been subject to criticism. Consumers may be misled in respect of the quality and content of food, much of which contains additives and preservatives which may damage their health (see, e.g., Cannon and Walker 1985; Croall 1987). Similarly, pressures on processing plants may lead to a neglect of safety considerations, contributing to the presence of "foreign bodies." Organizational "defects," such as communications failures, have also been isolated as factors in corporate offending (Hopkins 1980); and as explained above, other corporate policies may lead to neglect of regulations by employees.

It could of course be argued that the relative absence of corporate offenders provides another example of business avoiding the criminalization of its activities. While analysis of the relationship between business, the criminal law, and its enforcement lies beyond the scope of this paper, it is suggested that such an absence is not solely a result of corporate influence on lawmaking. On the other hand, it does not indicate high levels of "social responsibility" on the part of large corporations. Box (1988) argues that "corporate crime need not occur," in that in addition to influencing regulation itself, corporations may engage in law evasion—for example, manufacturing substandard goods in countries with less stringent regulatory codes. Similarly McBarnet (1988), discussing tax evasion, details many practices of large concerns which comply with the *content* but not the *intent* of the law. Many of the offences described occur at the fringes of the law, and one could point to numerous instances where "normal trading practices" adversely affect the consumer. There are many loopholes in the law which regulate some practices but not other, similar ones. Thus even "legal" bargain offers may be extremely misleading, water may quite legitimately be added to food through modern processing techniques, and some mass-produced food, consisting of little more than "additive cocktails," could well be said to involve legalized adulteration (Cannon and Walker 1985; Clutterbuck and Lang 1982). Deceptive packaging has often been criticized as the sale of "empty space," and is seen as one of the major gaps in consumer protection legislation (Smith 1982). Thus, consumers can be quite "legitimately" deceived by practices which routinely breach the "spirit" if not the letter of the law, yet the arguments often advanced that corporations are the "real" criminals due to their immunity from legal controls and enforcement may simplify an extremely complex relationship between criminal law and business.

The relative scarcity of corporate offenders renders problematic other assumptions about white-collar offenders. Such offenders are almost universally assumed to be treated more sympathetically in the criminal justice system due to their superior resources and status. In court there may be clear distinction between large and small businesses in terms of defences and mitigation offered, with larger businesses being more able to persuade the court of their responsibility (Croall 1988). Sentences, often described as "derisory" (see, e.g., Levi 1984), had differing impacts, as a "trifling" fine to a large corporaion could represent a substantial amount to a small business, even threatening its survival (Croall 1987). Thus the assumption that the white-collar offender enjoys "benign" treatment is not universally applicable to all offenders. Indeed, given the wide variety of offenders, for many the grounds for such sympathy may not exist.

In conclusion it can be argued that the predominating image of the "crimes of the powerful" perpetrated by the corporation or high-status, respectable business offender can both disguise the variety of white-collar crime and exaggerate the distinction between "conventional" and white-collar crime. Classifications differentiating between corporate and employee or small-business offending and distinctions between crimes against corporations, crimes by corporations, and criminal corporations may also be misleading, as any one category may include many varieties. In addition, attempts to explain offending in relation to market factors must recognize that these may have a differential impact on different groups of offenders within the same offence category. Box (1987) argues, for example, that the ability of large corporations both to affect regulations and to evade the law may produce higher levels of small-business crime related to the economic exigencies of the recession. Thus, models attempting to explain such crime must take account of the complexities of market and structural factors as they affect different groups of offenders—corporations, employees, small businesses, and indeed "criminal business."

REFERENCES

Aldrich, H. et al. (1981). "Business Development and Self-Segregation: Asian Enterprise in Three British Cities," in C. Peach et al., eds., *Ethnic Segregation in Cities.* London: Croom Helm.

———. (1984). "Ethnic Advantage and Minority Business Development," in R. Ward and R. Jenkins, eds.

Borrie, Sir G. (1984). *The Development of Consumer Law and Policy: Bold Spirits and Timorous Souls.* London: Stevens.

Box, S. (1983). *Power, Crime and Mystification.* London: Tavistock.

———. (1987). *Recession, Crime and Punishment.* London: Macmillan.

Braithwaite, J., and Condon, B. (1978). "On the Class Basis of Criminal Violence," in J. Braithwaite and P. Wilson, eds.

Braithwaite, J., and Vale, S. (1985). "Law Enforcement by Australian Consumer Affairs Agencies," *Australian and New Zealand Journal of Criminology,* 18/3: 147–64.

Cannon, G., and Walker, C. (1985). *The Food Scandal.* London: Century.

Clinard, M. B., and Yeager, P. C. (1980). *Corporate Crime.* New York: Free Press.

Clutterbuck, C., and Lang, T. (1982). *More Than We Can Chew: The Crazy World of Food and Farming.* London: Pluto Press.

Cranston, R. (1979). *Regulating Business.* London: Macmillan.

———. (1984). *Consumers and the Law,* 2nd edn. London: Weidenfeld and Nicholson.

Croall, H. (1987). "Crimes against the Consumer: An analysis of the Nature, Extent, Regulation and Sanctioning of Trading Offences," Ph.D. thesis, University of London.

———. (1988). "Mistakes, Accidents or Someone Else's Fault: The Trading Offender in Court," *Journal of Law and Society,* 15/3:293–315.

Director General of Fair Trading. (1979–83). *Annual Reports.* London: HMSO.

Ditton, J. (1972). "Absent at Work: Or How to Manage Monotony," *New Society,* 21 Dec. 1972.

———. (1974). "The Fiddling Salesman: Connivance at Corruption," *New Society,* 28 Nov. 1974.

———. (1977). *Part-time Crime: An Ethnography of Fiddling and Pilferage.* London: Macmillan.

Harvey, B. W. (1982). *Law of Consumer Protection and Fair Trading,* 2nd edn. London: Butterworths.

Hawkins, K. (1984). *Environment and Enforcement: Regulation and the Social Definition of Pollution.* Oxford: Clarendon Press.

Hopkins, A. (1980). "Controlling Corporate Deviance," *Criminology,* 18/2:198–214.

Hutter, B. (1986). "An Inspector Calls," *British Journal of Criminology,* 26/2:114–28.

Institute of Environmental Health Officers. (1981). "Briefing Notes on Food and Drugs Amendment Bill."

Lea, J., and Young, J. (1984). *What Is To Be Done About Law and Order?* Harmondsworth, Middx.: Penguin.

Leonard, W. N., and Weber, M. G. (1977). "Auto-makers and Dealers: A Study of Criminogenic Market Forces," in G. Geis and R. F. Maier, eds.

Levi, M. (1981). *The Phantom Capitalists.* London: Macmillan.

———. (1984). "Business Regulatory Offences and the Criminal Law," *Company Lawyer,* 5/6:251–58.

McBarnet, D. (1988). "Law, Policy and Legal Avoidance: Can Law Effectively Implement Egalitarian Policies?" *Journal of Law and Society,* 15/1:113–22.

McIntosh, M. (1974). *The Organisation of Crime.* London: Macmillan.

Mars, G. (1973). "Hotel Pilferage: A Case Study in Occupational Theft," in M. Warner (ed.), *Sociology of the Workplace.* London: George Allen and Unwin.

Mars, G., and Nicod, M. (1984). *World of Waiters.* London: George Allen and Unwin.

Nelken, D. (1983). *Limits of the Legal Process.* London: Academic Press.

Reiner, R. (1985). *The Politics of the Police.* Brighton: Wheatsheaf Books.

Rothschild, D., and Throne, B. (1976). "Criminal Consumer Fraud: Victim Oriented Analysis," *Michigan Law Review,* Mar., 661–707.

Smith, D., and Gray, J. (1985). *Police and People in London.* Aldershot: Gower.

Smith, G. (1982). *The Consumer Interest.* John Martin.

Sudnow, D. (1965). "'Normal Crimes': Sociological Features of the Penal Code," *Social Problems,* 12 (Winter), 255–70.

Sutton, A., and Wild, R. (1985). "Small Business: White Collar Villains or Victims?" *International Journal of the Sociology of Law,* 13:247–59.

Taylor, L., and Walton, P. (1971). "Industrial Sabotage: Motives and Meanings," in S. Cohen, ed., *Images of Deviance.* Harmondsworth, Middx.: Penguin.

Ward, R., and Jenkins, R., eds. (1984). *Ethnic Communities in Business: Strategies for Economic Survival.* Cambridge: Cambridge University Press.

Gender and Varieties of White-Collar Crime

KATHLEEN DALY

Studies of gender and crime draw primarily on official arrest statistics. From such studies we learn a good deal about the frequency, but almost nothing of the nature, of men's and women's illegalities. These gaps are especially acute for white-collar crime.

Scholars typically use Uniform Crime Reports (UCR) or Offender-Based Transaction Statistics (OBTS) arrest data on embezzlement, fraud, and forgery when assessing gender- or race-based rates of white-collar crime (e.g., Hirschi and Gottfredson, 1987; Manson, 1986; Simon, 1975), but their analyses are based on questionable assumptions. Simon (1975) argues, for example, that the increasing female share of embezzlement, forgery, and fraud arrests during the 1960s and early 1970s may be explained by increases in women's labor force participation rate. She assumes that all three offenses are occupationally related. Hirschi and Gottfredson (1987:967) assert that "by definition one must be in the white-collar world to be a white-collar offender." They apparently assume that all those arrested for fraud and embezzlement are

"Gender and Varieties of White-Collar Crime" from *Criminology* 27:4 (1989): 769–93. Reprinted by permission.

PANEL 15 An Economy of Fraud

Successful economies are built on trust and stability; individuals must be able to trust financial institutions and their representatives not to abscond with their investments while financial markets must have in place guidelines or rules that help to prevent substantial market swings, such as depressions. According to Kitty Calavita, Henry N. Pontell, and Robert H. Tillman, best known for their examination of the Savings and Loan debacle of the late 1980s and early 1990s, the rollback of federal regulation over thrifts, coupled with newly legislated financial incentives designed to aid thrifts, helped create an economy of fraud unparalleled in American history. The S&L disaster cost American taxpayers over 500 billion dollars; much of it going to already wealthy investors, political cronies, and even convicted felons. Their comprehensive analysis included interviews with industry and government insiders, as well as analysis of government records. Their findings showed that the Reagan and Bush administrations, responsible for much of the deregulation in the industry, chose to ignore the impending crisis and actively worked to blunt efforts to bring the fledgling crisis under control. The political connection to the Savings and Loan crisis also reached into the deep recesses of Congress, where congressmen received substantial economic inducements, in the form of campaign contributions, to block legislation and regulatory oversight into S&Ls. Once exposed, however, several members of Congress lost their seats on important committees, were investigated by the Department of Justice, or, in the case of Jim Wright, Speaker of the House and the third most powerful member of government, forced to step down from office under fire for their role in maintaining the crisis. Most, however, avoided scrutiny and condemnation for their roles. Similarly, most of the white-collar criminals who defrauded investors and institutions escaped serious charges and prison time. Only 1 out of 7 people suspected of committing a major thrift crime—that is, a crime involving the loss of $100,000 or more—will be charged for a crime in Texas (Jim Wright's home state), and only 1 in 4 will be charged in California. Of those charged and convicted, the median prison sentence was only 22 months, a sharp contrast to sentences received by individuals guilty of robbing banks of only a few thousand dollars. The majority of offenders in the S&L scandal, most of whom are well educated and the picture of success, escaped unpunished and substantially wealthier. In some cases, crime does pay.

Adapted from Kitty Calavita, Henry N. Pontell, and Robert H. Tillman, *Big Money Crime: Fraud and Politics in the Savings and Loan Crisis.* Berkeley: University of California Press, 1997.

white-collar workers.[1] Most research on the sentencing of white-collar offenders focuses on class-based disparities; however important that question, more basic questions are overlooked. Who are these white-collar offenders and what is the nature of their acts? Is there any relationship between celebrated cases of white-collar crime described in case studies (e.g., Geis and Meier, 1977; Geis and Stotland, 1980) and most defendants prosecuted for white-collar crime in the courts?

It is imperative that we understand the characteristics of acts falling in the presumptive "white-collar" statutory domain, how they are organized both within and outside workplace settings, and their class-, gender-, and race-specific nature. The aim of this paper is to begin that process. The focus of the analysis is 1,342 defendants (14% female) who were convicted of white-collar offenses in U.S. federal district courts during the late 1970s. This is a select group of white-collar offenders, those who were prosecuted and convicted; thus, the generalizations that can be drawn are limited. Despite these restrictions, which are addressed below, the data are useful for contrasting varieties of men's and women's white-collar crime.

RESEARCH LITERATURE AND HYPOTHESES

Disputes over defining white-collar have been with us for half a century (see reviews by Coleman, 1989; Geis and Goff, 1983). Rather than entering into the dissension over when an illegality is a white-collar offense, this section highlights the links between different definitions and themes in the literature on gender and white-collar crime.

The disagreement in defining white-collar crime revolves around whether characteristics of the offense or the offender should be primary. An offense-related approach focuses on how a crime is committed, while an offender-related approach focuses on a particular group of people—those in high-status or "respected" occupations or in positions of power. If one takes an offender-related approach, a Medicaid fraud is considered a white-collar crime if it is carried out by a doctor or nursing home owner, but not if it is carried out by a clerical worker or poor person. If one uses an offense-related approach, that distinction is not important.

The different definitions affect how scholars conceptualize gender and white-collar crime. One line of research is to analyze state- or federal-level arrest data for embezzlement, fraud, and forgery, a method using an offense-based definition of white-collar crime, that is, a crime committed by fraud or

---

[1] Hirschi and Gottfredson are inconsistent on this point. In a 1987 article, they suggest that "white-collar crimes [are] events that take place in an occupational setting" and that "obviously, only white-collar workers can commit white-collar crimes . . ." (p. 961). But in Hirschi and Gottfredson's response to Steffensmeier's (1989) critique, they say "we did not define for purposes of empirical work 'white-collar crimes' as crimes committed by employees" (1989:362).

deception. State data show that the female share of arrests for these three white-collar offenses is 35 to 40% (Bureau of Justice Statistics 1987a:298; Manson, 1986:3). At the federal level the female share of arrests for embezzlement and forgery is 30 to 40% (Bureau of Justice Statistics, 1987b:7). Because the female share of arrests has increased in the past two decades, some believe that men's and women's white-collar crime rates are converging.

Women's visibility in arrest data is not reflected in the second line of research, which focuses on major forms of organizational crime, workplace crime, or crimes committed by professional workers, such as doctors or lawyers. Few of these studies have a single woman in them. One explanation is that relative to men, few women are in positions of power. But there are other reasons for women's invisibility in this body of research: few researchers thought it important to interview female managers, professional workers, or business owners, or to pursue questions of how gender relations in the workplace may structure occupational or organizational crime.

These two lines of inquiry produce radically opposite images of gender and white-collar crime. The offense-based approach suggests a rising tide of "new" female white-collar criminals; the offender-based approach suggests that white-collar crime is a male-only domain. And in a nimble feat of journalistic ingenuity, selected cases of major embezzlements and frauds carried out by women are juxtaposed against female arrest rates for these crimes (Adler, 1975; Burrough, 1987; Kirschenbaum, 1987).

A review of the research literature reveals the paucity of evidence beyond statistical analyses of arrest data or sensational media stories. With the exception of some small-scale case studies (Carlen, 1985; Franklin, 1979; Mahan, 1987), Zietz's (1981) research offers the only sustained inquiry. Zietz wanted to determine if Cressey's (1953) generalizations for men who had "violated a position of financial trust" applied to women imprisoned for fraud and embezzlement. She found that the circumstances precipitating crime for her group of women differed from those of Cressey's men. The women were more often motivated by a need to meet their responsibilities as wives or mothers. Zietz (1981:58) says that women had a "Joan of Arc quality . . . a willingness to be burned at the stake" to obtain medical care for a loved one or to preserve a marital relationship and that they rationalized their crime on the basis of family need or maintaining relations with spouses. Cressey's men, in contrast, had a "non-shareable" financial problem stemming from business or gambling debts, poor judgment, or spending beyond their means. Virtually all rationalized their illegalities as "borrowing"; none of Zietz's women used that rationale.

What remains in the literature are hypotheses, speculations, and a debate over interpreting white-collar arrest data. Drawing from studies of sex segregation in corporations (e.g., Kanter, 1977) and in "underworld" crime. Steffensmeier (1983) outlines these hypotheses for men's and women's "upperworld" crime: an absence of women in corporate (or organizational) crime, a lower likelihood that women will work in organized groups or with others in comparison with men, and less lucrative economic gains from women's crimes. Steffensmeier suggests that men's sexism toward women in the "underworld" should also be seen in the "upperworld": men do not like having women as crime partners; they neither trust women nor think them capable in a jam.

But if men exclude women from upperworld crime groups, why don't women form their own groups? Messerschmidt (1986:116–121) attempts to answer this question by pointing to a "masculine ethic" in the corporate world. This ethic of success and achievement at all costs may propel more men than women who are in the middle and managerial ranks to become involved in corporate crime. Messerschmidt's explanation is echoed in Ghiloni's (1987) study of gender differences in the use of organizational power. Ghiloni finds that corporate women are more inclined toward a "morality of positive change" (p. 20) and more concerned with issues of social responsibility in comparison with men in similar corporate positions.

Sex segregation in the labor market or within work organizations is the basis for Box's (1983:181–182) assertion that the female share of occupational crime (crime against one's employer or that uses one's technical expertise) should also be low. Specifically, Box speculates that because women are subject to greater supervision in their jobs, their opportunities to engage in white-collar crime are restricted. He also points to women's shorter history of "collectivist" experiences in the workplace. One implication may be that workplace social bonds are stronger for men than for women, and thus occupational crime as a group activity is more likely for men.

The issue of gender differences in "workplace opportunities" to commit white-collar crime has sparked debate over interpreting UCR arrest data. Simon (1975:106) argues that as women move into "those types of jobs that will provide them with the opportunities to commit offenses that are important enough to report," the female share of arrests for forgery, fraud, and embezzlement will increase. Critics take Simon to task on several grounds. Chapman (1980) and Messerschmidt (1986) say that the increasing female share of UCR white-collar arrests reflects women's economic and occupational marginality, not mobility; and Steffensmeier (1978) suggests that women's frauds and forgeries may not be occupationally related at all.

Plainly, the literature on gender and white-collar crime is long on speculation and short on evidence. Hence, five hypotheses that consolidate some of the major themes reviewed are explored in this paper:

H1: The female share of corporate (or organizational) crime is very low.
H2: The female share of occupational crime is low.
H3: Women are less likely to work in crime groups than men.
H4: Women's economic gains from crime are less then men's.
H5: Men's and women's motives for criminal involvement differ.

But to analyze the data with only these hypotheses in mind is insufficient. We need a descriptive portrait of the defendants and the nature of their acts.

Thus, also sketched are the defendants' socioeconomic profiles, occupations, and occupational roles in the crimes, and how their crimes are organized.

THE DATA

The Wheeler et al. (1982, 1983) data set used in this analysis was gathered in the following way. At seven federal district courts a sample of cases was drawn for defendants convicted during 1976–1978 of bank embezzlement, income tax fraud, postal fraud, credit fraud, false claims and statements, and bribery. In addition, all antitrust and securities fraud convictions in these and other federal districts were selected.[2] The presentence investigation (PSI) report was obtained for each defendant, and a coding scheme was developed to quantify information in the PSI narrative.[3] In selecting cases, Wheeler et al. (1982:642) took an offense-based approach and defined white-collar crime as "economic offenses committed through the use of some combination of fraud, deception, or collusion." Thus, the sample is not restricted by any offender-based criteria.

Selection Bias and Generalization

Several features of the data warrant caution in the generalizations that can be drawn. First, these white-collar offenders have been subject to criminal prosecution and conviction. Katz (1979), Rabin (1972), and Shapiro (1985) show that the desire and investigative ability of federal agencies, departments, and attorneys to pursue cases as criminal matters are important questions. Sample selection bias looms large, but, at present, we do not know how this sample of cases differs from others in which civil or administrative action or no legal action was taken.

Second, because the cases were selected by a stratified random sampling procedure, the structure of offenses in the sample does not reflect the structure of white-collar convictions in federal courts during 1977. A comparison of the data with statistics complied by the Administrative Office of the U.S. Courts (1977:370–373) shows the sample has proportionally fewer convictions for income tax fraud, and to some extent, postal fraud and bank embezzlement; antitrust violations and, especially, securities fraud are overrepre-

---

[2]The federal districts and cities are Central California (Los Angeles), Northern Georgia (Atlanta), Northern Illinois (Chicago), Maryland (Baltimore), Southern New York (Manhattan and the Bronx), Northern Texas (Dallas), and Western Washington (Seattle). Unlike the analysis in Wheeler et al. (1982), but like that in Wheeler et al. (1988), the sample analyzed here includes *all* securities fraud and antitrust cases.

[3]A PSI report is written by a probation officer and describes the nature of the offense and characteristics of the offender. It includes the prosecuting attorney's and the defendant's description of the offense; the defendant's current and previous family history, occupational and financial status, physical and mental health, and other biographical elements. It also contains the probation officer's evaluation of the case and sentencing recommendation.

sented. Thus one can draw generalizations from the sample by using a weighting procedure or by analyzing each offense separately. The latter approach is taken here.

Third, the sample is bounded in time and place. The defendants were prosecuted in major urban areas in 1976 through 1978. Benson and Walker (1988) argue that the cases differ from those prosecuted in less urban federal districts. A comparison of conviction statistics compiled by the Administrative Office of the U.S. Courts for 1977 and 1985, however, reveals no major temporal shifts. During this period, there were increases in false claims convictions and decreases in tax fraud convictions; the remaining six offenses had about the same share in both years.[4]

Offense Variability

Each of the eight crimes encompasses diverse illegalities (Weisburd et al., 1989; Wheeler et al., 1988). The proscribed activities are outlined in the appendix, but because the offense categories are broad, they can be misleading. For example, postal fraud is a residual category because it includes any activity in which the U.S. mail or other federal communication systems are used to defraud persons, businesses, or state and federal agencies. Some drug traffickers may be convicted of tax fraud because prosecutors have insufficient evidence of a drug conviction, and bribery cases may be related to income tax fraud.

RESULTS

Features of the Eight Offenses

Sociodemographic measures are shown in Table 1. The proportion of female defendants in each offense category varies dramatically: women were 45% of convicted bank embezzlers, but their numbers were negligible for antitrust violations, bribery, and securities fraud (n's of 1, 4, and 5, respectively). Offense categories in which there was a moderate share of women were postal fraud (18%), credit fraud (15%), and false claims and statements (15%). Generally, the higher the percentage of women in each offense, the higher the fraction of nonwhites (predominantly Black) and those not completing four years of college. In fact, the results for the education variable are startling. If completing college is an indication of status or occupational power, then most of

---

[4]One cannot know from the mix of convicted offenses if the characteristics of acts prosecuted in 1977 differ from those prosecuted in 1985 or today. However, the analysis of federal court conviction statistics for 1977 and 1985 (table available from author) does not support the perception that U.S. attorneys are prosecuting more "real" white-collar crime (securities fraud or antitrust violations) in the 1980s than in the 1970s. My thanks to one reviewer who cites contradictory evidence from Justice Department officials and insiders on this issue.

the defendants, including those convicted of securities fraud and antitrust violations, do not fit a high-status profile.

Table 2 reports the offenders' occupations, whether an occupational role was used in some way to carry out the crime, and the corporate nature of the defendants' illegalities. The occcupations held by men and women when they committed the white-collar crimes are compressed into four groups: professional and managerial, other workers (sales, clerical, craft, operatives, laborers, service, and farm workers), unemployed, and illegal or unknown occupation. To simplify the discussion, defendants in the last two groups are described as having "no labor force ties."

Four findings are noteworthy. First, a high percentage of women (30 to over 40%) and about one-fourth of the men convicted of postal fraud, credit fraud, and false claims and statements had no labor force ties. Second, 40 to 85% of the male offenders were professional or managerial workers, but only a majority of the very small number of women convicted for tax fraud, bribery, securities fraud, and antitrust violations were professionals or managers. Third, there is offense- and gender-specific variability in whether an offender used an occupational role to carry out the offense. As one would expect, bank embezzlement, securites fraud, and antitrust violations were occupationally related. Postal fraud and false claims, however, were more likely to be occupationally related for men than for women, and credit fraud was somewhat more likely to be occupationally related for women than for men.

Finally, a higher percentage of men's (14%) than women's (1%) cases involved indictments against corporations or businesses. The corporate nature of defendants' illegalities is moderate to low for men, and almost negligible for women. Of the 194 women, only two cases had corporate indictments: the one woman convicted of antitrust violations and one of the five convicted of securities fraud. For the 162 men's cases involving corporate indictments, most were concentrated, not surprisingly, among the antitrust violators, and to a lesser degree, securities fraud offenders.

Gender Comparisons for Four Offenses

Because there are so few women in the sample who were convicted of tax fraud, bribery, securities fraud, and antitrust violations, this section draws gender comparisons for the remaining four offenses: bank embezzlement, postal fraud, credit fraud, and false claims.

Socioeconomic Profile. Table 3 shows that there are substantially higher proportions of nonwhite women than men for all but one offense, false claims. The women are somewhat younger than the men, they are much less likely to have completed four years of college, and they are more likely to have familial dependents outside a marital context. The economic circumstances of both the men and women are far from affluent. The median value of assets owned for women ranged from no assets to $2,500; and for the men, from $5,500 to

TABLE 1
Sociodemographic Features of the Sample

	Bank Emb. (N = 201)	Postal Fraud (N = 190)	Credit Fraud (N = 158)	False Claims (N = 157)	Tax Fraud (N = 210)	Bribe (N = 84)	Sec. Fraud (N = 225)	Anti-Trust (N = 117)
Female	45%	18%	15%	15%	6%	5%	2%	0.5%
White	74	77	72	62	87	82	99.5	97
Completing 4-yr. College	13	22	18	29	27	29	41	40

TABLE 2
Offenders' Occupations,* Occupational Roles in Offenses, and the Corporate Nature of Their Crimes**

	Bank Emb. (N = 90)	Postal Fraud (N = 34)	Credit Fraud (N = 24)	False Claims (N = 24)	Tax Fraud (N = 12)	Bribe (N = 4)	Sec. Fraud (N = 5)	Anti-Trust (N = 1)
Women								
Prof. & Mgr.	7%	12%	12%	12%	59%	50%	60%	100%
All Other Workers	91	44	59	59	33	25	40	0
Unemployed	0	35	20	21	0	25	0	0
Illegal or Unknown	2	9	9	8	8	0	0	0
Occupational Role Used % Yes	100	9	58	29	33	50	100	100
Corporate Indictment % Yes	0	0	0	0	0	0	20	100
	(N = 111)	(N = 156)	(N = 134)	(N = 133)	(N = 198)	(N = 80)	(N = 220)	(N = 116)
Men								
Prof. & Mgr.	51	43	45	39	59	66	62	84
All Other Workers	45	34	31	40	32	23	31	12
Unemployed	2	14	12	14	2	6	0	0
Illegal or Unknown	2	9	12	7	7	5	7	4
Occupational Role Used % Yes	89	54	43	54	14	61	91	99
Corporate Indictment % Yes	0	3	1	5	0	9	15	93

* The occupational classifications are professional, technical, managerial, and administrative workers; all other workers (sales, clerical, service, operatives, laborers, craft, and farm); unemployed; and illegal or unknown occupation. In Table 4 and the text, those not employed or having an illegal or unknown occupation are defined as having no labor force ties.
** Occupational role includes using a business identity or position of power, or using an occupational role in a workplace organization, to carry out the crime.

TABLE 3
Sociodemographic and Economic Indicators

	EMBEZZLEMENT		POSTAL FRAUD		CREDIT FRAUD		FALSE CLAIMS	
	Men (N = 111)	Women (N = 90)	Men (N = 156)	Women (N = 34)	Men (N = 134)	Women (N = 24)	Men (N = 133)	Women (N = 24)
Race (%)								
White	86	59	83	47	75	54	62	63
Nonwhite*	14	41	17	53	25	46	38	37
Age (Yrs.)								
Median	31	26	41	30	38	31	38	32
Range	18–62	19–50	20–69	20–36	21–64	22–38	21–70	22–68
Education (%)								
Did Not Complete High School	11	11	28	38	25	21	12	33
Completed High School	69	85	47	56	54	79	55	63
4-year College Degree or More	20	4	25	6	21	0	33	4
Family Circumstances (%)								
Married, Dependent(s)	55	24	55	18	51	29	52	25
Not Married, Dependent(s)	12	23	16	55	24	41	20	33
Married, No Dependents	5	18	2	3	1	4	1	8
Not Married, No Dependents	28	35	27	24	24	26	27	34
Value of Assets Owned ($)								
(can be determined from PSI)	(N = 95)	(N = 69)	(N = 113)	(N = 29)	(N = 106)	(N = 19)	(N = 113)	(N = 20)
Median Value Men	7,500		5,500		7,500		8,500	
Women		1,000		none		2,500		1,500
Primary Means of Support (%)								
Own Earnings	73	82	58	53	53	54	62	42
Welfare, Unemployment Benefits	0	1	3	18	2	4	5	17
Other (pension, social security, friends, relatives, uncertain)	2	1	10	6	8	8	5	4
Not in PSI	25	16	29	23	37	34	28	37

* Predominantly Black, but includes some Latinos and Asians.

$8,500. When they committed the offense, most men and women supported themselves by their own earnings. However, the primary means of support for about one-fifth of the women convicted of postal fraud and false claims was welfare or unemployment benefits. This and other tables report the percentage of data or number of cases "not in the PSI." This enables accurate interpretations of the data and flags those variables with gender differences in "missing data," which as discussed below, bears on the analysis of men's and women's motives.

Occupation and Occupational Role in the Offense. Table 4 provides detail on men's and women's occupations and whether and how they used their job to commit the crime. Turning first to the women, no matter what the offense, most employed women were clerical workers. Over 90% of the bank embezzlers were clerical workers, as were over half of the employed women in the remaining offenses. Few women were self-employed or owned a business; of the employed women, most worked in the private sector, with the exception of postal fraud offenders. For two offenses that are job related—bank embezzlement and, to a lesser extent, credit fraud—women used their access to documents to carry out the crime. It appears, however, that many women supplemented wage-earning income by engaging in illegalities that were not related to their jobs. This pattern holds for men, as well.

The majority of employed men were managers or administrators, and about 10 to 20% were sales workers. Like the women, but to a lesser degree, many men (about 20 to 25%) convicted of postal fraud, credit fraud, and false claims had no labor force ties. The proportion of men who were self-employed or owned their own business ranged from 10% of bank embezzlers to about 40% of postal fraud and credit fraud offenders. With the exception of false claims and statements, men were more likely than women to have used a business identity or position of authority to carry out their crimes.

Of the four offenses, bank embezzlement was the only one that was clearly occupationally related. Thus, the particular type of bank worker and how he or she embezzled funds is of interest (Table 5). In this sample, 60% of the convicted female embezzlers were bank tellers; few were bank officers or financial managers (7%). Thus, most women embezzled funds by taking cash or negotiable instruments or by manipulating bank accounts. For the men, about 40% were bank officers or financial managers, and 14% were bank tellers. Thus, in addition to taking cash and manipulating bank accounts, the men also manipulated documents.

Organization of the Offense and Attempted Economic Gain. There is a good deal of diversity within and across the four crime categories (Table 6). This occurs, in part, because each offense (except bank embezzlement) contains a mix of occupationally related and unrelated crime. Also, for the men's offenses there is a mixture of those using (or not using) their business or self-employment status as a conduit for crime.

The first variable in Table 6, resources used, reveals gender-based vari-

TABLE 4
Occupations and Occupational Roles in Offenses

	EMBEZZLEMENT		POSTAL FRAUD		CREDIT FRAUD		FALSE CLAIMS	
	Men (N = 111)	Women (N = 90)	Men (N = 156)	Women (N = 34)	Men (N = 134)	Women (N = 24)	Men (N = 133)	Women (N = 24)
Occupation Category								
Professional and Technical	0%	0%	9%	6%	7%	4%	17%	0%
Managerial and Administrative	51	7	34	6	38	8	22	12.5
Sales	5	0	18	0	17	13	12	8
Clerical	36	90	5	29	5	42	11	38
Other (service, operatives, laborer, craft, or farm)	4	1	11	15	9	4	17	12.5
No Labor Force Ties*	4	2	23	44	24	29	21	29
Class of Worker								
Employee in Private Company	84	99	31	24	37	63	37	59
Government Employee	1	0	8	32	3	8	10	8
Self-employed or Owns Business	11	0	40	0	38	4	29	4
No Labor Force Ties*	4	1	21	44	22	25	24	29
How Occupational Role Was Used								
Had Access to Documents; Job Facilitated Access to Documents	80	100	12	6	18	42	23	4
Used Business Identification or Position of Power	4	0	31	3	17	12	22	21
Combinations of Above	5	0	10	0	8	4	9	4
No Role, Not Employed, Not Known	11	0	47	91	57	42	46	71

V* No labor force ties includes those not employed, illegal occupations, or occupation is not known. Small discrepancies in this category for occupation and class of worker reflect the fact that occupation but not class of worker is known or vice versa.

TABLE 5
Bank Embezzlement: Occupational Detail and How the Embezzlement Was Carried Out

	Men (N = 111)	Women (N = 90)
Specific Job		
Bank Officer or Financial Manager	39%	7%
Other Type of Manager	12	0
Bank Teller	14	60
Bookkeeper	7	11
Other Type of Clerical Worker	15	19
All Other Types of Workers or Unknown	13	3
How the Offender Embezzled		
Took Cash	21	37
Stole Negotiable Instruments	3	14
Manipulated Bank Accounts	38	39
Manipulated Documents	29	8
Other Method	5	2
Not in PSI	4	0

ability in offense organization. One or more individuals using "personal" resources means that the crime was accomplished without the expertise of other workplace personnel or without using a business entity, whether one's employer or another business. One or more individuals using "organizational" resources is a more heterogenous category; it includes a business entity formed to sell nonexistent land to unwitting customers, as well as a bank manager who embezzled funds by seeking assistance from one of the bank's accountants.

For all four offenses, the majority of men and women did not use organizational resources, although more men than women did. Interpreting this finding for women is straightforward. When women used organizational resources, they did so in the context of wage-earning employment. But when men used organizational resources, they did so in one of two ways: either they used their own business or professional enterprise as a front or conduit for crime, or they drew from organizational resources in the context of wage-earning employment.

As for crime group size, most women worked alone in committing the offense, although the percentage varied from 50% of women convicted of false claims to almost 90% of bank embzzlers. For the men, with the exception of postal fraud, 50 to 60% worked alone. In general, men were more likely than women to have carried out their crimes with at least two other persons. In comparing the results for group size with the defendant's role in a group, the percentages for "worked alone" and "acted alone—no coordination with others" are slightly discrepant because some offenders knew that others were involved in the same illegal activity, but they did not plan or coordinate the activity with them.

TABLE 6
Offense Organization and Attempted Gains

	EMBEZZLEMENT		POSTAL FRAUD		CREDIT FRAUD		FALSE CLAIMS	
	Men (N = 111)	Women (N = 90)	Men (N = 156)	Women (N = 34)	Men (N = 134)	Women (N = 24)	Men (N = 133)	Women (N = 24)
Resources Used								
Personal Resources	86%	98%	61%	94%	74%	87%	71%	79%
Organizational Resources	14	2	39	6	26	13	29	21
Size of Crime Group								
Worked Alone	63	87	29	61	50	63	49	50
Worked with One Other	11	4.5	20	6	11	12	14	13
Small to Moderate (2–10 others)	13	6.5	27	27	18	8	12	8
Large (11 or more others)	13	2	24	6	21	17	25	29
Role Relative to Others								
Acted Alone—No Coordination	70	92	44	71	56	71	53	54
Acted with Others—Subordinate Role	14	3	21	14	16	12.5	12	30
Acted with Others—Primary Role	11	3	21	6	15	12.5	25	8
Uncertain or Not in PSI	5	2	14	9	13	4	10	8
Attempted Economic Gain (can be determined from PSI)	(N = 100)	(N = 82)	(N = 117)	(N = 23)	(N = 98)	(N = 19)	(N = 82)	(N = 15)
$1,000 or less	8	26	6	4.5	5	16	13	7
$1,001 to $10,000	40	55	29	78	35	37	46	73
$10,001 to $100,000	36	18	26	13	36	42	27	7
$100,001 to $500,000	8	0	17	0	17	5	5	13
$500,001 or more	8	1	22	4.5	7	0	9	0
Median (in thousands)								
Men	$10–25		$25–100		$10–25		$5–10	
Women		$1–2.5		$5–10		$5–10		$2.5–5

When women worked in groups, their leadership and subordinate roles varied by offense. For credit fraud, women were just as likely to be leaders as subordinates, but for false claims, more took a subordinate role. By contrast, more men took a primary role in false claims offenses; but for the remaining offenses, men were just as likely to be leaders as subordinates. There is no variable in the data file for the gender (or race) composition of crime groups; thus, the proportions of men and women working in same- or mixed-gender (or race) groups cannot be determined.

For each offense, the men's attempted economic gain was higher than the women's: by a factor of ten for bank embezzlement, five for postal fraud, and two for credit fraud and false claims. Note that the attempted economic gain variable is based on the whole offense, not on an individual's "take" when two or more persons were involved.[5]

The more grouped nature of men's bank embezzlements, coupled with the higher numbers of male bank officers and financial managers, likely explains men's substantially greater economic gains from embezzlement. Yet group size alone cannot explain why men's monetary gains from credit fraud, postal fraud, and false claims were higher than women's. An added ingredient is men's more frequent use of organizational resources to carry out their crimes. As one would expect, when organizational resources are used, the magnitude of white-collar crime is greater (Wheeler and Rothman, 1982). On average, the attempted gains for these four white-collar offenses are much higher than those for common crime, ranging from $1,000 to 10,000 for women and $2,500 to 25,000 for men. Compared with the gains from antitrust or securities fraud violations, however, they are trivial.[6]

Motives. Before examining men's and women's motives for criminal involvement (Table 7), several issues must be addressed: the higher proportion of "missing data" for men than women on this variable, the relationship between motive and rationalization, and interpretive problems.

Information on defendants' motives is missing for a higher proportion of male (about one-third) than female offenders (about one-fifth). Did the women more frequently give a motive or "explain themselves"? We cannot know from the data set, but a qualitative study of the same PSI reports by Rothman and Gandossy (1982) sheds some light. They found that in comparison with men, women more often admitted guilt, more readily acknowledged personal responsibility for the offense, provided stronger justifications for their crimes, and were more likely to express remorse. Their study suggests that women's

---

[5] It is not possible to construct a precise measure of an individual's take in an offense because the group size and attempted gain variables are coded in range form. The conceptual basis for the attempted economic gain measure is total impact or harm to victims, not the avarice of individual offenders.

[6] The magnitude of attempted economic gain could not be determined for most antitrust violators, but in the cases for which it could (n = 16), all cases exceeded $500,000. For the securities fraud cases in which attempted economic gain could be determined (n = 143), half exceeded $500,000.

accounts were more compelling than men's, and that a sense of shame or stigma was felt more deeply by women.

In the discussion of the defendants' stated motives, the words motive, justification, and rationalization are used interchangeably, but the imprecision is deliberate. It is simply the best way to represent what probation officers recorded from their interviews with defendants.

Finally, the interpretive layers in the PSI reports are many: the defendant's portrayal of his or her motives, the probation officer's account of what the defendant said, potential differences in what probation officers remember male or female defendants saying, and the like. To avoid convuluted sentence constructions, the defendants' motives are represented as what defendants said.[7]

Women's Motives. For the women giving motives, the most frequent was financial need for their families—30 to 35% of women gave this motive. In addition, 10 to 15% cited financial gain without any reference to need, and 15 to 20% gave nonfinancial personal reasons, such as frustration or some kind of distress. Different motives are apparent for women convicted of embezzlement and credit fraud and those convicted of postal fraud and false claims. More women in the first group said they were motivated from a financial need for themselves, while more in the second group said they were influenced by others, whether by coercion, following orders, or doing a favor. None of the women rationalized their crimes as stemming from "normal business practices."

Men's Motives. Need-based motives (financial need for their families or for themselves) were 25 to 40% of men's motives across the four offenses. For each offense, about 15 to 20% of men said they were influenced by others; financial gain (no need stated) and nonfinancial personal reasons each accounted for 10 to 20% of men's motives. Financial need for a business was the motive for about 20% of men convicted of credit fraud, but only 3 to 8% of men convicted of the other offenses.

Gender Differences in Motives. Men's and women's motives differ in two areas: (1) the relative importance of self and family in need-based justifications and (2) the degree to which being influenced by others varies by offense for women.

Although financial need for themselves or their families was the modal justification for men and women, family need dominated women's need-based motives more than men's (about 35% and 15%, respectively). By comparison, men were just as likely to say they needed money for themselves or for their families.

---

[7]When a probation officer described a defendant's motive but then challenged its veracity, the coders were instructed to code what the defendant said. The results therefore reflect what defendant said even when probation officers believed other motives were central.

For each offense, similar proportions (15 to 20%) of men said they were influenced by others. But for the women, the influence of others varied by offense: it was a more frequent rationale for postal fraud and false claims offenders (25 to 30%) than for the bank embezzlers and credit fraud offenders (5%). To interpret this finding, we must consider the organization of men's and women's bank embezzlements and credit frauds.

Recall that women's embezzlements were less likely to be coordinated with others than men's (6% and 25% respectively), and men more often played a subordinate role (14%) than women (3%). Thus, one would expect fewer women to say they were influenced by others. But this explanation does not satisfy for credit fraud. Similar proportions of men's and women's credit frauds were coordinated with others (25 to 30%), and similar proportions of men and women played a subordinate role (13 to 16%). Yet, few female credit fraud offenders said they were influenced by others. Although the number of cases is small, I would speculate that women's credit frauds are organized more along egalitarian lines than men's. Put another way, the composition of men's crime groups in workplace settings may be more hierarchical in nature, perhaps reflecting a mix of managers and clerical workers.

"His" and "Her" White-Collar Crime. The variable patterns in these four white-collar crimes defy any simple characterization of men's and women's crimes. It is possible, however, to identify some gender-specific elements. Three offenses—postal fraud, credit fraud, and false claims and statements—have a distinctive "his" and "her" flavor. Although men's and women's bank embezzlements differ, much of the variability is related to occupational location and, perhaps, to a cross-occupational composition of men's crime groups.

The crime patterns for men's and women's postal frauds are distinctive in the following ways. The men coordinated with others to defraud businesses and individuals; many of their offenses seemed to be fraudulent sales scams to unwitting investors. The women's postal frauds were not job- or business-related nor carried out with others; they involved receiving credit cards or government checks under false pretenses. Although postal fraud is known as a residual "garbage can" offense category, these differences are noteworthy.

The women convicted of credit fraud and embezzlement share similar crime patterns. Most were clerical workers who used their occupational access to documents to carry out the fraud or to embezzle. Women's credit frauds were more lilely than men's to be carried out by insiders in financial institutions. Men, on the other hand, more frequently tried to defraud as outsiders to lending institutions.

In contrast to credit fraud, men's false claims offenses were more likely to be occupationally related than women's. For these illegalities, the pattern for men was to inflate or falsify claims for reimbursement of goods and services; the pattern for women was fraudulently obtaining government benefits or loans.

DISCUSSION

It bears repeating that these white-collar offenders are a select group. They were criminally prosecuted and convicted in urban federal district courts during 1976–1978. Skeptical readers may question the utility of describing white-collar crime from this sample, but there are good reasons for doing so. Until we understand what offenses and people are subject to criminal proceedings, the parameters of discretion and selection bias will not be known. And until we have a grasp of the variable nature of crime in the statutory white-collar domain, theoretical efforts will founder.

This sample of white-collar cases supports hypothesis 1 that the female share of corporate (or organizational) crime is low. Only 1% of women's cases, but 14% of men's involved indictments against corporations or businesses. The rare presence of female corporate crime defendants can be interpreted in several ways. Women may be more averse than men to abusing positions of organizational power, or they may be excluded from men's corporate crime groups, or perhaps both. It is also possible that more women are in fact involved in corporate crime, but fewer are caught or criminally prosecuted.

As for the hypothesis that the female share of occupational crime is low, the results are mixed; hypothesis 2 cannot be supported fully. If occupational crime is defined broadly as crime committed for personal gain in the course of an "otherwise respected and legitimate occupation or financial activity" (Coleman, 1989:5), all but one of the eight offenses (antitrust violations) include forms of occupational crime. The female share was low or negligible for six of these seven offenses. But for bank embezzlement—an archetypal occupational crime—the female share was close to 50%. In suggesting that women's workplace jobs have a higher degree of surveillance than men's, Box (1983) ignored the possibility that enhanced surveillance may increase the likelihood of being caught for some occupational crimes, especially in banks or other work settings where there are daily checks of cashiers' or tellers' transactions. With 60% of the female bank embezzlers working as tellers, and 90% working in clerical jobs of some kind, the image of embezzlers as "aristocrats of chiseling employees" (Coleman, 1989:83) does not suit most female offenders.

The hypothesis that women are less likely than men to work in crime groups is supported for three of four offenses examined. With the exception of false claims, women were more likely to work alone and to not coordinate their illegalities with others. The average attempted gain from women's crime was less than men's, which confirms hypothesis four. Gender differences in group size, occupational location, and the greater use of organizational resources in men's crime likely explain the lower monetary gains in women's crime. But gender differences in need or greed cannot be discounted.

Finally, financial need for themselves or their families were more frequent rationales for women's involvement in crime than men's: over twice as many women as men cited financial need for families. Despite these differences, hypothesis five is only partially supported. Men's and women's motives do differ to some degree, but not as starkly as Cressey's (1953) and Zietz's (1984) studies suggest (see also Mahan, 1987). For example, although 30 to 40% of the women said their offenses were motivated by financial need for their families, most women gave a combination of other motives, including financial need for themselves and nonfinancial personal reasons. A good way to compare Cressey's and Zietz's findings with those presented here is to examine only those men and women convicted of bank embezzlement, the offense closest to what Cressey's men and Zietz's women were convicted of (and imprisoned for). Half the male embezzlers in this study cited motives that reflect a "nonshareable" financial problem, but about 40% of the female embezzlers also gave such motives. Family need, though a more frequently stated motive for the female bank embezzlers (36%), was also a motive among their male counterparts (18%). . . .

REFERENCES

Adler, Freda. 1975. Sisters in Crime. Prospect Heights, Ill.: Waveland Press.

Administrative Office of the U.S. Courts. 1977. Annual Report of the Director. Washington, D.C.: Government Printing Office.

Benson, Michael L. and Esteban Walker. 1988. Sentencing the white-collar offender. American Sociological Review 53:294–302.

Box, Steven. 1983. Power, Crime, and Mystification. New York: Tavistock.

Bureau of Justice Statistics. 1987a. Sourcebook of Criminal Justice Statistics—1986. Edited by Katherine Jamieson and Timothy J. Flanagan. Washington, D.C.: U.S. Department of Justice.

———. 1987b. White Collar Crime. Special Report, NCJ-106876. Washington, D.C.: U.S. Department of Justice.

Carlen, Pat (ed.). 1985. Criminal Women. Cambridge: Polity Press.

Chapman, Jane Roberts. 1980. Economic Realities and the Female Offender. Lexington, Mass.: Lexington Books.

Coleman, James W. 1989. The Criminal Elite: The Sociology of White Collar Crime. 2nd ed. New York: St. Martin's Press.

Cressey, Donald R. 1953. Other People's Money: A Study in the Social Psychology of Embezzlement. Reprinted 1973. Montclair, N.J.: Patterson Smith.

Franklin, Alice. 1979. Criminality in the work place: A comparison of male and female offenders. In Freda Adler and Rita J. Simon (eds), The Criminology of Deviant Women. Boston: Houghton Mifflin.

Geis, Gilbert and Colin Goff. 1983. Introduction to White Collar Crime: The Uncut Version (by Edwin H. Sutherland). New Haven: Yale University Press.

Geis, Gilbert and Robert F. Meier (eds). 1977. White-Collar Crime. 2nd ed. New York: Free Press.

Geis, Gilbert and Ezra Stotland (eds). 1980. White-Collar Crime: Theory and Research. Beverly Hills, Calif." Sage.

Ghiloni, Beth W. 1987. Power through the eyes of women. Paper presented at the annual meeting of the American Sociological Association, Chicago.

Hirschi, Travis and Michael Gottfredson. 1987. Causes of white-collar crime. Criminology 25:949–974.

———. 1989. The significance of white-collar crime for a general theory of crime. Criminology 27:359–371.

Howe, Louise Kapp. 1977. Pink Collar Workers. New York: Avon.

Kanter, Rosebeth Moss. 1977. Men and Women of the Corporation. New York: Basic Books.

Katz, Jack. 1979. Legality and equality: Plea bargaining in the prosecution of white-collar and common crimes. Law and Society Review 13:431–460.

Kirschenbaum, Carol. 1987. New white-collar criminals. Glamour Magazine (March): 306 ff.

Mahan, Sue. 1987. Opportunities for women in white collar crime. Paper presented at the annual meeting of the American Society of Criminology, Montreal.

Manson, Donald A. 1986. Tracking offenders: White-collar crime. Bureau of Justice Statistics, Special Report, NCJ-102867. Washington, D.C.: U.S. Department of Justice.

Messerschmidt, James W. 1986. Capitalism, Patriarchy, and Crime: Toward a Socialist Feminist Criminology. Totowa, N.J.: Rowman and Littlefield.

Rabin, Robert L. 1972. Agency criminal referrals in the federal system: An empirical study of prosecutorial discretion. Stanford Law Review 24:1036–1091.

Shapiro, Susan P. 1985. The road not taken: The elusive path to criminal prosecution for white-collar offenders. Law and Society Review 19:179–217.

Simon, Rita J. 1975. Women and Crime. Lexington, Mass.: Lexington Books.

Smart, Carol. 1976. Women, Crime and Criminology: A Feminist Critique. Boston: Routledge & Kegan Paul.

Steffensmeier, Darrell J. 1978. Crime and the contemporary woman: An analysis of changing levels of female property crime, 1960–75. Social Forces 57:566–584.

———. 1983. Organization properties and sex-segregation in the underworld: Building a sociological theory of sex differences in crime. Social Forces 61:1011–1032.

———. 1989. On the causes of "white-collar" crime: An assessment of Hirschi and Gottfredson's claims. Criminology 27:345–358.

Weisburd, David, Stanton Wheeler, Elin Waring, and Nancy Bode. 1989. Middle-Class Criminals: White-Collar Crime in the Federal Courts. Book Manuscript. School of Criminal Justice, Rutgers University.

Wheeler, Stanton and Mitchell L. Rothman. 1982. The organization as weapon in white-collar crime. University of Michigan Law Review 80:1403–1426.

Wheeler, Stanton, David Weisburd, and Nancy Bode. 1982. Sentencing the white-collar offender: Rhetoric and reality. American Sociological Review 47:641–659.

Wheeler, Stanton, David Weisburd, Nancy Bode, and Elin Waring. 1988. White collar crime and criminals. American Criminal Law Review 25:331–357.

Zietz, Dorothy. 1981. Women Who Embezzle or Defraud: A Study of Convicted Felons. New York: Praeger.

Corporate Control, Crime, and Compensation: An Empirical Examination of Large Corporations

DIANA BILIMORIA

Recently, much public concern has been directed toward a variety of corporate governance issues and the costs associated with effective control (e.g., Buckley, 1988; *Business Week*, 1986, 1987, 1988; Byrne, 1988; Crystal, 1986, 1988, 1989, 1991; *The Economist*, 1988; *Harvard Business Review*, 1992; Reynolds, 1987; Woodworth, 1987). When agency costs associated with information asymmetries are prohibitively high (i.e., when stockholders do not control the necessary information to verify the protection of their interests), effective monitoring and incentive alignment of executive compensation by boards of directors are jeopardized, and managerial action may not be consistent with ownership interests. Although previous research has examined executive compensation under different monitoring and incentive alignment conditions (e.g., Gomez-Majia, Tosi & Hinkin, 1987; Dyl, 1988; Tosi & Gomez-Majia, 1989), and theory suggests that the incidence of corporate illegal behavior varies with who controls the corporation (e.g., Blair & Kaserman, 1983), the issue of whether corporate illegal behavior leading to executive pay differs according to the level of monitoring and incentive alignment by the board of directors has not been separately investigated. Accordingly, this study specifically tests whether the association between corporate crime and executive compensation differs in owner controlled and manager controlled firms.

Control of the corporation refers to the power to determine the broad objectives and policies that guide the corporation in its activities (Mizruchi, 1983; Temporary National Economic Committee, 1940). It points to the discretion which the dominant coalition has to pursue its own objectives (Cubbin & Leech, 1983). Two controlling interest groups, managers and owners, have historically been identified as having differing preferences for corporate ends and activities (cf. Berle & Means, 1932). Owners desire to have the firm managed so that it provides a steady income from dividends and appreciation over time of the market price of the stock while managers act so as to maximize their own lifetime incomes (Monsen & Downs, 1965).

Ownership control of the corporation refers to the curtailment of managerial opportunism by the corporations' owners. Control over corporate policy is exercised by shareholders on account of their ownershp of significant blocks of outstanding stock which carry voting rights and permit occupation of seats on

"Corporate Control Crime, and Compensation" from *Human Relations* 48:8 (1995): 891–908. Reprinted by permission.

corporate boards. Ownership control includes increased top management compensation monitoring and incentive alignment activities by the board of directors (Dyl, 1988; Tosi & Gomex-Majia, 1989). Monitoring refers to the direct and indirect observation of top managers' behaviors (achieved through budgets, responsibility accounting, rules and policies) and incentive alignment refers to the design of pay packages so as to encourage managers to make decisions in the best interests of stockholders (Tosi & Gomex-Majia, 1989).

Managerial control of the corporation, referring to the domination of corporate agendas by managerial interests, suggests that in corporations with widely dispersed stock ownership, managers employ their strategic position to control their economic destinies, ensure their perpetuation and otherwise behave in ways that maximize their own welfare at the expense of shareholders (e.g., Berle & Means, 1932; McEachern, 1975; Rappaport, 1978; Bowen, 1981; Herman, 1981; Louis, 1984). Particularly as the chief executive officer (CEO) controls director selection and the board information apparatus, top management has *de facto* control of the board and the corporation (Vance, 1968; Mace, 1971; Herman, 1981).

In this study, the differences between owner controlled and manager controlled firms are examined in terms of the relationship between corporate crime and the compensation of top executives of the firm. It is important to investigate this relationship because executive compensation is a powerful mechanism to align managerial behavior with stockholder interests regarding the commission of corporate illegal behavior.

CORPORATE CRIME

The incidence of corporate illegality has been the subject of extensive public attention and concern in recent times. Popular and academic media have focused on corporate irresponsibility and the erosion of the fine line between legitimate business practices and corporate illegal behavior (Clinard & Yeager, 1980; Ross, 1989; *U.S. News and World Report,* 1982), and the enormous financial and non-financial costs to society from corporate crime. Widespread concern about the collapse of corporate ethics has been expressed (e.g., Becker, 1985; Crock, 1985; Metzenbaum, 1986; Berenbeim, 1988; Byrne, 1988). In the organizational theory literature, interest in the subject was spurred by Staw and Szwajkowski's (1975) study of the influence of environmental scarcity/munificence on the commission of illegal activities. Recently, others have examined the composition of boards of directors and the commission of corporate illegal acts (Kesner, Victor, & Lamont, 1986), the relationship between corporate legal violations, philanthropic acts, and organizational performance (Wokutch & Spencer, 1987), the impact of firm size on the commission of illegal acts (Dalton & Kesner, 1988), and the corporate and environmental antecedents of illegal behavior (Baucus & Near, 1991).

Attention by the board of directors to the issue of corporate crime is important for two reasons. First, issues of legality are a prominent area of board responsibility (Kesner, Victor, & Lamont, 1986). The board of directors determines the broad policies and guidelines regarding the legal stance of the corporation and for evaluating top managers in line with legal standards. In one study, board chairmen considered their primary role in relation to other board members to be that of ensuring the board's fulfillment of legal requirements (Chitayat, 1985). Other authors have pointed to the board's ultimate responsibility regarding the commission of corporate illegalities (The Business Roundtable, 1978; Louden, 1982; Vance, 1983; Nader & Andrews, 1984; Waldo, 1985). Since top management is considered to be the most important causal factor for corporate illegal behavior (see Clinard, 1983; Cochran & Nigh, 1987, and Frederick & Weber, 1987), and top management influences the organization's behaviors and outcomes (Child, 1972; Hambrick & Mason, 1984) particularly in situations of high managerial discretion (Hambrick & Finkelstein, 1987; Finkelstein & Hambrick, 1990), an important aspect of the board's oversight function is to ensure managerial and corporate actions in accordance with the requirements of the law (Hatfield, 1982; Louden, 1982; Vance, 1983). Second, enormous costs accrue to society each year on account of corporate misconduct. For example, price fixing practices alone are believed to cost consumers $60 billion a year (*U.S. News and World Report*, 6 September, 1982). Gautschi and Jones (1987) cite consumer advocates who estimate that corporate crime squanders as much as $200 billion a year in inflated prices, evaded taxes, corruption of government officials, and poisoned air, land, and water.

EXECUTIVE COMPENSATION

The board of directors is constituted to be the primary implementation mechanism of stockholders to monitor and align managerial behaviors with the interests of owners (Fama, 1980). In doing this, the board is faced with two important control options: altering the incentives of the managerial team or dismissing senior executives (Walsh & Seward, 1990). Previous research, however, suggests that dismissal is not a favored means to control managerial behaviors even though it is associated with stock price increases when used (Furtado & Rozeff, 1987). In contrast, despite the less than perfect correlation between executive compensation and firm performance noted in the popular press (e.g., Crystal, 1988, 1989, 1991), control over the rewards of key executives through monitoring and incentive alignment arrangements remains a more feasible mechanism for the board to ensure that managerial preferences do not overshadow the interests of owners (Lambert & Larcker, 1985). For example, Lewellen, Loderer, & Martin (1987) found that individual elements of corporate pay packages are designed to control for managerial limited horizon and risk exposure problems. Similarly, Coughlan and Schmidt (1985) found empirical support for the notion that boards of directors employ executive compensation plans to create managerial incentives consistent with the interests of the firm's owners.

HYPOTHESIS

Agency costs associated with information asymmetries occur from the separation of ownership and control (Fama & Jensen, 1983). When shareholders (principals) contract out control over the corporation's daily operations to managers (agents), they do not control the information necessary to verify that their interests are being protected (Eisenhardt, 1989). To constrain managerial opportunism, owners may initiate control mechanisms through the operation of the board of directors, as for example, increased monitoring and incentive alignment of executive pay (Dyl, 1988; Tosi & Gomez-Majia, 1989). However, where owners of the corporation are small and dispersed, and managers enjoy undisputed control over corporate affairs and resources, agency costs associated with information asymmetries may be prohibitively high, jeopardizing effective monitoring of managerial action and appropriate incentive alignment by the board of directors.

An agency cost arising from the separation of ownership and control is the cost of corporate crime leading to executive pay. This cost represents the cost to owners of ensuring that managerial interests regarding the association of corporate crime and executive pay do not supersede ownership interests. Certain benefits may accrue to powerful managers from the corporation's commission of legal violations. First, illegal activities are likely to increase the short run profitability of the firm by achieving higher revenues or lower costs than would otherwise be gained. For example, disregard of environmental protection laws with respect to the installation and continued operation of pollution control devices and processes may result in inflated current incomes. Managers' preferences for short run gains (Lambert & Larcker, 1985) would thus be serviced by engaging in such behaviors. Second, findings in the literature suggest that manager controlled firms engage frequently in firm-enlarging merger activities (Amihud & Lev, 1981; Stano, 1976), even when such diversification may be inconsistent with shareholder interests (Reid, 1968). Legal infractions resulting in form-enlarging and increased market power ends are attractive to managers since they service important non-pecuniary preferences for prestige and power. For example, collusive agreements, price fixing, illegal merger activities, and other violations of trade and antitrust laws may have outcomes that expand the firm's size or market share, and thereby yield greater power to the firm's managers. Third, since the probabilities of detection of corporate crime are low, and the size of the punishments handed down to executives is non-deterring, managers may not be averse to engaging in illegal behaviors (Becker, 1968; Conklin, 1977; Ermann & Lundman, 1982; Blair & Kaserman, 1983). In one study, firms convicted for illegalities encountered neither investors' nor consumers' negative reaction, possibly due to the large size of the firms involved, the delayed nature of the reaction, past reputation of the firms, and actions by top managers to mitigate the effects of a conviction (Baucus, 1989). In summary, these reasons suggest that managers may not be averse to corporate engagement in legal violations when such behaviors may service their short run and size-oriented ends with minimal risk.

In the absence of controlling ownership interests (i.e., where monitoring and incentive alignment by principals is low) the board of directors is unlikely to be capable of employing executive compensation to ensure managerial behavior consistent with ownership ends. Instead, executive compensation may be used to further managers' own ends. Previous research indicates that manager controlled firms exhibit unconstrained and excessive distribution of corporate resources as compensation to top executives (McEachern, 1975), loss of efficiency through disproportionate managerial compensation contracts (Herman, 1981), adoption of stable sources of income through the linkage of compensation with factors such as firm size and accounting rather than market indices of performance (Baumol, 1959; McEachern, 1975; see also Baker, Jensen, & Murphy, 1988; Murphy, 1985), and short run rather than long run compensation time horizons (see Lambert & Larcker, 1985).

Since positive consequences from corporate crime may accrue with low risks, powerful managers are likely to structure executive compensation so as to positively reflect the potential benefits from corporate illegalities when agency costs associated with information asymmetries are high (i.e., where owners cannot ensure managerial actions consistent with their own interests). In contrast, in firms where the agency costs associated with information asymmetries are low (i.e., where boards of directors engage in comprehensive monitoring and incentive alignment activities to ensure managerial action commensurate with ownership interests), executive compensation and corporate illegalities are not likely to be positively associated.

Hypothesis. Corporate crime and executive compensation will be positively associated in manager controlled firms but not in owner controlled firms.

METHODS

Sample

The objective of this research was to examine the relationship between corporate crime and executive compensation in manager and owner controlled firms. The sample consisted of the 100 companies comprising every fifth company in the 1984 *Fortune 500* list. Annual data were collected for each company and averaged over the 3-year period, 1984–86. Nine companies were dropped from the list on account of non-published data; the final sample consisted of 91 companies.

Measures and Data Sources

Executive Compensation. Compensation was measured as the annual salary and bonus received by the chief executive officer (CEO) and the top management team. Earlier research on compensation has focused exclusively on the compensation received by the CEO. These studies have drawn on the notion that organizational outcomes are in large part attributable to the CEO, who is therefore of primary interest to decision makers, market analysts, and corporate publics (Glover, 1976; Brady & Helmich, 1984). However, the study of the top management team is also important since the chief executive shares tasks and power with other executives (Bantel & Jackson, 1989; Finkelstein & Hambrick, 1990; Hambrick & Mason, 1984). In order to consider both these perspectives, two measures of compensation were employed in this study; cash compensation received by the CEO and the mean cash compensation received by all company executives as a set. Mean executive compensation was measured as the total cash compensation received by all executives as a group divided by the number of executives. Data for annual CEO and executive cash compensation were collected from corporate annual proxy statements.

To remove the effects on CEO compensation from a CEO change during the 3-year period, only firms without any changes in their chief executives were retained for the analyses of CEO compensation. This procedure yielded a total of 78 firms for the analyses of CEO pay and 91 firms for the analyses of mean executive compensation.

Corporate Control. Although the exact correspondence between corporate control and stock ownership is yet unknown, a long historical tradition initiated by the Patman Staff Report (1968) has indicated that even a 5% ownership of common stock is sufficient to exercise significant control in large firms. Subsequent research has established this 5% figure as the conventional demarcation of large owner control, without which managerial opportunism continues unabated (e.g., Davis & Stout, 1992; Gomez-Mejia, Tosi & Hinkin, 1988; O'Reilly, Main, & Crystal, 1988; Salancik & Pfeffer, 1980; Tosi & Gomez-Mejia, 1989). Accordingly, a firm was defined in this study as manager controlled if there was no non-management 5% stockholder and owner controlled if there was at least one non-management 5% stockholder.

Data on 5% common stock owners were collected from corporate annual proxy statements. In order to remove the effects of any changes in corporate control that may have occurred during the 3-year period, only those firms without any control changes were retained for the analyses. By this procedure, the final sample consisted of 62 firms without any control changes for the analyses of mean executive compensation (20 manager controlled and 42 owner controlled firms) and 53 firms without any control changes or CEO changes for the analyses of CEO compensation (15 manager controlled and 38 owner controlled firms).

Corporate Crime. In the broad usage of the term, corporate crime is any violation of administrative, civil, or criminal law committed by corporations

(Clinard & Yeager, 1980; Clinard, 1983). For this study, two aspects of corporate illegal behavior were employed: filings (initiated proceedings) against the firm and violations (negative judgments) legally determined against the firm. Whereas the filings measure used in this study represents the mere allegation of corporate misconduct, the violations measure captures the final judgment made or agreement reached about such an allegation. That is, filings measure the proceedings initiated against a firm while violations measure the decisions against the firm that end matters under dispute. Filings were included since previous research has noted that mere allegations of illegalities adversely impact equity return (Strachan, Smith, & Beedles, 1983).[3]

The final measures were computed as follows. First, data were collected on the annual total number of legal proceedings filed against and violations determined through a legal judgment against a corporation. Next, since previous research has indicated a significant positive relationship between corporate illegal behavior and firm size (Dalton & Kesner, 1988; Baucus, 1988; Hill, Kelley, Agle, Hitt, & Hoskisson, 1992), filings and violations were regressed on firm sales, with the standardized residuals (representing that portion of corporate illegal behavior not accounted for by firm size) being used as the final measures of corporate crime.

Data on corporate illegal behavior included unfair trade violations (e.g., price fixing), product violations (e.g., failure to warn consumers of potentially harmful side-effects), environmental violations (e.g., illegal dumping of waste materials), and labor violations (e.g., age discrimination). Data were obtained from two sources: corporate 10K statements and *The Wall Street Journal Index*.[4] A mandatory item in corporate 10K statements refers to the pending legal proceedings of a firm in a given year. The corporation is required to disclose all litigation that may have a significant adverse effect on the business and finances of the firm. Included within this disclosure is the concluding deci-

---

[3] Filings included lawsuits filed or investigations initiated against the corporation. Certain agreements or settlements entered by a corporation in the preliminary stages of actual or potential lawsuits or investigations were included in the total number of filings, if the time duration between the filing of the lawsuit or the institution of the investigation and the consent or litigation decree was short enough to warrant an attribution to the acts of the current management, while ensuring that no double counting of investigations, filings, and settlements occurred.

[4] Earlier studies (e.g., Staw & Szwajkowski, 1975; Kesner, Victor, & Lamont, 1986) had operationalized the commission of illegal acts as court decisions and consent litigation decrees that were listed in *Trade Cases* (Commerce Clearing House, Inc.), an annual publication on antitrust and trade violations. This measure was not employed in the present study for three reasons. First, the nature of violations listed in *Trade Cases* is limited to trade and antitrust actions, and it was desired to examine in this study a broader range of possible violations. Second, for this study, a measure of corporate misconduct was required that represented generally available information to the investing public. Trade publications such as *Trade Cases* have, by their very nature, much more selective audiences than those of less specialized business publications such as *The Wall Street Journal*. Third, the period between the commission of the activity and the decision reported in *Trade Cases* may stretch over several years. Including such decisions in a test of the effects of illegal acts on executive compensation would amount to examining current managements for the actions of their predecessors. Instead, a measure that more appropriately adjusts the time period of the illegality with the compensation of executives was desired.

sion of the case and investigations, stating the material costs to the corporation, the current legal status of pending litigation, and potential lawsuits and investigations. The second source of the data, the Index, lists all items appearing in *The Wall Street Journal* for a given corporation, including reports of lawsuits filed, investigations instituted, settlements reached, and judgments determined against the corporation.

In the present study, of the 91 firms in the original sample, 58.2% had at least one filing and 25.3% had at least one violation in the 3-year period. Of the 53 firms without any control changes or CEO changes during the period 1984–86, 60.4% had at least one filing and 32.1% had at least one violation in that period. Of the 62 firms without any control changes during the relevant 3-year period, 61.3% had at least one filing and 29.0% had at least one violation during 1984–86.

Size. Previous research has indicated the importance of including size in examinations of CEO compensation (Murphy, 1985; Gomez-Mejia, Tosi, & Hinkin, 1987). Size was operationalized as total sales of the corporation. Data were obtained from Fortune 500 annual surveys.

Performance. A firm's performance was defined as its return on equity (ROE). ROE is a measure of the firm's profitability. It reflects the utilization of the stockholders' investment in the firm. Return on equity has been frequently used in investigations of executive compensation (e.g., Dyl, 1988; Finkelstein & Hambrick, 1989; O'Reilly, Main, & Crystal, 1988). Data were obtained from Fortune 500 annual surveys.

Analyses

Multiple regression analyses for the 3-year period were conducted to test the hypothesis. The final sample consisted of 53 companies (15 manager controlled and 38 owner controlled) for the analyses of CEO compensation and 62 companies (20 manager controlled and 42 owner controlled) for the analyses of mean executive compensation. To allay concerns regarding the small sample size of the manager controlled firms, similar analyses were also conducted for each of the 3 years separately: 87 firms in 1984 (of which 35 were manager controlled), 85 firms in 1985 (of which 31 were manager controlled), and 80 firms in 1986 (of which 27 were manager controlled). These annual analyses are not reported in this study because of space considerations; however, the results were substantively similar to those reported below.

RESULTS

Table I reports the summary statistics and correlations for the variables.

The results of the multiple regression analyses of CEO and mean executive compensation are reported in Table II. Regressions were first performed

TABLE I
Summary Statistics and Pearson Correlations

Variable	ALL FIRMS						MANAGER CONTROLLED FIRMS						OWNER CONTROLLED FIRMS					
	Mean	SD	1	2	3	4	Mean	SD	1	2	3	4	Mean	SD	1	2	3	4
1984–86[a]	(N = 53)						(N = 15)						(N = 38)					
1. CEO pay[b]	655.21	260.82					805.80	354.60					595.77	187.62				
2. Sales[b]	3836.96	7878.37	.46**				9317.32	13326.13	.40				1673.65	1747.73	.43**			
3. Return on equity	12.67	6.43	.27	.16			14.78	6.98	.26	.17			11.83	6.10	.18	–.12		
4. Filings	.00	.99	.25	.00	–.00		–.05	1.49	.52*	–.02	–.03		.02	.74	–.06	.24	.01	
5. Violations	.00	.99	.18	.00	–.12	.70**	–.12	1.31	.46	–.03	.02	.88**	.05	.85	–.03	.35*	–.20	.49**
1984–86[c]	(N = 62)						(N = 20)						(N = 42)					
1. Executive pay[b]	237.28	82.62					284.93	111.14					214.59	52.90				
2. Sales[b]	3834.18	7386.01	.52**				7726.04	11806.15	.47*				1980.91	2380.00	.39*			
3. Return on equity	11.85	6.43	.26*	.15			12.52	7.41	.40	.25			11.53	5.98	.11	–.11		
4. Filings	.00	.99	.27*	.00	–.01		–.09	1.37	.48*	–.04	.03		.04	.77	.06	.31*	–.05	
5. Violations	.00	.99	.20	.00	–.10	.64**	–.08	1.23	.37	–.00	–.01	.82**	.04	.87	.08	.12	–.16	.43**

[a] Firms exhibiting no control change or CEO change over the 3-year period.
[b] compensation and sales are in $000s.
[c] Firms exhibiting no control change over the 3-year period.
* $p < .05$.
** $p < .01$.

on the sample as a whole to investigate whether filings and violations were significantly associated with CEO compensation. Subsequently, regressions were performed for the subsamples of manager controlled and owner controlled firms.

The results reported in Table II indicate that the variance explained by the independent variables (R^2) for the 12 analyses ranged between .17 and .54. In general, firm sales were positively related with CEO and mean executive compensation, as established by previous research (e.g., Baumol, 1959; McEachern, 1975; Murphy, 1985). Return on equity was marginally associated with CEO and mean executive compensation for all firms, but not for either manager or owner controlled firms, separately.

The results also indicate that for the undivided sample of firms, both filings and violations were significantly or marginally associated with CEO and mean executive compensation. When the sample was split on the basis of type of control, the hypothesized direction of the coefficients emerged. The results revealed positive and significant coefficients for the filings variable for both CEO pay and mean executive pay in manager controlled firms, and nonsignifi-

TABLE II
Regressions of 1984–86 CEO and Mean Executive Compensation on Filings and Judgments

	ALL FIRMS		MANAGER CONTROL		OWNER CONTROL	
	Beta	*T*	Beta	*T*	Beta	*T*
CEO compensation[a]	$N = 53$	$R^2 = .31$	$N = 15$	$R^2 = .47$	$N = 38$	$R^2 = .27$
Sales	.43	3.55**	.38	1.70	.50	3.29**
Return on equity	.20	1.69†	.19	.84	.24	1.61
Filings	.25	2.10*	.52	2.38*	−.18	−1.21
CEO compensation[a]	$N = 53$	$R^2 = .29$	$N = 15$	$R^2 = .42$	$N = 38$	$R^2 = .26$
Sales	.42	3.46**	.38	1.62	.52	3.28**
Return on equity	.23	1.86†	.19	.82	.21	1.38
Violations	.21	1.73†	.47	2.03†	−.18	−1.11
Mean executive compensation[b]	$N = 62$	$R^2 = .38$	$N = 20$	$R^2 = .54$	$N = 42$	$R^2 = .18$
Sales	.49	4.65**	.42	2.41*	.42	2.72**
Return on equity	.20	1.86†	.28	1.60	.15	1.01
Filings	.27	2.63*	.49	2.88*	−.07	−.44
Mean executive compensation[b]	$N = 62$	$R^2 = .35$	$N = 20$	$R^2 = .45$	$N = 42$	$R^2 = .17$
Sales	.48	4.53**	.40	2.06†	.40	2.67*
Return on equity	.21	1.98†	.30	1.59	.16	1.05
Violations	.22	2.07*	.38	2.04†	.05	.36

[a] Firms exhibiting no control change or CEO change over the 3-year period.
[b] Firms exhibiting no control change over the 3-year period.
† $p < .10$.
* $p < .05$.
** $p < .01$.

cant coefficients in owner controlled firms. The violations variable was positively and marginally associated with CEO pay and mean executive pay in manager controlled firms, and nonsignificantly related to compensation in owner controlled firms. In summary, the results reported in Table II indicate support for the Hypothesis in that the relationship between corporate illegal behavior (filings and violations) and the compensation of top executives, including the CEO, differs according to the nature of corporate control.

DISCUSSION

The results of this study indicate differences between manager and owner controlled firms in the compensation of CEOs and top executives. Pay was positively associated with corporate illegalities in manager controlled firms but not in owner controlled firms. These findings point to the continued importance of including corporate control in future studies of corporate governance issues. Even though this study employed a broad indicator of control—the 5% ownership cutoff—the results show differences among owner and manager controlled firms. The use of more fine grained measures of corporate control, such as various measures of ownership dispersion (e.g., Cubbin & Leech, 1983; Demsetz & Lehn, 1985; Hill & Snell, 1989), is likely to further current understanding of corporate level phenomena, particularly issues of executive pay.

The results also draw attention to the importance of examining the compensation of the top management team, not just CEO pay. While an extensive body of literature has focused over the decades on issues pertaining to CEO pay (Tosi & Gomez-Mejia, 1989), comparatively little work has been done on the compensation of the team of executives comprising the top of the corporation. The findings indicate that the study of top executives' compensation can yield substantial insights into the decision making of boards of directors, and that different mechanisms may, in fact, be in operation in the determination of CEOs' and top executives' pay. Future research should examine issues related to top management team compensaion more closely.

Four general caveats about this inquiry are important for consideration at this point. First, the sample size employed in this study was relatively small, especially in the cases of the separate tests of owner and manager controlled firms. The total sample was reduced considerably for the final analyses since multiple control and CEO changes had occurred over the 3-year period of the study. To alleviate concerns about sample size effects, individual analyses were conducted for each of the 3 years separately, allowing the investigation of larger group sizes (group sizes ranged from 80 to 87 for all firms, from 27 to 35 for manager controlled firms, and from 52 to 53 for owner controlled firms). In general, the pattern of results obtained from these individual year analyses was substantively similar to that reported in this study.

Second, the small number of cases employed in this study precluded a comprehensive treatment of executive compensation. Various other individual and corporate/industry factors may influence top management compensation, such as the executive's tenure, human capital, and level, and the corporation's and industry's complexity.

Third, a portion of the results of this study were obtained using the allegation or filing of legal proceedings as a measure of corporate crime. Frivolous, procedural, or purely legalistic claims against companies may be captured by this measure, as well as some bonafide claims that may later be dismissed. Some of this concern may be alleviated since the data sources of legal filings were either the corporations themselves (in their annual reports) or *The Wall Street Journal,* both of which are likely to publish this data only if they deem the accusations to be of sufficient material interest to stockholders and the general public.

Fourth, since the sample consisted of the largest U.S. corporations, generalizability of these findings is of concern. It is possible however, that ownership may have an even greater effect on top management compensation in smaller companies (Gomez-Mejia, Tosi, & Hinkin, 1987) while simultaneously, the possible costs and benefits of legal infractions may be magnified in them. For these reasons, it may be that the differences obtained in this study may, in fact, be heightened within a sample of smaller companies.

Policy Implications

The results of this study indicated that the illegal behavior-executive pay association was positive in manager controlled firms. This finding suggests important implications for the governance and conduct of manager controlled firms. The boards of these companies appear unable to appropriately engage in top management compensation monitoring and incentive alignment activities to reflect stockholder interests. If executives in manager controlled companies continue to remain unpunished or see positive benefits associated with engagement in croporate illegalities, it is unlikely that any serious efforts to curb corporate crime will succeed.

Cumulatively, these implications suggest that there is a strong need in manager controlled firms for top managers to be distanced from the compensation process. Current practices allow CEOs unconstrained influence on the determination of their own and their top executives' pay through their control over the selection of directors who serve on the board's compensation committee (Geneen, 1984; Kesner & Dalton, 1986), and their control of the board information apparatus through, for example, the selection of compensation consultants (Williams, 1985). Since the costs of organizing are prohibitive for dispersed owners, it is particularly difficult for companies without large owners to distance top managers from decisions regarding their own compensation; rather, policies enforcing such distancing should be designed and regulated by marketplace agencies such as stock exchanges. For example, restrictions may be imposed by stock exchanges on the composition, member selection and operation of the compensation committees of companies listed, analogous to current policies that regulate audit committees. Devices suggested in previous research to protect shareholder welfare by increasing the independent judgment of directors (e.g., Geneen, 1984; Lorsch, 1989) should be directed specifically at compensation committee members. Such policies mandated by market agencies should include increasing the power of outside directors to select compensation committee members, laying the responsibility for the selection of compensation consultants in the hands of the compensation committee, and increasing the firm ownership stake of compensation committee members.

Further, the results of this study indicated that although pay was not positively associated with the incidence of corporate crime in owner controlled firms, the boards of even these firms did not appear to be powerful enough to actively signal their displeasure with their executives for illegal corporate activities through a downward adjustment of top managers' pay. Thus, even in the case of owner controlled firms, although not as evident as in the case of manager controlled firms, the findings of this study provide some support for previous research that points to the apparent inadequacy of corporate boards of directors to ensure that owners are not shortchanged (e.g., Kerr & Bettis, 1987).

In summary, framers and regulators of corporate policy should recognize the different relationships between corporate behaviors and executive compensation in certain types of corporations more than in others. As Blair and Kaserman (1983) point out in the context of the design of antitrust policy, corporate policy framers should design deterrents and sanctions aimed at preventing the opportunistic use of managerial power, and should direct these specifically at executives of firms without large and concentrated stockholdings.

REFERENCES

Amihud, Y., & Lev, B. Risk reduction as a managerial motive for conglomerate mergers. *Bell Journal of Economics*, 1981, *12*, 605–617.

Baker, G. P., Jensen, M. C., & Murphy, K. J. Compensation and incentives: Practice vs. theory. *Journal of Finance*, 1988, *43*(3), 593–616.

Bantel, K., & Jackson, S. Top management and innovations in banking: Does the composition of the top team make a difference? *Strategic Management Journal*, 1989, *10*, 107–124.

Baucus, M. B. Why firms do it and what happens to them: A reexamination of the theory of illegal corporate behavior. In *Research in corporate social performance and policy* (Vol. 11). Greenwich, CT: JAI Press, 1989, pp. 93–118.

Baucus, M. B., & Near, J. P. Can illegal corporate behavior be predicted? An event history analysis. *Academy of Management Journal*, 1989, *34*(1), 9–36.

Baumol, W. J. *Business behavior, value and growth.* New York: MacMillan, 1959.

Becker, G. S. Crime and punishment: An economic approach. *Journal of Political Economy*, 1968, *76*, 169–217.

————. Tailoring punishment to white-collar crime: A mix of fines and lawsuits—with the occasional prison term—would remove the profit motive from corporate crime. *Business Week*, October 28, 1985, 20.

Berenbeim, R. E. An outbreak of ethics. *Across the Board*, 1988, *25*, 14–20.

Berle, A. A., & Means, G. C. *The modern corporation and private property.* New York: Commerce Clearing House, 1932.

Blair, R. D., & Kaserman, D. L. Ownership and control in the modern corporation: Antitrust implications. *Journal of Business Research*, 1983, *11*, 333–343.

Bowen, W. How to regain our competitive edge. *Fortune*, 1981, *103*, 9 March, 74–90.

Brady, G. F., & Helmich, D. L. *Executive succession.* Englewood Cliffs, NJ: Prentice Hall, 1984.

Buckley, W. F., Jr. Disgrace abounding (corruption and fraud in politics and business). *National Review*, 1988, 16 Sept., *40*, 65.

The Business Roundtable. *The role and composition of the board of directors of the large, publicly owned corporation.* New York: The Business Roundtable, 1978.

Business Week. The job nobody wants. 1986, 8 September, 56–61.

Business Week. The battle for corporate control, 18 May, 1987, 102–108.

Business Week. Businesses are signing up for ethics 101. 15 February, 1988, 56–57.

Byrne, J. A. Business are signing up for ethics 101. *Business Week*, Feb. 15, 1988, 56–57.

Child, J. Organization structure, environment, and performance: The role of strategic choice. *Sociology*, 1972, *6*, 1–22.

Chitayat, G. Working relationships between the chairman of the board of directors and the CEO. *Management International Review* (Germany), 1985, *25*(3), 65–70.

Clinard, M. B. *Corporate ethics and crime.* Beverly Hills, California: Sage, 1983.

Clinard, M. B., & Yeager, P. C. *Corporate crime.* New York: The Free Press, 1980.

Cochran, P. L., & Nigh, D. Illegal corporate behavior and the question of moral agency: An empirical examination. *Research in Corporate Social Performance and Policy*, 1987, *9*, 73–91.

Commerce Clearing House, Inc. *Trade cases: Trade regulation reports.* Chicago: Commerce Clearing House, Inc., annual.

Conklin, J. *Illegal but not criminal.* Englewood Cliffs: Prentice Hall, 1977.

Coughlan, A. T., & Schmidt, R. M. Executive compensation, management turnover, and firm performance: An empirical investigation. *Journal of Accounting and Economics*, 1985, *7*, 43–66.

Crock, S. How to take a bite out of corporate crime. *Business Week*, 15 July, 1985, 122–123.

Crystal, G. S. Too many make-any-excuse CEOs. *Fortune*, 21 July 1986, *114*(2) 116–117.

————. The whacky world of CEO pay. *Fortune*, June 6, 1988, 68–78.

————. Seeking the sense in CEO pay. *Fortune*, June 5, 1989, 88–104.

————. *In search of excess: The overcompensation of American executives.* New York: Norton, 1991.

Cubbin, J., & Leech, D. The effect of shareholding dispersion on the degree of control in British companies: theory and measurement. *The Economic Journal*, 1983, *93*, 351–369.

Dalton, D. R., & Kesner, I. F. On the dynamics of corporate size and illegal activity: An empirical assessment. *Journal of Business Ethics*, 1988, *7*, 861–870.

Davis, G. F., & Stout, S. K. Organization theory and the market for corporate control:

A dynamic analysis of the characteristics of large takeover targets, 1980–1990. *Administrative Science Quarterly,* 1992, *37,* 605–633.

Demsetz, H., & Lehn, K. The structure of corporate ownership: Causes and consequences. *Journal of Political Economy,* 1985, *93*(6), 1155–1177.

Dyl, E. A. Corporate control and management compensation: Evidence on the agency problem. *Managerial and Decision Economics,* 1988, *9*(1), 21–25.

The Economist. Incurable mergeritis. *The Economist,* 23 April, 1988, *157,* 14.

Eisenhardt, K. Agency theory: An assessment and review. *Academy of Management Review,* 1989, *14*(1), 57–74.

Ermann, M. D., & Lundman, R. J. *Corporate and governmental deviance* (2nd ed.). New York: Oxford University Press, 1982.

Fama, E. F. Agency problems and the theory of the firm. *Journal of Political Economy,* 1980, *88,* 288–307.

Fama, E. F., & Jensen, M. C. Separation of ownership and control. *Journal of Law and Economics,* 1983, *26,* 301–325.

Finkelstein, S., & Hambrick, D. C. Chief executive compensation: A study of the intersection of markets and political processes. *Strategic Management Journal,* 1989, *10,* 121–134.

————. Top-management-team tenure and organizational outcomes: the moderating role of managerial discretion. *Administrative Science Quarterly,* 1990, *35,* 484–503.

Frederick, W. C., & Weber, J. The values of corporate managers and their critics: An empirical description and normative implications. *Research in Corporate Social Performance and Policy,* 1987, *9,* 121–152.

Furtado, E. P. H., & Rozeff, M. S. The wealth effects of company initiated management changes. *Journal of Financial Economics,* 1987, *18,* 147–160.

Gautschi, F. H., & Jones, T. M. Illegal corporate behavior and corporate board structure. *Research in Corporate Social Performance and Policy,* 1987, *9,* 93–106.

Geneen, H. S. Why directors can't protect the sharehoders. *Fortune,* 1984, September 17, 28–32.

Glover, J. D. The many roles of the chief executive. In J. D. Glover and G. A. Simon (Eds.), *Chief executive handbook.* Homewood, Illinois: Dow-Jones Irwin, 1976, pp. 3–21.

Gomez-Mejia, L. R., Tosi, H., & Hinkin, T. R. Managerial control, performance, and executive compensation. *Academy of Management Journal,* 1987, *30,* 51–70.

Hambrick, D. C., & Finkelstein, S. Managerial discretion: A bridge between polar views on organizations. In L. L. Cummings and B. M. Staw (Eds.), *Research in Organizational Behavior* (Vol. 9). Greenwich, CT: JAI Press, 1987, 369–406.

Hambrick, D. C., & Mason, P. A. Upper echelons: The organization as a reflection of its top managers. *Academy of Management Review,* 1984, *9,* 193–206.

Harvard Business Review. How much is enough? 1992, *70*(4), 130–139.

Hatfield, R. S. The changing corporate environment: Problems and opportunities. In G. C. Greanias and D. Windsor (Eds.), *The changing boardroom: Making policy and profits in an age of corporate citizenship.* Houston: Gulf Publishing Co., 1982.

Herman, E. S. *Corporate control, corporate power.* New York: Cambridge University Press, 1981.

Hill, C. W. L., & Snell, S. A. Effects of ownership structure and control on corporate productivity. *Academy of Management Journal,* 1989, *32*(1), 25–46.

Hill, C. W. L., Kelley, P. C., Agle, B. R., Hitt, M. A., & Hoskisson, R. E. An empirical examination of the causes of corporate wrongdoing in the United States. *Human Relatios*, 1992, *45*(10), 1055–1077.

Kerr, J., & Bettis, R. A. Boards of directors, top management compensation, and shareholder returns. *Academy of Management Journal*, 1987, *30*, 645–664.

Kesner, I. E., & Dalton, D. R. Boards of directors and the checks and (im)balances of corporate governance. *Business Horizons*, 1986, September–October, 17–23.

Kesner, I. F., Victor, B., & Lamont, B. T. Board composition and the commission of illegal acts: An investigation of Fortune 500 companies. *Academy of Management Journal*, 1986, *29*(4), 789–799.

Lambert, R. A., & Larcker, D. F. Executive compensation, corporate decision-making and shareholder wealth: A review of the evidence. *Midland Corporate Finance Journal*, 1985, *2*, 6–22.

Lewellen, W., Loderer, C., & Martin, K. Executive compensation and executive incentive problems: An Empirical Analysis. *Journal of Accounting and Economics*, 1987, *9*, 287–310.

Lorsch, J. *Pawns or potentates: The reality of America's corporate boards*. Boston: Harvard Business School Press, 1989.

Louden, J. K. *The director*. New York: American Management Association, 1982.

Louis, A. M. Business is bungling long term compensation. *Fortune*, 1984, *110*(2), 64–69.

Mace, M. L. *Directors: Myth and reality*. Cambridge, MA: Harvard University Graduate School of Business Administration, 1971.

McEachern, W. A. *Managerial control and performance*. Lexington, MA: D. C. Heath Company, 1975.

Metzenbaum, H. M. Too soft on corporate crime. *Financial World*, April 15, 1986, 160.

Mizruchi, M. S. Who controls whom? An examination of the relation between management and boards of directors in large American corporations. *Academy of Management Review*, 1983, *8*(3), 426–435.

Monsen, R. J., Jr., & Downs, A. A theory of large menagerial firms. *The Journal of Political Economy*, June 1965, 221–236.

Murphy, K. J. Corporate performance and managerial remuneration: An empirical analysis. *Journal of Accounting and Economics*, 1985, *7*, 11–42.

Nader, R., & Andrews, K. R. Reforming corporate governance: Difficulties in overseeing ethical policy. *California Management Review*, 1984, *26*(4), 126–137.

O'Reilly, C. A., Main, B. G., & Crystal, G. S. CEO compensation as tournament and social comparison: A tale of two theories. *Administrative Science Quarterly*, 1988, *33*, 257–274.

Patman Staff Report. *Commercial banks and their trust activities: Emerging influence on the American economy*. U.S. Congress, House, Committee on Banking and Currency, Domestic Finance (1968). Committee, 90th Congress, 2nd session. Washington, D.C.: Government Printing Office, 1968.

Peltzman, S. The effect of FTC advertising regulation. *The Journal of Law and Economics*, 1981, *24*, 403–448.

Rappaport, A. Executive incentives vs. corporate growth. *Harvard Business Review*, 1978, July–August, 81–88.

Reid, S. R. *Mergers, managers and the economy*. New York: McGraw Hill, 1968.

Reynolds, L. Congress to corporations: Clean up your act! *Management Review*, 1987, *76*, 23–24.

Ross, I. How lawless are big companies? *Fortune*, 1 December, 1980, 57–64.

Salancik, G. R., & Pfeffer, J. Effects of ownership and performance on executive tenure in U.S. corporations. *Academy of Management Journal,* 1980, *23,* 653–664.

Stano, M. Monopoly power, ownership control, and corporate performance. *Bell Journal of Economics,* 1976, 672–679.

Staw, B. M., & Szwajkowski, E. The scarcity-munificence component of organizational environments and the commission of illegal acts. *Administrative Science Quarterly,* 1975, *20,* 345–354.

Strachan, J. L., Smith, D. B., & Beedles, W. L. The price reaction to (alleged) corporate crime. *The Financial Review,* 1983, 121–132.

Temporary National Economic Committee. *Investigation of concentration of economic power, monograph No. 29: "The distribution of ownership in the 200 largest non-financial corporation."* Washington, D.C.: U.S. Government Printing Office, 1940.

Tosi, H., & Gomez-Mejia, L. R. The decoupling of CEO pay and performance: An agency theory perspective. *Administrative Science Quarterly,* 1989, *34*(2), 169–189.

U.S. News and World Report. Corporate crime: The untold story. September 6, 1982, 25–30.

Vance, S. C. *Corporate leadership: Boards, directors and strategy.* New York: McGraw Hill Book Company, 1983.

Waldo, C. N. *Boards of directors: Their changing roles, structure and information needs.* Westport, CT: Quorum Books, 1985.

Walsh, J. P., & Seward, J. K. On the efficiency of internal and external corporate control mechanisms. *Academy of Management Review,* 1990, *15*(3), 421–458.

Williams, M. J. Why chief executives' pay keeps rising. *Fortune,* 1 April, 1985, 66–76.

Wokutch, R. E., & Spencer, B. A. Corporate saints and sinners: The effects of philanthropic and illegal activity on organizational performance. *California Management Review,* 1987, *29*(2), 62–77.

Woodworth, W. The scandalous pay of the corporate elite. *Business and Society Review,* 1987, *61,* 22–26.

Toward Understanding Unlawful Organizational Behavior

DIANE VAUGHAN

THE STRUCTURAL IMPETUS

The idea that the social structure generates the motivation for individuals to engage in deviance was suggested by Robert Merton.[2] The concepts central to

"Toward Understanding Unlawful Organizational Behavior" from *Michigan Law Review 80* (June 1982): 1377–1402. Reprinted by permission.
[2] R. Merton, *Social Structure and Anomie,* In Social Theory and Social Structure 185 (1968).

his thesis are competition, economic success as a culturally approved goal, and erosion of norms supporting legitimate procedures for achieving it.[3] Because Merton concluded that these factors differentially affect the lower class, empirical assessment of his ideas has been restricted to individual behavior. But the concepts that he identified in many ways seem more appropriate for understanding rates of misconduct among organizations than among individuals.[4]

Though organizations have many goals, economic success is imperative for organizational survival. In fact, organizations must seek profits regardless of variability in the values of a particular culture.[5] Not only is economic success critical to survival in the corporate world, but organizational wealth is also an indicator of prestige. The annual publication of Fortune's "Five Hundred"[6] indicates membership in the upper class of the organizational stratification system. How organizations are ranked within this stratification system is monitored through quarterly reports, earnings, dividends, and stock market transactions. The key to social mobility within the system is profit-maximization.[7] . . .

Financial success is a goal held out to be attained by all, but profit-seeking organizations must compete to attain it.[13] They compete not only for economic goals, but also for the resources that promote achievement of economic ends: personnel recruitment, product development, land acquisition, advertising space, and sales territory. An organization's ability to obtain requisite resources may be constrained by the source, nature, and abundance of the resource, by the behavior of other organizations in the environment in the roles of consumers, suppliers, competitors, and controllers,[14] by individuals in the role of consumers,[15] and by the resources already possessed by the organization and preexisting demands on those resources. As a result, attainment of economic goals may be obstructed in two ways. First, an organization may be

---

[3] More specifically, Merton suggested that the interplay between the cultural structure and the social structure plays a critical role in the production of deviance. He focused on two elements of the cultural structure: (1) culturally defined goals (ends) that are held out and accepted as legitimate objectives for all members of a society, and (2) norms that specify the allowable procedures (means) for attaining these objectives. When the achievement of the desired goals receives strong cultural emphasis, while much less emphasis is placed on the norms regulating the means, these norms will tend to lose their power to regulate behavior. A state of anomie (normlessness) develops. Given the culturally induced motivation to succeed and the decreased effectiveness of norms, the pursuit of desired goals by illegitimate means may be one response. *Id.* at 186–89.

[4] The precise relationship between Merton's concepts and the ideas presented here is elaborated in D. Vaughan, On the Social Control of Organizations ch. 4 (1983) (forthcoming).

[5] *See* Lemert, *Social Structure, Social Control and Deviation,* Anomie and Deviant Behavior 57, 62–66 (M. Clinard ed. 1964) (critiquing Merton's assumption of uniform values for individuals).

[6] *The Fortune Directory of the Largest U.S. Industrial Corporations,* Fortune May 3, 1982 at 258.

[7] *See e.g.,* M. Friedman, Capitalism and Freedom 133 (1962); Coffee, *"No Soul To Damn: No Body To Kick": An Unscandalized Inquiry into the Problem of Corporate Punishment,* 79 Mich. L. Rev. 386, 395 (1981) ("the economist assumes that firms universally seek to maximize profits").

[13] *Cf.* R. Merton, *supra* note 2, at 188 (discussing competition between individuals).

[14] J. Pfeffer & G. Salancik, *supra* note 1, at 39–59.

[15] A. Hirschman, Exit, Voice, and Loyalty 4, 21–54 (1970).

PANEL 16   Small Change

On July 6, 1999, Michael Wise, the former head of the Silverado Savings and Loan Association, was sentenced to three and a half years of prison after pleading guilty to two violations of the Federal wire-fraud law. Wise was ordered to repay nearly $9 million to swindled investors.

Source: New York Times; July 7, 1999.

On March 11, 1999, the Bankers Trust Company pleaded guilty to Federal charges. Senior bank officers illegally diverted over $19 million in unclaimed checks and other credits owed to customers. These monies were placed into a "slush" fund that was used to supplement income and offset expenses. The bank agreed to pay a $60 million Federal fine and a $3.5 million New York state fine.

Source: New York Times; March 12, 1999.

On August 2, 1999, John Sanchez, an assistant treasurer at the Bank of New York, was charged with defrauding his employer. Sanchez transferred hundreds of millions of fictitious funds into a time deposit account. Over the course of a year, Sanchez earned at least $700,000.

Source: New York Times; August 3, 1999.

In February, 1999, a federal appeals court ruled that bank officer Shaith Pharaon must pay interest on a $37 million fine for his role in the Bank of Credit and Commerce scandal. The fine against Pharaon is the largest the Federal Reserve has ever imposed on an individual.

Source: Wall Street Journal; February 26, 1999.

On February 24, 1997, Smith Kline Beecham, a British pharmaceutical company, agreed to pay the United States $325 million to settle charges that it had overcharged Medicare for patient services. This is the largest civil settlement in American history involving health care. Investigators said Smith Kline Beecham billed the United States government for millions of laboratory tests that were not medically necessary, were not ordered by a doctor, or were not performed.

Source: New York Times; February 25, 1997.

In 1999, Jay Fabrikant, former chief executive of the New York Health Plan, Inc., pleaded guilty to offering a false instrument for filing. The charge refers to the submission of false claims to Medicaid, which resulted in a $320,000 loss to Medicaid. After learning that the city planned to end his $4 million-a-year contract to treat 32,000 Medicaid recipients, Fabrikant instructed his staff to drop 6,700 Medicaid-eligible patients. A court settlement requires Fabrikant to pay Medicaid $375,000 and to perform 250 hours of community service.

Source: New York Times; May 25, 1999.

entirely excluded from the competition *(e.g.,* market entry is prohibited by controllers; resources are unavailable to devote to product development). Second, an organization might gain entry to the competition, but remain unable to attain its economic goals because supplies of the resources that represent the goals *(e.g.,* government contracts, customers for a particular product) are limited. Profit-seeking organizations, therefore, must compete for both economic goals and the means to those goals. The availability of both can be limited, or unwillingness to obtain a commodity at a given price. Thus, some scarcity can always exist. And when the scarcity of strategic resources threatens an organization with possible loss in legitimate competition, unlawful conduct may result.

The likelihood that an organization will act unlawfully is not, of course, determined solely by the availability of strategic resources. The effect of goal variability on the competition must also be considered. All organizations must maximize returns over costs to survive, but the more general goal of economic success will be reflected in differential standards in particular organizations. Economic success is relative and an organization's criteria for success are shaped by both financial conditions and by the other organizations with which it must compete. Standards for economic success reflect position in the organizational stratification system, and may take three forms:[16]

(1) A shift in economic and social position; higher status competitors.

(2) A Shift in economic position; higher status among same competitors.

(3) Maintenance of existing economic and social position.

For organizations already among the elite, an upward shift in social position may not be possible, though higher economic status within the same membership group may be. Organizations not among the elite may, at varying time, be concerned with all three standards for success. And *all* organizations, regardless of rank, must seek to maintain their existing economic and social position. To fail to maintain that position is to succumb to downward mobility. Consequently, scarcity, combined with the differential standards for economic success, raises the possibility of blocked access to resources *regardless of an organization's site, wealth, age, experience, or previous record.*

Economic goals vary in a second important way as well. Competitive pressures and the cultural emphasis on economic success typically lead organizations to establish new goals once one is achieve. A "maximum" profit, in the literal sense, becomes an infinitely receding possibility under these circumstances. Motivational tensions continue to operate, reinforcing the pursuit of success. Should a goal be attained, a new one is set, continually recreating the possibility of blocked access to resources and the consequent tensions to attain them unlawfully.

Unlawful conduct is most likely to be chosen as a survival strategy when support diminishes for legitimate procedures for reaching desired goals. The

---

[16]These standards for organizational success are based on the standards that Cloward and Ohlin presented for individuals. *See* R. Cloward & L. Ohlin, Delinquency and Opportunity 94–95 (1960).

erosion of normative support for legitimate conduct among organizations has been noted in the stratification systems of societies that become modernized.[17] The importance of family lineage as the basis of rank declines, while the rankings of organizations relative to one another become increasingly important. Organizational membership becomes an indicator of individual prestige. In this way, individuals' mobility becomes linked to improving the position of their organization relative to other organizations. In a society that is not experiencing major structural reorganization, the norms governing competition for rank among organizations usually obtain consensus. When modernization is underway, however, the established stratification principles are inappropriate. The units to be ranked are organizations, not families, and the ranking process is further complicated by the rapid multiplication of organizations. Consensus is absent on the ranks of organizations and how the ranks may legitimately be improved.

New organizations, moreover, tend to be led by new leaders, who did not previously occupy elite positions. Because of youth and their rapid rise to wealth and prominence, these new leaders tend to be "less committed to the norms of the system of stratification among organizations."[18] Unsocialized by the old elite, their behavior is guided by the principle that new organizations only rise rapidly if they have some disrespect for traditional standards.[19] In a period of rapid structural differentiation, "therefore *[w]hat is very generally at stake is the definition of what is deviant.*"[20] Under these circumstances, the means of organizational competition become unlimited.

The characteristics attributed to modernizing societies continue in highly modernized societies. Because some organizations cease to exist and others are constantly being created, the ranking of organizations remains in flux. Organizational membership continues to be a key element defining individual prestige. Perhaps most important, the definition of deviance remainsambiguous,[21] creating the possibility of a chronic state of anomie for all organizations, *regardless of rank in the stratification system.* Successful achievement of organizational goals through unlawful conduct tends to reinforce the occurrence of this behavior, so that what the society defines as illegal may come to be defined in the organization as normative. Choice is not simply an output of struc-

---

[17]*See* Stinchcombe, *Social Structure and Organizations,* in Handbook of Organizations 142, 169–80 (J. March ed. 1965).

[18]*Id.* at 174.

[19]*Id.*

[20]*Id.* at 175 (emphasis added).

[21]"On the top economic levels, the pressure toward innovation not infrequently erases the distinction between business-like strivings this side of the mores and sharp practices beyond the mores." R. Merton, *supra* note 2, at 195. *See also* Geis, *White Collar Crime: The Heavy Electrical Equipment Antitrust Cases of 1961,* in Criminal Behavior Systems 139 (M. Clinard & R. Quinney eds. 1967); Kramer, Corporate Crime: An Organizational Perspective 14 (Paper presented at the Conference on White-Collar and Economic Crime, Potsdam, N.Y., Feb 7–9, 1980) (copy on file with the *Michigan Law Review);* Corporate and Governmental Deviance, *supra* note 1.

ture, but a strategic input for the system as a whole.[22] The successful become models for others in their environment who, initially less vulnerable and alienated, now no longer keep to the rules that they once regarded as legitimate.[23] Decisions to use illegitimate methods to achieve desired goals thus feed back into the social structure, effectively maintaining the pattern "unless counteracting mechanisms of social control are called into play."[24]

The "counteracting mechanisms of social control," however, operate at less than maximum effectiveness because administrative rules and regulations and criminal and civil statutes that are directed at organizational behavior do not revolve around sacred values—in fact, in many cases represent no values of individuals—but instead result from compromises reached between agencies or legislatures and the firms that they regulate.[25] This situation arises because of the interdependence of controllers and controlled. Interdependence between two organizations means that outcomes for each are, in part, determined by the activities of the other.[26] The outcomes they reach are determined by the nature and distribution of resources between the two and the way in which the resources are used: Each has the potential to interfere with the other's activities.[27] Both have a vested interest in shaping a regulatory environment that enhances their own survival. Hence, they act in ways that maximize use of their resources to meet survival goals and minimize the other's ability to interfere with goal attainment. Since the information and wealth possessed by organizations can create obstacles to enforcement activities, agencies frequently fulfill their responsibilities through negotiation, internal proceedings, informal hearings, and mutually agreeable solutions. And business firms, similarly concerned with successful operation, soften the power of agencies by efforts to influence law-making and as a consequence, the nature of enforcement, and find equivalent gains to be had from negotiation. Compliance emerges as a product of the power-mediating efforts of both parties, as compliance demands fewer resources from both agencies and business firms than do adversarial activities to impose and thwart punitive sanctions.[28] In any given case, a course, a firm or agency may funnel all available resources into a full-fledged adversarial proceeding.[29] But when this occurs,

---

[22]Stinchcombe, *Merton's Theory of Social Structure*, in The Idea of Social Structure 11, 23–24 (L. Coser ed. 1975).

[23]R. Merton, *Anomie, Anomia, and Social Interaction: Contexts of Deviant Behavior* in Anomie and Deviant Behavior, *supra* note 5, at 235,.

[24]*Id.*

[25]Lemert, *supra* note 5, at 69.

[26]J. Pfeffer & G. Salancik, *supra* note 1, at 40–54, 113–42.

[27]*Id.*

[28]For a further explication of interdependence, with special attention to implications for social control, see D. Vaughan, *supra* note 4, at ch. 6.

[29]The recently settled IBM case provides one extreme example. *See* Gerhart, Corporate Giantism and Effective Antitrust Enforcement (Paper presented at the American Society of Criminology Annual Meetings, Philadelphia, Pa., Nov. 7–9, 1980) (on file with the *Michigan Law Review*). Gerhart notes, for example, that during the first three and a half years of trial in the monopoly case brought by the government against IBM,

the event will take place in a regulatory environment that has developed as a result of the interdependence of controllers and controlled. The institutionalized guidelines—laws, regulations, sanctions, and proceedings—have been shaped by the survival interests of both. And in many cases, these guidelines will inhibit the efforts of agencies to restrain unlawful organizational behavior in spite of their skills, resources, and commitment to an adversarial stance.

Unlawful behavior thus receives additional structural support, which aids in maintaining the pattern. The success of some organizations at attaining their goals unlawfully encourages others to follow the same path to success.[30] The absence of normative support for legitimate conduct is replaced by normative support for the illegitimate, but expedient. Carried to the extreme, norm erosion might become so extensive within an organization or subunit of an organization that unlawful conduct to attain goals occurs regardless of resource scarcity. Behavior that, if viewed by society, would be considered unlawful may come to be considered acceptable business practice and nondeviant within the organization.

As normative support for legitimate procedures for reaching organizational goals erodes, organizations motivated by the cultural emphasis on economic success and the need to survive, and unable to attain resources legitimately, may instead resort to technically expedient but unlawful behavior. Anticompetitive actions like price-fixing and discriminatory price-cutting, theft or trade secrets, false advertising, and bribery and payoffs to ensure market share could thus be described as the victimization of one organization by another to obtain resources that facilitate upward mobility in the organizational stratification system.[31] Similarly, organizations seeking either a change in economic position that will bring higher status among similarly situated organizations, or merely to maintain their economic position may also act unlawfully under these circumstances.[32]

These concepts, of course, do not explain all unlawful organizational behavior. As presented here, they are directed toward understanding the unlawful activities of profit-seeking complex organizations in the legitimate economic order.[33] The concepts fit the activities of organizations that violate the

---

the government presented fifty-one witnesses (one appearing for over a month), the trial transcript totaled 84 thousand pages, and 211,000 pages of documents were received as evidence. Equally prodigious work occurred before the trial even began. The parties took over 1300 depositions. IBM is said to have produced over 65 million pages of documents for review by the government and several private plaintiffs suing IBM, and the government produced approximately 26 million pages of documents for IBM's review, almost a million at which were copied by IBM.

    Id. at 5.

[30.]R. Merton, *supra* note 23, at 235; Stinchcombe, *supra* note 22, at 23–24.

[31]*See* Levine, *Empiricism in Victimological Research: A Critique,* 3 Victimology 77, 88 (1978).

[32]*See* R. Cloward & L. Ohlin, *supra* note 16, at 94–95.

[33]I suggested earlier, however, that the applicability of these concepts is not restricted to profit-seeking business organizations. A brief discussion at this point is worthwhile to demonstrate how other organizations may or may not be included. Three types of complex organizations

law in pursuit of culturally approved goals, broadly defined as economic success. This criterion excludes behavior that is not directed toward maximizing returns, such as violations resulting from mistakes.[34] A law or regulation may be violated because it is misunderstood, or because its existence is unknown. For other violations, such as sex discrimination in hiring, the linkage between the violation and profit-making remains a matter of empirical inquiry. Consider also violations that result from negligence. Because business firms do take risks in the name of profit, negligence may occur as a result of profit-seeking activity. If it can be determined that a firm negligently allocated resources to maximize profits at the expense of proper attention to some task, the concepts would be relevant to the organization's behavior. In this and similar situations, the inability to make the necessary empirical determinations may be a serious impediment. Nevertheless, current opinion on the link between objectives, regardless of diversity, and the need for organizations to

---

come to mind: (1) organizations designed to fail; (2) nonprofit organizations; and (3) organizations operating in the illegitimate economic order—organized crime.

Organizations designed to fail: Not all organizations seek profits. Some, in fact, are designed to accumulate losses, rather than profits. The individual owner or owners receive benefits, while the organization is the center of transactions and losses. *See* Shapiro, Detecting Illegalities: A Perspective on the Control of Securities Violations 259 (1980) (unpublished doctoral dissertation, Yale University). These organizations obviously do not fit a motivational scheme based on competition to acquire resources in order to survive.

Nonprofit Organizations: Some organizations are designed to seek neither profits nor losses (*e.g.,* churches, voluntary associations, government, state-supported universities, and community self-help organizations). Regardless of their diverse goals, they must acquire resources. In the acquisition of resources, as well as in other activities, nonprofit organizations do engage in economic activity encompassing the production, exchange, distribution, and consumption of goods and services. While necessary resources and other activities may not themselves be viewed as profits or mechanisms for obtaining profits, these organizations must maximize returns in order to exist.

Organizations operating in the illegitimate economic order: The organized crime enterprise engages in business activities that extend into both the legitimate and illegitimate economic orders. *See* J. Kwitny, Vicious Circles (1979). In both instances, organizational survival depends on the ability to maximize returns. Though the means used to seek profits may consistently be illegitimate, these organizations certainly engage in competition for economic success. The case of organized crime raises an interesting point for speculation. While the origins of organized crime may be attributed in part to blocked access to legitimate means, *see* Cloward, *Illegitimate Means, Anomie, and Deviant Behavior,* 24 Am. Soc. Rev. 164 (1959), the continued use of unlawful behavior may call for a different explanation. One principle behind organized crime is that illegitimate means have become institutionalized. Some organizations within the organized crime enterprise, therefore, may never find legitimate means blocked because once illegitimate means are institutionalized, legitimate means are abandoned. The continuation of unlawful behavior, then, may be better explained by blocked access to goals. But if one can assume that organized crime organizations are characterized by normative solidarity supporting use of illegitimate means to attain goals, these mechanisms may operate regardless of resource scarcity.

[34] Other unlawful organizational behavior that clearly does not fit within the conceptual scheme developed here includes conspiring to overthrow the government and the deprivation of members' liberty or lives by religious organizations. *See* Sherman, *Three Models of Organizational Corruption in Agencies of Social Control,* 27 Soc. Probs. 478 (1980).

maximize returns for continued existence[35] suggests that the model developed here is generally valid.

While no explanation has yet been found that encompasses all forms of organizational misconduct, the structural factors suggested in this part appear to apply to many instances of unlawful organizational behavior.[36] Admittedly, no single paradigm can serve as a tool for investigating the entire range of intriguing questions concerning organizational misconduct. A psychological explanation, for example, may provide acceptable answers to some questions.[37] Nonetheless, thinking about organizations in terms of structural pressures to engage in unlawful behavior explains a good deal of what is known and surmised about the phenomenon in question. The extent to which the fit is true, though, must be verified empirically.

II. OPPORTUNITIES FOR UNLAWFUL CONDUCT

While the social structure may produce tensions for organizations to seek desired resources by illegal methods, unlawful behavior cannot be explained by these structural tensions alone. Opportunities must be available to obtain resources unlawfully.[38] Opportunities to attain resources unlawfully but through legitimate mechanisms are inherent in all complex organizations operating in the legitimate economic order because of the nature of organizational processes and structure. Created for the purpose of conducting legitimate business activity, these same factors may also promote unlawful behavior by providing normative support for illegality, providing resources for carrying out illegal acts, and minimizing the risk of detection and sanctioning. As a consequence,

---

[35] See F. Scherer, *supra* note 8, at 38. For discussions of the methodologically based controversy on the diverse goals of organizations, see R. Hall, Organizations 94–96 (1972); Perrow, *The Analysis of Goals in Complex Organizations*, 26 Am. Soc. Rev. 854, 859–66)1961).

[36] See, e.g., C. Stone, Where the Law Ends 35–69 (1975); Geis, *supra* note 21; Gross, *Organizational Crime: A Theoretical Perspective*, in Studies in Symbolic Interaction 55 (N. Denzin ed. 1978); Staw & Szwajkowski, *supra* note 1; Vaughan, *Crime Between Organizations: Implications for Victimology*, in White-Collar Crime 77 (G. Geis & E. Stotland eds. 1980); D. Vaughan, *supra* note 4.

[37] See, e.g., Coffee, *supra* note 7, at 393–400, for an explanation of organizational unlawfulness which stresses the interrelation between psychological and structural influences. Discussing the pressures on middle-level managers. Professor Coffee observed:
> The middle manager is acutely aware that he can be easily replaced; he knows that if he cannot achieve a quick fix, another manager is waiting in the wings, eager to assume operational control over a division. The results of such a structure are predictable: When pressure is intensified, illegal or irresponsible means become attractive to a desperate middle manager who has no recourse against a astern but myopic notion of accountability that looks only to the bottom line of the income statement.

Id. at 398. See E. Shorris, The Oppressed Middle: The Politics of Middle Management (1981); Getschow, Overdriven Execs: Some Middle Managers Cut Corners to Achieve High Corporate Goals, Wall St. J., Nov. 8, 1979, at 1, col. 6; Editorial, Why Managers Cheat, Bus. Week, Mar. 17, 1980, at 196.

[38] See R. Cloward & L. Ohlin, *supra* note 16.

organizations may respond to blocked access to desired resources by turning to the opportunities within their own boundaries to attain them unlawfully.

Organizational characteristics have frequently been hypothesized to encourage unlawful organizational behavior.[39] The factors examined have included firm longevity, product diversification, financial performance, geographic expansion, market power, and size.[40] What these characteristics have in common is that they are researchable—this information is publicly available, through corporate financial statements and mandatory agency filing requirements. But, other organizational characteristics—processes and structure that are internal and, therefore, more elusive for research purposes—play an important role in the unlawful conduct of business firms and may complicate the findings concerning those factors that have been studied. Organizational size, for example, has been the most frequently investigated factor thought to be related to violations that are committed by one organization against another.[41] The larger the organization, it has been hypothesized, the more frequent the violations. The evidence, however, has been contradictory. Perhaps a more satisfactory hypothesis is that it is not simply size per se that facilitates the unlawful conduct, but the complexity of the internal processes and structure that *accompany* increased size that explains the behavior.[42]

This Part examines how structure and processes create opportunities for organizations to act as offenders. Before turning to this topic, I want to make three points. First, these same factors create an arena where individuals may readily engage in misconduct that is in their own interests, separate and distinct from the interest of the organization. Second, the opportunities inherent in business firms not only create the potential for an organization to engage in unlawful conduct, but also promote the possibility that an organization will be victimized—by other organizations as well as by its own members. Finally, although these same opportunities exist in general form for all organizations, the conditions and combinations of factors that do or do not result in unlawful behavior cannot yet be unraveled. They cannot, therefore, be discussed in the language of causality, but rather as factors that facilitate, generate, encourage, or present opportunities to obtain resources through unlawful conduct.

A. Organizational Processes

Processes are the dynamics of organizational life that affect individual members. While introducing the notion of organizations as actors is legitimate and

---

[39] *See, e.g.,* C. Stone, *supra* note 36; Gross, *supra* note 36.

[40] *See, e.g.,* M. Clinard & P. Yeager, Corporate Crime (1980); Perez, Corporate Criminality: A Study of the One-Thousand Largest Industrial Corporations in the U.S.A. (1978) (unpublished doctoral dissertation, University of Pennsylvania).

[41] *See, e.g.,* M. Clinard & P. Yeager, *supra* note 40; M. Clinard, P. Yeager, J. Brissette, D. Petrashek & E. Harries, *supra* note 1, Asch & Seneca, *supra* note 1; Perez, *supra* note 40.

[42] Though not addressing organizational misconduct, R. Hall, supra note 35, at 171, also states that complexity may be more important than size alone in understanding organizational behavior.

effectively accounts for certain actions, organizations must rely on individuals to act as their agents. To describe properly the behavior—lawful or unlawful—of organizations, therefore, we need an explanation that goes beyond the goals and actions of the organization to the nexus of the goals and actions of the organization and the goals and actions of its members.[43] This necessity draws attention to the internal processes of organizations and to the normative environment that results.

It is common knowledge that organizations selectively recruit new members who in many ways match those already there. But individuals come to business firms influenced by their affiliations with other organizations: families, churches, clubs, schools, trade unions, and previous employers. Because business firms depend on their members to attain goals, they must ensure that members' skills, motivations, and values are consistent with the organization's needs. To the extent that members subscribe to, support, and are willing and able to pursue organizational interests, the firm's chances for survival are enhanced.

The existence of these important characteristics of members is, not surprisingly, rarely left to chance. As Selznick has noted, "the more esoteric the activities of the organization, the less it can rely on the general education provided by the community, and the greater the need for internal orientation."[44] Most organizations, therefore, subject new recruits to education and training. Skills are taught, sharpened, and adjusted to meet organizational needs through both formal and informal mechanisms: training classes, apprenticeships, peer groups, and mentoring. Integral to the mechanisms operating to develop these skills are systematic socialization processes that attune members ideologically to the organization's goals.

Educational and training programs are supplemented, and perhaps eventually superseded, by an internal reward system incorporating both remuneration and prestige. The rewards are often formal, tangible, and obvious to other employees and even outsiders: promotion, bonuses, salary increases, profit-sharing, parking privileges, expense accounts, gold watches, company cars, employee-of-the-month awards, attractive offices, and assistants. In other cases, the rewards are informal and not so obvious, but are powerful incentives, especially in the upper echelon, because of their long-term impact on a career. Use of first names, inclusion in after-hours get-togethers with management officials, or an invitation to play golf with the boss reward the employee with admission to the informal organization of the firm. Behavior inconsistent with organizational goals typically leads to negative sanctions. These, too, can be formal—loss of parking privileges, a lateral transfer, or a shift to a dead-end position—or informal—exclusion from the boss's golfing clique. The ultimate sanction, of course, is a resignation or firing.

---

[43] Coleman, *Legitimate and Illegitimate Uses of Power,* in The Idea of Social Structure, *supra* note 22, at 221, 234–35.
[44] P. Selznick, The Organizational Weapon 36 (1960).

Large organizations, moreover, tend increasingly to absorb members, while at the same time insulating them from the outside world.[45] Skills and language for a particular task may be so specialized that an employee cannot find similar work in other organizations. Members with no alternative skills are tied to the firm by financial dependence. Accumulated retirement benefits and delayed remuneration also encourage long-term commitments to organizations. Profit-sharing not only encourages long-term commitments, but gives the individual a stake in the system. The luster of future financial rewards binds members to the organization like a pair of golden handcuffs, securing their continued affiliation with the firm. And recreational activities, committee work, company cafeterias and corporate dining rooms, long hours, special projects, and frequent transfers separate an organization's members from the outside community and foster a dependence on the organization that is social, as well as financial.

In these and other ways, the needs of the individual member eventually become linked to the organization's success. Because a primary criterion of individuals' status in highly modernized societies is the social status of the organizations to which they belong,[46] the individual identifies with the organization and the organization's goals. The organization's ability to attain desired resources affects the ability of members to be upwardly mobile, to improve their economic position while remaining in the same social class, or simply to preserve their existing position. Because the interests of members and organizations coincide, employees may engage in unlawful behavior in the organization's behalf, using the skills, knowledge, and resources associated with their position to do so.

Organizational processes, then, create an internal moral and intellectual world in which the individual identifies with the organization and the organization's goals. The survival of one becomes linked to the survival of the other, and a normative environment evolves that, given difficulty in attaining organizational goals, encourages illegal behavior to attain those goals. But some finer distinctions must be made. Not all agents of an organization will act illegally in the organization's behalf. The nature of the response—lawful or unlawful behavior—will be shaped by structural factors both internal and external to the organization.[47] While organizations may experience structural tensions to violate, variation in subunit membership,[48] position in the information system,[49] and in rewards and punishments[50] may undermine the organization's ability to unify the goals and actions of its members with its own goals and actions, producing either deviance or conformity to legal norms.[51]

---

[45] D. Margolis, The Managers: Corporate Life in America 41–66, 93–116 (1979).
[46] See Stinchcombe, *supra* note 17, at 164–80.
[47] Stinchcombe, *supra* note 22, at 17–23.
[48] *Id.*
[49] *Id.*
[50] See Lemert, *supra* note 5, at 70–73; Stinchcombe, *supra* note 22, at 17–18.
[51] Lemert, *supra* note 5, at 73–75.

Subunit membership Tensions to attain resources unlawfully differentially affect the various parts of the organization. The subunits with skills and resources most relevant to profit-seeking goals are most likely to be affected. Because of the many and changing goals of organizations, the subunits affected may vary over time, and some may never experience such tensions. Members of subunits not subject to these tensions will not be motivated to engage in illegal behavior in the organization's behalf.

Position in the information system Though working in a subunit that is experiencing tensions to act unlawfully, members without information about necessary resources and difficulties in attaining them will not be motivated to act illegally in the organization's behalf. For unlawful behavior to occur, the member's position must provide access to information regarding the organization's goals as they relate to the activities of the subunit in which the member is employed. The position, moreover, must entail some responsibility for goal attainment. Finally, the position must provide skills and resources that allow the individual to resolve the organization's difficulties.[52]

Rewards and punishments Even if subunit membership and position in the information system create tensions to engage in unlawful behavior in the organization's behalf, members thus situated may not do so. Norms and values learned through association with other organizations (both formal and informal) may compete with and contradict those learned while in the firm.[53] Should the norms be contradictory, members will make choices in accordance with the rewards and punishments accompanying the various alternatives.[54] Members will weigh the possibility of gaining rewards against the possibility of incurring punishment.

As the rewards and punishments accompanying the alternatives vary, the patterns of individual choice will vary.[55] Should the firm's rewards for gaining the desired resources outweigh the perceived costs of pursuing them unlawfully, members may commit violations on behalf of the organization despite competing norms. Again, position in the information system is relevant, for information flows affect the probability that rewards and punishments—both internal and external to the organization—will be meted out.[56] The significance of the organization's rewards and punishments, moreover, will vary as the individual's dependence on the firm varies. Alternative skills, alternative sources of income, and alternative validating social roles reduce financial and social dependence on the firm.[57] Consequently, external rewards and punish-

---

[52] *See* note 37 *supra.*
[53] Lemert, *supra* note 5, at 62–71.
[54] *Id.* at 70–73; Stinchcombe, *supra* note 22, at 17.
[55] As Lemert has noted, "[c]osts are important variables in analysis because changes in the costs of means can modify the order of choices, even though the 'ideal' value order of the individual remains constant." Lemert, *supra* note 5, at 63.
[56] Stinchcombe, *supra* note 22, at 21.
[57] P. Blau, Exchange and Power in Social Life 119–25, 140–42 (1964).

ments may reduce the organization's ability to mobilize individual efforts in its behalf, despite processes that produce a normative environment supporting unlawful conduct.

Although all organizations create normative environments that join the goals and actions of members to those of the firm, to assert that organizational processes produce a fertile atmosphere for illegality obscures the complexity that exists. The degree to which an organization experiences pressures to act unlawfully varies not only by subunit, but within subunits, and over time. The ability and willingness of members to act illegally in the organization's behalf depend on the subunit in which they work, their position in the information system, and the weighing of rewards and punishments. These factors may not only generate lawful conduct in the face of organizational pressures to violate, but may generate unlawful conduct despite a normative environment that supports compliance with legal norms. It is important to recognize, therefore, that the normative environment generated by organizational processes will have a variable relationship to unlawful conduct, and that the problem of measurement remains a powerful obstacle to a complete understanding of the relationship between internal environment and behavior.

B. Organizational Structure

The structure of complex organizations creates opportunities by providing many settings where unlawful behavior might occur, and by isolating those settings where unlawful behavior might occur, and by isolating those settings and masking organizational behavior. Size and the complexity that frequently accompanies size provide many locations in which unlawful behavior might take place. As organizations grow larger, specialized subunits result, each providing opportunities to engage in unlawful behavior on the organization's behalf. Not only are organizations internally diversified in ways that multiply the possible settings for illegality, but many organizations are geographically dispersed, with locations throughout the United States and the world, greatly expanding the number of locations in which unlawful behavior might occur.

These specialized subunits compete for resources with other organizations and with each other.[58] The need for a subunit to outperform other organizations, other units within the same organization, or even its own previous record to secure resources from the parent organization may generate illegality, such as falsification of records, or theft of trade secrets. Subunits' concerns about their own survival may or may not coincide with the interest of the larger organization, and if given an opportunity to exercise discretion, lower-level managers will tend to act not to maximize the firm's welfare, but rather

---

[58] For a dramatic example of intra-organizational competition, see Coffee, *Beyond the Shut-Eyed Sentry: Toward a Theoretical View of Corporate Misconduct and an Effective Legal Response*, 63 Va. L. Rev. 1099, 1135 (1977) (reporting a case where "two wholly owned subsidiaries of U.S. Steel . . . actively lobbied with regard to proposed legislation, *but on opposite sides*") (emphasis in original).

to enhance the interest of their own unit or division.[59] In a recent book on the internal workings of General Motors, for example, the corporation's continual competition with the Ford Motor Company bears striking similarities to the description of the rivalry between two divisions of General Motors, Chevrolet and Pontiac, as well as to the adversarial relationship between the divisions of the company and their respective dealers.[60]

Specialization not only generates opportunities for unlawful behavior by increasing the locations where it might occur, but also by obscuring organizational behavior, lawful and unlawful. Task segregation cloaks activities. No one individual or group can command all the knowledge pertaining to particular operations, materials, or technology.[61] This serves a protective function for the organization, increasing its ability to survive despite information leakage or personnel turnover.[62] The secrecy generated by task segregation, however, also creates the opportunity for misconduct. Specialization creates problems of coordination and control. Consequently, organizations develop rules and procedures to handle the various internal contingencies the organization faces by specifying how, when, and by whom tasks are to be performed.[63] The rules and procedures are expressed in a language common to all subunits of an organization, symbolically integrating the various parts. They seek not only to control and coordinate activities, but also to facilitate the systematic exchange of information that is necessary for decision-making.

Though directed toward integrating the separate parts of the organization, the potential for rules and procedures to achieve internal coordination and control varies considerably. Progressive loss of control over subunits seems to be a natural consequence of organizational growth. Structure interferes with the efforts of those at the top to "know" the behavior of the diverse parts by obscuring activity at other levels.[64] As the organization grows, and as the distance between subordinate units and those at the top likewise grows, "authority leakage" develops.[65] Authority leakage conveys an image of an or-

---

[59] O. Williamson, Markets and Hierarchies 125 (1975); O. Williamson, Corporate Control and Business Behavior 47–52 (1970) [hereinafter cited as Corporate Control]; Coffee, *supra* note 58, at 1135–36; Perrow, *The Analysis of Goals in Complex Organizations*, 26 Am. Soc. Rev. 854 (1961).

[60] J. Wright, On A Clear Day You Can See General Motors 73–97 (1979).

[61] Technology is used here to encompass operations technology, materials technology, and knowledge technology. *See* Hickson, Pugh & Pheysey, *Operations Technology and Organization Structure: An Empirical Reappraisal*, 14 Ad. Sci. Q. 378 (1969).

[62] *See* D. Nelson, Managers and Workers (1975).

[63] *See* R. Hall, *supra* note 35, at 173, 196.

[64] *See* Gouldner, *Reciprocity and Autonomy in Functional Theory*, in Symposium on Sociological Theory 241 (L. Gross ed. 1959); Weick, *Educational Organizations as Loosely Coupled Systems*, 21 Ad. Sci Q. 1 (1976).

[65] Studying governmental bureaucracies in the 1960's, Gordon Tullock observed the phenomenon of "authority leakage." He described this as a progressive loss of control over subordinate units within the same bureaucracy as the organization expanded and the distance between such units and those at the agency's top became greater. Subsequently, another student of bureaucracies, Anthony Downs, formalized Tullock's perception into a general law, the "Law of Diminishing Control," which states: "The larger any organization becomes, the weaker is the control over its actions exercised by those at the top." Both Downs and Tullock found one underlying cause of

ganization that has, by reason of increased size, hierarchical authority system, and specialization, become so unwieldy that the upper levels cannot control the subunits. The organization, in short, can diversify beyond the capability of those at the top to master it.

Authority leakage allows an organizational subunit—a subsidiary, the accounting division, or the research and development branch, for example—to engage in a fraudulent transaction with another organization and ensures that no countervailing intra-organizational authority can prevent or control the unlawful behavior. Specialized knowledge further complicates this problem. In an organization with highly specialized subunits, one may lack the expertise to detect ongoing violations in another. Interestingly, subgoal pursuit and authority leakage may also lead to *compliance* with legal standards in the face of organization pressures to violate. Nevertheless, these characteristics also should be considered as factors that may generate opportunities for violation.

Implicit in the concept of authority leakage is that an organization should be able to control its subunits. It might be thought, therefore, that authority leakage could occur only when an organization is operating irrationally or ineffectually, and that if a firm were operating in best form, information would flow smoothly (and accurately) from bottom to top and vice versa, maximizing the possibility of control. This notion is contradicted by both research and theory.[66] The result that may in some cases be described as inefficient or irrational behavior may thus in others be the rational institutionalization of systematic censorship procedures by those controlling the flow of information.[67]

While authority leakage is a consequence of structure that focuses attention on the inability of those at the top to control the organizational bureaucracy, systematic censorship procedures can originate at *any* point in the hierarchy and mask behavior throughout the organization. Units at the top may thus be encouraged to engage in unlawful conduct not only by their structural isolation, but also by systematic censorship of information that obscures misconduct from others. Furthermore, the hierarchical authority structure diffuses personal responsibility for decision-making throughout the organization.

---

this progressive paralysis to be the ease with which generalized orders and nonspecific policies imposed at the top could be successively reinterpreted, distorted, or qualified as the commands filtered downward through the organization.

Coffee, *supra* note 58, at 1136–37 (footnotes omitted). *See* A. Downs, Inside Bureaucracy 143 (1966); Corporate Control, *supra* note 59, at 26; G. Tullock, The Politics of Bureaucracy 142–93 (1965).

[66]*See* J. Emery, Organizational Planning and Control Systems 24–48 (1969); Coffee, *supra* note 58, at 1137–39.

[67]*See* K. Arrow, The Limits of Organization 73–75 (1974); C. Stone, *supra* note 36, at 43–44; Corporate Control, *supra* note 59, at 22, 25–26; Coffee, *supra* note 58, at 1134–47. Coffee points to the Theory of Cognitive Dissonance, which "simply states the much-observed phenomenon that recipients of information unconsciously focus on and relay only the information that reinforces their preexisting attitudes, while filtering out conflicting information." *Id.* at 1137. *See* L. Festinger, A Theory of Cognitive Dissonance (1957); M. Rokeach; The Open and Closed Mind (1960). For more recent revisions of this theory, see I. Janis & L. Mann, Decision Making 15–16, 82–85, 420 n.3 (1977).

Determining where within an organization a decision was made is difficult.[68] As a result, "[t]he delegation of responsibility and unwritten orders keep those at the top of the corporate structure remote from the consequences of their decisions and orders, much as the heads of organized crime families remain 'untouchable' by the law."[69] . . .

Characteristics and Sources of White-Collar Crime

NICOLE LEEPER PIQUERO AND ALEX PIQUERO

Investigators have outlined a number of theoretical models to account for white-collar offending including, among others, rational choice (Paternoster and Simpson, 1993; Cohen and Simpson, 1997), and integrative theories (Coleman, 1987; Finney and Lesieur, 1982; Braithwaite, 1989), as well as organizational strain perspectives (Vaughan, 1997; Simpson and Koper, 1997). These approaches have focused on both micro (Simpson et al., 1998) and macro levels (Vaughan, 1983, 1996) of analysis, and have exploited both quantitative (Clinard and Yeager, 1978; Weisburd et al., 1991) and qualitative approaches (Geis, 1967; Vaughan, 1983, 1996). While theorists and empiricists sometimes disagree about the meaning and interpretation of this line of research, all scholars agree that the breadth of white-collar crime, and the costs associated with such crimes, is worthy of continued and furthered empirical attention with an eye toward exploring and uncovering the sources and characteristics of white-collar and corporate offending. This is especially important, since the counting and recording of the number, sources, and characteristics associated with white-collar and corporate crimes are limited (Cohen, 1992; Simpson et al., 1993; Wellford and Ingraham, 1994).

INDIVIDUAL LEVEL

Sources

Opportunities to commit crime are differentially distributed within organizations; some opportunities are available to a range of individuals, while certain opportunities are made available only to individuals who hold positions of power. Nevertheless, while *some* type of opportunity to engage in *some* type

---

[68] For an extended discussion of how this organizational characteristic relates to legal issues of responsibility for organizational behavior, see C. Stone, *supra* note 36, at 60–69.

[69] J. Conklin, "Illegal But Not Criminal" 65 (1977).

PANEL 17   Violent Corporate Crime

On July 23, 1998, Odwalla, Inc., a juice manufacturer, pleaded guilty to 16 misdemeanor charges of delivering "adulterated food products for introduction into interstate commerce" and agreed to pay $1.5 million in fines, the highest criminal fine ever levied in a food-injury case. The company also was given five years probation. The adulterated product was unpasteurized apple juice containing a toxic form of the bacterium *E. coli.* In October 1996, 14 children became ill with a life-threatening kidney ailment, and a 16-month-old Colorado girl died after drinking the contaminated juice. It was reported that a safety inspector at Odwalla's Dinube, California, factory wanted to reject a load of the defective fruit but was overruled. It was thought by Odwalla officials that the bacteria could not survive in the acidic apple juice.

Sources: Denver Rocky Mountain News, July 24, 1998, p. 1A; *Denver Post,* July 24, 1998, p. B1; *Denver Rocky Mountain News,* July 27, 1998, p. 31A.

---

of white-collar or corporate crime is typically available, opportunities for the most serious forms of white-collar crime are quite limited.

Even with the availability of opportunities, however, not all individuals will recognize, much less act upon, the opportunities they encounter (Simpson, 1986; Sutherland, 1949; Clinard and Yeager, 1980). So, what separates those individuals who recognize and act on opportunities from those who do not? In other words, what motivates certain people to seize criminal opportunities that others would dare not think of?

Dennis Levine (1991:390), a former insider trader, characterized his seizing of opportunities like this: "Something deep inside me forced me to try to catch up to the pack of wheeler-dealers who always raced in front of me. . . . It was only in time that I came to view myself as an insider trading junkie. I was addicted to the excitement, the sense of victory." Stone (1990:45) also reports of a similar adrenaline rush enjoyed by Michael Milken and those who worked with him. The pursuit of fun and excitement that swept Levine into insider trading and Milken into junk bond trading is central to the reward component of rational choice models of criminal offending (Paternoster and Simpson, 1993) and is akin to the excitement described by offenders of various criminal domains (Katz, 1988; Wright and Decker, 1994, 1997; Nagin and Paternoster, 1993; Piliavin et al., 1986; Piquero and Tibbetts, 1996).

Much of what we know about motivation comes from the rational choice perspective. A premier example of this perspective has been advanced by Raymond Paternoster and Sally Simpson (1993, 1996). These scholars argue that individuals weigh the expected benefits from committing a crime against the expected costs. Costs include formal sanctions (probability of detection, severity of punishment), informal sanctions (loss of reputation for both the individual and the company and self-respect), and the cost of executing the crime (i.e., time, energy, know-how). Benefits include, among others, increased income, higher status within the organization, the thrill of engaging in the act, obtaining market share, and reducing organizational expenses. Opportunity is important in the rational choice model, as it varies by type of corporation and position of employment within the corporation.

In general, results from a series of studies employing hypothetical, third-person vignettes administered to business students and managers, suggest that white-collar workers are deterred by sanction threats and moral inhibitions. However, the opposite is true regarding the perceived benefit of offending: Individuals who see some gain in committing an offense are more likely than others to seize the opportunity and engage in criminal activity (e.g., Paternoster and Simpson, 1996; Simpson et al., 1998; Elis and Simpson, 1995).

Research employing other methodological techniques reach very similar conclusions. For example, Stanton Wheeler (1992:112) found that greed (i.e., one example of the pleasure component of the rational choice model) motivates people to engage in white-collar crime. In addition, he found that fear of losing what one already has (nice salaries and lifestyles) serves as an inhibitory factor in preventing white-collar crime. In this case, the commission of a white-collar crime serves to maintain their position in the corporate world (Weisburd et al., 1991:224). In another study, Dowie (1979:26) reported that executives of the Ford Motor Company in the 1970s decided to design and build the Pinto with a defective rear assembly in spite of their knowledge that even minor rear-end collisions would cause death, injury, and burned vehicles. Spending the $11 per vehicle that it would cost to correct the defect, they reasoned, would cut into profits and impair their competitive position. Similarly, in their seminal work on the Savings and Loans Crisis, Calavita and Pontell (1990:327) reported a variety of instances of coverup after crimes were committed. These actions can be considered examples of proactive detection avoidance. In sum, a focus on an individuals' self-interest, a central feature of other criminological theories (Gottfredson and Hirschi, 1990), appears to be a useful predictor of white-collar offending at the individual level.

Characteristics

Perhaps the best empirical description of white-collar offender characteristics has come from the research of David Weisburd and his colleagues (1991). In their detailed study of PSI's (presentence investigations), these authors examined the characteristics of several hundred individuals convicted of various forms of white-collar crime in seven districts throughout the 1970s. Although their analysis could do little to explore the motivation behind white-collar offending (Weisburd et al., 1991:188), they were able to provide several important findings regarding demographic characteristics of the offenders.

First, organizational complexity[1] was associated with white-collar crime. Second, they found that organizational complexity exerted different effects that were contingent on the level of offense. Third, their research revealed that individuals at the top of the serious crime list: (1) were middle-aged white males with stable employment in white-collar occupations, (2) were not owners or officers in their companies, (3) had college degrees, and (d) were well above average in socioeconomic status.

The importance of organizational position cannot be overstated. The most consequential of all white-collar crimes in terms of scope, impact, and costs appear to require for their commission that their perpetrators be well versed in the operational environment, know the key players within their own company as well as in other companies, and know the ebb and flow of money transactions. The key factor, then, is location in the organizational structure. Those who have positions as managers, officers, or owners are better suited to commit the most serious of all white-collar offenses because of the intimate knowledge of the business they possess (Weisburd et al., 1991:60–61).

More often than not, individuals occupying these powerful positions are educated, middle-class, white males. Since very few women occupy positions at the top of the hierarchy, they do not encounter the opportunities to engage in serious offenses. Thus it should come as no surprise that women comprise a large proportion of those arrested for embezzlement and fraud, since they are likely to occupy positions wherein opportunities for such crimes are commonplace. Thus offender traits such as social class, ethnicity, educational status, and gender are related to white-collar offending because these characteristics provide access to opportunities.

In this vein, Daly's (1989) analysis of the data of Weisburd et al. revealed that the women offenders were younger, less educated, and nonwhite; owned fewer economic assets; and had lower-status positions and incomes than their male counterparts. In addition, women were overwhelmingly under-represented among those charged with the two offenses that are most likely to be corporate crimes, antitrust and SEC violations. Almost all (98%) individuals charged with these violations were male; in contrast, 45% of those charged with bank embezzlement were female. Interestingly, the women charged with bank embezzlement were more likely to be bank tellers, whereas the men were more likely to be bank officers or financial managers.[2]

---

[1] Organizational complexity was defined on a scale that included offenses that: (1) have a discernable pattern, (2) use organizational resources, (3) are committed by a number of conspirators, and (4) take place over long periods of time (Weisburd et al., 1991:39).

[2] These findings raise the provocative hypothesis that once women occupy such positions, their involvement in serious white-collar crimes will mimic those engaged in by males (Weisburd et al., 1991). However, we cannot assume that men and women in the same occupational position are

Similar accounts of position and opportunity are relevant for race and age. For example, since there are few persons of color in high-level positions, members of minority groups are unlikely to engage in serious white-collar offending (see Weisburd et al., 1991:83). Similarly, the fact that many white-collar offenders are middle-aged is likely due to the normative status that age brings to the white-collar table. With age, argue Weisburd and his colleagues (1991), come special opportunities to develop social networks within organizations that can last over long periods of time. These networks are built and developed by a mutual trust and credibility.

In sum, one's structural position within an organization can determine an array of opportunities that are not afforded to all members of the organization. Vaughan (1983:85; see also Cloward and Ohlin, 1960) makes this point explicitly clear: "Because of task segregation in organizations, not all members have equal access to all opportunities (i.e., fix prices). Because members are differentially located in the organization by position, the motivation to engage in unlawful conduct will vary, and consequently the form of the violation will vary." As such, it appears that individual demographic characteristics are related to white-collar crime primarily as a function of structural position (and hence opportunity to offend) within the organization. Thus it is no surprise that white, college-educated, males are likely to engage in the most serious white-collar crimes because they are likely to hold positions that afford them the opportunities needed to undertake such acts (Weisburd et al., 1991).

ORGANIZATIONAL LEVEL

Sources

Why do some organizations, some of them powerhouses in their respective industries, engage in unlawful behavior?[3] Evidence for this is available on both

---

necessarily presented with the same opportunities for white-collar crime. Box (1983) argues that female workers are more closely supervised than males in the same job, and hence may have fewer opportunities. Taken in the context of findings showing that women managers are often excluded from the social networks of their male colleagues (Kanter, 1977), more research should be undertaken to examine the complex interaction between gender and opportunity to offend (see Zager, 1994). Even further, little research has explored gender differences in the motivation of white-collar criminals (Coleman, 1998:210–211). What we do know is that men and women appear to use different rationalizations in justifying their white-collar crimes. Zietz's (1981) study of embezzlers shows gender differences in reasons behind female criminality compared to Cressey's (1976) male embezzlers.

[3]To be sure, the motivation for organizational offending is not always profitability (Clinard and Yeager, 1978). Sometimes corporations attempt to shape external conditions, while other times they are concerned with size, stability, and prestige.

quantitative and qualitative levels. Across a number of quantitative studies, Sally Simpson (1986, 1987) has garnered much information as to what leads to and what prevents organizational offending. In one study, Simpson and Koper (1997) examined the antitrust offending of 46 U.S. manufacturing firms between 1963 and 1984 and found that offending levels were highest when firms were headed by CEOs from finance and administrative backgrounds, had prior offending backgrounds, and pursued product-dominant strategies. In another study, these same authors (Simpson and Koper, 1992) found that recidivism among antitrust companies was negatively related to the severity of the sanction, suggesting that corporate crime might be the outcome of a rational cost–benefit calculation, a finding that mimics research at the individual level.[4] Finally, in their most recent work, Simpson and Koper (1997) focused on international organizational characteristics and their relationship to antitrust offending. They found that CEOs from certain subunits (finance and administration) increased company involvement in antitrust offending. In addition, top management succession, with a new CEO coming on board, lessened offending levels.

Some of the most important qualitative work in this area has been carried out by Diane Vaughan. For some time, she has engaged in a program of in-depth, qualitative research that has attempted to explore the sources of organization offending in Revco Drug Stores (Vaughan, 1983), as well as within a branch of the federal government, NASA (Vaughan, 1996). She has linked a number of organizational characteristics to corporate offending including: firm longevity, product diversification, financial performance, geographic expansion, market power, and size.

Nevertheless, an interesting interplay occurs within organizations because most of them subject new recruits to education and training to meet organizational needs through both formal and informal mechanisms. New members are then attuned ideologically to the organization's goals (Vaughan, 1983:69). According to Blundell (1976), corporations can and do create a moral tone that influences the thinking, conduct, values, and even the personalities of the people who work for them. To the extent that this organizational culture is centered around illegality (Clinard and Yeager, 1978), individuals working for the corporation may be eased into an "established way of life" (Geis, 1973:109), equipped with all the rationalizations necessary to engage in crime.

In sum, the hierarchical structure of large corporations, and the diffusion of responsibility that arises out of the hierarchical structure, foster conditions conducive to deviance at the organizational level (Clinard and Yeager, 1978). Given the size of large corporations, decision-making has to be delegated to

---

[4]Other research has supported the inhibiting effect of government-supported enforcement activities (Cohen, 1987; Magat and Viscusi, 1990; Block et al., 1981).

various points throughout the organization, thereby creating the opportunity that many decisions go unchecked.

Characteristics

Unlike the individual-level research, much less is known about the characteristics of organizational offending. One consistent finding since Sutherland's (1949) seminal work has been that some major companies engage in various sorts of offending, and a good portion of these same companies are recidivistic offenders (Ross, 1980; Simpson and Koper, 1992; Clinard and Yeager, 1978; Sutherland, 1949). This finding replicates research on individual-level criminal careers in general (Wolfgang et al., 1972), and individual-level criminal careers in white-collar offending in particular (Weisburd, Chayet, and Waring, 1990).

For example, in their ground-breaking work, Clinard and Yeager (1978) calculated the number of criminal, civil, and administrative actions either initiated or completed by 25 federal agencies against the 477 largest publically owned manufacturing corporations in the United States during 1975 and 1976. They found that approximately 3/5 of the corporations had at least one action initiated against them. Interestingly, 8% of the corporations in the sample accounted for 52% of all violations charged in 1975–1976, an average of 23.5 violations per firm. In particular, large corporations (those corporations with annual sales of $1 billion or more) accounted for almost 3/4 of all violations, an average of 5.1 total violations, 3.0 of them serious or moderate (Clinard and Yeager, 1980).[5]

Moreover, these authors found that certain industries are more conducive to crime (see also Cressey 1976; Riedel 1968). They reported that oil, pharmaceutical, and motor vehicle industries were among the most chronic offenders. In fact, the oil industry accounted for 17.3% of all sanctions, an over-representation likely due to oil spills (Clinard and Yeager, 1980:121). Disproportionate percentages were found for environmental, manufacturing, administrative, and labor violations. Interestingly, within the two-year period studied by Clinard and Yeager, one firm had 54 environmental cases brought against it (p. 117).

More recent industry-specific studies also confirm Clinard and Yeager's

---

[5]This is not to say that white collar offending is relegated solely to large corporations. In her study of white collar offending in the form of consumer violations, Croall (1989) found that a substantial portion of white collar offenders were typically small businesses (i.e., individual food stores, restaurants, butchers, meat suppliers, market traders, and corner ships). She attributes the over-representation of small businesses in her sample to their inability, relative to larger corporations, of being immune from prosecution. As such, Croall (1989:158) cautions that reliance on formal enforcement data may reflect enforcement decisions rather than 'real' crime rates.

industry-concentration deviance finding. A 1985 General Accounting Office study of the top 100 defense contractors found that half of the firms had been the subject of criminal investigations by the Justice Department between 1982 and 1985. The cases involved varied offenses such as procurement fraud, overcharging, defective products, and conflicts of interest. Finally, 28 of the 100 contractors had been the target of multiple investigations (GAO, 1994). A 1992 study conducted by the Securities and Exchange Commission investigated trading practices at 161 branch offices of 9 large brokerage firms, the latter which accounted for 49% of all customer accounts in the United States. The SEC reported instances of excessive trading, unsuitable recommendations, unauthorized trading, and improper mutual fund switching at one-quarter of the offices it examined (GAO, 1994). In 8 of 14 offices of one of the firms studied, the SEC uncovered routine broker misconduct in the handling of elderly client accounts (Rosoff et al., 1998:15).

In another study, Jamieson (1994) collected data on antitrust case filings between 1981 and 1985 against companies listed in the 1985 Fortune 500. She found that alleged violators were over-represented in the petroleum industry, followed by the chemical and allied products industry. To explain involvement in antitrust offending, she relied on available information about internal characteristics of the corporation, including the number of employees, the ratio of nonmanagement staff to total employees, and the mean number of subsidiaries owned by the organization. She was also able to measure several environmental characteristics that were external to the corporation including five-year mean profit, absolute company profit, industry profit, relative profit (i.e., profit standing of the firm relative to the industry), and industry concentration with the expectation that serious violators will be found more frequently in highly concentrated markets than in less concentrated markets (Hay and Kelley, 1974).

Several findings from Jamieson's study are noteworthy. First, she found that nonviolators were generally smaller and had fewer production employees than the violator group. Second, when examining the characteristics associated with a favorable versus unfavorable charge outcome, she found that, when compared to guilty violators, nonviolating companies were smaller and had less industry profit. However, when compared to firms charged with horizontal offenses, manufacturers charged with less serious antitrust activity had greater absolute profit and greater profit in the product market involved in the conspiracy. Moreover, as the 20-firm concentration ratio increased, the more likely the firm was in the nonserious group. None of the internal structural characteristics of the corporation predicted alleged violation.

Three limitations prevent firm conclusions regarding the characteristics of offending at the corporate level. First, organizational data that tap into various theoretical characteristics, aside from objective indicators of size and earnings, are difficult to come by. Second, the data on organizational offending present a very selective sample in that most of the knowledge base at this level of analysis is a function of corporations that have been caught and sanctioned. Third, much disparity exists in how organizational characteristics influence offending across different types of corporations. Clearly, more empirical work and a cross-agency database would help scholars better understand the organizational characteristics of corporate offending.

A HIERARCHICAL UNDERSTANDING OF WHITE COLLAR CRIME

A complete understanding of the sources and characteristics of white-collar and corporate crime must not rely on one level of analysis to the exclusion of another; instead, scholars must recognize the potential usefulness of all levels of analysis, since by definition the study of white-collar crimes within organizations necessitates a hierarchical analysis. This is important for studies that examine the sources of offending *and* nonoffending.

The Savings and Loan looting can be used to highlight this multilevel perspective (Calavita and Pontell, 1990; Calavita et al., 1997). At the structural level, changes in the laws throughout the 1970s and 1980s regarding constraints on ownership and investment of thrifts created a window of opportunity for individuals (and corporations) to acquire ownership and/or managerial control of the thrifts, to bring in larger deposits, and to invest recklessly or engage in theft and fraud of the thrifts assets (Friedrichs, 1995). At the organizational level, the hierarchical structure of S&Ls allowed diffusion of responsibility across different components of the organization. At the individual level, some thrifters were risk seekers who were invested in acquiring material symbols of success.

We believe that the rational choice model of white-collar and corporate offending could be useful in the context of a multilevel process (see also Simpson et al., 1998). Rational choice identifies the main sources of corporate and white-collar offending as a result of decisions made by managers and individuals within an organization. Moreover, rational choice is also informed by a structuralist position in that the choice of crime occurs in the context of a business organization and is influenced by organizational factors, but in- and outside of the resident organization, that may affect the costs and benefits of individual actions (Cohen and Simpson, 1997:33).[6] As such, corporate leaders are able to persuade their subordinates to engage in illegal activities, often without ordering them to do so, because their position in the organization gives them control over the rewards and punishments that are important to those below them (Coleman, 1998:195). This necessitates an understanding of the wider business culture characterized by individualism, competition, and materialism (e.g., Messner and Rosenfeld, 1997; Coleman, 1987, 1998:180–181;

---

[6]On the other hand, Ermanm and Rabe (1997) argue that organizational processes, not rational choices, produce most corporate crimes.

Jackall, 1988). We hope that students of white collar and corporate offending begin to unravel the complexities and relationships across the various levels of analysis, and continue the task of painting a portrait of the sources and characteristics of white-collar and corporate offending.

REFERENCES

Block, M. K., F. C. Nold, and J. G. Sidak (1981) The Deterrent Effect of Antitrust Enforcement. *Journal of Political Economy,* 89: 429–45.

Blundell, W. E. (1976) Equity Funding: 'I Did it for Jollies.' In *Crime At the Top,* edited by J. Johnson and J. Douglas. Lippincott: Philadelphia:

Box, S. (1983) *Power Crime and Mystification.* Tavistock: London.

Braithwaite, J. (1989) *Crime, Shame and Reintegration.* Cambridge University Press: New York.

Braithwaite, J., and B. Fisse (1990) On the Plausibility of Corporate Crime Theory. In *Advances in Criminological Theory* (Vol. 2), edited by W. S. Laufer and F. Adler. Transaction Publishers: New Brunswick.

Calavita, K., and H. N. Pontell (1990) Heads I Win, Tails You Lose: Deregulation, Crime, and Crisis in the Savings and Loan Industry. *Crime & Delinquency,* 55: 309–41.

Calavita, K., H. N. Pontell, and R. Tillman (1997) *Big Money Crime: Fraud and Politics in the Savings and Loan Crisis.* University of California Press: Berkeley.

Clinard, M. B., and P. C. Yeager (1978) Corporate Crime—Issues in Research. *Criminology,* 16: 255–72.

Clinard, M. B., and P. C. Yeager (1980) *Corporate Crime.* The Free Press: New York.

Cloward, R. A., and L. E. Ohlin (1960) *Delinquency and Opportunity.* The Free Press: New York.

Cohen, L. E., and M. Felson (1979) Social Change and Crime Rate Trends: A Routine Activities Approach. *American Sociological Review,* 44: 588–607.

Cohen, M. A. (1987) Optimal Enforcement Strategy to Prevent Oil Spills: An Application of a Principal-Agent Model with Moral Hazard. *Journal of Law and Economics,* 30: 23–51.

Cohen, M. A. (1992) Environmental Crime and Punishment: Legal/Economic Theory and Empirical Evidence on Enforcement of Federal Environmental Statutes. *Journal of Criminal Law and Criminology,* 82(4): 1054–108.

Cohen, M. A., and S. S. Simpson (1997) The Origins of Corporate Criminality: Rational Individual and Organizational Actors. In *Debating Corporate Crime,* edited by W. S. Lofquist, M. A. Cohen, and G. A. Rabe. Anderson Publishing Company: Highland Heights, KY.

Coleman, J. W. (1997) Toward an Integrate Theory of White-Collar Crime. *American Journal of Sociology,* 93: 406–39.

Coleman, J. W. (1998) *The Criminal Elite: Understanding White-Collar Crime.* St. Martin's Press: New York.

Cornish, D. B., and R. V. Clarke (1986) *The Reasoning Criminal: Rational Choice Perspectives on Offending.* Springer-Verlag: New York.

Cressey, D. (1976) Restraint of Trade, Recidivism, and Delinquent Neighborhoods. In

Delinquency, Crime, and Society, edited by J. F. Short, Jr. University of Chicago Press: Chicago.

Cressey, D. (1988) The Poverty of Theory in Corporate Crime Research. In *Advances in Criminological Theory* (Vol. 1), edited by W. S. Laufer and F. Adler. Transaction Publishers: New Brunswick.

Croall, H. (1989) Who is the white-collar criminal? *British Journal of Criminology,* 29:157–74.

Daly, K. (1989) Gender and varieties of white-collar crime. *Criminology,* 27:769–94.

Dowie, M. (1979) Pinto Madness. In *Crisis in American Institutions,* edited by J. H. Skolnick and E. Curie. Little Brown: Boston.

Elis, L. A., and S. S. Simpson (1995) Informal Sanction Threats and Corporate Crime: Additive Versus Multiplicative Models. *Journal of Research in Crime and Delinquency,* 32(4): 399–424.

Ermann, M. D., and G. A. Rabe (1997) Organizational Processes (Not Rational Choices) Produce Most Corporate Crimes. In *Debating Corporate Crime,* edited by W.S. Lofquist, M. A. Cohen, and G. A. Rabe. Anderson Publishing: Cincinnati.

Friedrichs, D. O. (1995) *Trusted Criminals.* Wadsworth Publishing Company: Belmont, CA.

Finney, H. C., and H. R. Lesieur (1982) A Contingency Theory of Organizational Crime. In *Research in the Sociology of Organization* (Vol. 1), edited by S. B. Bacharach. JAI: Greenwich, CT.

Geis, G. (1967) White Collar Crime: The Heavy Electrical Equipment Antitrust Cases of 1961. In M. B. Clinard and R. Quinney (Eds.) *Criminal Behavior Systems: A Typology.* Holt, Rinehart, & Winston, Inc.: New York.

Geis, G. (1973) Deterring Corporate Crime. In *Corporate Power in America,* edited by R. Nader and M. J. Green. Grossman: New York.

Gottfredson, M., and T. Hirschi (1990) *A General Theory of Crime.* Stanford University Press: Palo Alto, CA.

Hay, G., and D. Kelley (1974) An Empirical Survey of Price Fixing Conspiracies. *Journal of Law and Economics,* 17: 13–39.

Jackall, R. (1988) *Moral Mazes: The World of Corporate Managers.* Oxford University Press: New York.

Jamieson, K. M. (1994) *The Organization of Corporate Crime: Dynamics of Antitrust Violation.* Sage Publications: Thousand Oaks, CA.

Kanter, R. M. (1977) *Men and Women of the Corporation.* Basic Books: New York.

Katz, J. (1988) *Seductions of Crime.* Basic Books: New York.

Levine, D. B. (1991) *Inside Out: An Insider's Account of Wall Street.* Putnam: New York.

Magat, W. A., and W. K. Viscusi (1990) Effectiveness of the EPA's Regulatory Enforcement: The Case of Industrial Effluent Standards. *Journal of Law and Economics,* 33: 331–60.

Messner, S. F., and Rosenfeld (1997) *Crime and the American Dream.* Wadsworth, Belmont, CA.

Nagin, D. S., and R. Paternoster (1993) Enduring Individual Differences and Rational Choice Theories of Crime. *Law and Society Review,* 27: 467–96.

Needleman, M. L., and C. Needleman (1979) Organizational Crime: Two Models of Criminogenesis. *Sociological Quarterly,* 20: 517–28.

Passas, N. (1990) Anomie and Corporate Deviance. *Contemporary Crisis,* 4: 157–78.

Paternoster, R., and S.S. Simpson (1993) A Rational Choice Theory of Corporate Crime. In *Routine Activities and Rational Choice: Advances in Criminological Theory* (Vol. 5), edited by R. V. Clarke and M. Felson. Transaction Publishers: New Brunswick.

Paternoster, R., and S.S. Simpson (1996) Sanction Threats and Appeals to Morality: Testing a Rational Choice Model of Corporate Crime. *Law and Society Review,* 30: 549–83.

Piliavin, I., C. Thornton, R. Gartner, and R. L. Matsueda (1986) Crime, Deterrence, and Rational Choice. *American Sociological Review,* 51: 101–19.

Piquero, A., and S. G. Tibbetts (1996) Specifying the Direct and Indirect Effects of Low Self Control and Situational Factors in Offenders' Decision Making: Toward a More Complete Model of Rational Offending. *Justice Quarterly,* 13: 481–510.

Riedel, M. (1968) Corporate Crime and Interfirm Organization: A Study of Penalized Sherman Act Violations. *Graduate Sociology Club Journal,* 8: 74–97.

Rosoff, S. M., Henry N. Pontell, and R. Tillman (1998) *Profit Without Honor: White-Collar Crime and Looting of America.* Prentice Hall: Upper Saddle River, NJ.

Ross, I. (1980) How Lawless are Big Companies. *Fortune,* December 1: 57–64.

Shover, N., and K. M. Bryant (1993) Theoretical Explanations of Corporate Crime. In M. B. Blankenship (Ed.) *Understanding Corporate Crime.* Garland Publishing: New York.

Simpson, S. S. (1986) The Decomposition of Antitrust: Testing a Multi-Level, Longitudinal Model of Profit-Squeeze. *American Sociological Review,* 51: 859–75.

Simpson, S. S. (1987) Cycles of Illegality: Antitrust Violations in Corporate America. *Social Forces,* 64: 943–63.

Simpson, S. S., and C. S. Koper (1992) Deterring Corporate Crime. *Criminology,* 30(3): 347–73.

Simpson, S. S., and C. S. Koper (1997) The Changing of the Guard: Top Management Characteristics, Organizational Strain, and Antitrust Offending: *Journal of Quantitative Criminology,* 13: 373–404.

Simpson, S. S., A. R. Harris, and B. A. Mattson (1993) Measuring Corporate Crime. In M. B. Blankenship (Ed.) *Understanding Corporate Criminality.* Garland Publishing: New York.

Simpson, S. S., R. Paternoster, and N. L. Piquero (1998) Exploring the Micro–Macro Link in Corporate Crime Research. In *Research in the Sociology of Organization* (Vol. 15), edited by S. B. Bacharach. JAI: Greenwich, CT.

Stone, D. G. (1990) *April Fools: An Insiders' Account of the Rise and Fall of Drexel–Burnham.* Donald Fine Company: New York.

Sutherland, E. (1949) *White Collar Crime.* Dryden Press: New York.

U.S. General Accounting Office (1994) *Defense Procurement Fraud: Cases Sent to the Department of Justices' Defense Procurement Fraud Unit.* SEC: Washington, D.C.

Vaughan, D. (1980) Crime Between Organizations: Implications for Victimology. In *White Collar Crime: Theory and Research,* edited by G. Geis and E. Stotland. Sage Publications, Beverly Hills.

Vaughan, D. (1983) *Controlling Unlawful Organizational Behavior.* University of Chicago Press: Chicago.

Vaughan, D. (1996) *The Challenger Launch Decision.* University of Chicago Press: Chicago.

Vaughan, D. (1997) Anomie Theory and Organizations: Culture and the Normalization of Deviance at NASA. In N. Passas and R. Agnew (Eds.) *The Future of Anomie Theory.* Northeastern University Press: Boston.

Weisburd, D., S. Wheeler, E. Waring, and N. Bode (1991) *Crimes of the Middle Classes: White Collar Offenders in the Federal Courts.* Yale University Press: New Haven.

Weisburd, D., E. F. Chayet, and E. J. Waring. (1990) White-collar crime and criminal careers: Some preliminary findings. *Crime and Delinquency* 36:342–55.

Wellford, C., and B. Ingraham (1994) *Toward a National Uniform White Collar Crime Reporting System.* National Institute of Justice: Washington, D.C.

Wheeler, S. (1992) The Problem of White Collar Crime Motivation. In *White Collar Crime Reconsidered,* edited by K. Schlegel and D. Weisburd. Northeastern University Press: Boston.

Wolfgang, M. E., R. M. Figlio, and T. Sellin (1972) *Delinquency in a Birth Cohort.* University of Chicago Press: Chicago.

Wright, R. T., and S. Decker (1994) *Burglars on the Job: Street Life and Residential Break-ins.* Northeastern University Press: Boston.

Wright, R. T., and S. Decker (1997) *Armed Robbers in Action: Stickups and Street Culture.* Northeastern University Press: Boston.

Zager, M. A. (1994) Gender and Crime. In *The Generality of Deviance,* edited by T. Hirschi and M. R. Gottfredson. Transaction: New Brunswick, NJ.

Zietz, D. (1981) *Women Who Embezzle or Defraud: A Study of Convicted Felons.* Praeger: New York.

Competition and Motivation to White-Collar Crime

JAMES WILLIAM COLEMAN

. . . The theory of white-collar crime presented here is based on the hypothesis that criminal behavior results from a coincidence of appropriate motivation and opportunity (Cantor and Land 1985; Vaughan 1983; Cloward and Ohlin 1960). The concept of motivation has been defined in many different ways, but this paper follows the definition most used in research on white-collar crime in holding motivation to consist of a set of symbolic constructions defining certain kinds of goals and activities as appropriate and desirable and others as lacking those qualities. An opportunity is defined as a potential course of action, made possible by a particular set of social conditions, which has been symbolically incorporated into an actor's repertoire of behavioral possibilities.

"Competition and Motivation to White-Collar Crime" is adapted from "Toward an Integrated Theory of White-Collar Crime" in *American Journal of Sociology* 93: 2 (September 1987): 406–39. Reprinted by permission.

Thus, a potential course of action becomes an opportunity only when someone is aware of it. In popular speech, the use of the word opportunity is generally restricted only to those things an individual actually wants to do. We speak of the opportunity to double an investment not the opportunity to have cancer surgery, but the definition given above would accept any possible course of action as an opportunity. An opportunity can, nonetheless, be characterized as attractive or unattractive from the standpoint of a particular individual. One opportunity may also be said to be more attractive than another, in a general sense, if it is more appealing to the majority of the individuals to whom it is available.

Because social structure becomes a reality only through its effects on the behavior of individual persons (Collins 1981), my analysis will begin with an examination of the motivational patterns of white-collar offenders. I will then consider the ways social structure influences motivation and determines the patterns of opportunities available to the occupants of different social statuses.

THE INTERACTIONIST THEORY OF MOTIVATION

There is a strong tendency among the general public and even many psychologists and criminologists to see the criminal as an abnormal individual with significant biological or psychological differences from other people. Yet, despite the popularity of such theories, they have seldom been applied to white-collar offenders. There have been virtually no scientific attempts to uncover a heredity component in white-collar criminality or to attribute it to a biological condition of some other origin. Nor has there been a significant effort to link white-collar crime to family background or abnormalities in early socialization. While somewhat greater attention has been given to the psychological makeup of white-collar offenders, this line of investigation has proved no more rewarding. Sutherland([1949] 1983; Cohen, Lindesmith, and Schuessler 1956) argued strongly for the psychological normality of white-collar criminals, and studies of different groups of white-collar offenders by Blum (1972, pp. 145–57), Bromberg (1965, pp. 377–400), Spelling (1944), and Spencer (1965) support this conclusion. Although those four researchers do posit some common psychological characteristics as causal factors in their subjects' criminal involvement, there is far too little consistency in their findings to conclude that such personality theories have much explanatory value.

Because there seems to be nothing unusual in the biological makeup or socialization of most white-collar criminals, researchers have had to look elsewhere to explain the motivation for their offenses. Although there are many social-psychological paradigms that might be applied to this problem, the interactionist approach has proved to be the best suited and has been used in the vast majority of the research on this question. Unlike psychiatric perspectives, which see motivation as the product of biological urges or unconscious desires, interactionists see motivation as a symbolic construct. The meaning that individuals attribute to a particular situation and to social reality in general structures their experience and makes certain courses of action seem appropriate while others are excluded or ignored. But socially created symbolic constructs not only define reality, they also allow individuals to anticipate the kinds of responses their behavior is likely to bring and adjust their actions accordingly. Thus, individual motivation is seen to include a general symbolic construction of reality, definitions of various individual situations, construction of some ends as valuable and others as undesirable, and a set of expectations about the kinds of responses different behaviors can be expected to evoke (Mead 1934; Mills 1940; Foote 1951; Cressey 1969; Coleman 1978).

Because behavior is evaluated in terms of the actor's symbolic construction of the responses anticipated from others, the expectations of significant others and the generalized expectations of society as a whole are critical elements in individual motivation (Mead 1934, pp. 152–63). But the fact that the generalized other is held to be a central element in thought and behavior poses a problem for an interactionist theory of white-collar crime because most criminal activities are likely to violate the societal expectations it embodies. Although Sutherland was the first to apply interactionist theory to the analysis of white-collar crime, he never explicitly recognized this contradiction. It was Cressey's ([1953] 1971) work on the way embezzlers "adjust" the symbolic construction of their behavior to conform to generalized social expectations that first came to grips with this problem. In his interviews with institutionalized embezzlers, Cressey found that his subjects used a number of common "techniques of neutralization" (Sykes and Matza 1957) to allow themselves to maintain a nondeviant self-image while still engaging in criminal activities. Most of the embezzlers interviewed by Cressey adjusted their construction of their criminal behavior by telling themselves that they were just borrowing the money and would soon return it. As one subject put it, "I figured that if you could use something and help yourself and replace it and not hurt anybody, it was all right" (Cressy [1953] 1971, p. 101). Cressey's respondents also reported using several other justifications, but the claim that they were just borrowing the money was by far the most common, probably because it is so well suited to neutralizing the definition of embezzlement as deviant behavior.

Such symbolic constructions are often referred to as rationalizations by interactionist theorists, but the term carries a different connotation in this context than it does in everyday speech. To interactionists, a rationalization is not an after-the-fact excuse that someone invents to justify his or her behavior but an integral part of the actor's motivation for the act (see Cressey 1969). Most of Cressey's embezzlers, for example, would not have committed their offenses if they had defined such activities as simple theft instead of as borrowing.

The borrowing rationalization so common among embezzlers is much less appropriate for most other kinds of white-collar crime. There are, however, ample data from both sociological research and the public statements of convicted offenders to construct a typology of the techniques of neutralization used by white-collar criminals. One of the most common of these techniques is the denial of harm. When convicted white-collar offenders are asked to explain their behavior, they frequently claim that their actions did not harm anyone, and they have therefore done nothing wrong. A Westinghouse executive who was one of the defendants in the 1961 heavy electrical equipment price-fixing trials expressed this justification when he was asked if he thought his behavior was illegal. He responded: "Illegal? Yes, but not criminal. . . . I assumed that a criminal action meant hurting someone, and we did not do that" (Geis 1977, p. 122) Similar justifications were expressed in Zeitlin's (1971) study of workers discharged for stealing from their employers. As one of his subjects put it: "It's not really hurting anybody—the store can afford it" (p. 22). Moreover, survey data show the public to be more tolerant of theft from large businesses and government than from smaller, more vulnerable organizations, probably because theft from a larger organization is perceived as less damaging to the victim (Smigel 1956).

Individuals involved in organizational crimes frequently justify their behavior by claiming that the laws they are violating are unnecessary or even unjust. Complaints about "government interference" in the free market are, of course, common in the business community, and business leaders often use the ideology of laissez-faire capitalism to criticize laws and regulations that they consider inappropriate. Because laissez-faire ideology holds many of the regulatory laws to be more harmful to the public than the business practices they prohibit, it can be used to justify a host of business crimes. Clinard (1952, p. 69), for example, concluded that gasoline dealers' belief that the wartime rationing of gasoline was unnecessary was a "rationalization for the violations which were occurring," and similar attitudes certainly play a role in many violations of worker safety, environmental, and antitrust legislation. However, ideological considerations are probably less important among small-business people than the perception of the fairness of the regulations in their individual cases. Ball's (1960) study of rent control in Honolulu found no significant difference in violation rates between landlords who felt that controls were necessary and those who felt they were not. But there were significantly higher rates among landlords who believed that the rent ceiling applied to their property was less than its "fair" value.

Another common rationalization holds that certain types of criminal behaviors are necessary to achieve vital economic goals or just to survive. Chibnall and Saunders (1977) cite the case of a former city councilman in Britain who justified his part in a corruption scandal in these words: "I am by nature a wheeler-dealer. How else can you be a successful politician . . . ?" The same Westinghouse executive quoted earlier also used the appeal to necessity to justify his participation in the price-fixing conspiracy:

"I thought we were more or less working on a survival basis in order to try to make enough to keep our plant and our employees" (Geis 1977, p. 122). The sales manager of a competing company made the same point: ". . . the spirit of the [price-fixing] meetings only appeared to be correcting a horrible price level situation. . . . There was not personal gain in it for me *[sic]*. The company did not seem actually to be defrauding [anyone]. Corporate statements can evidence the fact that there have been poor profits during all these years" (Geis 1977, p. 123).

This appeal to necessity is especially common among those who participate in illegal activities because their employer expects it. Sutherland cites the case of an idealistic young college graduate who reported losing two previous jobs because he refused to become involved in unethical activities. After finding that his third employer had the same expectations, he said, "I sometimes felt disgusted and wanted to quit, but I argued that I did not have much chance to find a legitimate firm. I knew the game was rotten, but it has to be played—the law of the jungle and that sort of thing" (Sutherland [1940] 1983, pp. 241–42). Employees in large corporate organizations may find the pressure to become involved in illegal activities particularly difficult to resist. A corporate manager's chances of finding another position with comparable pay and benefits depends on his or her record of success with previous employers, and the threat of dismissal is a powerful one. But fear of losing an important assignment or being passed over for promotion is nearly as strong a threat to achievement-oriented executives as outright dismissal. Another of the managers involved in the heavy electrical equipment price-fixing case justified his criminal activities by claiming: "If I didn't do it, I felt someone else would. I would be removed and somebody else would do it" (Geis 1977, p. 124). Moreover, there is ample evidence that such fears are often justified. A report to the Securities and Exchange Commission concerning Lockheed's involvement in foreign bribery states that "the Committee was told by several witnesses that employees who questioned foreign marketing practices damaged their claims for career advancement" (Clinard and Yeager 1980, p. 65).

A closely related technique of neutralization involves transfer of responsibility from the offender to a large and often vaguely defined group to which he or she belongs. When asked to explain their criminal activities, admitted offenders repeatedly claim that 'everybody else is doing it too.' As one embezzler put it: "In the real estate business you have to paint a pretty picture in order to sell the property. We did a little juggling and moving around, but everyone in the real estate business has to do that. We didn't do anything that they all don't do" (Cressey [1953] 1971, p.137). One of the major themes of the 'everybody's doing it' rationalization is that it is unfair to condemn one violator unless all other violators are condemned as well. The following statement of a defendant in a British corruption case is typical in this regard: "I will never believe I have done anything criminally wrong. I did what is business. If I bent the rules, who doesn't? If you are going to punish me, sweep away the system. If I am guilty, there are many others who should be by my side in the dock" (Chibnall and Saunders 1977, p. 142).

Such justifications imply that criminal behavior must be some sort of individual choice and that a person is not responsible for his or her behavior when merely conforming to the expectations of others. Thus, corrupt employees often claim that they have not done anything wrong because their actions were considered acceptable behavior by their peers (see Geis 1977, p. 142). These justifications are very important ones, for opinion polls indicate that business people not only believe that their peers are willing to commit unethical acts but that they are actually doing so. A study by the *Harvard Business Review* found that four out of five executives felt that some of the generally accepted practices in their industry were unethical and that four out of seven believed that other executives would violate a code of ethics if they felt they would not be caught (Baumhart 1961). A 1975 survey of top officials in America's 57 largest corporations found that they believed unethical behavior to be widespread in industry and that it had to be accepted as a part of everyday business activities (Silk and Vogel 1976). Another study concluded that: "Most managers believed that their peers would not refuse an order to market off-standard and possibly dangerous products (although a majority said they would personally reject such orders), and a majority thought young managers automatically go along with superiors to show loyalty" (Madden 1977).

Finally, occupational criminals commonly justify their offenses on the grounds that they deserve the money. Research shows this to be a particularly common rationalization for employee theft. Gerald Mars's (1974, p. 224) study of dockworkers found many types of pilferage were defined as a "morally justified addition to wages" or an "entitlement due from exploiting employers." Zeitlin (1971) found similar attitudes among employees who stole from retail stores. One of his subjects felt that the "store owed it to me," while another said, "I felt I deserved to get something additional for my work since I wasn't getting paid enough" (p. 22). Government workers also use these same rationalizations, especially since they often feel they are underpaid in comparison with their counterparts in private industry. One former city councilman gave the following account of his reasons for becoming involved in corruption: "People like me are expected to work full-time without salaries, without staff, or even postage stamps. I for one couldn't afford such a situation. And that is where Poulson [a businessman seeking special favors] filled the gap. . . . I came to the conclusion that I was missing out, that I could combine my real desire to give public service with what they call a piece of the action" (Chibnall and Saunders 1977, p. 143). Of course, many other justifications are also used by white-collar criminals, but the six rationalizations just discussed are by far the most commonly mentioned both in the public statements of accused offenders and in confidential replies to sociological investigators.

THE CULTURE OF COMPETITION

Although the existing body of interactionist research presents a convincing account of the motivations of white-collar offenders and the ways in which they neutralize the symbolic constraints on their behavior, it fails to explain the origins of the motivations it describes. Consequently, its attempt to explain the origins of white-collar crime fails as well. The answer to this question must ultimately be found on the structural, not the social-psychological, level, and the failure of interactionist theorists lies precisely in their failure to root their analysis in the political economy of industrial capitalism.

This is not to imply that current interactionist theory has no explanation of the origins of these motivational structures, for it clearly does. The problem is that the explanation it offers focuses so heavily on the social–psychological level that it breaks down when followed to its logical conclusion. Simply stated, the interactionist position is that the symbolic constructs that motivate criminal behavior are learned from association with others. Sutherland provides the most comprehensive statement of this idea in his theory of differential association: "The hypothesis of differential association is that criminal behavior is learned in association with those who define such behavior favorably and in isolation from those who define it unfavorably, and that a person in an appropriate situation engages in such criminal behavior if, and only if, the weight of favorable definitions exceeds the weight of unfavorable definitions" (Sutherland [1949] 1983, p. 240). In one sense, Sutherland denies the possibility of true deviance. He argues that individuals automatically conform to the expectations and definitions of their associates and that criminal behavior does not occur without such social support—certainly not a position Mead would have **accepted**.[3] The theory of differential association thus transforms crime from a problem of deviant individuals to a problem of deviant groups, but, in so doing, it still fails to answer the question of the origins of criminal motivation. Even if it could be shown that all criminal behavior is learned from association with others, we still must ask why certain groups foster criminal motivations and others do not. Current interactionist theory supplies no answer.[4]

In order to back out of this dead end, we need to reexamine how the con-

---

[3]Mead (1934) felt that the self contains two different components: the "I" and the "me." The me is a passive reflection of the responses an individual's behavior produces in others, but the I is the spontaneous, creative side of individual behavior that is capable of free action, independent of external pressure.

[4]Sutherland himself, clearly recognized the role of structural variables in the etiology of criminal behavior, but he failed to integrate them into his explanation of white-collar crime. The theoretical conclusions presented in chap. 15 of *White Collar Crime* (1983, pp. 240–57) place heavy stress on the importance of differential association. He also included a brief discussion of two facets of social disorganization that encourage white-collar crime—the anomie created by the transition from laissez-faire policies to a more regulated economic system and the conflicts between the business community, which is strongly organized for criminal activities, and the government, which is much more weakly organized to prevent them. But he did not seem as convinced of the value of the disorganization approach as he was in his earlier work n the origins of crime (see,

struction of the motivational patterns of white-collar offenders is handled in the interactionist literature. The taxonomy of rationalizations presented above provides a great deal of information about the way offenders justify their criminal behavior but tells us little about why that behavior is attractive in the first place. There is, however, no question in the public's mind about the attraction of white-collar crime. The respondents in Lane's (1954) sample of business and government leaders clearly reflected the consensus of the public when they claimed that white-collar criminals were simply out to make a "fast buck," and, for once, there is little reason to doubt the conventional wisdom. The desire for financial gain is indeed an obvious part of the motivation of most offenders. Perhaps too obvious, for interactionist theorists seem to have accepted the importance of financial self-interest as a motivation for white-collar crime with little critical analysis, and it is precisely such an analysis that provides the necessary link between structural and social–psychological variables.

The idea that wealth and success are central goals of human endeavor is part of a larger complex of beliefs that may be termed the "culture of competition." The foundations of this worldview can be traced at least as far back as the 17th century. Its reflections can be seen in the work of Hobbes, Locke, and other social thinkers of that era who formulated what MacPherson (1962) has termed the theory of possessive individualism. Reaching its peak in the 19th century, this vision of human nature is still deeply embedded in contemporary culture and supplies many of the key assumptions of the culture of competition (Lukes 1973). From this perspective, each person is seen as an autonomous individual with the powers of reason and free choice, who is, in large measure, responsible for his or her own condition. The pursuit of economic self-interest and the effort to surpass their fellows in the accumulation of wealth and status are of critical importance to these autonomous individual actors. As Wuthnow (1976, p. 105) puts it: "Becoming successful was more than simply one path a person could choose. It was in a very real sense a badge of one's intrinsic worth." In contrast to traditional values, the competitive struggle for personal gain is defined as a positive, not a selfish or harmful, activity. Competition is thus a builder of character, a test of personal worth, and a powerful stimulus to individual achievement that ultimately produces the maximum economic value for society as a whole. The competitive economic struggle typical of life in capitalist society is seen as a battlefield on which the most capable and the hardest-working individuals emerge victorious. Over the years, these beliefs have become a fundamental legitimation for social inequality because they imply that the poor deserve their inferior position because of laziness, incompetence, or some other personal failing (Feagin 1975). In con-

---

e.g., Sutherland 1934, pp. 63–74). He concluded that the explanation of crime in general in terms of social disorganization . . . has not proved to be a very useful hypothesis up to the present time" (1983, p. 257).

trast to the stigmatization of the poor, "winners" are admired for the ability and drive that made them successful.

One element of the culture of competition that the theorists of individualism have seldom discussed is the pervasive sense of insecurity that has always been a powerful undercurrent in the culture of industrial capitalism. This fear of failure permeates every stratum of contemporary society from the corporate leaders to the underclass. The following description of the subculture of lower-class street hustlers would, for example, apply equally well to the world of achievement-oriented business executives or to the culture of competition in general: "Full-time hustlers never can relax. . . . As is the case in any jungle, the hustler's every waking hour is lived with both the practical and subconscious knowledge that if he ever relaxes, if he ever slows down, the other hungry, restless foxes, ferrets, wolves, and vultures out there with him won't hesitate to make him their prey . . ." (Malcolm X 1965, p. 109). This same fear of failure in the competitive struggle for wealth and success is just as clearly reflected in the middle-class world of American television: "Television's world is relentlessly upbeat, clean, and materialistic . . . with few exceptions prime time gives us people preoccupied with personal ambition. If not utterly consumed by ambition and the fear of ending up as losers, these characters take both the ambition and the fear for granted" (Gitlin 1983, pp. 268–69). This fear of failure is the inevitable correlate of the demand for success, and together they provide a set of powerful symbolic structures that are central to the motivation of economic behavior.

This undercurrent of fear is nothing new to the culture of competition, and contemporary consumer culture is undoubtedly as materialistic and success oriented as any in history. But a number of social theorists argue that the growth of huge, impersonal bureaucracies and the increasing influence of the social sciences, which view individuals as partially or wholly determined by their social environment, have weakened the "rugged individualism" of the 19th century (Mills 1951; Riesman et al. 1950; Whyte 1957; Wuthnow 1976). There is little doubt, for example, that some persons become involved in organizational crimes because of their identification with the interests of their employer and not because of their desires for personal success. But, any weakening in the individualistic orientation of contemporary culture must be seen in the perspective of its original strength. The primary motivation of the vast majority of organizational criminals is still the personal rewards they expect from their employer, not an altruistic desire to help their organization. Moreover, the key components of the culture of competition in motivating the white-collar criminal—the desire for wealth and success and the fear of failure—have, if anything, grown stronger in the 20th century.

Yet human motivation is never a simple phenomenon, and those two desires cannot account for the motivation of all white-collar criminals. Some crimes result from the effort to live up to the expectations of friends and associates in the offender's occupational world or from an unreflective acceptance of a set of definitions that make certain criminal activities seem to be a normal part of the occupational routine. Examples include the bureaucratic functionaries who obediently carry out their superiors' orders with little or no thought about the consequences and members of occupational subcultures who participate in an pattern of illegal activities in order to win the acceptance and support of their peers. However, when analysis is extended beyond single individuals to encompass the entire group that sustains such criminogenic attitudes, the influence of the culture of competition reappears. While some of the lower-level functionaries involved in organizational crimes may be acting from a sense of conformity or obedience, executives usually make the decision to violate the law because of their desires for wealth and success. Similarly, individual members of a deviant occupational subculture may merely be going along with the expectations of their peers, but a collective desire for financial gain is the primary force creating and sustaining such expectations. . . .

The displacement of the open sharing of reciprocal exchange by the calculated self-interest of market exchange creates very different attitudes among those involved in economic transactions and, ultimately, in society as a whole (see Bonger [1905] 1969, pp. 37–38; Engels [1884] 1972; Leacock 1978). Market exchange is inevitably tied to ideas of profit and loss, and often the greater the gain of one trading partner, the lower the profit of the other. Thus, as production for market replaces production for immediate consumption, competition and the quest for personal gain tend to displace the cooperative sentiments fostered in reciprocal exchange. Of course, reciprocal exchange is still common among relatives and friends in even the most capitalistic industrial societies, but it is market exchange that predominates.

In addition to the accumulation of surplus wealth and the growth of market exchange, a third factor in the development of the culture of competition is the use of money as a medium of exchange. Because money provides an objective standard for measuring profit and loss, it further reinforces the spirit of competition and the depersonalization of economic exchange (Amsel 1973). Finally, the pervasive sense of insecurity so characteristic of the culture of competition reflects the underlying social and economic insecurity of industrial capitalism. Such societies are hierarchically organized, with great differences in status among their members. But, unlike traditional agricultural societies in which status is fixed largely by family background, there is far more mobility in industrial societies, and consequently an individual's status is far less secure. Employment, the single most important source of social status and economic reward, is subject to many unpredictable threats. Employees are often vulnerable to arbitrary dismissal or demotion at the whim of their superiors, and there is always the danger that the firm on which one's future depends may slip into bankruptcy or that the vicissitudes of the economy may force large-scale layoffs. The existence of a substantial group of the able-bodied unemployed serves as a constant reminder of the dangers of economic failure and the need to maintain one's competitive drive.

NORMATIVE RESTRAINTS AND THE DISTRIBUTION OF MOTIVATION

The culture of competition is an extremely important part of the culture of contemporary industrial capitalism. It is obvious, however, that modern life is not the Hobbesian war of all against all that such a system of values could be expected to produce if unfettered by other restraints. One such restraint comes from the influence of different social ideals, such as the values of cooperation and mutual support, which are so important in family and friendship groups. But, although very few people question the validity of those values in principle, their effectiveness as a constraint on white-collar crime is limited by the increasing segmentation of social life in industrial society (Bellah et al. 1985, pp. 27–51). The economic sphere is usually constructed as a separate realm from the world of home, family, and friendship, and both worlds contain their own values and operative principles. In the social world of economic activity, the culture of competition is the dominant cultural force, and the idea that one must look out for the well-being of one's competitors is considered hopelessly naive.

A more important barrier to the formulation of motivation for white-collar crime lies in the normative restraints on economic life that attempt to provide rules of the game within which the struggle for personal gain is expected to be waged. These normative restraints include such things as the need for honesty, fair play, and ethical practices in business, as well as the injunction to follow the laws and standards imposed by government authority. But, like the culture of competition itself, these norms can be understood only in the context of the structural forces in which they have their roots. Despite the strong support the economic system provides for the ideals of competitive individualism, it is clear that the pursuit of economic self-interest must be contained within some normative boundaries—or social and economic chaos would be the ultimate result. The economic rationality necessary to industrialism demands that exchange relationships be based on some set of mutually accepted standards. Without these rules, exchange relationships would become vastly more difficult for all parties involved, and many of the complex economic relationships characteristic of modern society would be virtually impossible to maintain. By making the struggle for personal gain appear fairer to its participants, these standards also help to legitimize the economic order in the eyes of the majority of people who do not stand out as particularly successful competitors. The demands of social life outside the economic realm also require normative restraints, and some of those are inevitably applied to economic behavior in even the most segmented societies. The restrictions placed on activities that are seen as wantonly destructive of human life or a physical danger to the community are typical examples.

These ethical standards for economic behavior are easily combined with the values of competitive individualism on the theoretical level, but in actual practice there is often an obvious contradiction between the two. While the pronouncements of public figures tend to emphasize theory and ignore the practical contradictions, there is little doubt in the public's mind that those who are willing to violate ethical standards enjoy a significant competitive edge over those who are not. In the words of the popular homily: "Nice guys finish last." This contradiction is a major source of tension in modern society that is not only reflected in the survey research on the ethical standards of business managers (Baumhart 1961; Silk and Vogel 1976; Madden 1977) but also in countless literary and artistic works. Indeed, the laws, regulations, and standards defining white-collar crime reflect this contradiction and the effort to demand compliance with ethical standards for economic behavior in the face of the extreme pressures of competitive individualism. The rationalizations examined by the interactionist theorists represent a different approach to resolving this contradiction, one that tends to weaken the normative restraints rather than reinforce them.

The relative strength of these two cultural forces and the way the contradictions between them are resolved are, therefore, critical factors in determining the motivation for white-collar crime. The purveyors of mass culture expose virtually everyone to both sets of values through the expectations and assumptions they weave into their vision of taken-for-granted reality. Yet, despite such general societal influences, individuals in different statuses are still exposed to every different constructions of reality. Of particular relevance to the study of white-collar crime are the work-related subcultures that expose their members to a particular worldview while providing some degree of insulation from the generally accepted definitions of social reality. As Holzner (1972, p. 95) puts it, the "epistemic communities that provide the locus for specialized reality construction in society on the basis of work concerns or ideological commitments [often] show tendencies toward isolation and segregation from the rest of society, and thus isolation from the generally shared reality of the interpretive order."

There are at least three distinct types of these subcultures that may be interwoven in various occupational settings. First, every complex organization has its own distinctive subculture. Not only do such subcultures promote attitudes and definitions that help shape the motivation for specific offenses, but there is also an "ethical tone" in an organization that, in a general way, either reinforces or opposes the normative standards for economic behavior (Clinard and Yeager 1980, p. 60). Over and above the organizational subculture, there are industry subcultures that express the attitudes, beliefs, and definitions common to organizations in a particular subsector of the economy (Barnett 1984). Finally, there are occupational subcultures among those who work in the same careers. Because persons in the same profession work in different organizations and in different industries, occupational subcultures crosscut the other subcultures, providing a different channel for diffusion of new ideas, information, and definitions.

These work-related subcultures tend to isolate their members from the mainstream of social life and its construction of reality. As Peter Drucker (1972, p. 88) writes of corporate executives: "Contacts outside of business tend to be limited to people of the same set, if not to people working for the same organization. The demand that there be no competing outside interests and loyalty . . . not only breeds a parochialism of the imagination comparable to the 'military mind,' but places a considerable premium on it." Members of professions such as law, medicine, and law enforcement are subject to similar pressures. They are expected to identify with their profession, to support their colleagues, and to work to advance their common interests. Like the executives Drucker describes, a disproportionate number of these professionals' everyday social interactions are with others who share the same subculture.

Because of this isolation, work-related subcultures are often able to maintain a definition of certain criminal activities as acceptable or even required behavior, when they are clearly condemned by society as a whole. There are numerous examples of executives who expressed genuine surprise and even shock that other people looked at their illicit activities as criminal behavior. Typical is the statement by one General Electric executive that price fixing "had become so common and gone on for so many years that we lost sight of the fact that it was illegal" (Geis 1977, p. 123). Carey's (1978, p. 384) description of the attitude of Richardson-Merrell Company employees, who concealed tests showing the dangerous side effects produced by one of their company's drugs, reflects this same normative isolation: "No one involved expressed any strong repugnance or even opposition to selling the unsafe drug. Rather, they all seemed to drift into the activity without thinking a great deal about it." But the influence of such subcultures works both ways and may also discourage criminal behavior. For example, the same police subcultures that defined some types of corruption as providing a kind of harmless fringe benefit also condemned the acceptance of "dirty money" from narcotics dealers (Knapp Commission 1972; Pennsylvania Crime Commission 1974). Subcultures in such professions as medicine and dentistry have a similar dual influence. Strongly held sentiments of group solidarity and collegial support make it much more difficult for enforcement agents to punish wrongdoers, yet at the same time those subcultures still hold out high standards of ethical behavior as the ideal for their members.

Of course, the formulation of criminal motivation depends on far more than the definitions to which an individual is exposed by virtue of his or her occupational position. The ideas, values, attitudes, and beliefs individuals bring into the workplace play a decisive role in determining which of the definitions that they learn on the job become part of their taken-for-granted reality, which are given only tentative acceptance, and which are rejected out of hand. Early socialization is especially important in shaping an individual's vision of the world, but many other experiences are a part of this ongoing process of reality construction. Membership in groups such as those based on kinship, religion, or friendship often serve as a counterbalance to the influence of occupational associations. But their importance depends on the way an individual actor goes about the task of constructing a meaningful world. Some persons maintain a highly integrated definition of self and the reality it inhabits, and their behavior is guided by a symbolic network that weaves together elements from all the social worlds in which they participate. But others have a far less global sense of reality and experience no difficult in following one set of standards and definitions on the job and a contradictory set in other social relationships. The increasing segmentation of personal reality is an often-noted characteristic of industrial society (Holzner 1972; Bellah et al. 1985), and contemporary men and women are probably more comfortable with a multidimensional view of self than was true in the past (Ogilvy 1977). Yet, at the same time, what Wuthnow (1976, pp. 70–71) terms "the quest for wholeness" and the "desire that one's experiences somehow make sense in relation to one another" remains an important force in all social life.

THE STRUCTURE OF OPPORTUNITY

Any analysis of the motivation of white-collar offenders can be of only limited explanatory value unless it is placed in the context of the actual opportunities available to individual actors. No matter how strong an individual's motivation may be, if there is no opportunity, there will be no crime. The variations in the menu of opportunities presented to the occupants of different social statuses are one of the principal ways structural constraints shape individual behavior, and the distribution of such opportunities plays a major role in the etiology of white-collar crime. Moreover, motivation and opportunity are often closely associated in a particular setting. Many of the rationalizations that are such an important part of symbolic motivations structures are formulated in response to a particular set of structural opportunities and have little meaning in another context. And, by the same token, an opportunity requires a symbolic construction making that particular behavioral option psychologically available to individual actors, and that construction may also include potential rationalizations. Thus, an individual may learn of both the opportunity for a particular offense and at least part of the motivation for committing it at the same time in the same setting. The two are, nonetheless, clearly distinct, for a motivation is a subjective construction of an individual's personal desires, while an opportunity is rooted in a set of objective social conditions.

Opportunities may be characterized as attractive or unattractive from the standpoint of a particular actor (or group of actors). An opportunity's attractiveness is determined by at least four factors. The first is the actor's perception of how great a gain he or she might expect to reap from the opportunity. Second is the perception of potential risks, such as the likelihood that a criminal; act will be detected and the severity of the sanctions that would be invoked if detection indeed occurs (Hollinger and Clark 1983a, 1983b). The third factor is the compatibility of the opportunity with the ideas, rationalizations, and beliefs the individual actor already has. Finally, the evaluation of an illicit opportunity is made in comparison with the other opportunities of which the actor is aware and is therefore influenced by the actor's entire opportunity structure. A decrease in the availability or attractiveness of legitimate opportunities will normally increase the attractiveness of illegal opportunities. The attractiveness of an opportunity for white-collar crime is not, however, an inherent characteristic of the opportunity structure, the opportunity itself, or of the motivation of the individual actor; it arises out of the relationship among them. . . .

CONCLUSIONS

The objective of this paper has been to create a unified theoretical framework to explain the causes of white-collar crime. However successful this endeavor has been, much remains to be done. Existing research has established the general outlines of the rationalizations used to justify white-collar crimes, but larger and more comprehensive quantitative studies are needed to determine more clearly the distribution and relative importance of the different rationalizations and to search for other common justifications that may have been overlooked. Scientific attention should also be directed to the variations in the original motivations for white-collar offenses. A good place to start such investigations would be a quantitative exploration of the relative strength of the culture of competition and the normative restraints on it among different groups and different organizational segments of society. An examination of the developmental changes in the balance of these two forces as individual actors respond to different environmental influences and career contingencies may also yield valuable information. Another fruitful area for research lies in the comparative study of the culture of competition. A quantitative assessment of the relative strengths of this system of beliefs in capitalist and communist nations would be particularly interesting because industrialized communist nations share many of the structural characteristics that gave rise to the culture of competition (great surplus wealth, monetarized market exchange, and a high degree of social inequality), yet their official ideology condemns most of the central tenets of the culture of competition as the product of a corrupt capitalism. A comparative analysis of the opportunities for white-collar crime created in those two types of societies would also be valuable if reliable quantitative measures could be used. Much more work must also be done to clearly delineate the structure of opportunities for white-collar crime in capitalist societies. Broadly based studies of the variations in opportunities among different occupational statuses and in different industries would be particularly useful in this regard.

REFERENCES

Amsel, Hans Georg. 1973. "Money and Criminality: A Reorientation of Criminological Research." *International Journal of Criminology and Penology* 1:179–87.

Ball, Harry V. 1960. "Social Structure and Rent Control Violations." *American Journal of Sociology* 65:598–605.

Baumhart, Raymond C. 1961. "How Ethical Are Businessmen?" *Harvard Business Review* 39 (July–August): 6–19, 156–76.

Bellah, Robert N., Richard Madsen, William M. Sullivan, Ann Swidler, and Steven M. Tipton. 1985. *Habits of the Heart.* Berkeley and Los Angeles: University of California Press.

Blum, Richard C. 1972. *Deceivers and Deceived.* Springfield, Ill.: Charles Thomas.

Bonger, Willem. [1905] 1969. *Criminality and Economic Conditions.* Bloomington: Indiana University Press.

Bromberg, Walter. 1965. *Crime and the Mind: A Psychiatric Analysis of Crime and Punishment.* New York: Macmillan.

Cantor, David, and Kenneth C. Land. 1985. "Unemployment and Crime Rates in the Post-World War II United States: A Theoretical and Empirical Analysis." *American Sociological Review* 50 (June): 317–32.

Carey, James T. 1978. *Introduction to Criminology.* Englewood Cliffs, N.J.: Prentice-Hall.

Chibnall, Steven, and Peter Saunders. 1977. "Worlds Apart: Notes on the Social Relativity of Corruption." *British Journal of Sociology* 28:138–53.

Clinard, Marshall B. 1952. *The Black Market: A Study of White-Collar Crime.* New York: Rhinehart.

Clinard, Marshall B., and Peter C. Yeager. 1980. *Corporate Crime.* New York: Macmillan.

Cloward, Richard A., and Lloyd E. Ohlin. 1960. *Delinquency and Opportunity: A Theory of Delinquent Gangs.* New York: Free Press.

Cohen, Albert, Albert Lindesmith, and Karl Schuessler, eds., 1956. *The Sutherland Papers.* Bloomington: Indiana University Press.

Coleman, James William. 1978. "The Dynamics of Narcotic Abstinence: An Interactionist Theory." *Sociology Quarterly* 19:444–64.

Collins, Randall. 1981. "On the Microfoundations of Macrosociology." *American Journal of Sociology* 86:984–1014.

Cressey, Donald R. [1953] 1971. *Other People's Money: A Study in the Social Psychology of Embezzlement.* Belmont, Mass.: Wadsworth.

———. 1969. "Role Theory, Differential Association and Compulsive Crimes." Pp. 1115–28 in *Delinquency, Crime and Social Process,* edited by Donald R. Cressey and David Ward. New York: Harper & Row.

Drucker, Peter F. 1972. *Concept of the Corporation.* Rev. ed. New York: John Day.

Engels, Frederick [1884] 1972. *The Origin of the Family, Private Property, and the State.* New York: International press.

Feagin, Joe R. 1975. *Subordinating the Poor: Welfare and American Beliefs.* Englewood Cliffs, N.J.: Prentice-Hall.

Foote, Nelson. 1951. "Identification as the Basis for a Theory of Motivation." *American Sociological Review* 16:14–21.

———. 1977. "The Heavy Electrical Equipment Cases of 1961." Pp. 117–32 in

White Collar Crime, rev. ed. Edited by G. Geis and R. F. Meier. New York: Free Press.

Gitlin, Todd. 1983. *Inside Prime Time.* New York: Pantheon.

Hollinger, Richard D., and John P. Clark. 1983a. *Theft by Employees.* Lexington, Mass.: Lexington.

————. 1983b. "Deviance in the Workplace: Perceived Certainty, Perceived Severity and Employee Theft." *Social Forces* 62:398–418.

Holzner, Burkart. 1972. *Reality Construction in Society.* Rev. ed. Cambridge, Mass.: Schenkman.

Knapp Commission. 1972. *The Knapp Commission Report on Police Corruption.* New York: Braziller.

Lane, Robert E. 1954. *The Regulation of Businessmen: Social Conditions of Government Control.* New Haven, Conn.: Yale University Press.

Leacock, Eleanor. 1978. "Women's Status in Egalitarian Society. Implications for Social Evolution." *Current Anthropology* 19:247–55.

Lukes, Steven. 1973. *Individualism.* Oxford: Blackwell.

Macpherson, C. B. 1962. *The Political Theory of Possessive Individualism:* Oxford: Clarendon.

Madden, Carl. 1977. "Forces Which Influence Ethical Behavior." Pp. 31–78 in *The Ethics of Corporate Conduct,* edited by Clarence Walton. Englewood Cliffs, N.J.: Prentice-Hall.

Mars, Gerald. 1974. "Dock Pilferage: A Case Study in Occupational Theft." Pp. 220–32 in *Deviance and Social Control,* edited by P. Rock and M. McIntosh. London: Tavistock.

Mead, George H. 1934. *Mind, Self, and Society.* Chicago: University of Chicago Press.

Mills, C. Wright. 1940. "Situated Actions and Vocabularies of Motive." *American Sociological Review* 5:904–13.

————. 1951. *White Collar.* New York: Oxford University Press.

Ogilvy, James. 1977. *Many Dimensional Man: Decentralizing Self, Society and the Sacred.* New York: Oxford University Press.

Pennsylvania Crime Commission. 1974. *Report on Police Corruption and the Quality of Law Enforcement in Philadelphia.*

Riesman, David, et al. 1950. *The Lonely Crowd.* New Haven, Conn.: Yale University Press.

Silk, Howard L., and D. Vogel 1976. *Ethics and Profits: The Crisis of Confidence in American Business.* New York: Simon & Schuster.

Smigel, Erwin O. 1956. "Public Attitudes toward Stealing as Related to the Size of the Victim Organization." *American Sociological Review* 21:320–27.

Spelling Lonell S. 1944. "Specific War Crimes." *Journal of Criminal Law and Criminology* 34:303–10.

Spencer, John C. 1965. "White Collar Crime" Pp. 233–266 in *Criminology in Transition,* edited by E. Glover, H. Mannheim, and E. Miller. London: Tavistock.

Sutherland, Edwin H. [1949] 1983. *White Collar Crime: The Uncut Version.* New Haven, Conn.: Yale University Press.

Sykes, Gresham K., and David Matza. 1957. "Techniques of Neutralization: A Theory of Delinquency." *American Sociological Review* 22:667–70.

Vaughan, Diane. 1983. *Controlling Unlawful Organizational Behavior: Social Structure and Corporate Misconduct.* Chicago: University of Chicago Press.

Whyte, William H. 1957. *The Organization Man.* Garden City, N.Y.: Doubleday.

Wuthnow, Robert. 1976. *The Consciousness Reformation.* Berkeley: University of California Press.

X, Malcolm. 1965. *The Autobiography of Malcolm X.* New York: Grove.

Zeitlin, Lawrence R. 1971. "A Little Larceny Can Do a Lot for Company Morale." *Psychology Today* 14:22 passim.

6

Controlling White-Collar Crime?

Introduction

Seen through the lens of rational-choice theory, the key to controlling crime lies in escalating the perceived risks of committing it while increasing legitimate opportunities and the estimated payoffs from noncriminal conduct. The risks of crime include not only legal sanctions but also the disapproval of others and self-rejection caused by a guilty conscience. What is known about decision making by street offenders, however, shows their rationality is bounded severely by age-related lifestyle and situational factors. Clearly, there is not a simple, one-to-one relationship between the schedule of threatened penalties and the criminal calculus.

In contrast to the chaotic lifestyles of street criminals, most white-collar workers live and work in worlds structured to promote, to monitor, and to reward prudent, deliberate decision making. In support of this contention, recall from the paper by Frank Pearce, which was included in Section 1, that corporate officers and managers assert that their organizations are rational actors. Some of the consequences of their rationality and planning can be seen in Panel 17, reprinted here from the work of Mark Dowie. In order to get dangerous products to market without violating the letter of the law, companies willfully violate its spirit in order to evade environmental and consumer regulation. These actions are not criminal, but they exemplify a rational indifference to potential harm.

Although few investigators have explored criminal decision making by white-collar offenders, it is widely believed that clearly articulated threats coupled with swift detection and certain and severe panalties may produce substantial specific and general deterrence among them. The rationale for this is set forth here by John Braithwaite and Gilbert Geis in the paper "On Theory and Action for Corporate Crime Control."

Despite belief in the potential deterrent effects of legal threats and punishment, the cultural and financial resources available to the respectable and privileged combined with the advantages that accrue to them at successive stages of the criminal process produces a capacity to resist, to delay, or to best control efforts that is available to few street criminals. Respectable offenders and their representatives play an active—many believe dominant—part in crafting the private standards, regulatory rules, and laws that circumscribe their conduct. And they do not sit idly by when the state and other parties try to curb their criminality; SLAPP lawsuits (Strategic Litigation Against Public Participation) and retaliatory actions against whistleblowers stand as powerful reminders of the determination of the privileged and powerful to conduct their affairs as they see fit. What is known about corporate codes of ethics gives reason also for concern about their willingness to regulate their own behavior; codes generally emphasize the importance of employee fidelity to organizational policies and norms but say remarkably little about the importance of compliance with legal norms. There appears, moreover, to be little realtionship between the presence of these codes and firm-level regulatory compliance.

The level of state commitment to and resources invested in rule enforcement plays an important part in shaping collective shared assessments of the risks of criminal behavior and, therefore, criminal opportunities. When the agencies and personnel nominally charged with curbing white-collar crime lack enthusiasm for the task or receive only minimal political and fiscal support for doing it, inevitably the belief grows among the privileged that they can break the law with impunity. As Henry Pontell, Kitty Calavita, and Robert Tillman point out, this was true of state capacity to respond decisively to massive crime in the savings and loan industry in the 1980s. The net result was that large numbers of corporate pirates either escaped punishment entirely or received little more than a slap on the wrist for their crimes.

The practical challenges of detecting, investigating, and convicting white-collar criminals are considerable, and this is true particularly where organizational offenders are the target. The organizational context of crime can make it extremely difficult to identify culpable individuals and to collect evidence sufficient for conviction. This raises investigatory and preparation costs. Drawing from his multistate research into corporate crime prosection, Michael Benson reinforces what was made apparent in screening and prosecuting S&L frauds: Decisions to prosecute are made in a complex calculus constrained by whether or not available resources are adequate to the challenge.

Despite the belief by many that white-collar offenders are responsive to the threat of criminal sanction, the bulk of state and private effort to control white-collar misconduct is rules that carry minimal professional or civil penalties for most forms of white-collar rule breaking; the body of statute law that citizens in their occupational roles and the organizations that employ them are expected to meet is small when compared with the volume of regulatory rules that confronts them. Regulatory enforcement, however, suffers from most of the same problems faced by police and prosecutors. Largely because of this, an alternative perspective on and approach to regulation and enforcement has gained support for state officials, for industry, and from regulatory investigators. Known as the compliance approach, advocates for this system of regulation and control of business interests suggest that regulatory enforcement is best accomplished when the enforcers work flexibly and cooperatively with those subject to regulation. The Australian government is engaged in a series of initiatives to maintain or enhance tax revenue streams, one of which is adoption of a compliance approach to enforcement. Valerie Braithwaite and John Braithwaite note the characteristics of their proposal for responsive tax enforcement and show how it will be applied in efforts to stem the loss of revenue to the cash economy and to gain greater compliance from corporations and high-wealth individuals.

The potential shortcomings of compliance strategies remain worrisome to many, however. Laureen Snider notes some of the reasons for these concerns, including that cooperative regulation takes place in a world of structured inequality and power that is not altered by the new regulatory approach. When they sit down with regulators to discuss cooperation and compliance, the privileged do so from a position of strength while agency personnel work under severe resource and political constraints. The bottom line on cooperative or responsive regulation has yet to be written.

Both the faces of white-collar crime and the control challenge it presents have altered fundamentally with the growth of the global economy and transnational corporations (TNCs). Although the signatories to international trade agreements typically pledge to adopt and enforce in their home countries elementary regulations for worker and product safety, the willingness of states to confront white-collar crime has waned substantially under the exigencies of competition and reassurances from business that oversight is heavy-handed, unnecessary, and costly. Police and prosecutors in most nations and local jurisdictions lack the budget, expertise, and other resources to pursue these cases. In addition, corporate owners and managers bent on gaining or maintianing weak regulatory oversight threaten relocation to countries with less restrictive regulatory regimes and the loss of jobs and tax revenues this would produce. States have moved significantly in the direction of strategies of cooperative regulation. The question raised by this development and by the growing dominace of large corporations is whether or not they now are beyond the law.

On Theory and Action for Corporate Crime Control

JOHN BRAITHWAITE AND GILBERT GEIS

. . . Criminal justice interventions to reduce street crime, whether mediated by principles of deterrence, rehabilitation, or incapacitation, can at best have

---

"On Theory and Action for Corporate Crime Control" from *Crime & Delinquency* (April 1989): 292–314. Reprinted by permission.

only modest effects on the rate of offending. It will be argued in this paper that, in contrast, deterrence, rehabilitation, and incapacitation are viable strategies for fighting crime in the suites. . . . This argument will be advanced in the context of a more general set of propositions asserting that the conventional wisdom of criminology with respect to traditional crime should be inverted with corporate crime.

There also is a broader purpose in our presenting the six propositions which follow. We seek to establish that corporate crime is a conceptually different phenomenon from traditional crime. Corporate crime is defined as conduct of a corporation, or of individuals acting on behalf of a corporation, that is proscribed and punishable by law.[7] . . . The propositions that follow specify reasons why principles developed in relation to traditional crime should not be assumed to apply to corporate offenses. Once the domains are accepted as conceptually separate, the burden of proof shifts; the opponent of legislation to control corporate crime must show why caveats from traditional criminal law should be regarded as relevant to the control of corporate crime.

SIX BASIC PROPOSITIONS

Proposition 1

With most traditional crimes, the fact that an offense has occurred is readily apparent; with most corporate crimes, the effect is not readily apparent.

When one person murders another, the corpse is there for people to see; or at least the fact that a person has disappeared is readily apparent. When, on the other hand, a miner dies from a lung disease, people may never appreciate that he has died because his employer violated mine safety regulations. Inevitably, most such violations are undetected.[8] People who pay more to go to a movie because of price fixing among theater owners will not be aware that they have been victims of a crime. When taxes go up because Defense Department officials have accepted bribes to purchase more expensive ships or missiles than the country needs, no one knows that a crime has occurred and that we all have been its victims.

Such is the limited power of individuals for ill that when they perpetrate a traditional crime there is usually only one victim (or, at most, there are only a few victims) for each offense. These individual victims become acutely aware

---

[7] Following Sutherland (*White Collar Crime*), we take the view that to exclude civil violations from a consideration of corporate crime is an arbitrary obfuscation because of the frequent provision in law for both civil and criminal prosecution of the same corporate conduct. Conduct subject only to damages awards without any additional punishment (e.g., fine, punitive damages) is, however, not within the definition of corporate crime adopted here.

[8] Joel Swartz, "Silent Killers at Work," *Crime and Social Justice*, Summer 1975, pp. 15–20; W. G. Carson, "White-Collar Crime and the Enforcement of Factory Legislation," *British Journal of Criminology*, October 1970, pp. 383–98.

that another person has dealt them a blow. The structural reality of much corporate crime, in contrast, is one of diffuse effects. A million one-dollar victimizations will not generate the kind of public visibility that a single million-dollar victimization will.

Even when the effects of corporate crime are concentrated rather than diffuse, victim awareness is often not there. If a consumer pays an extra thousand dollars for a used car that has had its odometer turned back, he will almost never be aware of the fraud.[9] The consumer might think that he has been sold a lemon, but not that he has been a victim of business crime. Similarly, when patients die from using a dangerous drug that was approved by health authorities on the strength of a bribe from a pharmaceutical company, a practice common in many countries,[10] the crime is not apparent. Low visibility also follow from the fact that often the only witnesses to a crime are themselves implicated in the offense.[11]

This first proposition has important implications for the difference between how law enforcers must go about controlling corporate versus traditional crime. Traditional crime control is reactive. The police normally do not investigate until a citizen reports a victimization.[12] For corporate crimes, whose visibility is almost invariably masked through being embedded in an ongoing transaction, the reactive model must be discarded for a proactive enforcement stance.[13]

Proposition 2

Once an offense becomes apparent, apprehending a suspect can be difficult with traditional crime, but is almost always easy with corporate crime.

When a house is robbed, or when a car is reported as missing, it is often a difficult job for the police to find the burglar or the car thief. Great public ex-

---

[9] John Braithwaite, "An Exploratory Study of Used Car Fraud," in *Two Faces of Deviance*, Paul R. Wilson and John Braithwaite, eds. (St. Lucia, Australia: University of Queensland Press, 1978), pp. 101–22.

[10] John Braithwaite, *Corporate Crime in the Pharmaceutical Industry* (London, England: Routledge and Kegan Paul, in press), ch. 2.

[11] John Hagan, Ilene H. Nagel, and Celesta Albonetti, "Differential Sentencing of White-Collar Offenders," *American Sociological Review*, December 1980, pp. 802–20.

[12] Albert J. Reiss, Jr., *The Police and the Public* (New Haven, Conn.: Yale University Press, 1971) ch. 2.

[13] Carson ("White-Collar Crime and the Enforcement of Factory Legislation, p. 390) found that only 5 percent of Factories Act violations in Britain were reported to as opposed to discovered by, the Factories Inspectorate. Even with consumer affairs offenses in which there are victims who become aware of their victimization, a proactive approach is typically required to stop the offense before the offender disappears and aggrieved consumers begin to trickle into the agency. (See Philip G. Schrag, "On Her Majesty's Secret Service Protecting the Consumer in New York City," *Yale Law Journal*, July 1971, p. 1586). On proactive enforcement tactics generally, see Herbert Edelhertz, *The Investigation of White-Collar Crime: A Manual for Law Enforcement Agencies* (Washington, D.C.: Department of Justice, Law Enforcement Assistance Administration, 1977).

pense is incurred to achieve unremarkable clearnace rates for these types of offenses.[14] In contrast, in the unlikely event that a sick worker discovers his illness is the result of an industrial health violation at work, almost by definition the law enforcement agency can identify a corporate suspect—the worker's employer. Similarly, if it is discovered that a bribe has been passed to secure a particular defense contract, there is an immediate suspect, the corporation that benefits from the contract. There was no need for the police to print "Wanted" posters or to set up roadblocks to find the corporate suspect when it was discovered that bribes were accepted in many countries throughout the world to secure sales of Lockheed aircraft.

This second proposition more than counterbalances the first in its implications for the potential effectiveness of corporate crime control. Corporate crime investigators cannot enjoy the luxury of sitting back in their offices waiting for the telephone to ring to notify them of the offense, but they are saved the tribulations of identikit photos, fingerprinting, and all the other paraphernalia that burden police in pursuit of traditional types of suspects.

With the use of proactive enforcement, there are many ways in which the disadvantage of invisibility could be swamped by the advantage to the enforcement agency of not having to apprehend the suspect. Although odometer frauds are invisible to the victims, representatives of law enforcement agencies could readily observe the mileage readings of cars standing in used car lots and then check back with the former owners to establish the mileage readings at the time of sale. If the enforcement agency were in a position to deliver the cars to the company itself, it would not even have to rely on the memory of the former owners.[15]

Our first two propositions together may constitute an argument for tactics that might involve or border on entrapment.[16] Nevertheless, it is an argument that demands consideration in corporate crime cases. Under the reactive enforcement model for traditional crimes, entrapment is hardly necessary. Law enforcement agencies have quite enough offenses reported to them and need not create more. Should they decide that they do want to create more offenses, given how little the police know about who is committing most of them, deciding whom to entrap would be difficult.

In contrast, if one accepts the inevitability of a proactive enforcement model for white collar crime, investigators may have little choice but to create

---

[14] In 1976 in the United States, only 14.4 percent of motor vehicle thefts were cleared by arrest. For property crimes generally, the clearance rate was 18 percent; for violent offenses, it was 45.6 percent. *Sourcebook of Criminal Justice Statistics—1978* (Washington, D.C.: Law Enforcement Assistance Administration, 1979), p. 502.

[15] Ogren is one advocate of auto repair fraud targeting by undercover operations with rigged vehicles. Robert W. Ogren, "The Ineffectiveness of the Criminal Sanction in Fraud and Corruption Cases: Losing the Battle against White-Collar Crime," *American Criminal Law Review,* Summer 1973, pp. 959–88.

[16] On entrapment, see Sorrells v. U.S., 287 U.S. 435 (1932).

their own offenses. For some types of white collar crimes, entrapment may be one of the few ways of doing this. The present authors differ with respect to the FBI's tactics in the ABSCAM case; but consider the options available for the conviction of political bribe takers. The FBI does not have citizens calling the agency claiming to be victims of political bribes, yet it does have intelligence on who the corrupt politicians are. Such intelligence rarely is sufficient to sustain criminal charges. The use of entrapment ruses for corrupt politicians may be more necessary and less indiscriminate than is the entrapment of, say, drug users by the offer of a deal. It can also be argued that holders of public office and the primary beneficiaries of the economic system have a special obligation to obey the law and to resist temptation.

Readers may conclude that entrapment is unacceptable with respect to either white collar or traditional crime. However, the balance of considerations that lead to this conclusion under the proactive model of white collar crime enforcement should be very different than the factors weighed for the types of offenses that can be handled under the reactive model.

Proposition 3

Once the suspect has been apprehended, proving guilt is usually easy with traditional crime, but almost always difficult with corporate crime.

Especially for less serious traditional crimes, the police have little difficulty in obtaining a conviction, particularly when they are willing to plea bargain. Once the police have made up their minds that a person is guilty and deserves to go to court, a conviction usually will follow.[17] When enforcement officers decide that a corporation probably is guilty of an offense and deserves to go to court, a conviction is usually *not* the result. Indeed, it does not normally eventuate that the matter *will* go to court.[18] The high costs to the state of corporate prosecutions, which work against pursuing the case in court, may be not only financial (e.g., legal fees) but also political (e.g., votes and campaign contributions, which may produce understandable caution among conservative bureaucrats in dealing with powerful actors).

Even where these costs are deemed to be bearable, the government will often lose in court because the complexity of the law[19] or the complexity of the

---

[17] Only 2.8 percent of defendants in cases terminated before United States district courts in 1977 were found not guilty, *Sourcebook of Criminal Justice Statistics—1979* (Washington, D.C.: Law Enforcement Assistance Administration, 1980), p. 555.

[18] See Clinard et al., *Illegal Corporate Behavior,* p. 291; Carson, "White-Collar Crime and the Enforcement of Factory Legislation"; Ross Cransten, *Regulating Business: Law and Consumer Agencies* (London, England: Macmillan, 1979).

[19] See Adam Sutton and Ron Wild, "Corporate Crime and Social Structure," in *Two Faces of Deviance,* Wilson and Braithwaite, eds., pp. 177–98; John Braithwaite, "Inegalitarian Consequences of Egalitarian Reforms to Control Corporate Crime," *Temple Law Qaurterly,* vol. 53, no. 4 (1980), pp. 1127–46.

company's books[20] makes it impossible to prove the case beyond reasonable doubt. There is a considerable difference, for instance, between convicting a corporation that takes money by fraud and convicting an individual who takes it at the point of a gun: "Criminal intent is not as easily inferred from a taking executed through a market transaction, as it is from a taking by force."[21] Corporations, unlike individuals, have the resources to employ the legal talent to exploit this inherent complexity. Good lawyers who use complexity to cast "reasonable doubt" on the applicability of existing statutes to the behavior of their client also use complexity to protract proceedings and thereby push up the cost disincentives for the prosecution to continue with formal proceedings.[22]

In addition to the complexity of the law and the complexity of the books, there is the complexity of the organizational reality of corporate action. Every individual in a large organization can present a different version of what company policy was, and individual corporate actors can blame others for their own actions (x says he was following y's instructions, y says that x misunderstood instructions she had passed down from z, ad infinitum). So how can either company policy or any individual company employee be guilty?[23] Even if this is not what actually happened,[24] it is difficult for the prosecution to prove otherwise.

There is, in addition, the complexity of science. Pollution, product safety, and occupational safety and health prosecutions typically turn on scientific evidence that the corporation caused certain consequences. In cases that involve scientific dispute, proof beyond reasonable doubt is rarely, if ever, possible. Science deals in probabilities, not certainties. The superstructure of science is erected on a foundation of mathematical statistics which estimate a probability that inferences are true or false. Logically, proof beyond reasonable doubt that a "causes" b is impossible. It is always possible that an observed correlation between a and b is explained by an unknown third variable, c. The scientist can never eliminate all the possible third variables. Hence, to require proof beyond reasonable doubt that a violation of the Food, Drug and Cos-

---

[20]See Adam Sutton and Ron Wild, "Companies the Law and the Professions: A Sociological View of Australian Companies Legislation," in *Legislation and Society in Australia*, Roman Tomasic, ed. (Sydney, Australia: Allen and Unwin, 1979), pp. 200–13; Abraham J. Briloff, *Unaccountable Accounting* (New York: Harper and Row, 1972).

[21]Gilbert Geis and Herbert Edelhertz, "Criminal Law and Consumer Fraud: A Sociolegal View," *American Criminal Law Review*, Summer 1973, p. 1006. See Holland v. U.S., 348 U.S. 121, 139–40 (1954); U.S. v. Woodner, 317 F.2d 649, 651 (2d Cir. 1963).

[22]For various examples of the use of delaying tactics by company lawyers, see Mark J. Green, *The Other Government: The Unseen Power of Washington Lawyers*, rev. ed. (New York: W. W. Norton, 1978).

[23]It may be that individual corporate actors are following standard operating procedures which were written by a committee, many of whose members are now retired, deceased, or working elsewhere. Consider Simeon M. Kriesberg, "Decisionmaking Models and the Control of Corporate Crime," *Yale Law Journal*, July 1976, pp. 1091–129.

[24]In *Corporate Crime in the Pharmaceutical Industry*, Braithwaite concludes that many corporations present to the outside world a picture of diffused accountability for law observance, while ensuring that lines of accountability are in fact clearly defined for internal compliance purposes.

metic Act caused an observed level of drug impurity, which in turn caused fifty deaths, is to require the impossible.[25]

The problem is illustrated by the federal OSHA statute. It requires proof that the violation was willful and caused death before a criminal conviction can stand. OSHA counsel explained to one of the authors that when fifty-one Research-Cottrell workers were killed by the collapse of scaffolding for a water tower, the fact that OSHA regulations had been violated was clear, the fact that workers died was clear, but proving beyond reasonable doubt that it was the violations (rather than other factors) that caused the scaffolding to collapse was another matter. The complexity of the forces that caused the scaffolding to collapse was such that it was represented by a computer simulation. OSHA counsel decided, undoubtedly correctly, that a computer simulation was more complexity than any jury could stand.

That the complexity of corporate crime and the power and legal resources of the defendants make convictions much more difficult than with traditional crime hardly needs to be labored.[26] This difficulty rather than the low visibility of offenses (Proposition 1) is the real stumbling block to effective corporate crime control. Consequently, it will be the barriers to conviction rather than those to discovery and apprehension that will be the focus of reforms considered in the final part of the paper.

Proposition 4

Once an offender has been convicted, deterrence is doubtful with traditional crime, but may well be strong with coroporate crime.

Specific must be distinguished from general deterrence. The former refers to the deterrence of the offender who is actually convicted. The case for specific deterrence is weak with traditional crime. Offenders who are incarcerated may be more embittered than deterred by the experience. They appear less likely to learn the error of their ways while in prison than to learn better ways

---

[25]See the discussion of this problem in relation to the Abbott case study, ibid., ch. 4.

[26]Compare Herbert Edelhertz, *The Nature, Impact and Prosecution of White-Collar Crime* (Washington, D.C.: National Institute of Law Enforcement and Criminal Justice, 1970); Christopher D. Stone, *Where the Law Ends: The Social Control of Corporate Behavior* (New York: Harper and Row, 1975); Sanford Kadish, "Some Observations on the Use of Criminal Sanctions in Enforcing Economic Regulations," *University of Chicago Law Review,* Spring 1963, pp. 423–26; "Comment: Increasing Community Control over Corporate Crimes: A Problem in the Law of Sanctions," *Yale Law Journal,* September 1961, pp. 280–93; Ralph Nader, Mark Green, and Joel Seligman, *Taming the Giant Corporation* (New York: W. W. Norton, 1976); Developments in the Law: "Corporate Crime: Regulating Corporate Behavior through Criminal Sanctions," *Harvard Law Review,* April 1979, pp. 1243–61; Ogren, "Ineffectiveness of the Criminal Sanction in Fraud and Corruption Cases"; Saxon, *White-Collar Crime.* In civil law, note also Wanner's evidence that corporate plaintiffs, in a sample of 7,900 cases, win more, settle less, and lose less than do individual plaintiffs (Craig Wanner, "The Public Ordering of Private Relations: Part One: Initiating Civil Cases in Urban Trial Courts," *Law & Society Review,* Summer 1974, pp. 421–40; Craig Wanner, "The Public Ordering of Private Relations: Part Two: Winning Civil Court Cases," *Law & Society Review,* Winter 1975, pp. 293–306).

of committing crimes.[27] This is not likely to be true of persons convicted of corporate crime. A feature that distinguishes traditional from corporate crime is that the illegitimate skills (e.g., safe-cracking) involved in the former are learned in criminal settings (e.g., prison), while the illegitimate skills (e.g., concealing transactions in books of account) of the corporate criminal are learned in legitimate noncriminal settings. While the illegitimate skills of burglars may be developed while they are incarcerated, those of crooked accountants will simply become increasingly out of date as they languish in prison.

A major risk in apprehending the traditional criminal is that the stigmatizing process will push him further and further into a criminal self-concept. This is the contention of labeling theory.[28] Evidence such as that from the Cambridge longitudinal study of delinquency[29] has been interpreted as support for the labeling hypothesis. This study showed that boys who were apprehended for and convicted of delinquent offenses became more delinquent than boys who were equally delinquent to begin with but who escaped apprehension. West and Farrington note about their findings,

> Court appearances may aggravate already tense family situations, alienate youths still further from their teachers and employers, and discourage their more respectable companions of either sex from continuing to associate with them. The sanctions imposed by the courts in the shape of fines are likely to increase the delinquent's debts, thereby increasing the temptation to dishonesty, while doing nothing to teach him to manage his finances better. Even supervision by a probation officer can be a mixed blessing, if it helps to confirm the youngster's self-identification with delinquent groups.[30]

These labeling arguments cannot readily be applied to corporate offenders. They are likely to regard themselves as unfairly maligned pillars of respectability, and no amount of stigmatization is apt to convince them otherwise. One does meet people who have a mental image of themselves as a thief, a safecracker, a prostitute, a pimp, a drug runner, and even a hit man, but how often does one meet a person who sees himself as a corporate criminal? The young black offender can often enhance his status back on the street by having done some time, but the reaction of the corporate criminal to incarceration is shame and humiliation.[31]

---

[27] Peter Letkemann, *Crime as Work* (Englewood Cliffs, N.J.: Prentice-Hall, 1973).

[28] Edwin Lemert, *Social Pathology* (New York: McGraw-Hill, 1951); Howard S. Becker, *Outsiders: Studies in the Sociology of Deviance* (London, England: Collier-Macmillan, 1963); Erving Goffman, *Stigma* (Englewood Cliffs, N.J.: Prentice-Hall, 1963).

[29] Donald J. West and David P. Farrington, *The Delinquent Way of Life* (New York: Crane Russak, 1977).

[30] Ibid., p. 162.

[31] Marshall B. Clinard, *The Black Market: A Study of White Collar Crime* (New York: Rinehart, 1952); Gilbert Geis, "The Heavy Electrical Equipment Antitrust Cases of 1961," in *Criminal Behavior Systems: A Typology*, Marshall B. Clinard and Richard Quinney, eds. (New York: Holt, Rinehart and Winston, 1967), pp. 139–51; Kenneth Mann, Stanton Wheeler, and Austin Sarat, "Sentencing the White-Collar Offender," *American Criminal Law Review*, Spring 1980, pp. 479–500.

Such an observation has important implications. Although the labeling hypothesis makes it unwise to use publicity as a tool to punish juvenile delinquents, it is sound deterrence to broadcast widely the names of corporate offenders. Corporations and their officers are genuinely afraid of bad publicity arising from their illegitimate activities.[32] They respond to it with moral indignation and denials, not with assertions that "if you think I'm bad, I'll really show you how bad I can be," as juvenile delinquents sometimes do.

Chambliss argues that white collar criminals are among the most deterrable types of offenders because they satisfy two conditions: They do not have a commitment to crime as a way of life, and their offenses are instrumental rather than expressive.[33] Corporate crimes are almost never crimes of passion; they are not spontaneous or emotional, but calculated risks taken by rational actors. As such, they should be more amenable to control by policies based on the utilitarian assumptions of the deterrence doctrine.[34]

Individual corporate criminals are also more deterrable because they have more of those valued possessions that can be lost through a criminal conviction, such as social status, respectability, money, a job, and a comfortable home and family life. As Geerken and Gove hypothesize, "the effectiveness of [a] deterrence system will increase as the individual's investment in and rewards from the social system increase."[35] Clinard and Meier, moreover, place particular emphasis on the "future orientation" of white collar criminals:

> Punishment may work best with those individuals who are "future oriented" and who are thus worried about the effect of punishment on their future plans and their social status rather than being concerned largely with the present and having little or no concern about their status. For this reason gang boys may be deterred by punishment less strongly than the white-collar professional person.[36]

In general, the arguments about the deterrability of individuals convicted of corporate crimes are equally applicable to the corporations themselves. Corporations are future oriented, concerned about their reputation, and quintessentially rational. Although most individuals do not possess the information necessary to calculate rationally the probability of detection and punish-

---

[32] W. Brent Fisse, "The Use of Publicity as a Criminal Sanction against Business Corporations," *Melbourne University Law Review*, June 1971, pp. 250–79.

[33] William J. Chambliss, "Types of Deviance and the Effectiveness of Legal Sanctions," *Wisconsin Law Review*, Summer 1967, pp. 703–19.

[34] See Developments in the Law, "Corporate Crime," pp. 1235–36.

[35] Michael R. Geerken and Walter R. Gove, "Deterrence: Some Theoretical Considerations," *Law & Society Review*, Spring 1975, p. 509. See also Franklin E. Zimring and Gordon J. Hawkins, *Deterrence: The Legal Threat in Crime Control* (Chicago: University of Chicago Press, 1973), pp. 127–28; Johannes Andermes, "Deterrence and Specific Offenses," *University of Chicago Law Review*, Spring 1971, p. 545.

[36] Marshall B. Clinard and Robert F. Meier, *Sociology of Deviant Behavior*, 5th ed. (New York: Holt, Rinehart and Winston, 1979), p. 248.

ment,[37] corporations have information-gathering systems designed precisely for this purpose. Hence, conclude Ermann and Lundman, "business concerns have regularly engaged in price fixing . . . under the correct assumption that the benefits outweigh the costs."[38]

The specific deterrent value of fines can be questioned for both traditional[39] and corporate[40] offenders. A large fine imposed upon a poor property offender might leave him little option but to steal again so as to be able to pay the fine. With corporations the problem is to be able to set a fine large enough to have a deterrent effect.

> The $7 million fine which was levied against the Ford Motor Company for environmental violations was certainly more than a slap on the wrist, but it rather pales beside the estimated $250 million loss which the company sustained on the Edsel. Both represent environmental contingencies which managers are paid high salaries to handle. We know they handled the latter—the first seven years of the Mustang more than offset the Edsel losses. One can only infer that they worked out ways to handle the fine too.[41]

Although the fine itself may be an ineffective deterrent when used against the corporate criminal, other sanctions associated with the prosecution—unfavorable publicity,[42] the harrowing experience for the senior executive of days under cross-examination,[43] the dislocation of top management from their normal duties so that they can defend the corporation against public attacks[44]—can be important specific deterrents.

---

[37] Dorothy Miller et al., "Public Knowledge of Criminal Penalties: A Research Report," in *Theories of Punishment*, Stanley Grupp, ed. (Bloomington: Indiana University Press, 1971), pp. 205–26.

[38] M. David Ermann and Richard J. Lundman, "Deviant Acts by Complex Organizations: Deviance and Social Control at the Organizational Level of Analysis," *Sociological Quarterly*, Winter 1978, p. 64.

[39] Jocelynne A. Scutt, "The Fine as a Penal Measure in the United States of America, Canada and Australia," in *Die Geldstrafe im Deutschen und Auslandischen Recht*, Hans-Heinrich Jescheck and Gerhardt Grebing, eds. (Baden-Baden, Germany: Nomos Verlagsgesellschaft, 1978), pp. 1062–181.

[40] Trevor Nagel, "The Fine as a Sanction against Corporations" (Ph.D. diss., University of Ademide Law School, 1979); Laura Shill Schrager and James F. Short, "Toward a Sociology of Organizational Crime," *Social Problems*, April 1978, pp. 407–19.

[41] Edward Gross, "Organizations as Criminal Actors," in *Two Faces of Deviance*, Wilson and Braithwaite, eds., p. 202.

[42] Fisse, "Use of Publicity as a Criminal Sanction against Business Corporations"; Wayne L. Pines, "Regulatory Letters, Publicity and Recalls," *Food, Drug and Cosmetic Law Journal*, June 1976, pp. 352–59; John Braithwaite, "Transnational Corporations and Corruption: Towards Some International Solutions," *International Journal of the Sociology of Law*, May 1979, pp. 125–42; John E. Conklin, *"Illegal but Not Criminal"* (Englewood Cliffs, N.J.: Prentice-Hall, 1977), p. 132.

[43] Hopkins, in a personal communication concerning his interviews with Australian Trade Practices Act offenders, pointed out that executives reported the experience of testifying in court to be grueling. Andrew Hopkins, "Anatomy of Corporate Crime," in *Two Faces of Deviance*, Wilson and Braithwaite, eds., pp. 214–31. See also the Abbott case study in Braithwaite, *Corporate Crime in the Pharmaceutical Industry*, ch. 4. One informant said of his fellow executives who were acquitted in this case, "The guys who were defendants in that case some of them are basket cases today. They've never been the same since."

[44] This dislocation is even worse when top management is actually replaced because of a corporate crime scandal, something that happens not infrequently when the scandal is of major proportions.

General deterrence is an effect more difficult to establish empirically. General deterrence refers to the consequences of a conviction for those who are not caught, but who through observing the penalties imposed on others decide not to violate the law. The state of the evidence on general deterrence for common crime, and how scholars interpret that evidence, is in turmoil.[45] It seems fair to say, however, that there has been a growing disillusionment with how much crime prevention can be achieved through deterrence, particularly of offenders from lower socioeconomic levels. Disillusionment has progressed so far that, whereas once the conventional wisdom of conservative criminology demanded that high imprisonment rates be justified by deterrence, now incarceration conventionally is based on the idea of just deserts.[46]

The evidence on the deterrent effects of sanctions against corporate crime is not nearly so voluminous, but the consensus among scholars is overwhelmingly optimistic concerning general deterrence.[47] This may in part reflect an uncritical acceptance of the empirically untested assumption that because corporate crime is a notably rational economic activity, it must be more subject to general deterrence.

However, the faith in the efficacy of general deterrence for corporate crime is not totally blind, as can be illustrated by a number of instances of corporate reaction to enforcement strategies. For example, business executives in Australia were asked whether the introduction of the Australian Trade Practices Act of 1974, with its relatively severe penalties, affected their behavior.[48] Survey respondents claimed that the legislation caused them to abandon certain price-fixing agreements with competitors and introduce antitrust "compliance programs." A more sophisticated study by Block et al. found that U.S. Justice Department antitrust prosecutions in the bread industry had significant and notable specific and general deterrent effects on price fixing. The degree of deterrence was surprising, given that bread price fixers have never

---

[45] Alfred Blumstein, Jacqueline Cohen, and Daniel Nagin, eds., *Deterrence and Incapacitation: Estimating the Effects of Criminal Sanctions on Crime Rates* (Washington, D.C.: National Academy of Sciences, 1978); Jack P. Gibbs, *Crime, Punishment, and Deterrence* (New York: Elsevior, 1975). For an innovative perspective on the practical constraints of system capacity in making deterrence work in practice, see Henry N. Pontell, "Deterrence: Theory versus Practice," *Criminology*, May 1978, pp. 3–30.

[46] See Ernest van den Haag, *Punishing Criminals* (New York: Basic Books, 1975); James Q. Wilson, *Thinking about Crime* (New York: Basic Books, 1975); Andrew von Hirsch, *Doing Justice: The Choice of Punishments* (New York: Hill and Wang, 1976); Richard G. Singer, *Just Deserts: Sentencing Based on Equality and Desert* (Cambridge, Mass.: Ballinger, 1979).

[47] See Clinard, *Black Market;* Marshall B. Clinard and Peter C. Yeager, *Corporate Crime* (New York: Free Press, 1980); Saxon, *White-Collar Crime;* Gilbert Geis, "Criminal Penalties for Corporate Criminals," *Criminal Law Bulletin,* June 1972, pp. 377–92; Developments in the Law: "Corporate Crime"; Richard A. Posner, *Antitrust Law: An Economic Perspective* (Chicago: University of Chicago Press, 1976); Kenneth Elzinga and William Briet, *The Antitrust Penalties: A Study in Law and Economics* (New Haven, Conn.: Yale University Press, 1976); Stephen A. Yoder, "Criminal Sanctions for Corporate Illegality," *Journal of Criminal Law and Criminology,* Spring 1978, pp. 40–58.

[48] G. JeQ. Walker, "The Trade Practices Act at Work," in *Australian Trade Practices,* John P. Nieuwenhuysen, ed. (London, England: Croom Helm, 1976), pp. 46–47. Walker refers to an unpublished survey by the Macquarie University School of Economic and Financial Studies.

been sent to jail and that fines average only 0.3 percent of the annual sales of the colluding firms. The Block et al. data suggest that deterrence is mainly mediated by civil treble damage suits that follow in the wake of criminal conviction.[49]

The most impressive evidence is from Lewis-Beck and Alford's study of United States coal mine safety enforcement.[50] Using a multiple interrupted time series analysis, these authors were able to show that the considerable increases in enforcement expenditure which followed the toughening of the mine safety legislation in 1941 and 1969 were both associated with dramatic reductions in coal mine fatality rates. The cosmetic 1952 Federal Coal Mine Safety Act, which actually arrested the rate of increase in Bureau of Mines enforcement expenditures, had no effect on fatality rates. Controls introduced into the regression models refute an interpretation that the historical trends are the result of technological advances in mining, changes in mine size, or variations in the types of mining operations. The most parsimonious interpretation of the data is that the rate of deaths from coal mine accidents is less than one-quarter of the rate of fatal accidents occurring before the 1941 legislation because of the deterrent effects of law enforcement.

Proposition 5

Although incapacitation is not apt to be very effective or acceptable for controlling traditional crime in a humane society, it can be a highly successful strategy in the control of corporate crime.

Traditional criminals can be incapacitated if the society is willing to countenance severe solutions. If we execute murderers, they will never murder again; or we can lock them up and never let them out. Pickpockets can be incapacitated by our cutting off their hands. Most contemporary societies are not prepared to resort to such barbaric methods. Instead, the widely used punishment is imprisonment for periods of months or years. Yet only partial incapacitation is in effect while the offender is incarcerated. Offenders continue to murder, to rape, and to commit a multitude of less serious offenses while they are in prison. Indeed, the chances of being a victim of homicide in the United States are five times as high for white males inside prison as for those outside.[51] And the partial incapacitation of prison lasts only as long as the sentence.

The limits of incapacitation as a policy become more apparent when we ask who is to be incapacitated. A substantial body of evidence shows that no matter how we attempt to predict dangerousness, the success rate is very

[49] Michael K. Block, Frederick C. Nold, and Joseph G. Sidak, "The Deterrent Effect of Antitrust Enforcement," *Journal of Political Economy,* June 1981, pp. 429–45.

[50] Michael S. Lewis-Beck and John R. Alford, "Can Government Regulate Safety: The Coal Mine Example," *American Political Science Review,* September 1980, pp. 745–56.

[51] Marvin Wolfgang, personal communication.

low.[52] Any policy of selective incarceration to "protect society" will result in prisons full of "false positives."

The most sophisticated study of the reduction in crime that might be achieved by incapacitation is by Van Dine, Conrad, and Dinitz.[53] For their Ohio cohort, a severe sentencing policy of a flat five-year term for any adult or juvenile convicted of a felony would have prevented only 7.3 percent of the reported crimes of the cohort. Such estimates are of limited value, of course, because there is no way of knowing how many unreported crimes might also have been prevented. Nevertheless, even under generous assumptions about the prevention of unreported crime, Van Dine et al. conclude that incapacitation can never be a cost-effective rationale for a tough sentencing policy. Notwithstanding this conclusion, Van Dine and his colleagues fail to take account of a variety of homeostatic forces, more recently considered by Reiss,[54] which further weaken incapacitative effects. For example, to what extent do criminal groups recruit new members to replace those who are incarcerated, or increase their own rate of offending to make up for the shortfall in criminal production arising from the absence of one member from the group? More fundamentally, studies such as that of Van Dine et al. make the false assumption that if 1,000 offenses were committted by offenders during a period of freedom, then 1,000 crimes would have been prevented if those people had been in prison for that period. The assumption is false because most offenses are not committed by lone offenders.[55] If the man who drove the getaway car in a robbery had been in prison, the robbery might still have gone ahead without him. For these additional reasons, we are even more strongly inclined to agree with the conclusion of Van Dine et al. that "we do not know how to bound a whole class of wicked people, and the evidence of this research suggests that we never will."[56]

Incapacitation is more workable with corporate criminals because their kind of criminal activity is dependent on their being able to maintain legiti-

---

[52]Ernst A. Wenk, James O. Robison, and Gerald W. Smith, "Can Violence Be Predicted?" *Crime and Delinquency,* October 1972, pp. 393–402; John P. Conrad and Simon Dinitz, eds., *In Fear of Each Other: Studies of Dangerousness in America* (Lexington, Mass.: Lexington Books, 1977); Joseph Cocozza and Henry J. Steadman, "Prediction in Psychiatry: An Example of Misplaced Confidence in Experts," *Social Problems,* February 1978, pp. 267–76; Murray L. Cohen, A. Nicholas Groth, and Richard Diegel, "The Clinical Prediction of Dangerousness," *Crime & Delinquency,* January 1978, pp. 28–39; Simon Oinitz and John P. Conrad, "Thinking about Dangerous Offenders," *Criminal Justice Abstracts,* March 1978, pp. 99–130; John Monahan, "The Prediction of Violent Criminal Behavior: A Methodological Critique and Prospectus," in *Deterrence and Incapacitation,* Blumstein, Cohen, and Nagin, eds., pp. 244–69.

[53]Stephen Van Dine, John P. Conrad, and Simon Dinitz, *Restraining the Wicked* (Lexington, Mass.: Lexington Books, 1979), pp. 17–34.

[54]Albert J. Reiss, Jr., "Understanding Changes in Crime Rates," in *Indicators of Crime and Criminal Justice: Quantitative Studies,* Stephen E. Fenberg and Albert J. Reiss, eds. (Washington, D.C.: Govt. Printing Office, 1980).

[55]Reiss points out that National Crime Survey data indicate that only 30 percent of offenders in victim-reported crime incidents were lone offenders. Ibid.

[56]Van Dine et al., *Restraining the Wicked,* p. 125.

macy in formalized roles in the economy. We do not have to cut off the hands of surgeons who increase their income by having patients undergo unnecessary surgery. All we need do is deregister them. Similarly, we can prevent people from acting in such formal roles as company directors, product safety managers, environmental engineers, lawyers, and accountants swiftly and without barbarism. Should we want only short-term incapacitation, we can, as Stone advocates, prohibit a person "for a period of three years from serving as officer, director, or consultant of any corporation. . . ."[57] Moreover, an incapacitative court order could be even more finely tuned. The prohibition could be against the person's serving in any position entailing decision making that might influence the quality of the environment. Corporate crime's total dependence on incumbency in roles in the economy renders possible this tailormade incapacitation. It makes the shotgun approach to incapacitation for common crimes look very crude indeed. However, the substitution problems that plague traditional incapacitative models are also a major constraint on the efficacy of incapacitating individuals who have been responsible for corporate crime. If, for example, the corporation is committed to cutting corners on environmental emissions, it can replace one irresponsible environmental engineer with another who is equally willing to violate the law.

This is where court orders to incapacitate the whole organization become necessary. Capital punishment for the corporation is one possibility: The charter of a corporation can be revoked, the corporation can be put in the hands of a receiver, or it can be nationalized. Although corporate capital punishment is not as barbaric as execution of individual persons, it is an extreme measure which courts undoubtedly would be loath to adopt, especially considering the unemployment caused by terminating an enterprise (although this does not apply to nationalizing it). Even though court-ordered corporate death sentences may be politically unrealistic, there are cases where regulatory agencies through their harassment of criminal corporations have bankrupted fairly large concerns.[58]

A less draconian remedy is to limit the charter of a company by preventing it from continuing those aspects of its operations where it has flagrantly failed to respect the law. Alternatively, as part of a consent decree, a corporation could be forced to sell that part of its business which has been the locus of continued law violation. The participation of the regulatory agency in the ne-

---

[57] Stone, *Where the Law Ends*, pp. 148–49.

[58] Schrag ("On Her Majesty's Secret Service") recounts how Detective, a publicly traded company which was defrauding consumers, was bankrupted in the aftermath of a "direct action" campaign by the New York City Department of Consumer Affairs. See below for a discussion of Schrag's "direct action" tactics against corporate offenders. Industrial Bio-Test, one of the largest contract testing laboratories in the United States, was bankrupted by the Food and Drug Administration after allegations had been made that it fudged data on the safety testing of drugs. Pharmaceutical companies ceased giving their toxicology testing contracts to IBT after the FDA warned them that data submitted to the agency that had been collected by IBT would be subjected to a special audit.

gotiations would serve to ensure that the sale was to a new parent with an exemplary record of compliance.[59] This kind of remedy becomes increasingly useful in an era when the diversified conglomerate is the modal form of industrial organization. Forcing a conglomerate to sell one of its divisions would, in addition to having incapacitative effects, be a strong deterrent in cases where the division made sound profits. Deterrence and incapacitation can be achieved without harm to the economy or to innocent employees.

Effective incapacitative strategies for corporate crime are, therefore, possible. All that is required is for legislatures, courts, and regulatory agencies to apply them creatively, to overcome the conservatism that leaves them clinging to the failed remedies carried over from traditional crime. The goal of incapacitation illustrates better than any other how the effective and just means for achieving criminal justice goals cannot be the same with corporate crime as with traditional crime. Consider, for example, the application to the Olin Mathieson Chemical Corporation of a law that forbids offenders convicted of a felony from carrying guns. Mintz has described what happened after Olin Mathieson was convicted of conspiracy concerning bribes to get foreign aid contracts in Cambodia and Vietnam:

> It happened that there was a law which said in essence that a person who had been convicted of a felony could not transport a weapon in interstate commerce. This created a legal problem for Olin, because it had been convicted of a felony, was in the eyes of the law a person and had a division that made weapons for use by the armed forces. Congress resolved the dilemma by enacting a law that, in effect, got Olin off the hook.[60]

Here we are struck by the absurdity of automatically applying to corporations an incapacitative policy designed for individuals. It will be argued later that this absurdity of applying law governing the behavior of individuals to the crimes of collectivities is the fundamental impediment to effective corporate crime control.

Proposition 6

Even though rehabilitation has failed as a doctrine for the control of traditional crime, it can succeed with corporate crime.

The disenchantment of criminologists in the past two decades with rehabilitation as a response to traditional crime has been even more profound than has

---

[59]The coal industry is a classic illustration of how some corporations are well known to have a superior record of compliance compared with the performance of others. Generally, it is the mines owned by the large steel corporations, with the safety compliance systems they bring from their parent industry, that have superior safety performance. In 1978–79 Westmorland Coal Co. had an injury incidence rate seven times as high as the rate in mines owned by U.S. Steel. Ben A. Franklin, "New Effort to Make Mines Safer," *New York Times,* Nov. 22, 1980, pp. I.29, I.32.

[60]Morton Mintz, *By Prescription Only* (Boston: Houghton-Mifflin, 1967), p. 383).

the disillusionment with deterrence. The high tide of this change was the publication of the massive and detailed review of the efffectiveness of correctional rehabilitation programs by Lipton, Martinson, and Wilks.[61] Even though Martinson stated at a later time that the review should not be used to justify a wholesale rejection of rehabilitation as a goal for the criminal justice system, the raw data which aroused the mood of pessimism are still there for all to see; and since the publication of the review there has hardly been a flood of studies showing that rehabilitative programs really do reduce crime.

There is little reason to suspect that individuals responsible for corporate crime, or white collar crime generally, should be any more amenable to rehabilitation than are traditional offenders. As Morris noted,

> What would Jimmy Hoffa discuss with his caseworker, in or out of prison, relevant to Hoffa's psyche or the manipulation of power within a union? A discussion between Spiro Agnew and his probation officer, had any unfortunate been appointed to that task, is even more mind boggling.[62]

Althopugh rehabilitating individuals would seem as unpromising with corporate as with traditional offenders, rehabilitating the corporation itself is a different matter. Many corporate crimes arise from defective control systems, insufficient checks and balances within the organization to ensure the law is complied with, poor communication, and inadequate standard operating procedures which fail to incorporate safeguards against reckless behavior.[63] Sometimes these organizational defects are intentional, manifesting a conscious decision by the corporate hierarchy to turn a blind eye to corner cutting in order to get results.[64] Sometimes the defects reflect sloppiness or managerial negligence. The chief executive of a pharmaceutical company, for example, might consciously ignore a situation in which his quality control director was overruled by the production manager when a batch of drugs was rejected for want of purity. If the organization were reformed so that the person responsible for achieving production targets was no longer able to overrule quality control, and if only the chief executive officer could reverse a quality control finding, and then only in writing, the chief executive could no longer turn a blind eye to avoid the situation.[65]

Regulatory agencies have an arsenal of weapons with which to force corporations to correct criminogenic policies and practices. They can insist upon,

---

[61] Douglas Lipton, Robert Martinson, and Judith Wilks, *The Effectiveness of Correctional Treatment: A Survey of Treatment Evaluation Studies* (New York: Praeger, 1975).

[62] Norval Morris, *The Future of Imprisonment* (Chicago: University of Chicago Press, 1974), p. 20.

[63] Hopkins, "Anatomy of Corporate Crime"; Braithwaite, *Corporate Crime in the Pharmaceutical Industry.*

[64] Stone, *Where the Law Ends*, pp. 199–216.

[65] For a more detailed discussion of this kind of organizational defect, see Braithwaite, *Corporate Crime in the Pharmaceutical Industry*, chs. 3, 4, and 9.

for example, abolition of off-the-books accounts, multiple approvals for specified actions, routine reporting of certain matters to committees of outside directors, and the establishment of internal compliance groups who report directly to the board with recommendations for sanctioning individuals who fail
to abide by corporate policies. Rehabilitation is a more workable strategy with
corporate crime than with traditional crime because criminogenic organizational structures are more malleable than are criminogenic human personalities. A new internal compliance group can be put in place much more readily
than can a new superego. Moreover, state-imposed reorganization of the
structure of a publicly traded company is not so unconscionable an encroach-
ment on individual freedom as is state-imposed rearrangement of a psyche.[66]

Hopkins, in the only systematic published study of the rehabilitation of
corporate offenders, concluded that most companies prosecuted under the
consumer protection provisions of the Australian Trade Practices Act introduced at least some measures to ensure that the offense did not recur.[67] Case
studies based on interviews by Fisse and one of the present authors with executives involved in major corporate crimes in America confirm Hopkins's finding.[68] In the aftermath of public disclosure of corporate crimes and the ensu-
ing scandals, many, although not all, corporations changed internal policies
and procedures to reduce the probability of reoffending. Much of this corporate rehabilitation undoubtedly took place because of prodding by regulatory
agencies. Large corporations tend to be responsive to the demands of regulators in making internal reform following the unveiling of a corporate crime in
part because they want the pressure exerted by regulators to cease.[69]

A number of formal mechanisms can be used to bring about corporate rehabilitation: consent decrees negotiated with regulatory agencies,[70] probation
orders placing the corporation under the supervision of an auditor, environmental expert, or other authority who would ensure that an order to restruc-
ture compliance systems was carried out;[71] or suspended sentencing of con-

---

[66]For a criticism of the rehabilitative model in these terms for individual deviance, see Philip
Bean, *Rehabilitation and Deviance* (London, England: Routledge and Kegan Paul, 1976).

[67]Hopkins, "Anatomy of Corporate Crime."

[68]These data will be published in a forthcoming book by Fisse and Braithwaite on the effects of
adverse publicity on corporate crime.

[69]As Galbraith points out, "In the American business code nothing is so iniquitous as government
interference in the *internal* affairs of the corporation." John Kenneth Galbraith, *The New Industrial State*, 3d ed. (Harmondsworth, England: Penguin, 1978), p. 81.

[70]This technique has been particularly popular with the United States Securities and Exchange
Commission. For a more refined version of this general approach, see Fisse's development of
the idea of court-imposed "preventive orders." W. Brent Fisse, "Responsibility, Prevention and
Corporate Crime," *New Zealand Universities Law Review*, April 1973, pp. 250–79.

[71]Comment: "Structural Crime and Institutional Rehabilitation: A New Approach to Corporate
Sentencing," *Yale Law Journal*, December 1979, pp. 353–75; John Collins Coffee, Jr., "Corpo-
rate Crime and Punishment: A Non-Chicago View of the Economics of Criminal Sanctions,"
American Criminal Law Review, Spring 1980, pp. 419–78.

victed corporations by the courts, contingent on their producing a report on the weaknesses of their old compliance systems and implementing new ones.[72]

DISCUSSION

It has been argued that the largely discredited doctrines of crime control by public disgrace, deterrence, incapacitation, and rehabilitation could become highly successful when applied to corporate crime. More generally, it has been argued that when the accumulated insight of criminology tells us that something is true of traditional crime, in many respects we can expect the opposite to be true of corporate crime.

Hence, there is reason for optimism that where we have failed with street crime, we might succeed with suite crime. . . . Because corporate crime is more preventable than other types of crime, the persons and property of citizens can be better protected; and restitution is a more viable goal for corporate than for traditional criminal law. Convicted corporations generally have a better capacity than do individuals to compensate the victims of their crimes.

Even though corporate crime is potentially more preventable and its victims are more readily compensated, there is no guarantee that either prevention or restitution will happen under traditional legal systems. This is because of our third proposition: Convictions are extremely difficult in complex cases involving powerful corporations. There are at least two ways of dealing with this problem. One is for regulatory agencies to achieve the goals of deterrence, incapacitation, and rehabilitation by nonprosecutorial means. They readily can do this if they have sufficient bargaining power. Consider the tactics of the Securities and Exchange Commission in the foreign bribery scandals of the latter half of the 1970s. In many cases the agency may have effected significant deterrence through the adverse publicity that followed public disclosure of the largest scandals,[73] a modicum of incapacitation in cases where corporations forced responsible senior executives into early retirement,[74] and a considerable amount of rehabilitation through consent or-

---

[72] Fisse suggests adjournment of sentence as a "back-door to enter the internal affairs of an offender" by reference to Trade Practices Commission v. Pye Industries Sales Pty. Ltd., A.T.P.R. 40-089 (1978); W. Brent Fisse, "Criminal Law and Consumer Protection," in *Consumer Protection Law and Theory,* Anthony J. Duggan and Leanna W. Darvall, eds. (Sydney, Australia: Law Book Co., 1980).

[73] While this adverse publicity may have had effects on company morale, such effects in most cases did not filter through to depress stock prices significantly. The stock market effects were somewhat more notable, however, with the companies named early in the foreign bribery campaign. Paul A. Griffin, "Sensitive Foreign Payment Disclosures: The Securities Market Impact" (mimeo; Graduate School of Business, Stanford University, June 1977).

[74] In some corporations (e.g., Lockheed, Northrop, Gulf) these included chief executive officers. The new chief executives in some cases really did seem to act as if they were the new broom attempting to sweep things clean.

ders that mandated audit committees of outside directors, outlawed off-the-books accounts, and led to other reforms which, although far from eliminating the prospect of bribery, certainly made it a much riskier and therefore less rational business practice.[75] At the same time, criticism of the agency on a number of grounds regarding the small number of cases referred to the Justice Department for prosecution assuredly was justified.[76]

In an illuminating article detailing why law enforcers so often choose to practice informal enforcement, Schrag discusses why he abandoned the prosecutorial stance that he brought to his position as head of the enforcement division of the New York City Department of Consumer Affairs.[77] A variety of frustrations, especially the use of delaying tactics by company lawyers, led to substitution of a "direct action" model for the "judicial" model. Nonlitigious methods which were increasingly used included threats and use of adverse publicity, revocation of licenses, direct contact of consumers to warn them of company practices, and pressure exerted on reputable financial institutions and suppliers to withdraw support of the targeted company. As Schrag points out, the dilemma of the direct action model is that it gets results without any regard for the due process rights of targeted "offenders."

An alternative to substituting the direct action for the judicial model is to reform the law so that the conviction of guilty corporations is made easier.[78] The precise nature of such reform is beyond the scope of the present paper. What we have attempted is to establish a case for the premise to undergird such a program of law reform: *The fact that a principle has been found to be justified in dealing with traditional crime is not a satisfactory rationale for its application to corporate crime.* If valid, the six propositions in this paper force the conclusion that corporate crime is a conceptually quite different domain from traditional crime. Consequently, we should never reject a strategy for controlling corporate crime merely because that strategy has been found wanting, on the grounds of either justice or efficacy, with traditional crime.

---

[75] Edward D. Herlihy and Theodore A. Levine, "Corporate Crisis: The Overseas Payment Problem," *Law and Policy in International Business,* vol. 8, no. 4 (1976), pp. 547–629. Note also Arthur F. Mathews, "Recent Trends in SEC Requested Ancillary Relief in SEC Level Injunctive Actions," *Business Lawyer,* March 1976, pp. 1323–52.

[76] Bequai, for example, says, "The SEC has been firing blanks. Who gets hurt in consent settlements? The SEC gets a notch on its gun. The law firm gets money, the public is happy because they read 'fraud' in the newspaper and think criminality right away. The company neither admits nor denies anything. It's the perfect accommodation. And it's all one big charade." August Bequai, "Why the SEC's Enforcer Is in Over His Head," *Business Week,* Oct. 11, 1976, p. 70.

[77] Schrag, "On Her Majesty's Secret Service."

[78] It is interesting to juxtapose this alternative against the "direct action" approach with respect to the due process protections available to targets of government sanction. Perhaps if corporations are not stripped of some due process protections so that convictions can become more possible, governments will increasingly be forced to take the "direct action" route, with its total absence of due process.

PANEL 18   Strategies for Getting Dangerous Products to Market

The Name Change
When a product is withdrawn from the American market, receiving a lot of bad publicity in the process, the astute dumper simply changes its name.

The Last Minute Pullout
When it looks as if a chemical being tested by the Environmental Protection Agency will not pass, the manufacturer will withdraw the application for registration and then label the chemical "for export only." That way, the manufacturer does not have to notify the importing country that the chemical is banned in the United States.

Dump The Whole Factory
Many companies, particularly pesticide manufacturers, will simply close down their American plants and begin manufacturing a hazardous product in a country close to a good market.

The Formula Changes
A favorite with drug and pesticide companies. Changing a formula slightly by adding or subtracting an inert ingredient prevents detection by spectrometers and other scanning devices keyed to certain molecular structures.

The Skip
Brazil—a prime drug market with its large population and virulent tropical diseases—has a law that says no one may import a drug that is not approved for use in the country of origin. A real challenge for the wily dumper. How does he do it? Guatemala has no such law; in fact, Guatemala spends very little each year regulating drugs. So, the drug is first shipped to Guatemala, which becomes the export nation.

The Ingredient Dump
Your product winds up being banned. Do not dump it. Some wise-ass reporter from *Mother Jones* will find a bill of lading and expose you. Export the ingredients separately—perhaps via different routes—to a small recombining facility or assembly plant you have set up where you are dumping it, or in a country along the way. Reassemble them and dump the products.

Adapted from: Mark Dowie, "The Corporate Crime of the Century," *Mother Jones*, November (1979): 23–79.

Prosecuting Corporate Crime: Problems and Constraints*

MICHAEL L. BENSON

This paper explores problems that local prosecutors confront in responding to corporate crimes. It is based on field studies conducted in Chicago, Illinois, Los Angeles, California, Duvall County, Florida, and Nassau County, New York in 1988 and 1989. At each site, attorneys in the local prosecutors office and representatives from the state attorney general's office were interviewed as well as officials from law enforcement and regulatory agencies. The interviews focused on the factors that constrain prosecutorial decision making and discretion in corporate cases.

Most illegal corporate conduct does not result in criminal prosecution (Clinard and Yeager, 1980; Sutherland, 1949). The reasons why corporate crimes often go unprosecuted and unpunished are complex. The special institutional features of business corporations make control of businesses a distinct problem from that of individuals in ordinary situations (Stone, 1975:7). Corporate offenses pose special investigatory and prosecutorial problems that make the successful application of the criminal law complicated and difficult (Shapiro, 1990; 1984; Levi, 1987; Rakoff, 1985; Stone, 1975). In addition, corporate crimes often are viewed as less serious than other crimes, especially those involving drugs, gangs, or violence. Finally, corporate offenders sometimes escape the criminal law because of their economic and political power (Reiman, 1979:139). Access to money and political pull enables corporations and the financial elites who run them to exert significant influence on law enforcement agencies. The failure of prosecutors to apply the criminal law to corporate crimes is caused by insufficient resources, competing priorities, legal constraints, the availability of alternative sanctions, and the political and economic influence of corporations.

INSUFFICIENT RESOURCES

Like most organizations, the prosecutor's office must pursue multiple objectives with limited technical, budgetary, and personnel resources. These resources can be severely taxed by the difficult and time-consuming process of

---

* Adapted from *Combating Corporate Crime: Local Prosecutors at Work*, by Michael L. Benson and Francis T. Cullen. Copyright 1998 by Michael L. Benson and Francis T. Cullen. Used with permission of Northeastern University Press. The data used for this paper come form a project supported by grant number 88-IJ-CX-0044 from the National Institute of Justice. Points of view or opinions expressed in this paper are those of the author and do not represent the official position or policies of the U. S. Department of Justice.

investigating, preparing, and prosecuting a case against a corporation (Bequai, 1978). The evidence in these cases may be little more than an elusive "paper trail" of memoranda and files. Organizations and individuals often go to great lengths to control the prosecutor's access to this crucial information (Mann, 1985). For example, documents may be destroyed or deliberately hidden from investigators, or the corporation may hire skilled defense attorneys to restrict the government's access to information. The difficulty of gathering evidence buried in corporate files severely limits the ability of prosecutors to investigate corporate crimes and to convict corporate criminals (Cullen et al., 1987; Rakoff, 1985; Schudson et al., 1984; Vaughan, 1983).

According to many local prosecutors, the difficulties of investigating and convicting corporate offenders make them reluctant to invest scarce resources in these cases. Resources tend to be invested mainly in criminal investigations where evidence can be easily gathered, especially evidence that incriminates a sepecific individual who can be sentenced to prison. If it appears unlikely that an individual can be convicted, civil proceedings are favored.

> If there's a feeling that you can get the evidence fairly easily, and if the case is easy to explain to a jury, and if the person is likely to get a good sentence, I think they'd go criminally.

But in cases where the evidence is hard to locate, where the offense is complex and not easy to explain to lay persons, and where the offender is unlikely to receive a sentence of incarceration, the likelihood that the local prosecutor will "go criminally" drops precipitously.

Precisely how inadequate resources are at the local level became obvious during the case study visits. Prosecutors and investigators in these relatively large, relatively well-to-do offices have to make do without the most basic equipment. For example, prosecutors in Chicago lamented that they did not even have dictaphones. Memoranda, briefs, and other documents had to be written in longhand before office secretaries could type them. An investigator pointed out that simply having a car phone and an answering machine would greatly improve her efficiency and productivity. It would enable her to make and return calls as she traveled around the city working her cases. Without the phone, her time in the car was, as she put it, "mostly wasted." The interviewees noted that these simple items are standard equipment in all but the smallest private law firms.

On a more substantial level, prosecutors in one district commented that their ability to develop and properly to dispose of environmental crimes was seriously diminished by lack of access to adequate laboratory facilities. A long delay in having a substance identified can limit the prosecutor's options in responding to cases of illegal disposal of toxic wastes. As one prosecutor explained, to

> . . . find out what's in a substance six months later is too late in an environmental case you're dealing with. How can you walk in [to a court] and [ask] for injunctive relief and say there's an immediate need to close this [business]

down when you've waited six months . . . how can you really do anything criminally and talk about how bad this is if we let it go six months at a time?

COMPETING PRIORITIES

When undertaking corporate cases, prosecutors must consider not only their own resource constraints but also those faced by judges and correctional system officials. What the corporate crime prosecutor views as a serious case may not be regarded as seriously by others in the justice system who see a different mix of cases. Almost without exception, the prosecutors noted that their corporate crime cases receive lower priority than drug or gang cases. In every jurisdiction, prosecutors noted that the war on drugs, for all its intrinsic merit, was devouring resources at a tremendous pace and severely undermining law enforcement in all other areas. In the words of one prosecutor who commented on the effect of the war on drugs on corporate prosecutions,

> . . . the system is finished. It's kaput. It's over. The game, the war? There is no war. We've filed them to the max on these drug things. We've allocated all our resources for drug things. The judges can't review the court calls for four or five hundred cases . . . and you try to talk about corporate prosecutions. The judge is going to say, "I don't have the time. I got thirty drug dealers."

Indeed, according to some prosecutors, drugs and violence have become such high priorities in large cities that environmental crimes actually receive more attention in rural areas than in urban areas. In urban jurisdictions, the press of violent and drug-related offenses is so great, that prosecutors with environmental cases have difficulty getting judges to take their cases seriously. A New York prosecutor described the situation in this way.

> Within the state we have rural counties upstate that are much more attuned to environmental problems. Because, let's say, they're a rural county and if there's a landfill or a factory that's polluting, it becomes a major political issue. That'll be front page news. New York City has such a terrible crime problem in terms of regular street crime, and violent crime, and drugs, murders [that] when you go to court in a New York City criminal court with a polluter, unless it is a major, major case, the courts are so overwhelmed by the drug problems, they are so understaffed, so crowded, . . . [and] the judges are so hardened by what they are seeing, because they deal with such a huge quantity and overwhelming amount of violent crime that . . . it's hard for them to take this [the polluter] seriously. And although they many be a committed environmentalist, they're not going to waste a lot of court time or what they deem is a waste of court time, because they don't even do it in the serious felonies. [Even] the serious violent felonies go assembly-like justice, because it's the only way the system can manage. And if you come in with a complex environmental case, which nobody in the court system is familiar with, no judge has an idea what you're talking about. They don't know anything about any of the statutes or regulations.

Thus prosecutors recognize that judges always assess the seriousness of a case relative to other cases. From the prosecutor's perspective, it makes little sense to pursue environmental offenses aggressively, if judges do not treat them seriously.

The justice system has been described as a loosely linked system (Hagan et al., 1979). This characteristic means that lack of resources is best viewed as a constraint that affects priorities in the entire justice system, not just the prosecutor's office. Beginning with the police and continuing through each stage of the justice process, caseload priorities set at one stage are, at least in part, determined by the priorities nad capabilities of the following stage. For example, before the police decide to crack down on a particular form of crime, they must have some reasonable assurance that their cases will be accepted and pursued by the prosecutor. Prosecutors, in turn, would be unwise to bring cases that judges are not interested in hearing. Sentencing judges must keep in mind the capacity of the prison system to absorb convicted offenders. This is not to suggest that prosecutors have absolute veto power over decisions made by police or that judges can override prosecutors with impunity. A certain amount of give and take between stages in the justice process always exists; prosecutors cannot simply ignore the police, and neither can judges simply ignore cases brought by prosecutors. Nevertheless, actors at one stage can make it more or less difficult for actors at another stage to do their job.

Local prosecutors are situated within a set of nested contexts that influence their decision making. The prosecutor's most immediate context consists of other actors in the justice system—police, regulatory officials, and judges. These actors influence prosecutors through their ability to affect the prosecutor's workflow. They either bring cases to prosecutors (as do police and regulators) or take cases from them (as do judges). The context of the justice system, itself, is then situated within the larger community context. And this larger context influences not only the prosecutor but all other stages of the system as well. This point was particularly well illustrated by two prosecutors in the New York state attorney general's office. They explained how environmental cases are treated differently in New York City as opposed to their treatment in upstate jurisdictions.

> I could tell you that it's very difficult to bring any white-collar criminal cases into the court system in New York City because of the drugs and the street violence. They just don't want to deal with that. They just feel that it's not . . . I mean unless it's a real celebrated type of case, they're just not going to really put that much attention to it. Upstate (since we do handle cases outside of the New York City area all over the state) you can see the difference. It's black and white. An environmental case in an upstate county that has very few violent crimes and not a terrible drug problem, all of a sudden that case is much more important, and that case becomes front page news. . . .

Later the prosecutors referred to a specific case in which a judge in an upstate county apparently had not been sympathetic to the prosecution's recommendation that an executive convicted of an environmental violation receive jail time. The judge's statements generated enormous local interest and publicity.

> Now it seems the fact that the judge himself expressed a lot of hostility towards the case and towards the prosecution in that case . . . it was a front page story every day throughout the trial, before the trial, at the sentencing. That's the kind of treatment it gets in those area as opposed to New York City, where, I mean unless it's a major action involving city landfill or something, if we were to bring a criminal case against a company in criminal court it's not going to make the *New York Times*. I mean, if it does, it's going to be a tiny little word or filler material and that's it. These cases are not going to generate publicity down here.

LEGAL CONSTRAINTS

Prosecutors also must contend with legal constraints. Legal constraints are features of the law that make it more or less difficult for legal actors to apply. For example, the legal standard of probable cause makes it harder for police to conduct legal searches than would be the case if only a reasonable suspicion were required. In corporate criminal cases, prosecutors frequently face legal constraints of a conceptual, constitutional, and evidentiary nature.

Conceptually, courts have encountered difficulties transferring traditional, individualistic notions of the criminal law to nontraditional, corporate settings. For example, indictments against corporations have been dismissed because of restrictive judicial interpretations of the legal meaning of "person," the appropriateness of existing criminal sanctions for corporate actors, and the need to prove *mens rea* (Maakestad, 1981; 1986; Fisse, 1983; Coffee, 1981). These concerns may limit the perceived options available to corporate criminal prosecutors.

Corporations may raise constitutional arguments that threaten the viability of prosecutors' cases. For example, for many years, considerable confusion existed over whether Federal OSHA regulations preempted state prosecution of unlawful conduct in the workplace. That issue has now largely been settled in favor of the states. Local prosecutors no longer have to worry that their cases involving workplace-related offenses will be thrown out of court because of lack of jurisdiction. But corporations continue to make similar arguments that Federal regulatory law preempts state law in other areas, making the job of the local prosecutor that much more difficult.

Prosecutors also must contend with evidentiary constraints. Seldom is it possible for a prosecutor to offer dramatic, "smoking gun" proof of criminal knowledge or intent in a corporate context. Proof of such knowledge or intent is critical, for it is the element of *mens rea* that can turn what might have been a civil suit into a criminal proceeding. In today's complex and often labyrinthine corporate structures, it can be extremely difficult to pinpoint individual responsibility for specific decisions. In addition, large-scale organizations develop mechanisms for shielding their members from responsibility for corporate actions (Katz, 1977; 1979; Gross, 1978). These problems in developing evidence seriously complicate the prosecutor's decision-making calculus.

In discussing the impact of legal constraints on prosecutorial decision making, some care must be exercised. The law never stands still; it continually evolves and changes. Legislatures can draft new statutes that ease the legal burdens prosecutors face. Courts can render decisions that clarify the meaning of ambiguous legal relationships. Legal constraints also can vary dramatically from one jurisdiction to another. A constraint in New York may not be one in California. Thus any description of the legal constraints faced by local prosecutors should not be taken as the last word, or as an entirely accurate description of the current state of affairs nationwide.

A major constraint on the decision to prosecute a corporate criminal case is the burden of proof required to win a conviction. This burden is especially hard to meet in the case of individual executives in large organizations. The fragmented and hidden character of decision making in large organizations makes it difficult to locate a responsible person. The person truly responsible is difficult to pin down without some form of documentation, documentation that often is absent. As one prosecutor put it,

> If you can show some document tying somebody high enough in the organization . . . I mean when you sue a company for selling sugared water as apple juice and you've got documents showing the heads of the company knew this was occurring and had to know, you got a criminal case. You don't have that and you [can only] show somebody below did it and there's no indication they knew of it, [then its] very difficult.

The general view seemed to be that securing convictions was harder against individuals than corporate entities. But in the case of corporate entities, convictions often were regarded as not worth the effort because no person would be exposed to a sentence of incarceration. without the possibility of someone doing some time, the deterrence potential of a case was seen to decline, and hence the expenditure of resources became less justifiable.

In some cases, the difficulty of establishing *mens rea* arises out of poorly drafted statutes. Statutes can be poorly drafted in a variety of ways. They may require the prosecutor to prove something that is nearly impossible to prove. In New York, for example, a prosecutor complained about an unreasonable burden of proof in a case involving water pollution.

> We're working on a case now that [it's obvious] this statute was never drafted by someone that had proved a case in court. Seventy-one dash nineteen dash thirty-three is a water pollution statute, and it subscribes a [class] C felony, a highest felony, to one who knowingly pollutes, or puts a pollutant into a sewer, which subsequently causes a serious physical injury, i.e., down the stream to the sewage treatment plant. [Now] how are you going to prove that causal relationship up here and down here without intermingling forces, other reactions, [affecting] the integrity of this stuff? How do you know it's the same

stuff? How do you know somebody else didn't double-quantity down the pipe? It's ludicrous.

The problem is that to obtain a criminal conviction the prosecutor must show a direct connection between the illegal emission and a specific injury. It is nearly impossible to demonstrate this connection given the physical distance between the polluter and potential victims.

Statutes can be poorly drafted in other ways besides posing an unreasonable burden of proof. They may be ambiguous as to exactly what is being declared illegal. Ambiguity creates problems for prosecutors with respect to "prior notice." An example of this situation also comes from New York. Two prosecutors complained that the environmental law had evolved in disorganized fashion. the result is "a hodge-podge or patchwork quilt," which made it extremely difficult for prosecutors and potential violators to know exactly what is illegal. As the two prosecutors put it:

> *First prosecutor:* They [the state legislature] criminalized the regulatory scheme.

> *Second prosecutor:* Right, so now we have a statute that says anybody having any degree of culpable mental conduct, whether it's negligence, recklessness, knowingly, intentional, any degree whatsoever, any of those culpable mental states, who violates any of your regulations found in blah, blah, blah, blah is guilty of a misdemeanor. You now have a statute that says it. Now that presents a lot of problems for a prosecutor, because you have to give the defendant notice of what he's being charged with. Is he being charged with being reckless? Negligent? Intentional? And here you have a statute that doesn't even differentiate. Any of those mental states is fine. Or it violates any of these regulations, and then you have set of regulations that's this thick. . . .

> *First prosecutor:* That's not an exaggeration. The regulations are impenetrable, a great disservice.

> *Second prosecutor:* By scientists, by anybody. They're impossible no matter how well-intentioned you are, really. When you say any violation of that complex set of regulations with any state of mind, there's a crime.

According to these prosecutors, some of these problems can be ameliorated by drafting what are called "endangering statutes." Such a statute makes it a crime to release a toxic substance in such a manner as to endanger public health safety and the environment. It does not require the prosecutor to show that the release resulted in a specific injury or harm. Instead, the prosecutor only must show that a toxic substance was released in such a manner as to endanger public health.

Simple as they may be, endangering statutes can still have problems if they are not carefully constructed. Endangering statutes may be drafted by environmental law specialists instead of criminal law specialists. Specialists in environmental law may draft laws that are difficult to use, because they lack experience with proving criminal cases in court. As the prosecutors quoted above see it:

They [environmental law specialists] really don't understand the due process requirement, and the problems of proof, and the problems of notice to the defendant of what he's being charged with. . . . You have to charge them under the specific section of the crime that puts them on notice of what . . . the prescribed conduct is. And when you have a section, a single section of a statute, that, let's say, has several different mental states, you have a problem there.

ALTERNATIVE REMEDIES

A welter of federal and state regulatory agencies have jurisdiction over various aspects of corporate conduct. Prosecutors must depend on those agencies both for technical expertise and for the development of crucial evidence. Traditionally, regulatory agencies have been more concerned with encouraging compliance than with punishing wrongdoing. They do not see themselves as law enforcers and often are reluctant to use the criminal law in response to corporate misconduct (Levi, 1987:163; Braithwaite, 1985b:10). Given the difficulty of getting regulators to cooperate in criminal proceedings against corporations, prosecutors may opt for alternative, noncriminal rather than criminal sanctions.

The problem of deciding what type of remedy to pursue can be further complicated when the interests of victims conflict with broader social interests. Sometimes victims are more interested in restitution than retribution and may oppose the use of criminal proceedings. Yet prosecutors may believe that failure to respond sternly to corporate crimes undermines belief in equal justice under law. The tension between community and victim interests may complicate the choice or remedy for prosecutors.

POLITICAL AND ECONOMIC CONSTRAINTS

Two important and controversial issues regarding prosecutorial decision making involve the politics of law enforcement and the impact of prosecution on the community. As elected officials, most local prosecutors are members of the local political establishment. They know and interact with local political leaders, some of whom also may be leading figures in the local business establishment. To conduct election campaigns, local prosecutors, like all elected officials, must raise money, some of which comes from corporations or their executives and leaders. It is reasonable to wonder whether the prosecutor's links to the political and business establishment influence how the law is enforced against other members of the establishment.

Corporations often make valuable contributions to community well being in the form of employment and taxes. Some communities are dependent on particular corporations or businesses for their economic livelihood. This dependence provides a source of power for those who own or manage these organizations, power that, it has been argued, enables them to break the law with impunity.

The complaints that justice is not blind and that the well-to-do and powerful fare better than others in the justice system are old and hotly debated matters. White-collar crime scholars from Sutherland's time on to today's conflict theorists have argued that economic and political elites receive special consideration in the justice system (Reiman, 1979; Barnett, 1981; Snider, 1982). Naturally, this issue is sensitive for prosecutors, one they do not discuss enthusiastically. Nevertheless, on several occasions the prosecutors we interviewed openly addressed the influence of political and economic constraints on their decision making.

As noted earlier, in the 1980s the war on drugs had top priority for many law enforcement agencies. At the same time that the national war on drugs was consuming the lion's share of criminal justice resources, other developments on the national political scene reduced local prosecutor's effectiveness against corporate crime. The election of Ronald Reagan as president ushered in an era of pro-business and anti-regulation politics. In this new era, local prosecutors found that they could no longer automatically count on federal agencies for support of their enforcement efforts. According to some local prosecutors, federal agencies such as the Environmental Protection Agency (EPA) and Federal Trade Commission (FTC) became much less aggressive, and in some cases actually hostile, toward law enforcement against business. One discouraged local prosecutor described the situation this way:

> Without getting excessively political about this, there was a clear sea change in the 1980s as a result of the Reagan administration's policies. . . . [T]he attorneys general through the National Association of Attorneys General and the district attorneys have been very critical of the federal administration in the last nine years for failing to prosecute consumer and anti-trust and environmental cases. EPA and FTC and the Anti-Trust Division of the Justice Department have done much less than they did historically to aggressively pursue these arease. Now partly it's a philosophical difference, and I understand that when you win the White House you have the right to bring in a new prosecutorial philosophy. But without waxing at great length on a subject that's of great sensitivity to us here in the state and local prosecution business, I'll say that many of us of all political stripes have been very disappointed by the retrenchment of these federal enforcement agencies.

This prosecutor went on to describe how the state attorneys general and local district attorneys have been forced to step in and take over responsibilities once assumed by federal agencies. In some cases, local prosecutors even found themselves fighting against the federal government in court. Needless to say, these developments had detrimental effects on relationships between local and federal agencies.

> I could name a dozen areas including environmental prosecution where AGs and the large DAs have gotten involved in what I consider filling the vacuum of the void left by the federal agencies. In fact, for a while there, and I do see

this changing, for a while there some of the federal agencies were actually entering on the sides of the defendants. The US Anti-Trust Division would file *amicus* briefs repeatedly on the side of defendants to ease the anti-trust law. I understand that there's a philosophical difference there and such, but you must know—in your study you might want to reflect in a footnote someplace—how enormously demoralizing it is for state and local officials to have the feds do a complete about face and change their prosecutorial standards dramatically, cease prosecuting certain kinds of things, and actually file *amicus* briefs for defendents. I mean that's just horrible for our relationship with those agencies.

CONCLUSIONS

Local prosecutors strongly believe in the general deterrent effects of corporate criminal prosecutions (Benson and Cullen, 1998). Nevertheless, not all corporate cases that come to light are brought before a jury or judge. In many instances, prosecutors elect not to file charges or, after charges are filed, not to bring cases to trial. These decisions are made on a case-by-case basis and in light of the unique set of facts presented by each case. Nevertheless, the field studies permit some generalizations about the exercise of prosecutorial discretion in corporate cases.

The decision not to prosecute is shaped primarily by legal and resource constraints. Lack of cooperation from victims, the availability of alternative regulatory remedies, insufficient investigatory personnel, and the difficulty of establishing *mens rea* in a corporate criminal context, all limit the willingness of local prosecutors to prosecute corporate criminal offenses. Prosecutors and investigators often spoke at length about the difficulty of successfully prosecutintg corporate case without sufficient technical and personnel resources. Clearly, they desired to do more. But the reality of limited resources prevented them from doing so. In brief, local prosecutions of corporate crimes are relatively rare not because local prosecutors regard these offenses as harmless violations of technical regulations or as someone else's problem, but rather because the offenses at times are simply too complex and difficult to handle.

REFERENCES

Barnett, Harold. 1981. "Wealth, Crime and Capital Accumulation." Pp. 182–88 in *Crime & Capitalism*, edited by David Greenberg. Palo Alto, CA: Mayfield.

Benson, Michael L., and Francis T. Cullen. 1988. *Combating Corporate Crime: Local Prosecutors at Work*. Boston: Northeastern University Press.

Bequai, August. 1978. *White-Collar Crime: A 20th-Century Crisis*. Lexington, MA: Lexington Books.

Braithwaite, John. 1985. "White-Collar Crime." *Annual Review of Sociology* 11: 1–25.

Clinard, Marshall B., and Peter C. Yeager. 1980. *Corporate Crime.* New York: Free Press.

Coffee, John C. 1981. "'No Soul to Damn, No Body to Kick:' An Unscandalized Inquiry into the Problem of Coroprate Punishment." *Michigan Law Review* 79:386–459.

Cullen, Francis T., William J. Maakestad, and Gray Cavendar. 1987. *Corporate Crime under Attack.* Cincinnati, OH: Anderson.

Fisse, Brent A. 1983. "Reconstructing Corporate Criminal Law: Deterrence, Retribution, Fault and Sanctions." *Southern California Law Review* 56:1141–246.

Gross, Edward. 1978. "Organizational Crime: A Theoretical Perspective." Pp. 55–85 in *Studies in Symbolic Interaction,* edited by Norman Denzin. Vol. 1. Greenwood, CN: JAI Press.

Hagan, John, John Hewitt, and Duan Alwin. 1979. "Ceremonial Justice: Crime and Punishment in a Loosely Coupled System." *Social Forces* 58:506–27.

Katz, Jack. 1977. "Legality and Equality: Plea Bargaining in the Prosecution of White-Collar Crimes." *Law & Social Review* 13:479–500.

Katz, Jack. 1979. "Concerted Ignorance: The Social Construction of Cover-Up." *Urban Life* 8:295–316.

Levi, Michael. 1987. *Regulating Fraud.* London: Tavistock.

Maakestad, William J. 1981. "A Historical Survey of Corporate Homicide in the United States: Could It Be Prosecuted in Illinois." *Illinois Bar Journal* 69:772–79.

Maakestad, William J. 1986. "State's Attorneys Stalk Corporate Murderers." *Business and Society Review* 56:21–25.

Mann, Kenneth. 1985. *Defending White-Collar Crime: A Portrait of Attorneys at Work.* New Haven, CT: Yale University Press.

Rakoff, Jed S. 1985. "The Exercise of Prosecutorial Discretion in Federal Business Fraud Prosecutions." Pp. 173–86 in *Corrigible Corporations & Unruly Law,* edited by Brent Fisse and Peter A. French. San Antonio: Trinity University Press.

Reiman, Jeffrey H. 1979. *The Rich Get Richer and the Poor Get Prison.* New York: John Wiley & Sons.

Schudson, Charles B., Ashton P. Onellion, and Ellen Hochstedler. 1984. "Nailing an Omelet to the Wall: Prosecuting Nursing Home Homicide." Pp. 131–46 in *Corporations as Criminals,* edited by Ellen Hochstedler. Beverly Hills, CA: Sage.

Shapiro, Susan P. 1984. *Wayward Capitalists.* New Haven: Yale University Press.

Shapiro, Susan P. 1990. "Collaring the Crime, Not the Criminal: Reconsidering 'White-Collar Crime.'" *American Sociological Review* 55:346–65.

Snider, Laureen. 1982. "Traditional and Corporate Theft: A Comparison of Sanctions." Pp. 235–58 in *White-Collar and Economic Crime,* edited by Timothy Wickman and Peter Dailey. Lexington, MA: Lexington Books.

Stone, Christopher D. 1975. *Where the Law Ends: The Social Control of Corporate Behavior.* New York: Harper & Row.

Sutherland, Edwin H. 1949. *White-Collar Crime.* New York: Holt, Rinehart and Winston.

Vaughan, Diane. 1983. *Controlling Unlawful Organizational Behavior.* Chicago: University of Chicago Press.

PANEL 19   Legal Responses to Corporate Crime

The state response to corporate crime tends toward the noninvasive and low-key and to sanctions that generaly amount to little more than a slap on the wrist. While enforcement officials can impose a number of legal actions on corporate offenders, only the most egregious and harmful offenses result in criminal prosecutions. Marshall Clinard and Peter Yeager report that 1529 sanctions were imposed on the 477 largest publicly owned manufacturing corporations during 1975 and 1976. For the most serious violations, approximately two-thirds of penalties were administrative, one-fourth were civil, and slightly more than 10% were criminal. Generally, violations that affected the economy recieved harsher santions than other kinds of violations, particularly those that affected the environment or product quality. During the two-year study period, 118 cases of antitrust and trade violation against manufacturing corporations were successfully prosecuted. Of these cases, 49 (41.5%) involved administrative panalties; 44 cases (37%) were given civil penalties; and 25 cases (21%) were responded to with criminal sanctions. In only 19 cases of antitrust violations were corporate officials criminally convicted, 5 of which resulted in the incarceration of officials and 11 of which resulted in probation. Those sentenced to confinement were given terms averaging six days (excluding suspended portions of the sentence), while the average length of probation was less than 10 months. Serious criminal sanctions are rarely imposed on corporate offenders, and corporate defendants, if convicted, can expect either modest fines or probation.

Source: Marshall B. Clinard and Peter Yeager, *Corporate Crime.* New York: Free Press, 1980.

Corporate Crime and Criminal Justice System Capacity: Government Response to Financial Institution Fraud

Henry N. Pontell, Kitty Calavita, and Robert Tillman

Fraud in financial institutions currently poses one of the most serious problems in the history of American law enforcement. The unprecedented scale of the savings and loan crisis . . . severely strains the state's responsive capac-

"Corporate Crime and Criminal Justice System Capacity" from *Justice Quarterly* 11:3 (September 1994): 383–410. Reprinted by permission.

ity. Recent government reports attest to the immense scale of the thrift debacle. The Resolution Trust Corporation (RTC), which is responsible for taking over failed savings and loans, reports that from its inception in 1989 through July 1992, it resolved (merged, sold, or assumed management of 652 failed thrifts (RTC 1992). The estimated losses to taxpayers from failed thrifts reached almost $84 billion during the same period, and the government spent close to $196 billion to resolve these institutions (RTC 1992). The U.S. Department of Justice reports that between October 1988 and February 1992, 2,942 defendants were indicted, resulting in 2,300 convictions in major financial institution fraud cases.[1] More than 1,100 of these defendants were associated with savings and loans, and over 800 were convicted. In 1992 almost 500 S&L offenders had been sentenced to prison and jail terms. (U.S. Department of Justice 1992).

White-collar crime contributed significantly to the insolvencies that constitute "the thrift crisis." Some government reports suggest that fraud was a central factor in 70 to 80 percent of thrift failures. (U.S. Congress, House 1988:52; U.S. General Accounting Office 1989). Government hearings have pointed to the backlog of extremely complex criminal cases and to the potential inability of federal enforcement agencies to respond effectively. In April 1990 there were 1,298 "inactive cases," each involving more than $100,000; such cases, under current official definitions, are designated as "significant," but there were not enough FBI agents or U.S. Attorneys to investigate or prosecute them (Rosenblatt 1990).

The amount of fraud uncovered will increase as more institutions come under government control and as the remains of insolvent institutions are scrutinized carefully by regulators. Investigators from the Resolution Trust Corporation have uncovered elaborate schemes in their review of seized thrift documents that were designed to keep examiners in the dark, to misrepresent the financial health of the organization, and to hide fraudulent transactions. Such postmortem investigations will never show the complete extent of fraud in the industry, but these autopsies confirm (1) that fraud is far more pervasive than some current estimates suggest (see, for example, Ely 1990; White 1991) and (2) that the cover-ups and complex transactions designed to keep regulators at bay were often themselves an integral part of the fraud.

. . . Specifically, we note that the complexity of these crimes and the fact that they are well disguised within ordinary business transactions complicate enforcement efforts and strain further a response system already stretched beyond capacity.

The paper is organized as follows. First, we discuss the methodology of the study. Next, we present a short historical overview of government efforts to clean up the thrift industry, focusing on new mechanisms of enforcement

---

[1] The Department of Justice defines "major cases" as those involving more than $100,000, tied to the insolvency of an institution, involving directors or officers, or having other significant aspects."

and coordination designed to further tighten the connections among the different agencies involved. After this, we examine the loose coupling (Hagan 1989) and the system capacity (Pontell 1982, 1984) perspectives, and discuss their utility in understanding the control of white-collar crime. Then we illustrate the value of the notions of loose coupling and system capacity for understanding government response to the S&L debacle, using statements from enforcement officials involved in the thrift industry cleanup. Salient issues include (1) the extraordinary complexity and hidden nature of such crimes and the difficulties inherent in detecting and investigating them, (2) the degree of coordination among enforcement and regulatory agencies, (3) the adequacy of resources, and (4) obstacles to successful investigation, prosecution, and sentencing. Finally, we consider how these microlevel responses relate to theories regarding the control of white-collar and corporate crime.

METHODOLOGY

The data for this stydy come from interviews with key enforcement and regulatory personnel, government reports and documents, and Congressional hearings. Interviews took place over a period of $2^1/2$ years in Washington, DC, Florida, Texas, and California. The selection of these sites was based on the following considerations. First, California and Texas experienced the greatest number of thrift failures and frauds. Thus they were the most "consequential areas," and provided numerous interview opportunities with experienced fieldworkers. As the study was about to begin, a number of savings and loan executives in Florida were indicted, and that state's thrift industry began to crumble. We chose Washington, DC because it is home to numerous federal agencies whose staffs we interviewed. At each site we determined, through contacts with various officials, the position of the key locations and persons in the agencies most deeply involved with thrift regulation and enforcement.

We conducted 98 in-depth personal interviews (usually lasting one to two hours); almost all of these were tape-recorded. The total number of persons interviewed was 105; 18 of these individuals were interviewed more than once.[2] . . .

. . . [A]lmost all the interviewees agreed to being tape-recorded. We agreed not to name them if excerpts were used, and to keep the tapes secure and coded by number to protect confidentiality. We conducted the following numbers of interviews with various agency officials: FBI, 20; Office of Thrift Supervision, 13; Resolution Trust Corporation, 11; U.S. Attorneys, 11; Federal Deposit Insurance Corporation, 7; Secret Service, 10; General Accounting Office, 4; Justice Department 3; Office of the Comptroller of the Currency 3; Executive Office of the United States Attorneys, 2; Congressional Committee

---

[2]The breakdown of the 18 multiple interviewees is as follows: 13 persons had one follow-up interview; 3 had two follow-ups; 1 had three follow-ups; and 1 had five follow-ups.

Staff, 4; IRS, 1; Treasury Department, 6; Federal Reserve, 1; and other non-government), 4.[3] The interviews were conducted from January 1990 through August 1992. . . .

Although the interviews were unstructured and "conversational," we asked a number of standard questions, depending on the respondent's agency affiliation and duties. The following represent a sampling of the points covered: At the investigation stage, what are the main obstacles to assembling a successful case? How problematic is the need for extensive documentation? To what extent do evidentiary requirements hold up investigations? Could more interagency cooperation improve investigative capacities? Are there any drawbacks to interagency action, in terms of overlapping responsibilities? At the filing stage, what factors determine whether an indictment is sought? How are the cases of savings and loan fraud generally charged? What factors determine whether criminal or civil actions are taken? How much funding and time will the RTC need to complete the job it was created to do—i.e., finish the cleanup of the savings and loan industry? Is there an opportunity for a second round of fraud due to the possible corruption of RTC employees?

In the interviews we obtained law enforcers' and regulatory officials' perceptions of the savings and loan crisis and the role of fraud in that crisis. In addition, we gained perspectives on the effectiveness of various enforcement and regulatory actions and how these response strategies interact in dealing with savings and loan fraud. The taped interviews were transcribed by research assistants and entered into a computer. Each interview was read and coded into topical and conceptual categories. Those relating to government responses to fraud in the thrift debacle are presented here.

NATURE AND TYPES OF THRIFT FRAUD

The hidden and complex nature of bank fraud is described in detail by Alt and Siglin, who use the term broadly to include frauds against "all depository institutions, including banks, thrifts, and credit unions" (1990:1).

The Federal Home Loan Bank Board (FHLBB) describes savings and loan fraud as follows:

> . . . individuals in a position of trust in the institution or closely affiliated with it have, in general terms, breached their fiduciary duties; traded on inside information; usurped opportunities or profits; engaged in self-dealing; or otherwise used the institution for personal advantage. Specific examples of insider abuse include loans to insiders in excess of that allowed by regulation; high risk speculative ventures; payment of exorbitant dividends at times when the institution is at or near insolvency; payment from institution funds

---

[3]These numbers do not add up to the interview figure of 98 because two agencies were represented at some interviews. Thus they are counted as interviews in separate agencies on this list, but together make up only one interview in the total interview count.

for personal vacations, automobiles, clothing, and art; payment of unwarranted commissions and fees to companies owned by the shareholder; payment of "consulting fees" to insiders of their companies; use of insiders' companies for associated business; and putting friends and relatives on the payroll of the institutions (U.S. General Accounting Office 1989:22).

In 1989 a U.S. General Accounting Office (GAO) study of 26 of the most costly thrift failures found that every one of the institutions was a victim of fraud and insider abuse. Evidence presented by the FHLBB to the GAO indicates that fraud was not confined to these 26 thrifts. In fact, the Bank Board referred more than six thousand cases for criminal investigation in 1987 and another five thousand during 1988, a significant increase over 1985 and 1986 (434 and 1,979 respectively; GAO 1989). The weaknesses at the 26 failed thrifts investigated by the GAO included (1) "inadequate board supervision and dominance by one or more individuals" (73% of failed thrifts); (2) "transactions not made in thrift's best interest"; (3) "inadequate underwriting of loan administration"; (4) "appraisal deficiencies"; (5) "noncompliance with loan terms"; (6) "excessive compensation and expenditures"; (7) "high risk ADC [acquisition, development, and construction] transactions"; (8) "loans to borrowers exceed[ing] legal limits"; (9) "inadequate record keeping"; and (10) "transactions recorded in a deceptive manner" (GAO 1989:18–49).

The GAO (1989) cites one thrift that paid a chairman of its board a $500,000 bonus in a year when the thrift lost almost $23 million; this expenditure, according to thrift regulators, violated the federal regulation against "excessive compensation." At another thrift, regulators told management that a bonus of more than $800,000 (one-third of the institution's earnings) paid to one officer was a waste of assets; the management paid the individual in question $350,000 to relinquish his right to future bonuses, and increased his salary from $100,000 to $250,000. The GAO also found that extravagant expenditures were made to officers and their families for private planes, homes, and expensive parties. In one case a majority stockholder used $2 million of thrift funds to buy a beach house and spent another $500,000 for household expenses, none of which were business-related.

The varieties of thrift fraud are limitd in some ways only by the perpetrator's imagination. These crimes, however, display distinct patterns, which often appear to be variations on a number of recurring themes. Elsewhere we have classified thrift crimes as belonging to three types: unlawful risk taking, collective embezzlement, and covering up (Calavita and Pontell 1990). . . .

THEORETICAL BACKGROUND: CRIMINAL JUSTICE COUPLING, PUNISHMENT CAPACITY, AND WHITE-COLLAR CRIME

How are formal state policies regarding fraud in financial institutions translated into concrete organizational action by social control agents? Borrowing from the literature on organizational environments, Hagan (1989) points out that the loose form of organization among criminal justice agencies is a central concept in understanding formal responses to crime. Hagan states, "[I]n the absence of political power that is directed toward particular crime-linked goals, American criminal justice systems and subsystems tend to be loosely coupled. This is a common condition in the U.S. federal, state, and local systems of criminal justice . . ." (1989:118). Loose coupling allows criminal justice agencies to adapt to environmental changes when necessary. Such organizations "have a unique capacity to absorb changes in the surrounding political environment" (Hagan 1989:119).

Looseness of organization, however, does not guarantee effective social control when agencies are subjected to rapid changes in their environments and when enforcement response demands much greater coordination, not only among criminal justice agencies but also with outside regulatory subsystems. The enforcement environment becomes highly problematic, for example, when the scale of crime and the corresponding workloads increase suddenly, threatening to outstrip the government's capacity to respond and maintain order. Such a situation calls for "tighter" coupling among agencies in order to process cases. . . .

System capacity (Pontell 1976, 1982, 1984) refers to the ability of formal agencies of social control to sanction crime. One way to examine the concept of criminal justice coupling is through the idea of organizational capacity, whereby institutions of social control respond and adapt to environmentally induced workload demands. . . . It seems clear that institutional capacity is tied inextricably to the degree of coupling among agencies; both may be regarded as affecting social control efforts.

In view of the exceedingly high workload demands in criminal justice agencies, institutional limits to crime control are present for all offenses. Yet perhaps they manifest themselves most clearly in the case of white-collar and corporate crime. . . .

Katz (1980) views the institutional capacity to investigate and prosecute such crimes as a function of practical limitations on resources, given the overall responsibilities of the prosecutor's office and the existing institutional arrangements. At least equally important, resources and institutional arrangements are affected by the laws governing white-collar and corporate crime, by the complex nature of corporate crime, and by the political milieu in which such laws are enforced and resources are distributed. White-collar crime enforcement, which involves proactive policing, ordinarily requires tighter coupling among agencies for successful investigation, prosecution, and sentencing. . . .

We focus here on organizational relations, particularly issues of limited capacity. We argue that the response to S&L crime can be viewed in microorganizational terms, as expressed by regulators and criminal justice workers who deal directly with financial institution fraud cases. In the following analysis we . . . show that enforcement is necessarily limited by the complexity and the massive scale of thrift crime relative to available resources and to the level of coordination possible among agencies. The following section illustrates these systematic limitations, using statements from regulators and law enforcement officials.

GOVERNMENT RESPONSES TO FINANCIAL INSTITUTION FRAUD

Criminal justice case loads in financial institution fraud are enormous. Assistant Attorney General W. Lee Rawls reported to Congress that the FBI received 28,150 criminal referrals involving banks and thrifts in fiscal year 1991, resulting in 5,490 FBI investigations. By the end of 1991, almost 9,000 financial fraud investigations were being conducted. During the first quarter of 1992, 7,491 criminal referrals for financial fraud were received, triggering nearly 2,000 new FBI investigations (U.S. Congress, Senate 1992:117). . . .

Enforcement agents' responses are limited by the scale of the S&L crisis, the complex and time-consuming nature of fraud cases, the alternative administrative and civil routes for dealing with them, and the high degree of interagency dependence necessary for bringing successful cases. These agents recognize that not all crimes will be discovered and that many which are discovered will not be prosecuted; if they are prosecuted, they will not result in full sanctioning on the original charges.

·   ·   ·

Because crimes remain hidden within business transactions and because ferreting them out can take years, financial institution fraud presents formidable obstacles to enforcement officials. One regulator commented simply, "The criminal justice system is not going to be able to handle this problem."

Many of those convicted of fraud wrought havoc in thrifts by engaging in complex schemes designed to cover their fraud and to keep regulators and enforcement personnel at bay by claiming superior knowledge of financial transactions and by keeping their own boards of directors in the dark. . . .

Regarding the complexity of these cases, one FBI agent related a theme popular among officials:

> I have been in the Bureau for about fifteen years and have worked a lot of political corruption, and these things, as far as just getting the pieces straight, you don't know where they are going to lead. You just don't know.

Because of the complexity of [these] cases, federal investigators often find it difficult to present them to a judge or jury. As a result, cases are made as simple as possible to increase the certainty of conviction. . . .

The nature and the unprecedented scale of financial institution fraud, however, limit the government's ability to contain damage to the thrift industry, despite an enormous influx of enforcement resources. The government is limited to reacting to major frauds that occurred years earlier in now-insolvent institutions.

·   ·   ·

One of the intended cnsequences of FIRREA was to increase the degree of interagency coordination in processing financial institution cases. Although a "tighter coupling" among agencies certainly has resulted in some areas, control agencies' actions reveal that much maladjustment still exists because of a number of factors. Not the least of these involve strong political pressure to produce results, the differences in organizational mandates, lack of sufficient resources, and various other legal and organizational obstacles. . . .

Perhaps the largest organizational obstacles concern parallel civil and criminal proceedings and the disparate functions of regulatory and enforcement agencies. Regulatory agencies such as the RTC and FDIC, although necessarily concerned with enforcement, investigations, and criminal referrals, nonetheless are not responsible for criminal investigations or proceedings. Their primary responsibility following an insolvency is the recovery of assets and the achievement of civil remedies. Conflict sometimes may arise if a defendant is named in both civil and criminal proceedings. If the defendant is convicted first of a crime related directly to the civil case, the civil case may achieve little if it seeks to recoup funds through professional liability insurance, because most such insurance policies are nullified if a crime is involved.

Knowledgeable defense lawyers also can use the discovery process to their benefit if a civil case precedes or is contemporaneous with a criminal case. This conflict about which case to make first not only may affect the timing of parallel cases, but also may impede the timely referral of a case for criminal prosecution. Furthermore, communication gaps appear periodically, partly as a result of this potential conflict and the differences between regulatory and law enforcement agencies' priorities. Although a number of enforcement officials report improvements, the sharing of information among agencies occasionally has been problematic. More significant to the criminal sanctioning of financial institution fraud, however, are organizational mandates that lead regulatory investigators to approach civil matters first. One RTC investigatory chief commented:

> We're driven so heavily by the civil statutes that we probably have a balance of focus of about forty percent of our time devoted to fraud, about sixty to the civil. What I'm hoping to be able to do, once we successfully meet the deadline for the civil statutes, is to go back to these hot, smoldering ashes—because they are by no means cold, they are still very active—sift through them deeper, get into what I think are the very sophisticated, convoluted fraud schemes that I believe are there, and pull together the network of fraudulent schemes between these incestuous relationships of these various institutions that I believe are there. But unfortunately, resources and time constraints have let us take a big chunk and look at only pieces of it. But I still think that there is more there to be found. It is my fervent wish that they'll let RTC continue its effort after the civil statutes expire to go back and really look at the fraud.

A larger structural conflict in the nature of the banking system also precludes close interagency relations. This conflict revolves around the essential ingredient of trust, which is necessary if financial institutions that handle other people's money are to thrive, versus the apparent need to regulate these institutions tightly. If accusations are made against management, a solvent institution soon may lose capital and fail. In other words, interagency cooperation may be thwarted by regulatory actions that ignore crime in order to prevent further damage to the industry. . . .

Sometimes direct conflicts arise among agencies in their attempt to coordinate their activities. One example demonstrates an irony in the way enforcement is currently organized. In requesting information from the RTC, the FBI contacted a private attorney who was handling the case for the RTC under contract ("fee counsel"). The attorney then billed the RTC (at $350 per hour) for the time he spent squabbling with federal agents over their right to receive such information. . . .

Lack of strong central leadership that would pull together the various independent agencies is a major factor in the malcoordination of these efforts. United States Attorneys are perhaps the most independent of all agencies responding to financial institution fraud, and their level of participation can very greatly from one office to another. Moreover, their pivotal role in bringing criminal cases into federal courts weighs most heavily in the sanctioning of these frauds. One expert, who has worked in both criminal and regulatory enforcement agencies, stated:

> The agencies did things differently from each other in working with Justice. We kept pushing Justice, but we really should do things to coordinate the government better in making cases. You've got to work with the prosecutors and regulators together, but the other agencies were not doing it. . . . For years we have tried to create working groups to work together, and it never really got off the ground. . . . One of the problems with the Justice Department is that they have ninety-four prima donnas, U.S. Attorneys that take orders from 1600 Pennsylvania Avenue, and while they work ostensibly for the Department of Justice, they are really their own fiefdoms out there. If there is any coordination problem, we can work it out. One of the problems, though, still happens to be the independence of the United States Attorneys.

· · ·

Adequate resources remain a problem for many agencies, given the massive task before them. . . . An enforcement official in Washington, DC remarked on the importance of resources in controlling such crimes:

> I don't think it is a question of better or more laws at the moment, it's the resources to use these laws. The greatest stumbling block is the lack of resources within the criminal justice system as a whole. It's not just the lack of agents investigating. It's lack of prosecutors, lack of judges, lack of places to book.

To some officials, the lack of sufficient resources is a major factor limiting enforcement. . . .

The time required to conduct an investigation is often exrtremely long, and limited resources do not allow for a full discovery of wrongdoing. [An FBI agent comments]: . . .

> There's no question [as to available resources playing a major role]. You are in a situation now when many of those cases that are being adjudicated—and the Bureau, I think, is very much up front on this—that you could stay in there with a bevy of agents for four or five years and still not investigate every criminal allegation because many of these places were such rats' nests. You could investigate them for a decade and still not be sure that you got everything that they were involved in. So, you have to (with the resources you have) say, "All right, this guy's a bad actor. We want to be able to go in and get to the meat of the problem, and we want to be able, in the prosecution of this individual, to see that he gets a substantial criminal sentence without having spent an inordinately long amount of time, because we've got these other cases that are backing up over here."

Other indications of resource problems were noted by respondents who believe that the more professional crooks will be able to exploit the government's limited capacity to respond:

> There's so much of it going on. You have to think, and a lot of these people are very bright, exceedingly bright people. You easily catch the dumb ones and some of the bright ones, but the exceedingly bright ones . . . I have to believe it continues. They outfund us. They have more money to do it, to outstrategize us, and it contines. I know they're there.

Some law enforcement officials already are looking ahead to what they regard as an even greater strain on resources, as formidable tasks appear on the criminal horizon. Control agents believe that more proactive enforcement is a key element to stretching already thin sanctioning resources. . . .

Thrift fraud cases often involve complicated transactions that must be investigated thoroughly before charges can be brought. Investigations are extremely labor-intensive, and the more creative criminals are particularly adept at covering their "paper trails," thus making the task of law enforcement much more difficult. Much potential criminal activity is relegated to the category of administrative violations or civil wrongdoing, where the burden of proof is lighter. Thrift investigators try to limit uncertainty in their work and to increase the likelihood of a succssful prosecution, given the complexity of the frauds they are addressing. Consequently they tend to focus on narrow aspects of a case, for which they will be able to produce unimpeachable evidence of wrongdoing. . . .

In simplifying cases for judges and juries, the investigators, who work closely with prosecutors (U.S. Attorneys) throughout a case, take a "rifle-shot" approach, picking only the strongest charges and focusing only on certain aspects of an entire set of fraudulent transactions. This piecemeal strategy can greatly reduce uncertainty and produce faster results. It also allows prosecutors to return and charge on additional counts if they are not satisfied with the initial results. The disadvantages of such a strategy are more conceptual than real in regard to prosecutors facing large caseloads: not all crooks will be labeled as such, and not all charges will be brought. This mode of enforcement evolved as officials realized the magnitude of their workloads. [One reports]: . . .

> One of the suggestions to Justice, that they already know of, is that they really ought to make simpler cases, two-or 3-count indictments. That is a very simple case, and you ought to do it faster. One of the questions that everyone asks me is why is it taking so long to make a criminal case on some of these guys like the Keatings of the world. The answer is because it's very complicated, and can you find two or three transactions that you can prosecute that person on rather than put together the entire story. The problem with not putting together the entire story is if he only pleads guilty to one or two counts, he may not get significant jail time. We're not going to try to bring every count of every potential crime because to do so confuses the jury, stretches out the cases, and you start to lose in the process. So we're going to look for four-five strong counts with substantial amounts of money involved, very specific criminal activities, and pursue those.

A major obstacle for enforcement personnel concerns the age of the cases. The reactive mode of enforcement and the late start on addressing these crimes exacerbate an already serious situation and further limit the capacity of control efforts. The older a case grows, the harder it is to acquire evidence. . . .

To make matters worse, in many cases the financial institution involved has disappeared or has changed management: . . .

Coupling among agencies is perhaps least highly developed in relation to sentencing. Norms regarding the punishment of convicted defendants, according to many enforcement experts, are not yet shared equally. The window of time within which this recognition must take place further reduces the capacity of the criminal justice system to punish violators. An FBI agent explains:

> There's more crime than we can address, but we will certainly not walk away from a key figure who's gotten a six-month sentence. When we find additional criminal culpability, it will be up to the U.S. Attorney to pursue additional counts. Now it is the judge's opinion that counts as far as the sentence, but the judge doesn't control our investigation in bringing additional counts. As he cannot tolerate us in his business, we will not accept any guidance by the judge if we have any additional counts to pursue. That's not their business. Their business is to try the case before them. We would pursue if we found a situation with a key figure receiving an unduly light sentence. With additional criminal culpability, we'd pursue that.

Declination of cases by prosecutors is another area of potential conflict or loose coupling among agencies. U.S. Attorneys decline cases for various reasons, and policies vary across the country. In most areas, however, U.S. Attorneys have established "prosecution thresholds" that are well known to investigators. Prosecutors must set minimal requirements for taking cases; in cases of financial institution fraud, the requirement usually is related to the dollar amount involved. . . .

Finally, investigative effectiveness is hampered severely by barriers to information. The FBI was not geared to handle these kinds of complex financial cases and the change came quite abruptly with the sudden appearance of massive numbers of criminal referrals for insider fraud in banks and S&Ls. To compound this early lack of FBI training in complex financial cases, the thrift insiders responsible for producing records and documents are often themselves under investigation. . . .

DISCUSSION

The current crisis in U.S. financial institutions provides an excellent case study for examining the government response to corporate and white-collar crime. . . .

Extreme situations that involve tremendous workloads or strains on enforcement resources . . . can aid in examining how government response is organized and how limits to such enforcement are structured.

The savings and loan crisis is an almost unparalleled situation; this fact helps to underscore the limits to government control. The unprecedented scale of fraud in financial institutions that play a central role in distributing government-insured capital probably explains the relatively strong response to these frauds, in contrast to other white-collar crimes. As shown by the responses of enforcement personnel, however, these efforts are severely limited and do not approach the level of response necessary for control or deterrence of crime. Even though the coupling among agencies has become somewhat tighter, the complexity and the magnitude of thrift fraud severely limit the capacity of the criminal justice system to respond. . . .

. . . [S]ome scholars believe that "cooperative models," involving regulatory agreements and persuasion, should be used in lieu of criminal sanctions to control corporate crime because many areas of organizational violation lie beyond the reach of the law (Stone 1975). . . .

In the case of savings and loan fraud, it is uncertain that self-regulation would have been effective. First, there is some doubt about whether self-regulation alone can be effective as a mechanism of social control (Levi 1984). Second, and more important, the fraud perpetrated in the thrift industry in the 1980s, unlike traditional corporate crime, was often the product of deliberate strategies to loot the institution (Calavita and Pontell 1990). Appeals to institutional interests, including the business's reputation and long-term profitability, conceivably may work in an environment in which corporate actors are committed to the institution's survival; they are largely irrelevant, however, to the prevention of such insider abuse and executive looting. Moreover, in view of the nature of these crimes and the historical precedent, adding internal control personnel would appear to do little more than extend the network of fraud to include them (Pontell and Calavita 1993) . . .

Although the government has mounted a relatively strong response to the unprecedented fraud in financial institutions in the United States, the success of this effort has been severely limited. Most enforcement officials recognize that a reactive approach, taken long after the complex and numerous frauds were committed, limits their effectiveness as social control agents. Although criminal justice and regulatory agencies now are coupled more tightly, major structural and organizational obstacles remain. More generally, this study highlights the limitations inherent in reactive state policies designed to control white-collar and corporate crime. . . .

REFERENCES

Alt, K. and K. Siglin (1990) Memorandum on bank and thrift fraud to member and staff of Senate Banking Committee, July 25.

Calavita, K. and H. N. Pontell (1990) "'Heads I Win, Tails You Lose': Deregulation, Crime and Crisis in the Savings and Loan Industry." *Crime & Delinquency* 36:309–41.

Ely, B. (1990) "Crime Accounts for Only 3% of the Cost of the S&L Mess." Unpublished manuscript, Ely and Company.

Hagan, J. (1989) "Why Is There So Little Criminal Justice Theory? Neglected Macro- and Micro-Level Links between Organization and Power." *Journal of Research in Crime and Delinquency* 26:116–35.

Katz, J. (1980) "The Social Movement against White-Collar Crime." In E. Bittner and S. Messinger (eds.), *Criminology Review Yearbook 2*, pp. 161–84. Beverly Hills: Sage.

Levi, M. (1984) "Giving Creditors the Business: The Criminal Law in Action." *International Journal of the Sociology of law* 12:321–33.

Pontell, H. N. (1978) "Deterrence: Theory versus Practice." *Criminology* 16:3–22.

——— (1982) "System Capacity and Criminal Justice: Theoretical and Substantive Considerations." In H. E. Pepinsky (ed.), *Rethinking Criminology*, pp. 131–43. Beverly Hills: Sage.

——— (1984) *A Capacity to Punish: The Ecology of Crime and Punishment.* Bloomington: Indiana University Press.

Pontell, H. N. and K. Calavita (1993) "The Savings and Loan Industry." In M. Tonry and A. J. Reiss Jr. (eds.), *Beyond the Law: Crime in Complex Organizations. Crime and Justice*, Vol. 18, pp. 203–46. Chicago: University of Chicago Press.

Resolution Trust Corporation (1992) *RTC Review*, August. Washington DC: Resolution Trust Corporation.

Rosenblatt, R. A. (1990) "1,000 Bank, S&L Fraud Cases Go Uninvestigated, Lawmaker Says," *Los Angeles Times*, March 15, p. D1.

Stone, C. (1975) *Where the Law Ends: The Social Control of Corporate Behavior.* New York: Harper and Row.

U.S. Congress, House: Committee on Government Operations (1988) "Combatting Fraud, Abuse and Misconduct in the Nation's Financial Institutions: Current Federal Reports Are Inadequate." 72nd Report by the Committee on Government Operations, October 13.

U.S. Congress, Senate: Subcommittee on Consumer and Regulatory Affairs, Committee on Banking, Housing, and Urban Affairs (1992) "Efforts to Combat Criminal Financial Institution Fraud." Hearing before the Subcommittee, February 6.

U.S. Department of Justice (1992) "Attacking Financial Institution Fraud." Second Quarterly Report to Congress, Fiscal Year 1992.

U.S. General Accounting Office (GAO) (1989) "Thrift Failures: Costly Failures Resulted from Regulatory Violations and Unsafe Practices." Report to Congress, June 1989.

White, L. J. (1991) *The S&L Debacle.* New York: Oxford University Press.

An Evolving Compliance Model for Tax Enforcement

VALERIE BRAITHWAITE AND JOHN BRAITHWAITE

Decades of research on regulatory rule enforcement prompted a battle of sorts between those who favor a deterrence approach and those who promote compliance approaches, between punishment and persuasion (Reiss, 1984; Hawkins, 1984; Pearce and Toombs, 1990; Snider, 1990). In some areas, evidence suggests that deterrence works, if only modestly, as in the area of occupational health and safety (Scholz, 1991; Braithwaite, 1985). In nuclear safety and other realms, a shift away from a rule enforcement approach toward a more communitarian style of self-regulation improves complicance (Rees, 1994). In other domains, however, it is unclear whether the effect of increased deterrence is positive or negative (Makkai and Braithwaite, 1994).

PANEL 20   Critics Beware

In 1998, Beverly Enterprises, one of America's largest nursing home operators, filed a defamation suit against Kate Bronfenbrenner, a Cornell University labor researcher. Months before the suit was filed, at the request of several congressmen, Dr. Bronfenbrenner spoke at a town hall meeting in Pittsburgh, Pennsylvania, on unfair labor practices by employers to curb organizing efforts by employees. She called Beverly Enterprises "one of the nation's most notorious labor law violators." In May 1998, Beverly's suit was dismissed by a U.S. District Court judge, who ruled that Bronfenbrenner's statements were protected by legislative immunity under Pennsylvania state law.

Source: Cornell University, News Release, May 27, 1998.

Tax enforcement is an area where the effects of deterrence and compliance approaches are unknown (Andreotti, Erard, and Feinstein, 1998). When taxpayers are audited, for example, and a penalty imposed, it is unclear whether they learn that they got away with a lot of things that the audit did not detect. The deterrence sign will be positive if this is the bigger lesson than the lesson that cheating will be punished. Sometimes an audit succeeds in deterring cheating in the long run, but in the year or two after audit taxpayers believe they are unlikely to be audited, and this has a dramatic negative effect on compliance in those two years.

This and other kinds of complexity have moved the compliance literature over the past decade away from a crude contest between punishment and persuasion. Rather the debate has been about how to get the right mix of the two. In the case studies discussed in this essay, the Australian Taxation Office (ATO) became persuaded to an enforcement pyramid approach to regulation (Ayres and Braithwaite, 1992; Gunningham and Grabosky, 1998). This means regulatory staff prefer the low-cost option of persuasion first and escalate to more deterrence-oriented options (and ultimately to incapacitation), as less interventionist strategies successively fail.

In this essay, we first consider the history of the development of an Australian Taxation Office compliance model out of the work of the Cash Economy Task Force. Ultimately, the responsive regulatory model developed by this group was adopted as policy for all ATO operations. We consider how the model has begun to be applied in three domains: with large corporations, with high wealth individuals, and in the cash economy. In each of these three domains taxpayer complicance is becoming more challenging.

THE TAX COMPLIANCE PROBLEM

Like all nations, Australia has many large corporations that pay no company tax or very little. Data available from the Organization for Economic Cooperation and Development (OECD) suggest that Australia's problems of large corporate compliance may be somewhat below the average for OECD nations, but it is enormous nonetheless (Slemrod, 1996:290). Along with emergence of e-commerce and other developments, the enhanced capabilities of big players in the world system to engage in financial engineering is a growing threat to the corporate tax base. Sophisticated accounting firms, for example, can engineer new derivative products for their largest clients that are not countenanced by existing tax law. Thus, if the Australian subsidiary of a transnational corporation wishes to buy components from another subsidiary of the same corporation in Mexico, computer software is available to show exactly how to route the purchase through a chain of subsidiaries to minimize tax liability. Increasingly, the problem for large business firms is not tax evasion, but adoption of sophisticated strategies for circumventing tax laws. Tax avoidance, but not tax evasion.

The problem of corporate tax compliance is exacerbated by a cultural shift in the global elite of the accounting profession. In the United States, the Big Five accounting firms seem to have been able to increase their profits substantially through shifts towards more aggressive tactics. Individual staffers can secure bonuses up to $US400,000 for landing deals such as those pursued by Deloitte & Touche in the following letter to two middle-sized U.S. firms in 1998:

> Dear ____
>
> As we discussed, set forth below are the details of our proposal to recommend and implement our tax strategy to eliminate the Federal and State Income taxes associated with [the company's] income for up to five (5) years ("the Strategy").

Ernst & Young and Deloitte & Touche reported a 29% jump in revenues from tax services in the United States in 1997 (Novack and Saunders, 1998). Since 1993, tax revenues for the Big Five have grown at twice the pace of audit revenues. The worry is that when elite firms play the game in this way, lesser players will increasingly assume that promotion of aggressive avoidance is the only way to stay competitive. In turn, management and directors of firms who receive letters such as the above, begin to worry that they will come under fire from shareholders if they pay some tax in circumstances where a Big Five accounting firm is telling them that they do not have to. The culture change is well grasped by the fact that tax departments today are viewed as profit centers in some large corporations.

What is true for the largest corporations is also true for the wealthiest individuals. Throughout the world, paying tax for them is increasingly optional. Again, the reason is not primarily tax evasion but the fact that the most sophisticated advisers can engineer a way around the need to pay any tax. This works until the taxation authority discovers it, and, if it responds competently and decisively, new legislation will ban the new path around the law. At this point, the adivser forges a new financial product that will successfully put the wealthy client back in a grey area until *it* is made black by adjustment to the law. The game is much more destructive of the integrity of the law than outright evasion.

The "cash economy" refers to economic transactions that are conducted via cash payments without payment of applicable taxes. In nations like Nigeria, Thailand, Egypt, the Phillipines, and Mexico, this shadow economy predominates, and it is estimated to be near that in Russia and other transition economies (Schneider and Enste, 1999). Best estimates suggest that Australia has less of a problem than developing economies; in common with other Anglo-Saxon countries, Australia's shadow economy seems to be somewhat below the average of all developed countries, around 14% of the economy (Schneider and Enste, 1999).

THEORETICAL BACKGROUND

In *Punish or Persuade,* Braithwaite (1985) first argues that compliance is mot likely when an agency displays and employs an explicit enforcement pyramid. An example of an enforcement pyramid appears in Figure 1. Most regulatory action occurs at the base of the pyramid, where attempts are initially made to coax compliance by persuasion. The next phase of enforcement escalation is a warning letter; if this fails to secure compliance, imposition of civil monetary penalties; if this fails, criminal prosecution; if this fails, plant shutdown or temporary suspension of a license to operate; if this fails, permanent revocation of license. This particular enforcement pyramid might be applicable to occupational health and safety, environment or nursing home regulation, but inapplicable to banking or affirmative action regulation. It is not the content of the

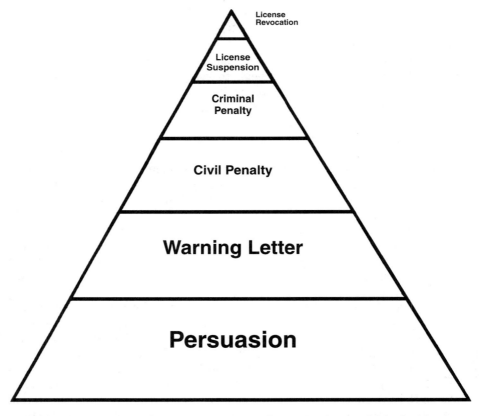

FIGURE 1 A pyramid of enforcement responses. (*Source:* Ian Ayres and John Braithwaite, *Responsive Regulation: Transcending the Deregulation Debate.* New York: Oxford University Press, 1992, page 35).

enforcement pyramid but its form. Different kinds of sanctioning are appropriate to different regulatory arenas.

Defection from cooperation is likely to be a less attractive proposition for business when it faces a regulator with an enforcement pyramid that when confronted with a regulator having only one deterrence option. This is true even where the deterrence option available to the regulator is a powerful, even cataclysmic, one. It is not uncommon for regulatory agencies to have the power to withdraw or suspend licenses as the only effective power at their disposal. The problem is that the sanction is such a drastic one (e.g., putting a television station off the air) that it is politically impossible and morally unacceptable to use it with any but the most extraordinary offenses. Hence, such "or else" has little credibility. This is one case of the paradox of extremely stringent regulatory laws causing under regulation. Regulatory agencies have maximum capacity to lever cooperation when they can escalate deterrence in a way that is responsive to the degree of uncooperativeness of the firm, and to moral and political acceptability of the response. It is the same point as in strategic deterrence in international affairs; a country with a nuclear deterrent but no conventional forces may be more vulnerable than one that can bargain with a limited range of conventional escalations. And it is the same point that has been demonstrated empirically in the domain of criminal justice: if death is the sentence for rape, juries that think this excessive will not convict rapists; if mandatory imprisonment is provided for drunk drivers, many police officers will decline to arrest them (Ayres and Braithwaite, 1992).

The logic and the use of regulatory pyramids are compatible with several theoretical perspectives. From a rational-actor point of view, the expectation of increased regulatory sanctions with repeated failure to cooperate provides an incentive for all players to economize on time and effort and settle differences sooner rather than later. For the tax officer working from a rational actor perspective, implementing the strategy involves three objectives: (1) to ensure that the full range of credible sanctions are known to the taxpayer, (2) to clearly signal a willingness to cooperate initially with the taxpayer, and (3) to make clear the intention to escalate in the event that cooperation is not forthcoming.

Social theories that understand compliance from the perspective of institutional legitimacy and procedural fairness are also given effect in the formulation of a regulatory pyramid. The argument is that taxpayers will regard tough enforcement action as more procedurally fair when persuasion has been tried first. Citizen perceptions of procedural fairness are more than just a political asset to an embattled tax authority; they are likely actually to increase voluntary compliance (Tyler, 1990; Makkai and Braithwaite, 1996). Moreover, when regulated actors believe they are treated as someone who is trusted, compliance increases (Braithwaite and Makkai, 1994).

According to the responsive regulatory strategy, trust works even better when verification–distrust–enforcement lurks in the background. One way of framing the responsive regulatory aspiration is to have most taxpayers believe that tax officers trust *them* at a personal level, but to want tax officers to keep distrustful enforcement strategies at the ready because *others* cannot always be trusted. Knowing that the institutional mechanisms are in place to deal with those who cheat builds community confidence and the legitimacy of the tax system. Regulatory pyramids provide tax officers a set of tools that can be applied without regard to reasons for noncompliance. One starts with the expectation of cooperation, and escalation on the pyramid occurs only when one or the other becomes noncooperative or defaults.

This analysis, however, denies something that is at the core of every regulatory encounter, whether it is personal or impersonal, tax focused or not tax focused, and that is the human quality of making attributions about why others behave as they do. Attributions about other's behavior is at the heart of communication and social relationships (Heider, 1958), and in the area of regulation, the type of attribution that looms large is the underlying motive (Kagan and Scholz, 1984). The advantage of the regulatory pyramid is that its use is not dependent on a correct diagnosis of the motives of the taxpayer. All one needs to do is to look for cooperation in correcting the problem at hand. Yet the reality is that tax officers, like other regulators, are human and "think" motives.

Understanding the motives of another is difficult at the best of times. In the case of regulation, problems are created not only by the inaccessibility of motives, but also by the demands of the social situation, specifically, the imperative to present oneself as a model citizen of compliance. Motives, however, while hidden, are not without influence on more observable phenomena. Motives shape the values and attitudes we publicly espouse to defend our position to ourselves and others (Schwartz, 1992). We all approach regulators with our own world view of how we want to and ought to engage with the regulatory system. These orientations are generally knowable because they are freely expressed. They have been termed motivational postures (V. Braithwaite et al., 1994).

The individual is capable of adopting any of the four motivational postures to be described; they can be held simultaneously, and can be brought into play in a relatively short space of time, depending on the nature of the social interaction. Motivational postures are not fixed characteristics of a person, but are the result of the dynamic interplay between persons or groups and those who want to influence their behaviors.

In the taxation context, the motivational posture of resistance would describe a confrontational approach to tax officers and the tax system. From this perspective, the tax system is likely to be seen as oppressive and burdensome, inflexible and unforgiving, and punishing rather than helping taxpayers. Tax officers are likely to be construed as unhelpful, incompetent, mistrustful, and unwilling to consult with taxpayers.

The posture of disengagement incorporates a spirit of hopelessness on top of resistance. The state of disengagement is accompanied by nonresponsiveness. The system is viewed as one that should be avoided at all cost, and any demands for compliance should be dealt with in a minimalist fashion. Cynicism about the tax system is likely to be matched by cynicism about the power of government. From the disengaged perspective, there is little tax officers can do to harm citizens who do not comply. According to this world view, there is nothing that anyone can do to make a noncomplier comply.

Both postures have been linked with noncompliant behaviors, but with one important difference. Whereas the posture of resistance is associated with a desire to be respected by the authorities, disengagement is not. Research on nursing home compliance has shown that those who adopt a resistance posture are more likely to comply at a future state. Those who have disengaged, however, remain noncompliant (V. Braithwaite et al., 1994).

The noncompliant motivational postures are balanced by two compliant postures, accommodation and capture. Accommodation describes an explicit commitment to doing the right thing, supporting the system, accepting responsibility for compliance, and managing compliance demands conscientiously and effectively. From the perspective of this motivational posture, the tax system would be seen to have power that is legitimate, and that will be used against those who do the wrong thing. At the same time, tax officers would be seen as respectful of taxpayers, treating them as trustworthy, and consulting them when appropriate.

While the posture of accommodation involves deliberate and conscious commitment to satisfying the demands that are being made, the posture of capture is more laissez faire. The tax system is likely to be seen as something of which one is part, and tax officers are not to be feared, nor their approval cultivated. The posture of capture would be associated with the expectation that trust and cooperation will prevail, and that nothing too terrible would happen if one owns up to mistakes and remedies them.

Common to these postures is social distancing or the manufacturing of social rift, a phenomenon that, as it increases, makes voluntary compliance less achievable. Capture and accommodation are postures of minimal social distance in that they signal belonging to the regulatory community. Resistance is the posture of those who want to be respected by the community, but feel apart. The social distance is greater, but can be reversed. Disengagement, on the other hand, represents psychological separation without feelings of loss: A wall has been constructed between the regulated and the regulator.

The significance of social rift is best understood through theories of shame and identity (Braithwaite, 1989; Lewis, 1971; Tajfel, 1978). As regulators expose behavior that is noncompliant, those being regulated protect themselves from disapproval by placing more social distance between themselves and their accusers. Through construing the situation in terms of "us" and "them," the noncompliers are able to hide in the safety of an identity that is at odds with the "demonic" other. To sustain this protective mechanism, the social rift must be allowed to continue and grow. When noncompliers pursue this path, cooperative resolution of the problem is difficult. The challenge for the regulator then becomes one of changing the motivational posture.

According to the responsive regulatory strategy, trying cooperation remains the best first choice for achieving this goal. To the extent that social rift is manufactured through feelings of shame, offering cooperation displays the elements of social reintegration that are a necessary part of eliciting compliance in the future. Offering cooperation to resistant and disengaged noncompliers, however, may not always be the response that regulators feel like making. If regulators respond to resistance and disengagement in a like manner, they may exacerbate the social rift already in existence. In such circumstances, the risk is that regulatory activity will spiral up the pyramid, driven more by emotional volatility than reasoned action. The responsive regulatory strategy cautions against emotional reactivity. The reasoned response is to try cooperation first, regardless of the posturing of the noncompliers.

The ATO Compliance Model

In 1996, the Australian Commissioner for Taxation created and appointed members of a Cash Economy Task Force. Research presented to the Task Force showed that there was widespread acceptance in the community that not paying tax on cash income was acceptable and that there was no certainty in the community that the ATO could detect tax evasion through the cash economy (Cash Economy Task Force, 1997). In 1997, Valerie Braithwaite was invited to join the Task Force as an academic advisor on compliance issues and community values. In preparing for its second report, the committee examined and assessed strategies that would enable the ATO to (1) better understand the dynamics of the cash economy, (2) build partnerships with the community, (3) introduce incentives to improve compliance, and (4) enforce compliance through a greater variety of, and more flexible, sanctions tailored to particular industries and cash practices, and to individual circumstances. In 1998, the Task Force recommended that these objectives be achieved through the development of a model of compliance behavior that would complement the existing Taxpayers' Charter (Cash Economy Task Force, 1998). The Charter assures citizens of their right to being treated fairly and reasonably, having their privacy respected, and receiving timely and helpful advice and information.

The Australian Taxation Office Compliance Model has three key features, each feature represented on a side of the pyramid (Fig. 2). The front side contains the "menu of options" for dealing with noncompliance. They range from learning, educating, and persuading at the base through to prosecuting at the top. In between is a range of sanctioning options that are tailored to the particular industry or tax.

The pyramid face to the right represents the type of regulatory encounter in which tax officers might be engaged. At the base of the pyramid, the activities are self-regulatory. As sanctions increase, the self-regulation may be enforced, and eventually, the style of engagement has more of a command and control quality. Setting out styles of regulatory interaction was important for

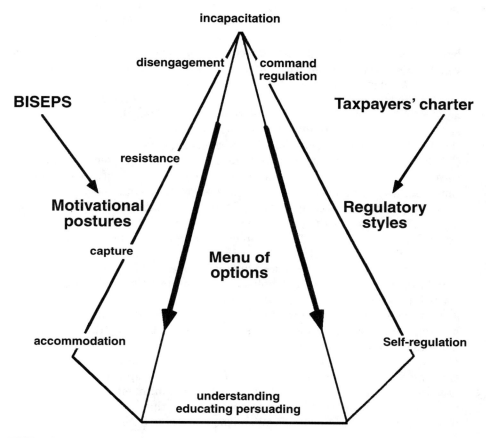

FIGURE 2   The ATO Compliance Model.

ATO staff. Different groups dealt with problems at different levels, and each group had its own culture and set of beliefs as to the "correct" regulatory style. Recognizing a range of regulatory styles, while reinforcing the importance of taxpayers having an opportunity to cooperate initially, communicated an important message to ATO staff: Each subculture contributed to overall tax compliance; the "soft approach" of persuasion and dialogue being as important as the "tough talk" of the court room. One context for these efforts is the *Taxpayers' Charter* ensuring protection of the rights of citizens.

The model of the regulatory pyramid suggests regulatory strategies, while the social rift model describes the posturing of those subject to regulation. The ATO Compliance Model brings these different sides of the regulatory relationship together to summarize the process of conflict escalation, not with the intention of avoiding conflict so much as managing it. As one goes up the regulatory pyramid, sanctioning mechanisms increase in severity. When sanctioning strategies communicate increasing disapproval to the taxpayer, the social rift between noncompliers and the regulatory culture likely increases, and the entrenchment of noncompliant regulatory postures is more likely to follow. The ATO Compliance Model thereby reflects the ways in which the costs associated with enforcing sanctions are magnified by the antagonisms unleashed by resistant and disengaged taxpayers.

On the left face of the pyramid are the motivational postures of taxpayers and/or their agents from accommodation at the bottom through capture, resistance, and at the top, disengagement. Overarching all these postures are the business, industry, sociological, economic, and psychological signs (BISEPS) that might explain why taxpayers present themselves to tax officers as they do. The ATO Compliance Model requires staff to investigate these factors to gain insight into how they might engineer a more cooperative regulatory encounter. Furthermore, systematic attention to the BISEPS over an extended period of time is believed to enhance ATO understanding of the structural underpinnings of noncompliance and provide the necessary intelligence for its early prevention.

According to the responsive regulatory model, ever-increasing sanctions may have to be used to gain compliance. At the same time, dialogue and persuasion must be pursued to draw out a more cooperative regulatory posture so that negotiations can be resumed as soon as possible at the bottom of the pyramid. For a taxpayer showing disengagement, a strategy that results in a move to resistance would improve the tax officer's prospects for gaining compliance. A further move in the right direction would be achieved through a strategy that harnessed the motivational postures of capture or accommodation. Accommodation implies a deeper level of commitment than capture, and would be regarded as the motivational posture that is most conducive to processes of thoughtful persuasion and rich dialogue, both of which are desirable at the bottom level of the regulatory pyramid.

The effectiveness of strategies of dialogue and persuasion rest heavily on a strong and cohesive regulatory culture. The ATO compliance Model captures the importance of investing heavily in building a broad base to the pyramid, a base where there is considerable consensus on what compliance means, strong commitment to doing the right thing, and communication networks that reinforce the importance of law-abiding behavior. Such bases cannot be taken for granted. Nowhere is this more apparent than in relation to the cash economy (Cash Economy Task Force, 1998).

RESPONSIVE REGULATION AND TAX COMPLIANCE

Large Corporations

John Braithwaite has been working with the ATO in adapting the cash economy compliance model to large corporate compliance. The Compliance Model objective of understanding taxpayer behavior has involved the ATO's Large Business and International business line in a variety of sophisticated exercises in risk assessment. As mentioned earlier, this had led them to the position that the main risks to compliance with the intent of tax laws comes not in the form of tax evasion but in tax avoidance. It has instituted a Business Systems Development Project (Bruce-Smith and Pegler, 1998) to build the hard and soft networks for knowledge coaches to mobilize the mentoring needed to advance contextual understanding of taxpayer behavior.

A Strategic Intelligence Network has been put in place. An example of how it has transformed the understanding of taxpayer behavior is through the insight that there are only a handful of tax advisers who have the capability and aggressiveness to promote the tax shelters that are most damaging to the revenue. It follows that it may be more strategic to target this handful of advisers than to target taxpayers with a high risk profile. Strategic Intelligence Analysis developed an "AAA list" strategy. For a major aggressive adviser, an AAA list of the adviser's key clients would be discovered. When these were revealed to be repeat users of tax planning schemes, they would remain on the AAA list for special-purpose audits until they changed to a more conservative approach to tax compliance. In some cases, targeted clients actually called the ATO to advise that they were switching tax advisers and to please take them off the AAA list.*

Risk leveraging is a creative activity. It is a bad idea to provide a formula for how to do it because advisers will soon learn that formula. Continuous reinvention of risk leveraging is what will keep would-be avoiders guessing and therefore, complying. A culture of continuous reinvention of risk leveraging requires taking storytelling seriously. The ATO has decisively moved away from being a business run according to a Procedures Manual. At the level of informal staff interaction, ATO culture is no longer a rulebook, it is a storybook (Shearing and Erickson, 1991). A storybook orientation helps with another objective of the Compliance Model: increased flexibility in operations to support compliance. Best Practice Workshops to share success stories is an important part of the staff morale game in revenue authorities who feel embattled in their dealings with powerful corporate taxpayers. So too is recognition in performance reviews for the heroes of risk leveraging success stories.

Strategic Intelligence Analysis (SIA) seeks to build community partnerships, among other initiatives, through a 250 Financial Planners Project to create an informal soft network to open communication channels between SIA and 250 of the largest financial planning institutions. Another SIA initiative is for a soft network with a group of 15 large corporate tax managers who represent a slice of corporate Australia.

A growing source of flexibility in the ATO's approach to compliance is to

---

*Since this paper went to press, decisions in the Australian courts have obstructed the ATO's access to client lists of tax advisers that the strategy requires. Consequently, this particular way of targeting advisers has been abandoned.

take problems to international forums. The Advance Pricing Arrangement (APA) is one approach to locking in higher tax receipts from transnational corporations that has been enabled by cooperation through the OECD (Killaly, 1996). APAs are negotiated agreements between the ATO and corporations on a transfer pricing methodology that will result in an appropriate allocation of income and expenses between related parties that are selling goods or services between different countries. Negotiating APAs is painstaking work. Because they lock in higher returns much more than audits do and because they shift the rules of the game to more cooperative ones with business, the investment may be well justified. On the other hand, the ATO needs to monitor the cost of keeping APAs up to date in the face of company-, product-, and time-specific changes that make the parameters of the APA obsolete. In addition, there is a worry that only "squeaky clean" companies will ask for APAs, hence skewing ATO activity to areas of low risk. Often companies are reluctant to enter into APA negotiations because they fear this may reveal tax liabilities going back over many years. The kind of flexibility of ATO response required here is for the ATO to be willing to grant an amnesty on tax liabilities going back more than two years as part of the incentive for entering into negotiations. International tax competition can cause compliance problems that can only be addressed through international cooperation. The practice of enlisting cooperative strategies to solve competitive problems is not only relevant to APAs. The approach extend to tax havens and e-commerce as just two examples.

In effect, amnesties on back taxes use reward as a compliance strategy at the base of an enforcement pyramid. The Canadian Audit Protocols (Revenue Canada, 1996) that the ATO is piloting also reward cooperative relationships between the ATO and its clients with negotiated audit protocols that reduce compliance costs for business and increase compliance effectiveness for the ATO. This may include scheduling visits by different areas of the ATO so that disruption to business is minimized, doing concurrent audits, discussing in advance the form that efficient record keeping might take, and the like. The key idea is that Revenue Canada and participating corporations jointly produce a written framework that established guidelines for the relationship and the audit process. The ATO is also increasing the number of escalation options in its enforcement pyramid by innovating with a variety of audit products short of full-scale audits (e.g., special-purpose audits, real-time enquiries). Above audit, it has the capacity to submit cases to the superior investigative powers and criminal punishment orientation of the National Crime Authority.

High-Wealth Individuals

The High Wealth Individuals (HWI) Taskforce commenced work in 1996 simultaneously with the work to develop the ATO compliance model. The objective was an enhanced compliance management strategy for HWIs. In the first year of operation, 180 HWIs received a questionnaire about the groups of entities they control or from which they receive income. These were formalized in subsequent years into expanded tax returns. This was an important innovation to enhance flexibility of response. The inflexibility problem being responded to was that previously either a single individual or a single corporation was a case. The HWI Taskforce made a single case of one of the highest-wealth individuals in the country and all the entities (trusts, corporations) under that individual's control. To stay on the program, HWIs also had to be paying very little tax. The Task Force therefore enabled a more holistic view of tax planning by the rich. One HWI adviser explained why this strategy might be effective with this kind of taxpayer: "The more information he's [the Commissioner's] got, the less aggressive they will be in their tax planning." This adviser explained that notifying X in 1999 reduces the taxpayer's degrees of freedom to reconfigure his 2000 affairs in such a way that not-X appears to be the case in 1999. "Changes each year will be noticed." So HWIs must keep their affairs consistent with the underlying truths of earlier declarations. Moreover the holistic surveillance of the HWI's diaspora of entities means that it is harder to pretend X in the return of one trust and not-X in the return of another. The Task Force may have had modest success in this kind of way. Private companies controlled by individuals in the HWI program paid 17% less tax than non-HWI companies in 1994, 12% less in 1995, 23% more in 1996, and 20% more in 1997. In other words, companies controlled by high-wealth individuals in the project changed from being below-average to above-average taxpayers.

Cash Economy

To date, the impact of the Compliance Model as a response to the cash economy has been in building a stronger community base. Partnerships have been built with industry associations to improve the flow of information and to find ways of making compliance easier. A theme common to many of the industry-based projects is better record keeping. The ATO, for instance, has designed and published a restaurant record keeping booklet, freely available and successfully marketed not only as a tax aid but also as an aid to better business practice. Industry benchmarking has also been important for educating tax agents and the public as to ATO expectations of taxable income from different industry groups. Real-time reviews have been introduced as well in certain industry segments to improve knowledge of and practices in keeping track of cash transactions. The activity at this level is providing the ATO with valuable feedback concerning appropriate incentives for recording cash transactions, intelligence regarding tax evasion schemes, and strategies that may discourage some kinds of evasion in the future.

CONCLUSION

A holistic understanding of taxpaying behavior is necessary to improve compliance. It will not be accomplished by considering individual or corporate taxpayers one at a time as value-maximizing unitary actors. We can learn from investment in evidence-based tax administration that industry associations, families, advisers, tax managers, tax agents, and international organizations like the OECD, among others, are loci of influence over tax compliance. The drivers of complicance at these different loci are plural. By seeing and managing compliance appeals in pyramidal fashion so that reward and trust are favored strategies at the base and tough enforcement at the peak, we can move responsively to improve tax compliance by mobilizing appropriate drivers at propitious moments.

REFERENCES

Andreoni, James, Brian Erard, and Jonathan Feinstein. 1998. "Tax Compliance." *Journal of Economic Literature* 36:818–60.

Ayres, Ian, and John Braithwaite. 1992. *Responsive Regulation: Transcending the Deregulation Debate.* New York: Oxford University Press.

Braithwaite, John. 1985. *To Punish or Persuade: Enforcement of Coal Mine Safety.* Albany: State University of New York Press.

Braithwaite, John. 1989. *Crime, Shame and Reintegration.* Cambridge: Cambridge University Press.

Braithwaite, John, and Toni Makkai. 1994. "Trust and Compliance." *Policing and Society* 4:1–12.

Braithwaite, Valerie. 1995. "Games of Engagement: Postures within the Regulatory Community." *Law and Policy* 17:225–55.

Braithwaite, Valerie, John Braithwaite, Diane Gibson, and Toni Makkai. 1994. "Regulatory Styles, Motivational Postures and Nursing Home Compliance." *Law and Policy* 16:363–94.

Cash Economy Task Force. 1997. "Improving Tax Compliance in the Cash Economy." Report to the Commissioner of Taxation, Australian Taxation Office. Canberra, ACT.

Cash Economy Task Force. 1998. "Improving Tax Compliance in the Cash Economy." Report to the Commissioner of Taxation, Australian Taxation Office, Canberra, ACT.

Gunningham, Neil, and Peter Grabosky. 1998. *Smart Regulation: Designing Environmental Policy.* Oxford, U.K.: Clarendon.

Hawkins, Keith. 1984. *Environment and Enforcement: Regulation and the Social Definition of Pollution.* Oxford, U.K.: Clarendon.

Heider, Fritz. 1958. *The Psychology of Interpersonal Relations.* New York: John Wiley.

Kagan, Robert, and John Scholz. 1984. "The Criminology of the Corporation and Regulatory Enforcement Strategies." Pp. 67–97 in *Enforcing Regulation,* edited by Keith Hawkins and John M. Thomas. Boston: Kluwer-Nijhoff.

Killaly, Jim. 1996. "Advance Pricing Arrangements: The Australian Position: Practical Issues Relating to Australia's APA Program." OECD Working Paper No. 6, 18–19 April. Paris: OECD.

Lewis, Helen. 1971. *Shame and Guilt in Neurosis.* New York: International University Press.

Makkai, Toni, and John Braithwaite. 1994. "The Dialectics of Corporate Deterrence." *Journal of Research in Crime and Delinquency* 31:347–73.

Makkai, Toni, and John Braithwaite. 1996. "Procedural Justice and Regulatory Compliance." *Law and Human Behavior* 20:83–98.

Novack, Janet, and Laura Saunders. 1998. "The Hustling of X Rated Shelters." *Forbes* 14(December):2.

Pearce, Frank, and Steve Toombs. 1990. "Ideology, Hegemony, and Empiricism: Compliance Theories of Regulation." *British Journal of Criminology* 30:423–43.

Rees, Joseph. 1994. *Hostages of Each Other: The Transformation of Nuclear Safety Since Three Mile Island.* Chicago: University of Chicago Press.

Reiss, Albert J. 1984. "Selecting Strategies for Social Control over Organizational Life." Pp. 23–35 in *Enforcing Regulation,* edited by Keith Hawkins and John M. Thomas. Boston: Kluwer-Nijhoff.

Revenue Canada. 1996. "RC4024 The Audit Protocol." Ottawa: Revenue Canada.

Schneider, Friedrich, and Dominik Enste. 1999. "Shadow Economies around the World—Sizes, Causes and Consequences." Paper to Center for Tax System Integrity. September 8.

Scholz, John T. 1991. "Cooperative Regulatory Enforcement and the Politics of Administrative Effectiveness." *American Political Science Review* 85:115–36.

Schwartz, Shalom. 1992. "Universals in the Content and Structure of Values: Theoretical Advances and Empirical Tests." Pp. 1–65 in *Advances in Experimental Social Psychology,* edited by M. P. Zanna. Orlando, FL.: Academic Press.

Shearing, Clifford D., and Richard V. Erickson. 1991. "Towards a Figurative Conception of Action." *British Journal of Sociology* 42:481–506.

Slemrod, Joel. 1996. "Tax Cacophony and the Benefits of Free Trade." Pp. 283–309 in *Fair Trade and Harmonization: Prerequisites for Free Trade? Volume I,* edited by Jagdish Bhagwati and Robert E. Hudec. Cambridge, Mass.: MIT Press.

Snider, Laureen. 1990. "Cooperative Models and Corporate Crime: Panacea or Cop-Out?" *Crime & Delinquency* 36:373–90.

Tajfel, Henri. 1978. *Differentiation between Social Groups: Studies in the Social Psychology of Intergroup Relations.* London: Academic Press for the European Association of Experimental Social Psychology.

Tyler, Tom. 1990. *Why People Obey the Law.* New Haven, Conn.: Yale University Press.

Cooperative Models and Corporate Crime: Panacea or Cop-Out?

LAUREEN SNIDER

. . . The orientation that regulatory agencies should adopt and the weapons they should use have become central issues in the policy literature on corpo-

"Cooperative Models and Corporate Crime" from *Crime & Delinquency* 36:3 (July 1990): 373–90. Reprinted by permission.

rate crime. The debate has come to revolve around a basic disagreement over control strategies. Whereas many continue to argue for more intense regulation and more severe sanctions, others call for "realistic" measures that take into account the powers and the limitations of regulatory regimes in the industrialized democracies as well as the problems of the corporate sector in complying with regulatory law. Such "cooperative models" argue against the use of criminal law, which advocates see as an inappropriate and ineffective tool against corporate crime, and in favor of a combination of persuasion, education, and civil/administrative remedies to secure compliance (Bardach and Kagan 1982; Jamieson 1985; Kagan 1978; Peltzman 1976; Scholz 1984a, 1984b).

This . . . argues that cooperative models have become popular politically because they recognize and legitimate the existing relations of power, the status quo under which regulatory forces are outmatched by the powerful corporate sector. The result of enshrining this disparity in official policy is to stabilize it, weakening thereby the forces that seek to strengthen regulation. By ignoring the corporate political, ideological, and economic dominance that creates regulatory ineffectiveness in the first place, cooperative models set themselves up to be the victims of this dominance. . . .

PANEL 21　Criminal Interference?

On March 5, 1999, a Miami, Florida, jury awarded $37 million to the family of a 12-year-old girl who was killed in a traffic accident after Florida Power & Light Co. (FPL) turned off the electric power to a traffic light in Pinecrest, Florida. The award was reported to be the largest in U.S. history for the death of a minor, and the company subsequently filed multiple requests with the trial court to set aside the verdict. In April 1999, investigators hired by the company contacted the jury foreman and, according to the girl's parents, offered to pay him to help determine whether the jury acted improperly in reaching its decision. FPL admitted its investigators contacted the juror, but it denied doing so in hopes of overturning the jury award. It also denied offering money to the juror. Post-trial contact with jurors is a violation of Florida's ethics rules for lawyers and, when it is done with intent to tamper with a verdict, is a felony punishable by five years in prison and/or a $5,000 fine. It was learned subsequently that a second juror also was contacted by FPL investigators. The second juror had admonished the company after the verdict was announced by turning to its lawyers in the courtroom and saying, "Shame on you." The judge in the case had warned FPL at the end of the trial not to interview jurors about the verdict.

Source: Miami Daily Business Review, May 20, 1999, p. A1, and May 26, 1999, p. A1.

MODELS OF REGULATION

Corporate crimes are white-collar crimes committed with the encouragement and support of a formal organization, and intended at least in part to advance the goals of that organization (Coleman 1985, p. 8; Edelhortz 1970, p. 3; Meier and Short 1982, p. 24). In the majority of Western democracies, corporate crime has been regulated by some combination of civil, administrative, and criminal procedures, enforced by special regulatory agencies acting under federal, state/provincial, or municipal law. Regulatory enforcement is the consistent application of formal rules and sanctions to secure compliance with the enabling legislation and promulgated regulations. . . .

Criminalization

From Sutherland in 1938 to Clinard and Yeager in the late 1970s, investigators have documented the minuscule role criminal sanctions play in the control of corporate criminality and called for an increase in their frequency and severity. To summarize this literature: full enforcement is neither the goal of regulatory agencies nor the reality; penalties are handed out in inverse proportion to offending firms' size and power; and sanctions are so small that they hardly qualify as licensing fees, let alone as deterrents. Regulators prefer persuasion and education to laying charges; often their official mandate directs them to balance the benefits of enforcement against the drawbacks, assessing whether or not enforcement is in "the public interest." (For example, will it have negative consequences such as loss of jobs in a community, or loss of votes for a particular incumbent or party?) Dozens of studies, in Canada, Britain, Australia, United States, and elsewhere, document this reluctance to invoke formal procedures against corporate offenders (e.g., Carson 1970; Clinard and Yeager 1980; Downing and Hanf 1983; Goff and Reasons 1978; Grabosky and Braithwaite 1986; Cunningham 1974, 1984; Hawkins 1984; Morgenstern 1982; Shover, Clelland, and Lynxwiler 1986).

The tendency to focus on offenders who do the least amount of damage also has been documented. The largest and most powerful organizations are the least sanctioned; the smallest and most peripheral are treated most severely, in both quantitative (number of visits, summonses) and qualitative (criminal versus civil law sanctions) terms. Evidence comes from a number of areas: Food and Drug Laws, False Advertising and Anti-combines in Canada (Snider 1978; Snider and West 1980), tax violations in the United States (Long 1979); coal mining violations in United States (Lynxwiler, Shover, and Clelland 1984); and assorted other countries and fields (for example, Fellmeth 1973; Fisse and Braithwaite 1983; Reasons, Ross, and Patterson 1981, Thomas 1982).

The paucity of sanctions is similarly well established empirically. Civil and criminal fines, for large organizations, typically represent a fraction of the profits made in 1 hour of operation, and imprisonment is virtually unknown. . . .

Identifying this reluctance to "get tough" with corporate offenders as the problem, many scholars see increased use of imprisonment and higher criminal fines as the remedy. . . . The fact that increasing the number and severity of criminal laws has not provided better control over corporate crime is explained by focusing on insufficient utilization. If criminal sanctions were to be deployed regularly, if corporations knew that their chances of escaping criminal conviction were slight, if fines commensurate with the size of the firm and the profitability of the crime were imposed, if jail sentences were given, if these procedures were coupled with more enforcement personnel and more punitive laws, backed by civil and administrative remedies where appropriate, then criminalization and deterrence would be effective (Coffee 1984; Elkins 1976; Watkins 1977).

In recent years, however, the results of increasingly sophisticated studies of regulatory agencies have subjected criminalization models to heavy attack. The first and most serious charge has been simply that criminal law does not work against corporate offenders. Regulatory law is different from traditional criminal law because its goal is not to punish, but to secure compliance and educate. Corporate offenders may lack the technical competence required for compliance, they may be ignorant of the law, or unintentional organizational (system) failures may lead them to offend. Moreover, charging corporations and executives and pursuing them through the criminal courts creates antagonism, threatening the cooperation and goodwill that are crucial to the effectiveness of regulation because so many areas of corporate misbehavior are beyond the purview of law (Stone 1975).

A second charge is that criminalization actually increases the amount of harm produced by corporate crime. The strict evidentiary requirements of the criminal courts mean that a regulatory agency, rather than stepping in when it first hears of an offense, has to allow it to continue long enough to gather evidence. The high cost of using criminal justice procedures is also an issue. . . .

Empirical studies show the merit of these criticisms.

Rankin and Brown (1988) compared two agencies in the province of British Columbia, one using administrative penalties and the other criminal sanctions. The Waste Management Branch, using criminal law, filed an average of 44 charges annually from 1984 to 1986, and convicted an average of 16 per year, with an average fine of $565 each. The Workman's Compensation Board, by contrast, issued 300 administrative penalties and a mean fine of $5000 in the first half of 1986 and $3100 in 1985 (p. 6). Jamieson's study (1985) of British factory regulation identified four components of inspectors' beliefs that make them unlikely to use punitive measures: (a) industry is powerful enough to resist regulations it defines as overly restrictive; (b) regulations that threaten economic viability will not be passed in the first place; (c) society only wants the harmful side effects of industry restricted, as it approves of the corporate sector in general; and (d) societal consent for the regulatory function would be withdrawn if policing were seen as overzealous.

Increasingly detailed knowledge about the nature of regulatory agencies also weakens the case for criminalization. The factors that create and nourish regulatory agencies (theories of origins), their advantages and disadvantages, and their various constituencies (from the general public to producers, competitors, and government itself), all have been studied now (Fels 1982, p. 32; Kagan 1978, pp. 13–15; Mitnick 1980). And the more we find out, the more limited the ability of the typical regulatory agency to employ a criminalization strategy appears to be. Consider, for example, the phenomenon of "capture," the process whereby the regulatory agency takes on the perspective of the industry it is supposed to regulate. Capture is thought to be both recurring and inevitable. Regulatory agencies historically have displayed a pattern of long-term growth that has outstripped growth in the industry they were set up to regulate (Noll 1978; Meier and Plumlee 1978; Stigler 1975). This growth is associated not with more efficient control of corporate crime, however, but with greater rigidity of decision making. An agency's creative youth is no defense against a rigid and captured old age (Anderson 1975; Cobb and Elder 1972; Sabatier 1975, 1977).

Cooperation

In light of such studies, cooperative models begin to look appealing, and they have come to dominate discussions of policy and reform in popular and business forums. . . . Braithwaite's cooperative proposals represent his continuing efforts to surmount the weaknesses of criminalization models and to find an effective sanctioning mechanism for corporate crime. In 1982 he suggested government enforced self-regulation, whereby all organizations would be required to file, and have approved, their own proposals for policing potentially troublesome areas of operation. Such areas include the control of pollution, standards for worker safety, and provisions for the legal distribution of company shares. There would be strict minimum standards and criteria for each organization, and each plan would be monitored periodically even after approval. This cooperative system, Braithwaite argued, would have several advantages. Inspectors hired by the corporation to enforce the industry-generated standards would be insiders, not outsiders as regulatory agency employees are, and would therefore have access to all kinds of formal and informal sources of information presently denied to outsiders. Also they would have the technical knowledge effective regulation requires, and would be less likely to be seen by fellow employees as "the enemy." The regulated organization would pay most of the costs of the scheme, and each firm could make sure that the rules it drew up fitted its organizational structure. Moreover, standards and procedures could be tightened as technical advances allowed. Braithwaite conceded that company inspectors would be even more subject to capture than state-employed inspectors are, but thinks this could be overcome by laws requiring a public report if management overruled its inspectors (Braithwaite 1982).

Braithwaite and Fisse (1983) next developed a model of "informal social control," defined as "behavioral restraint by means other than those formally directed by a court or administrative agency" (p. 1). Informal social control relies heavily on stigma and adverse publicity as disincentives to antisocial corporate conduct. Provided there were mechanisms to increase public access to and knowledge of corporate crimes, it could be, they argued, a useful deterrent. As evidence, they cited the complete about-face on the asbestos issue that characterized James Hardie, formerly a major asbestos manufacturer in Australia. They do recognize its limitations, however, admitting at one stage: "Perhaps the real lesson . . . is that informal social control can work when structural realities make is possible" (Braithwaite and Fisse 1983, p. 76).

Building on these schemes, Braithwaite (1988, 1985b) more recently suggested a pyramid approach based on a hierarchy of penalties. Assuming that industrial self-regulation is absent or has failed, the regulatory agency would be required to pursue a fixed sequence of options when it suspects laws have been breached: (a) attempts would be made to persuade the organization to comply; (b) official warnings would be delivered; (c) compulsory civil charges leading to monetary penalties would be assessed; and (d) criminal prosecution would be accompanied by mandatory sanctions ranging from prison sentences for executives to removal of the operating license and plant shutdown. The system is intended to overcome problems which have been caused, Braithwaite argued, by exclusive reliance on either civil/administrative penalties or criminal sanctions (or, indeed, problems caused by using persuasion/education as exclusive strategies).

A political scientist has developed another variation of cooperative regulation. Based on the "prisoner's dilemma" logic game, Scholz (1984a, 1984b) demonstrated, mathematically and logically, that cooperative strategies are advantageous to both regulators and regulated. He assumed that both sides have a common interest in minimizing costs, and the regulated corporation seeks also to minimize sanctions. Cooperative strategies are normally best for both, but only if both sides adhere to this policy. When one player abandons it, the other, to maximize benefits, must defect immediately as well. Thus, if the defector is a firm, the regulatory agency should instantly abandon persuasion/education and move to a deterrence strategy through the appropriate legal mechanisms. (If it is the regulatory agency that abandons the cooperative mode, the firm should immediately, according to this model, adopt avoidance/evasion strategies.) With such a model, the firm derives minimum benefit from cheating, and the regulators are caught out or "suckered" only once before moving to more punitive rules of play. A strategy whereby regulatory agencies use only the criminal law/deterrence orientation, Scholz argued, makes law evasion on the part of the regulated a rational strategy. Illustrative of the increasingly powerful law and economics movement, this scheme appeals for two reasons: (a) it is grounded in mathematical symbols rather than words, and (b) it demonstrates that cooperation represents a sensible economic strategy, a rationale much more persuasive than "soft" concepts such as values and morality.

Comparing this model with his pyramid proposal, Braithwaite (1988) pointed to advantages and disadvantages. On the plus side, Scholz's model has a political advantage for regulatory agencies, as it allows them the moral upper hand—they do not opt for punitive methods until the regulated organization has demonstrated bad faith. Thus they are responding to antisocial corporate behavior that has already occurred, not singling out for special treatment "law-abiding corporations which are minding their own business." It also has the virtues of simplicity and flexibility, in that the agency can revert to cooperative strategies once the industry signals its desire to do so by complying with the law. The negatives are that it cannot easily be used with individuals and organizations that are "one-shotters" as opposed to "repeat players" (Galanter 1974); and it provides no comparable way of dealing with situations where cooperation cannot ever be expected to develop.

Cooperative models . . . try to get around the demonstrated pitfalls of criminalization by putting in place flexible schemes that are purportedly in the interests of both the regulated and the regulators. They have been received with considerable enthusiasm and are said to embody philosophical change that has occurred in regulatory law, especially in United States and Great Britain . . .

PITFALLS OF COOPERATIVE REGULATION

Both criminalization and cooperative models can be faulted for recommending remedies without fully taking into account the broader socioeconomic realities of life in a capitalist system. Advocates of criminalization call for stricter enforcement, higher fines, and prison sentences. However, since regulators choose not to use the considerable arsenal of sanctions they already possess, getting even more punitive laws on the books is surely not the answer.

Advocates of cooperative models, on the other hand, fail to deal with the implications of class-based power. They recognize that the overwhelming opposition of the corporate sector has invitiated efforts at criminalization, but they ignore its potential effect on cooperative regulation. It is corporate power that makes regulatory agencies and remedial measures ineffective, not the measures themselves; and corporate power will make cooperative models at least equally futile. In fact, I argue that these models will be much less effective than criminalization in controlling corporate crime (though they may well be more efficient in the sense that the gap between what they attempt and what they achieve is less). Indeed, it is this increased potential to make regulation ineffective that has caused corporate analysts, the business press, and allied politicians to embrace cooperative models with such enthusiasm.

To understand where cooperative models go wrong, one must start by examining their origins. Like criminalization models, they are deeply rooted in mainstream Western thought, part of a pluralist tradition that has championed the continuing extension of social control through the institution of law. Dominant ideology stresses that law is a universalistic instrument that treats all classes, gender, races, and religions alike, and looks with the same disfavor on predatory acts of the rich as those of the poor. Under these circumstances, the virtual exemption corporations and the rich originally enjoyed from coercive legal regulation became a threat to the legitimation and consent essential for the operation of the modern state. Discipline and legal regulation, used originally to transform a pre-industrial peasant class into a functional working class, soon spread to encompass virtually all classes and behaviors (Cohen 1979, 1985; Foucault 1979; Melossi 1980). Once the antisocial acts of the upper classes and corporate elites became visible (with the development of mass media and literacy), and once the lower and working classes gained power (through the universal franchise and working-class organizations), it was inevitable that the former would be called to account. From the 19th century on, reformers, working-class groups and, later, scholars called for greater control over corporate misconduct.

Scholars advocating cooperative models are well grounded in the discourse of increased social control, but here it becomes regulatory and not criminal law that is advocated. And a new twist has been put on the concept of universalism with the argument that treating corporate criminals the same as traditional ones is not necessary, as long as the end result is to produce more and not less control over the wrongdoers. They are not, then, arguing for increased tolerance. Criminal law is rejected by cooperative models not because it is too punitive or controls too heavily, but because it controls too little. Criminalization models are punitive only in theory, only in the law books, because laws are not enforced. Indeed, they cannot be enforced because criminal law itself is seen as a flawed technique. Cooperative models, then, are philosophically very much in tune with dominant ideological currents of the 1980s wherein moves towards "liberalization" or "permissiveness" are greeted with horror (Snider 1985), and moves to "clamp down" are hailed.

However, the reception accorded cooperative models in the public arena in the 1980s must be understood not in the context of scholars' intentions, but in the declining light of liberalism and the dramatic rise of the New Right. These conservative forces, quiescent during the prosperous 1960s and 1970s, came into their own during the 1980s with the election of Ronald Reagan in the United States and Margaret Thatcher in Britain and the advent of fiscal crises in both countries. The capitalist class and its allies in government have promoted an economic agenda that favors austerity capitalism and monetarist policies. The goal, to legitimate a smaller share of national wealth for the working and lower classes and a larger one for the corporate sector, is sold by reason-based appeals to remain competitive combined with emotional appeals to religion and nationalism. In the area of crime, this means a law-and-order agenda attacking Blacks, feminists, homosexuals, and any other group that can be used to symbolize decline, decay, and the loss of traditional White male authority (Comack 1988; Horton 1981).

Corporate crime, however, is treated differently. Here, the New Right advocates deregulation, the removal of government "fetters" over business.

Neoconservatives see the shortcomings of criminalization as confirmation of their position. They argue that the arguments favoring cooperative models put forth by the Law and Economics groups (Lewis-Beck and Alford 1980; Smith 1976, 1979; Whiting 1980) confer scholarly blessings on their ideologically motivated attempts to represent the corporate sector as the beleaguered scapegoat of social democracy in the postwar period. They contend that respectable business people do not commit crimes intentionally, that their crimes are victimless bookkeeping errors too trivial to merit criminal prosecution, and that the importance of business to the development of the capitalist economy warrants overlooking any minor excesses that might occur. The movement, then, seeks to rescue capitalism from the ideological and financial threats represented by the 1960s, Watergate-type scandals, and looming fiscal crises.

Scholars supporting cooperative models may have no desire to convey such a message, and may disapprove of the political uses to which their work is put. However, neoconservative use of the movement to cooperative regulation was not foreseen and its implications are still not recognized. Given that the original purpose of cooperative reforms was to increase control over the corporate sector, not decrease it, such a reception should have been a dramatic signal that something was wrong. Scholarship is neither produced nor received in a political and economic vacuum. This is not to say that scholars are unconscious tools of an all-powerful ruling class; merely that, out of all the ideas produced in a given time period, those consonant with and useful to powerful groups will be the ones most likely to be heralded as significant, and incorporated into the commonsense notions by which people make sense of the social world. The popularity of cooperative models does not surprise those who have studied the social diffusion and transmission of ideas. At particular ideological junctures, ideas are seized upon, disseminated, popularized, and thereby transformed into instruments that increase the power of the dominant class.

Dominant ideological currents are continuously being disseminated in this way, though they are met in democratic societies by dissenting groups that oppose them. This is an ongoing but unequal struggle because antithetical ideologies are simultaneously created out of the same contradictory processes as dominant ones. Such opposing ideas, supported by groups outside the hegemonic consensus (such as labor unions, feminist groups, or environmental lobbies), meet with heavy resistance, and have a much more difficult time commanding a mass audience and securing acceptance.

Examples of the speed and enthusiasm with which ideas consonant with dominant ideological currents are adopted would include, in the area of criminal law, the reception and distortion of Martinson's critique of offender rehabilitation programs, commonly and erroneously summed up in the phrase "nothing works." This came along just when the public sector was feeling the fiscal crunch associated with changes in the structure of monopoly capitalism, and was consonant with a hardening of attitudes toward traditional crime

(Walker 1985; Martinson 1974). In a field like corporate crime, in which the ideological and financial implications of ideas and the social policies they spawn directly affect the profitability of major corporate actors, the significance of a shift in the assumptions underlying social policy can be enormous. Changes directly affect the interests of the most powerful groups in the society, the corporate elites and the two main levels of the state (federal and provincial/state). When Yeager (1986) said that calling corporate misbehavior criminal was resorting to an unnecessary "linguistic flag," he was forgetting all that we know about the political economy of regulation and enforcement. Obscuring the link between corporate crime and traditional crime may have a profound and deleterious impact on the already weak structure of regulation.

It should also be clear that the emphasis these models place on cooperation with the targets of regulatory law is nothing new—it has always been the dominant strategy regulators actually employed. In fact, it plays a major role in all law enforcement, since every law requires those who would control to negotiate some minimal level of consent from the targets of the law. The limits of this negotiation are set by a constellation of factors: (a) the enabling legislation and precedents; (b) the power of targeted groups; (c) and the subjective and objective relevance of structural variables (such as the interests affected, national policies, and the like). Obviously, this process grants considerably more leverage to the corporate executive than to the armed robber. As we noted previously, cooperative regulators in the area of corporate crime have been the rule not the exception, even where legislation specifically directs enforcers to the contrary. If there is evidence that criminalization does not work, there is equally compelling evidence that cooperation does not either.

It may be, then, that even the best of the cooperative schemes. . . . do no more than describe the operational procedure that good regulatory agencies generally follow. A sequence from persuasion to civil to criminal sanctions is common (Rankin and Brown 1988; Shapiro 1985; Shover et al. 1986; Tucker 1987). Regulatory ineffectiveness was—and is—the result of agencies being hemmed in by structural factors, and the ideological, political, and economic consequences of this. One result of this power is that regulators themselves often "buy" the dominant ideology and see corporations and their executives as non-criminal entities who offend through ignorance rather than design. But even with zealous regulators, the typical disparity in resources between them and the regulated means it often is more efficient, in the narrow sense of the word, for regulators to choose strategies that gain them the support and trust of the more powerful group (as all supplicants must do). Because they lack anything approaching equal power, this is one of the few ways that regulators can influence corporate behavior. From the regulators' point of view, these tactics make good sense. However, to persuade scholars that the stratagems regulators have developed to survive in a hostile regulatory climate are actually and intrinsically the best ones is a surprising development.

The acceptance of this conclusion comes directly out of the aforementioned academic failure to recognize the implications of this overwhelming disparity in power for cooperative models. Class power has shaped the laws that regulate corporate crime; it has a major impact on the behavior of state officials; and it is responsible for most of the difficulties they face in regulating effectively. At the risk of oversimplification, the entire agenda of regulation is the result of a struggle between the corporate sector opposing regulation and the much weaker forces supporting it. Cooperative models allow scholars to conceptualize the existing balance of power between regulators and the corporate sector as a fundamental and acceptable constraint on the state's ability to regulate corporate crime. The acceptance of "the hegemony of corporate ideology" (Pearce and Tombs 1988, p. 8) makes this dominance the starting point for regulators rather than a barrier that must be challenged and overcome. This in turn sets very low limits for regulators, and signifies an acceptance by scholars of the position that really effective regulation of corporate crime is not possible.

IMPLICATIONS

It must be clear by now that securing effective regulatory enforcement is going to be very difficult. If this analysis is correct, change will require strategies that weaken the economic and ideological power of the corporate sector while simultaneously strengthening that of oppositional forces. Given present-day economic exigencies and the antiregulatory climate still dominant in the major Western democracies, this will be a major challenge.

It should also be clear, however, that repealing criminal law and substituting the goal of cooperation with regulators can only weaken further proregulatory forces. . . .

Since securing even minimal regulatory effectiveness requires constant vigilance and political struggle, those who want effective control should look for ways to increase the power of pressure groups and focus media attention on the frequency (great) and the human consequences (immense) of corporate crime. This necessitates confronting prevailing cultural assumptions that attribute all social evils to the criminality and drug habits of the poor and powerless, and shifting the political spotlight onto those who do the most damage and cost the most lives. The result of continuing along our present path will be to undermine, not assist, the struggle for effective control of corporate crime.

REFERENCES

Anderson, J. E. 1975. *Public Policy-Making.* New York: Praeger.

Bardach, E. and R. A. Kagan. 1982. *Going by the Book.* Philadelphia: Temple University Press.

Braithwaite, J. 1982. "Enforced Self-Regulation: A New Strategy for Corporate Crime Control." *Michigan Law Review* 80:1468–1507.

———. 1985b. *To Punish or Persuade*. Albany: State University of New York Press.

———. 1988. "Toward a Benign Big Gun Theory of Regulatory Power." Canberra: Australian National University, Australian Institute of Criminology.

Braithwaite, J. and B. Fisse. 1983. "Asbestos and Health: A Case of Informal Social Control." *Australian-New Zealand Journal of Criminology* 16:67–80.

Carson, W. G. 1970. "White Collar Crime and the Enforcement of Factory Legislation." *British Journal of Criminology* 10:383–398.

———. 1982. "Legal Control of Safety on British Offshore Oil Installations." In *White Collar and Economic Crime*, edited by P. Wickman and T. Dailey. Toronto: Lexington Books.

Clinard, M. B. and P. Yeager. 1980. *Corporate Crime*. New York: Free Press.

Cobb, R. W. and C. D. Elder. 1972. *Participation in Politics*. Boston: Allyn & Bacon.

Coffee, J. C. 1984. "Corporate Criminal Responsibility." Pp. 253–264 in *Encyclopedia of Crime and Justice*, Vol. 1, edited by S. Kadish. New York: Free Press.

Cohen, S. 1979. "The Punitive City: Notes on the Dispersal of Social Control." *Contemporary Crises* 3:339–363.

———. 1988. *Visions of Social Control*. Cambridge, U.K.: Polity Press.

Coleman, J. 1985. *The Criminal Elite*. New York: St. Martin.

Comack, L. 1988. "Law and Order Issues in the Canadian Context." Paper presented to the American Society of Criminology, Chicago, November.

Downing, P. and K. Hanf. 1983. *International Comparisons in Implementing Pollution Control Laws*. Boston: Kluwer-Nijholl.

Edelhertz, H. 1970. *The Nature, Impact and Prosecution of White-Collar Crime*. Washington, DC: U.S. Department of Justice, National Institute on Law Enforcement and Criminal Justice.

Elkins, J. R. 1976. "Decision-Making Models and the Control of Corporate Crime. *Hobart Law Journal* 85:1091–1129.

Fellmeth, R. 1973. "The Regulatory-Industrial Complex." In *Common and Corporate Accountability*, edited by R. Nader. New York: Harcourt Brace Jovanovich.

Fels, A. 1982. "The Political Economy of Regulation." *University of New South Wales Law Journal* 5:29–60.

Fisse, B. and J. Braithwaite. 1983. *The Impact of Publicity on Corporate Offenders*. Albany: State University of New York Press.

Foucault, M. 1979. *Discipline and Punish*. New York: Pantheon.

Galamer, M. 1974. "Why the Haves Come out Ahead: Speculations on the Limits of Legal Change." *Law & Society Review* 9:95–160.

Goff, C. and C. Reasons. 1978. *Corporate Crime in Canada*. Toronto: Prentice-Hall.

Grabosky, P. and J. Braithwaite. 1986. *Of Manners Gentle*. Melbourne: Oxford University Press.

Gunningham, N. 1974. *Pollution: Social Interest and the Law*. Oxford: Centre for Socio-Legal Studies, Oxford University.

———. 1984. *Safeguarding the Worker*. Sydney: Law Book Company.

Hawkins, K. 1984. *Environment and Enforcement*. Oxford: Clarendon.

Horton, J. 1941. "The Rise of the Right: A Global View." *Crime and Social Justice* 15:7–17.

Jamieson, M. 1985. *Persuasion in Punishment*. Master's thesis, Oxford University, United Kingdom.

Kagan, R. 1978. *Regulatory Justice*. New York: Russell Sage.

Levi, M. 1981. *The Phantom Capitalists*. London: Heinemann.

————. 1984. "Giving Creditors the Business: The Criminal Law in Inaction." *International Journal of Sociology of Law* 12:312–333.

Lewis-Beck, M. S. and J. R. Alford. 1980. "Can Government Regulate Safety? The Coal Mine Example." *American Political Science Review* 74:745–781.

Long, S. 1979. "The Internal Revenue Service: Examining the Exercise of Discretion in Tax Enforcement." Paper presented to the Law and Society meetings, May.

Lynxwiler, J., N. Shover, and D. Clelland. 1984. "Determinants of Sanction Severity in a Regulatory Bureaucracy." Pp. 147–165 in *Corporations as Criminals,* edited by E. Hochstedler. Beverly Hils, Calif." Sage.

Martinson, R. 1974. "What Works? Qustions and Anmswers about Prison Reform." *The Public Interest* 35:21–54.

Meier, R. and T. P. Plumlee. 1978. "Regulatory Administration and Organizational Rigidity." *Western Political Quarterly* 31:80–95.

Meier, R. and J. F. Short. 1982. "The Consequences of White Collar Crime." In *White-Collar Crime: An Agenda for Research,* edited by H. Edelhertz and T. Overcast. Toronto: D. C. Heath.

Melossi, D. 1980. "Strategies of Social Control in Capitalism: A Comment on Recent Work." *Contemporary Crises* 4:381–402.

Mitnick, B. M. 1980. *The Political Economy of Regulation.* New York: Columbia University Press.

Morgenstern, F. 1982. *Deterrence and Compensation.* Geneva: International Labor Organization.

Noll, R. 1978. *Reforming Regulation.* Washington, DC: Brookings.

Pearce, F. and S. Tombs. 1978. "Regulating Coroprate Crime: The Case of Health and Safety." Presented to American Society of Criminology meeting, Chicago, November.

Peltzman, J. 1976. "Toward a More General Theory of Regulation." *Journal of Law and Economics* 19:211–240.

Rankin, F. and R. Brown. 1988. "The Treatment of Repeat Offenders under B. C.'s Occupational Health and Safety and Pollution Control Legislation." Presented to the Canadian Law & Society Association meeting, Windsor, June.

Reasons, C., W. Ross, and C. Patterson. 1981. *Assault on the Worker.* Toronto: Butterworth.

Sabatier, P. 1975. "Social Movements and Regulatory Agencies: Toward a More Adequate and Less Pessimistic Theory of Clientele Capture." *Policy Sciences* 6:301–341.

————. 1977. "Regulatory Policy-Making: Toward a Framework of Analysis." *Natural Resources Journal* 17:415–460.

Scholz, J. 1984a. "Deterrence, Cooperation, and the Ecology of Regulatory Enforcement." *Law & Society Review* 18:179–224.

————. 1984b. "Voluntary Compliance and Regulatory Enforcement." *Law and Policy* 6:385–404.

Shapiro, S. 1985. "The Road not Taken: The Elusive Path to Criminal Prosecution for White Collar Offenders." *Law & Society Review* 19.

Shover, N., D. A. Clelland, and J. Lynxwiler. 1986. *Enforcement or Negotiation: Constructing a Regulatory Bureaucracy.* Albany: State University of New York Press.

Smith, R. J. 1976. *The Occupational Health and Safety Act.* Washington, DC: American Enterprise Institute.

————. 1979. "The Impact of OSHA Inspections on Manufacturing Injury Rates." *Journal of Human Resources* 14:145–160.

Snider, L. 1978. "Corporate Crime in Canada: A Preliminary Report." *Canadian Journal of Criminology* 20:142–168.

————. 1985. "Legal Reform and Social Control: The Dangers of Abolishing Rape." *International Journal of the Sociology of Law* 18:337–356.

Snider L. and W. G. West. 1980. "Social Control, Crime, and Conflict in Canada." In *Power and Change in Canada,* edited by P. J. Ossenberg. Toronto: McClelland and Stewart.

Stigler, G. 1975. *The Citizen and the State.* Chicago: University of Chicago Press.

Stone, C. 1975. *Where the Law Ends.* New York: Harper & Row.

Thomas, J. 1982. "The Regulatory Role in the Containment of Corporate Illegality." In *White-Collar Crime: An Agenda for Research,* edited by H. Edelhertz and T. Overcast. Toronto: D. C. Heath.

Tucker, E. 1987. "Making the Workplace Safe in Capitalism: Enforcement of Factory Legislation in Nineteenth Century Ontario." Paper presented to the Canadian Law and Society Association meeting, Hamilton, June.

Walker, S. 1985. *Sense and Nonsense about Crime.* Monterey, CA: Brooks/Cole.

Watkins, J. C. 1977. "White Collar Crimes: Legal Sanctions and Social Control." *Crime and Delinquency* 23:290–303.

Whiting, B. J. 1980. "OSHA's Enforcement Policy." *Labor Law Journal* 31.

Winter, G. 1985. "Bartering Rationality in Regulation." *Law & Society Review* 19:219–250.

Yeager, P. C. 1986. "Managing Obstacles to Studying Corporate Offenses: An Optimistic Assessment." Paper presented to the American Society of Criminology meeting, Atlanta, November.

About the Editors

Neal Shover is professor of sociology at the University of Tennessee. His principal interests are criminal organization and criminal careers, macro-level sources of punishment variation, and white-collar crime. Dr. Shover's latest book is *Great Pretenders: Pursuits and Careers of Persistent Thieves* (Westview, 1996). He is completing *"Doing Deals" and Making "Mistakes,"* which is scheduled for publication in 2001.

John Paul Wright is associate professor of criminal justice at the University of Cincinnati. His current research interests focus on the effects of family and labor market participation on criminal offending across the life-course. Dr. Wright has also published in the areas of white-collar crime, crime control policies, and general criminological theory. Currently, he is completing a book on *Life-Course Criminology.*